MARKETING PRINCIPLES AND PRACTICE

S.A. CHUNAWALLA

B.Com. (Hons.), D.Pharma, MBA (Marketing)

Communication Consultant,
Benzer, Borivali (W), Mumbai - 400 103.
E-mail: chunawalla@yahoo.com

Himalaya Publishing House

ISO 9001:2015 CERTIFIED

First Edition	:	**1997**
Reprint	:	**1999, 2002**
Second Revised Edition	:	**2006**
Third Revised Edition	:	**2013**
Reprint	:	**2017**
Reprint	:	**2020**
Reprint	:	**2024**

Published by : Mrs. Meena Pandey
for **HIMALAYA PUBLISHING HOUSE PVT. LTD.,**
"Ramdoot", Dr. Bhalerao Marg, Girgaon, Mumbai - 400 004.
Phone: 022-23860170, 23863863; **Fax:** 022-23877178
E-mail: himpub@bharatmail.co.in; **Website:** www.himpub.com

Branch Offices :

New Delhi : "Pooja Apartments", 4-B, Murari Lal Street, Ansari Road, Darya Ganj, New Delhi - 110 002.
Phone: 011-23270392, 23278631; Fax: 011-23256286

Nagpur : Kundanlal Chandak Industrial Estate, Ghat Road, Nagpur - 440 018.
Phone: 0712-2721215, 2721216

Bengaluru : Plot No. 91-33, 2nd Main Road, Seshadripuram, Behind Nataraja Theatre,
Bengaluru - 560 020. Phone: 080-41138821; Mobile: 09379847017, 09379847005

Hyderabad : No. 3-4-184, Lingampally, Besides Raghavendra Swamy Matham, Kachiguda,
Hyderabad - 500 027. Phone: 040-27560041, 27550139

Chennai : No. 34/44, Motilal Street, T. Nagar, Chennai - 600 017. Mobile: 09380460419

Pune : "Laksha" Apartment, First Floor, No. 527, Mehunpura,
Shaniwarpeth (Near Prabhat Theatre), Pune - 411 030.
Phone: 020-24496323, 24496333; Mobile: 09370579333

Cuttack : Plot No. 5F-755/4, Sector-9, CDA Markat Nagar, Cuttack - 753 014,
Odisha. Mobile: 09338746007

Kolkata : 3, S.M. Bose Road, Near Gate No. 5, Agarpara Railway Station,
North 24 Parganas, West Bengal - 700 109. Mobile: 09674536325

DTP by : Sudhakar Shetty

Printed at : Geetanjali Press Pvt. Ltd., Nagpur. On behalf of HPH (P).

PREFACE TO THE THIRD REVISED EDITION

We are in a globalised small world with markets integrated to one another and an array of products of wide variety. Marketing, as we know, creates customers within the country and across the world for these products. It is fascinating to learn how these products are planned, how new products are developed and launched and how these are maintained over their life cycle. The whole area of product management has been thoroughly revised. The concept of brand equity has been dealt with in detail. Similarly, these products are promoted aggressively through advertising and other means. A new chapter of advertising decisions has been added. Pricing decisions are important. These have been thoroughly revised. The chapter on consumer behaviour has been recast. Viral marketing concept has been explained. In short, this is an altogether a new enriched book for readers who study this subject as a compulsory foundation course. It paves the way for further advanced study of the subject. The previous chapters of sales force management, marketing research and marketing environment have been retained after minor modifications.

I am sure the present book will prove to be immensely useful to the readers.

— AUTHOR

PREFACE TO THE SECOND REVISED EDITION

Marketing management has changed a lot in India since the first edition of this book appeared way back in 1997. There are now competitive markets, global brands, strong national and regional brands and new media options like the internet. The emphasis today has shifted to brand management and new product management. Customer relationship is more important since it is easier to retain customers than to acquire new ones. Markets have changed and so does marketing management. The new edition reflects these contemporary realities. I am deeply indebted to the research work that has gone into making Marketing a respectable profession. I am sure this edition will fulfil the needs of the readers. I welcome constructive criticism and suggestions.

— AUTHOR

Mumbai
January 2006

EXCERPTS FROM THE PREFACE OF THE FIRST EDITION

Marketing as a formal discipline was recognised in the US and Europe only in the forties. Prior to that, it was believed that if the goods are produced, they will be sold and there is no need to study the methods of selling them. Indian economy was protected till eighties, and it was only in 1992 that the focus shifted from the producer to the consumer. Indian students learnt marketing in business schools till then, but as a practice it emerged only in this decade.

As a teacher of marketing, I had a strong urge to write on this subject, but resisted the temptation till marketing comes of age in India, and Indian firms start practising marketing. Indian economy now has enough challenges and opportunities both for the domestic and global marketers. Perhaps if I had penned something on marketing prematurely, it would not have gone beyond cloning the works of my American counterparts. The decision to put a marketing book now in this competitive market-driven environment is an appropriate response to the changing scenario and the author has the satisfaction of incorporating the Indian examples to illustrate the theory wherever possible.

Apart from a sea-change in environment which motivated me to write on marketing, there is also a desire to serve a large body of management students who learn marketing as a compulsory subject. Majority of these students are located in university-affiliated courses or autonomous courses recognised by AICTE and are striving to get either a postgraduate degree or diploma. Foreign texts are too exhaustive for them and are too far removed from Indian realities. This book intends to help them in mastering the compulsory marketing paper.

I have used lively and interesting prose which invites the students to read. Without diluting academic integrity, the book makes the important concepts enjoyable. It is a fun-filled learning experience.

I wish you a very glorious future in the field of management in general and marketing in particular.

— AUTHOR

Mumbai
15th August, 1997
50th Anniversary of Independence

CONTENTS

1 WHAT IS MARKETING?

Each decade presents its own opportunities and challenges to a company management. Till the 1980s, Indian companies operated in highly-regulated protected environment. It was mostly a seller's market. Whatever was being offered to consumers, however shoddy, was being sold. Then the winds of liberalisation started blowing, exactly at the fag end of the premiership of Mrs. Gandhi and continued to blow during the stewardship of Mr. Rajiv Gandhi. By the time Mr. Narasimha Rao was catapulted to centre-stage by a quirk of fate, the Soviet empire disintegrated and socialism crumbled in Eastern Europe. In a unipolar world, a new order came into existence, and countries vied with each other to open up their economies and be market friendly. India adopted liberalisation of economy from the 1990s. India made a serious effort to integrate her economy with global market place and deregulated on a massive scale. In a sense, we could get huge opportunities for companies in the basic infrastructural sector like civil works and construction, transport, telecommunications and power. There was expansion of the market in terms of domestic potential and going international. It also, however, means a fiercely competitive scene, where multinationals compete with Indian companies, in what they describe as a playing field that is not level.

One message comes loud and clear. Companies have to adapt to this new environment in order to survive and grow. The rapid technological advances in the fields of IT and telecom, robotics, Artificial Intelligence (AI), molecular designing, super-conductivity and genetic engineering offer unheard of business opportunities.

What is required is a set of new strategies to deal with the new environmental opportunities and challenges. The very purpose of business is to create a customer and for this, the companies have to understand his needs, wants and desires in a sharp manner. Gone are the days, when Indian customers had only Bajaj scooters, Ambassadors and Fiats for his automotive needs. The wider choice available today cater to the gaps in his personal transportational needs and also tries to match his personality profile. There are vehicles suitable for men and women, vehicles for teenagers, vehicles to shuttle in the city and vehicles for small families. There are hatchbacks, sedans and SUVs. These vehicles are not only functional, but they are aesthetically built too. Technologically, they are aerodynamic and fuel efficient. The moral is to keep on changing so as to keep pace with the changing needs of customers. The winning formula cannot be the same for all time to come.

❖ Globalisation

The world has become a small village, thanks to the rapid means of transportation and telecommunications. Satellite transmission has widened the geographical markets. The countries have become interdependent, both in purchases as well as in sales. In India, we have cars and TV sets with many Korean, Taiwan and Japanese components. An aircraft has parts from as far as Italy, Canada, England and Japan — though the finished product may be American. The book that you are reading is composed on an American computer and printed on a German press. The finished products are thus a combination of made and bought parts and the bought parts may come from different countries of the world. "Buy Indian" may be, a good slogan. In practice, however, it may lead to our buying a calculator that was actually made in China and only assembled in India. On the contrary, we may avoid buying Kellog's cornflakes and Domino's Pizza though the products in this millennium are essentially produced in India.

Indian companies use not only imported components, but are also selling their finished products to markets abroad. To take advantage of global markets, Indian companies are making strategic alliances with foreign companies. Global networking of suppliers, distributors, technical collaborators, ad agencies is being created. The winners of this millennium will rely more and more on global integration and networking.

There are trends towards universal free trade. At the same time, regional trading blocs like NAFTA (North Atlantic Free Trade Agreement) amongst the U.S., Canada and Mexico are emerging. The ECM: European Common Market is a trading bloc of 12 countries. These blocks want the elimination of the barriers to the free movement of goods and services. The SAARC and Far East countries may form trading blocs soon. The economic map of the world will change beyond recognition very soon.

❖ Income Gap

In spite of India's adopting a socialist democracy model with the motto of maximum benefit for the maximum number of people, we still find that large sections of her population live below the poverty line. After the liberalisation of economic policy, there is a clamour for reforms with a human face in view of the hardships they have caused to the common people. Though wage incomes have risen the real income has declined due to inflationary pressure, that erodes the purchasing power of the rupee. In a market friendly economy that we are creating, the needs of the consumers have multiplied, but they lack the purchasing power to pay for the needed goods. We observe a strange paradox of *poverty amidst plenty.* India has a great scope to sell the *products in volume* but at attractively low prices. Of course, there is scope to sell premium products at high prices to the suitable market niches, *e.g.*, a high quality lipstick for the affluent at a price of ₹ 150 – ₹ 250 whereas a fairly reasonable quality of lipstick for a large number of women at a price of ₹ 30 – ₹ 35. The consumers in India have a greater need to get VFM (Value-For-Money). This is true whether we sell a soap or a luxury car.

India still has a large population below the poverty line and close to half the women population who is to a large extent illiterate. India enters this millennium with proper investment in the social sector of education, health and rural development.

❖ The Environmental Imperative

India woke from its slumber when Bhopal gas tragedy owing to methyl isocyanide leak at the Union Carbide plant killed many and incapacitated many others. Each company must now examine the overall impact of its operations on the surrounding environment. The environmental regulation by the government has come to stay. Soon there is going to be an environmental audit. What has emerged as an accepted principle is the element of accountability of a company for the maintenance of a healthy environment. The Earth Summit (1992) at Rio de Janeiro and the recent Copenhagen Summit considered the environmental threats, and how to ward them off. The companies have also started *going green.* In India, there is growing consciousness about environment in the industry and at the governmental level. Our Supreme Court has done the greatest service to protect the environment. In fact, it is the most environment-friendly court in the world. There is a concept of carbon credits in operation now.

❖ A New Perspective

No longer can the firms have a cloistered existence and sheltered environment. They are facing more and more domestic and international competition. Domestic firms rely more upon the purchases from abroad and sales in the foreign markets. Hence, they have to be on par with international firms in terms of the wage costs and material costs. Indian companies must take cognisance of the rapidly advancing technologies and should learn new ways of organising and marketing.

Without understanding the rapidly changing environment, the companies cannot remain profitable. We must bid good bye to the *marketing myopia* which so far has afflicted us. There is no dearth of counselling on the ways to do business. Each expert has his own prescriptions. Douglas McGregor's *theory* in the 60's asked the companies to treat employees as individuals who do not need coercion but an environment conducive to foster their creativity. Later in the 70s, the time had come for *strategic planning* teaching us how different business units can be managed strategically in a turbulent environment. In the 80s, we started concentrating on *management excellence* and *quality.* All these are inspiring themes. But 90s have ushered in an era of *customer-oriented* and *driven* companies, replacing the product driven or technology driven approach of the past. Too many companies lack the input of customer needs while designing the new products. Some companies consider the sale as the ultimate transaction beyond which customer need not be remembered. Clearly 1990s have taught the firms a market-based view of business success.

Drucker reminds us that a superstar company of yesterday finds itself stagnating and frustrated because the assumptions on which the organization has been build and is being run no longer fit the reality. These assumptions are about the markets, competitors, technology and company's strengths and weaknesses.

❖ Key Concepts in Marketing

There are as many definitions of marketing as there are authors on this subject. We endorse the following definition of marketing:

Marketing is the process that facilitates the exchange of valuable products created and/or offered to consumers so as to satisfy their needs and wants and demands.

The above definition puts forward several key concepts: *needs, wants and demands, value, products, exchange* and *satisfaction.*

The following diagram illustrates the linkage between these concepts:

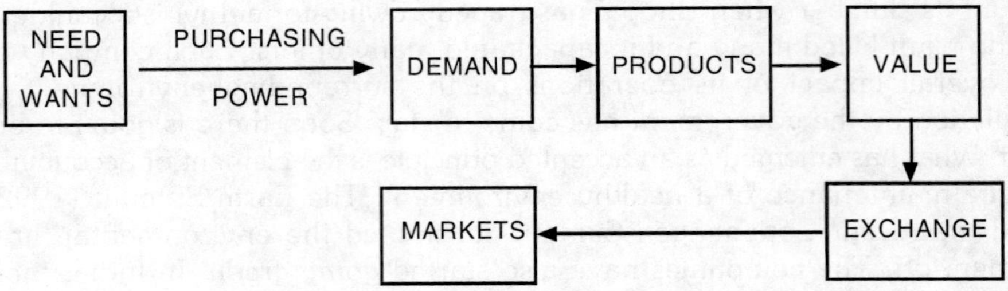

Fig: 1.1 Key Concepts in Marketing

These concepts have been discussed below.

❖ Needs and Wants

The starting point of any marketing activity is the human needs and wants. We, as human beings, need certain basic necessities like air, food, water, clothing and shelter. These needs ensure our survival. Beyond these basic needs, we aspire to have good education, some recreation and would like to have certain services. Basic human needs exist in the biological condition of the human beings. They are not created by the marketers. Our needs feel us deprived of some basic satisfaction: To satisfy our basic needs, we show strong preferences for certain product versions, *e.g.*, South Indians prefer rice and North Indians like wheat.

Wants are our desires for specific satisfiers of our basic needs. Thus, we need Basmati rice and we want Kohinoor. We need entertainment and we visit a cinema hall to see a movie. We need status and we may buy a Maruti delux. While our basic needs are few, our wants have no end. Our wants are shaped continuously by the environment in which we live, and the institutions with which we interact — schools, families, religious orders, business organisations.

❖ Basic States of Consumer Psyche

It is necessary for a marketer to recognise two basic states of the consumer psyche which are relevant to his needs — the actual state and the desired state. Need recognition is a result of knowing these two states. If there is a gap between these two states, it provides an opportunity to the marketer to fulfil these needs and bridge the gap. Let us take the example of a washing machine.

The *actual state* is an urban nuclear family with no support system, which struggles to carry out household chorus all on its own, including clothes washing. The contributing factor is non-availability of domestic help and even if available, her *kat-kat* and absenteeism. Another contributing factor is the working woman, who keeps away from home, along with her husband who also works. This leads to the *desired state* of having washing machine which washes reasonably well, rinses and even dries the clothes any time. It is essential to know the 'states' by doing research. The desired state may not be a specific benefit always. It could just be an extension of the brand personality e.g. Pepsi's endorsement by young celebrities projects it as a drink which is 'young and lively', and this gets associated with the desired state. Marketing communication tries to create a 'desired state' by combining functional and/or emotional benefits. It is to be appreciated, however, that these 'states' are not static and keep on changing. We have to cater to the changing 'desired states'. Hero Honda motorcycles marched ahead of Bajaj to cater to the changing 'desired states' of consumers.

❖ Demands

When wants are backed by purchasing power and a willingness to buy, they become demands. So many of us may desire to have a bungalow at a hill station, but only a few can afford it and are willing to buy it. Companies thus basically concentrate on demand management — how many people have the ability and willingness to buy the products. Marketers try to influence the demand by offering a suitable product at an affordable price and make it available to people who demand it.

❖ Products

Goods and services available in the market place are the means by which we satisfy our needs and wants. Product is a comprehensive term that includes both goods and services. Anything that satisfies needs and wants qualifies to become a product. Our demand for products has not much to do with acquisition, but with the benefits they offer. A car is just not a possession but it enables us to move from place to place. An oven provides us the cooking service and thus it does not just remain an object of admiration. Physical products are the medium through which benefits sought by us are offered.

Benefits are also offered by products other than physical products — thus a *place* like Kashmir rejuvenates us when we visit it as tourists and *activity* like a literacy mission keeps us occupied in productive work, an *organisation* like Poona Club provides us a forum of social interaction and an *idea* like Transcendental Meditation leads us to an enlightened life and a *person* like a comedian makes us laugh and drive away our blues. The term "product" thus encompasses not only physical products, but also all other media through which our needs and wants are satisfied. We also use the term *offerings* in lieu of *products*.

Product is not just a bundle of some physical and chemical attributes. Manufacturers view products in this fashion. Products are really speaking a bundle of benefits and services. They are to be seen as a solution to our problems. A young girl using lipstick is in fact buying the concept of *beauty*. Tonics give us a *hope* of being healthy. Hair dyes offer us *youthfulness*. No carpenter buys a drill, he buys a *hole*. Physical objects just package the benefits. Our definition of products should be need-oriented or benefit-oriented, or else we would suffer what Levitt calls *marketing myopia*.

❖ Value

Many products satisfy our given needs and we have to choose from among them. An employee who has to reach his office in Bombay's central business district can think of taking a suburban train, ride a mobike or a scooter or board a BEST bus or hire a taxi cab or use a car. All these products fall into his *choice set*. While travelling can be undertaken in any of these products, the employee has to satisfy several additional needs — to reach as quickly as he can, to have a comfortable journey, to have a safe journey and above all, to economise on the cost of transport. The products available have a different capacity to satisfy each of his variegated needs. The product that is ultimately chosen should deliver the maximum total satisfaction in respect of his various needs.

The criterion is *customer value*. We have to assess the capacity of each product to satisfy our *need set*, thus mentally ranking the products from the most satisfying ones to the least satisfying ones. What is value then? It is an assessment that the customer makes about the overall capacity of the product to satisfy his/her needs.

An *ideal product*, though Utopian, enables us to place the available products against this benchmark. Ideal transport makes us reach the place of work in a jiffy, with utmost comfort safety and without paying anything at all. We have to see how closer the available products are to the ideal one.

Again, we have to consider what value we get and at what price we get it. To be frank, one would love to commute in an automobile, but the initial investment and the recurring maintenance cost and the problem of parking may make us opt for another product, say, a first-class suburban train travel. The product that is chosen must give the most value per rupee spent.

Further details of consumer behaviour, we shall examine in a separate chapter. The whole marketing plan rests on our assumptions about the way the consumers choose their products.

All these three concepts, *viz.* value, cost and satisfaction are of utmost importance for a marketer.

Marketing links two basic functions *viz.* those of *production* and *consumption*. Marketing is an activity which is directed at satisfying customer needs and wants through exchange transaction in the market.

❖ Exchange

The availability of products that have value and a set of people having needs and wants do not necessarily lead to marketing. Marketing is an outcome of the process of exchange — "The process of obtaining a desired product from someone by offering something in return" (Kotler). Apart from exchanges, we can get products by charity, by force or by self-production. But the most widely prevalent method of obtaining products is through exchanges. In return, we may offer another product or service or money. These days money is the most common medium of exchange. In any exchange, there are at least two parties, with each having something of value for the other. There is freedom to both the parties either to accept or reject the offer. The offer is capable of being communicated and delivered. The parties find the dealing mutually desirable/beneficial. The actual exchange is a value-creating process. On accomplishing the exchange, they are said to have entered into a transaction — a trade of values between two parties. When money is offered as consideration for a product in a transaction, it is called a monetary transaction. Each transaction is governed by agreed-upon conditions. Agreed transactions are legally enforceable through a law of contract. A transaction differs from a transfer where nothing tangible is offered in return. A gift from X to Y is, thus, a transfer.

Marketing is all about eliciting the desired responses from our customers for effecting successful exchanges. This is called transaction marketing. But transaction marketing occurs within the broader relationship marketing, based on mutual trust, respect, credibility and win-win situations. No marketer can afford to stop at just concluding a deal. He has to offer quality, after-sales-service, support service, fair price to other parties over a period of time. He has to build strong bonds with all concerned so as to facilitate transactions to the point of making them routine and automatic.

What is the result of a marketing activity? It is a *marketing network* consisting of the firm, its suppliers, its intermediaries and its customers who are bound together in a beneficial business relationship. Marketing has shifted its focus from profit-from-each-transaction to long-term beneficial relationship. What matters are relationships — transactions are incidental?

The UK Chartered Institute of Marketing defines marketing as:

Marketing is the management process responsible for identifying, anticipating and satisfying customer requirements profitably.

❖ Markets

These are the logical extensions of the concept of exchange. Markets are made up by customers. All of them have certain needs and wants. They try to satisfy these through the exchange mechanism. Market size is thus given by the persons having particular needs/wants and who are ready to exchange their resources for want of satisfying products.

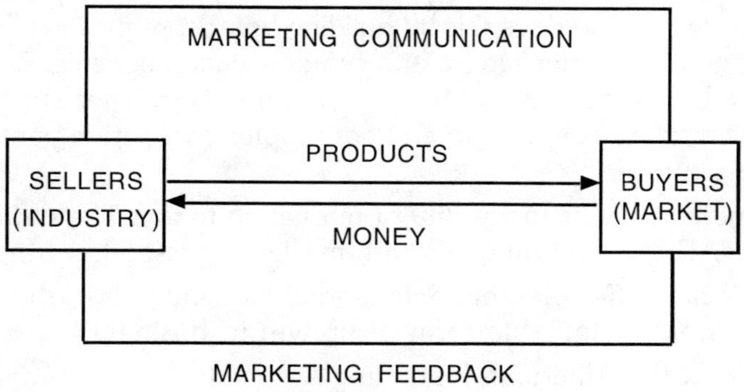

Fig. 1.2 Marketing System

Formerly, markets were considered to be certain geographic locations. To the economists, market is a group of buyers and sellers who enter into transactions for certain goods/services. To the marketers, the sellers are the *industry* and the buyers constitute a *market*. Sellers offer products to the market. To inform and persuade the buyers in the market, they communicate with the buyers, say, through advertising. Buyers from the market offer money as consideration to the sellers. They also give feed-back to the sellers about their experience with the consumption.

Modern economy is based on the concept of market. Division of labour leads to specialisation. These specialists produce a number of goods. They sell off these to receive money. They use the same to finance their purchases. There are a number of intermediaries between the Manufacturer and the Customers, *e.g.*, wholesalers, retailers, departmental stores, super-markets etc. The government itself is a very large producer and seller of goods/services. The government receives taxes both from the producers and customers to run its affairs. Two or more firms engaged in the same type of business are competitors.

Let us chart out a modern marketing system:

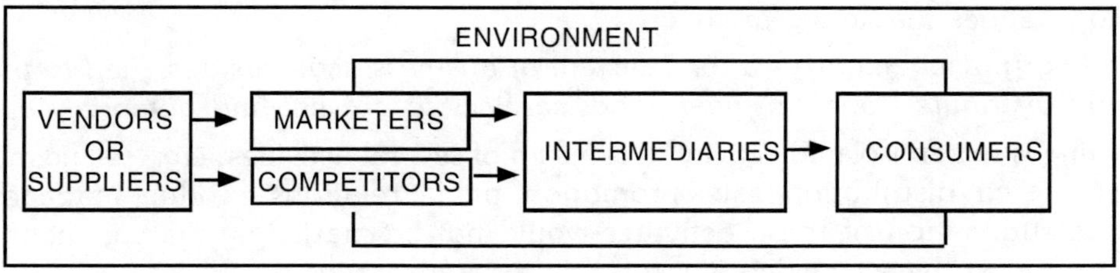

Fig. 1.3 Modern Marketing System

❖ Marketing Defined

The Chartered Institute of Marketing defined marketing in 1976 as 'the management process responsible for identifying, anticipating and satisfying customer requirements profitably'.

Since then, the world has changed a lot. The above definition was formulated in the pre-internet pre-globalisation age. There were few channels and there was no relationship marketing. Marketing is no longer a one-way process. There is social marketing and marketing for no-profit organisations. All these factors make the above definition anachronous. A new definition of marketing has been put forward by the institute.

Marketing is "the strategic business function that creates value by stimulating, facilitating and fulfilling customer demand. It does this by building boards, nurturing innovation, developing relationships, creating good customer service and communication benefits. By operating customer-centrically, marketing brings positive return on investment, satisfies shareholders and stake-holders from business and the community and contributes to positive behavioural change and a sustainable business future."

The above definition reflects the reality of marketing today. The definition expands from 12 words to 60 words. The definition deals with marketing as both a function and a process.

The Marketing Society offers another definition of marketing. It is 'the creation of customer demand which is the only sustainable form of growth in business'.

The definition from the American Marketing Association (AMA) reads: 'Marketing is an organisational function and a set of processes for creating, communicating and delivering value to customers and for managing customer relationships in ways that benefit the organization and its stakeholders'.

❖ Marketing Management

The American Marketing Association defines marketing management as follows:

Market management is the process of planning and executing — the conception, pricing, promotion and distribution of goods, services and ideas — to create exchanges — with target groups — that satisfy customer and organisational objectives.

This definition acknowledges the significance of exchange process of goods, services and ideas. It recognises that marketing management is a process of planning and implementation. Analysis precedes planning and controlling follows implementation. The ultimate aim is consumer satisfaction.

Marketing management, traditionally has been associated with consumer or customer markets, though there can be dealings in labour market, money or capital market and raw materials market.

Stanton defines marketing as follows:

Marketing (management) is a total system of business activities designed to plan, price, promote and distribute want-satisfying goods/services to present and potential customers.

Marketing is not an isolated activity. It is a sum of several activities. *e.g.*, selling, advertising, marketing research, distribution, sales promotion, public relations, product management etc. Even a mere summation of these activities would not be marketing management. There is *interaction* amongst these, making it a total, integrated process.

Marketing starts with the conception of product idea. It does not end with the sale of a finished product. It aims at consumer satisfaction and hence continues even after the sale is made.

In its broadest sense, marketing management is essentially demand management. It influences the level of demand, *e.g.*, the actual demand is less than the desired demand and marketing management has to stimulate demand. Marketing management also influences the timing and the composition of demand, *e.g.*, telephone services have low demand at night, and so concessions are offered in tariff to stimulate the demand during these lean hours. Sometimes, instead of stimulating demand, we have to discourage it. Thus we have anti-drug ads and ads to conserve water and electricity. Thailand puts a warning on cigarette packets that smoking cause sexual impotence.

By using marketing resources like marketing research, sales force and advertising, marketing managers develop *marketing programmes.* These planned programmes need implementation so as produce a desired level and mix of transactions with the target markets.

❖ What does marketing actually do?

Marketing performs a number of activities which are listed below:

(*a*) *It identifies marketing opportunities*

(*b*) *It manages existing products and develops new products*

(*c*) *It chooses and motivates channels of distribution*

(*d*) *It advertises and promotes products and services*

(*e*) *It sets prices and terms of supply*

(*f*) *It plans the marketing activity*

The following diagram captures these activities:

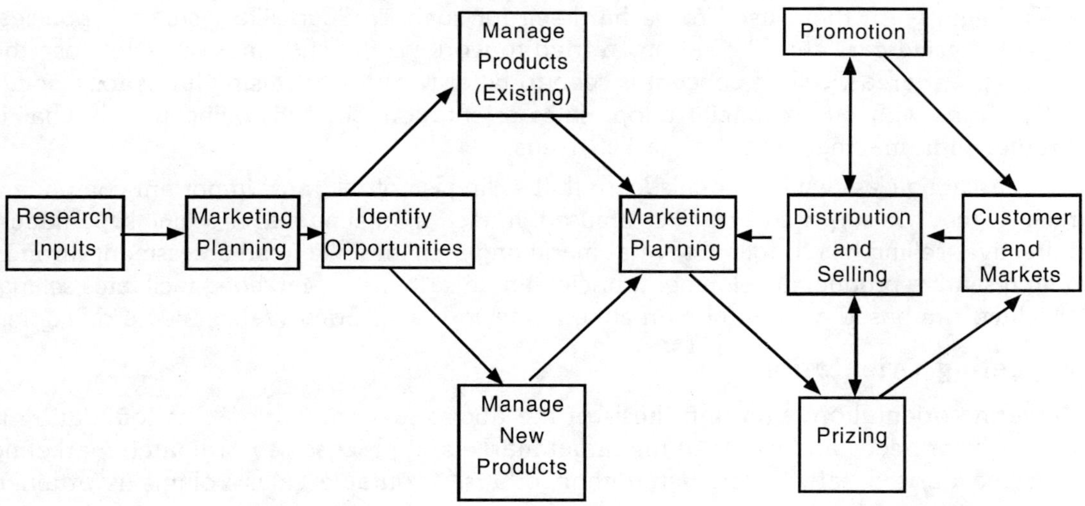

Fig. 1.4 What does marketing activity do?

❖ Evolution of Marketing Management

Marketing management, as we have already stated, is an attempt to get the desired response from our target audience towards our offering. The overriding consideration is what influences marketing philosophy the most.

❖ Production Orientation

This is a very common orientation to be seen. The whole company is engineering driven. Production is considered to be an ultimate aim. Whatever is produced is fed into the market. The emphasis is on production efficiency. Later, the efforts are concentrated on distributing widely the available production. There is no marketing effort worth the name, the assumption being any well-made and reasonably priced product will find its own market. In the U.S. Texas Instruments sells a large volume of instruments at rock bottom prices. It has a typical production orientation. Many Japanese companies also have production orientation. This type of orientation works when demand exceeds supply. Most of the technocrats tend to be obsessed with production. Indian companies prior to liberalisation operated under licence permit raj and in a protected environment. They tended to be production centred.

Production-centred firm at a later stage does attempt to improve product design as far as possible by engineering skills, without any input from the customers. It leads to marketing myopia where railroads concentrate on trains, rather than on transportation needs.

❖ Sales Orientation

When we find that simply making a better product is not enough guarantee of market success, we turn to sales orientation, believing that the output must be sold by conscious efforts. To begin with, there used to be hard-sell for such products like insurance policies, encyclopedias, used cars etc. The salesmen tried to work up the customer so as to close the sale. In non-profit areas, selling concept is seen to be at work, *e.g.*, raising funds for a social cause. The firms with over-capacity adopt sales orientation, the aim being to sell what is made, rather than making what the market needs.

In a marketing class when students learn that selling is not the most important component of marketing, they are surprised as well as amused. In fact, marketing makes selling superfluous. To be effective, selling has to follow several marketing activities like need assessment through marketing research, product development, pricing and distribution. Marketing facilitates selling. Right products are based on careful marketing homework *e.g.*, Sony Walkman, Xerox copier.

❖ Marketing Orientation

Marketing-orientation is an anti-thesis of the above two orientations. Its foundation is the assessment of needs and wants of the target markets. It practises co-ordinated marketing to deliver the desired satisfaction better than others. Profitable sales volume is attained through customer satisfaction.

The key-concepts are: the target market, customer needs, co-ordinated marketing and profitability. The following diagram illustrates the distinction between the Sales-orientation and the Marketing-orientation.

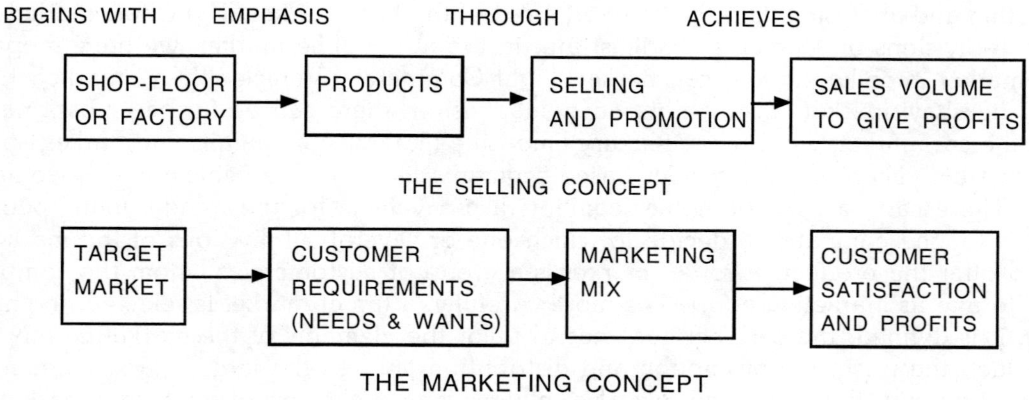

Fig. 1.5 Marketing Orientation

❖ Distinction between Marketing and Selling

Many amongst us are still confused about the distinction between Marketing and Selling. Many tend to equate these terms, as if they are synonymous. However, these two concepts have exactly opposite connotations.

As we have already observed, the selling concept comes in when a product is first made and then an attempt is made to sell it by various methods so as to motivate people to buy it. As a matter of fact, the company tries to manipulate the demand in such a way that it suits the supply made available by it.

Under the marketing concept, the company first identifies its customers or its target market and then identifies what these customers want. The product is developed so that it satisfies these wants and still yields profit. Here the company is manipulating its supply so that it subserves the consumer demand.

In short, we can put the distinction in the form of a table as follows:

Selling	*Marketing*
1. Emphasis on the needs of the seller.	1. Emphasis on the needs of the buyer.
2. First, a product is made. Then efforts are taken to sell it.	2. First, target market and its wants are identified. The product is made to satisfy these wants.
3. The company's goal is to convert the product into cash by selling a large volume.	3. The company's goal is to satisfy the needs and wants of customers by means of the product. Profitable sales volume is incidental.
4. Short-term results are expected from planning. Only current products and markets are considered.	4. Long-run strategic planning. New products and new markets are considered. Future growth is an ultimate aim.

Let us now examine, in detail, the key concepts in marketing orientation.

❖ Target Market

As we have already observed, a market consists of people with needs and wants, with money to spend, and with a willingness to buy. An organisation starts its marketing planning by selecting and analysing its target market(s) out of the total market. The whole market has many sub-divisions or segments. To illustrate, in the automobile market, we have mopeds/ scooty market, mobike market, car market, Light Commercial Vehicles (LCV) market, truck market, rickshaw market. Even within each subdivision, there can be further subsegments, *e.g.*, in the car market, we can have luxury limousine market, small family car market, sports car market etc. There can be gender-based segments like a man's vehicle and a woman's vehicle. There can be psychographic segments like a vehicle for the trendy young people. Thus it is for the company to decide to which one or several subdivisions of the market it wants to offer the product. A *target market* is a group of customers at whom the company intends to aim its marketing effort. The more carefully, a target market is selected, the more sharply, it is defined, the easier it becomes to tailor the elements of the marketing mix like the product, the price, the promotion and distribution. Just as the target market influences the marketing mix, the marketing mix also influences the selection of the target market.

❖ Customer Needs

Despite the selection of the target market, the company may fail to understand the needs of its customers. To illustrate, an economy car may mean fuel efficient car, low maintenance car or initially low investment car. An 'attractive swimwear' might be interpreted as a good-looking swimwear or sexy swimwear or fashionable swimwear. We have to probe the needs deeply to understand them properly. The needs which are stated are as important as the needs which are unstated, *e.g.*, a customer buying car's economy model expects good after sales service from the dealer, though he explicitly does not say so. There are also hidden needs, *e.g.*, a car buyer desires that he is considered to be a modern savvy consumer or a mobike buyer needs identification as a macho man.

The customer may have a real need which is far different from the stated need, *e.g.*, a customer demanding computer education needs employability. Maybe, a TV Advertising Course covering Computer Graphics may satisfy his need better than the ordinary computer fundamentals course.

Customer driven companies think everything from the customer's point of view. A customer's buying decision is a result of balancing and counter balancing of several alternatives. A car has to be low cost, safe, good performance car, which is at the same time eye appealing. All these attributes are needed in a car within an overall price of ₹ 2.5 lakh. The car marketer has to incorporate these trade-offs of desirable features while designing the car.

Every marketer thus satisfies needs and wants — real needs and wants — hidden needs and wants. While doing so, the marketer has to be one-up than the competitor.

The sales of a company originate from existing customers and new customers. Existing customers must keep on buying, they should do repeat purchasing. It is a question of retaining them. Attracting new customers is a costly proposition.

Customer retention is thus crucial. It is ensured by customer satisfaction. How does a satisfied customer help a company?

(*i*) He continues to buy, shows loyalty and buys more and more.

(*ii*) He buys product-brand extensions from the same company.

(*iii*) He gives good word of mouth publicity.

(*iv*) He is less vulnerable to competitive advertising and brands. He is less sensitive on the price front.

(*v*) He costs less to serve.

(*vi*) He is a good source of ideas to the company.

A satisfied customer is more effective as an advertiser than the media advertising. It is advisable for a company to conduct regular research to assess customer satisfaction. The irritants can be removed and corrective action can be taken, if there is some dissatisfaction.

Though customer complaints are a good index of dissatisfaction, all dissatisfied customers do not complain. Some may stop dealing with the company. The company should actively encourage customers to complain and to give suggestions. Many of the great product improvement ideas come by listening to customers carefully. Mere listening is not sufficient. The company must come out with a positive and constructive response. It is foolish to lose customers for trivial things. Tracking customer satisfaction continuously is a must for every marketer. Profitability with declining customer satisfaction is a serious thing. Long-term profits come through customer satisfaction.

❖ Co-ordinated Marketing

All the employees may not be inclined to work for the customers. In a branch of nationalised bank, the counter clerks offer less than courteous, prompt and satisfactory service to the customers. They feel customers are too demanding. The supervisory staff and the manager, however, wish they could help customers transact their business with the branch as smoothly as possible. There is lack of co-ordination in the approach towards customers between the Managers and the Staff. Internal co-ordination is a must for a marketing oriented company. First, there should be co-ordination between sales, advertising, marketing research, product management and distribution. Secondly, there should be co-ordination between Marketing and other Departments of the company like production, personnel, finance, purchase and materials. It is not desirable to keep top management isolated from customers. Middle and front-line people who interact with the customers far more must keep top management posted with what the customer perceptions are. The top management must analyze these perceptions, and support the middle and front-line managers in their efforts to satisfy the customers. All levels of management must be geared to serve the customers.

❖ Profitability

Profit is a major goal for any company in the private sector. This is to be achieved incidentally while serving the customer. It should be an index of how well the company is serving the customers in the long-run. Marketing offers profits, market share and growth on a platter to those who keep customers' interest in mind. Different marketing opportunities have different profit potential and hence a good marketing manager analyzes each marketing opportunity for what it is worth.

❖ Acceptance of Marketing Concept

Of late, marketing has come to be accepted all over the world. Even in India, companies have started acknowledging the importance of the marketing concept. But when it comes to practising it, very few companies can really be labelled as master marketers. Only a handful of companies in India focus on the customer and respond positively to his needs.

What are the criteria to judge a good marketing-oriented company?

First and foremost, it has a well-staffed marketing department.

Secondly, all the other departments of such a company like production, materials, personnel, finance, R & D accept the marketing philosophy of being consumer oriented.

Thirdly, the organisational culture has a typical marketing ethos that pervades the whole organisation.

Mere presence of a formal marketing department or appointment of a few marketing functionaries do not make a company market focused or customer driven. The acid test is how they respond to the customers' needs, and that too in relation to the competitors. The failure to adapt to the changing environment and losing the focus on customer show that the company lacks marketing maturity.

What are those factors which lead companies to the adoption of marketing concept?

1. To begin with, *heavy marketing expenditure* by itself leads to the adoption of a systematic marketing programme. The media tariff for advertising inflates every now and then. Space and time buying for advertising have become expensive. The compensation of the sales force, the expenditure on marketing communications, the sales promotion expenses, the public relations exercises, publicity campaigns — all these need more and more money. It is necessary to undertake marketing planning and marketing audit.
2. Another factor that prods the company to accept marketing is the *competitive environment.* Indian firms have now to face both domestic and foreign competition. India has opened up her economy. In the consumer electronics sector, we now find many TV companies, especially the foreign brands like Panasonic, Akai, Samsung, Thomson, and LG. The automobile sector has changed its complexion and there are many two-wheelers and four-wheelers in the market. Telecom and power sector are being exposed to foreign competition. In such a competitive environment, it becomes necessary to learn marketing in order to survive and grow.
3. *Stagnation* also leads to acceptance of the marketing philosophy. Companies will have to seek new markets, launch new products, stimulate demand for the new products in the new markets to ward-off stagnation.
4. *Changes in consumer behaviour* also act in favour of the marketing concept. The needs and wants of consumers have undergone a sea change. The phenomenon of working women, for example, makes it necessary for companies to tap markets for an entirely new range of products like instant foods, kitchen equipment and labour saving devices. To match the product to the changing consumer wants and needs, it becomes necessary to adopt marketing.
5. *Declining sales* also spur companies to marketing action. With the onslaught of TV and satellite TV, the magazines were compelled to redesign their marketing strategies to arrest their declining sales. Thus we have *niche* magazines, regional editions, better editorials etc.

To begin with, most of the companies are production oriented. They gradually evolve to have sales-orientation. Certain factors discussed above lead them to adopt marketing orientation ultimately.

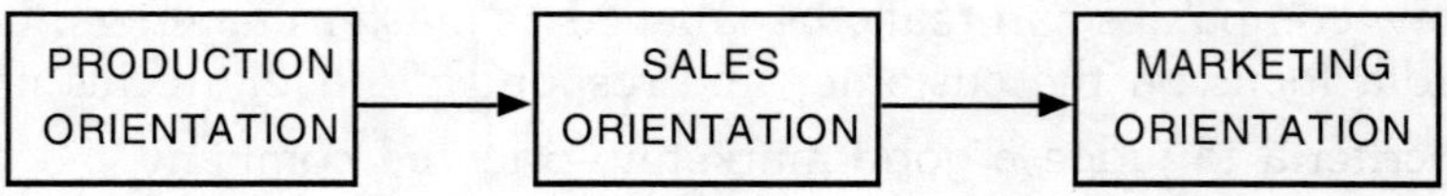

Fig. 1.6 Stages in the Evolution of Marketing Management

In its widest amplitude marketing concept represents a philosophy of doing business. The firm accepts customers' want satisfaction as the *raison de taire* of its existence. The whole business is viewed as a result, from the customer's point of view. While satisfying the customers, the firm has still to make profits in the long-run. As Stanton observes, "the key to implementing the marketing concept successfully is a favourable attitude on the part of top management." Chase Bank stated, "Marketing begins with top management. Only top management can provide the climate, the discipline and the leadership required for a successful marketing programme."

Though companies have started adopting the marketing concept owing to a variety of factors, the actual implementation of the concept still leaves much to be desired. There are several degrees of marketing orientation. At one extreme there are firms who just pay lip sympathy to this concept and establish marketing department only in name. To them marketing is just a fancy label given to selling. At the other extreme, there are firms where pre-eminence of the customer permeates every nook and corner of the company. The whole organisation becomes marketing oriented. In between these two extremes, there are several possibilities of differing marketing orientations.

According to Al Ries and Laura Ries, management and marketing are perpetually at war. The management people are left brained, whereas marketers are primarily right-brained. As a CEO, the decisions made are based on facts are figures and research data. A CEO is thus left-brained. As a marketer, the chances are that the divisions are based on gut instinct, with little or no supporting evidence. It could not be otherwise in creative disciplines like marketing. As left-brains, CEOs often want to build sales, whereas marketers want to build brands.

It has been accepted now that if there are no customers and no sales, the company's assets have no value. Creating customers and retaining them are the key tasks of marketing. The product offerings should satisfy customers' needs so as to satisfy them. Marketing function of satisfying the customers is to be shared by other departments like production, finance and personnel. Marketing department should influence the decisions in other departments in such a way that the concerted action of the firm is for the satisfaction of the customer. In the early stages, the firm gives equal importance to all functional areas like production, finance, marketing and personnel. Several factors, as we have seen, make it adopt marketing orientation, thus gradually increasing the importance of the marketing function. A stage is soon reached where all other functions sub-serve the marketing function, which occupies a central position. When the marketing orientation becomes 100%, the customers' sovereignty is accepted, and the whole business is seen an organised from his viewpoint. Ultimately marketing becomes a bridge between the customer and all other functions of business.

The adoption of marketing is a slow process. It starts as a sales department in an organisation. Later on, other functions like advertising and sales promotion are added to the marketing department. Consumer orientation slowly creeps in and emphasis is placed on feedback and marketing research. The target market is defined by segmenting the market and selecting some specific segments for product offerings. The product, price, promotion and distribution make up the marketing mix which is adapted to suit the specific segments. A specific consumer benefit is then selected to appeal to a large section of the market, thus paving the way for market positioning. In its highly evolved form, marketing acquires a managerial orientation with elements of analysis, planning and control. It is a very slow journey from sales department to an integrated marketing department with managerial orientation. Kotler calls this the law of *slow learning.* Though marketing evolves slowly, many organisations slip back to the old ways of doing business and tend to neglect the customers once again. This tendency is called by Kotler as the law of *fast forgetting*.

❖ Social Orientation

Marketing has now acquired an added dimension — social responsibility. Marketing executives are expected to act in a socially responsible manner. They have to trade-off between the consumer wants and interests and the long-term social welfare. External pressures of diverse nature influence the marketing programme of a firm. Marketing has to show concern for natural resources, shortages, deleterious effects of certain products, non-biodegradable materials, pollution, environment etc. Marketing has to offer a better quality of life — rather than a mere standard of living.

❖ Spread of Marketing

Marketing has been adopted not only by the business organisations, but also by the Non-Profit Organisations (NPOs) like hospitals, universities, churches and performing arts groups. In India, NGOs (Non-Government Organisations) which are voluntary groups to promote a social cause use marketing campaigns for loss prevention, cancer detection, energy saving etc. International business has made marketing an international discipline. It has spread along with the multinationals all over the world. The western firms have entered the huge Indian, Chinese, South-East Asian markets. Marketing has registered its presence in these countries. Multinationals are also exploring marketing opportunities in East European countries, whose economies had so far remained *'closed'*.

❖ Relationship Marketing

It is an attempt at a long-term relationship and is an exercise in brand building, with interaction between the Brand and the Consumer. It goes beyond conventional marketing and seeks to establish an enduring relationship with the consumers. It is not just one transaction. It is an antithesis of sales promotion which is a short-term exercise — a temporary incentive for people to buy.

To institute relationship marketing, we have to start with the data on consumers.

Companies may offer schemes to its regular customers during sales and special offers.

Service industry like banks and hotels can also make effective use of relationship marketing. Communication here is more focused and effective.

Relationship marketing opens a two-way communication channel with consumers. It has the potential to win their loyalty.

❖ Recession Marketing

In recession, the demand is low. The sentiments are uncertain. Consumers demand value-for-money and emphasise safety and security. Budgets are strained. Consumer non-durables must be marketed aggressively. New segments can be tapped. Trials are induced by sampling. Multiple-media approach is used. Rural markets are tapped. Small packages are preferred. Consumer durables are badly hit. The functional aspect of the product are emphasised. Sales promotion is on the basis of exchange offers. There are many announcements regarding products. Products are sold directly. Credit facilities are made available. Services are priced lower to improve usage. Direct marketing is used to market services. Payment terms for services are made easier. Industrial products in recessionary times are sold through intensive direct marketing. Credit availability becomes the main criterion. Brand building around USP is done. In recessionary times, many new products are launched providing key customer benefits. Differentiation becomes key to survival. Brands are build around price. Commodity status brands use price promotions. Brand's value chain is rewritten to ward off the evil effects.

❖ Pareto Principle

Pareto principle gives the famous 80:20 ratio. Most companies know that 80 per cent of their profits come from 20 per cent of their customers. These are super-profitable customers. The cost of reaching them is the same as that of reaching other not-so-profitable customers. We can afford to pay less attention to these 80 per cent, and give more attention to the top 20 per cent. It is a good cost reduction exercise. We should not follow the carpet bombing strategy, but should identify our targets precisely. This is possible, by doing proper consumer and media research. What we need is focused marketing. In the 'Bag It' contest, Shoppers' Stop identifies regular spenders in the stores and invites them to join their First Citizens Club (FCC), entitling them to special offers and discounts.

❖ Home Delivery

The neighbourhood grocery store was the first to provide the home delivery facility to the consumers. But these days a wide range of companies and retailers are using it. Hindustan Lever has opened Sangam outlets which take orders of groceries on the phone. It acts as a differentiator and gives a larger market share. Food Bazaar uses this channel extensively. Fast food chains like Pizza Hut, Nirula's and McDonald's use this method. Cinema halls and multiplexes provide home delivery of tickets. Poultry sellers like Godrej Agrovet also provide this service. It helps consumers when they don't want to step out, say in monsoons or are too tired to do so. Sometimes, the unexpected guests are also taken care of. Working couples like home deliveries. Families with younger children also like this method. Home delivery is encouraged by high disposable incomes. It saves us the trouble of lugging heavy bags. Besides driving to mall in India is not easy. Home delivery makes the product more accessible. It is a push strategy. Retail bankers deliver DDs and cash at home. The service logistics should be worked out or else it may affect the brand image. Home delivery generates a data base useful to the company for research purposes.

❖ Viral Marketing

Viral marketing is a marketing activity in which the participants become the unpaid salesmen of the organization. Hotmail enlisted over 12 million users within the first 18 months of its operation. Each of the users filled up a detailed profile in exchange for a free e-mail account. The simple promotional tagline was getting your free, private email at www.hotmail.com. Google g-mail asked for referral, its USP being exclusivity. It made the numbers to stack up. Viral marketing works best for internet brands and dot coms. The jokes we forward to our friends over email is an example of viral marketing. A good viral triggers a chain reaction. Mass mailing is not viral, strictly speaking.

APPENDIX

Marketing to Children

Small kids are fussy while selecting their outfits in the retails stores. They may demand an outfit resembling that of a popular star in a recent movie. The search may last the whole day. Some kids may want a leather jacket similar to one Shah Rukh wears in a particular movie.

Children influence the buying decisions in almost a third of all purchase decisions taken for FMCG products. Children influence the decisions not only for kid products but also for products used by the family. Mostly, children affect decisions of buying toys and sports shoes. Of course, their opinion is valued for buying all other products. Children accompany their parents when they buy cars. Children love to use Titan watches, LG TVs, Coke, Cadbury chocolates and Santro Cars. Their favourite snacks are Britannia and Lays.

Parents love to get an opportunity to spend time with them. They also wash their guilt by spending for children. In small families with one or two kids, there is scope for doting on them. Children these days have their own independent identity. They love to have their own study-cum-bed room. They are better exposed to products thanks to Internet and satellite channels. When children participate in the decision, the parents feel proud. Children boast of the products their parents buy and this encourages their peers to exercise pressure on their parents to get similar products.

There are 32 million children between 8 and 19 in Sec. *A, B* and *C* in India. India's child population is 18.7% of the world's child population of 315 millions. A third of this child population in is below 15 years. In India, there are 47 million children below 15. They are part of *C* & *S* homes estimated to be 44 million. *C* & *S* home figure is growing by 15-20% TV channels. Children are exposed to these channels at an impressionable age. There is a special children channel 'Hungama' TV. ICCI Prudential Life Insurance sponsored Captain Hunt, a kids programme. It has a product Smartkid Insurance Policy. The protagonist in this commercial was a child. They received many calls from children on their helpline. They took the initiative in motivating the father to buy this policy. Even mothers were interested in this policy. There is a big connect between the Mother and the Child. ICCI Prudential therefore, directed its message towards both the mother and the child.

There are children's channels like Cartoon's Network, Pogo, Animax and Nickelodeon.

Companies direct their ad messages to children. Asian Paints have special shades for children's rooms. Malted beverages are targeted towards children. Goodlass Nerolac uses children in its commercial.

Children are emerging as the power centre. They deserve the marketer's attention.

Customer Relationship Management (CRM)

These days the companies have realised that success in today's competitive market place is by providing customer service of quality and their grievance redressal mechanism. A contact centre is one such mechanism which handles customer calls and complaints. It is a third-party customer contact desk. It goes beyond call handling, and tries to establish comprehensive customer relationship management system. These services are outsourced. Many companies from abroad are outsourcing significant amount of customer contact services from India. If companies just rely on their internal resources it may result in customer dissatisfaction. A plethora of communication devices may not be helpful. There should be a single response number. Customer contact centres are common in service industries like credit card companies, banks and cellular phone companies. Third party customer contact centres are increasingly being used by FMCG companies, consumer durable companies and insurance companies. These centres also provide telemarketing solutions. Some companies get forms filled up on-line, courier them to be signed, collect them with supporting documents and submit them. A call centre enters into an agreement with the company. In centralised model all calls across various cities are handled by Customer Service Representatives (CSR) in a single location. If the central location is at place called *X* and calls originate from *Y* and *Z* centres, they are received at the respective local switches to be re-routed to *X*. In distributed option, the local centres take care of the calls. The hybrid model is a mixture of the two. Companies improve brand perception by employing the services of call centres. A company will have to advertise a customer service number.

CRM is not just managing a call centre. It is a core business process which integrates various functions like call centre, marketing, sales, support, manufacturing and billing. We also use e-CRM which is internet-based. Small businesses thrive on personal touch *e.g.,* a local book-seller or a grocer CRM enables a large business to practise that personal touch. Business becomes fleet-footed and customer-oriented.

CRM application has three major segments — sales automation software, marketing automation software and customer support/call centre software.

Neuro Marketing

We come across a consumer who visit a hypermarket to buy a particular brand of jeans, but picks up just another brand on the spot since the physical characteristics of that brand were found to be more appealing. These last minute changes in consumer behavior can be explored by Functional Magnetic Resonance Imaging (FMRI). How the brain picks up signals from the environment becomes the subject matter of neuro marketing. Neuro marketing studies the marketing stimuli. It brings the understanding of the human brain to the marketing field. A negative attitude towards brands can be studied by FMRI test. It can separate the risk takers and the conservatives. It can guide marketers to design campaign that stimulate the risk takers to take action in favour of the brand. Imaging techniques capture the neural activity through sensors. The signals are processed, and a pattern established. All this is non-invasive.

Neuromarketers are also interested in deciphering the code passed by the optical nerve to the brain. It can answer questions related to the exposure either to the brand or its campaign and its buying. It also explores the possibility of the off-the-shelf buying in the retail environment.

Neuromarketing studies the marketing mix elements in terms of their being stimuli — packaging, pricing and distribution and the response to these.

In neuromarketing the areas of brain showing maximum activity while choosing or not choosing a brand are studied. The influencing factors are thus known and the products can be better positioned.

Industrial Marketing

Industrial marketing till recently was considered just a selling function. However, it has now emerged as a critical function, much more then mere selling. Prices are not just cost-plus, but are dictated by competition. This is one of the reasons for the shift of emphasis from selling to marketing. Technological advantage does not always give the competitive edge. It calls for a marketing approach. Many companies are keeping in touch with the market and the consumer. They are setting up Market Development Groups. These monitor the market and spot the opportunities for new and better products. Gabriel discovered through such a group that its shock absorbers have a new market, that of washing machines and exercise assignments. Product upgradation is also necessary. The manufacturing process should be geared to provide better values to the consumer. In purchasing, product features and specifications are the key factors. The industrial market is also being segmented e.g. high, medium and low voltage switchgears. There are image building corporate campaigns. Prior to selling, a presentation of the corporate profile is made. Mainstream advertising is used to project a corporate image.

The product information is critical and selling is based upon it, rather than emotional appeals. There is generic promotion. As the buyers are well-informed, there is no place for hard sell. The concept of consultative selling is growing. Though personal selling is still a major element of promotion, we come across seminars, exhibitions, business-to-business interactions and direct marketing. Companies like to cater to OEM market (Original Equipment Manufacturer). There is also a replacement and spares market. In selling to OEMs, the key factors are the quality and cost. The nature of the buying organisation also matters — whether it is the government, the private sector or the public sector. Public sector selling involves tendering. In defence selling, the quality and reputation of the manufacturer matter more. In government buying, two committees are involved in decision-making technical committee and price committees. The buying decision is based on purchase negotiations, the price, credit period, spares availability and after-sales-service. Service is emerging as a vital component of the marketing mix. Service has been made a revenue centre by many organisations. Channel decisions are also important in industrial marketing. Some companies operate through dealers or stockists. Some operate through distributors. When distributors are appointed, we have to deal with a small number of people and receiving payment is quite easier. But a dealer network ensures that the company is in touch with the marketing realities. A dealer provides valuable feedbacks.

Industrial marketers should not be limited to a small product range. They are vulnerable in a turbulent environment. They should resort to market segmentation. Industrial markets tend to be seasonal, affecting demand. Besides, technological advances change the consumer requirements. The reliability is a key factor in building reputation.

A single order in industrial markets could be worth several crores.

Several industrial marketers have ventured into consumer marketing with varying degrees of success *e.g.* The Tatas, Wipro, HMT, Andrew Yule, Crompton Greaves and TVS.

Evangelism Marketing

It is an advanced form of Word Of Mouth Marketing (WOMM) in which companies develop customers who believe so strongly in a particular product/service that they try to convince others to buy and use it.

Niche Marketing

Premium brands are marketed to the chosen few through exclusive events and entertainment programmes. This is a route that takes 'class media' rather than 'mass media'. It is essential to find a match between the event and target audience. A mismatch results in a failure. The real measure of success is how far the brand can leverage from the event.

There are children's channels like Cartoon Network, Pogo, Animax and Nickelodeon. Companies direct their ad messages to children. Asian Paints have special shades for children's rooms. Malted beverages are targeted towards children Goodlass Nerolac uses children in its commercial. Children are emerging as the power centre marketers they deserve the marketer's attention.

Marketing to Senior Citizens

Marketing opportunity	*Products patronized*
Leisure	Use leisure resorts and clubs.
Finance	Investments — fixed deposits, mutual funds, shares and securities.
Travel	Pilgrimage, Domestic Travel, International Travel, visit to Children, Holidaying
Consumer Goods and Durables	Buy durables products like garments, chocolates, natural products.

Customer Lifetime Value

Customer Lifetime Value (CLV) is the present value of the likely future income stream generated by an individual purchaser. Managers seek out more refined measures of CLV, using data-intensive procedures to identify top customers in terms of their likely future purchasing patterns.

The aim is not just the identification of customers. It goes beyond that — how to reach these customers through cross-selling, up-selling multi-channel marketing and other tactics. These are tied to metrics on attrition, retention and churn. These statistics are known as RFM — regency, frequency and monetary value. RFM has its roots in direct marketing, one of the most progressive industries to use CLV concepts. This method uses purchase transaction history.

CLV looks upon customer as a resource from whom companies try to derive as much value as possible. CLV is one component of Customer Relationship Management (CRM). It is difficult, however, to calculate CLV and more difficult to use it.

The easily available number is that of customer's current profitability. It can be used to design different programmes for different segments. But this may displease some customers.

It is difficult to predict retention of a customer and his growth. Therefore, we also really do not know how profitable our customers are.

The identification of key customers still has a strong intuitive component.

Tradition CLV considers the net present value of all income generated by one customer. We assume here that at some point the customer will defect. It leads to underestimation of the database. Though there is attrition, at the same time, we have to consider acquisition of new customers while valuing the database. It is important to maximize the database value and not the customer value.

There can be a strong increase in the expected time a customer will stay with you as you improve the average service quality. There are other factors too — competitor's strategy, cost of switching services for a customer, the evolution of technology. There is a natural service level standard. In call centres, for example, answering 80 p.c. of calls in 20 seconds or less is a common standard. The more the competition, the higher the industry standard.

* * *

2 MANAGERS AND ENVIRONMENT

All business organisations operate in an environment. The environment has several distinct components: political, economic, demographic or social, legal, public, technological and others. Business activities should be adjusted to these components of the environment and changes in these components. All these components interact and affect one another and in turn a business organisation. To some extent, a business organisation also affects the environment.

The environment is constantly changing. The change may be relatively faster for some industries and slower for some others. The change may be faster for some components of the environment and slower for some other components. All this needs the adaptation of the organisation to its environment. The environment is also full of business opportunities and poses some threats to the organisation. It is thus obvious that constant monitoring of the environment is necessary for business planning. In fact, the study of the prevailing environment and the environment of near future form an integral part of business planning.

Success or failure in business depends upon a variety of factors, some of which may be beyond our direct control. These factors beyond our control arise from the work environment. Business operates always in an environment and not in vacuum. Business managers while taking decisions always have to take into account their environment. It is, therefore, necessary to know precisely the meaning of the term "environment."

❖ Meaning

The word "environment" is a collectivity of all the factors within the control of the business and beyond the control of the individual business.

Environment is a macro-concept and a business unit is a micro-concept. In the given environmental factors, the firm operates. These environmental factors may be political, economic, legal, technological etc. Some factors may be static, some dynamic. Some factors may be quantitative, whereas some are qualitative. Environment is, therefore, a complex phenomenon.

The environmental factors vary from country-to-country, region-to-region and time-to-time. Environment could be the present environment or future environment.

Environment could be market environment or non-market environment. The former is influenced by market forces. The latter is influenced by non-market factors like social, cultural, government's laws etc.

Broadly, environment is economic, but we cannot neglect the non-economic environment which has economic implications, *e.g.*, social and cultural environment.

❖ Environment in India

Indian environment has undergone rapid changes. India has allowed the private sector's entry into infrastructural sector like power, telecommunications, roads and transport. Rupee has been made convertible on current account. The Tarapore Committee has recommended full convertibility in the next three years. The fiscal deficit stands at 5.5 per cent of GDP in 2012. There is a record food production — 185 million tonnes and stocks of 30 million tonnes.

In future, it is expected that both domestic and foreign trade will be freer. There will be more agrarian reforms. The excise duty structure will be revamped. The customs duty rates will be brought on par with other Asian countries. Petroleum and coal prices will be decontrolled. The inflation rate has dropped to single digit. India expects an average growth rate of 8.1 per cent thus coming out of the Hindu growth rate of 3.5 per cent after a long spell. Even during this slow down, experts estimate a growth rate between 6-7 per cent.

India has concentrated now on infrastructure like power, transport and communications. There is a power shortage now in certain areas and plans are afoot to reduce the shortfall by sanctioning and setting up new power plants by inviting private sector and by improving the plant load factor of existing power plants. India imports around 50 per cent of its total consumption of crude oil. Railways are state-owned and account for 77 per cent of passenger traffic and 55 per cent of total freight traffic. India handles around 95 per cent of her 100 million tonnes of two-way cargo through 12 major ports — Mumbai, Chennai, Kandla, Marmagao, Vizag, Kolkata, Haldia, Cochin, Tuticorin, New Mangalore, Paradip and Nhava Sheva. Containerisation is picking up, but still it is only 7 per cent of the total cargo handled. India's merchant fleet has 800 ships. India is slowly moving to 'open skies' policy in respect of civil aviation. Private airlines like Jet Airways, SpiceJet and Kingfisher are operating for the last several years. Recently, they have been allowed to fly to foreign destinations. No-frills low-cost air-lines like Air Deccan and Spice Jet have also started their operations. India happens to be a major buyer of aircrafts such as Boeing and Air Bus, Air freight accounts for 25 per cent of total export freight by value, though less than 8 per cent by tonnage. India has around 150 thousand post offices across the country. Of late, the private courier system is developing well. Telecom revolution has just begun in India with rural telephones, cellular phones, STD centres, more PCOs, videophones etc. India has both the GSM and CDMA: Code Division Multiple Access phones. Both Reliance and the Tatas offer Fixedtime Wireless Telephones (FWT). Cellular phones have outstripped the landline phones. Media scene has shown a tremendous growth of electronic media recently, with as many as 500 plus channels available through satellite TV. India has recently permitted DTH: Direct to Home TV. We have several DTH players — Tata sky, Dish TV, DD Direct, Big TV, Videocon and Airtel Bharati. Industrial production has picked up of late. Agriculture shows healthy growth due to good monsoons. Presently, its growth rate is 3 per cent plus. Despite the general economic slow down, one encouraging trend which is visible since 1991-92 in continuation of economic reforms process since 1991-92 irrespective of political changes in the country. Exports now account for close to 20 per cent of GDP, and currency has appreciated almost 10 per cent against the dollar. During the current slowdown, exports in 2008-09 have fallen down to 3.4 per cent. This is the lowest rate in seven years. Our savings rate continues to be high and healthy. It grow from 10% in 1950s to 24% in 2000, to around 34% in 2008. It is only second to China's, where it is 50% of GDP. Besides 65% of Indian GDP stems from private consumption, unlike the Chinese model. In these challenging times, India is among the only two countries to grow between 6.5% and 8%, the other being China.

❖ Nature and Scope of Environment

The organisational environment is anything and everything external to it. But it is difficult to delimit an organisation's boundary — where it ends and the environment begins. An organisation itself is having its own internal environment which is penetrated by many external factors and its own specific environment of suppliers, dealers and competitors. All this is surrounded by general environment of many macro-factors like economic, politico-legal, technological, demographic, socio-cultural factors etc.

ENVIRONMENT

External Macro-Environment	**Specific Task Environment**	**Internal Environment**
1. Political	1. Input suppliers	1. People
2. Economic	2. Output mechanism	2. Culture
3. Legal	3. Marketing intermediaries	3. Their work ethos
4. Social	4. Competitive Environment	4. Attitudes and values
5. Technological		
6. Natural		
7. International etc.		

Fig. 2.1 Nature and Scope of Environment

What is then environment of business?

❖ Internal Environment

Though we appreciate the blanket of the external environment consisting of several components like social, political, technological and the like, we tend to neglect the internal environment of the organisation consisting of its people, their work ethos and culture. The major participants in the organisation share a set of attitudes towards what they want to accomplish and what they think of, is of value. The Organisation Culture (OC) may be favourable or unfavourable to the total overall development. All this constitutes organisational environment. The organisation's internal environment interacts with the whole of external environment.

Let us now acquaint ourselves with the task environment of business.

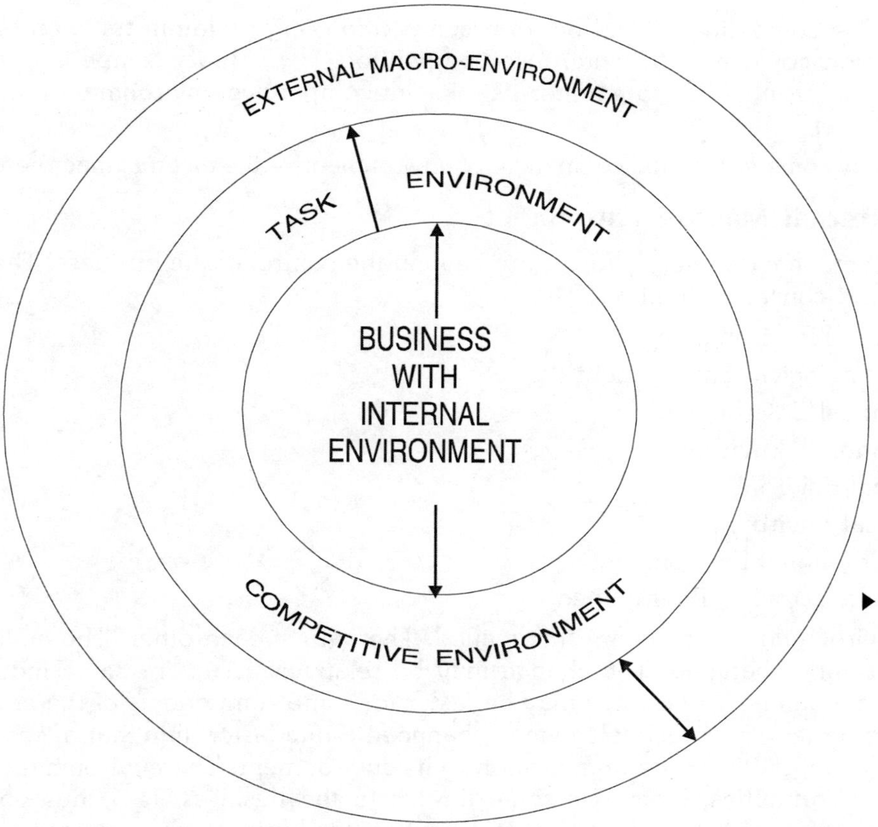

Fig. 2.2 Business Environment: Interactions

❖ Task Environment

It is the environment for an individual business. It consists of those forces outside the organisation which are directly relevant to the decision-making and transformation process of the individual organisation.

Most organisations are resource conversion machines where inputs from the environment are converted into outputs of products to be carried to the market either directly or through marketing intermediaries (dealers, distributors, retailers etc.). A typical organisation thus accomplishes its purpose by operating through its task environment.

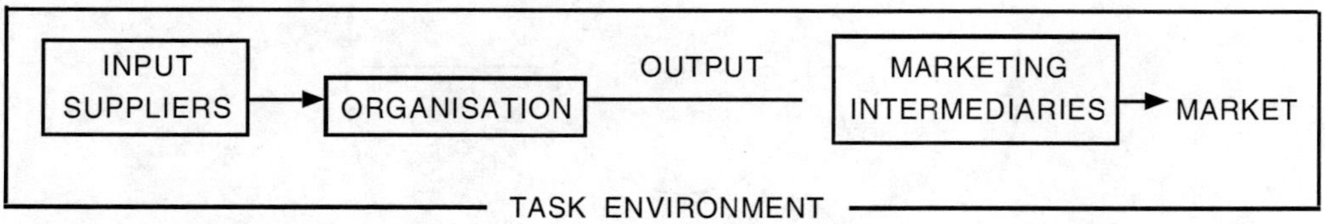

Fig. 2.3 Task Environment

The task environment is surrounded by competitive environment which interacts with it. The competitors could be generic competitors, *e.g.*, for a tonic, a yoga class is a generic competitor. The competition could be form competition, *e.g.*, vitamin tonic and iron tonic. The competition could also be enterprise competition, *e.g.*, Boots competing with Glaxo. Each individual business has to monitor its relevant competitive environment and formulate suitable strategies.

Let us now come to the final component of environment — the external macro-environment.

❖ The External Macro-Environment

The external environmental forces are beyond the control of the business. The following factors demand constant attention.

1. Natural Environment
2. Technological Environment
3. Political Environment
4. Economic Environment
5. Legal Environment
6. Social Environment
7. International Environment
8. Other factors of Environment.

The environmental factors are intertwined. They affect each other. The environmental trend is constantly changing. The change may be relatively faster for some industries and slower for some others. The change may be faster for some components of the environment, and slower for others, *e.g.*, technology may change at a rate faster than that of social change. All this needs adaptation of the organisation to its environment. The environment is also full of business opportunities and poses some threats to the business. It is thus obvious that constant monitoring of the environment is necessary for business or corporate planning.

We shall now examine some of the components of the external environment of business. We propose to study chiefly the following components:

(1) Demographic Environment, (2) Economic and Legal Environment, (3) Cultural Environment, (4) Technological Environment, (5) Natural Environment and (6) Social Environment.

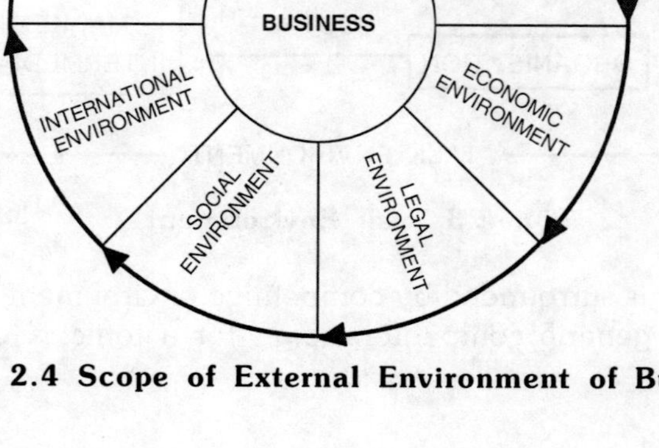

Fig. 2.4 Scope of External Environment of Business

1. Demographic Environment

The population in the country and its growth rate, the trend towards urbanisation, the vast untapped rural market with peculiar characteristics, the unemployment level, the literacy level, the technical manpower, the managerial manpower, the brain drain, the ratio of men to women, the occupational and agewise composition of population, the consumption pattern and reading habits of population, the labour market and its unionisation, the life-styles of people — all these demographic aspects of population greatly influence the decision-maker in a business enterprise.

Indian Demography: India is the second largest country in Asia. She is also the second most populous country in the world. With a population of approaching 900 million, it ranks next only to China. The population is growing at around 2 per cent per annum. More than 70 per cent of the people live in the rural areas.

Over 80% of the people are Hindus, and around 11% practise Islam. Other religions represented are Christianity, Sikhism, Buddhism, Jainism and Zoroastrianism.

More than 700 languages and dialects are spoken in India. There are 15 scheduled languages. Hindi is the most widely understood language (40%). English is widely used in commerce, government, courts, media, higher education, along with Hindi and the regional language of the respective state.

India has a strong educational infrastructure, and third largest pool of technical manpower. The average literacy rate is 53% (1991) as compared to 44%. (1981). Very small section of population takes higher education, but the quality of education is competitive.

India has a burgeoning middle class, estimated at over 150 million people, with a significant buying power, constituting a market larger than many European countries. The disposable income of this group is estimated at around ₹ 1,000 billion or about US $ 30 billion.

India's rural market of 6 lakhs villages and small towns has become an important segment for the sale of prepacked consumer goods. Apart from the consumer market, there are opportunities in capital goods market and services market.

India has a vast pool of scientific and technical talent, a dynamic entrepreneur class and a well-developed managerial base. India has both technical and non-technical labour base. Some 30 million people are engaged in manufacturing, 40 million in services such as transport and trading.

2. Economic and Legal Environment

The broad characteristics of the economic system in which the business operates constitute the macro-economic environment.

Today's economic environment is complex where business interfaces economically with the government, the capital market, the household sector and the foreign sector. All these sectors of the economy collectively affect the trends and structure of the economy.

The design and structure of the economic system relevant for the macro-economic decisions is a result of socio-political conditions. In a democracy, the government is accountable to people through Parliament. The cabinet is the decision-making body in a parliamentary form. In the presidential form, the President is the decision-maker. The federal structure allows more decentralised decision-making than the unitary form. Political environment and political decisions are associated with economic implications. After all, the government manages the economy. The government's political ideology guides its policies regarding the ownership, control and regulation of economic activities, *e.g.*, capitalist government allows full scope to the private sector, communist government makes all economic decisions by itself, a mixed economy allows the private sector and the public sector to co-exist.

Whatever may be the form of the government, certain economic problems of choice of the alternative use of scarce economic resources are common. Just allocation of resources and subsequent optimum production is the common concern everywhere. Economies function by solving problems of product mix, technology adopted, distribution suggested.

Most economies function by having a mix of "free market mechanism" and "centralised planning". In most economies government intervention is on the increase in the field of economic activities. Each state now tends to become a 'welfare state' for which it brings forth economic legislations. Modern economies, being open, are actively engaged in international trade and co-operation.

The above is a broad framework of the economic environment, which changes continuously. Even the non-economic factors also have economic implications. Business has, therefore, to monitor the environment vigilantly.

The following are the critical elements of the economic environment:

Critical Elements	*Definitions*
Economic System	Institutional framework of the environment. Indian economy operates through a combination of planning and pricing as it is a mixed model.
Nature of Economy	Physical framework of the environment. Consider the level of development and structure, level of per capita income, composition of per capita income, saving and investments. Occupational structure etc.
Anatomy of the Economy	Physical anatomy. Our economy consists of household sector, the corporate business sector, the administration of government, the capital market and the foreign sector.
Functioning of the Economy	The role of money, the role of planning, administered prices, free market prices and central banking.
Economic Planning	It is supposed to give direction to the changes in economic environment. Ours is planning by incentives.
Economic Policy Statements and Proposal	The implementation of planning is through the mechanism of economic policy, statements and legislations.
Economic Controls and Regulations	Thus we have: 1. Industrial Policy 2. Agricultural Policy 3. Fiscal-cum-Budgetary-Policies 4. Money & Credit Policies of the Central bank. 5. Physical policies of controls and regulations 6. Import-Export Policy 7. Price Control, Trade Control & Exchange Control etc.
Economic Legislations	These give effect to certain policies like: 1. Industrial Development and Regulation Act. 2. Company Act. 3. Minimum Wages Act etc.

Critical Elements	*Definitions*
Economic Trends & Structures	: The functioning of the economy is reflected in the long-term trends in the macro-economic variables like income, money supply, price, balance of payment, employment etc.
Economic Problems & Prospects	: Some of the trends are indicative of the problems. Problems like inflation, unemployment, recession, etc.

Background of Indian Economic Environment: India is a mixed economy, where private and public sectors co-exist. There are many sectors in India.

1. Amongst the private sector, we have organised and unorganised sectors. Then we have the tiny and village industries sector, the Small Scale Industries (SSI) sector, the medium and large industries sector. Private sector and public sector have joined hands (as in Maharashtra Bajaj Scooters and Government of Maharashtra) and formed the joint sector. Some private undertakings are foreign multinationals (MNCs).
2. Amongst the public sector, we have companies, corporations and departments. Public sector could be state government sector or the central government sector or could also be a joint sector.
3. We also have a network of co-operatives — industrial, housing, consumer, tribal, sugar, dairy etc.
4. We have heavy industries and light industries. We have the core sector and national sector. We have licensed and delicensed sectors. It is, in short, a whole complex of sectors.

   In Indian economy, we find a great variety of mechanism for working out our planning and pricing. Five Year Plans (FYP), annual plans, decentralised plans, plan holidays, rolling plans, qualitative plans mark our planning system.
5. Technology upgradation.
6. Quality orientation.
7. Re-orientation of the public sector including the development of its managerial cadre.
8. MRTP Act Amendment taking assets of dominant industry to 100 crores and then removing this ceiling also from 1991.
9. Taxation reforms as per the recommendations of Chelliah Committee. Kelkar Committee has suggested removal of a whole lot of deductions.
10. Full convertibility of rupee on the trade account and for NRI transactions and also on current account.
11. Foreign companies can invest in Indian companies' equity liberally.
12. Import duties have been slashed, and so also the excise duties.

Effects: Indian economy is becoming more and more outward oriented and is opening up. It has to be integrated to the global economy. It should, therefore, be a market-friendly economy.

1. Indian business received a new lease of life. Public sector undertakings are now expected to bring in adapted technology and wed to the concept of modernisation. There is disinvestment of a portion of equity holdings in select public sector undertakings. The banks have started offering their equity to the general public.
2. Human resource development has received the attention it deserves.

3. Private sector has been assigned a more challenging role. There are more joint sector plants. The areas reserved for core sector have been thrown open in some selected cases to the private sector. Heads of private corporations have been inducted into the Boards of Air India and Indian Airlines. Licensing has been liberalised. A new ministry of Information Technology (IT) has been set up. It has been given special attention.
4. The government wishes to build a capital market (cf. G.S.Patel Committee).
5. There is a march towards 'efficiency-oriented system'.
6. The stifling controls of IDRA, MRTP and FERA have been dispensed with and developmental aspects of these legislations have been emphasised.
7. Taxation policy is now growth oriented. Export orientation and quality orientation have been emphasised.
8. All manufacturing industries have recorded a growth rate of almost 8 per cent.
9. LTFP has introduced an element of openness in the system and business planning has become sharper than ever before.
10. Priority sector is receiving all encouragement after branch expansion of Indian banks (52000 from 8000 in 1969).
11. VAT is being introduced in 22 states from April 1, 2005.
12. Fiscal deficit in budgets have been controlled at 6 per cent of GDP and have been curtailed further to control inflation.
13. Private banks have been given licenses. Banking reforms are on the card. Private firms have entered the insurance sector. Insurance Regulatory Authority has been set up.

Capital Issues Control: Formerly, Controller of Capital Issues exercised control over big issues, bonus shares, premiums, convertible debentures etc. CCI's office has now been made redundant after recent policy changes announced to liberalise the capital market. SEBI has been given more powers.

Indian Economic Environment: In the mid-80's India's growth slowly started by liberalising her economy, and by the time Rajiv Gandhi took over as PM, the winds of liberalisation blowed strongly. It goes to the credit of Narasimha Rao and Dr. Manmohan Singh that they deregulated the economy a great deal, set in motion a process of reforms and made every effort to integrate our economy to the global market trends.

In this millennium, the economy did show the fastest growth — growth accelerated to the extent of 8.1 per cent. There was broad based industrial growth to the extent of 8 per cent supported by a robust agricultural performance. Food grains production attained 185 million tonnes.

From a level of hardly one billion dollars in June 1991 today by mid-Feb 1995, we have burgeoning foreign exchange reserves in excess of US $ 80 billion plus. In 2006, they stand at $144 billion or ₹ 6,48,000 crore, covering imports for 13 months.

Over the decades between 1950 to 1990, the real national income has grown at the rate of 3.9 per cent per annum, and per capita income at 1.7 per cent per year. In the 80s, there was accelerated growth (growth rate rising to 5.4 per cent in national income and 3.2 per cent in per capita income). The share of agricultural sector in national income has sharply declined. The share of industrial sector has nearly doubled.

The following industries are reserved for the public sector:

1. Arms and ammunition and allied lists of defence equipment, defence aircraft and warships.
2. Atomic energy.
3. Coal and lignite.
4. Mineral oils.
5. Minerals specified in the schedule to the Atomic Energy (Control of production and Use) Order, 1953.
6. Railway Transport.

During 1994-95, the National Mineral Policy was reviewed and the Mines and Mineral Development Act amended, to open up this sector to private and foreign investment. Thirteen minerals have been dereserved for exploitation by the private sector. The RBI based automatic approval policy for foreign investment was made applicable to mining (except for atomic minerals and minerals fuels), subject to a limit of 50 per cent on foreign equity.

The power sector, so far the preserve of the public sector, has been thrown open to private sector. It has received 138 private proposals for creating 58,745 mega-watts of capacity.

The National Telecom Policy, 1994 allows private provision of basic telecom services. The National Telecom Regulatory Authority (TRA) has now been set up.

The new Air Corporation Act, 1994 enables private air taxi companies to operate as regular domestic airlines. In 2005, private airlines have been allowed to operate international flights.

The National Highway Act is proposed to be amended to allow private participation in the construction, maintenance and operation of roads on Build-Operate-Transfer (BOT) basis. Private participation is allowed in port-related activities. The NDA government started the Golden Quadrilateral project of building road infrastructure to connect the four metros. The UPA government has decided to continue this project. The national highway development authority has been set up.

Tax Reforms: Import duties have been gradually reduced since 1991, in keeping with the government policy. Peak tariff levels have been reduced from 150 per cent in 1991-92, to 85 per cent in 1993-94, and further down to 25 per cent now. Import duties on most capital goods are down to 25 per cent. However, on several items, a Counter Vailing Duty (CVD) on capital goods has been re-imposed.

Excise duties are collected on MODVAT basis and it has been extended to capital goods to boost domestic production.

Shri Chidambaram introduced the lower direct tax rates. The minimum income-tax to be paid was brought down to 30 per cent. Voluntary Disclosure of Income Scheme (VDIS) was introduced, which became a grand success with tax collection close to ₹ 10,000 crores (1997). People in the metro occupying flats, having telephone connections undertaking foreign travels and owning cars are expected to file returns. Income-tax rates, both for the individuals and corporations, have been reduced. There is an attempt to broad-base the tax basket. Assumptive taxes have been introduced. Direct Tax Code is being proposed.

Financial Sector Reforms: Several private banks have been given licences like the HDFC Bank Ltd., Ind-Indus Bank etc. In 1994-95, six private banks were set up. Public sector banks were given additional capital. The ratio between capital to assets in 1993-94 was four. Nationalised banks offered a part of their share holdings to public. Prudential norms were announced for non-banking financial companies. They are now to be registered with the RBI. There was complete decontrol of interest rates on large loans. Institutional reforms for strengthening the financial systems continued. Cash reserve ratio stands at 5 per cent in 2006. The Government has recently amended the Banking Law to enable the RBI to issue new banking licences from 2013.

Capital Market: SEBI has been set up as a regulatory body. Greater transparency of transactions was its avowed aim. Rules have been announced for private placement and for allotment of shares to promoters. A new take-over code has been announced. The National Stock Exchange of India commenced operation in June, 1994. (Wholesale debt market segment). It started equity trading from November 1994. It has screen-based scripless trading system, and VSAT satellite links. Foreign institutional investors rose from 158 to 286 during 1994-95.

There is a very large Foreign Direct Investment (FDI) in Indian capital market though it is not as good as that in China. Foreign equity inflow has been of three types and in roughly equal measure:

(*i*) Direct foreign investment in Indian ventures.

(*ii*) Purchase of Indian stocks by overseas mutual funds and investment companies, and

(*iii*) Indian issues in overseas markets.

Mutual funds which were a state monopoly have been thrown open to private parties. SEBI has approved several private sectors sponsors to set up mutual funds in India.

Indian firms, aggressively tapped Euro dollar markets. India's current preference is for equity, rather than debt. Most issues were for Global Depository Receipts (GDRs) held in trust by off-shore managers on behalf of individual investors. There are three credit rating agencies in India — Credit Rating Information Services of India (CRISIL), Investment Credit Rating Agency (ICRA) and Credit Research and Analysis (CRA). Rating is mandatory for debt obligations such as debenture issues and fixed deposits and short-term instruments such as Commercial Paper (CP). Indian companies can now invest upto $ 15 million in overseas joint ventures without waiting for any clearance from the government. The first Indian MNCs might be on the way soon.

Small Sector: Small-scale industries in India employ 14 million workers and account for 40 per cent of our total manufacturing output and 35 per cent of our exports. This sector needs a strong marketing orientation to avoid sickness and to help it grow from small to medium to large-scale.

Foreign Trade: India's foreign trade accounts for $ 80 billion. International trade has assumed an increasing role in the Indian economy.

Major imports are fuels, capital goods and manufactured inputs. Until recently exports lagged behind the imports, resulting in an adverse balance of payment situation. The trade deficit has now fallen.

In recent years, exports growth is spectacular. Indian's export basket is versatile. It has a wide variety of products and caters to a wide variety of markets. There is a good export potential, particularly for value-added goods as compared to commodity exports. To acquire competitive positioning in global markets, India needs a strong expertise in international marketing.

The government remains committed to driving modernisation process and continues to reduce tariff barriers whilst making meaningful strides in moving the rupee towards full convertibility.

The burgeoning foreign exchange reserves, in excess of US $ 80 billion, is another record for India. The reserves have been built up by the capital inflows and a substantial reduction in the trade deficit.

The five-year Export-Import Policy signifies dismantling of import controls over a large number of products. The import duties have been rationalised. Exports have been encompassed by policy modifications, especially of agricultural products and services. Imports duties have been brought down from the peak levels of 150 per cent to 25 per cent today. Import duties on most of capital goods are down to 25 per cent The government is moving towards full convertibility of the rupee. Exporters can now retain 25 per cent of forex earnings in foreign currency accounts to meet business related expenditures.

The government proposes the announce steps for Capital Account Convertibility (CAC) shortly. It will give freedom to buy shares, mutual funds, deposits in overseas banks, real estate, gold, silver etc. for public at large and corporate and financial institutions without any currency restrictions by the RBI. Currently, the rupee is fully converted for trade in goods and services, but restrictions placed on international asset acquisition by way of various limits set by RBI.

Economic and Non-Economic Environment Interface: It may be noted that economic environment influences the sociological environment and vice versa. The work ethos of Japan, a part of social environment, results in high productivity, a part of economic environment. Similarly, education — cultural environment and economic environment are inter-related. For example, there is no educational background in the gulf countries and so to build their economic environment, they import manpower from other countries. The political stability makes way for business expansion and growth and allows entrepreneurs to take risks and invest money. Socialistic leanings or leftlist policies may harm business interests. Legislations hamper as well as promote business interests. All these legislation are socio-economic politico-economic in character. Business also decides the role of the rulers, just as rulers decide that of the business. The historical environment and business environment are also interdependent. We have inherited the present economic environment from past historical environment. There is also an interface between our natural resources and economic environment. We are thus a country exporting tea and importing capital goods. Business may improve the physical environment or may destroy it. Everywhere, a stand has been taken against pollution and business is expected to be anti-pollutant and pro-(physical)-environment.

Liberalisation: The 90s unfettered Indian industry. With this, the power and aspirations of billion people were unleashed. The freedom experienced by people is just over a decade old. In post-independence India, the first 40 years were years of large scale state intervention. There was a small private sector, who had learnt to live with and exploit the licence and quota raj. Competition was an alien word. The consumer suffered in the process.

Liberalisation witnessed an end to all this. Moreover, it ushered in the freedom of mind. A billion people rose to release their potential. There is a feeling that Indian can do it. Just see how the BPO industry has emerged creating jobs for 17 lac people and generating a revenue of ₹ 5,500 crores.

India has to stake the baggage of 40 years such as low manufacturing scales, lack of branding and marketing and poor processes. We have to leverage its low-cost but skilled work-force.

India was bound within the confines of an artificial economic wall. The walls have fallen. The world is for India's taking.

Liberalisation of Different Sectors: We shall briefly consider the liberalisation of different sectors.

Finance:

- In 1992, Indian companies were allowed access to foreign funds.
- Banking was thrown open to private parties in 1993-94. Even mutual funds were thrown open to private parties.
- Foreign institutional investment was permitted in Indian debt and equity in 1994.
- Since 1995, the process of freeing the interest rates charged by banks was initiated by the RBI. Interest rates have fallen down considerably.
- Insurance has been opened to the private sector in 2000.

Petroleum:

- In 1992, oil exploration and refining was opened up to foreign investment.
- ONGC has been corporatised (1993). LPG distribution was opened to the private sector. (1993)
- Petroleum distribution has been thrown open to private players. (1998)
- Administered Price Mechanism (APM) has been dismantled (2002).

Automobiles: This is the most liberalised sector of the economy. It started with the permission to foreign investors to have 40 per cent equity in joint-ventures to manufacture 100-cc mobikes. (1993). The sector was opened to licence free investment both Indian and Foreign (1993). The indigenisation stipulation on foreign companies were axed. (2001). Maruti's control was handed over to Suzuki. (2002). The government disinvested Maruti by selling a quarter of stake to Indian public (2003).

Telecom: Private operators were given licence for cellphone and landline services (1994). Private ISPs were allowed in 1998, breaking the monopoly of then public sector company VSNL. Cell licences switched over to revenue sharing (1999). In 2001, limited mobility (WLL) services were allowed to landline operators. There is a switch to unified licence now. There was allocation of 2G spectrum on first-cum-first-served basis, and then for 3G on competitive auction basis.

Aviation: Though this sector has seen some liberalisation, much needs to be done. In 1992, under the Open Sky Policy, air taxi operators were issued licences. They have been given the status of airline in 1997. Till 1993, IA was the only domestic sector carrier with a flight schedule. There are several private airlines now. *e.g.*, Jet Airways, Kingfisher etc.

Infotech: Like automobiles, this is another most liberalised sector of Indian economy. Software companies were given a tax holiday in 1991. In 1998, the government created an information technology ministry. In 2000, the government enacted cyber-laws. Infosys, TCS, Wipro, HCL are well-established IT companies of India. Satyam has been taken over by Mahendra Tech in 2009.

Legal Environment: Right from the time of locating the business, till the distribution of dividends amongst the shareholders, the activities of a corporation are controlled and regulated. The legislations that make up the legal environment of business in India can be listed here; the list, however, is illustrative and not exhaustive:

- Companies Act, 1956
- Capital Issues Control Act, 1947
- MRTP Act, 1969

- FERA, 1970 which is replaced by Foreign Exchange Management Act (FEMA)
- Trade Unions Act
- Factories Act
- Bonus Act, 1961
- Social Security Enactments
- Laws for Consumers' Protection
- Law for Managerial Remuneration
- Essential Commodities Act, 1974
- COFEPOSA. The Conservation Of Foreign Exchange and Prevention Of Smuggling Activities Act, 1974
- Sick Industrial Companies Act, 1985

The students should also note that there is Packaged Commodities Act, Misrepresentation of Women (Indecent Ads) Act, Consumer Protection Act, 1986 which also form the legal environment of business.

3. Cultural Environment

Culture is a part of the social environment of business. Business cannot afford to neglect cultural trends. Culture differs over space, time and societies.

It may be noted that what we call culture is socially transmitted, rather than genetically. Culture is a complex wholly made up of knowledge, beliefs, art, morals, law, customs and conventions, other capabilities and habits. Culture is acquired by man as a member of society.

In short, culture refers to the following:

1. Social interaction's product.
2. Means to fulfil our social and biological needs.
3. Transmitted from generation-to-generation in a given society. It is therefore cumulative.
4. Symbolic and hence meaningful.
5. Learned and acquired as a part of socialisation.
6. Basic characteristic of personality.
7. Society should function continuously to make a culture survive.

Culture, however is independent of any individual or group.

We can describe culture as either material culture of concrete objects or non-material culture of abstract things like values, beliefs, ideals etc.

Core Cultural Values have High Persistence: Many beliefs and values of people are not equally important. Those that are steadfastly followed can be called their *core beliefs* and *values* and have a high degree of persistence.

For example, most Indians believe in working for livelihood, in getting married, in giving to charity and in being religious. These beliefs influence through everyday life. Core beliefs and values are inherited and are always reinforced by other institutions of society.

Secondary Beliefs and Values: People also hold secondary beliefs and values. These are subject to change in the wake of new social forces. Believing in the institution of marriage is a core belief, but believing people ought to marry within caste is a secondary belief.

Managers and business are well-advised not to violate the core beliefs but can hope to modify the secondary cultural values.

Secondary Cultural Values Undergo Shifts through Time: Although core culture values are fairly persistent, there are shifts occurring during a time frame. We have seen hippies, Beatles and Playboy lifestyles. We have seen long hair, jeans life style. Over a period of time, these life-styles have changed, leading to changes in behaviour.

The measurement and forecasting of cultural change is still highly speculative. Some big organisations, MR firms and futurists release periodic reports to summarise cultural trends.

Culture shows Preferences: Society decides which things in life are attractive and unattractive as objects of desire. This is called preferences. Preferences are not the same from culture-to-culture, time-to-time, and region-to-region. Culture decides our taste standards (in specific lines of human activity). A street urchin enjoys beating a dog; it is his culture. A music lover enjoys Bhimsen Joshi; it is his culture. Tastes are seen in food, housing and its decor, clothing, sexual practices, a great variety of our possessions and activities.

Product development and design, branding, packaging, labelling, promotion, distribution — all these are greatly affected by cultural preferences.

Each Culture Consists of Sub-Cultures: A society consists of people who share the same core beliefs and values. Yet there are always certain groups of non-conformists, such as criminals and saboteurs. Furthermore, there can be much diversity in the secondary beliefs and values people hold, giving rise to sub-cultures. For example, ethnic groups, caste groups, the elite groups, the intelligentsia are sub-cultures within a culture because they display somewhat different systems of beliefs and values.

A clear articulation of different secondary patterns of belief and behaviour is seen in *life-style groups.* A life-style group is one whose members share similar attitudes, interests and opinions. The persons making up a life-style group are similar in likes, wants and needs. The various life-style groups have somewhat different product, brand and media preferences. Thus business makes life-style segmentation a very important marketing tool for certain products like cigarettes and soft drinks.

Cultural Pattern: Social structure is an important determinant of the cultural pattern. Society is stratified into upper middle class, middle class and lower class people. Each strata has unique cultural characteristics. Social and economic institutions also affect cultural pattern. The caste system, the joint family system, the child marriage, the patriarchal family: all these are examples of social institutions and systems. India had till recently an occupational caste system. Joint family had the Karta — the decision-maker. Social set up defined the position of women and children.

In India, most of the age-old institutions are crumbling under the pressure of changed social values and attitudes. Individualism is now more important than collectivism. Women of today no longer want to remain confined to the four walls of the house. Business is also not a prerogative of any caste or community. Customs have become flexible.

Cultural pattern is also decided by traits — a unit of observation or normative behaviour. TV announcer wishing us 'namaste' is a trait. Traits form a larger trait complex — a collection of inter-related traits. Many of our promotional methods do rely upon our trait.

Education and Culture: Education is expected to bring about positive cultural values. Business has to understand the significance between Formal literacy and the Level of culture. Spread of education also helps in developing sound business ethics, but it also may lead to more economic offences, computer frauds, etc. Materials progress and business morality are closely related.

4. Technological Environment

The present-day civilisation owes much to technology. It is technology which has given wonder drugs like ampicillin norfloxacillin, pelox, coronary bypass surgery and oral contraceptives. It also led to nuclear stockpiling and star wars. It has released such mixed blessings as the automobile, tele-video sets, and white bread. We may have either a positive or a negative attitude towards technology.

Every new technology may herald the coming of a major industry. We only have to imagine transistors, xerography, microprocessors, computers, robotics, antibiotics and bio-technology. These industries not only create but destroy. Transistor damaged the vacuum-tube industry and xerography damaged the carbon paper business. Technology is a force for "creative destruction." Every enterprise must watch what is new in the environment, for this might eventually destroy it. If it has the imagination, the innovation may redeem it.

The correlation of growth rate of economy and technological innovation will be established in the coming years. Unfortunately, technological innovativeness of breakthrough are sporadic — there is a gap or time lag between the Railroad and Auto industry, Radio and TV. In the absence of technological breakthrough an economy can stagnate. Technological forecasting is thus of crucial importance. New technology creates some major long-run consequences that are not always foreseeable at the time.

Accelerating Rate of Technological Change: Most of the technological products we take for granted today were not present even one hundred years ago. Automobiles, airplanes, phonographs, radio or the electric light are recent products. Television, aerosol sprays, refrigerators, automatic dishwashers, room air-conditioners, antibiotics or electronic computers are all new products. Xerography, synthetic detergents, tape-recorders, many synthetic drugs, or geostationary satellites do not have a long history. Freeze-dried coffee, fuel injection engines or laser technology are totally new. As much as 20 per cent of our products and brands were not around a decade earlier.

Toffler sees an accelerative thrust in the invention, exploitation and diffusion of new technologies.[1] There are more product ideas; the time lag between the idea and the successful implementation is falling rapidly and the time between introduction and peak production is shortening considerably.

Unlimited Innovational Opportunities: There are plenty of novel ideas for new products. Only the technical and commercial feasibility of these ideas is limited. Among the most important things researchers are working on are cancer remedies, psychiatric medicines, AIDS remedies geriatrics, electric cars, desalinisation of sea water, home computer systems, butler robots and non-fattening foods. Researchers are also working on a host of other innovations, including small flying cars, lightweight single person rocket belts, commercial space shuttles, space colonies.[2]

The areas of research are: transportation, energy, life-extension research, new materials, instrumentation, mechanisation of physical activities and mechanisation of intellectual activities.

High R and D Budgets: Though India spends less on *R* and *D* by world standards, there is now a trend towards spending more on *R* and *D*.

The Union government is the largest supplier of *R* and *D* funds, and industry and the government-funded laboratories are the largest users. Almost 90 per cent of the funds go to

1. Toffler, *Future Shock,* pp. 25-30.
2. For a long list of possible innovations, see Dennis Cabor, *Innovations: Scientific, Technological and Social* (London; Oxford University Press 1970).

applied *R* and *D*. The remainder is spent on basic research, almost half of which takes place in colleges and universities.

Research today is team-work in government-aided or industry-sponsored laboratories. Managing research scientists poses major challenges. They are professionals who resent too much cost control. They are more interested in solving scientific problems than in coming up with marketable products. Yet companies are making some progress in impressing a stronger marketing orientation on their science manpower.

Concentration on Minor Improvements Rather than on Major Discoveries: Credit squeeze of late has led many companies to concentrate more on pursuing minor product improvements than staking on major innovations. In the drug industry, new drugs are now made by modifying chemically a parent drug. Most companies deploy finances to improve such things as cleaning power of detergents, antiseptic properties of tooth pastes, putting new flavours into soft drinks and restyling the automobiles. Some part of every *R* and *D* budget is spent simply to produce or copy 'me-too' products, rather than in striving to surpass them.

Increased Regulation of Technological Change: Technological change being controlled more today than ever before, with increased complexity the public needs assurance of their safety. Government agencies have responded by arrogating power to scrutinise new products that might be directly harmful or have questionable side effects. Thus FDA (Food and Drugs Administration) has issued elaborate regulations governing the scientific testing of new drugs.

Technological change is also meeting opposition from those who see large-scale technology destroying many of the values they cherish. Medha Patkar opposes the Sardar Sarovar Project for the perceived disastrous effects it might have on population being uprooted by it. There is opposition to creation of cities, which are like 'concrete jungles.'

5. Natural Environment

In recent years, there is an increased concern over whether the natural environment was being irreparably damaged by industrial activities. It is pointed out that there is environmental damage to water, earth and air caused by industrial activity of certain kinds. This has led to the formation of various groups of environmentalists.

No government worth its salt can afford to remain a silent spectator to the threat of environmental pollution. The governments are attempting to monitor environmentally damaging actions. Ironically, the effort to protect the environment often runs counter to the attempt to generate more employment and increase economic growth. From time-to-time, conservation politics theme subserves the economic growth theme. Management must be alert to that regulatory developments and the opportunities that open up with the effort to protect the natural environment.

6. Social Environment

It has come to be accepted today that being a part and parcel of society, business does have a social purpose so as to enjoy social acceptance. Social environment of business consists of a whole lot of cultures, beliefs, values, traditions, attitudes, institutions, stratification, social groupings etc.

There are several social movements which draw their form and content from the nature of social objectives and constraints. For example, we have trade union movement, the consumers movement, the managers' movement, the shareholders movement etc. Business ethic gets very much affected by these social movements.

Business has to balance the aspirations of various interest groups with its own achievements. Only this balancing results in social harmony.

Sociological environment is a complex resulting form of operation of many forces — political, ecological, geographical, historical, ethical, moral, institutional etc. In social harmony, an end is achieved by different methods & means and social environment differs from place-to-place, from time-to-time.

Social and business environments are hand in glove. All social movements do have economic content and intent that economic growth and social justice are to keep pace with each other. Socio-economic problems are like the Siamese twins, to be tackled simultaneously. Economic planning has social welfare as an ultimate goal. SR (Social Responsibility) is now a part of business vocabulary and practice. There is no social progress till economy is significantly developed structurally.

We have in India "family business" which is slowly getting professionalised. We have a recruitment policy where all other factors being equal, caste may be a critical factor for selection. With growing professionalisation, things are changing fast.

Let us see a few current social movements facing us here in India.

❖ The Trade Union Movement

Workers have organised themselves into unions as a reaction to industrialisation where their large numbers and denial of their just interests made them feel to go in for this mechanism. Indian trade union history begins in the first quarter of this century. The formation of All India Trade Union Congress (AITUC) in 1920 and the passing of the Trade Union Act, 1926 are two important milestones of this movement. Soon the movement splintered into several groups and the same trend continues even after Independence. INTUC (Indian National Trade Union Congress) backed by Congress in 1947, the HMS (Hind Mazdoor Sabha) backed by PSP in 1948, the BMS (Bharatiya Mazdoor Sangh) in 1955, UTUC (United Trade Union Congress) in 1949, the HM (Hind Mazdoor). The membership of the union is about 5 million.

The shortcomings of our Trade Union (TU) movements are:

1. Smaller in size, nearly 75% of them have membership of less than 500.
2. Financial difficulties due to smallness of size and insignificant contributions.
3. No paid officers on full-time basis.
4. Inter-union and within-the union rivalries.
5. Peculiar labour profile — illiterate, migratory etc.
6. Obsession with strikes.
7. Multiplicity of unions.

Weak unions are much more militant to assert themselves. We have to strengthen our trade union movement to improve our social and economic environment. We have to build unions whose bargaining power equals that of the management.

Again, in India, we have a vast unorganised sector, especially in agriculture and construction industries. Some leaders have started organising the farmers, like Sharad Joshi in Maharashtra and Tikait in Northern India. We have to carry forward this trend. Even the present labour minister's concern for construction workers is praiseworthy. We have to have public sector and the government as model employers.

A new trend called managerial unionism is emerging in India. They are called Officers'. Associations. We have many such associations in the banking industry. This is the outcome of growing service sector. Just as the industrial revolution heralded blue-collar unions, the post-industrial society is to herald white-collar unions. The challenge so far was to manage the workers. The challenge of the future is to manage the managers.

❖ Consumer Movement

Along with the trade union movement, the consumer movement also affects the social environment tremendously. Strong consumer movement leads to a healthy household sector in the economy.

A consumer faces a number of problems in his day-to-day life. Most of the problems relate to adulteration, short weights and measures, excess price, unfair trade practices, misleading advertisements etc. Over the years, these problems have assumed an alarming proportion.

Aware of these problems, the Government has accorded priority to the programmes of consumer protection. It has taken a number of measures to promote a strong and broad-based consumer movement in the country. The most significant of these is creation of a suitable legal and administrative framework which is within easy reach of consumers. Some of these steps, are as follows:

(*i*) Consumer Redressal Forums have been set up at district, state levels and a national forum has been setup at Delhi. This has become grievance handling machinery for the consumers.

(*ii*) A promotional programme for consumer education has been undertaken.

(*iii*) National awards for consumer protection are given.

❖ Management Movement

In our society, besides employees and consumers, one more group that matters is that of the managers. Though Indian consumer movement and the trade union movement are not so strong, the management movement is very distinct and very strong. After the advent of freedom, our management complexion has changed for the better. From the managing agency system created to solve the problem of finance and management, we have travelled to Board Management, though many of these Boards still retain some of the characteristics of the old system. The domination of big business houses has remained.

There is a distinct trend towards Indianisation, with many multinationals now having Indian chairman and MD's and the board composed of Indians. Indian management in the private sector excluding multinationals is the hereditary management of the families. In the public sector, it is bureaucratic management 'participative' these days and there were schemes of workers' participation in management. However, participation has remained passive participation and not active participation in decision-making.

Though family-managed businesses are still on the scene, there is an increasing tendency towards professionalisation of management. Professionalisation is understood as management divorced from ownership, availability of management training and education, attitudes and value system of a professional not geared only to profit, but loyalty towards the profession. Indian professional managers of the early periods were all promoters with little educational background. In the sixties, engineers became professional managers. In the 80s though MBAs continued to dominate as professional managers, many companies had reservations about them and embarked upon their own management development programmes. Indian professional managers have formed an elitist class and have remained confined to private sector, thus leaving the vast public sector and co-operative sector under managed. We need more of a barefoot manager — the type IRMA produces at Anand to go to rural India and manage the rural projects. Professional managers and the lowly workers are poles apart and in such a situation there is a mismatch between the Professional manager and the Organisational culture. We have to Indianise the management education for this purpose, for which a close link between the Industry and the Academics is needed.

In short, India has a professional management cadre of three varieties — multinationals, the private sector and the public sector. Professional managers also feel insecure just like the rank and file. Management's professionalisation has made it a specialised branch and a whole lot of consultants have appeared on the scene to sell their expertise.

❖ Shareholders' Movement

As a corollary of the professional management movement, of late, there has been shareholders' movement in the socio-economic environment. There were many shareholders associations from the beginning. But the Annual General Meeting (AGM) was taken as a more legal formality, a ritual that must be gone through. Shareholders were unaware of their rights for a long time.

In recent past, all this is changing. Capital market has attracted widely awakened investors and the companies will no longer be able to treat AGMs lightly. Leave apart the closely held companies where majority of shares are within a family or group, but even in widely held companies with a large number of shareholders, the minority shareholders continue to run the companies and perpetuate a dynastic family rule with a typical management culture. Shareholders have not only been kept out of management, but have never exercised their rights.

AGMs are a good forum for shareholders to participate in management decision-making, but shareholders waste this opportunity by being after the small token gifts given as complementaries. Even attendance at AGMs is meagre.

Times are changing. Shareholders have become more knowledgeable and eager to exercise their rights. They have realised that they have a power to destabilise the present management by take over bids and that the majority shareholders like the financial institutions keep their options about strategic alignment open. AGMs of late have become crucial battle grounds. The Escorts experience is not too old to be forgotten. Shareholders' movement now realises that AGMs can decide issues one way or the other.

Another important factor of social environment is the eagerness with which business has embraced its social responsibilities. No longer business has remained just a money-making machine. Much more than money is at stake. Business has to be innovative, a public benefactor, and one that serves the public. The public it serves are owners/shareholders, managers, workers, distributors, suppliers, consumers, government and the like. Business is expected to fulfil its social commitments to all these.

❖ International Environment

Those industries which have inputs from imports and outputs which are sold as exports, have greater concern with international environment, both economic and non-economic. The foreign trade policies directly affect such a business in India. Major international developments do affect business, *e.g.*, oil prices affected the whole world's economy. Recently political developments in Eastern Europe will have repercussions everywhere. Little tiger countries (South Korea, Taiwan, Hong Kong and Singapore) have emerged as economic powers in their own right. Of late, these so-called economic tigers faced devaluation of their currency and a crash of their stock prices. Japan is the new economic power. Yen's changed valuation affected many automotive collaborations in India. Foreign policies of outside government also affect the business environment. The basic question for multinationals is to monitor what a particular government thinks of foreign investment and on what terms it is allowed. India is being asked to respect the intellectual property rights especially in the field of pharmaceuticals where process patent is adopted in India rather than product patent. India has become signatory to GATT. India has recently amended its Patent Act to move to Post-GATT regime. Export marketing to the extent of 70-80 per cent or 100 per cent makes a business vulnerable to foreign environment of the importing country; *e.g.,* Japanese cars in the United States.

There is a trend towards Business Process Outsourcing (BPO) for both voice and data related world. India has generated jobs for several lac people in the BPO sector for the US and UK companies on the strength of cost advantage and trained manpower.

High tech industries like informatics and biotechnology have created 5 million jobs.

Venture capitalists are seriously considering the biotechnology companies, nano technology firms, IT and ITES firms, anti-AIDs research, genetic engineering and such other new areas.

In other words, here we get a picture of business opportunities and growth area. International environment seems to favour the small business which has a competitive edge in growth.

The students have to keep abreast of international environment by reading literature and books like Batra's *Great Depression* which predicted a slump on the stock exchange in the United States.

The liberalisation of the Chinese economy and the opening up of the Russian economy have a great potential for a country like India. East European countries will offer many business opportunities. The reconstruction of the Gulf after the war is also a consideration. China is already competing with India for foreign investment. The European Economic Community is unified, presenting a vast market. North Atlantic Treaty is also a consideration.

To sum, let us put the nature and scope of business environment in some precise statements.

1. Business environment means surroundings, conditions, situations, trends within which business has to operate.
2. General environment or macro-environment is created by many factors or forces which act upon business — political, economic, social, technological etc.
3. Business has internal as well as external environments.
4. There is procurement of inputs, processing of inputs into outputs by using equipment, material, information, money etc. The output could be products or services. These are carried by marketing intermediaries to the market. There is competition in the market.

   All this collectively constitutes the task and competitive environment specific to an individual business. It considers materials, production, marketing and finance functions.
5. Business environment changes. Organisations seek to fit their environment. For this, they monitor and adapt to it.
6. Business environment is the foundation of corporate planning.

❖ Manager and Environment

An organisation's performance is a matter of the degree of alignments between the organisation's environmental opportunities, objectives, strategies, structure and system.

Environment → Objectives → Strategies → Structure → System

The task is complex because these various components alter at different rates, resulting in a non-optimal alignment. Thus we have in 2005 environment objectives which were set in 1995, strategies which were developed in 1993. We still have not changed the organisation structure of 1995 which the founding fathers established and the systems introduced in the same year. This then is the tragedy of many organisations. Progressive companies bring about an alignment in the above components and go a step further. They will forecast the environment of 2010, for which they develop objectives and strategies describing where they would like to be in 2010 and begin to change the organisation and its systems so that they become supportive for the new objectives and strategies in 2010. The manager operating in a stable environment is fortunate, but one who operates in a turbulent environment must scan the environment systematically, must identify environmental threats and opportunities, and must take intelligent adaptations to the changing environment.

❖ Survival in a Turbulent Environment

It is widely believed that corporations live for ever. Legally, it has perpetual existence, survive even when all its shareholders die. But in reality most corporations have a life of 40-50 years. Only those corporations which continuously adapt themselves to the changing environment have a longevity beyond 40-50 years. In this book *The Living Company* de Geus, an executive from Shell cites the example of Stora which began business more than 700 years ago of copper mining in Sweden. In 15th Century, when Stora was 270 years old, the king of Sweden threatened its existence. In response to this, this company became a powerful military guild. Later, it shifted its business continuously, from copper to forestry to iron smelting to paper, wood pulp and chemicals. Its survival is attributed to its adaptation to the changing environment.

❖ Services Sector

Indian economy was predominantly agrarian in the 80s, but its face has changed in the 90s and in this new millennium by becoming the world largest service provider — software, back office operations, contract research, engineering design, medical consultancy, entertainment software, financial services, equity research, even publishing. Though industrial and agricultural growth remained slow in the 90s, it was the services sector that kept the growth rate of about 6 per cent a year, raising its share in the GDP from 40 per cent to 50 per cent.

Services sector has added an estimated five million jobs every year, making even those who lived on economic fringes truely prosperous. Today, an estimated 45 million people are employed in the organised services sector. Their purchasing power is an estimated ₹ 450,000 crore, assuming an average annual income of ₹ 1 lac. Out of this, ₹ 1 lac crore is in the hand of a young work force between the age of 20 and 30. There are lacs of others employed in services as humble as laundry, car garages, running telephone booths, hair cutting etc.

This growth is propelled by competition in the wake of liberalisation. India has a vast pool of economical, skilled and English-speaking work-force. Every year India adds 1.5 million graduates through colleges and technical institutes. These graduates no longer are solely dependent on domestic growth. They can tap the opportunities being offered by foreign firms, even though they remain physically in India.

Indian industries till early 90s earned major portion of revenue from manufacturing activities, but this has changed in favour of the services sector. For example, the Tata group earned 90 per cent of its revenues from the manufacturing activities. Today, IT and hospitality brings 40 per cent of its revenues. Reliance is also going the same way, by diversifying into life sciences, education, retail and telecom.

If done right, services can add one percentage point to the annual GDP growth rate by 2010.

To sustain the growth of services, India should continue to liberalise more and keep its manpower resource pipeline flowing by focusing on higher education. India should not encourage services at the cost of manufacturing or agriculture. There has to be a balance between Manufacturing and Services. Most of all, India must let entrepreneurs be.

JAWA: A Case of Marketing Myopia

Original Company	: Jawa Motors, ((then) Czechoslovakia
First Model of Jawa	: October 23, 1929
Sales Elsewhere	: Popular all over the world. Gradually manufactured or assembled outside Czechoslovakia
Indian Plant	: The largest production plant under license.
Mid-1950s	: Motor cycle imports were prohibited by the Government. Assembly of foreign machines in India continued.
Motor Cycle Production	: Under license, the first motor cycle left the Ideal Jawa plant, Mysore on Mach 5, 1961. The plant was under license. The plant was established by Rustom Irani, an import agent from Mumbai.
Performance	: Technical collaboration of Jawa Ltd. Czechoslovakia. Good performance. The collaboration ended in 1968. The Indian plant developed indigenous technology.
1970s	: Yezdi was launched.
1980s	: Japanese bikes entered the Indian market through JVs. 100 cc bikes, fuel-efficient and easy-to-ride.
Adaptation	: Jawa could not adapt to the changing marketing environment. Japanese bikes offered better mileage, style and comfort.
Design changes by Yezdi	: They put Road King but it was too little too late.
End	: Yezdi was laid to rest in 1996.

****

3 STRATEGIC PLANNING

Keeping a customer satisfied is the secret of business success. However, as we have seen, a company has to operate in an ever-changing environment. Its success in a large measure, is also attributable to its adaptation to this changing environment by practising *strategic planning*. It is through strategic planning that the company creates a viable fit between its resources, skills and objectives and the changing marketing opportunities. Strategic planning involves shaping and reshaping a company's business and products so as to obtain the desired profits and growth.

Strategic planning is best tackled at the top levels of corporate management and as such is also called corporate planning. By its very nature, it influences every level of a corporation. It extends to every part and activity. Its prime function, however, is to examine corporate strategy at the top. It came into being in the US in the fifties. It came of age in the seventies. It has evolved a great deal over a period of time. It has spread geographically to all industrial societies.

Strategic planning has three important dimensions:

(*a*) *Investment portfolio approach* in which a company decides which business it is doing needs building up, maintenance or phasing out.

(*b*) *Growth-share matrix approach* where future profit potential of each business is considered.

(*c*) Formulation of a *strategy* to realise our objectives.

Marketing provides a very important input to strategic planning. The very foundation of any strategic plan is the definition of business mission. Business missions are marketing oriented. The environmental scanning is done with a view to seeking marketing opportunities. Marketing plays a vital role in formulating strategies, objectives and goals. It also helps in implementing the strategies by defining the product, the market, the distribution and the quality level. Strategic plans generate operating plans which again lean heavily on marketing.

❖ Evolution of the Planning Function

Let us examine the evolution of strategic planning functions:

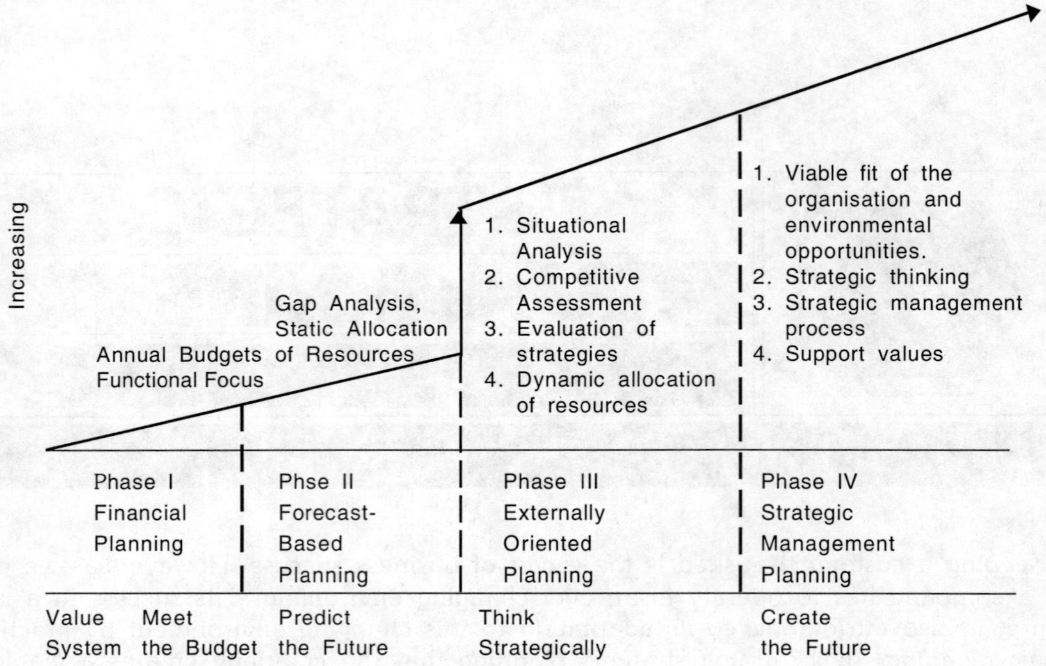

Fig. 3.1 Evolution of Strategic Planning
(Gluck, Kaufman & Walleck, 1978 McKinsey & Co.)

From the above diagram, it is obvious that planning in the beginning is financial planning where budgets are made.

Later, for planning we start making use of forecasting methods to understand the strategic planning gap. When business becomes complex and operates in a dynamic environment, a need is felt to monitor the environment. We also have to respond to competition. Previously, we used to allocate resources as a convention. Now environmental analysis calls for dynamic allocation of resources. Planning becomes externally oriented and we start thinking strategically.

Sophistication in planning further leads to make our planning a *strategic management process* of developing and maintaining a viable fit between the Organisation's objectives and Resources and its environmental opportunities. It is concerned with managing organisation in such a way that it keeps the company going, even when some of its businesses are hurting. Strategic management planning is concerned with the creation of the future of the company.

Planning is like a learning process, rather than a state of being. It is like learning to ride a bicycle, as opposed to producing a year's balance sheet.

The following table gives the evolution of planning terms and concepts:

Term	*Basic Definition*	*Evolution*
Planning	Setting goals and preparing programmes to achieve them typically at the functional and sub-functional levels.	Used by Taylor. Emerged in fifties with professional management. Embodied in MBO in the sixties.
Business Planning	Combining the plans of each function into a business plan.	Decentralised organisations of the fifties adopt it. George Steiner popularised it in the sixties.
Strategic Business Planning	Business plan focused on the utilisation of resources to achieve competitive success in attractive markets of the future.	Emphasis changed in the seventies.
Corporate Strategic Planning	Integrating business strategic plans so that performance of the whole is greater than the sum of its parts.	Portfolio Analysis of late seventies. Role and content in response to environment and organisation.

❖ Levels of Strategic Planning

Any large corporation of today has four levels of organisation and each level has its own strategic planning. At the top, the corporate headquarters consisting of top management formulate a *corporate strategic plan* for the entire organisation. This plan is a guide to where we are today and where we are heading to. We, in other words, are exploring where we need to go to make our future rewarding. It also guides us whether we are prepared for the trip from the present into the future. The corporate plan decides the deployment of resources to each division and also decides which business to be in and which business to be out.

Next to the corporate level at the top, we have business divisions for which *strategic divisional plans* are made. Here a decision is taken for the deployment of funds in to *Strategic Business Units* (SBUs) within that division. Each SBU in turn makes a *strategic marketing* plan for the product line or brands for activating its objectives.

The entire planning process at each level is implemented by suitably organising and later controlled by measuring the results and taking corrective action. The following diagram illustrates the hierarchy of strategic planning.

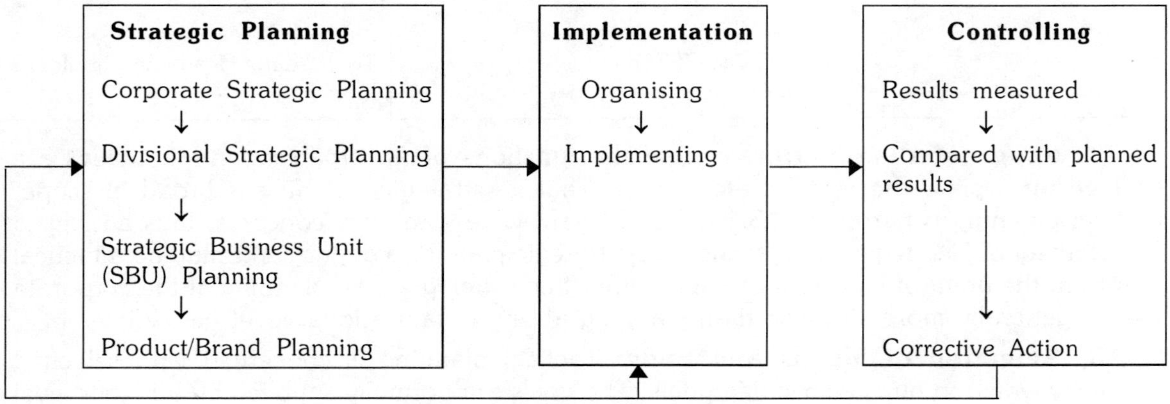

Fig. 3.2 Strategic Planning Hierarchy

❖ Tactical and Strategic Planning

As far as formulation of a corporate plan is concerned, the distinction between Tactical and Strategic planning is often made but is seldom made clear. Decision that appear strategic to the one person may appear tactical to another. This suggests that the distinction is relative rather than absolute. Indeed this is so. Much of the confusion and ambiguity derive from the fact that the difference between Strategic and Technical planning is three-dimensional. The three dimensions are:

1. Duration of Impact: The longer the effect of a plan and the more difficult it is to reverse, the more strategic it is. Therefore, strategic planning is concerned with decisions that have enduring effects that are difficult to reverse; for example, next week's production planning is more tactical and less strategic than planning a new plant or a new distribution system. Strategic planning is long-range planning. Tactical planning is of another range. But "long" and "short" are relative terms and so are the terms "strategic" and "tactical". In general, strategic planning is concerned with the longest period worth considering for planning while tactical planning is concerned with the shortest period worth considering. Both types of planning are necessary. They complement each other. They are like the head and tail of a coin: we can look at them separately, even discuss them separately, but we cannot separate them in fact. A brilliant strategy is not enough. The day-to-day response to the market called tactics pushes a brand. Strategy is brand's long-term decision, chosen and defined. Tactic is here and now. Tactics can become strategy if it defines the brands decision in the long-term. Tactics believe in quick advantages. Tactics should, however, not violate the brand's essence. Tactics can indicate the change or shift in strategy.

TACTICS USED IN INDIAN MARKET

Organisation	*Short description of Tactics Used*	*Name of the Tactics used*
LG Electronics	Marketing of colour televisions without sales promotion or exchange offers	Price tactic
Coca-Cola	Signed cricketers for promotion	Take on Pepsi promotion
Hindustan Lever	Pepsodent 102 per cent better	Comparative advertising
	Clinic ZPTO All Clear	To pre-empt Head and Shoulder's launch

2. Scope of Planning: The more the functions of an organisation's activities are affected by a plan, the more strategic it is. That is, strategic planning is broad in scope. Tactical planning is narrower. "Broad" and "Narrow" are relative concepts, thus adding to the relativity of "strategic" and "tactical". A strategic plan for a department may be a tactical plan from the point of view of a division. Other things being equal, planning at the corporate level is generally more strategic than planning at any organisational level below it.

3. Selection of Means and Ends: Tactical planning is concerned with selecting means by which to pursue specified goals. The goals are normally supplied by a higher level in the organisation. Strategic planning is concerned with both the formulation of the goals and selection of the means by which they are to be attained. Thus, strategic planning is oriented to ends as well as to means. However, "means" and "ends" are also relative concepts; for example, "advertising a product" is a means to the end of "selling it". "Selling it" however is a means to the end "profit" and profit is itself a means to many other ends.

To put briefly, strategic planning is long range corporate planning that is ends oriented (but not exclusively so). It should be apparent that both strategic and tactical planning are required in order to maximise progress.

❖ Steps in Strategic Planning

Strategic planning has several distinct steps. We shall examine these steps one by one.

1. Environmental Scanning: A corporation can be effective only if it can grapple successfully with the external environment in which it functions. While coping with the environment, it has to consider the macro-factors like:

(*a*) economic environment;

(*b*) political environment;

(*c*) social environment;

(*d*) regulatory environment;

(*e*) technological environment.

To deal with the external environment, it collects data on a continuous basis. The trends and mega-trends are noted. The factors are inter dependent. To set our objectives and develop our strategies, we need information from environmental scanning.

2. Company's Mission: Taking the interactions with the external environment into account, the planning process is started by determining the company's mission and objectives.

The *raison d'etre* of an organisation is some accomplishment in the environmental context. Its specific *mission or purpose* is crystal clear, usually right from the start. Over a period of time, its mission may become hazy as the organisation expands and puts forward new products and enters new markets. Another possibility is that its mission may remain clear, but some managers may lose interest in it. In some cases, the mission, howsoever clear, is rendered irrelevant under the changed circumstances. In such a contingency, the organisation must rediscover its purpose.

Peter F. Drucker advises to answer some pertinent questions while defining the mission:

1. What business are we in?
2. Who is our customer?
3. What value is delivered to the customer?
4. What business are we going to be in?
5. What business ought we to be in?

Apparently simplistic though this analysis may seem to be, it is one of the most arduous exercises, that a corporation is expected to perform. Successful companies give considerable thought and attention to the answers of these questions.

Elements of Company's Mission: The building blocks of the organisation's mission will be examined here. The first is the *history* of the organisation. Every organisation has a set of traditional values and policies which are reflected in its purpose or mission. The Tatas will not be prudent to be film producers like R.K. Studios even when such a move constitutes a growth opportunity. The second is the consideration for *current preferences* of management. Those who pilot the company guide it by their personal goals and vision. For instance, the Walchand Group which owns a sugar factory with attached distillery do not enter into alcoholic beverages industry despite the bright prospects as it will collide with their personal ethos as Jains. On the other hand, then Sahu Jain company like Carona Sahu ventures to make and market footwear made out from animal hides. Thus it all depends upon the management's preference or dislike for a particular line. The *environmental considerations* also shape the mission. The environment defines the threats and opportunities which merit attention while deciding the mission. A theological political party will not survive in an environment substantially committed to secularism, socialism and egalitarianism. The *resources* make certain missions possible and others not. Lastly, the organisation bases its purpose on its *distinctive competence* to handle a particular business. Gits Foods could probably enter the solar energy business but that would not be making use of its main competence — providing low-cost instant vegetable food to individual and bulk buyers.

These days organisations share their mission statements with departmental heads, employees, and also in many cases with customers and the public at large. A well-developed mission statement invests the corporate personnel with a sense of opportunity, direction, importance and achievement. It plays the role of an *invisible hand* that directs the corporate employees to strive towards the corporate objectives. A formal mission statement is easy to draft and evolves over time after a process of investigation about what the organisation stands for.

The mission statement, in order to be of maximum use, must show several characteristics. It should not be too wide and sweeping in its scope. A statement like: "We want to be market leaders with premium quality product-line backed up by extensive distribution channel which makes the products available at the lowest possible prices" sounds good but lacks the clarity necessary while deciding tough business options. The purpose preferably should define externality. Market leadership and profitability are an effect of the corporate purpose, rather than the purpose itself.

The mission statement should give specificity to business domain, preferably in three dimensions: customer groups to be served, customer needs to be met, and the technology to be employed to meet these needs. The organisation is at liberty to either expand or contract its business domain. In his "Marketing Myopia", Levitt recommends market-oriented definitions of business rather than product-oriented definitions. However, while formalising the market-oriented definition, the organisation should avoid a definition that is too narrow or too broad.

The mission statement should make the work of the employees meaningful and purposive and should be motivating enough. It should also reflect the major policies to which an organisation stands committed. The company draws its strength from its mission for the next ten or twenty years and so it should not be subject to frequent revisions. It can, however, be amended when it has lost credibility and no longer remains an optimum course for the company.

3. Corporate Objectives or Goals: For setting objectives/goals of planning, we undertake a SWOT (Strengths, Weaknesses, Opportunities and Threats) analysis. The main purpose of environmental scanning is to spot the opportunities and identify the threats. Opportunities and threat analysis is thus an external environmental analysis. To exploit these opportunities, we must have the competence to do so. The business, therefore, undertakes an internal environmental analysis called strengths and weaknesses analysis. After undertaking a SWOT analysis, a business can develop specific objectives and goals and can identify different strategies to achieve them.

4. Key Areas of Corporate Goals: Planning is a goal oriented process. Hence, unless the goals are defined, planning becomes impossible. Thus the definition of corporate goals becomes necessary and essential first step in corporate planning. Since survival and growth are universally recognised as the basic goals of an organisation, they constitute the basic goals of a corporation as well, as corporation is essentially a social organisation. However, a corporation has multiple goals as objectives need to be identified in every single area in which the quality and effectiveness of performance of a corporation directly and vitally affects its chances of survival and growth. Peter F. Drucker has identified eight such key areas as follows:

(1) Market standing
(2) Innovation
(3) Productivity
(4) Resources: Physical, financial and technological
(5) Profitability
(6) Managerial performance and development
(7) Workers' performance
(8) Public responsibility and attitude.

5. Strategic Planning Gap: Forecasts are very good inputs to the planning process. They give us a projected figure, say, for example, of sales over a period of time.

Now our objective is to achieve a desired sales level over a period of time.

The gap between our objective (of desired sales) and the projected sales is called the strategic planning gap.

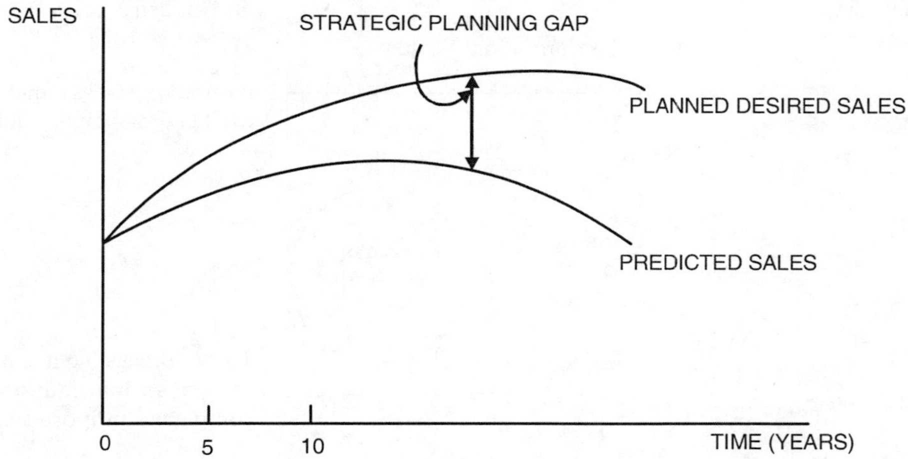

Fig. 3.3 Strategic Planning Gap

We are now in a position to fill up this gap by deciding our task or by setting up a *plan*. There can be four strategies to fill this gap.

(*a*) Market-Penetration Strategy; (*b*) Market Development Strategy; (*c*) Product Development Strategy and (*d*) Diversification strategy.

The following matrix explains these strategies:

	Current Products	**New Products**
	Market Penetration Strategy	*Product Development Strategy*
Existing Markets	Management increases the market share of its existing products in the existing markets. (*a*) Increase frequency of buying (*b*) Increase consumption quantity (*c*) Lure non-users.	New products are developed
	Market Development Strategy	*Diversification Strategy*
New Markets	Enter the new markets with existing products (*a*) add new segments (*b*) add new geographical areas.	Enter a new business and a new market

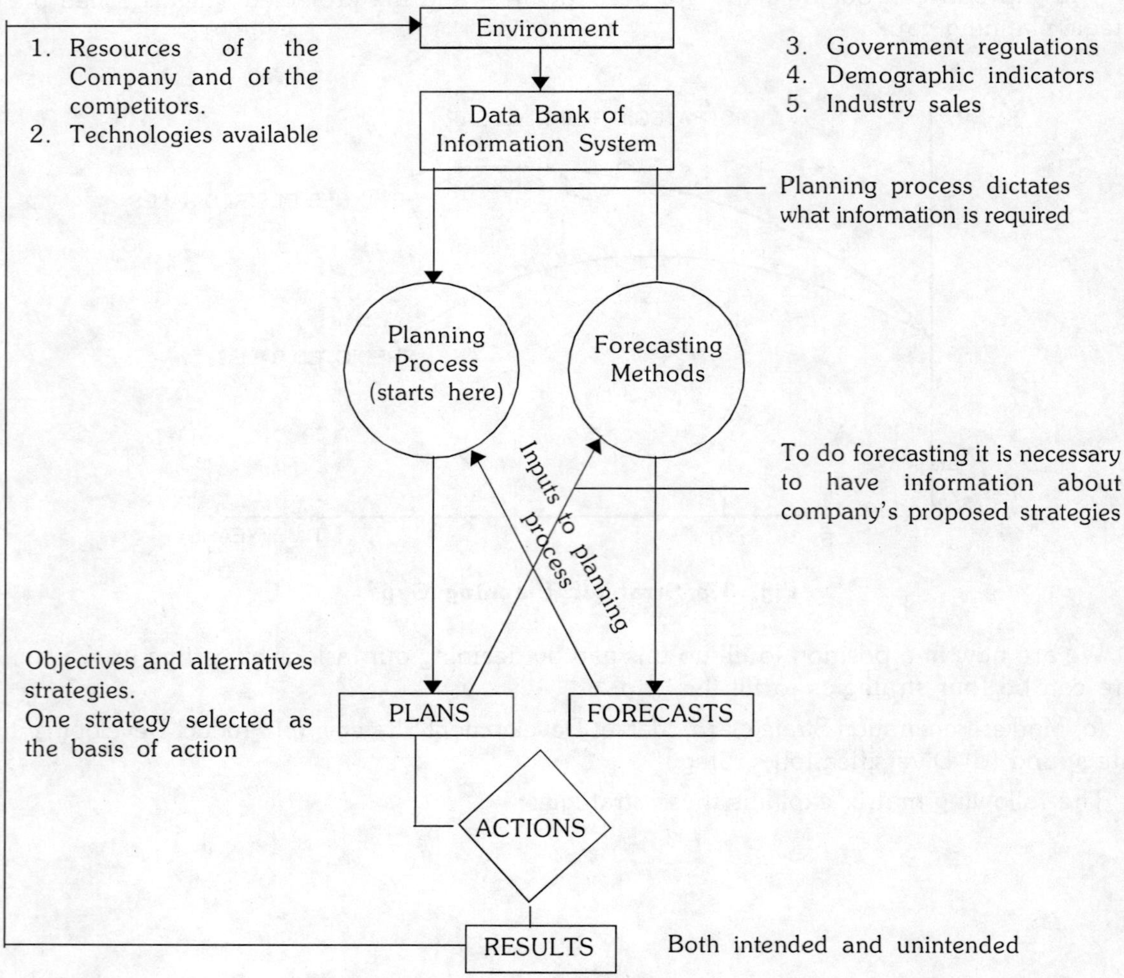

Fig. 3.4 Strategic or Corporate Planning Process

The company's strategies of market penetration, market development, product development are called intensive growth strategies. Diversification growth strategy stands in a class by itself. The company can also choose growth by integration which can be backward integration (petrochemicals → PFY → Textiles) or forward integration (TV software → satellite channel) or horizontal integration (by acquiring competitive business).

6. Implementation and Feedback: This plan of action is implemented after taking into account the constraints and the means. We are then left with results. They may be as per our expectation or they may not be. It then makes necessary to monitor the environment in the light of these results.

To summarise the planning process, we can say that a firm determines its overall objectives first. Then it generates alternative strategies to achieve the objectives. Later, it evaluates these strategies and develops a systematic procedure to monitor the results. (See Fig. 3.4)

❖ Strategy

As we have seen, corporate planning involves the formulation of objectives and their achievements by means of a strategy. A strategy in this sense is a route to the destination — corporate objectives. The strategies adopted at the top provides strategies for managers down the line. Strategies are means and objectives are ends and the means-ends chains tie the organisations into a purposeful whole. The managers become strategic managers when they have a *strategic vision* — a profound scanning ability of the environment.

Strategy is derived from the Greek *strategia.* It is the art and science of directing the military forces. Strategies exist at all levels, though the most important are the overall organisation strategies. In long range planning, the focus is on forecasting the future. It led to first generation plans, wherein the firm chose the most probable appraisal of the future environment and of its own strength and weaknesses. Then strategy evolved out of the organisation-environment fit. Strategic planning which is today's approach focuses on second generation planning — a mix of several future scenarios. Contingency strategies are then prepared for each of these likely future scenario.

Strategies may exist at three levels in an organisation — corporate level, business level and operating level. The business level strategies are for a unit or division in business which can be strategically managed (SBU). Operating level strategies are concerned how the different business functions, *e.g.,* marketing, finance etc. can contribute to the strategies of other levels. These strategies may depend upon strategic decisions — market entry, price, product offer, investment in plant, financing pattern, manpower etc.

Strategic management decides the strategy and its implementation and consists of three elements —

1. *Strategic analysis:* Organisational environment and changes, their impact, SWOT, effects of changes on manpower.
2. *Strategic choice:* Possible courses of action are arrived at. They are evaluated. The choice is made. Strategic options are evaluated to select a strategy.
3. *Strategic implementation:* Here the general direction is translated into action. While implementing the strategy, we have to do resource planning. We have to consider organisation structure, systems and people.

Strategic management is flexible, ensures consistency, makes managers proactive, reduces conflict and improves corporate communication.

In short, strategy is a unified, comprehensive and integrated plan that relates the strategic advantage of the organisation to the challenges of environment.

❖ Policy and Strategy

Andrews views words like "strategy", "policy" and "objectives" like keys of an accordian. They shed into each other. Policy is a guideline to the thinking and action of decision-makers. Strategy is the direction in which human and physical resources are deployed. Policy is a contingent decision — a decision for a repetitive occurrence or contingency in advance. Strategy is a rule for making decision under the conditions of partial ignorance about certain environmental variables for which assumptions are made. Policies can be delegated downwards in the organisation. Strategy may require last minute changes and cannot be so delegated.

❖ Strategic Thinking: An Attitude to Life

Kenichi Ohmae is too well-known a name in corporate planning to need any formal introduction. With five books to his credit, the latest and the fifth is entitled *The Mind of the Strategist,* published by Penguin Books. It happens to be his first English book. As an international management consultant, he has drawn invaluable experience while heading McKinsey's Japanese operations, in which assignment, he has handled accounts of top corporations in Japan — either indigenous or American or European corporations working in Japan. His is a formidable name as a creative strategist who has also develop organisational concepts to implement his creative strategies.

In his latest book. Ohmae is highly readable and makes no pedantic pretensions of being original. His strategic concepts are "the common intellectual property of informed business people for many years," and he simply claims to have put theory in its place — a place distinctly secondary to creative intuition.

❖ Strategy Formulation

The first step, according to Ohmae, is *analysis.* In his words, "The first stage in strategic thinking is to pinpoint the critical issue in the situation." The method follows a step by step and analysis and oversteps instinct. He recommends an *issue diagram* to have a full analysis of the problem.

❖ Four Basic Ways to Get Competitive Edge

The main objective of strategic planning is to establish superiority over competition. Ohmae sees four ways to do so.

(i) *Key Factors of Success (KFS).* The strategy should be based on the key factors for success. The strategist first determines the KFS for the business he is in. It can be done by two methods.

(a) Dissect the market as imaginatively as possible and identify its key segments.

(b) Analyse what differentiates winner companies from loser companies.

On identifying the KFS, the company should reallocate corporate resources and fortify the relevant corporate capabilities.

(ii) *Product Comparison:* This is the second way to gain competitive advantages. By comparing your product with that of the competitor, you can assess the product's strengths and weaknesses.

(iii) *Perusal of Aggressive Initiatives and Challenge the Established Notions of Doing Business:* The strategist is not a conformist. He challenges the established practices by a simple word: why? In this way, he realises the bottlenecks to fundamental improvement. The business can achieve major breakthrough by this method.

(iv) *Degrees of Freedom:* This is the final route based on his concept of strategic degrees of freedom which determines the amount for freedom for strategic moves that surrounds a particular key factor — say technology. A particular direction of success can be chosen from this set of possible moves.

❖ Customers-Based Strategies

Ohmae emphasizes the need for all strategies to be based on the customer.

❖ Selectivity and Sequencing

He recommends selectivity and sequencing of the improvement of functional competence rather than a shot-gun strategy.

❖ Cost-Effectiveness

Being cost-effective is only one way to develop strategy. There is at times a real trade-off to be made between the Cost of a function and Superiority in functional performance over a competitor.

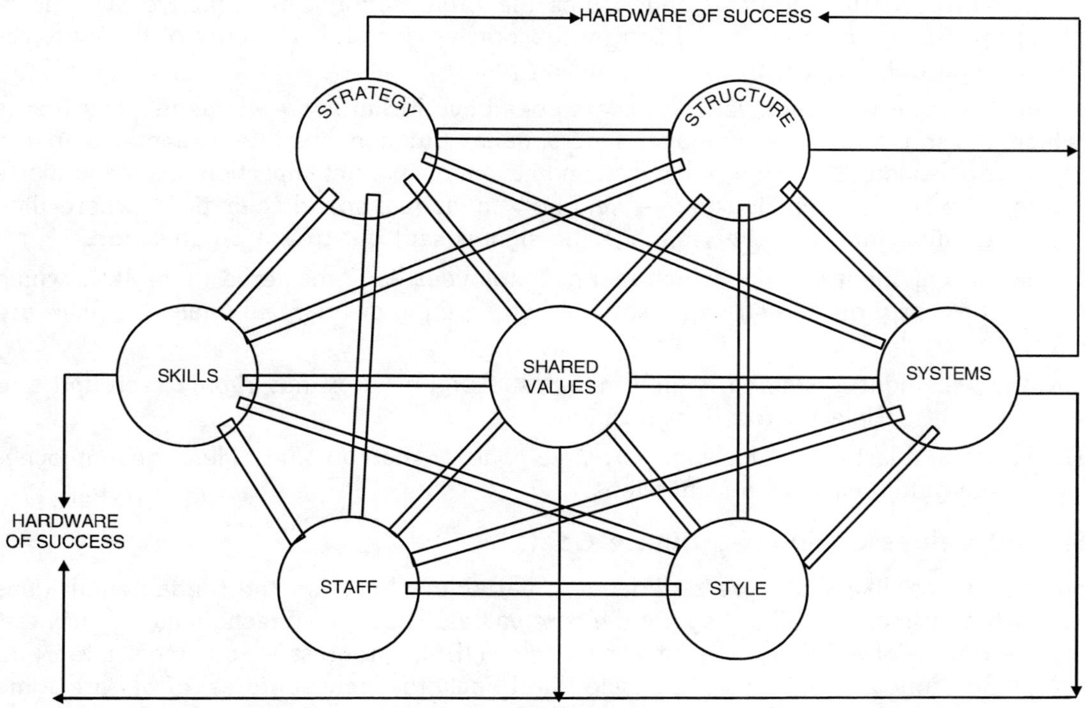

Fig. 3.5 The 7-S Model

❖ Creative Insight

Without a spark of creative insight, all methods to develop business strategy can be successful only up to a point. Creative insight is not teachable, but can be cultivated consciously in the presence of ingredients like sensitivity, will and receptiveness to be nurtured by example, direction and conditioning. Ohmae eloquently puts a grand finale: the strategist has to live, think and dream strategy. To a strategist, strategic thinking is an attitude to life.

STRATEGY IS NOT ENOUGH

❖ McKinsey 7-S Framework

Strategy is given too much importance these days. But even when the organisation has a clear strategy, it is not enough. After a study of 75 particularly successful and well-regarded companies. McKinsey and Co., USA identified six other elements over and above strategy which together constitute an effective organisation.

The first three elements — strategy, structure and systems — are called hardwares of success.

The next four — style, staff, skills and super-ordinate goals or shared values — are the software.

It is not clear which of the seven elements will be the *driving force* in managing a change in a specific organisation at a *given point of time.*

Most management literature has stressed the hardware elements. Accordingly, an organisation which develops an appropriate *strategy* to reach its goals, builds an appropriate organisational *structure* to carry out this strategy and equips the organisation with effective *systems* of information, planning, integrating and control, becomes successful. The crux of the matter is that *strategy* and not the *structure* is the starting point.

In some organisations, however, success goes beyond hardware elements. The first is *style* which doesn't refer to a manager's personality but concerns such elements in the *management's* behaviour that can be controlled and have an important impact on an organisation's functioning. The key element is style — *i.e.*, how managers spend their time, where they focus their attention and how they manage the signals sent out to the organisation.

The second element is *skills*, which means employees have mastered those skills which are necessary to carry out the strategy (say market planning or financial analysis). Skills are a dependent variable.

The third element is *staffing,* which means the organisation has rightly recruited and selected, the right people for the right positions.

The fourth and last element is *super-ordinate goals* or *shared values*. Here the employees share the same guiding values and missions.

❖ Shared Values or Super-ordinate Goals

Shared values, like skills, are a dependent variable. These are the fundamental ideas around which a business is built. They are the core values. They give directionality to business. 'Universal services' of AT & T, 'customer service' of IBM, 'progress — our most important product' of GE, 'innovative people' of Hewlett and Packard, 'new ventures' of 3M are some cogent examples of shared values. These are abstractions, which may mean little to others, but which propel the inside staff to peak levels. These values are to be properly articulated. They stabilise an organisation in turbulent environment.

❖ Implications

1. There are four variables which can be described as *change levers* — structure, systems, style and staff.
2. The strategy of an organisation can both lead to or be the result of these variables.
3. At any given time, an organisation fits with its relevant environment may be excellent. The 7-S's are in alignment.
4. Consequent upon on environmental change, the company will be compelled to make appropriate adjustments in one or more of the seven S's if it is to continue to prosper.
5. The extent of these adjustments depends on the degree, speed and complexity of environmental change.
6. The underlying problem is that the relevant environment may change faster than the organisation's seven S's. There are many Indian companies in a 2013 environment with left-overs of 1980's strategy, structure, systems, style, staff, skills and shared value. In such a case, the company may be efficient but not effective.
7. Though a powerful expository tool, changing the shared values of the organisation which is the central task in this model is a difficult task.

❖ Corporate Strategic Planning Process

Each business, as we have seen, can be narrowly defined in terms of physical products or can be broadly defined in terms of its market. Revlon, thus, is not a cosmetics company but is a company that sells hope. A broad definition makes the company alive to the overall opportunities it can tap. Each company has to identify the businesses it wants to be in. A business, say of cosmetics, can be planned separately from the rest of the company. When it has its own distinct competitors and is managed as a profit centre, such a single business (or collection of related businesses) can be developed as *Strategic Business Unit (SBU)*. These SBUs have their own goals. They are funded appropriately. These SBUs can be built or maintained. They can be harvested or divested. It all depends upon their performance, especially their profit potential. While assigning resources to these SBUs, we make use of either the Boston Consulting Group (BCG) approach or General Electric Company (GEC) approach. Taj Hotel Group in India has been structured into five strategic business units (SBUs) — luxury hotels, business hotels, leisure hotels, international operations and the air catering business.

❖ Corporate Planning Model

Boston Consulting Group (BCG) Growth/Share Matrix: Boston Consulting Group is a renowned management consultancy from which has evolved a model of *growth-share matrix*.

In this matrix, the market growth rate is shown on the vertical axis. It denotes the annual growth rate of the market in which the corporation operates. It could be within the range of 0 – 20 per cent, though a larger range could also be shown. Any rate above 10 per cent is considered high.

The *relative market share* is shown on the horizontal axis. It shows how strong a company relatively is. Here the market share of the strategic unit is shown with reference to the market share of the largest competitor. A relative market share of 0.1 means that the strategic unit of the product has only a 10 per cent of the leader's share. The relative market share is bifurcated into high and low market shares, using a market share of 1.00 as the bench-mark. Log scale is used to mark the relative market share. The growth share matrix is made up of four cells In diagram 3.6, there are two question marks. They are in a high growth market but the relative market share is low. Several new entrants in Credit Card market can treat this business, as a question mark. They are a high growth business and can become tomorrow's bread-winners. Just now the banks continue to pour money into credit card business. Out of the two question marks of the above company the company has to deploy more resources into one business rather than putting meagre resources into both of them.

There are two stars in the following diagram. A business which was a question mark yesterday can become a star today. As the growth rate of a star is high, the company has to deploy large resources to the stars. This is necessary to ward off competitive assault also. Though stars do not generate cash today they may become cash-generating cows in future. Each company must have some stars. Each cell represents a different business unit.

- *Question Marks* are those business/products which have high market growths but relatively low market shares. It requires a lot of cash.
- *Stars* are successful question marks. Star is a market leader in a high growth market. They are often cash using rather than cash generating. They are however profitable. They have the potential to become future cash cows.
- *Cash Cows* show growth rate of less than 10 per cent These provide a lot of cash. Since market growth rate is low, it does not require commitment of finance to expansion. The business/product is the market leader and hence enjoys economies of scale and higher profit margins. A manufacturer 'milks' this product even at the cost of endangering its brand equity.
- *Dogs* describe weak business products. They typically generate low profits/losses or they may throw-off some cash.

The following diagram of BCG analysis for a multi-product company illustrates this model:

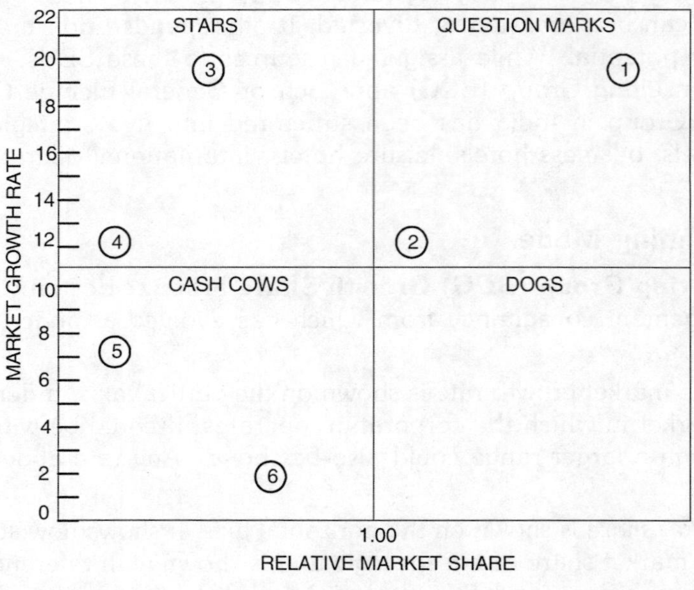

Fig. 3.6 BCG Approach

Our company has two cash cows. Here there is less market growth. But there is huge cash generation. Being the market leaders, cash cows are highly profitable on account of economies of scale. The cash generated is deployed to keep up our stars, questions marks and dogs which are always cash hungry. To illustrate, soaps and detergents are cash cows for the market leader Hindustan Lever Ltd. This cash-cow supports their stars like personal care products and chemicals and question marks like polymers. Our company has only two cash cows. The position is vulnerable. If these cows lose the market share, we will have to inject more money here itself to maintain our share. If this does not happen, cash cow can become a dog.

In our example, there is no dog. For a bank, priority sector advances have low margins though these generate some cash. The banks justify their holding on to these businesses on social justice grounds. Priority sector advances being dogs consume more of management time than they are worth.

It is for the company to have a healthy business portfolio. When a company has too many dogs and too many question marks and too few stars and too few cash cows, the portfolio is considered unbalanced. Each business in the portfolio is assigned a budget, has to achieve certain objectives and formulates strategies to achieve them. The basic objectives are to increase the market share (or building the business), to maintain the market share (or holding the business), or to increase the short-term cash flow (or harvesting the business) and to withdraw from the business by taking resources away from it (divesting the business).

With advancing times, SBUs undergo a metamorphosis. What started as a question mark becomes a star? A star of today may become a cash cow tomorrow. Finally, the SBU fades out by becoming a dog. The travelling route of SBUs must be taken into account while planning for them. Even a healthy portfolio is no guarantee of success. Each SBU must have the right objectives and strategies to succeed. SBUs cannot be treated uniformly for planning purposes. The very idea behind SBU analysis is to exploit their differing potential to realise profits. Cash cows must be supported by funds, or else they get enfeebled. It is not correct to have too many question marks, each underinvested. It is also not correct to commit to dogs hoping to turn them around.

❖ Corporate Planning: The GE Model

General Electric Company pioneered the corporate planning model much before it came into vogue in the USA. In 1970, GE divided its 200-odd department into Strategic Business Units. (SBUs)

A unique feature of GE's planning process in the sixties was the development of the concept of business differentiation. In the mid-sixties when GE's top management had to make some tough decisions about which lines of business to persist with and which of them to divest; a clear perception that each business was different in nature and needed to be viewed quite differently from the rest emerged, the concept of differentiation then came to the forefront and continues to be an underlying feature of GE's planning.

Since then the basic feature of GE's corporate strategic planning is that the management recognises that each of its business is unique and its operations need to be reviewed separately. Nevertheless, at the same time the company is fully aware that since each business unit forms a part of the whole and the SBUs cannot be isolated from the rest of the company and that at a certain level the strategies of the SBUs need to be integrated with the remaining business of the company. In June every year, each SBU submits a detailed strategic plan to the corporate policy committee. Some SBUs are basically composed of only one line of business while other may include several related lines of business.

Each business is rated against two variables *industry attractiveness* and the *company's business' strengths.* The success of company depends to the extent it enters the attractive industries and has the requisite amalgam of business strengths to succeed. If either of the variables is wanting, the success is affected adversely. In GE model, the planners identify the factors underlying each variable, measure them and combine them into an index.

To illustrate, the following table will make the multi-factor portfolio analysis clear:

Variable	*Factors underlying*	*Weight*	*Rating (1 – 5)*	*Value (3 × 4)*
1	2	3	4	5
Industry Attractiveness	Overall market size			
	Growth-rate of market (annual)			
	Profit-margin competitiveness.			
	Technological requirements			
	Vulnerability to inflation			
	Energy requirements			
	Environmental impact			
	Social/Political/Legal	Must be acceptable		
		1.00		
Business Strength	Market share, Share growth			
	Product quality, Brand image			
	Distribution network			
	Promotional effectiveness			
	Productivity, Unit costs,			
	Material supplies, *R* and *D* performance			
	Managerial Personnel			
		1.00		

Source: Hosmer, *Strategic Management,* Englewood Cliffs, N.J. Prentice Hall, 1982, p. 310. Adapted.

After carrying out the above exercise, the planner places an SBU into a matrix as shown in Figure. 3.7. The SBU is placed as a point, around which a circle is drawn. The size of the circle represents the size of the market. Inside the circle, a shaded portion is shown to show its market share.

The GE matrix is divided into three zones, consisting of nine cells. The three cells at the upper left show any SBU falling in this region should *invest/grow.* The diagonal cells which are unshaded in the above diagram are medium in overall attractiveness. The companies SBU if placed in this region could pursue *selectivity/earnings.* The three cells at the lower right shaded vertically indicate *harvest/divest* strategy. The three zones are described as Green zone, Yellow zone and Red Zone respectively. The matrix is known as General Electric multifactor portfolio matrix. The model is discussed elaborately by Derek Abell in *Strategic Market Planning,* Prentice Hall, 1979, Ch. 4. It is refined further by Shell Company, which calls it the directional policy matrix.

Given the current strategy, management is in a position to forecast the placement of an SBU in the next three to five years. Depending upon the placement of the SBU, the demand or revenue is managed to the targeted level. Each SBU's sales/profit potential are assessed. After setting the budget and objectives, marketing managers carry out the plans for each SBUs.

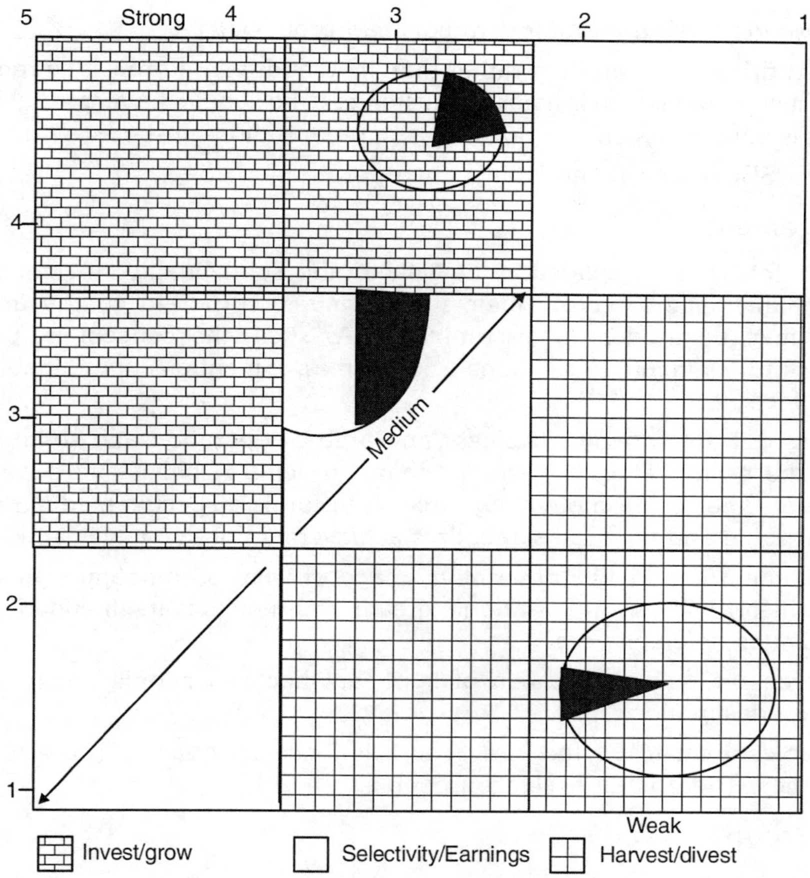

Fig. 3.7

❖ Strategic Considerations

Marketing is losing sheen since it is too much occupied with the 4 Ps led tactical marketing. Chief Executive Officers are not as much impressed by marketing executives as they are by their finance and production executives. Though CEOs are customer oriented, they feel marketing to be the guiding philosophy pervading the whole organisation, rather than as a narrow function limited to one department. Marketing can be referred to it original glory if it becomes strategic, cross-function and profit driven.

According to Nirmalya Kumar, an organisation must take strategic initiatives such as

- *brand rationalisation* where focus is on core brands and others are sold off to those for whom they are valuable. A brand is milked till it dies a natural death. Some brands are phased out.
- *strategic segmentation* must be practised instead of market segmentation e.g. a low cost airline which involves total make-over of operations, purchasing and marketing.
- *providing solutions* rather than products.
- *channel migration* from traditional channels to newer options of organised retailing and internet.

- *reorganisation around customers* rather than products.
- be market driving organisation rather than market driven. Ford wittily remarked that had he just remained a listener to customers, he would have produced a faster horse. It is only incremental innovation. An organisation must educate the customer.
- shift from SBU - centric marketing to corporate marketing.

❖ Vision Statements

Vision statements were articulated in the wake of the Total Quality Movement (TQM) of the 1980's. Companies like to codify their ethics, values, corporate culture and goals. A vision statement may be used as a discriminator. As such, the concept is fuzzy, says a cosmetic manufacturer claiming 'to sell hope'. Sometimes, it mentions unattainable goals like 'attaining zero defects.'

Mission spells out a company's business and area of operation and some generalized goals like 'to be the best.' Values are strong, common veins of belief and drive which run through a company. They are a motivating force. A vision is a specific medium range goal, measurable, deliverable and timed. It symbolizes achievement of the values and the mission.

A vision statement is a vividly descriptive image of what a company wants to be and wants to be known for. It is an organisation's dream and indicates its intended direction. It inspires and motivates its employees.

A vision statement is like a beacon of light that beckons people in an organization towards a common destination.

Most companies want to be the best. There is focus on quality. There is a quest to delight the customer. There is an accent on people.

❖ The Tata Group

At the Tata Group, our purpose is to improve the quality of life of the communities we serve. We do this through leadership in sectors of national economic significance to which the group brings a unique set of capabilities. This requires us to grow aggressively in focused areas of business.

"Our heritage of returning to society what we earn evokes trust among consumers, employees, shareholders and the community. This heritage will be continuously enriched by formalizing the high standard of behaviour expected from employees and companies."

"The Tata name is a unique asset representing leadership with trust. Leveraging this asset to enhance group synergy and becoming globally competitive is the route to sustained growth and long-term success."

❖ The Aditya Birla Group

Our vision:

To be a premium conglomerate with a focus at every business level.

ADITYA BIRLA GROUP

Our mission:

To pursue the creation of value.

Our aim:

To deliver value for our customers, shareholders, investors, employees and society at large.

Management ethos:

Focus on value-added growth through:

- Strategic thrust: Fundamental value-creation and sharper business focus.
- Structural initiatives: Internalising the concept of value-creation.

❖ Godrej Consumer Products

We shall operate in existing and new businesses which profitably capitalize on our corporate image of quality and integrity.

Godrej Consumer Products Ltd.

"Our objective is to delight both in India and Abroad.

"We shall achieve this objective by re-engineering our business and through continuous improvement in quality, cost and customer service.

"We shall strive for excellence by nurturing, developing and empowering our employees and suppliers. We shall encourage an open atmosphere, conducive to learning and teamwork."

Vision statement for Tata Steel

Tata Steel enters the new millennium with the confidence of a learning organization, a knowledge-based and happy organization. We will establish ourselves as the supplier of choice by delighting our customers with our services and products. In the coming decade, we will become the most cost-competitive steel plant and so serve the community and the nation.

Reliance does not have a formal, written mission statement.

Infosys has three principle corporate objectives:

- To be a world-class software house in the global market.
- To be one of the first names to come to mind for software solutions.
- To create wealth for the company, shareholders and employees by the legal and ethical means.

Infosy's vision is:

We will be a globally respected corporation that provides best-of-breed software solutions delivered by the best-in-class people.

* * *

4 MARKETING PROCESS AND MARKETING PLANNING

As we are already aware, business success is guaranteed by strategic orientation and marketing savvy. Strategic planning initiates marketing planning. Each marketing plan has strategic and tactical dimensions. The former is based on environmental analysis and the latter, on marketing specifics like promotion, pricing, distribution and merchandising. Marketing plan is a part of the overall business plan, consisting of production plan, purchase plan, manpower plan, financial plan etc. Marketing plan becomes a key plan for many businesses. It also directs and co-ordinates the marketing effort of the firm.

To understand, marketing plans, we shall first study the marketing process and the steps it involves.

❖ Marketing Process

Marketing process is a part of overall business activity consisting of making and selling value-added products to the target market. Traditionally, business manufactured what it could, and markets absorbed all its production. This may be true in a situation of scarcity. But in competitive markets, marketing homework starts while designing the products for manufacture itself. The right values are chosen for a select target market which is then provided to the target market. Product development, pricing, sourcing and making, distribution and servicing are part of value provision process. The built-up value in the product is then communicated by means of the sales force, sales promotion and advertising.

Marketing managers carry out the marketing process having the following steps:

(*i*) Analysing marketing opportunities.

(*ii*) Target market selection.

(*iii*) Formulation of marketing strategies.

(*iv*) Making marketing programmes. and

(*v*) Organisation, implementation and controlling of the marketing effort.

Diagrammatically the marketing process is given below:

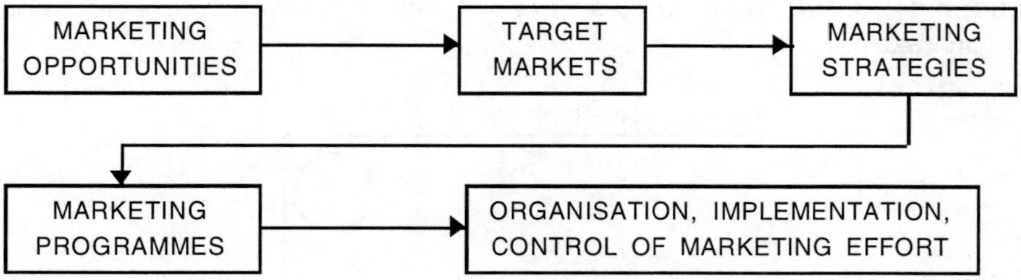

Fig. 4.1 Marketing Process

❖ Marketing Opportunities

We have to spot the marketing opportunities in tune with our business mission. Thus, an entertainment company can make movies and distribute them so as to exhibit them in cinema halls. However, as video cassette recorders enter the consumer homes, it can sell-off video rights of the movie to other companies or can itself undertake to produce video cassettes. In the changing environment, it can see further opportunities for itself. Already the satellite channels have started beaming round-the-clock programmes. The movie company has the infrastructure and the know-how to produce TV programmes. It, therefore, can enter into this field. Since music has become an integral part of Indian movies, a movie company can think of selling the audio rights to a music company. Business opportunities are thus to be spotted in the environment that is shaped by social, technological, economic, cultural, legal and demographic forces. A British condom manufacturer bagged a major contract during the Gulf War to supply 5 lac condoms to Saudi Arabia which were used to ship over the end of rifle barrels to keep sand from entering them. The opportunities chosen are those that fit with our business mission and which we can exploit profitably due to our expertise in that particular area — our *distinctive* or *core competence*. To evaluate these opportunities, we can make use of marketing research. While tapping the opportunities, we must think of our competitors. Their strengths and strategies do affect our business moves.

❖ Target Markets

The market that we shall cater to should be defined. It could be an overall market or just a small segment of it, consisting of homogeneous buyers. Thus, we can put a soap for all those who take a bath, or can restrict the soap for babies only like Johnson and Johnson Baby Soap or Wipro's Baby Soap. The size of the market, the growth of the market, the profitability of a market and the risk involved must be carefully assessed. Each segment of the market is also evaluated. Only that market segment which the company selects is called its target market. There are various methods of segmentation which are dealt with later. Markets are broadly segmented on the basis of customer groups or customer needs. Our market segment should suit our objectives and resources.

❖ Marketing Strategies

Suppose a food manufacturing firm wishes to offer its beverage. It has decided to segment the market into two broad groups — individual buyers and institutional buyers. It has now to position its beverage — it can be a taste-additive powder to be added to milk or it can be a health food for old people or it could be growth food and nutrient for growing children. The position taken by the company decides its formulation and the competition it will face. Which position a company generally adopts? It all depends upon the attributes chosen for positioning and the competitive scene. Consider the following product positioning map for a book on taxation:

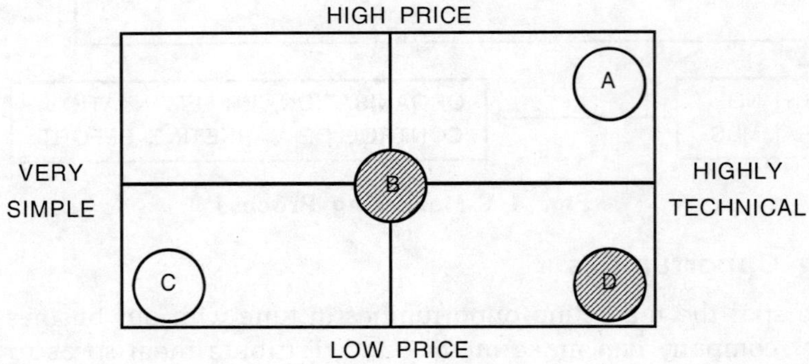

Here two attributes relevant to a book on taxation are chosen. The complexity of the subject matter and the price are the two attributes. Book *A* is a highly technical book and is highly priced too. It is meant for seasoned professionals perhaps who are practising taxation law. Book *B* is moderate in complexity and moderately priced. It is meant for learners who can grasp the subject matter and who can afford the price. Book *C* seems to be a trash available at a throw away price just to pass the examination. The new publishing company can think of a *gap* in this space map. It is given by *D* where a sufficiently high quality text is made available at a low price. Alternatively, the newcomer can just put any product in the position map near *A*, *B*, or *C*. But in that case, it must have better marketing resources and capability.

Once the position is thus decided, we have to develop our product. New product development is done in several stages. The new product developed is then launched. Once the product is launched, it passes through several stages of its life-cycle — introduction, growth, maturity and decline. Both new product development and PLC are considered in separate chapters later. Each stage of its life cycle calls for a different strategy. Strategy formulation, in the ultimate analysis, is a result of the changing business environment that throws off different business opportunities.

❖ Marketing Programmes

Marketing strategies are ultimately converted into marketing programmes. Any marketing programme has to first decide about the *marketing spend* — expenditure necessary to achieve the marketing objectives. Mostly marketing budgets are set as percentage of sales — its own sales and those of the competitors. Sometimes more than the budgeted ratio may be spent in order to attain a desired market share. In the final analysis, the budget is set in relation to marketing task on hand — a given sales volume or market share for which costs are ascertained. The total budget is allocated towards the various elements of the marketing mix.

❖ Marketing Mix

The foundation of modern marketing management is put on the concept of marketing mix. It was McCarthy who identified the four inputs that make up an organisation's marketing system. They are the product, the price, the place (or distribution) and the promotion. They are called the four Ps. Marketing mix is a combination of these four Ps. Mostly, these four

Ps are within the control of the organisation, but they are subject to the external environmental forces. The various marketing variables under each P are shown in the following table:

MARKETING MIX

Product	**Price**	**Place**	**Promotion**
Design	Retail price	Channels	Advertising
Features	Wholesale price	Locations	Salesforce
Brand name	Discounts	Transport	Sales Promotion (SP)
Variety	Allowances	Coverage	Public Relation (PR)
Quality	Payment period	Inventory	Direct Marketing (DM)
Sizes	Credit terms	Assortments	
Services			
Warranties			

The marketing mix of a company for each product at a particular time can be represented (2.00, ₹ 6,000, ₹ 1,00,000, ₹ 1,50,000) where each figure stands for (P_1, P_2 P_3 and P_4). In this case the average product quality is given by 1.00 and good product quality by 2.00. The price per piece of say a washing machine is ₹ 6,000. The amount spent on distribution per month is 1 lakh and the amount spent on promotion per month is 1.5 lakhs. It will be appreciated by students that marketing mix is selected from several possibilities. If there are 2 product qualities, 10 different product prices, and 5 different expenditure levels of distribution and promotion, then the marketing mix combinations which are possible are ($2 \times 10 \times 5 \times 5$) = 500. Besides, one set of marketing mix is selected for the distribution channel and one for the final consumers. All the variables in the marketing mix cannot be adjusted in the short-run. Of course, prices, promotion and distribution can be changed in the short-run, but not the new product development and distribution channels. Marketers have to allocate marketing rupees is different promotional media, sales territories, products and channels. Each of the four Ps have been separately considered in this book in detail.

The four Ps are inter-related. Any decision pertaining to one variable affects the other variables. Management seeks a mix that will lead to optimal synergistic results.

Product: It involves planning and development of the right products. Strategies for existing products and new products are needed. There are decisions regarding branding, packaging and product features.

Price: Here the right price for a product is determined, then there are decisions regarding discounts, transportation charges and credit terms.

Place (Distribution): Here trade channels are selected for distributing the product. The firm must understand the different types of wholesalers, retailers and distribution firms.

Promotion: Here the product is brought to the notice of the target market favourably. It not only informs but also persuades. Advertising, personal selling, sales promotion, direct marketing and public relations are the major promotional activities.

The concept of marketing mix is applicable to non-business organisations, too. For a university, the products are the various courses, which are offered at a price (fee) and are distributed in the classrooms or by post and are promoted by media advertisements and counsellors.

The mix is both influenced and supported by a company's non-marketing activities like production, finance, personnel and by non-market resources like location, public image etc.

❖ Four Cs of Marketing

According to Kotler, though four Ps remain a useful organising framework for planning, these Ps could be further translated into the four Cs which take a customer-based rather than a seller-based view. Product becomes Customer Value, Price becomes Customer Costs, Place becomes Customer Convenience and Promotion becomes Customer Communication. Buyers, according to Kotler, want customer value, lower total costs, more convenience and honest communication. The starting point is not the 4 Ps but Segmentation, Targeting and Positioning (STP). STP is strategic marketing and the 4 Ps are tactical marketing.

❖ Marketing Effort: Organisation, Implementation and Controlling

The last step of the marketing process is to make use of marketing resources to implement the marketing plan and then to control it. The marketing plan is implemented through the mechanism of a marketing organisation. In a smaller organisation, there is too much centralisation of the marketing functions. In a larger organisation, there are different specialists in charge of different marketing tasks. At the top of the marketing organisation, there is the marketing manager. Essentially, he co-ordinates the efforts of the different marketing functionaries working under him. To illustrate, he ensures that the sales manager makes the best use of the product strategies formulated by the product manager and the product manager, in turn, exploits the feedback given by the field salesforce. Beyond this, a marketing manager co-ordinates with other functional heads like the production manager, finance manager, purchase manager etc. Marketing department's effectiveness is ultimately a function of how well the marketing personnel are recruited, selected, trained, developed and compensated. A motivated team can work out the magic needed for success. There should be constant communication between the Subordinates and the Managers. In the implementation of a marketing plan, there are going to be certain bottlenecks. The company seeks feedback and institutes control procedures.

There are three ways to control the marketing effort. First it is seen every year whether goals set for the marketing function are being met or not. If there are gaps between Goals set and Achieved, we must find the causes and take corrective action. Secondly, control is kept on the profitability of the different marketing activities. Control has to be strategic to make marketing effective. *Marketing audit* is used to exercise strategic control. The following table summarises the above discussion.

❖ Marketing Plan: Nature and Contents

At the end of the marketing process, what we get is a marketing plan. As we know, marketing plan is a part of overall corporate and divisional plans. In the marketing plan, we have product-line plans, brand plans and market plans. There are integrated brand-market plans, too. We also have promotional plan, distributional plan and price plans. In the section of promotional plans, we have advertising, media and sales plan. Each marketing plan has the following major heads:

Section	*Purpose*
(*i*) Executive Summary	Overview of the entire plan for the benefit of the executives.
(*ii*) Background	Prevailing situation of the market, product, competitive scene and overall environment.
(*iii*) Opportunities Analysis	Opportunities and threats of major nature are identified. Strengths and weaknesses and issues facing the products are jotted down.

Section	Purpose
(*iv*) Objectives	Goals are set for: (*i*) Sales volume, (*ii*) market share, and (*iii*) Profits
(*v*) Marketing Strategies	Strategies desired to meet the objectives.
(*vi*) Action Programme	The line of action proposed, the person taking the decisions for the same, the time of the decisions and the cost of this.
(*vii*) Projected Profit and Loss Statement	Profit and loss forecast
(*viii*) Controls	Monitoring of the plan

The above sections have been illustrated by taking the case of Essar Cellophone — the company that has introduced mobile phones in Delhi and its satellite towns.

❖ Executive Summary

It condenses the whole plan into some major goals and recommendations. Here is a concise example.

❖ Background

The market is analysed in terms of the competitive scene, distribution pattern, physical characteristics, qualitative aspects, products available and the broad environmental factors.

Market Situation: The data on the target market are given and market growth is shown. These data are on the needs of customers.

There are people who are willing to spend on cameras if the right type of product is available. Cameras can become popular in India as they are elsewhere. The cameras are for people who want to have fun. The cameras are meant for all age groups.

Product Situation: Here the data about the sales, prices, margins and profits are given.

Competitive Situation: All major companies offering competitive products are identified. The data regarding competition are collected.

Distribution Situation: The data regarding the channels of distribution are presented here.

Macroenvironment: Here the factors like demography, economic situation, technological conditions, socio-political conditions having influence on the product in question are considered.

❖ Opportunities Analysis

The marketing department has to identify the major *opportunities* in the market place, and the *threats* it faces. It has to identify the *strengths* the organisation possesses and its *weaknesses.* Ultimately, the company formulates the *issues* the product line faces.

Objectives and Marketing Strategy: Each plan is committed to some objectives. A marketing plan has financial and non-financial objectives.

❖ Action Programmes

Each element of strategy given above must be studied in the context of 3 Ws and 1 H. *What* is to be done? *When* is it to be done? *Who* will do it? *How* will it be done?

❖ Projected Profit and Loss Account

The sales forecast will appear on the credit side. The projected sales are the number of units multiplied by estimated price. To the debit side, we will show the total cost of production, distribution and marketing. The difference is the estimated profit. The projected statement is studied and approved by the management.

❖ Controls

The goals set, may or may not be attained. We have to monitor the progress of the plan for each goal set and take corrective action if necessary. There are contingency plans also, if there are some adverse developments.

❖ Stick to the Basics

According to Jack Trout, marketers should stick to the basics which means focusing on a constant or unique message followed by a coherent marketing direction, so that every element of marketing mix focuses on a main differentiating idea and moves in unison. The next step is changing people's mind. It is more challenging. By altering information on which the beliefs rest, one can change the belief system. One can also alter public's perception of the competition.

* * *

5 COMPETITIVE ENVIRONMENT

❖ Competition

Marketing is consumer-focused. But only the study of one's consumers is not sufficient. We have to study our competitors. In the late 90s what we face is fierce competition. These are the days of globalisation in which companies are moving across national boundaries and entering into alien markets. Each company must, therefore become *competitive* — they have to consider both the target customers and the competitors. We often read about marketing wars, say, for example, Cola wars in India. Yet many companies do ignore competitors perhaps under a mistaken notion that they know everything there is to know about their competitors. Competitive intelligence is a must for any sensible organisation. It is an important input for marketing planning. A comparison of our products, prices, promotion and channels with those of our major competitors gives us an added insight. We are able to judge our competitive advantage (or disadvantage conversely speaking). It enables us to meet competition effectively and defend our position in the market place.

What do we gather in any study of our competitors? We must first identify them (*who* are they?), then study their *strategies* and *objectives.* We must also know their *strengths* and *weaknesses.* At last we must knowhow they *respond* to our marketing presence. This information allows us to frame our marketing strategy.

❖ Who are Our Competitors?

Sometimes, it is easier to identify our competitors. Pepsi considers Coke as its competitor in India. Videocon knows Philips, BPL and Onida are its competitors in the TV market. However, we must go beyond this obvious analysis, and identify the hidden competitors. An ultrasonic washing machine using sound waves to clean the garments is a greater threat to detergents.

There are four types of competitive levels; based upon product substitution.

Brand Competition: Similar brands compete with each other — thus Surf Excel competes with Ariel Micro-shine as both are enzyme-based detergents. However, Surf Excel does not see Nirma detergent as a competitor.

Industry Competition: Similar industries (making the same product class) compete with each other. A TV manufacturing company, thus, competes with all other TV manufacturing companies.

Form Competition: These companies satisfy the same basic need. Thus an automobile company satisfying transportation need competes with other companies making mopeds.

Generic Competition: These companies compete for the same consumer rupees (disposable income). An auto company competes with all consumer durables, holiday packages and housing.

Competition can be studied in terms of *industry* and *market* place.

❖ Concept of Competition

First, we will understand the concept of competition from the view point of *industry.* Industry denotes a group of firms producing closely substitutable products or product classes. *e.g.,* pharma industry or automobile industry. Closely substitutable product have high cross-elasticity of demand — a rise in price of one product leads to the rise in demand of another product. Thus if the price of Videocon washing machines rise, there is going to be a greater demand for BPL washing machines due to people switching over from Videocon to BPL.

Each industry is governed by the demand and supply factors. These together affect the *structure* of that particular industry. The factors which affect the structure of an industry are:

Ease of Entry: Firms get attracted to attractive industries. The ease with which they can enter into an industry determine the industry's structure. Free entry leads to increased supply and a fall in prices. The returns become normal. Some industries have created *entry barriers.* Maybe they are too capital intensive. Maybe, they require too large a volume of production to seek economies of scale. Perhaps, the marketing muscle and savvy required is not so easy to acquire. There are certain intrinsic barriers and there are certain barriers created by the actions of the individual firms or their collective cartels. In certain industries, we cannot exit once we enter, even when the bottom-line is not so healthy. Maybe, there are legal, moral, technological restrictions. There may be sentimental barriers too.

Cost Structure: Each industry does its own unique cost structure. The cost mix gives a strategic average to the firms. The greatest costs are pruned. Some raw material consuming industries will become competitive when the material costs are reduced by a particular percentage. In the pharma industry, the marketing and promotional costs are too high. Perhaps a lean force of medical representatives cutting down the wage bill will make the industry competitive.

Vertical Integration: Integration in the backward or forward direction may prove advantageous. Reliance is a good example. It started producing PFY: Polyester Filament Yarn by backward integration. PFY is the basic raw material for its finished products. It went further backwards and started petrochemical industry to give inputs to its PFY producing plant. Reliance also integrated in forward direction by establishing retail outlets to sell its textiles and ready-to-wear fabrics. Vertical integration gives a greater control or value add-ons. It lowers costs, too. There are tax benefits also.

Global Reach: By their very nature, some industries are local like the distribution of newspapers by a vendor. Some industries are global like aircraft, cameras, pharmaceuticals. Global presence induces competitiveness.

Another way to look at competition is from the viewpoint of the customer need. A movie moghul may consider another movie moghul as his competitor, but from the customer's viewpoint, he is in the entertainment industry and thus his competition expands to cover TV serial producers, stage and theatre shows, folk dances, mimicry etc. This broader perspective gives a new insight to the company and makes strategic planning meaningful.

We shall now see how to identify our competitors.

❖ Competitor's Strategies: Identification

Close competitors cater to the same target audience and do follow more or less the same strategy. When a group of organisations follow the same strategy in a given market, they form a strategic group. Each firm has to identify as to which strategic group it belongs to. Each group follows a particular strategy. To illustrate, we shall take the case of electrical appliances. The dimensions on which each group is considered are the level of quality and the level of integration in production.

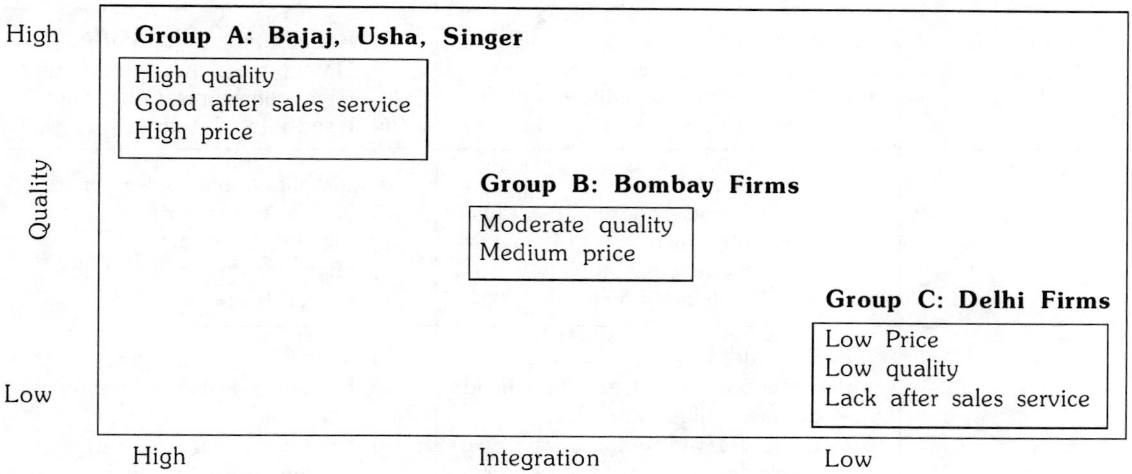

Group A and B are not so easy to enter. Any company entering these groups will have to compete with the existing group members. Unless there is some competitive advantage, it is difficult to succeed against the existing members. Competition is not only restricted to within the group but there is inter group competition also. For example, both group A and B firms go in for the upper middle class customers in a big way. Perhaps, even customers find the offers from these two groups one and the same. Each group wants to expand its market base. We can take a number of other dimensions to identify strategic groups like the production technology employed, the sophistication of technology employed and so on. We compare two banks here — one nationalised bank and the other a private sector bank. Both of them have a different strategic make up. Their customer groups are also different. Much more detailed profiles can be drawn up to cover many other aspects of management.

A company always considers the competitive strategies and revises its own strategies over a period of time. The turbulent marketing environment itself demands certain changes in the strategies.

Factor	*Nationalised Bank*	*Private Sector Bank*
Business strategy	Mass based wide network of branches	Concentrated marketing in selected markets; class-based banking.
Marketing	(*i*) Procedure-oriented (*ii*) Cross-subsidisation between Low-yield priority sector and high-yield general advances. (*iii*) Retail-banking (*iv*) Emphasis on interest income (*v*) Less innovation in products (*vi*) Less personal (*vii*) Service leaves much to be desired.	(*i*) Customer-oriented (*ii*) High-yield advances (*iii*) Wholesale banking (*iv*) Emphasis on interest as well as non-interest income of fees (*v*) High product innovation (*vi*) Relationship banking (*vii*) Service to the customers is of utmost importance.
Human Resources	(*i*) Non-professional (*ii*) Clerical manpower dominant (*iii*) Communication skills poor (*iv*) Training unrelated to needs.	(*i*) Professional, more MBAs (*ii*) Officer manpower dominant (*iii*) High communication skills (*iv*) Need-related training.
Operations	(*i*) Cumbersome (*ii*) Manual. Less computerisation (*iii*) Rigid approach (*iv*) Authority-responsibility link poor at the officer-clerk level	(*i*) Simplified and streamlined (*ii*) Highly computerised. (*iii*) Flexible approach. (*v*) High accountability at the officer level.
Organisation	(*i*) Pyramidal (*ii*) Functional heads and line heads do not collaborate (*iii*) Unnecessarily lengthy chain of command.	(*i*) Matrix (*ii*) Functional-line coordination very good. (*iii*) No unnecessary tiers in the organisational structure.

❖ Competitors Objectives

Each competitor has a unique set of objectives. However, out of the multiple objectives like profitability survival, market growth, there may be varied emphasis on each of these objectives. The weightage assigned by a competitor to any given objective helps us to know his reaction towards our particular strategies. A low-cost leadership firm will react more strongly to a technological break-through that reduces prices. Perhaps a larger ad budget of the competitor might not affect the low-cost leadership firm. The competitors objectives are formulated keeping in mind its size, the philosophy of the parent firm, current management, history and economics. Single-product dominant firms are very hard to attack. We have to assess the competitor's expansion plans also. That keeps the other firms battle ready.

Competitors Strengths and Weaknesses: We have to collect financial data about the competitor's business. We would like to know his capacity utilisation. Even market data like the marketing share of the competitor must be collected. Most of the data can be collected through secondary sources. Even some primary data may be collected through salesmen, distributors and suppliers. Each competitor is assessed on a rating scale of several key attributes — quality of products, quality of sales efforts, product availability, technical back-up. A competitor can be attacked on its weak spots. A competitor may make wrong assumptions, *e.g.*, price is not important as long as service is delivered or the sales — force is the most important part of promotion and marketing. A firm can take advantage of a major wrong assumption.

Competitor's Response Pattern: Any action on the part of the organisation leads to a response pattern on the part of competitors. This response pattern depends upon the objectives set by the competitive firms, and it strengths/weaknesses. The ethos of the competitive firm and its organisational culture also shapes the response pattern. Some competitors are slow to react as they believe in the loyalty of their customers or they lack the funds to react. Some competitors are selective in their response pattern — they do not react to all the moves of the organisation but only to some select moves. Some competitors ferociously guard the ground by reacting strongly to any move. Standard Chartered found that their credit card members are being approached by Citi Bank agents in Bangalore. They inserted ads in the media inviting Citi card-holders and Diner's Club members to secure SCB cards on the strength of three previous statement of accounts. In some competitors, the reaction pattern is along predictable line.

One industry might have competitive harmony while the other may have a history of competitive discord. Competitive equilibrium is governed by several factors.

Homogeneous firms selling the same commodities are subject to disturbance of competitive equilibrium if there is any such move like a lowering of price by one firm. For those firms where cost reduction is possible by economies of scale or technology or learning curve, lowering of prices is possible, giving an enormous advantage to the firm so doing. Here a single dominant factor like cost has disturbed the equilibrium. Those industries where multiplicity of factors distinguish the firms, each competitor can have it own edge and many of them can co-exist, catering to specific segments. In case there are several critical factors associated with these firms, there will be a great many competitors, each having its own niche. If, on the other hand, there are few critical factors, there will be fewer competitors, who will co-exist. A market share ratios of 2:1 between two competitors is roughly the equilibrium point. It is not practical either to increase or decrease this share.

Competitive Intelligence: As we have already observed, it is necessary to know several things about the competitors for which data must be collected, processed, interpreted and used. There should be a trade-off between the cost of information collected and the cost associated with not getting it. The firm must design its own competitive intelligence system.

Facing Competition: A firm decides to take shots at the weak competitors, but it does not add anything to its capabilities. The firm has to face strong competitors. It should identify the weak spots of strong competitors and attack them. A firm likes to compete with competitors having a similarity, *e.g.*, Videocon TV and Onida TV. In competition, we should support good competitors who abide by the rules of the game and are reasonable. The company should attack only the bad competitors.

❖ Competition-centered Vs. Customer-Centered Firms

Tracking competitors is sensible, but an obsession with competitors should not dilute our customer focus. All our actions should not be in response to competition only. We have to shape the policies on our own keeping consumers in mind. It is necessary to keep an eye on competition without losing our customer focus. This balanced attention to both is the real *marketing orientation.*

* * *

6 MARKETING RESEARCH AND MARKETING INFORMATION SYSTEM

❖ What is Marketing Research?

These days the markets are flooded with products and services from a large number of companies. The buyers have become choosy. While buying they are affected by the opinions of their friends, the proddings of their kids and the dotingly fond talk of their wives. Besides, they see glittering advertisements in glossy magazines, view enchantingly beautiful models using the products on the small TV screen and once inside the shop are advised by the well-meaning dealers and distributors. There are people who love freedom, some who love adventure, and some an aristocratic lifestyle. People show negative attitudes to certain products (like vegetarians showing aversion to eggs) and show positive attitudes to some other products (like jeans, jogging shoes and lipsticks). We have buyers scattered all over the country, at times abroad also. In other words, these days, marketing has become a specialised activity which keeps the buyer or consumer in the centre while designing a product mix. The physical products as such are not important these days, but it is their capacity to satisfy the buyer's needs and wants like his need to have health, entertainment, transportation, speed, convenience etc. Marketing, therefore, starts much before the actual selling of the product by doing an analysis of the needs and wants of buyers and continues even after the selling of the products again by seeing whether the product offered gives complete satisfaction to the buyer or not.

In order to understand the needs of buyer and his behaviour, we have a tool; that of marketing research. Marketing research means finding out who the customers are, what are their needs and what they buy. It provides an organisation with basic information. It generates information for the decision-makers to design a suitable product, to further develop it, to price it properly, to promote it effectively and to distribute it for the convenience of the buyers. It helps the decision-maker to understand, to explain, to describe and to evaluate the marketing programme.

Marketing research is the systematic collection of information for the purpose of decision-making.

Against this background, we can say, marketing research is research pertaining to any problem in the area of marketing. Let us study some formal definitions.

> "Marketing Research (MR) is the systematic, objective and exhaustive search for and study of the facts relevant to any problem in the field of marketing."
>
> — *Crisp, R.D.*
>
> Marketing Research is "the application of scientific method to the solution of marketing problems." — *Luck, Wales, Taylor.*
>
> Marketing research is "the systematic and objective search for the analysis of information relevant to the identification and solution of any problem relating to marketing."
>
> — *Green and Tull.*
>
> "Marketing research is the systematic recording and analysing of data about problems relating to marketing." — *American Marketing Association.*

Let us now understand the salient points given by the above definitions.

1. Marketing Research Consists of Findings Based on Data: These data relate to any area of marketing function — from a study of the market place to a study of buyer behaviour. They cover an expanse of products, prices, distribution and promotion. The data collected are analysed and interpreted for the use of the decision-makers.

2. Systematic Collection of Data: The data are collected by following a systematic procedure. First of all, a problem is identified. For example, the problem is that of declining sales. Perhaps on further examination, we feel the declining sales are due to poor advertising. So the real problem that emerges is that of measuring our ad effectiveness and then if necessary to improve it. Keeping this problem in mind, research objectives are formulated and a sample selected to collect data, which are recorded, analysed and interpreted and presented in the form of a report.

3. Marketing Research is Objective: We do not presuppose things. We just put forth a hypothesis, collect data and either accept the hypothesis or reject it. While doing problem oriented research also, we do not allow subjective bias to creep in. The research is never carried out to support a predetermined result.

4. Marketing Research Converts Data into Information: Data as such are not meaningful. But on processing by systematic record, analysis and interpretation, they become useful information for the decision-maker.

5. Marketing Research is a Continuous Process: Since marketing activity is a continuous one where there are changes in product mix, promotion mix, distribution channels and prices. Marketing research also is carried out on a continuous basis. Yes, one project of the M.R. is isolated. But in the light of changed environment the data also change, and so continuous monitoring is called for. These days the TV market and so also the toothpaste market have become so dynamic, that market shares of different brands do change month to month and a constant marketing research is needed. In such cases, however, marketing research is integrated to Management Information System (MIS).

6. Marketing Research Draws Heavily from Different Disciplines: By its very nature, marketing research draws heavily from economics, psychology, sociology, statistics, operation research, computer science and such other subjects. Marketing research is a multi-dimensional cross-disciplinary subject.

7. Marketing Research is only a Tool to the Decision-Maker: Marketing research does not supplant or replace decision-making process. It only serves as an input to the decision-making process. It is at best a tool that guides the decision-maker. However, certain other variables may make the decision-maker take a decision contrary to findings of marketing research, and he may like another marketing research study to be conducted for confirming or ruling out his decision. The judgement is always that of an executive.

(*i*) Who are those young ladies who prefer to apply lipstick and put nail enamel as a matter of routine in their lifestyle?

(*ii*) When most of the people are glued to their TV sets? Why do the programmes interest them?

(*iii*) Why some people avoid flying even when they are sufficiently rich to afford it?

(*iv*) Is Lalitaji, the Surf model creating enough of impact on the viewers when she compares "sasti chiz and mehangi chiz"?

(*v*) Is the time right to launch a Hot-Shot-like amateur camera where you just aim and shoot?

(*vi*) What are the occasions to use Vicks herbal drops?

(*vii*) Is Rasna properly positioned? Does it compete effectively with remote substitutes like tea and coffee?

(*viii*) What do people feel about public hospitals, airports and nationalised banks?

(*ix*) What are the prospects of exporting our handicrafts items?

(*x*) Why our youngsters prefer romantic and/or thriller paperbacks?

These questions are related to marketing mix, sales, marketing environment, competition, market forecasting, buyer behaviour etc. Marketing research does not answer technical/engineering questions like why this car is not fuel-efficient (but yes, of course, it can answer question like: why people prefer bright red-coloured Maruti cars?)

The manager has to decide when to initiate research and how much to invest on it. He may opt for low cost techniques providing crude estimates or costly sophisticated techniques yielding highly refined estimates. It depends upon the purpose of the research and the available funds. It also depends upon the cost-benefit analysis of the research.

❖ Need for Marketing Research

Let us now see what is the need of marketing research:

1. There cannot be a real marketing activity without the backup of the marketing research function. It ultimately determines the customers' satisfaction. The very *raison d'etre* of an organisation is the customer's satisfaction.
2. Marketing research is a critical element that makes our marketing effort effective.
3. The transition from a seller's market to a buyer's market makes it necessary to have marketing research.
4. Marketing research makes an organisation prepared to changing turbulent business environment.
5. As our markets have expanded geographically, there are attended risks. So, marketing research comes handy to reduce these risks.
6. Product innovation, distribution problems, price-sensitive Indian market have all made marketing research essential.

Formerly advertising was not research based. The philosophy was that of selling rather than marketing. Slowly, complexity of business, growing competition, increasing marketing expenses, national and international distribution made marketing important. In the fifties, there was only Wood's survey of rural market. The real shift came in the sixties when marketing orientation came. Advertising agencies became professionalised. Research data were generated. ORG came up on the scene. IITA set up IMRB, a research outfit, in 1971. Then came MARG. Most of the agencies started relying upon marketing research. The companies also adopted strategic marketing. The advertising agencies did research on target audience. To begin with, the research studies were quantitative. These extended to product studies and consumer studies. Slowly the behavioural and psychographic studies came up and made popular lifestyle advertising. Media did its own research, mostly demographic for its target audience. NRS I, II, III, IV, V are already with us, while the VI and IRS-98, NRS-99 and NRS 2000 have been is published recently. There are further readership surveys called IRS conducted twice every year. The era of positioning had arrived and so researches became all the more necessary. Computer software packages have given a further fillip to research agencies and research departments.

The sector has two distinct segments – the customized survey business and the panel-based business. The panel segment provides media audience and consumption measurement, and requires upfront investment in measurement devices. The customized survey segment includes qualitative and quantitative methods that provide understanding of markets and consumers. As per European Society for Opinion and Marketing Research (ESOMAR), the Indian market for MR is estimated at $151 million (around *A* 744 crore in 2009).

❖ Scope of Marketing Research (MR)

Marketing research is used to find solutions to any problem of marketing. It anticipates a problem or can diagnose any existing problem. Marketing research for the purpose of advertising and other marketing decisions generally cover the following areas:

MARKETING RESEARCH

Advertising Research	*Product Research*	*Consumer Research*	*Sales Research*	*Corporate Research*
Advertisement Effectiveness Studies	Competitive Product Studies	Panel Research	Sales Analysis Tests	Trend Analysis
				Forecasting
Media Research	Product Testing	Diary Research Consumer Profile	Marketing Distribution Channel Studies	Pricing Studies
Readership Surveys	Concept Testing	Behaviour Prospecting	Market Analysis	Product Mix Studies
	Positioning Studies		Market Potential	Environmental Analysis
Motivation Surveys			Sales Research	
	Packaging Research			Consumer Studies
	Brand Profile			Corporate Image

Fig. 6.1

Marketing research can be quantitative or qualitative. Marketing research concerns itself with any problem of marketing mix (the four Ps of marketing — product, price, promotion and place). It brings corporate research also within its ambit.

Marketing research is comprehensive term, with a very wide scope. Market research, is, however, a part of marketing research. Market research is a research of the market place — its characteristics, size, potential etc. whereas marketing research is a broad-based term covering advertising research, product research, consumer research, sales research and corporate research. Quantitative research generalises for the population in the basis of a sample study. Qualitative research is exploratory or diagnostic in nature. The sample is non-random. It is impressionistic. Projective techniques are used in which people express their feelings indirectly. Depth interviewing is used where an analysis of attitudes and beliefs of participants is made. Both qualitative and quantitative research is necessary in advertising profession.

Marketing research is comprehensive in its scope and has application in all areas of the marketing mix *i.e.*, product, promotion, place and price.

Thus we have:

Product Research: Here studies can be conducted regarding concept and positioning of the products. Sales potential and sales forecasting for different products and market trend analysis form the major activities in this area. It also includes packaging research and best marketing of new products. MR is increasingly used to understand factors like brand equity, brand power and brand loyalty.

Promotion Research: Promotion research is related to personal selling research, advertising research public relation research and sales promotion research. In advertising, there is media research and pre-testing and post-testing of the ads. In personal selling research, activities like analysis of the sales force effectiveness, analysis of selling practices and establishment of sales quotas are included.

Distribution Research: The research activities under this head include location and design of distribution outlets, transportation and logistics studies, dealer surveys etc. MR also studies distribution coverage and dealer goodwill.

Price Research: It includes pricing studies about elasticities, marginal analysis, cost analysis and perception regarding prices.

Apart from the above major areas, the following two areas at the macro-level also has market research application.

Business Economics and Corporate Research: Here, macro-level forecasting studies for short, medium and long-term are undertaken. Business trends are analysed. Macro-level pricing studies are undertaken. There are studies of plant location, acquisition and export market studies.

Corporate Responsibility Research: In this age, environment friendly organisations are accepted. We have ecological impact studies.

Apart from these, there are studies on consumers' rights, social values, social change, legal constraints studies. Since all marketing decisions are ultimately geared towards consumers, we have a major research area called *Consumer Research*.

Consumer Research: Who is our target audience? What do they expect? How do the consumers behave? Why do they behave like this? All these and related questions about consumers are answered by consumer research studies. Though quantitative studies of consumers were the norm so far, these days psychological studies of consumers called qualitative research are made by using special techniques.

Qualitative Research (QR): Qualitative research has been accorded the respect it deserves in the recent past. The focus of qualitative research studies is consumer products. Media research is also no more a numbers game. Psychographic and life-style studies are common. Qualitative research is a step towards further quantitative research. Qualitative research is an understanding of the perceptions, altitudes and predispositions of a certain target segment towards a product, service, advertising concept or a need area. Qualitative research is based on assumption that a common thread pervades through every segment of consuming public. A small sample of say 4 groups of 8 respondents each is enough to appreciate this common thread. Qualitative research selects a few focus groups *e.g.,* say of those who use conventional blades and those who use twin blades. We then study the motivation of these groups.

QR budgets are being increased by the companies. HLL now sets aside a third of its budget for QR.

❖ New Frontier of Marketing Research

1. Until a few years ago, there was a reluctance to go in for syndicated studies. Now syndicated studies are commissioned by MNCs.
2. Marketing research is moving away from its problem solving role and is playing a strategic role. Research is being used from a strategic perspective.
3. Growth areas are: (*i*) New product research, (*ii*) Financial research, (*iii*) Economic research, (*iv*) Social sector research, (*v*) Company image research and (*vi*) Industrial products research.

Marketing Research as a Dynamic Function: A dynamic function shows a change for the better in terms of its scope, contents, techniques, designs and applications. Marketing research is truly dynamic. Traditionally, marketing research covered only limited problems in marketing. These days marketing research has become very comprehensive. It is useful for concept testing. For example, a malt-based drink which gives nutrient value and which is pleasantly flavoured is a product concept. Whether this concept is acceptable or not can be gauged by marketing research. Similarly, marketing research is very useful for the right positioning of the products. Alcohol-based antiseptic lotion can be marketed as antiseptic lotion (*e.g.,* Dettol) and can be perfumed and be sold as After Shave Lotion (*e.g.,* Old Spice of Cosme Matias, Goa). Positioning changes the competition for the product. Using the technique of Product Space Maps by attribute listing, we can position products. Washing machine can be positioned as highly automatic integrated unit of high price, or semi-automatic unit of moderate price or non-automatic unit of low price. Similarly, malt-based drink can be sold as health food for all or children's food for growing babies, or geriatric food for the elderly people. Marketing research is thus useful right from the concept to the commissioning of products these days and also is a useful tool to evaluate different marketing strategies. It has incorporated into its corpus many statistical tools and techniques. It has also incorporated experimental techniques. It undertaken attitude surveys by scaling methods and analyses personality by Thematic Apperception Test (TAT). It also conducts depth interviews where a subject is probed psychologically. It is both quantitative and behavioural. Marketing research has not kept the romance between Mathematics and Management confined to the four walls of the class-room, but has made practical use of this blending in its day-to-day applications. We have regression analysis techniques, discriminant analysis, sampling techniques, Markov chain analysis, factorial analysis, multi-variate analysis etc. Marketing research is not confined to manufacturing industries alone — it extends its sphere to service industries like airlines, banks and insurance and other Non-Profit Organisations (NPOs). Marketing research in fact has entered our national life in the form of Gallup polls prior to elections, opinion surveys of public opinion on men and matters, exit polls, after the elections are just over. Marketing research also studies social awareness regarding national problems of family welfare etc.

Thus, marketing research is progressive — it has become broad-based, technique-oriented, behaviourally inclined multi-dimensional discipline which richly deserves to be called dynamic. The following table illustrates how marketing research has evolved over the years and have shown dynamism.

DYNAMIC EVOLUTION OF MARKETING RESEARCH

Period	*Techniques Used*
Before 1910	Observations, elementary surveys
1910-20	Sales analysis, operating cost analysis
1920-30	Questionnaire construction, survey techniques
1930-40	Quota sampling, correlation analysis, distribution cost analysis, store-audits
1940-50	Probability sampling, regression, statistical inference, consumer and store panels.
1950-60	Motivation research, OR, multiple-regression, attitude measuring instruments
1960-70	Factor analysis, mathematical models, decision theory, scaling EDP, simulation, information storage and retrieval
1980-90	Mathematical models (advanced), qualitative research (advanced)
1990 onwards	Tracking studies, brand equity, new research models

After Kotler, *Marketing Management* (3rd Ed. Prentice Hall).

Results of Marketing Research: Marketing research seeks to find answer to some of the following questions:

- Who our customers are, where they are and what they are like?
- Who our non-customers are, and why so?
- What makes up the market?
- What segments are seen in the market?
- What is the behaviour of our customers, and why so?
- What is the pattern of market demand?
- What products/services are in demand, in what quantities and qualities?
- What changes are occuring in the market place?

  and so on and so forth.

❖ Growing Importance of Marketing Research

Contributions of Marketing Research: As you are aware, marketing research covers a very wide area and concerns itself with every phase of marketing activity. It is a tool that pervades every marketing activity. Its need and importance can be judged from the following discussion:

Enhances Marketing Effectiveness: Marketing research helps decision-making in the marketing area. It provides a logical basis for decisions. Marketing research covers both internal and external data. In the absence of marketing research, the decisions tend to be intuitive and based on hunches. Intuitive decisions are based on emotions, prejudices and personal experience. They are subjective. Research-oriented decisions are based on concrete data, tests, experiments and expert opinions.

The following summarises the contribution of marketing research by way of illustration: (*a*) There is research of consumer preferences for product design, (*b*) There is research for acceptable attributes of the product, (*e.g.*, flavour of the tooth-paste), (*c*) There is research on product quality, (*d*) There is research to determine our target audience, (*e*) There is research to profile the target audience, (*f*) There is research to determine an effective media mix for advertising, (*g*) The advertisement effectiveness is judged against predetermined criteria, (*h*) There is research on package size, design. (*i*) There is price research studies to optimise ROI and to determine discount policy, (*j*) The different propositions of channels of distribution are examined. There is research on exclusive basis distribution or decentralised distribution, (*k*) There is research on market segments, the appeals by which they can be approached.

1. Intuitive decisions are good in routine situations: In a competitive environment, the marketing performance may remain poor. Marketing research based decisions are effective, and enhance marketing effectiveness.

Marketing research brings about a near perfect (if we may be permitted to use this term) matching between the Consumer needs and the Decisions made. Marketing research makes us conversant with marketing environment, together with opportunities and threats it offers. Marketing research tells us about the constraints under which we operate. Marketing research enables us to examine alternative proposals.

2. Marketing research measures and therefore, improves marketing effort: (*a*) Marketing research makes us realise the types of products that are in demand or have potential demand. Marketing research makes us price these products rightly. Marketing research enables us to offer these products to the right customers, (*b*) Marketing research improves sales performance. It tells us how best to promote the products, (*c*) Marketing research curtails the marketing costs by making our marketing effective, (*d*) Marketing research compels us to revise and examine our policies and strategies in the light of the changed environment, and (*e*) Marketing research builds up the confidence amongst personnel when they are rest assured that the marketing effort is placed on sound footing.

3. Marketing research these days has become more or less compulsory because of a host of other factors: (*a*) Modern organisations are multi-product, multi-locational complex entities which operate under competitive and diverse marketing environments, (*b*) The environment is turbulent. There are constant changes — sociological, economic, technological, legal and political. To cope with this, we need constant monitoring of the markets. Environmental factors are uncontrollable. They can be exploited to the benefit of the firm by doing marketing research, (*c*) Marketing research helps a manufacturing firm to improve profitability by the choice of a right product mix. Marketing research helps the manufacturers to price the products in relation to their perceived value (this calls for psychological research).

4. Marketing research helps us to formulate our marketing strategy: Marketing research helps us to formulate product strategy: (*a*) How to have a right product mix? (*b*) How to do SBU (Strategic Business Unit) analysis? (*c*) How to do BCG (Boston Consulting Group) analysis? (*d*) How to formulate a new business plan?

While formulating a new business plan, we can have market penetration (current products to have more market share) strategy. We can also think of developing new geographical markets or market segments for current products. Or else we can have product development strategy where new products are launched in current markets. Or else we can have diversification strategy where both products as well as the markets are new. Diversification is related or unrelated to the present line of business. Diversification takes into account company's mission and its distinctive competence. All the above are in other words, *growth strategies*. Integrative and diversification growth is the choice before the company.

5. Marketing research helps us to research and select the target markets: We can for example decide whether we have to market manual typewriters or electronic typewriters or both and whether these are to be sold to small customers, medium customers or large customers. It helps us to determine our market coverage strategies, (*e.g.*, single market concentration). We can also choose between product specialisation (only electronic typewriters for all customers) or market specialisation (both electronic and manual machines but only for small customers). There can be selective specialisation (to tap an attractive strategy). There can be full market coverage strategy. Besides for each segment of market, we have positioning strategies. Marketing strategies in other three Ps of marketing mix (price, promotion and place) are also helped by marketing research. Marketing research equips us with tactical marketing also. It helps to implement and control our marketing effort.

❖ Functions of Marketing Research

Marketing research is a valuable tool to assist the marketing manager to take marketing decisions. While doing so it performs five major functions.

1. *Marketing research is descriptive:* Marketing research describes the situation, the background of any marketing problem. It helps us to understand in a preliminary manner the underlying marketing problems.
2. *Marketing research is exploratory:* It explores the various decision alternatives and examines them either to confirm/rule out them.
3. *Marketing research is evaluatory:* Marketing research compares two or more marketing strategies, for the selection of the best amongst them.
4. *Marketing research is predictive:* Marketing research prepares us for the future both in terms of risks and opportunities. Marketing research forecasts the future demand and market trends.
5. *Marketing research is an essential input* (given cost effectiveness) for decision-making.

Marketing research makes the total gamut of marketing activity more effective, it results into a right product mix with fair pricing, good distribution and effective promotion.

To sum up, the functions of marketing research are essentially what marketing research is capable of doing for modern business.

❖ Market Research and Marketing Research

These days both these terms are used interchangeably and mostly lay people use the term *market research* when what they actually have in their mind is *marketing research*. Before the 40s, marketing was not developed as a discipline and it was then that the term *market research* was used for collection and analysis of limited data from a particular market.

Thomas C. Kinnear and Jamse R. Taylor feel that emphasis has changed from market research to marketing research. Market research implied that the focus of research was on the analysis of markets. The shift to marketing research broadened the nature and role of research with emphasis on contact between the Researcher and the Marketing management process.

Strictly speaking, market research is narrow in its scope and remains confined to a particular market itself and the consumers who constitute that particular market. Marketing research, however, is a broad and comprehensive term and is related to research on any problem in the marketing area — product, price, distribution, promotion, consumers and macro-level studies. Market research was a haphazard attempt to collect and analyse the data, whereas marketing research is a systematic process.

MARKETING INFORMATION SYSTEM AND MARKETING RESEARCH

❖ Introduction

Marion Harper has aptly remarked that managing a business well means to manage its future and managing future means managing the information. Prudent managers have to anticipate the changes in environment, assess the direction and extent of these changes and reconcile their marketing planning to these changes. To fulfil this function, what is needed is information and its effective management. Information is available both internally and externally. To sort out a mass of information and put it to effective use is the role of a marketing information system. This system is an aid to managers in decision-making. Marketing information system is comprehensive and includes marketing research as one of its components.

❖ Why We Need a Marketing Information System (MkIS)?

Fast Decisions: Today, executives have less time to take decisions and are expected to react fast to changes and manage new product launches.

Complexity of Marketing: Marketing as a function has become more comprehensive and broader. Transnational and global marketing makes it imperative to have good information system.

Era of Shortages: Shortages of resources like energy and other raw materials make it compulsory for management to keep only viable products in its product line.

Consumer Awareness: Consumer expectations are high and to live up to these, managements need information.

Information Explosion: Makes it necessary to process it so that the best use is made of it.

❖ What is a Marketing Information System (MkIS)?

Samuel Smith and James Stafford define MkIS as follows:

"MkIS is an interacting, continuing, future-oriented structure of people, equipment and procedures. It is designed to generate and process an information flow to aid decision-making in a company's marketing programme."

❖ Elements of MkIS

MkIS has inputs from the macro, micro and internal environment. It processes these inputs and generates output in the form of periodic reports and special reports.

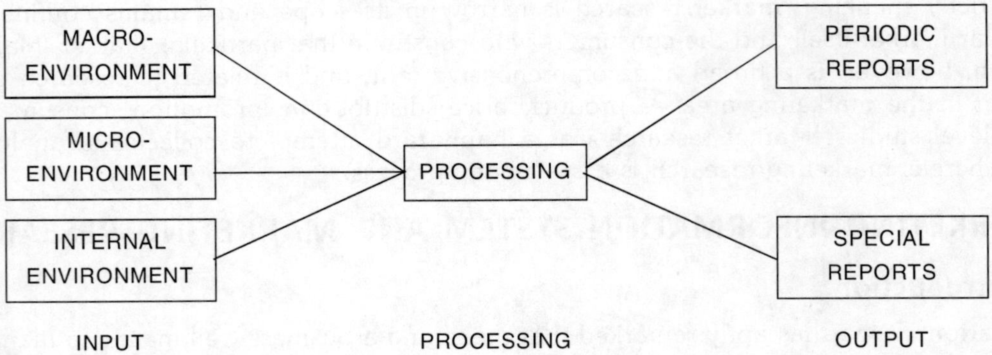

The system has to decide:

(*i*) What data are needed?

(*ii*) How to gather these data?

It then processes the information data:

(*i*) By making use of quantitative/analytical techniques.

(*ii*) By using computers.

It can also store/retain the data for future use. MkIS is future oriented and continuous. It has the potential, therefore, to prevent future problems (prophylactic) and to cure present problems (therapeutic). It has to use information processed which is wasted if not put to use. MkIS is modified in terms of the feedback received.

❖ Benefits of MkIS

1. It makes possible effective use of information gathered.
2. It provides faster, less expensive and more complete information flow.
3. Executives receive reports more often and in detailed form.
4. Makes possible retrieval of data.
5. Constant monitoring of marketing mix possible.

❖ Relationship between MkIS and Marketing Research

Many consider MkIS as just an extension of Marketing Research which is computer-based. Marketing research has a long history, whereas MkIS was first developed in the 60s. Both are distinct entities for some, though they essentially deal with the management of information. Those companies which do not have MkIS installed assign a broader role to their marketing research function. A company having MkIS on the other hand, treats marketing research as one of its component. To border on MkIS, marketing research should be systematic, which unfortunately traditionally practised marketing research is not. Marketing research is conducted on the basis of separate projects, each with a start and an end. On the contrary, MkIS presupposes a continuous flow. Marketing research is also more or less a post-mortem whereas MkIS is future oriented. However, modern day practitioners of marketing research are already doing what an information system entails; *e.g.*, forecasting, sales volume analysis, marketing cost analysis etc. In those firms which have formal MkIS, marketing research projects serve as major inputs. The distinctions are tabulated below:

Marketing Research (MR)	Marketing Information System (MkIS)
1. Mainly externally-oriented.	Handles both internal as well as external data.
2. Problem solving.	Prophylactic as well as problem solving.
3. Project-to-project intermittent basis.	Continuous.
4. Emphasis on past.	Future-oriented.
5. May not be computer-based.	Computer-based.
6. Becomes input for MkIS.	Has other sub-systems besides MR.

❖ Present Position of MR in India

So far MR has been used by reputed multinationals, like Lever giving the lead and others like Procter and Gamble, Bayer and so on following suit. Lever has an MR budget of *A* 10 crores so does ITC. Indian companies of late have started accepting MR: the Tatas, the Mafatlals, Asian Paints, HMT etc. Pepsi, Coca-Cola and Smithkhine Beecham (SKB) have MR budgets ranging from *A* 4 to 5 crores. Now, even smaller companies have started taking to some rudimentary MR. MR's use has spread but at a very slow pace. It is due to non-professionalised management also. With more professionally trained managers around, there is a possibility of greater receptivity being shown to MR.

Indian companies so far relied more on internal sources and marketing intermediaries and on secondary data that served the purpose. With seller's market and assured sales, no need for MR was felt.

However, market competition at least in consumer goods industry brought in advertising and for doing effective advertising, a need was felt of a good MR-base. Ad agencies like Hindustan Thompson set up separate marketing research subsidiaries like IMRB which later led to MARG. It has now merged with ORG. It accounts for nearly half the industry's business. Even Pathfinders of Lintas had that umbilical relationship. Independent MR agencies now have also come up on the scene. Government organisations like Institute of Public Opinion, National Council of Applied Economic Research Studies (NCAER) also took upon themselves the MR function. ORG (Operations Research Group) Baroda, became known for its retail shop audits of pharmaceutical preparations. We already have 5 NRS (National Readership Surveys).

Marketing research could not be popular for a variety of reasons in India. Demand here exceeded supply (Bajaj scooters till 70s). The profits were assured. The information collected without systematic MR was adequate. MR's value could not outweigh its cost. Indian industry lacked operational independence and relied more on government policies and foreign collaborators. Despite MR, there is no guarantee against product failures. Though in money terms, MR still has not attracted a respectable proportion of the operational cost, it is showing signs of growth in recent times. Almost 80 per cent of MR business is client specific. The rest is accounted for by syndicated MR products.

❖ Advantage and Limitations of Marketing Research

Advantages: The following are the major advantages of marketing research:

(*i*) Marketing research makes situational analysis and thus puts the problem in proper perspective.

(*ii*) Marketing research begins the marketing activity by assessing consumer needs and aspirations. It further assists product development right from concept testing to test marketing.

(*iii*) Marketing research helps to formulate hypotheses for further research.

(*iv*) Qualitative marketing research throws open consumers' inner-most motivations.

(*v*) Marketing research is predictive.

(*vi*) Marketing research helps advertising process in the following areas: (*a*) Identification of target audience, (*b*) Identification of theme, (*c*) Pre-testing of copy, (*d*) Post-testing of copy, and (*e*) Media effectiveness.

(*vii*) Marketing research helps the formulation of marketing strategies.

(*viii*) MR is seen by companies as marketing investment.

❖ Limitations of Marketing Research

The following are the major *limitations* of marketing research:

(*i*) Marketing research is not an exact science and cannot claim the accuracy of the physical sciences.

(*ii*) Marketing research is conducted in a marketplace where several variables are at work. The conditions are not controlled, as in laboratory experiments.

(*iii*) Since marketing research deals with human beings, it cannot rule out an element of artificial response from them when they are subjected to the process of marketing research.

(*iv*) Marketing research findings are difficult to verify. They may be subjective also.

(*v*) Marketing research becomes dated by the time the project is over; because the market situation is dynamic.

(*vi*) Marketing research findings may be biased on account of the research workers or on account of the respondents.

(*vii*) Lack of training to the researchers may generate faulty MR findings. Sometimes, preconceived notions are to be supported by the research data. Many times, research problem and objective are not properly identified. Marketing research requires time as well as money. Due to resource crunch, good marketing research may not be possible. Many researchers are not computer literate.

(*viii*) MR can tell you whether a product is likely to succeed or fail. It can never tell us whether it will be a success or failure. It is always an *indecisive estimate.*

❖ Consumer-orientation to Marketing Research

The basic reason for any company's being in business is to serve the consumer — to satisfy his needs by offering him suitable products and services. This is the essence of the marketing concept. As a result of this philosophy, all company activities like production, finance, personnel, purchase, selling etc., must be devoted to the satisfaction of consumers, while still making a profit over the long-run. Once this philosophy is accepted, the company starts with the basic question what business we are in. The traditional product-oriented answers like 'we make this..' or 'we sell that..' are replaced by consumer benefit oriented answers like 'we sell hope' or 'we sell entertainment'. Basic marketing research thus revolves around the motivations of consumer buying. The buying behaviour of consumers are studied in terms of its components like life-style, personality, social class, family life-cycle, reference groups, attitudes etc. Product development process requires research on concept development *e.g.,* a nutritious drink can be sold as an afternoon mid-day meal supplement for the office goers' or 'as a good-night drink for the aged' or 'as a health drink for the ill'. We have to formulate the product after concept testing. Even prior to that product ideas are generated by brain-storming and only those ideas which are feasible are developed into concepts by a suitable MR programme. While screening the ideas, the consumer-orientation is kept in mind. The prototype developed is tested again on a select audience and suitably modified. The product developed is rated as per consumer feedback. Further, packaging, branding, pricing and distribution are carried out keeping consumers in focus.

Advertising messages are directed towards company's target audiences. Market research helps to identify the target audience. Media research helps to maintain a fit between the Product and the Consumers targeted, pre- and post-testing of ads is also a consumer-related exercise.

The emergence of qualitative research for studying the psyche of the consumers has strengthened the consumer-orientation of marketing research.

Marketing research has to be consumer oriented because it is an aid to marketing decision-making which revolves around consumers.

❖ Increasing Need of Marketing Research

There has been a phenomenal growth in marketing research and the sophistication with which it is being conducted. The need for marketing research has been felt on account of the following five factors:

1. Transition from Local to National and from National to International Markets: As the geographical coverage of markets expands, there is an increasing need for marketing Research.

2. Transition from Buyer Needs to Buyer Wants: When more disposable income is placed in the hands of buyers, they become choosy. Sellers find it difficult to predict the buyer's response to their offering. They have to adopt marketing research to do so.

3. Transition from Price to Non-price competition: Commodities undergo branding. There is product differentiation, advertising and sales promotion. Companies want to know-how all these are working.

4. Technological Strides: Computers, micro-films, CCTV, photocopiers, recording machines, faxes, E-Mail and such other devices have revolutionised information handling. It has become sophisticated. Marketing research department on a formal basis is the best organisational device to keep pace with information explosion by making use of modern gadgetry.

5. Growth of Rural Markets: Our rural markets are growing four times as fast as the urban markets. The need to figure out what the rural consumer wants is fast becoming the focus of all the marketers.

❖ Which areas will make use of Marketing Research?

1. Marketing research will be used increasingly not only by consumer companies but also by consumer durable companies, industrial product companies and the services sector.
2. Social research will also become significant.
3. Marketing research in ad agencies will be integrated to broader account planning function.
4. Marketing research will tend to be more specialised – media research, children's research and financial research.

❖ Marketing Research Billings

In 1970, marketing research billings were a trifle ₹ 2.5 crores.

In 1980, they doubled to ₹ 5.1 crores.

In 1990, they touched ₹ 18 crores.

In 1997, MR industry has a total turnover of ₹ 170 crores.

It has grown at the rate of 20-25 per cent in 1997.

❖ Marketing Research's Acceptance

As more and more companies professionalise, research becomes an integral part of their marketing strategy. (Priya Tandon, Probe). Under the new liberalised environment, the demand for marketing research has gone up. Until now, the advertising industry with a turnover of *A* 20,000 crores was the Big Brother. In comparison, marketing research's turnover is just a speck. All over the world, as a rule of thumb, marketing research constitutes about 2-10 per cent of advertising turnover. Indian marketing research agencies have still a long way to go.

❖ Methods of Conducting MR

As we have seen already, marketing research is based on data which must be collected by a suitable method. We can collect data from two sources — we can collect primary data from the field itself or we can make use of published secondary data. We can also make use of a judicious combination of both primary and secondary data. While collecting primary data, we can use any of the following methods:

(*i*) Field investigation through surveys.

(*ii*) Observation.

(*iii*) Experimentation.

While doing field investigation, our study could be restricted to a selected sample or to a consumer panel.

We shall study these marketing research methods in this chapter in some details.

Collecting Primary Data: Primary marketing research data, as mentioned at the outset, refer to the data collected by a researcher for the particular marketing research project currently being undertaken. They are the most widely used marketing data.

There are basically three alternatives in collecting primary data: observation method, experimental method and survey method. Observation method and experimental method are discussed here.

❖ Observation Method

Observation is the process of recognising and recording the behaviour of people, objects, and events rather than asking for information. For example, instead of asking consumers what brands they buy or what television programmes they view, the researcher arranges to observe what products are bought and what programmes are watched.

Observational techniques can be classified in five ways as follows:

1. Natural Vs. Contrived: Natural observation involves observing behaviour as it takes place normally in the environment, *e.g.*, shopping in a grocery shop. Contrived observation involves creating an artificial environment and observing the behaviour patterns exhibited by persons put in this environment, *e.g.*, having people shop in a simulated grocery store.

2. Disguised Vs. Undisguised: "Disguise" refers to whether or not the respondents are aware they are being observed. The role of the observer should be disguised where people would behave differently if they knew they were being observed. Various approaches such as two-way mirrors, hidden cameras and observers dressed as sales clerks can be used to disguise the observations.

3. Structured Vs. Unstructured: Structured observation is appropriate when the decision problem has been clearly defined and the specification of information needs permits a clear identification of the behaviour patterns to be observed and measured. Unstructured observation is appropriate in situations where the decision problem has yet to be formulated and a great deal of flexibility is needed. Structured observation is more appropriate for conclusive research studies. Unstructured observation is preferred for exploratory studies.

4. Direct Vs. Indirect: "Direct observation" refers to observing as it actually occurs. Indirect observation refers to observing some record of past behaviour. Here, the effects, of behaviour are observed rather than the behaviour itself. The involves the examination of physical traces, a process which includes such things as counting the number of empty liquor containers in trash cans to estimate liquor consumption of houses.

5. Human Vs. Mechanical: In some situations it is appropriate to supplement or replace the human observer with some form of mechanical observer. The reason could be increased accuracy, lower costs or special measurement requirements. The major mechanical devices used in observation include the (1) Motion picture camera; (2) Audiometer; (3) Psycho-galvanometer; (4) Eye-camera and (5) Pupilometer. The *motion picture camera* can be used to record shopping behaviour in supermarkets, drug store and the like. The audiometer is a device to record when radio and television sets are turned on and the stations to which they are tuned. The psycho-galvanometer measures changes in perspiration rate from which inferences are drawn regarding a person's emotional reaction to stimuli present at the time of measurement. The stimuli presented might include brand names, copy slogans, etc. It is assumed, the stronger the reaction, the more favourable the person's attitude. The eye-camera measures the movement of the eye. It is used to determine how a person reads a magazine, advertisement, package and the like. The *pupilometer* measures changes in the diameter of the pupils of the eyes. An increase in pupil diameter is assumed to reflect on a person's favourable reaction to the stimuli being observed.

The observation method has several advantages. First, it does not rely on the respondent's willingness to provide the desired data. Second, the potential bias caused by interviewing methods is reduced or eliminated. Third, certain types of data can be collected only by observation.

The observation method has two major *limitations.* First, the inability to observe such things as awareness, beliefs, feelings and preferences it is difficult to observe a host of personal and intimate activities such as family games with children and late evening TV watching. Second, the observed behaviour patterns must be of a short duration, occur frequently, or be reasonably predictable if the data collection costs and time requirements are to be competitive with other data collection techniques. This requirement limits the observation method to a unique set of circumstances.

❖ Experimental Method

The second and least-used method of collecting primary data is that of controlled experiments. To date, the most common use of this method by marketers has been interest marketing.

Experimental method allows a maximum degree of control in comparison with other methods of collecting primary data. The method is also ranked as relatively high with respect to data accuracy since the ability to control the variables of interest tends to produce relatively error-free data. However, experimentation is limited to the collection of primary data on current behaviour and is, therefore, most restricted to primary data collection method in terms of flexibility and applicability. Besides, experimental method is usually costly and complex.

SURVEY TECHNIQUES

❖ Questionnaire or Survey Method

The survey technique is intended to secure one or more items of information from a sample of respondents or informants who are representatives of a larger group. The information is recorded on a form known as a questionnaire or a schedule or a blank form of inquiry. As data are gathered by asking questions from persons who are believed to have the desired information, the method is also known as the *questionnaire technique.*

The survey method is the most widely used technique in marketing research. It may be used at any one or more of the levels in the marketing process — at the consumer level, at retail, wholesale or manufacture level.

Reasons for Wide Use of Survey: There are a number of reasons for the very wide use of the survey techniques.

(*i*) It can secure both quantitative and qualitative information directly from the respondents, individuals or business consumers.

(*ii*) It is the only method of directly measuring attitudes and motivations.

(*iii*) It is quite flexible in terms of the types of data to be assembled, the method of collection or the timing of research.

It is presumed that respondents know the answers to the questions; have the authority to answer these questions and are willing to co-operate in answering these questions in the best manner.

The versatility of the survey method, its speed, its relatively lower cost are its selling points when it is compared with the observation method.

Surveys are an effective way of gathering information (not already available) for the following marketing problems:

(*a*) Planning product features.

(*b*) Advertising copy.

(*c*) Media of advertisement.

(*d*) Sales promotion.

(*e*) Channel choice.

(*f*) Consumer research.

(*g*) Dealer research.

Use of Survey Method: There are three main uses of the survey or questionnaire method:

(*i*) We can have a factual survey together with facts; *e.g.*, "What brand of tea or soap do you use?"

(*ii*) We can have an opinion survey to secure personal opinions or thinking on a particular matter; *e.g.*, "Which design of the ornaments do you think is the most beautiful?"

(*iii*) Interpretative survey can be conducted to probe into the personal feelings, motives, attitudes, etc., of the respondent, who is not only a reporter but also an interpreter; *e.g.*, "Why do you use Brand *X* detergent?"

Types of Survey: In the questionnaire or survey method, we can have communication with the information in three alternative ways:

1. Through the mail or post-office.
2. On the telephone.
3. At a personal interview.

1. The Mail Survey by Questionnaire: This is a very effective and cheap method of conducting surveys. The contact is made by mail. An up-to-date mailing list is prepared. A printed copy of the questionnaire, with a covering letter and a stamped reply paid envelope, is mailed to the respondent on the mailing list. The covering letter, as a silent salesman, should create interest, convince and motivate or induce the informant to send prompt and accurate replies. A gift incentive is provided to enlist co-operation and get a quick return of the duly completed questionnaire. A follow-up by a sweet reminder is necessary to secure the maximum response within a reasonable period.

The mail survey has no geographical limitation. It can reach even hard-to-reach respondents. It has, however, a few drawbacks. The response may be high as well as low. The questionnaire may not be carefully and completely answered. A higher rate of refusal and a lower degree of accuracy are the other important weaknesses of the mail survey.

2. Telephone Survey: In big urban areas, we can interview the respondent on the telephone. It is an ideal method of communication when you need information on current activities; *e.g.*, on radio listening or TV viewing, while these activities are actually being carried on. If you need factual answers to a few questions, this method is very suitable. We can also have a large number of interviews in a short period. The telephone survey is quick and cost very little. The data collected are usually accurate. If respondents are concentrated in a city and are available on the phone, and if you require simple information, the telephone survey is the ideal choice. Of course, on the phone, people give non-committal answers and they are unwilling to give personal information. Nor is a detailed investigation possible on the telephone. In India, this method has a limited scope, except in very big cities.

3. Personal Interview or Field Survey: It is a direct form of investigation, involving face-to-face communication with a free feedback of information. It offers a sense of participation to the respondent. It is a more flexible form of data collection. The use of unstructured, open-end questions is possible. The rate of refusal is low. Depth interviews are possible. Complex questions can be asked. The interviewer may ask additional questions to secure more information. The observation approach may be combined to verify age, income, status, standard of living, etc. We can get accurate information. Visual aids in the form of pictures, advertisements, exhibits, etc., can be used to get views and opinions and determine attitudes of the respondents. Literacy is not essential.

However, we need trained, experienced and competent interviewers. This method, moreover, is a costly and time-consuming method of data collection. Special supervision is needed. The interviewer must be honest and loyal. It is possible that the data collected in an interview may be vitiated by the interviewer's bias.

❖ Field Investigation

Field work is the most important method of data collection. Basically, it is the communication between the Researcher and the Respondent. Communication can collect a wide range of data (not possible by any other method). Here the researcher does not have to predict when and where the behaviour will occur or wait for it to occur.

For example, it is easier to ask a respondent about his purchase planning for a dishwasher or a refrigerator than to guess or try to anticipate and observe the purchase. This fact is what makes the communication method more useful than the observation method. But it suffers from some limitations. A. N. Oppenheir says "The respondents' unwillingness and/or inability to provide the desired data is the chief drawback of the communication method."

However, it is a proven fact that more than 60 per cent of the data collection programmes are possible with a questionnaire which is an effective tool of the communication method. Half or more of the U.S. population has participated in one or more research studies — a fact which spotlights the tremendous applicability and wide acceptance of the communication method. Even in our country, most of the research work is facilitated by the use of this method of gathering data.

❖ Media Used to Collect Data

When a questionnaire is fully structured, the next decision for the marketing researcher is to undertake a survey and collect accurate and valid information. The required information can be gathered with the help of the following three types of media:

(*i*) Personal contact.
(*ii*) Mailing of the questionnaires and
(*iii*) Contact on the telephone.

We shall now discuss: Personal contact, an important fieldwork method.

1. Personal Contact: Here, the selected sources are interviewed personally either at their residential places or at their places of work. The form of gathering data may be verbal, or the data may be acquired in writing. The instrument invariably used is the questionnaire. The interviewer presents the questionnaire to the selected respondents and covers the various topics included therein. The success of the personal contact method depends on the extent to which the interviewer is able to establish rapport with the respondent and motivate him. We must remember that the importance of sufficient training can never be underestimated, and even the smallest matters, like how to introduce oneself to the respondents, play a significant role in data collection in personal interviews. Unless interviewers are properly selected, trained and instructed, a lot of bias may occur in the data collected. That is why it is desired to have a significant supervision of the interviewers. The interviewers work in the field by themselves, enjoy plenty of latitude and possess enough scope to bend instructions, to twist verbal questions, to change their sequences, to record their own versions of the respondents' replies and, at times, to cheat by falsifying a part of the whole interview. This temptation can be curbed by proper supervision.

❖ Advantages

The *advantages* of this method are:

(*a*) Personal contact is considered to be the most important and is superior to the other two methods, mainly because it combines two features of getting information: questioning and observation.

(*b*) It is feasible to collect the maximum information from most of the selected respondents. Maximum information can be had from each respondent because the method is adaptable and flexible. Information can be obtained from the maximum number of the selected respondents because interviewers go the places of the respondents at a time convenient to the latter. The rate of the response and the accuracy of reporting are the highest in personal interviewing.

(*c*) The interview can be longer when the questionnaires are long. More points can be covered by asking a larger number of questions in the shortest possible time.

(*d*) The interviewer is an active participant. He can regulate the order of the presentation.

(*e*) Accurate data, which have more likely to be accepted, are likely to be generated by this method.

❖ Limitations

The *limitations* of the personal contact method are:

(*a*) It is the most expensive and most time-consuming method. An individual interview may last only for half an hour; but travelling, locating the respondent and submitting the report — these do take a considerable time.

(*b*) Administrative problems are enormous. The personal contact method needs a large organisation of investigators, supervisors, interviewers, statisticians and other experts. Besides, it needs large sized office staff. The control of scores of these persons, who are widely scattered in the field and office, is very difficult.

(*c*) Bias may play a central role. It very badly affects the overall research task. In a personal interview, distorted and erroneous information may be obtained because of the bias introduced by both the interviewer and the respondent. Moreover, studies have shown that most interviewers do not confine themselves to the instructions given to them. In all probability, they are interpreted to suit their own convenience. Biased information also occurs from the desire of the respondents to influence the interviewer by supplying information that raises the prestige of the respondent.

❖ Desk Research

Out of the two most important methods of marketing research, field research is meant to collect primary data and desk research is meant to collect secondary readymade data. Desk research is a library-oriented activity. Enough of desk work publications are available. Even commercial research agencies sell many types of marketing research data.

Secondary data have some significant advantages when compared to primary data. Secondary data in general.

1. Are relatively less expensive.
2. Take relatively less time.
3. Provide information which may be difficult or unfeasible for the average company to collect (*e.g.*, census data).
4. Desk research is less cumbersome.

However, desk research is preferable only under certain circumstances. It is not preferred when:

1. Data is obsolete.
2. Irrelevant.
3. Hidden in pile of data.

DISTINCTION BETWEEN DESK RESEARCH AND FIELD RESEARCH

Desk Research	*Field Research*
1. It is done indoors.	1. It is done outdoors in the field.
2. The sources are trade publications, journal, books, directories, research reports, libraries etc.	2. Field research includes communication methods by personal, mail or telephonic interview.
3. Relatively less expensive, less time consuming and easy.	3. Expensive, time-consuming, difficult.
4. Based on available data. Not verified	4. Based on actual fieldwork. Verification possible.
5. No interviewers' bias	5. May be tainted with interviewers' bias.
6. Supplementary to field research.	6. Extensively used technique.

DISTINCTION BETWEEN HUMAN OBSERVATION AND MECHANICAL OBSERVATION

Human Observation	*Mechanical Observation*
1. Observation by a human being (investigator).	1. Observation by mechanical means (eye-camera).
2. Simple, economical.	2. Complicated, expensive.
3. Limited reliability, less speed.	3. More reliability, speedy.
4. Subjective, biased.	4. Not subjective or biased.
5. Comprehensive.	5. Less comprehensive.
6. Widely used here.	6. Widely used in the West.

❖ Other Research Methods

Panel Research: When a researcher interviews the *same sample* group *two or more times* or secures data from them on two or more occasions, we say we have panel research. Respondents may be individual consumers, retailers, wholesalers (dealers) etc. Panel research enables the researchers to measure small changes in purchases, habits and other activities over a period of time. This is in contrast to the non-panel type of surveys where entirely different group is measured, each time a study is conducted.

Panels are made up of respondents who regularly and routinely report their buying behaviour. They keep a *diary* of purchases, advertising exposure, shopping activity or any other item under research.

(a) Consumer Purchase Panel: The consumer purchase panel (continuing) is widely used. A sample of family units keeps a diary and reports on a weekly or monthly basis the product purchases from their immediate use. The data include types, the number of units, prices, brands and sources of buying. Gift or cash prizes are given to members of the panel with a view to motivating them to maintain diaries honestly. The consumer panel (non-continuing) is used to test and evaluate a new product, a new package etc., or to answer questions relating to a particular investigation.

❖ Uses of Consumer Panel

(*i*) To determine consumer attitudes, preferences and changes in demand relating to a particular demand.

(*ii*) To test samples of products.

(*iii*) To assess market trends.

(*iv*) To ascertain brand share and brand switching.

(*v*) To estimate consumer response to package.

(*vi*) To know the importance of retail outlets of different types.

(*vii*) To set consumer reaction to prices and to advertising.

(*viii*) To have a marketing test while launching a new product.

Panels offer three benefits. They facilitate acquisition of knowledge of:

(*i*) Buyer behaviour, which can be related to the buyer characteristics.

(*ii*) Changes in buyer behaviour, which can be related to changes in the marketing mix.

(*iii*) Changes in buyer behaviour, which can be monitored over a period of time.

Examples: IMRB has set up consumer panels of males (for cigarette and razor blades research) in seven cities. The male panels in the metros have 1000 members and elsewhere 700 members. The female panel consists of housewives in 2000 household in four metros. The housewives report on household purchases of soaps, detergents, shampoos, hair oils, creams, toothpastes, cooking oils etc.

(b) Dealer Panels: Panel research at the retail level may be conducted by employing the technique of store audit (shop audit). It provides extensive information about retailers. A bimonthly check on inventory or stock in retail stores will give us particulars of the sales volume at the retail level. A physical audit of sales records by trained observers will throw light on purchases by retailers, sales to their customers, inventories, prices and related information by individual brands, package sizes etc. A shop audit of a sample of retailers will yield the measurement of the flow of goods at the retail levels. To illustrate, ORG conducts retail audits in India. It consists of two separate audits — one for pharmaceutical formulations and the other for consumer products. Sales and distribution data are published monthly, based on a sample of retail outlets all over India.

Parfitt, a market research expert, mentions the following merits of panel research:

1. There is less reliance on memory than in an interview call. There is continuity of information.
2. Research organisation in the West use diaries more and more.
3. There is no exaggeration of data.

❖ Selection of a Suitable Method for Marketing Research

There are a variety of methods to conduct marketing research like Desk Research, Field Research, Experimentation and Observation. However, the choice of a particular method is guided by a number of factors. It is understood that there are no hard and fast rules and one set of methods cannot be prescribed for all types of projects.

1. Nature of Research: A survey can be ambitious in scope covering national market or could be confined to a small area. Perhaps, mailing questionnaires could be a way out when a large population is to be contacted. A small sample could be covered by personal contact.

2. Nature of the Industry: We could operate in fashion goods or in pharmaceuticals. We have to design the method accordingly. A small sample of the elite could be useful for fashion goods, whereas a stratified random sample of physicians is required to research the pharmaceutical industry.

3. Accuracy: Accuracy wanted determines the method of research. Desk research gives less accuracy. Field research of desired accuracy can be planned.

4. Organisation: An organisation with an independent marketing research department may prefer field research immediately. Others have to seek services of outside research agencies.

5. Analytical Machinery: Primary data can be subjected to rigorous statistical analysis for which necessary staff is called for. If such facilities are non-existent, then it is better to have desk research.

6. Time: Time is a necessary ingredient of fieldwork research. The availability of time determines what method of data collection we should adopt.

7. Approach: What is our business philosophy? If it is totally market or customer-oriented, we shall try to do in depth analysis of a customer by undertaking motivational and behavioural research.

8. Top Management Attitude: The top management should support marketing research, its work and its findings. Marketing research is to be integrated into organisational needs. It should be inter-linked with other departments of the organisation.

9. Cost: Cost is an important constraint on the choice of method. Field investigation is the most expensive method. Experimentation is costlier than observation. Other physical resources are also considered along with the cost.

❖ Marketing Research Process

Marketing research has slowly acquired the status of a science. We call it a science for three reasons:

1. It follows a systematised step-by-step method to study a given problem. It verifies the hypothesis in the light of the data.
2. It is an objective study, free from subjective bias. It sets out its objectives and methodology objectively. It presents its findings objectively after an objective analysis of data.
3. It uses may sophisticated tools like Latin Squares; Markov Chains, Likert and Thurstone Scales, Multi-dimensional sealing like other sciences which also use some of these tools.

❖ What are Some of These Tools?

What is to be appreciated is to do marketing research, we adopt a scientific approach. These days, like physical sciences, we do conduct marketing research experiments under controlled conditions, thus giving marketing research an additional respectability as a science.

Let us now study the steps of the marketing research process.

Marketing Research Process: In general, there are *five major activities* that collectively serve to define the marketing research procedure. Each stage consists of sub-activities to be performed and decisions that need to be made. The figure shows these activities in the form of activity stages.

Marketing Problem or Opportunity Identification consists of several interrelated tasks and activities. It is perhaps the most crucial stage in the marketing research process. Identification of a marketing problem begins with a *problem audit.* It is a comprehensive and systematic examination of a marketing problem with the objective of understanding its origin and nature.

Often conducted concurrently with a problem audit is a background analysis frequently termed *exploratory research*. This is an exploratory analysis devoted to placing the problem in perspective and perhaps even providing sufficient information for resolving the problem. A complete background analysis consists of a *situation investigation, literature review, expert opinion sampling* and one or more case studies. The keys to successful problem identification are creativity and flexibility.

If a problem audit and background analysis reveal that further marketing research is required, the marketing problem need to be translated into an operational marketing research task. This requires specifying research objectives, research questions and research hypothesis.

1. Task: Typically, a marketing research task is expressed in terms of a specific set of marketing research objectives. These objectives delineate the scope of marketing research

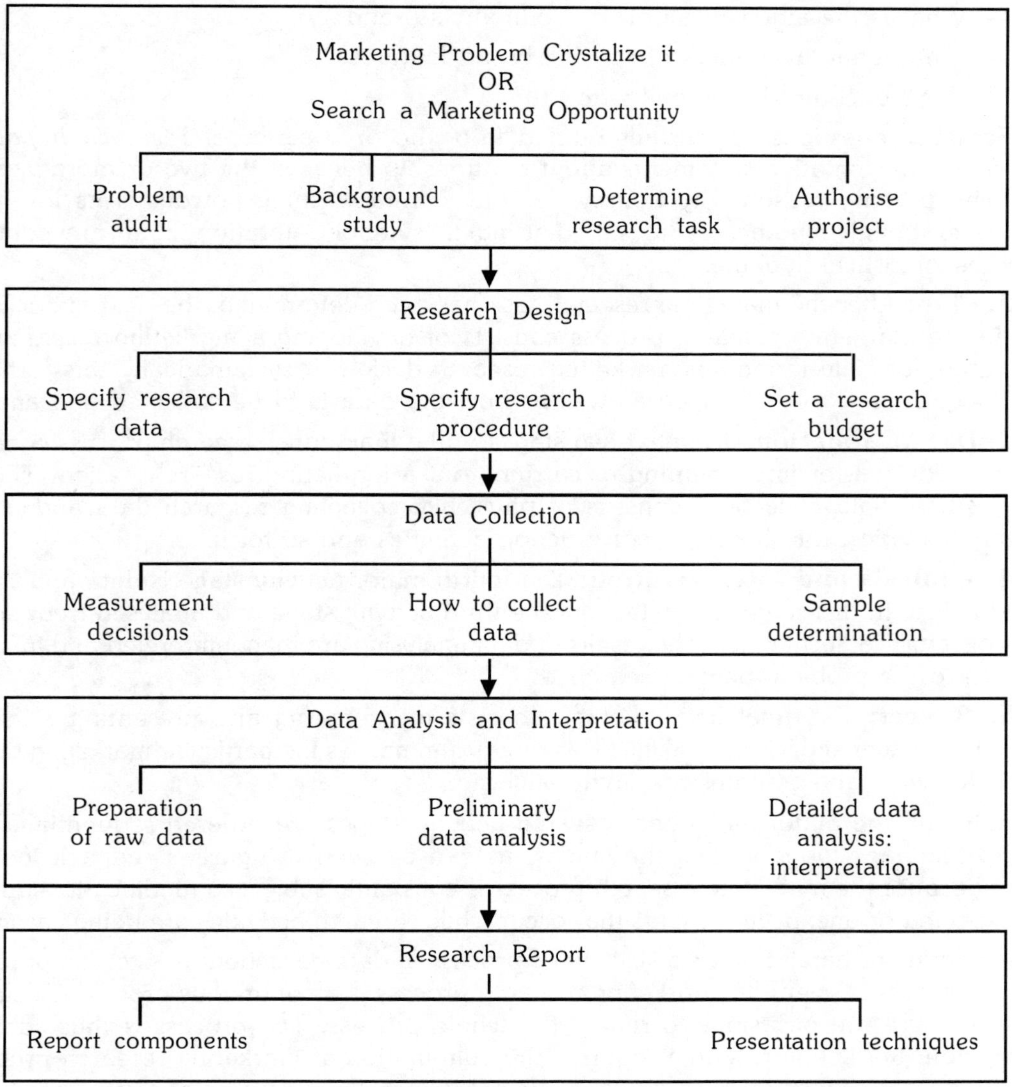

Fig. 6.2 Marketing Research Process

effort and specify what particular information needs are to be met by research results. In particular, the kind of information required for decision-making, whether it is on the external environment (*e.g.*, competitors, market) or on the organisation itself (*e.g.*, sales levels, distribution network) has to be specified in detail.

Research Questions are refined statements of research objectives. This may be illustrated with an example. An advertising manager may want a marketing researcher to investigate perceptions of industrial buyers regarding a new line of office furniture the company is considering to introduce. A specific research objective may be to determine the awareness level of potential buyers of the proposed office furniture with respect to the furniture brand currently being offered by the company. This research objective could be translated into several specific research questions:

— What is the unaided recall of the company's brand?

— What is the aided recall of the company's brand?

— What is the awareness of specific brand features?
(*e.g.*, price level, durability etc.)

Research questions are further refined into one or a series of *research hypotheses.* Hypotheses are tentative statements about relationship between the two or more variables, *e.g.*, "The primary reason why housewives buy Nirma washing powder is its low price." When operational hypotheses are stated using a 'symbolic notation, they are commonly termed as 'statistical hypotheses'.

2. Plan: After the marketing research task has been determined, the next major activity stage in the marketing research process consists of developing a marketing research plan. This plan is formally termed as marketing research design. It systematically sets forth what research data are to be collected as well as how the data is to be collected and analysed.

3. Data Collection: The next two stages of the marketing research process consists of activities required for implementing or carrying out a marketing research design. The third activity stage, data collection, consists of physically collecting research data and includes sampling activities, questionnaire construction activities and so forth.

4. Analysis and Interpretation: The fourth major activity stage is data analysis and interpretation. In this stage raw data from the third activity stage and analysed frequently by means of statistical techniques. The results of data analysing are then interpreted and inferences drawn as to the problem being researched.

5. Report: The final activity stage consists of preparing and presenting a research report for managerial decision-making. This report summarises the particular marketing research process followed and contains research conclusions.

Although the major marketing research activity stages are ordered sequentially, there are also feedback loops among the stages, as can be seen in figure. Feedback loops are present because the marketing research process is constantly subject to modifications resulting from expected or unexpected events that occur while research activities are being carried out.

Marketing research follows a systematic process of data collection. It is to be appreciated that this process is scientific. Marketing research process is a continuous process. Because of feedback, there are occasions to repeat the whole process. The process is thus subject to modification. Marketing research report is the culmination of marketing research process. It gives the operative part of the process — the recommendations which are actionable. These days we are marching towards a design of Marketing Information System (MkIS), of which marketing research is a part.

❖ Synopsis of Marketing Research Procedure

Marketing research is undertaken in the effort to learn something reliable about a marketing problem facing management. The value of the results depends upon the skill with which the marketing research project is designed and implemented.

Effective marketing research involves the following five steps:

(a) *Problem Definition:* The first step in the conduct of research calls for a careful definition of the problem. If the problem is stated vaguely, if the wrong problem is defined or if the uses of the research are not made clear, then the research results may prove useless to the manager.

(b) *Research Design:* The problem definition stage should lead to the development of a clear set of research objectives stated in writing if possible. The marketing research manager faces a choice among many alternative ways to collect the information that will satisfy the research objectives. He must decide on the data collection method, research instrument and sampling plan.

(c) *Fieldwork:* After the research design has been finalised, the research department must supervise or subcontract the task of collecting the data. This phase is generally the most expensive and the most liable to error.

(d) *Data Analysis:* The fourth step in the marketing research procedure is to attempt to extract meaningful information from the data. Anyone who has had the experience of massing data knows that further work has to be done to reveal underlying magnitudes and patterns of associations or casualty.

(e) *Report Preparation:* The last step is the preparation of a managerial orientated report presenting the major finding and recommendation coming from the study. The report should begin with a short statement of the problem and the major findings. A brief description of the research method should then be given with the more technical details being saved for an appendix. Many of the data should also be appendices. In general, the report should be written to facilitate the understanding and interest of the marketing executives and their ability to derive actionable information.

❖ Research Design

Research design is the basic plan which guides the data collection and analyses the phases of the project. It is the framework which specifies the type of information to be collected, the sources of data and data collection procedure.

Research Design Process: The research design process may be described in terms of the following sequential series of steps:

The above steps represent the general order in which decisions are made in designing a research project. However, we must emphasise the fact that steps in the design process interact and often occur simultaneously.

Like other communications the structure and coverage of a research proposal must be tailored to the situation. However, the following content outline is generally considered.

Step	*Description*
(*i*) Define the problem.	Determine the decision(s) facing management and the type(s) of information relevant to those decisions.
(*ii*) Specify the approximate value of information.	Determine the amount that can be spent on the project.
(*iii*) Select the data collection method(s).	Determine whether secondary data, a survey or experimentation will produce the required data and choose the form of the selected method(s) to use.
(*iv*) Select the measurement technique.	Determine whether and how to use questionnaires, attitude scales, observation, etc.
(*v*) Select the sample.	Determine who and how many respondents or objects to measure.
(*vi*) Select the analytical approach.	Determine the appropriate means of analysing the data to provide the required information.
(*vii*) Specify the time and financial cost.	For each research approach, develop time and financial cost estimates.
(*viii*) Prepare the research proposal.	Summarise the results of the preceding seven steps in the form of a research proposal.

BASIC CONTENTS OF A RESEARCH PROPOSAL

1. Executive summary	A brief overview of the contents of the proposal. This may be the only part read by some executives, so it should be sufficient to give them a basic understanding of the proposal.
2. Purpose and scope	A description of the management problem, possible reasons for the problem and the decision alternatives being studied.
3. Objectives	Defines the information to be obtained in terms of research questions to be answered. This information must be related explicitly to the management problem.
4. Research approach	Presents the important features of the research methods to be used, with justification of the strengths and limitations of the chosen method relative to the alternatives. All aspects of the research should be discussed such as sample size, quality control procedure and data collection method. Details of questionnaire format, sample selection procedures and so forth to be confined to an appendix.
5. Time and cost estimates	This encompasses all negotiated aspects, including fees, payments, provisions for contingencies and the schedule for submission of interim draft and final reports.
6. Appendices	Any technical matters of interest to a small minority of readers should be put at the back end of the proposal.

❖ Types of Research Design

Marketing research designs can be classified on the basis of the fundamental objective of the research. While this classification is far from perfect, consideration of different types of designs, their applicability, their strengths and their weaknesses will help us in selecting the design best suited to a specific problem. Two general types of research design are: (1) *Exploratory* and (2) *Conclusive.* The conclusive research can be subclassified into *descriptive research* and *causal research.*

❖ Need for Research Design

1. A good design will make sure that the information gathered is consistent with the study objective and that the data have been collected by accurate and economical procedure.
2. It helps the researcher to formulate, implement and control marketing research project.
3. The study remains on the right track.
4. It makes the research clear, compact and efficient. It provides a master-plan for an investigation.
5. It helps the appraisal of the project.
6. It ensures the requirements of staff and money at various stages of the project and prepares us for deviations.
7. Research design makes room for flexibility.

❖ Problem Formulation and its Importance

The first step in the conduct of research calls for a careful definition of the problem. If the problem is stated vaguely, if the wrong problem is defined or if the use of research is not made clear, then the research results may prove useless to the manager.

The problem definition stage leads to the development of a clear set of research objectives. To satisfy these objectives, alternative methods of collecting data is possible. The research method of data collection and sampling plan depend upon the research objectives.

It is thus obvious that crystalisation of is a problem is of utmost importance to give direction to further research.

Now we formulate the problem on the basis of a preliminary background study of the industry concerned, the product on hand, the marketing mix adopted, the environment around, the changes in the market etc. It is conducted informally to understand the problem environment.

Once we understand the background, we can appreciate the problem better. For example, an auto manufacturing firm was facing a problem of declining sales. But when the environment was studied, it was revealed that the dealers' salesmen were expected to give a free ride in the auto to prospects for demonstration purposes, which they were reluctant to offer because such an exercise had no incentive for them. So the real problem was how to motivate dealers' sales force to come forward to give free rides to prospective buyers and not the apparent symptoms of decline in sales. It is obvious here that may times we confuse the symptoms as problems but a preliminary study allows the real problem to emerge before us. Maybe, decline in sales is related to poor advertisement and then the problem would be to measure the effectiveness of advertisements and ways to enhance it.

Research objectives, research design and research findings all follow the problem. In other words, problem formulation helps us plan the research project itself.

Preliminary study to understand the problem in its correct perspective brings clarity and direction and unity of purpose into research work. There may be several problems, each is defined sharply, each is translated into research problem for further investigation.

❖ Objectives of Marketing Research Study

Problem defined gives us an idea of the research objectives. It is in fact the beginning of marketing research on correct lines. The marketing research procedure that follows is dependent upon the research objectives.

Research objectives which are ultimate are to be attained in the long term *e.g.*, we want to bring an awareness in 25% of target population about the existence of Wadilal brand of ice-cream in the 5 years. Now the same can be subdivided into an immediate objective of awareness in the first year. Now to attain 5% of this immediate objective, we have to formulate supplementary objective of:

1. Putting our message across in print media, the budget being 1.5% of total sales.
2. Covering an area to the extent of 40% geographically through the appointment of x no. of wholesalers and y no. of retailers.
3. Servicing this territory by a field force of x no. of sales people where each pays y no. of calls to all the parties.
4. Introduce dealer contest and consumer contest to motivate them to share and buy repeatedly, respectively Wadilal ice-cream.

So, as you will appreciate, the ultimate objectives are to be attained through immediate objectives, which are attained through supplementary objectives. The former are long-term, and the latter short-term. The former are strategic, the latter tactical. But they are all integrated.

In research work, for example, the ultimate objective is to find the cause of reduced sales. But the immediate objective could be to expand the market geographically by adding new customers, and by adding new segments. Another immediate objective could be to improve advertisement effectiveness and sales promotional methods. This will put him on the path of encountering the least consumer resistance. So, the hierarchy of objectives ultimately lead to the solution of the company's large problem.

Objectives thus give direction to research. They call for concerted action on certain specific issues. It mobilises the work of the research team towards pre-determined goals. They act as motivators. Research objectives are nothing but translation of a marketing problem into a research problem. In answers to the question: Why this study? The research methodology adopted depends upon the objectives stated.

❖ Check-list

We have seen that before a problem is formulated and survey conducted, a preliminary survey is done. Check-list is a substitute for preliminary survey, where a series of questions are asked covering various dimensions of the business. It gives direction to the thinking process and brings clarity in answering by tapping sources available. Check-list is then based on all points expected to be covered during the survey. All points are covered with great care, not omitting any important point. Check-list ideally is complete, correct and comprehensive. It embraces the marketing mix and production.

❖ Importance

1. Check-list is a substitute for preliminary survey.
2. Standard check-lists for various industries and research problems make survey work quick and easy.
3. It is a facilitative tool for marketing research.
4. It encourages a researcher to think from all possible angles.
5. Check-lists are prepared for all types of products and their marketing effort.
6. Check-list confines a research problem to limited answers.
7. Questionnaire later used in the survey becomes compact and comprehensive.
8. Model check-list can be used to revise the questionnaire to be used in survey.

Illustration

❖ Major Questions in a Concept Test

Concept of the Product: City Shuttle (Spark) which is something less than a mobike but more than a moped (Luna).

❖ Check-list

1. Is the concept of city shuttle clear and easy to understand?
2. Is it more useful than mobikes and mopeds?
3. Is the claim that city shuttle is the best for the city riders who have to speed up and down and ride through the narrow lanes believable?
4. Would you like to buy a city shuttle?
5. Would you replace your mobike, scooter or moped with a city shuttle?
6. Does city shuttle satisfy your need as a city dweller?
7. What improvements can you suggest in city shuttle?
8. Who would use city shuttle in your family?
9. What do you think the price of a city shuttle should be?

❖ Sources of Data

Types and Importance of Data in Marketing Research: We have already examined, though somewhat briefly, the nature and scope of marketing research and its applications. But it must be borne in mind that without any data, no research can be meaningful. We should, therefore, have sufficient data. In this section, we shall discuss the types of data and their application in marketing research.

The kinds of facts or data used in marketing research are many and varied. One useful classification divides marketing data into primary data and secondary data.

Primary data are the data that have been observed or recorded by researchers for the first time to their knowledge.

Secondary data may be described as those data that have been compiled by some agency other than the user. But the issue is not so simple. For example, if a company subscribing to one of the syndicated data services requests special information that is not ordinarily tabulated but is available in the data collected by the services, is the company seeking primary or secondary data? If the available data are secured rapidly and at low cost, there is no sense in spending time and effort to acquire primary data. Such considerations as the availability of experienced personnel and access to the sources of data materially affect the decision to collect primary data. Most marketing decisions do not warrant the time or cost involved in the collection of primary data. Even when it is necessary or desirable to obtain original information in a research project, secondary data are still useful in the total research effort. The secondary data are useful in the exploring research, especially for the hypothetical solutions of problem, suggested or inspired by other publications or data. Secondary data are essential in planning the sample from which primary information is to be obtained. They maybe used to describe the target population that is to be sampled as parameters and guide in the actual sample selections process and are a base for validating the obtained sample. Moreover, secondary data often enables us to carry out conclusive research to verify the expected effect of hypothesis under consideration.

The sources of secondary data are many and varied. They may be grouped into two general kinds:

(*i*) Internal data — that is, data available within the organisation for which the research is being done.

(*ii*) External data which are obtained from outside sources.

Internal Sources: Secondary data may be gathered from within the organisation for which the marketing research programme is carried out. A giant firm would have sufficient sources for the generation of secondary data in the form of customer billing, sales activity, information by selling activity, stock availability and product costs. When the information listed on a product, customer and/or area basis is available, we can examine the changes between areas, products and customers overtime. Standards or norms may be established to evaluate different parts of the marketing programme. There are various and obvious methods by which internal data may contribute to research studies. Most of the basic data are available in the accounting department, but co-ordination is essential between their Recording procedures and the Needs of marketing administration. Other types of data are not available from the accounting records. These data are frequently neglected, although they can be compiled and reported or at least filled in a manner which facilitates retrieval. Public utility firms often keep files of customer complaints that are analysed periodically. Marketing management also obtains important clues to protect deficiencies by examining service records which, in the absence of these records, would require large expenditure before the same information can be tabulated by collection of customers' views as primary data.

External Sources: External sources are numerous and obvious. Some of these are:

Libraries: Libraries are useful sources of information. Most universities have schools of business and have special divisions or room to serve these schools. Various institutions and large concerns maintain libraries with an excellent collection of information in the fields of their individual activity. They may be found in leading research institutions, banks, insurance companies, public utilities and manufacturing concerns.

Literature: A great volume of literature is published on the various subjects with which the marketing researcher may be concerned. Even a librarian has difficulty in keeping abreast of all the new writings and the accumulated writings of the past. When research is undertaken in some area of marketing in a particular industry, a sizeable task in involved in gathering these materials.

Trade Associations: For the collection of data relating to a particular industry, its trade association, if one exists, may be an excellent source. The trade association may have basic information that is not available in libraries. In the Indian context, you can approach a specialised board for a particular industry and the chambers of commerce with a view to collecting the relevant data.

Publishers: The leading publishers of general magazines and newspapers as well as television networks have been highly enterprising in collecting data or conducting marketing research.

State and Central Governments: Governments also provide useful data. Often, different government departments have information that rarely find its way into public or private libraries.

Other external sources are private sources, such as specialised marketing research firms, statistics available with private institutions or specialised agencies and so on.

DISTINCTIONS BETWEEN PRIMARY AND SECONDARY DATA

Primary Data	*Secondary Data*
1. These are first-hand original data collected by the researcher through various methods.	1. These are second-hand ready-made data collected by some other agency but not by the researcher.
2. Collection is time and cost consuming. It is complicated too.	2. Easy and quick collection at less cost.
3. Sources of primary data are the sampling units chosen.	3. Sources could be internal or external records.
4. Primary data are reliable and accurate when properly collected.	4. Supplementary to primary data.
5. Primary data affect the research directly	5. They provide secondary information.
6. Primary data are the latest useful for current problems.	6. Secondary data are historical.
7. Research related and relevant.	7. We have to modify it and be selective about it.

❖ Steps in Preparing a Questionnaire

Designing Survey Questionnaire: Of all the vehicles utilised to gather marketing information the questionnaire is probably the most used. The construction of questionnaire is one of the most delicate, yet critical research tasks. It is more of an art than a scientific operation. What we do know about questionnaire design comes from the experience of researchers who have specialised in this area. From this accumulated experience has emerged a series of rules or guidelines which can be useful to the new researcher. These are dealt with in this chapter.

1. Nature of Questionnaire Design

A questionnaire is simply a formalised set of questions for eliciting information. As such, its function is measurement and it represents the most common form of measurement in marketing research. A questionnaire can be used to measure: (1) *Behaviour:* Past, present, or intended; (2) *Demographic characteristics:* Age, sex, income occupation; (3) Level of knowledge and (4) *Attitudes and opinions:* The four areas are frequently measured by the questionnaire and often on the same questionnaire. Measurement of attitudes has become so important, both to marketing and behavioural sciences in general, that a number of specialised questioning techniques have been developed to measure them. These specialised techniques are treated in some detail in the next lesson.

Questionnaire construction is an essential part of any survey, but it must be done with more painstaking care for mail survey than for any other data gathering method. This is necessary because no interviewer will be present to answer questions or prevent any misunderstanding. A mail survey questionnaire, in its clarity, must perform both these functions itself.

There is another important difference between questionnaire for mail surveys and those administered by an interviewer. The mail survey questionnaire has to 'sell' itself. There is no particular pressure on the recipient of a mail questionnaire to fill it in. Therefore, the appearance and contents of the form itself must encourage the respondents to start doing so and it must hold their interest until they have completed it.

2. Elements of Questionnaire Design

The construction of questionnaire focuses on seven major areas. These areas and the major issues under each are listed below:

(1) *Preliminary Consideration.*

— Exactly what information is required?

— Exactly who are the target respondents?

— What method of communication will be used to reach these respondents?

(2) *Question Content:*

— Is the question really needed?

— Is this question sufficient to generate the needed information?

— Can the respondent answer the question correctly?

— Will the respondent answer the question correctly?

— Are there any external events that might bias the response to the question?

(3) *Question Wording:*

— Do the words used have but one meaning to all the respondents?

— Are any of the words or phrases loaded or leading any way?

— Are there any implied alternatives in the question?

— Will the respondents approach the question from the frame of reference desired by the researcher?

(4) *Response Format:*

— Can the question be asked as an open-ended, multiple-choice of dichotomous question?

(5) *Questions Sequence:*

— Are the questions organised in a logical manner that avoids introducing errors?

(6) *Layout of the Questionnaire:*

— Is the questionnaire designed in a manner to avoid confusion and minimise recording errors?

(7) *Pre-test:*

— Has the final questionnaire been subjected to a thorough pre-test?

3. Developing an Effective Questionnaire

One of the major frustrations of inexperienced market researchers is the development of a sound questionnaire. Too often the questionnaire is prepared, the survey is started and about halfway through the third or fourth interview, it becomes apparent that respondents do not understand what information is being sought. Even worse is the case where the survey is completed and it is then realised that an important piece of information was inadvertently left out. In either case, the problem usually lies with the questionnaire.

Entire books have been written about how to develop questionnaires. The following is simply a check-list of those things which are often overlooked or neglected by new researchers:

- Understand the research objectives. Listing the objectives help to prevent the inclusion of extraneous materials or questions that "would be interesting to know the answer to" but are not germane to the actual study.
- Write the actual points to the determined by the questionnaire. Be sure the description of the information is clear and concise. Avoid long questionnaires that tax the

patience of the respondent. When this happens, careless or flip answers often result, or the respondent finds reasons not to answer the questions fully.

- Break the items to be determined down into specific questions. Questions must be stated so that they are clear to the respondents and there is not a chance for misunderstanding. Avoid generalities and ambiguous terms.
- Write a rough draft first. Polish it after you have made all your points.
- Use a short opening statements. Include your name, the name of your organisation, and the broad purpose of the questionnaire.
- Open with one or two easily answered, interesting and in offensive questions. This tends to put the respondents at ease.
- Structure the questions so that they flow logically and easily from one to another. Ask general questions before the more detailed ones.
- Have a few 'closed' questions as possible. Use 'open-ended' questions where possible, although there are some problems with them.
- Avoid questions that suggest an answer or that could be considered 'leading' questions. Let the respondent answer fully and honestly. Do not use words with strong favourable or unfavourable connotations. They tend to bias results.
- Make the questions easy to answer. Do not use long detailed questionnaires which may confuse the respondent.
- When possible, include a few questions which will serve as cross-check on earlier answers. This aids in ensuring validity.
- Put the demographic questions (*e.g.*, age, income, education) and other personal questions at the end of the questionnaire.
- Pre-test the questionnaire to get out the bugs. Twenty of thirty persons in the proposed respondent group are usually a sufficient sample for a pre-test.

In the following sections, we will discuss further types of questions sequences of questions and layout and pre-testing of questionnaire.

4. Pre-testing Questionnaire

Although the art of writing questions may seem simple, every experienced researcher knows that it is full of pitfalls. It is, therefore, essential that a questionnaire is thoroughly pre-tested before it is administered the chosen sample.

In the first instance, this pre-testing generally takes the form of asking clients, informed colleagues their opinion and of obtaining critical appraisal from experts in the particular field under study.

The next stage is to construct a representative sub-sample of the target population of perhaps 25 to 30 individuals and, in the case of personally administered questionnaire, use senior research personnel to interview these respondents. Their answers, their queries or requests for help in interpretation, signs of confusion, boredom, etc. should be carefully noted. This will help to identify major shortcoming in the questionnaire. In addition, data from the pre-test should be processed according to research design specifications and even tentative conclusions reached. This might highlight superfluous information or information that does not contribute towards the achievement of the initial survey objectives. It will be self-evident that ultimate validity of pre-test will be maintained only in so much as the subsample used in a randomly determined subset of the sample proper.

❖ Sources of Bias

Bias is inclination, predisposition, influence in a certain direction, prejudice or preformed notions. Marketing research ought to be free from bias. Biased conclusions are wrong and may prove disastrous. The sources of bias are described hereunder:

Bias Through Questionnaire: Misleading or ambiguous questions allow bias to creep in. Some words are not understood by the respondents. The multiple choice questions are to be framed very carefully. Or else certain choices, usually at the top, get selected, thus introducing bias. The general form of questionnaire can also lead to bias. A questionnaire as a whole should be interesting to elicit responses. A dull questionnaire is not able to evoke the right response. Bias can also be due to faulty layout of the questionnaire — no adequate space to record the answers.

Bias Through Interviewer: Unwillingly, the interviewer can introduce bias. It is because of age, sex, dress manners, habits, personality etc., of the interviewer. Lack of integrity and interest can also bring in bias. Sometimes, he falsely claims to have collected data, which in reality he has not. He may omit questions. He may be suggestive about the answers to the respondent. All this leads to bias.

Bias Through Respondents: A wrong sample may lead to bias. Response that is not full or no-response can also lead to bias. Refusal or wrong responses also lead to bias. Biased answers may be given due to personal factors.

The other prominent sources of bias are: data collection method, complication and/or analysis of the data.

❖ How to Reduce Bias in Questionnaire?

1. The questions themselves should be free from bias. They should be properly worded and constructed with due attention and care.
2. Questions should be sequenced properly. Multiple choices should be carefully selected. Easy questions come first. Important questions are taken first.
3. The layout and design and construction of the questionnaire should be impressive. The respondents must get a feeling of importance while answering the questions.
4. Pre-testing of a questionnaire is advised to ascertain the problem areas and improve the questionnaire.
5. Positional bias is to be reduced by changing the order of answers provided.
6. Enough space should be provided to record the answers.
7. Too long and complicated questions are better avoided ambiguous and unfamiliar questions/words are omitted.
8. Those questions where the respondent is likely to refuse to answer are better avoided, (*e.g.*, highly personal questions, encroaching upon the privacy of persons concerned).
9. Suggestive questions and questions likely to cause misunderstanding are avoided.
10. Questionnaire should be as brief as possible.
11. Respondents are to be given a proper briefing.
12. Interviewers are to be trained properly.

DISTINCTION BETWEEN RESEARCH DESIGN AND RESEARCH PROCESS

Research Design	*Research Process*
1. Research design has two aspects: anticipation and specification.	1. It follows the anticipated plan and specified details of the research design.
2. Research design is basically a plan.	2. It is implementation of the research plan.
3. Research design is formulated after stating the research problem.	3. Research process starts as soon as the decision to conduct research is taken.
4. Research study's framework is given by research design.	4. Research process is lengthy. Research design is an important step in the whole research process.

DISTINCTION BETWEEN OPEN-ENDED QUESTIONS AND LIMITED-CHOICE QUESTIONS

Open Ended Questions	*Limited Choice Questions*
1. It is free answer questions. It shows free responses. It also includes some probing questions.	1. It offers limited choices as responses. They may be dichotomous or multiple choice questions.
2. There is great freedom and degree of openness in answering these questions. They are difficult to answer.	2. These questions are easy to ask and generally easy to answer.
3. They can be used for qualitative research.	3. They are used for eliciting simple factual answers which are likely to be biased.
4. They are used as an introduction to a topic.	4. They are helpful in obtaining classification data about a respondent.
5. They make the questionnaire interesting.	5. They make the questionnaire strait jacket.
6. They are good for educated respondents.	6. They can be answered by an average individual.
7. Interviewer should be well trained to avoid bias.	7. Interviewer can record answers even when not well-trained.
8. Difficult to analyse and interpret.	8. Easy analysis and interpretation.
9. Good as openers, pilot, exploratory and problem-identification studies.	9. Appear to be a better substitute for free answer questions.
10. Good in personal interviews (but not in mail surveys).	10. Suitable in mail surveys.
11. Answers may not be precise, relevant and correct.	11. Objective-type precise answers.

DISTINCTION BETWEEN AMBIGUOUS AND FILTERED QUESTIONS

Ambiguous Questions	*Filtered Questions*
1. Here, the language or words used are confusing, *e.g.*, theatre (whether a theatre for staging dramas or a cinema hall is not understood by the respondent).	1. It filters out answer to subsequent questions.
2. Ambiguous questions are avoided.	2. Filtered questions are included so as to ensure the omission of those respondents for whom the questions are not meant.
3. They are troublesome.	3. They provide convenience to respondents.

DISTINCTION BETWEEN OPENING QUESTIONS AND MULTIPLE-CHOICE QUESTIONS

Open Questions	*Multiple Choice Questions*
1. They are extremely good for qualitative and behavioural research.	1. They are appropriate when the respondents hold well-crystallised opinions.
2. Maximum freedom and openness in answering.	2. Some limited freedom given by "Any other ... Please specify" choice.
3. Not standardised always can be framed on the spot.	3. They are called cafeteria questions. Here, the answer is selected approximating to our own answer. Suitable for eliciting either opinions or motives.
4. Interviewer goes deeper into the subject of the respondent's opinion. There are varying responses.	4. The replies are easily recorded. Questions can be easily asked. Vocabulary raises no problem.
5. Time consuming.	5. More questions can be asked in less time
6. Spontaneous.	6. Kills spontaneity.
7. No positional bias.	7. Positional bias likely.
8. Not encouraging response. Good for the elite and educated lot.	8. Response encouraging. Good for less educated even.

❖ 'Why' Programme?

The questionnaire is a valuable data collection tool. In order to increase the usefulness of the questionnaire, it is subjected to a 'Why' programme so as to test the questions that have gone into making the questionnaire. Each question is subjected to this test. Some of the points raised about each question could be:

Is the question appropriate?

Is it clear and unambiguous?

Is it relevant?

Will it evoke a response?

Why is it included? etc., etc.

In other words, the why programmes critically evaluate each question. This prunes down the questionnaire, leaving finely worded important questions and omitting the rest. Even the types of questions to be included are subject to a 'why' test. 'Why' programme gives an ideal and effective questionnaire. It brings clarity to the questionnaire and renders it easy and convenient for the respondents.

Pre-testing: Before a final questionnaire is administered to the sample, the first draft is always tested upon a small sample. It is prior to the actual survey. When the questions are put to a small group, the deficiencies in the draft come to the surface. Then the questions are revised, re-examined and the questions are re-drafted. There may be more than one pre-tests. Ultimately, the final questionnaire emerges. Those who do the pre-testing job should be highly skilled. Experts on that question design are appointed for this purpose. Sometimes, a check-list comes handy to ensure:

1. Whether the questions are in harmony with the stated objectives of the research?
2. Whether the questions will elicit the responses intended?

3. Whether the questions are rightly worded, are intelligible, and are rightly sequenced?
4. Whether some additions/deletions are called for. In other words, pre-testing is a process which generates and ideal questionnaire for marketing research?

❖ Phrasing of Questions in a Questionnaire

The language used in a questionnaire should not be confusing. If the respondents assign different meanings to the words or sentences used, the collected information will be incorrect. Clear wording should be our goal. Words should be understandable. The interviewer should explain the question properly to the respondent.

Biased and loaded words are avoided. Questions which are phrased faultily make the whole research process meaningless.

❖ Features of a Good Questionnaire

1. Determine the area to be covered by the questionnaire, keeping in mind the research objectives.
2. Order the questions properly. Also word them properly.
3. Make a proper lay-out of a questionnaire.
4. Give straightforward and clear instructions.
5. Avoid asking the impossible.
6. Avoid asking offensive or antagonising questions.
7. Create permissive atmosphere.
8. Be unambiguous.
9. Pitch the question at right level of intelligence.
10. Be careful about loaded questions.
11. Be careful about leading questions.
12. Guard against contamination due to conditioning of prior questions.
13. There are no questions which tax the memory of the researcher too much.
14. Questions to which motives can be imputed are better avoided.
15. Questions are either coded or numbered for ease of further analysis.

❖ Multiple-Choice Questions

When the respondents hold well crystallised opinions, the multiple-choice questions are very appropriate; *e.g.*, "How often do you purchase your provisions?"

(*a*) Less than once a month; (*b*) Once a month; (*c*) Once a fortnight; (*d*) Once a week and (*e*) More than once a week.

Do you think your pen gives you satisfactory service?"

(*a*) Most satisfactory; (*b*) Quite satisfactory; (*c*) Satisfactory; (*d*) Slightly satisfactory and (*e*) Most unsatisfactory.

"Are you in favour of prohibition?"

(*a*) Definitely in favour; (*b*) Probably in favour; (*c*) Neither in favour nor against; (*d*) Probably against; (*e*) Definitely against and (*f*) No opinion.

In the multiple-choice questions, after various alternatives have been covered, space is left for any other opinion by providing for "Any other ..." (Specify). The respondent can, therefore, express any other opinion not covered by the alternatives provided.

These questions list a number of answers and permit the subjects to select the answer that best approximates to their own. This is sometimes known as the cafeteria question and is suitable for eliciting either opinions or motives. Its advantages lie in enabling a person to express herself or himself and in being easy to tabulate. Obviously, all significant degrees of the answer must be offered if it is to be a valid question.

Advantages:

As compared with open-ended questions, fixed alternative questions are easier to work. The replies, too, can be easily recorded. The interviewer can ask the questions quickly and without much effort and the respondent can also answer them quickly, without thinking much about them. He has only to choose the alternative that matches his opinion or attitude or experience. The vocabulary raises no problems here. A proper frame of reference is evident from the alteratives provided and appropriate information is obtained by the researcher. More questions can be asked in less time. The respondents are more willing to co-operate, for they don't have to tax their brains. Moreover, there is no scope for interviewer bias as the respondent chooses the alternative he wants. The responsibility for judgement lies with the respondent, not the interviewer. Again, the coding, classification, tabulation and analysis of these questions become easy and quick.

Disadvantages:

It is a difficult task to provide for all possible alternatives to fixed alternative questions. The framing of multiple-choice questions with an exhaustive list of sound requires not only considerable effort, but also a good deal of prior research. If all the alternatives are not provided, the answers are likely to be distorted.

Moreover, the respondent may be forced to choose an alternative which does not exactly correspond with his experience or opinion. The standardised response may kill the spontaneity of the respondent. Furthermore, position bias is an important problem in multiple choice questions. Researchers find that respondents tend to choose the middle alternative — there is a strong middle position bias. The researcher, therefore, can continue to influence the results by positioning the expected reply in the middle. Another important issue concerns the order of the alternatives.

There are no hard and fast rules governing the format on which responses should be based. The ultimate criterion of the suitability of the format is its capacity to obtain the required information accurately, correctly and without distortion.

❖ Depth Interview and Focused Interview

Motivational Research Techniques: The motivational research techniques can be broadly classified as depth interviews and projective techniques. These techniques are designed to uncover information that direct questioning and observation methods cannot bring out. Their focus is on the reasons why individuals buy or use various products and what the act of buying, owning or using the product, means to them.

In the discussion that follows, these two techniques are described briefly.

Depth Interview: Depth interviews are designed to uncover basic predispositions — unconscious feelings, needs, conflicts and the like. They achieve this result by creating a completely permissive atmosphere, in which the subject is free to express himself without fear of disapproval, admonition or dispute and without advice from the interviewer. Depth interviews can involve one respondent and one interviewer or they may involve a small group of respondents and a single interviewer. The latter type is called focus group interview and the former category is termed individual depth interview or just depth interview.

1. Individual Depth Interview: Such interviews may be described as less-structured and more intensive than a standardised questionnaire — administered interview. There are three broad types of individual depth interviews:

(*a*) *True Depth or Clinical Interview* that corresponds to the psycho-therapeutic interview and requires far longer than a single session and is, strictly speaking, outside the scope of conventional marketing research.

(*b*) *Non-directive Interview* where, although the interviewer retains the initiative during the course of the interview, the respondent is given maximum freedom to respond in the manner he wishes, within reasonable bounds of relevance.

(*c*) *Semi-structured or Focused Interview* where the interviewer is required to cover a specific list of points and although the respondent is allowed to respond freely, a much tighter control is exercised by the interviewer in order to maximise the collection of relevant data. Specific areas may be focused upon.

Individual depth interviews require great skill and considerable time. There are difficulties not only in establishing the right degree of confidence and eliciting answers but in interpreting the qualitative information provided. Analysis and interpretation are highly subjective. The technique is obviously expensive and in practice, group rather than individual interviews are more common place.

2. Focus Group Interview: A variation of the depth interview is the focus group interview. A number of individuals (usually 8 to 12) are brought together rather than being interviewed one at a time as in the individual depth interview. Each group is designed to reflect the characteristics of a particular market segment of interest. The interaction among the group members is only loosely directed by the group interviewer, called the moderator. The moderator attempts to develop three clear stages in the group interview: (*i*) Establishing rapport with the group, structuring the rules of group interaction and setting objectives; (*ii*) Provoking intense discussion in the relevant areas: and (*iii*) Summarising the groups' responses to determine the extent of agreement. The moderator requires to perform the difficult task of guiding the discussion into the relevant areas while exerting minimum influence on the content of the discussion.

Focus group interviews are currently one of the most frequently used techniques in marketing research. They have been applied to: (*i*) Generate idea of new products; (*ii*) Explore consumer reaction to new product concepts; (*iii*) Explore consumer response to both advertising concepts and finished advertisements; (*iv*) Explore consumer response to package design and labellings and (*v*) Develop consumer vocabulary as a preliminary step in structuring questionnaires and so on.

The Carnation Company (USA) provides an interesting example of the type of information focus group interviews can provide. Past research had revealed that many people did not drink powdered milk because of a perceived taste deficiency when compared with fluid milk. Carnation decided to reposition the brand to make it more appealing. First, Carnation conducted focus group interviews separately with users and non-users. Discussion with non-users confirmed that taste was a major barrier to use. Sessions with users revealed that a large percentage of them solved the 'taste problem' by mixing powdered milk half and half with fluid whole milk.

Thus, producing a cheaper, better-tasting low-fat milk. Carnation hypothesised that non-users would be more likely to be converted if the company repositioned its product as milk extender. Quantitative research confirmed this hypothesis and Carnation executed the strategy with an advertising and promotion campaign that told the milk extender story.

There are a number of *advantages* of focus group interviews over individual depth interviews. Each respondent is able to expand and refine his or her opinion in the interactions with the other members. Thus, the interaction process provides more detailed and accurate information than could be derived from individual depth interview. Snow-balling occurs when a comment, perhaps random, by one member triggers an idea or similar feelings in others. A group interview situation is generally more exciting and offers more stimulation to the participants than individual depth interviews. The heightened interest and excitement make more meaningful comments likely. In addition, the security of being in a crowd encourages some members to speak out when they otherwise would not. Because any question raised by the moderator is to the group as a whole rather than to individuals, the answers contain a degree of spontaneity not produced by other techniques. Furthermore, individuals are not under any pressure to 'make up' answers to questions.

However, there are a number of *disadvantages.* Both non-participation and non-response can be serious sources of error. Focus groups are expensive on a per respondent basis. Without a sensitive and effective moderator, self-appointed participant will dominate the discussion. Participants may react negatively toward the dominant member and this may have a 'halo' effect on attitudes toward the concept or topic of discussion.

Advantages and Disadvantages:

(*a*) Personal interview.
(*b*) Telephone interview.
(*c*) Mail interview.

❖ Market Survey Techniques

Advantages and Disadvantages of Personal, Telephone and Mail interview.

	Advantages	*Disadvantages*
(*a*) Personal interview	• Most reliable of the survey methods because of face-to-face contact. • Questions can be longer and more complex than with other methods. • With skilled observations and probing, respondent can be encouraged to answer questions fully. • Representative of sample can be well-controlled.	• Most costly method. • Some respondents such as high level business executives may be difficult to contact. • Personal bias of individual interviewers can affect results. • Reliability of face-to-face interviewing depends on integrity and skill of interviewers, which in some cases may be lacking.

	Advantages	*Disadvantages*
(*b*) Telephone interview	• Fast, convenient method of obtaining even large number of responses in short time. • Relatively low cost per interview. • Sometimes good for reaching important people who are inaccessible. • Respondents can be contacted at specific times of the day. • Interviewer bias is eliminated since no interviewer is present.	• Poor for obtaining large amount of information or for asking difficult questions. • Securing co-operation not always possible. • Obtaining a random sample may be difficult. • Respondents cannot be observed while giving answers. • Extensive or complex questionnaire usually yield poor result.
(*c*) Mail interview	• Questionnaire may be answered more accurately since respondents can fill out forms at their leisure. • Good for reaching people who are sometimes inaccessible • Comparatively low cost for reaching small and widely scattered groups.	• Respondent's interest in the subject under investigation has a direct effect on returns. • Good possibility of biased or non-representative return. • Respondents may be unable or unwilling to give answers without probing or stimulation from the interviewer.

❖ Sampling

Sampling Procedures: Sampling is a procedure of using a small number of units of a given population as a basis for drawing conclusions about the whole population. Advantages of sampling over a census are: reduced costs, reduced time and accuracy of results. Sampling process involves seven steps: defining the population, specifying sampling frame, specifying sampling unit, selection of sampling technique, determination of sample size and selecting the sample.

The two major sampling methods are probability and non-probability sampling techniques. Probability samples are based on chance selection procedures. This permits an evaluation of the precision of techniques derived from the sample. There are four basic Probability Sampling Procedures: simple random sampling, stratified sampling, systematic sampling and cluster sampling. Non-probability sampling techniques are convenient, but there are no statistical methods to measure their sampling error. The non-probability procedures include convenience sampling, judgement sampling and quota sampling.

The statistical determination of sample size requires specification of the error that can be tolerated, the confidence level and estimation of standard deviation.

(i) Sampling Defined: Once the researcher has clearly specified the problem and developed an appropriate research design and data collection instrument, the next step in the research process is to select those elements from which the information will be collected. It is in this, context that an understanding of the sampling procedures becomes important.

The process of sampling involves any procedure using a small number of items or parts of the whole population to make conclusions regarding the whole population. A sample is a subset or some part of a larger population. The purpose of sampling is to estimate some characteristics of the population. In research parlance characteristics of a population are termed parameters whereas the sample estimates of the population are termed parameters whereas the sample estimates of the population parameters are termed statistics.

We have defined sampling in terms of the population to be studied. A population or universe is any complete group of people, sales territories, stores, etc., sharing some common set of characteristics. When a distinction is made between Population and Universe, it is made on the basis of whether the group is finite (population) or infinite (universe). The term population element refers to an individual members of the population. A census is an investigation of all individual members of the population. A census is an investigation of all individual elements making up the population, that is, it involves a total enumeration rather than sampling.

The relationships among population parameter, sample and statistics can be illustrated by means of a Schematic diagram as follows:

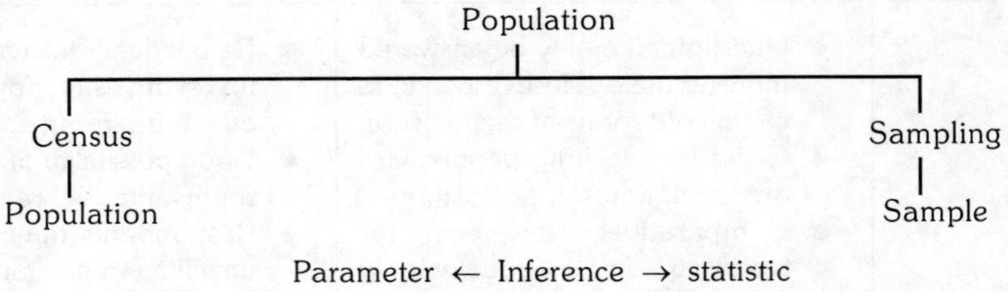

(ii) Why Sampling? It is sometimes possible and practicable to take a census. For instance, surveys of industrial consumers or of distributors of consumer products are frequently in the form of a census. More often than not, however, one or more of a number of reasons make it impracticable or even impossible to take a census. These reasons basically involve considerations of cost, time and accuracy.

Assuming a relatively large population, which is normally the case in marketing research, sampling offers obvious economic savings in time and money. It is simply less time-consuming and less expensive to collect data from a portion of the population then from the entire population. Moreover, because of time and cost limitations, sampling usually permits a more indepth investigation of individual study objects than would a census. Likewise, there are opportunity costs associated with census since any research-based decision would have to wait the added length of time required to conduct a census.

In certain circumstances a research project employing sampling might provide more comprehensive and more accurate data than one employing a census. With a small number of study objects a researcher is frequently able to maintain better control over the research process and ultimately obtain higher quality data than if a census were conducted.

Associated with every research project is a certain amount of total error. The error consists of two distinct components, sampling error and non-sampling error. Sampling error is not an error in the usual sense of mistake. Rather, it is a statistical term that refers to the precision with which a sample statistic is calculated. It results from the fact that data are being collected from less than an entire population of study objects and this introduces random variability into the statistic. Because of its random nature, as the size of the sample increases, sampling error decreases and precision increases. Briefly, then sampling error is essentially a function of sample size. If a census were conducted, all study errors would be non-sampling errors, since by definition, sampling error would not exist.

Non-sample error includes a wide variety of errors that can creep into a research project at nearly every stage. Non-sampling errors have up impact directly on the quality of research data.

(iii) Sampling Process — An Overview: Once a researcher has determined that sampling is more appropriate than conducting a census, several sampling decisions need to be made. These usually involve seven sequential steps which are briefly described below. A somewhat detailed treatment of some of these steps is given in the sections that follow:

Step 1: *Defining the Population:* A properly designated population must be defined in terms of elements, sampling units, extent and time. For example, a survey of consumers might specify the population as:

Element: Men and women

Sampling units: Households

Extent: Delhi metropolitan city

Time: During the period February-July 1997.

It is sometimes difficult to define the population properly. For example, how would a researcher define the population for a survey to determine the best features to promote a children's cereal? In such instances, one would have to know the role played by each family member in the purchase of the product as well as what types of families constitute the primary market.

Step 2: *Specifying the Sampling Frame:* A sampling frame is a means of representing the elements of the population. A sampling frame may be a telephone directory, list of registered voters, city directories, etc. Maps also serve frequently as sampling frames.

One of the researcher's more creative tasks in sampling is developing an appropriate sampling frame when the list of population elements is not readily available.

Step 3: *Specifying Sampling Unit:* We have already used the term "sampling unit" in defining a relevant population. It is now time to define it more explicitly.

The sampling unit is the basic unit containing the elements of the population to be sampled. It may, of course, be an element itself or a unit in which the element is contained. For example, if an airline wishes to sample passengers, every twenty fifth name on a complete list of passengers may be taken. In this case the sampling unit is the same as the element. This is a direct sampling procedure. Alternatively, the airline could resort to some indirect method of sampling. The airline could first select flights as the sampling unit. Then subsequently select certain passengers on the flights already selected. Here the sampling unit and the population element are not the same.

The sampling unit selected is often dependent upon the sampling frame and the design of the project. If a telephone survey is to be conducted, the sampling unit will necessarily be telephone numbers. A mail questionnaire requires a sampling unit of addresses. Personal interview studies, on the other hand, permit considerably more flexibility in choosing the sampling unit.

Step 4: *Selection of Sampling Method:* The sampling method is the way the sampling units are to be selected. A useful way of classifying them is shown below:

Sample Methods

Non-probability Sampling	**Probability Sampling**
Convenience	Simple random
Judgement	*Stratified Sampling:*
Quota	Proportionate
	Disproportionate
	Systematic Sampling
	Cluster Sampling

As shown above, sampling technique can be broadly classified as probability and non-probability sampling. In probability sampling, each element of the population has a known, non-zero chance of being selected in the sample. The sampling is done by mathematical decision rules. In non-probability sampling, chance selection procedures are not used. Thus, selection of sample is based in some part on the judgement of the researcher.

There are a number of different sampling procedures that fall into these two categories. We will discuss them separately.

Step 5: *Determination of the Sample Size:* When asked to evaluate a marketing research project, even those with little marketing research training, will begin by asking: How big was the sample? Intuitively, we know that the larger the sample, the more accurate the research results. Although sample size determination is perhaps as much an art as questionnaire construction, there are formulae available that can be used as guidelines. The subject is dealt within a separate section.

Step 6: *Selecting the Sample:* The final step in the sampling process is the actual selection of the sample elements. This requires implementation of each of the decisions made thus far.

(iv) Sampling Techniques: (*a*) *Probability Vs. Non-probability Sampling:* A brief comparison of the two procedures can be made on two broad dimensions — statistical and operational.

From a statistical perspective, probability sampling is preferable to non-probability sampling because it permits statistical evaluation of sampling error — the precision of sample statistics. Also, because of chance or randomisation device employed, probability sampling procedures tend to lead more objective sampling since relatively little discretion is left to a researcher when selecting a sample. Finally, probability sampling procedures serve as the basis of most common statistical techniques.

Though probability sampling procedures permit estimates of sampling error, there is no guarantee that they will produce more accurate results than non-probability sampling procedures. This is because both types of sampling are subject to same kinds of non-sampling errors. Non-probability sampling technique, on the other hand, permits more "hands-on" control by a researcher, in certain researcher situations it may actually yield more accurate results than a probability sampling procedure.

For operational reasons also, non-probability sampling techniques tend to be used as frequently as probability sampling or perhaps even more so, in marketing research. In certain marketing research applications, probability sampling procedures are not simply required. If, for instance, a researcher merely wants too learn whether people can taste the difference between two packaged food formulations, it may not be necessary to use sophisticated probability sampling provided that non-probability sampling procedures result in a sample that is not a typical of the population of interest. Thus, for some type of research tasks, especially where precise population inferences are not desired, non-probability sampling procedures are more than sufficient and much less expensive than sampling techniques.

Usually, the final choice of a specific sampling plan will depend on individual judgment. When a non-probability design must be used, the researcher will frequently be able to adopt some of the features of probability sampling to improve results. Conceptualisation of a design in probability sampling terms helps to structure the sampling issues and identify options more clearly than unaided intuition.

(b) Probability Sampling Techniques: As mentioned earlier, there are several probability sampling techniques which are outlined below:

1. Simple Random Sampling

This is unrestricted probability sampling technique wherein all study objects in a sampling frame possess an equal chance of being included in a sample. In addition, for a given sample size *n*, all combination of study objects possess an identical probability of being in the sample selected.

The sampling process is simple because it requires only one stage of sample selection. A frequently employed procedure to select random samples is to use random numbers, either generated by computer or found in a table known as random numbers table.

Despite being basic probability sampling techniques, sample random sampling is not widely used in marketing research. There are two major reasons. First, relative to some other probability sampling techniques, simple random sampling can be more expensive and administratively difficult to implement. Second, for a given sample size, there are other probability sampling techniques that can yield smaller standard errors and have greater precision than simple random sampling.

2. Stratified Sampling

A stratified sampling is distinguished by the following two step procedures: (*i*) the parent population is divided into mutually exclusive and exhaustive subsets and (*ii*) a simple random sample of elements is chosen independently from each group or subset. The subsets into which the universe elements are divided are called or sub-populations.

Stratified samples are of two types — proportionate stratified sample and disproportionate stratified sample. If the number of sampling units drawn from each stratum is in proportion to the relative population size of the stratum, the sample is a proportional stratified sample. On the other hand, in a disproportionate stratified sample, the sample size for each stratum is not allocated on a proportional base with the population size but dictated by analytical considerations. The essential difference between these types is how the total sample size is allocated among various sample strata. An example would clarify the points. Suppose the population consists of 1000 wholesalers and a total sample size of 100 wholesalers is desired. The wholesalers are divided into three strata, since the total sample size is 10 per cent of the population, for proportional stratified sampling a 10 per cent simple random sample would be selected from each strata as shown below:

Wholesaler strata	*Strata size*	*10 per cent directly proportional stratified sample size*
Large	50	5
Medium	300	30
Small	650	65
Total	1,000	100

Another possible allocation scheme would be to sample 33 wholesalers from each strata. The sample size would be close to 10 per cent, while equal allocation would facilitate interstrata comparisons. This is a common type of disproportionate stratification.

A major goal of stratified sampling is to increase sampling precision by eliminating or at least controlling, one or more sources of extraneous sampling variation that systematically increase the standard error of statistic. This comes through meeting the stratification criterion of "homogeneity and heterogeneity." Stratification must result in study objects being as homogeneous as possible within the strata, while across the strata study objects must be as heterogeneous as possible.

In stratified sampling, the costs of sampling are greater than those of simple random sampling because of the added step of stratification. However, if properly carried out, the resulting increased precision of stratified sampling more than offsets its additional costs.

3. Systematic Random Sampling

Suppose one wishes to take a sample of 1000 from a list consisting of 200,000 names. One-way of doing this is as follows: (*i*) draw a random number between 1 and 200, suppose the number chosen is 30 and (*ii*) then starting with 30 every 200th name from the list may be drawn. This is an illustration of systematic sampling.

While this procedure is not actually a random selection procedure, it yields random results if the arrangements of the items in the list are random in character. The problem of periodicity if a list is not random in character. However, periodicity is rarely a problem for of most sampling in marketing research.

In one form or another, wide use is made of systematic sampling. The principal advantage of this technique is its simplicity. It is often found that systematic sampling is somewhat more efficient statistically than simple random sampling.

4. Cluster Sampling

Suppose an investigator wishes to measure certain characteristics of industrial sales representatives such as their earnings, attitudes towards the job, hours worked and so on. It would be extremely difficult and certainly costly to develop an up-to-date list of sales representatives. Yet such a list would be require for a simple random sample. A stratified sample would rather required that the investigator possesses knowledge about some additional characteristic of each sales representative, for example, education or employer, so that the population could be divided into mutually exclusive and exhaustive subsets. With a cluster sample, on the other hand, one could use the companies as sampling units. The investigator would generate a sample of companies from the population of companies of interest. The investigator could then obtain a list of sales representatives working for each of the selected companies. If it is a one-stage cluster sampling, each sales representative of cash selected company would be studied. If the researcher sub-sampled sales representatives from each company's list, it would be two-stage cluster sampling.

While it may appear that cluster sampling is analogous to stratified sampling, there exists some basic differences between the two. The goal of stratified sampling is to increase precision more than the cost involved. The goal of cluster sampling is to decrease cost than the associated decrease in precision. Moreover, in stratified sampling, the strata should be homogeneous within and heterogeneous among, while in cluster sampling the clusters should be heterogenous within and homogeneous among. Finally, the two steps in stratified sampling can be characterised as "census, then sample," while in cluster sampling they can be characterised as "sample, then census."

Other probability sampling techniques exist which are basically extension of the four methods discussed above. Many of this techniques such as multistage sampling, double sampling, sequential sampling and multiplicity sampling techniques, are potentially useful in marketing research.

5. Non-probability Sampling Techniques

There are essentially three distinct non-probability sampling techniques. These are briefly described below:

1. Convenience Sampling: This is the least expensive and least time-consuming of all sampling techniques. As its name implies, convenience sampling refers to obtaining a sample of convenient study objects. In convenience sampling a researcher merely sample those study objects that are readily accessible with a minimum amount of effort. Typically, no explicit sampling frame is used. For example, it may be consumers at shopping centres. During election times, television stations often report "man-on-the-street" interviews that are presumed to reflect public opinion.

Perhaps the only research situation in which a convenience sample may be justified is during the exploratory stages of research project when a researcher is searching for ideas or attempting to generate hypotheses.

2. Judgment Sampling: A slightly more sophisticated sampling technique is judgment or purposive sampling. In judgment sampling, the sample is still essentially a convenience sample. However, in judgmental sampling, all study object selection decision are tempered by a researcher's judgment as to whether a particular study object should or should not be in the sample. Hence, *a criterion in addition to convenience* is used in selecting a judgmental sample. For example, test markets often are selected because they are viewed as typical cities with demographic profiles, closely matching the national profile. A fashion manufacturer regularly selects a sample of key accounts that he believes are capable of providing the desired information to predict what will sell during a festival period.

Ultimately, the value of a particular judgmental sample is determined by judgment, insights, expertise and creativity of a researcher.

3. Quota Sampling: Quota sampling is the most sophisticated non-probability sampling technique. The first stage consists of developing categories or quotas of study objects from which to collect data. These categories are based upon knowledge that a researcher has obtained previously. For example, census data may be used to develop demographic categories. Collectively the resulting categories comprise the *quota matrix*. In the second stage, study objects are selected for sample inclusion to the exact extent the investigators desire.

It is important to distinguish between Quota sampling and Stratified random sampling. In stratified random sampling, the sample within each stratum is chosen at random. In quota sampling, however, the sampling within each quota is not done at random, the field representatives are given wide latitude in the selection of respondents to meet their quotas.

Speed of data collection, lower costs and convenience are the major advantages of quota sampling. However, because study objects are selected according to convenience sampling procedure, rather than on a random basis, selection may introduce bias.

DISTINCTIONS BETWEEN SAMPLING ERRORS AND NON-SAMPLING ERRORS

Sampling Errors	*Non-Sampling Errors*
1. It is an error related to sample size.	1. If there is census, sampling error by definition, is out of question. The error may be due to poor arithmetic or poor record of data.
2. Sampling error is a matter of serious concern.	2. It is a minor error.
3. It is possible to determine sampling error accurately.	3. It is difficult to locate.

DISTINCTIONS BETWEEN PERSONAL INTERVIEW AND MAIL QUESTIONNAIRE

Personal Interview	*Mail Questionnaire*
1. It is directly conducted.	1. It is sent by post. It requires a brief covering letter of request.
2. Instructions are given to investigators.	2. Detailed instructions and self-addressed envelope called for.
3. Questions can be explained by the interviewer, if need be.	3. Questions should be crystal clear.
4. Questions, arranged as per interview's smooth progress.	4. Questions arranged as per respondent's convenience.
5. To be completed quickly.	5. Could be a little lengthy.
6. Better response.	6. Response rate is poor.

DISTINCTIONS BETWEEN AREA SAMPLING AND QUOTA SAMPLING

Area Sampling	*Quota Sampling*
1. In area sampling, out of a wide geographical area, a sample of some area is chosen.	1. In quota sampling, based upon experience of the researcher, a non-probability sample is chosen in a given class.
2. Area sampling is probability sampling.	2. It is non-probability sample.
3. It is objective.	3. It is subjective.
4. Information collected is non-biased.	4. It may be biased. To what extent, we cannot say.

DISTINCTION BETWEEN SURVEY METHOD AND OBSERVATION METHOD

Survey Method	*Observation Method*
1. Information is collected through respondents by means of a questionnaire.	1. Information is recorded as per observations of an observer.
2. Survey method is having wide scope (personal, phone, mail, panel, focus interview etc.).	2. The scope is not so wide (personal or mechanical, stock audit, dust-bin checks etc.).
3. Accuracy wise better.	3. Not so systematic.
4. Sophisticated.	4. Evolving.
5. Objective.	5. Subjective.

❖ Sampling in Marketing Research

Sampling: Sampling is based on the law of statistical regularity and the law of inertia of large numbers. Under the first law, if a small number of items (called a sample) are picked up from a large number of items (the larger group called the universe or population), the sample will tend to possess almost the same characteristics as the large or the whole group of items. Under the second law, large groups are more stable than small groups because we have the compensating effect of deviations in opposite directions. Of course, our sample should be large enough to represent truly the entire population or the universe.

A sample is a selection of units from the entire group called the population or universe of interest. In marketing, a sample is a particular segment or part of the market and it is the focus of the marketing decisions which may be applied to the entire market. The units included in the sample may be individual respondents, housewives, families, dealers, firms, city blocks and so on. The units included in the sample may be easily approached to obtain the desired information with a view to taking marketing decisions.

A sampling plan is a vital element of a research design. It must indicate:

(*i*) The sampling unit, *i.e.*, who is to be our respondent or who is to be surveyed?

(*ii*) The sample size, *i.e.*, how many respondents are to be contacted under the survey?

(*iii*) The sampling procedures, *i.e.*, how many respondents are to be contacted under the survey?

(*iv*) The sampling media, *i.e.*, how they are to be approached with a view to obtaining the desired information?

The person who is most likely to have the desired information will be our respondent or unit in the sample. This person may be the housewife, the husband, the family or the retailer. The sample size must be sufficiently large so that we may have a representative sample. The sampling procedure gives use different types of samples, *e.g.*, random sample or convenience (non-random) sample. In the sampling method or media, we have three alternatives to reach our respondents, *viz.*, mail or post-office, telephone and personal face-to-face interview.

Simple Random Sample: It is drawn by selecting every n^{th} item in the sampling frame. This is determined on the basis of the desired size of the sample. A number is drawn at random, usually a number between 1 and 10. For example, we have one lakh items in the universe and we want a sample size of 10,000 items. In our case, it is equal to 10. We have to select every 10th item from the universe, such as 4, 14, 24, 34 etc.

Stratified Random Sample: It is a sample in which the population is divided into groups. The groups are different from each other on relevant variables. For instance, the factor of willingness to purchase a certain brand is under our consideration. We may study this factor by grouping or stratifying the population on the basis of age, sex and income. We may select the sample from each of the strata in relation to its importance. Each stratum is represented in the sample on the basis of its importance. A stratified random sample may reduce the sampling error and is more representative sample.

Area Sample: We prepare a list of all the blocks in a big city and then select at random a certain number of blocks to be included in our sample. Every household or alternate household in the sample block may be approached to secure the desired information.

Quota Sample: It is the best example of the non-random or convenience sample. A research worker is given a quota of respondents with particular characteristics; for example, instead of instructing an interviewer to interview 500 housewives, he is called upon to interview 300 housewives living in chawls or tenements and 200 housewives living in flats or apartments. He is required to interview 50 per cent of the housewives who are 40 years old or less and 50 per cent of the housewives who are over 40 years of age. In a quota sample, we have sources of errors, *e.g.*, the interviewer's preferences, prejudices and his desire minimise his effort. Even then, convenience samples may be enough for many research purposes. For the exploratory and qualitative type of research, convenience samples are adequate.

Note: (*i*) A probability or random sampling enables us to measure the reliability of results with a mathematical exactness. But it is costly and time-consuming.

(*ii*) In quota sampling or convenience sampling, we have no mathematical device to measure the accuracy of the results. It relies considerably on the judgment of those in charge of designing and selecting the samples.

* * *

7 CONSUMER BEHAVIOUR

❖ Customer Analysis

A business exists for the sake of the customers. Though this is gospel truth, there is sometimes no appreciation for customer-orientation while developing the products, though there is enough lip sympathy for the marketing concept. In automobile markets, models for women buyers were unavailable despite MR suggesting that there is a strong market for this.

Customer analysis is thus a very useful topic for all the product managers. Customers here refer to the existing as well as potential customers These could be customers for competing products and currently non-customers or non-users for the product category.

Each customer has his unique requirements. It is, however, not possible to customize the marketing and product programme always for each customer. We, therefore, group these customers into homogenous groups called segments. It is as such a compromise between customisation and homogenization of all customers. Total homogenization is *mass marketing* as opposed to segmented marketing. Segmentation makes marketing more effective.

In this chapter, we have systematic analysis of the customers. The major areas of interest are:

- Who are our customers?
- What do they buy?
- How do they select?
- Why do they select (or customer value)?
- Where do they buy?
- When do they buy?

In all these six questions confront any product manager.

❖ Who buys the Product?

Previously, we have defined a product and analysed its competition. Product buying leads us to the definition of the product category. This category can be generically defined which widens the customers who could buy the product. A mutual fund buyer is also a share buyer, insurance buyer and real estate buyer. He is an investor.

❖ Buyers and users

A product category has customers. There may be several different buyers such as —

- *initiator* who identifies the need of the product.
- *influencer* who influences the buying decision.
- *decider* who makes the final decision by approving the budget.
- *user* who actually uses/consumes a product.

Toys may be bought by parents, but they are used by children. Such distinction is all the more important for industrial products.

Consumer behaviour, by definition, is a decision process and physical activity of making a purchase. The ultimate purchase activity is preceded by an interplay of several variables, and some of the variables also affect after the purchase has taken place. All these variables are a part of the decision process. The mental activity resulting in the final purchase may be complex and may happen over a period of time or it may be quick and simple.

❖ Decision Process

The consumer, as a first step, recognises his unfulfilled need or want. It is called problem recognition. It actually leads to information search and evaluation. The information search can be deliberate or prolonged or can happen without the consumer being even aware of it. He can rely on past experience or can seek information from external environment, *e.g.*, friends, shopkeepers and advertisements. The consumer evaluates the collected information to arrive at a purchase decision. Then having decided to buy, he makes the actual purchase, making a choice regarding the outlet to buy from. He consumes the product which either satisfies him, confirming correctness of his decision or dissatisfies him, leading to a search for alternative choices and evaluation afresh.

❖ Individual Determinants

Two individuals from one family may show entirely different purchase preferences. One may like Marathi theatre, novels of Khandekar and Phadke, humour of P.L. Deshpande and Neem soap. The other may like Debonair, English dramas and Mills and Boon romances and uses Dove soap. Why do they show variations, though the family environment is the same? The answer may be their individual motivation and involvement, attitude, self-concept, personality, learning, memory and information processing.

❖ Motivation and Involvement

Each of us is unique. We have a unique set of needs, aspirations and motivations. Motivation is an internal force which stimulates action in response to some need and sustain the same till the need is fulfilled. Physiological motivation satisfies biological needs of hunger and thirst. Psychological motivation satisfies social and prestige needs. Each one of us has both the physiological and psychological motivational force. We fulfil each of these motivations by different means. Someone seeks status by enrolling for an MBA programme and someone else by acquiring membership of the best-known club in the town. There may be someone who becomes a Diner Card holder to satisfy his need for status or may buy a Maruti Delux car to do so. We may satisfy our thirst by plain water or by mineral water or by a soft-drink like Thums Up or Pepsi.

Differing motivations are a functions of differing level of personal involvements. Involvement here means relevance or importance of a product perceived by the consumer in a given situation. For a professional musician, the choice of a music system is a situation of involvement, since it helps him immensely in his profession. He will be motivated, therefore, to buy the best state-of-the-art music system, irrespective of the price-tag. For another consumer, a music system is just a means of recreation after the office-hours and just about any system which is convenient and moderately priced might suffice his need.

High involvement leads to highly motivated state of mind. The behaviour process is distinctly different from that of low involvement and consequently low motivation. Maslow's and Herzberg's theories of motivation have been given as appendices.

❖ Attitudes

Attitudes are predispositions towards people, objects, events. They are learned. Our orientation towards people, objects, events is guided by attitudes. Attitudes are learnt from our socialisation process. A large section of Indian population have a negative attitude towards non-vegetarian dishes. Attitudes may change, *e.g.*, we loved savings previously, but now prefer to splurge our income for a better life-style. Canned foods were frowned upon a few years ago. But now we have come to accept them. Attitudes influence purchase decisions. Investment in stocks is preferred by risk-taking individuals.

❖ Beliefs

Rotler describes belief as a descriptive thought that a person holds about something. People carry beliefs about products and services. Foreign banks are believed to be customer friendly. Nationalised banks are believed to be lethargic in rendering service. These beliefs contribute to brand images. If the beliefs held are mistaken they should be corrected by suitable communication and action.

❖ Personality and Self-concept

The sum total of unique individual characteristics make up a personality. It is what we are. It is framework within which a consistent behaviour is shown.

Self-image or self-concept is our perception of ourselves in the social context. The products should match our self-concept. Product image should be close to self-image of target consumers, *e.g.*, royalty endorsing worsted suitings project an image of class and exclusivity. This matches well with the self-concept of the target consumers.

❖ Learning and Memory

In this age of information explosion, we tend to remember only relevant and important information. We tend to remember where we have a motivation to remember. Everyone is aware about the clutter of ads before a Hindi movie is shown on the T.V. Now the husband remembers the ad of Dunlop tyres, the wife that of Dabar Amla hair oil and the daughter that of Rasna concentrate. This is because they all have a motivation for different products. Learning and perception have been discussed is detail in appendices.

Attitudes, motives, personality act as filters. They let in relevant information, keeping out the other information. Our retention is selective.

❖ Information Processing

The same information may be evaluated in a different manner by different individuals. The response may also differ.

❖ External Environment

The external environment consists of five components and all other remaining influences are grouped under 'miscellaneous influences.'

(i) Culture: Culture is a complex term. It is the sum total of the process of socialisation — knowledge, beliefs, traditions, morals, art, customs, law and all other habits as a part of being one of society. Culture is restricted to a particular society and differs from society to society. Many of our action patterns and behaviour patterns are rooted in our cultural background, *e.g.*, a feeling of gratification when we sustain our parents in old age or when we save for a darling daughter's wedding. Within a particular culture, there may be groups of people with distinct customs, tradition and behaviour called subcultural groups. Thus, all Indians have a common cultural heritage, but still Maharastrians as a group are far different from Gujaratis as a group and Palghat Brahmins are not the same as Goud Saraswat Brahmins. Each subcultural group has a distinct life-style — food habits, dress habits, rites and traditional. These have definite inclinations for marketers and advertisers, *e.g.*, Gharghanti or home grinding mill is promoted amongst Gujaratis in Chitralekha since they are fond of fresh chapatis from home-made flour. In the South, on the contrary, stone-grinders for rice items like idlis and dosas are being promoted. The promotion of pain balm has to take into account the fact that Northern Indians like a burning sensation after its application, whereas in the South it is not so. The branded spices should be formulated to suit the regional tastes.

(ii) Social Class: 'Class' means a distinct position in society and consists of people of more or less equal position. It is more related to income and people of the same class show a distinct consumption pattern. Social classes are related to occupation also. From society-to-society, social classes differ. The standing of a social class does not remain the same over a period of time. The choice of residence, leisure time enjoyed, recreational habits, holidays availed of are all guided by the social class to which we belong.

(iii) Social Groups: Primary social groups such as family and our work groups do affect our decisions of consumption. Since we interact with them on a continuous basis. The interaction with primary groups is face-to-face.

Impersonal, formal groups are the secondary groups which affect our consumption pattern.

Politicians don khaddar clothes as a result of social group influence. People from South Canara prefer Safaris.

(iv) Family: The greatest influence on an individual is the family which helps him to inculcate several values right from childhood. These tend to stay later. Family decisions are group decisions and individual members contribute to it, though to differing extents. The break-up of joint family system to make way for a large number of single nucleus families also affect our consumption pattern, *e.g.*, demand for creche. The Family Life-Cycle (FLC) has been discussed in an appendix.

(v) Personal Influences: All other factors of the external environment do affect consumers, but, at the same time, his own personality affects him greatly, *e.g.*, his being an innovator makes him try new products. Besides, product rating depends upon the personality of the consumer, *e.g.*, for some price may be a critical factor and for other status symbol value may be most important.

❖ Miscellaneous Influences

Olympics or Asiads or World Cup make us go in for the TV sets. Sports events also lead to a greater consumption of sports goods.

Situational effects like a premium offer also affect our purchase decisions. Lipton's offering a mug autographed by the tabla maestro Zakir Hussain on each purchase of the Taj Mahal brand of tea when it completed 25 years must have tempted many to brand switch.

Each of the variables affect other variables and in turn is affected by other variables. The external environmental influences do not affect decision-making directly but they filter through the individual determinants and indirectly affect decision-making.

❖ Types of Purchase Decision Behaviour

Consumer behaviour changes depending upon the nature or type of buying — a razor blade may be purchased without much fuss but a colour TV set purchase takes time and deliberation. The nature or type of purchases give rise to three types of buyer behaviour:

(*a*) RR (Routinised Response) behaviour.

(*b*) LPS (Limited Problem Solving) behaviour.

(*c*) EPS (Extended Problem Solving) behaviour.

RR occurs where there is low product involvement, the consumer knows the brands available and criteria of choice and the stakes are not so high in terms of price; *e.g.*, bread, soft-drinks, pastes, soaps etc. Here the customer expects a consistent quality in the products. New customers are drawn by sales promotion and product improvements.

PLPS occurs when the consumer knows the brands available, but still needs additional information to make a correct choice, especially when a new or unfamiliar brand confronts him. Thus, Ariel or Surf Ultra enzyme detergents must convince the housewife that they are superior to conventional detergents due to the presence of enzymes and so the housewife feels the necessity of searching additional information. The marketer here has introduced a new brand in a well-known product category. The promotion here should explain complete features of the new brand and build up consumers' confidence to facilitate the purchase decision.

EPS occurs when a new product category comes on the scene. Here extensive information is needed on both the product category and the brand being made available, *e.g.*, micro-wave ovens introduced by Kelvinator first explain the concept of micro-wave cooking as distinguished from conventional cooking and then sell the brand. Colour TVs as a product category, a particular brand of TV (say Onida or Videocon) and a particular model (say PIP: Picture-in-Picture or Surrounded Sound System) do need information at three levels. Promotion should satisfy the needs of information at these three levels and especially, how the advertised brand has a unique set of positive attributes. This concept is most applicable to new products, maybe new to consumers. For a tribal, even purchase of a toothpaste may involve EPS, whereas for us it is just RR.

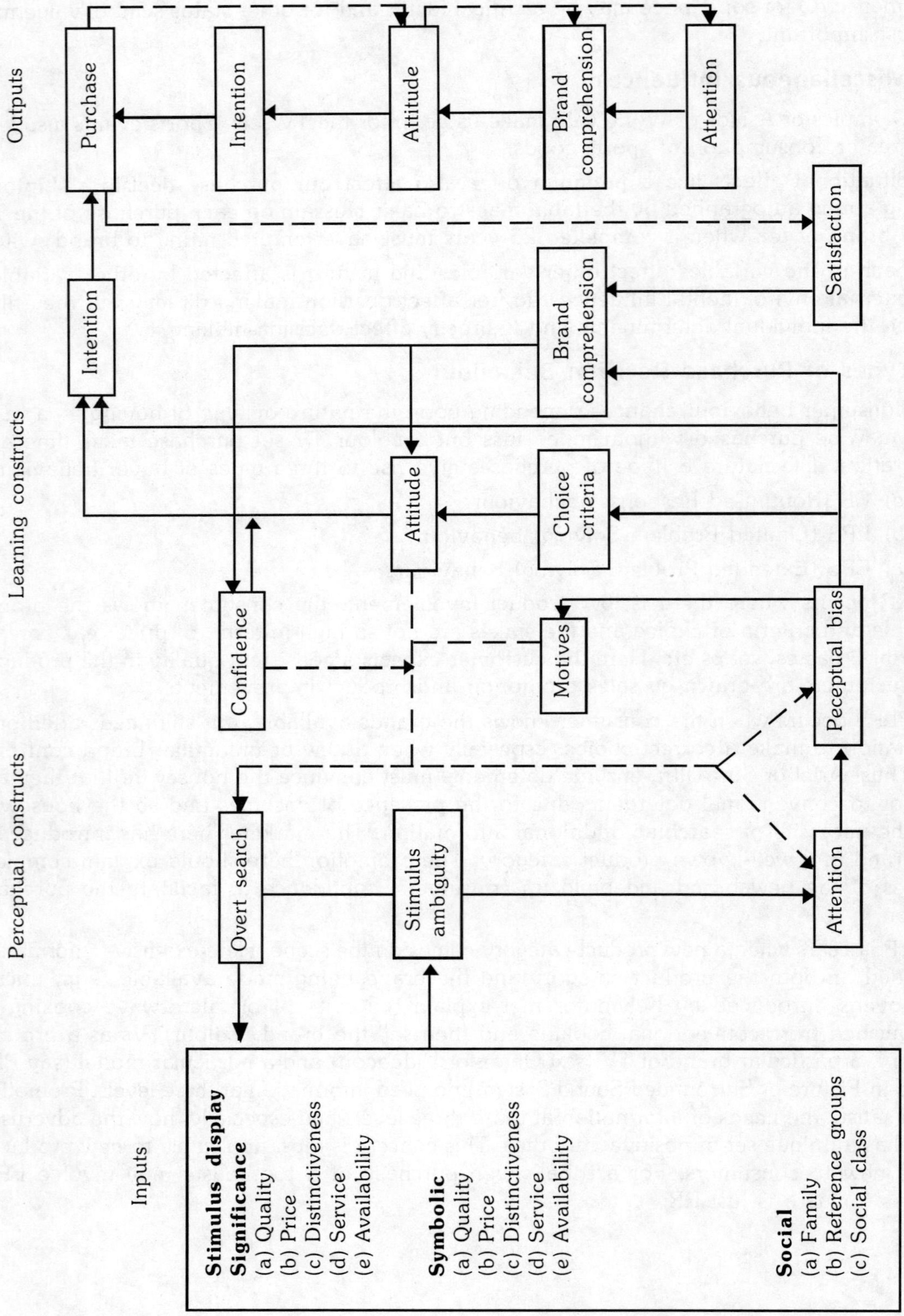

Fig. 7.1 Howard-Sheth Model: Simplified Adaptation

❖ Model of Buyer Behaviour

Research workers have developed various models to explain the influences on buyer's behaviour of purchase. Howard-Sheth model which has been developed by an Indian Jagdish Sheth in collaboration with Howard explains the behaviour of an individual consumer. There are separate models for group consumer behaviour and organisational buying behaviour.

❖ Howard-Sheth Model

The decision process is influenced by four major sets of variables, *e.g.*, (1) Inputs, (2) Perceptual and Learning Constructs, (3) Outputs and (4) External Variables.

(1) Inputs: These are stimuli to purchase decision. Significative stimuli are tangible product characteristics provided by the marketer. Symbolic stimuli are intangible or perceptual characteristics of the product, *e.g.*, the overall quality. The actual price may be significative stimulus and the price being on high or low side for the bargain is symbolic stimulus. Social groups like the family, reference groups and social class are the social stimuli.

(2) Perceptual and Learning Constructs: These are psychological variables, *e.g.*, motivation, attitudes and perceptions affecting the buyer. The interpretation of the stimuli are influenced by stimulus ambiguity and perceptual bias. Ambiguity of stimulus means the consumer is not sure of the meaning of the stimulus and his response thereto. Perceptual bias makes him distort the information received to fit his previous experience and his established needs.

His interpretation of the stimuli results in brand comprehension — his understanding of the brands and their ratings. High rating build up his confidence, resulting in the purchase decision.

(3) Outputs: The purchase decision itself is an output. Product trial may give him satisfaction. It reinforces his positive attitude. Then there is reinforcement of purchase intent and brand. He is favourably inclined to receiving stimuli which further improves his brand comprehension. On getting dissatisfied with the product, he may develop negative attitude, insensitivity to stimuli, poor brand comprehension and negative intention to purchase.

(4) External Variables: These are not part of the decision process in the model, but are improvement to the extent they influence a buyer. These differ from buyer-to-buyer and include, status, relevance of the product, social class, personality traits etc.

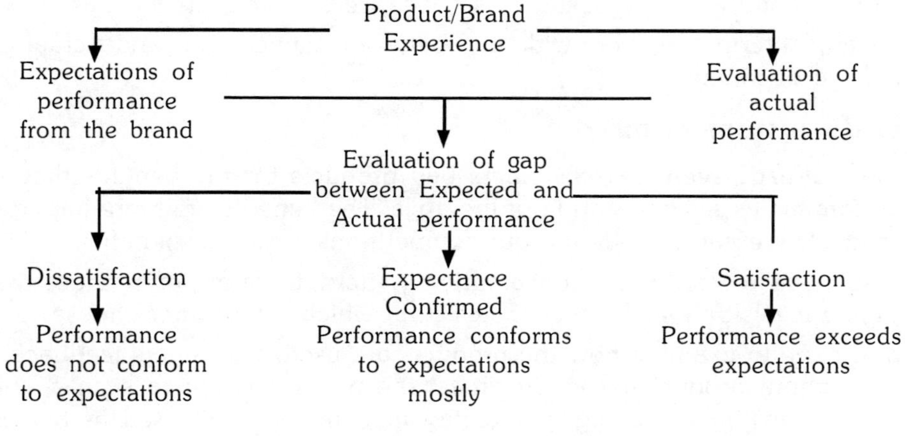

Fig. 7.2

❖ Post-Purchase Behaviour

The desire to study the behaviour of consumers after the purchase has been made is a 'true' marketing orientation, an identification with the consumers and seeing things from their perspective. Purchases are purposive and motivated. Post-purchase behaviour indicates to what extent these purposes have been met and motives achieved. Post-purchase activity gives an indication as to whether the customers are going to again patronise a firm in future and also whether they will be in a mood to recommend a product to potential customers.

❖ Formation of Satisfaction/Dissatisfaction

A purchase may lead either to satisfaction or dissatisfaction. Satisfaction is a result of expected outcome — when the product meets our expectations. Dissatisfaction means it does not perform as per our expectations. Dissatisfied customers may discontinue their association with the company, may spread negative word of mouth, may send a formal complaint or in extreme cases, may sue the company. The communication strategy depends upon the expectation-performance disparity.

Disparity	*Communication Strategy*
Minimised by adjusting perceived expectations with performance	Overstate product claims
Magnified	Reasonably undertake product claims
Negative feeling	Consistent claims with performance
Minor disparities minimised Major disparities magnified	State product claims above the actual performance marginally but within the overall acceptance range of the consumer.

The other tips for advertisers to avoid dissatisfaction:

1. State the facts. Execute the factual promotion creatively.
2. Help the consumer on product use by giving adequate instructions or information.
3. Promotion should be solution-based rather than product-based. Emphasis products' performance.
4. Assure the customers even when the purchase is over. State in your ads the fact — many have used the product and are satisfied. Write thank you letters. Make the technical staff visit the customer's residence to assess his feelings.

The technical term for a very wide gap between Expectations and Actual performance is post-purchase dissonance.

❖ What do customers buy?

We have already seen that customers buy products for the benefits they derive from them. Thus companies sell holes and not the drills. The benefits are more important than the physical product. We can thus define our competitions based on benefits.

We also have to study the consumption pattern in terms of product assortment of models, quality levels and such other things from which a customer chooses.

We also have to examine how the products are used. Customers feedback provides us valuable data about product usage. At times, the product is put to such a use which the companies have not imagined e.g. a washing machine may be used as a mixer-blender, churner by dairy owners for milk products. The context of a product usage also helps us to understand our customers better *e.g.*, what are those situations that provoke customers to send cards.

❖ How do customers choose?

Consumer behaviour is an exciting area of study. There is enough research work on consumer buying decisions.

❖ Multi-Attribute Model

This conceptualizes customer decision-making in a concise manner. It has several dimensions. Here products or alternative products in a category are considered to be bundles of attributes. Attributes could be either physical characteristics or benefits sought. Each consumer is assumed to have a perception of the quantum of attribute an alternative product possesses. Each consumer is assumed to rank the attributes in terms of value/weight it has while choosing. The ranked attributes are chosen according to some rule. Thus, we are concerned with four aspects.

- attributes
- amount of attributes possessed by a product
- weightage
- preferred choice

Attributes are chosen through focus group research or by survey-based methods. Perceptions about the amount of each attribute possessed by each product/brand is done by perceptual mapping. If we take two attributes for a marketing management text-book such as complexity of content and simplicity of presentation, we get the following perceptual map of the books in the market.

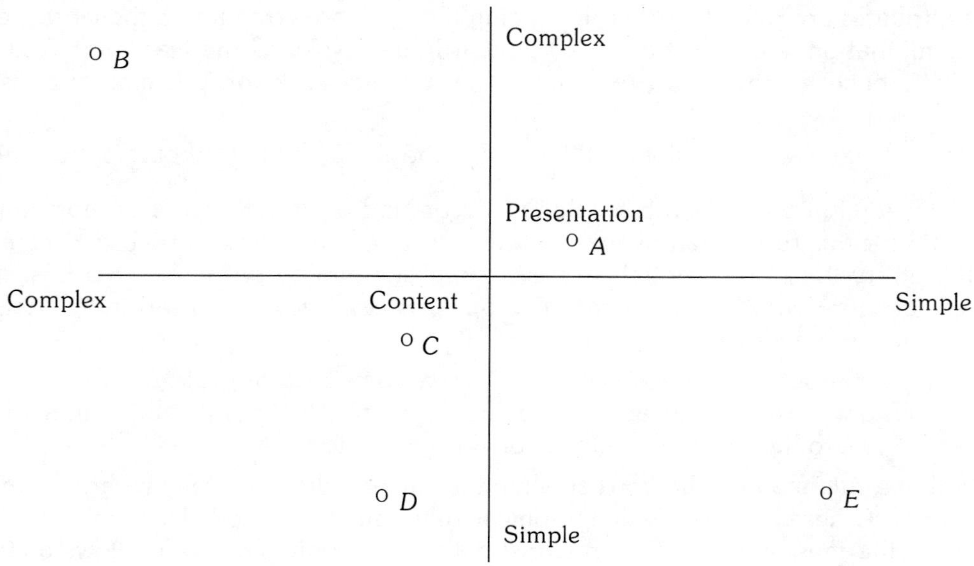

Book *A* is easily understandable format and has moderately complex content. Book B is complex in terms of presentation as well as content. Book *C* is moderate in understanding and content. Book *D* is complex content-wise but simple presentation-wise. Book *E* is for beginners, too simplistic content-wise and presentation-wise.

We can take several attributes and do multi-dimensional scaling in perceptual mapping.

All the attributes can be rated and can be ranked in terms of importance. Conjoint Analysis is another important MR technique that allows us to draw inferences about the significance of different product attributes from customer rank orderings of alternative packets of attributes.

Let us assume a cell phone's weight, battery life and brand name are being considered in terms of importance. We shall have two levels or values. The eight combinations can be rank ordered. (most preferred to least preferred)

Cell Phone: Three attributes.
Weight (100 gms or 120 gms)
Battery Life (4 hours or 6 hours)
Brand Name (Nokia, Sony Ericson)
Task: Rank order the following combinations of characteristics from 1 to 8.

Combination	**Rank**
100 gms, 4 hours, Nokia	4
120 gms, 6 hours, Sony Ericson	5
120 gms, 4 hours, Nokia	8
100 gms, 6 hours, Sony Ericson	3
100 gms, 4 hours, Sony Ericson	2
120 gms, 6 hours, Nokia	7
120 gms, 4 hours, Sony Ericson	6
100 gms, 6 hours, Sony Ericson	1

The attributes are rated to 1-8 scale 1 being the most preferred and 8 the least preferred. The last combination is the best and 120 gms, 4 hours, Nokia is the least preferred. There are trade-offs between these two extremes. The average rank for 100 gms options is 2.5 $\left(\frac{1+2+3+4}{4}\right)$. The average rank for 120 gms options is 6.5, for the 6-hours options, 4.0 and for the 4-hour option 5.0. It is 3.5 for Sony Ericson and 5.5 for Nokia. The most important characteristic for this respondent is weight (difference = 4.0) followed by brand name (2.0) and lastly battery life (1.0). Though this is a simplistic model, the working is basically the same even for more complex problems. The analysis can be done for an individual, but is generally done for a segment.

Information about attributes is combined by a compensatory rule where a product of attribute importance weight and attribute value is taken. All attributes are summed up for each person and product. It can be done for a segment too.

The above rule may not be correct when the ranking does not tally with the ranking of market shares. Other rules like lexicographical rule can be applied. Here all products are compared on the most important characteristic alone. A conjunctive rule allows a customer to reject a product which does not meet minimum cut-offs on different dimensions.

Compensatory rule implies that when all attributes are considered the weakness in one gets compensated by the strength in another. Conjuctive rule is not compensatory at all.

❖ Customers as Problem-solvers

Consumer behaviour changes depending upon the nature or type of buying – a razor blade may be purchased without much fuss but a colour TV set purchase takes time and deliberation. The nature or type of purchases gives rise to three types of buyer behaviour:

(*a*) RR (Routinised Response) behaviour.

(*b*) LPS (Limited Problem Solving) behaviour.

(*c*) EPS (Extended Problem Solving) behaviour.

RR occurs where there is low product involvement, the consumer knows the brands available and criteria of choice and he stakes are not so high in terms of price; *e.g.*, bread, soft-drinks, pastes, soaps, etc. Here the customer expects a consistent quality in the products. New customers are drawn by Sales Promotion and product improvements.

LPS occurs when the consumer knows the brands available, but still needs additional information to make a correct choice, especially when a new or unfamiliar brand confronts him. Thus, Ariel or Surf Ultra enzyme detergents must convince the housewife that they are superior to conventional detergents due to presence of enzymes and so the housewife feels the necessity of searching additional information. The marketer here has introduced a new brand in a well-known product category. The promotion here should explain complete features of the new brand and build up consumer's confidence to facilitate the purchase decision.

EPS occurs when a new product category comes on the scene. Here extensive information is needed on both the product category and the brand being made available, *e.g.*, micro-wave ovens introduced by Kelvinator first explain the concept of micro-wave cooking as distinguished from conventional cooking and then sell the brand. Colour TV's as a product category, a particular brand of colour TV (say Onida or Videocon) and a particular model (say PIP: Picture-In-Picture or Surround Sound System) do need information at three levels. Promotion should satisfy the needs of information at these three levels, and especially how the advertised brand has a unique set of positive products. This concept is most applicable to new products, may be new to consumers. For a tribal, even purchase of a toothpaste may involve EPS, whereas for us it is just RR.

❖ Why they prefer a product? Customer Value

Customer value is at the root of product preference. To a customer, the value constitutes the benefits derived over the costs incurred. A cheap product may have great value if it solves an important problem, and a very expensive product may have little value. The value customers place on products facilitates product pricing.

Value has three basic components: the usage, the effectiveness and the relative effectiveness. Value can be absolute or relative. There are no competing brands when it is absolute value, and relative value assumes comparison with other brands.

The relative effectiveness of brand is related to competitive scene. It is also necessary to determine the usage situations.

❖ Sources of Value

The *functional* characteristics or performance features of the product determines its utility or value to a customer. The service before the sale, at the time of sale and after-sales is another source of value. The image of the product and its matching with the self-image of the customer is the third source of value. Brand equity is the value of a product beyond all the three sources listed above. It is denoted by the premium a customer would pay.

❖ Manifestation of Customer Value

Some obvious manifestations of value are:

Price: It is the company's assessment of product value.

Price elasticity: A product that withstands price increase has greater value.

Satisfaction: A satisfaction survey can be taken. A satisfying product has value.

Complaints and compliments: The number indicates product's value.

Buzz: Word-of-mouth indicates a product's worth.

Profit contribution: Higher margins indicate greater value.

Rupee sales: It indicates an aggregate value.

Competitive activity: Entry of competitors and innovation on their part indicate lucrative marketing opportunities.

Repeat purchase rate: Loyalty indicates value.

❖ Value of a Product Category

We can assess the value of the product category by different methods. One way is to assess the various applications of a product category. We have to estimate the importance of these uses and determine competition usewise. We have to determine the relative effectiveness of the product category for each usage situation. Mathematically,

Value of a Product Category (VPC) = Σ (Importance) $\times$ (Relative Effectiveness)

Let us understand the value of the PCs.

They can be put to a number of uses — gaming, office, accountancy, data analysis and multi-media. The importance of each of these usages could be low, moderate or high. Each usage has competitive products e.g. gaming has competition from stand-alone gaming consoles, x-boxes and play-stations, accountancy has competition from accountants, office has competition from secretaries, word-processors, etc. We can spell out relative effectiveness for each usage as marginal, fair, good and very good. The category value could be low, moderate and high. It is the product of imp & rel. Here we have used adjectives rather than numbers, and the analysis is to provide broad indicative guidelines.

❖ Where do customers buy?

Channels of distribution are very important. These are not stagnant. These are dynamic, and evolve with the product and the market. We used to buy electronics from wholesale agencies and departmental stores like the Akbarallys. These days we have supermarkets and specialized electronic supermarkets like Croma. We used to buy our groceries from the neighbourhood kirana stores. These days we visit hyper-markets like Spencers and Big Bazaar. We have to tack trends in the retail market. There are migrations of customers from one channel to the other. There are new technologies for shopping. We have e-shops and home shopping channels.

❖ When customers buy?

The timing of purchase — year, month, day and the time of the day — is important. Fast food can divide the day into day parts. There are breakfast, lunch and dinner times. There are special occasions to buy — festive season, sales, discount sales, seasonal sales. The nature of the product leads to some sales variations. Fridges are sold more in summer and so do the ACs. Capital equipment is bought at the end of the financial year to utilize the budgeted amount. Cars are bought to avail of the depreciation benefit. Seasonal sales must be evened out by taking special efforts.

❖ Generation

Generation Y is passe. These are the days of i Generation of young people between 16-28 years of age. They are comfortable with technology driven products such as i Pods, cellphones and gaming consoles. Half the population in India is below 25. It is a post-liberalisation generation. It is friendly with TV and Internet. They believe in sharing books, movies, music and games on Internet. They want to stand apart. If they have money, they will spend. They are not averse to credit. Their purchasing power is increasing. They are customers for home loans and car loans. They use plastic extensively. They use new and innovative products. They are 'me and mine' generation. They spend on clothing especially T-hirts, jeans and accessories. There is a desire to show-off to peers and so the look of the product is important. They switch brands to keep pace with the times. They write their grievances on blogs — on-line communication. Youthshut.com aggregates consumer opinions and rates products. Compareindia.com allows users to select features of 37 products and lists the brands as per their prices. This provides valuable feedback to marketers. It democratises the media. i Generation expresses its opinion freely on internet with a reach to millions of people across the globe. This vests them with the ability to 'control' the media.

APPENDIX I

PERCEPTION

It is a very important psychological variable affecting the buyer behaviour. It is 'our way of looking at' objects, individuals, events and world in general. Our sense organs keep on receiving messages such as sight, smell, sound, taste and sensation. All these are stimuli. We recognise these stimuli, select them and organise them. These are ultimately interpreted in our own way, depending upon our expectations, needs and values. This process is known as perception. Since each individual is unique in his needs, expectations and motivations, each person's perception is also unique.

We observe that the responses to two individuals to the same set of stimuli may be different, because their perception maybe different. Each product is a bundle of stimuli of shape, size, colour, fragrance, feel and taste. The promotion of the product — its packaging, advertising — is like providing stimulus to the consumer. If we understand the different perceptions with the above stimuli, we can emphasise those stimuli which provoke the most favourable response in most people. In respect of cosmetics, quality is perceived in terms of company image, good packaging and price.

Countless stimuli bombard us daily. It is not possible to subject all of them to analysis. We have a screening system built into us that selects and rejects stimuli. The relevant stimuli are selected and recognised to the exclusion of all others. Advertisers like to have the stimuli provided by them to be recognised, interpreted and retained in memory. The following aspects of perception, therefore, need closer examination.

Selective Exposure

The consumer durables like colour TV, fridge or music system, we might intend to purchase are widely advertised. The moment we intend to purchase these, we become conscious of these ads, which hitherto we might have ignored. This is called selective exposure where people are more likely to notice stimuli which relate to their immediate needs. The advertisers have, therefore, to tap the segment of customers correctly, since other segments are not likely to notice the stimuli. Once the customer segment is properly identified, the advertiser has to ensure that the stimuli are interesting enough to attract and hold attention.

Selective Distortion

Suppose a customer decides to buy brand *A* of a music system. Since now the decision has already been made, the customer seeks only that information which confirms the correctness of his decision to buy brand *A*.

On coming across some positive remarks regarding brand *B*, the customer tends to pick up some holes here and there to get a feeling that he is right in his selection of brand *A*. When in this fashion, we slot the information to our own ideas or meaning, selective distortion occurs. The advertiser might find his message is twisted in different ways by different customers.

Selective Retention

We tend to remember only the positive features of brand *A*, confirming the correctness of our decision and tend to forget the rest of the stimuli. The retained information confirms our values and decision.

Illustration of Cadbury: Change in Consumer Perception

Market stagnation was a major problem for Cadbury. In order to tackle this, it is attempting to change the consumer perception of chocolates. They wish to position chocolates as universal products any one can enjoy. Amul tried to reposition chocolates by promoting them as gifts to someone you love. The focus remains on gift and does not cross across the age barrier. Cadbury is promoting chocolates by equating its consumption with natural spontaneous behaviour on the part of adults. The commercial lasting 60 seconds has the following clips:

(*i*) Overweight mother in her 30s playing hopscotch with her daughter with gusto.

(*ii*) A middle-aged executive kicking out at a football on his way home from work.

(*iii*) An old grandfather slowing bubbles with his little grandchildren.

Adults across different age groups are shown in their uninhibited moments.

The cadbury consumption clips are integrated:

(*i*) A man walking on a crowded pavement is about to cut a piece of chocolate when someone bumps against him, making him drop it. He picks it up, looks around of someone is watching him and pops it into his mouth.

(*ii*) Pregnant wife pointing to chocolate bars and then to her belly.

(*iii*) A sailor relishing a cadbury bar while perched on his suitcase.

The message is "the real of taste of life". Bring out the real self in you by natural spontaneous behaviour.

APPENDIX II

LEARNING

A baby sucking her mummy's breast is instinctive behaviour, but a grown-up child's demand for a chocolate is the result of learned behaviour. Much of the adult behaviour is learned.

The fact that most of the behaviour is learned teaches advertisers a lesson that consumers can be made to learn the desired behaviour, bringing into play a set of motives, stimuli, cues, responses and their reinforcement. Learning is a process of applying results of past experiences to evaluate a new situation or modify future behaviour.

A housewife has the need to grind so many things in the kitchen. When the need grows stronger, it becomes a motive. The motive is directed towards a stimulus object — a grinder-mixer of say Sumeet. The stimuli are the various advertisements she reads, sees and hears. Cues are minor stimuli determining her response in terms of time, place and method. Positive feedback about the mixie from her friend, watching it on display in a shop-window, a scheme reducing price during festive season, are the cues which influence her response to the motive of buying a mixie. Once she buys it and satisfactorily uses it, she would continue to use it as often as possible, and may be in future, buy another mixie or a better product like a food processor. Her response thus has been reinforced. Her decision to go in for Sumeet food processor is a result of her inference that this company making good mixers must be making good food processors also. It is thus a generalisation of response.

A marketer can build up this bond by making the consumer learn that the brand is worth. He, therefore, associates his brand with strong motives and uses the apt stimuli and cues, and provides positive reinforcements.

APPENDIX III

LIFE STYLE MARKETING

Life-style analysis makes our understanding of demographic groups sharper. In India, the marketers these days are tapping 'the young and upwardly mobile' group that cuts across many barriers. Many advertisement appeals are meant for this group. The behavioural differences do not come alive in demographic descriptions, but do show various aspects of life. It implies a central life interest such as family, leisure, religion, politics, sexual exploits etc. and this interest fashions our interaction with the environment. Variations in lifestyle are as a result of social change. Working women and working couples do have very distinct lifestyles.

In India, one of the agencies is trying to build a psychographic profiles of Indian children. Pathfinders have identified 8 types of Indian housewives.

VALS Systems of Classification

Values and Life Style (VALS) classification was developed by Arnold Mitchell. The adults (18 plus) are classified into distinctive life style groups. Each group has psychological needs (values) and behavioural response patterns (life styles). Much of VALS, is based on Maslow's *Need Hierarchy*. VALS blends together demographics, attitudes, activities, consumption pattern, brand preferences and media graphics.

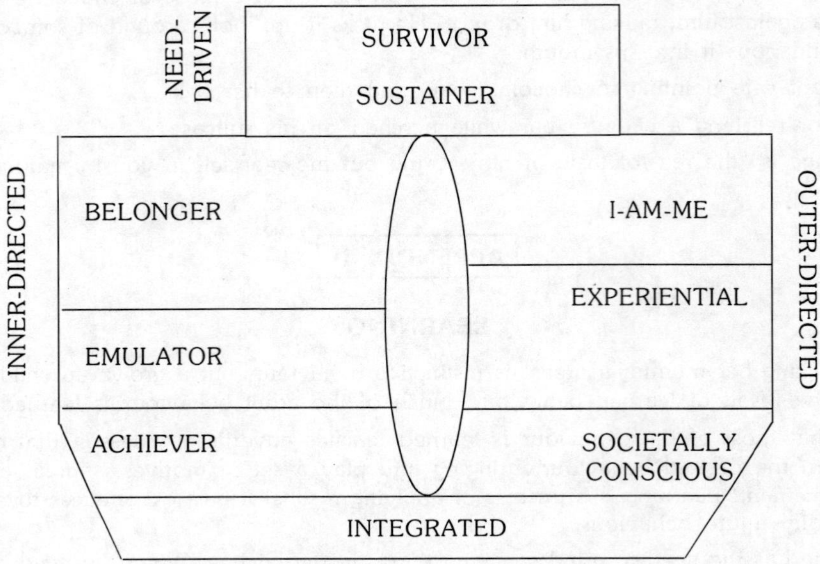

Fig. 7.3

Four Major Groups in VALS

(*a*) Need-driven poor and uneducated.

(*b*) Outer-directed upper and middle-class.

(*c*) Inner-directed due to inner-motivations.

(*d*) Integrated — a combination of both outer- and inner-directed values.

The above model of Thomas puts these groups into nine specific VALS segments.

Survivors are price-conscious and not very knowledgeable shoppers. Sustainers are swayed by brands and guarantees and are impulse buyers. Emulators buy to impress others, and to announce their status. Achievers buy high teach items and original top of the line products. Experiential buy for experimenting. Societally conscious want value for money.

Survivors are depressed; sustainers are strugglers. Belongers are conventional, emulators, are status-conscious. Achievers are leaders and I-am-me are young, impulsive people. Experiential pursue a rich inner life and are interested in life's offerings. Societally conscious people are socially responsible and integrated mature psychologically. Thus an individual passes through several developmental stages. In India, we are now targeting at selected life style groups for a suitable niche for our product.

Applications of life style Marketing

It is useful for:

(*a*) positioning of new products.

(*b*) re-positioning of old/existing products.

(*c*) developing new product inputs.

(*d*) creating promotional strategies.

Life style Advertising

A product which would add to the perception of one's life is a potential candidate for life style advertising. Life style advertising tend to be equal for different products and to break this parity requires time and effort of agencies. Genuine life style advertising makes an aspect of a life style intrinsic to the brand position and personality. In India, textile firms resort to life style advertising that is not distinctive. Good life style advertising should not become advertising for a good life. We should, therefore, focus on perceived product differentiation. Then only, life style imagery works. In most cases, life style advertising seems to be a safe, easy way out by creative people, without bothering to think of fresh ideas. Many have started using life style advertising for me-too products. Sometimes, life style portrayed are absolutely unrelated to the target audience. They tend to become visual cliches.

APPENDIX IV

FAMILY LIFE CYCLE

Concept of Family Life Cycle

People go through several phases in their lives. Family Life Cycle (FLC) refers to the series of life stages through which individuals proceed over a period of time.

In other words, FLC describes the process of family formation and dissolution.

To illustrate, a young man or a woman marry to form a family, in which children are born and live with the family till they grow up and later move out. At last, the couple grows old and fends for itself. Each life cycle stage differs from the previous stages in terms of (*a*) structure, (*b*) financial position, (*c*) consumption pattern and (*d*) product need and preferences.

Traditional or Conventional FLC

The FLC is a progression of several stages:

1. *Young and single bachelor stage.* The career has just started. However, in the absence of burdens, they are free to spend as they wish. They tend to buy personal consumption items of food and clothing, are fun-loving and buy entertainment, have time to be on vacations and tours, move about on bikes and other two-wheelers, read novels and thrillers. They buy some basic utensils and furniture.
2. *Newly married couples* have household burdens and go through an expenditure phase in life. They generally buy consumer durables like furniture, wall paints, refrigerators, TVs etc.
3. *Young married couples with child* direct their income to bringing up the child. They buy toys, medicines, tonics, baby foods, formula milk etc.
4. *Older married couples with children* are fairly stable income wise. They like food products, music, educational services and a wide variety of other products.
5. *Older married couples with dependent children* have high income, but do rational purchases. There is replacement buying.
6. *Older, married couples with no children* become interested in self-education, saving schemes, hobbies, luxury appliances, magazines, health products.
7. *Old, single, retired people* lead an economic life style. They are interested in health care and other services. They've budget constraints.

Revised FLC Concept for the 90s

Conventionally, family was considered a single unit throughout the life time of an individual. However, this assumption is not true these days. There are families due to second marriages, with a legacy of children from previous marriages. There are deserted wives. There are divorcees. Several families are single parent family, where the parent could be either a father or a mother. Again, the ubiquitous working woman makes the traditional FLC model invalid.

Let us consider the following dimensions of Indian families in 90s.

Young, Married, with Child and Dual Income

Here both the husband and the wife work and get two income cheques. The pace of life is faster and there is less time for children and also for one another. The consumption pattern, therefore, shows preference for convenience goods like washing machines, grinder-mixers, rice cookers, grinding mill (gharghanti) etc. Women manage on two fronts — domestic chores and work. Husbands share the responsibilities of running the house to some extent. Instant foods, creches etc. appeal to such families. To compensate for the time babies miss with parents, there is a tendency to buy costly garments for kids, games for kids, prams etc.

Single Parent Families

The single parent family needs security and buys all the products that offer physical and psychological and financial securities — *e.g.*, burglar alarms, teddy bears, insurance, saving certificates etc. When the child grows, he may be put in boarding school/public school.

Divorced

They buy money saving products, lease or rental housing, child care, time saving appliances, instant foods. They are short of cash.

Older People, Married or Single

They are also cash poor and health conscious. They need security. They also need recreation.

Middle-aged

They buy children's lessons (dance, music), dental care, furniture, autos, houses, dining out.

If there are no children, they are interested in luxuries, travels, gift products etc. Their cash position is good.

SEGMENTATION STRATEGY ON THE BASISS OF FLC

Product	*Segment*
(*i*) Cosmetics	Young single and young married women who are cash rich and are a potential segment for beauty products like face creams, moisturisers, compacts, foundation make up etc.
	Middle-aged families need facials, sauna baths and such related products.
(*ii*) Vacations	Newly married couples are sold vacations at the time of marriage in the form of honeymoon packages.
	Middle-aged couples with no responsibility of children are the most attractive segment to sell vacations in the form of packaged tours. They are cash rich and free from encumbrances.
(*iii*) Housing	Young, married with children need starter housing. Middle-aged couples need housing — 2 bedroom flats etc.
(*iv*) Education	Bachelors need liberal and professional education. They are career minded. They can be sold courses like private secretary, computers etc.
	Middle-aged with children buy education for their children home tuitions, coaching classes, public schools etc.
	They buy education for self also to improve their career — *e.g.*, distance education programmes of IGNOU.

APPENDIX-V

MASLOW'S THEORY OF NEED HIERARCHY

Very seldom an attempt has been made to understand Maslow's theory of need hierarchy beyond a narrow perspective. It is important to look at from a situational perspective and develop a frame of reference within which it would be possible to analyse specific situations. Maslow first presented this basic ideas on motivation when he addressed a psychoanalytic society and stated that he wanted to "integrate into a single theoretical structure the partial truths I saw in Freud, Ald - Jung, Levey, Fromin, Honey and Golstein", Maslow's thinking was also affected by the works of Murray, Gorden, Allport, Rogers and others.

Maslow's Need Hierarchy

Human motives can be put into five distinct categories in the form of a pyramid as shown in Fig.7.4 Perhaps, the five categories over simplify the human motives. This need hierarchy theory was the result of Abraham Maslow's work; and hence the name Maslow's Need Hierarchy. In fact, human behaviour is directed by several other needs and need combinations at a given point of time. It is, however, difficult to pinpoint them separately and so a need hierarchy as shown in Fig. 7.4 simplifies the problem for our understanding.

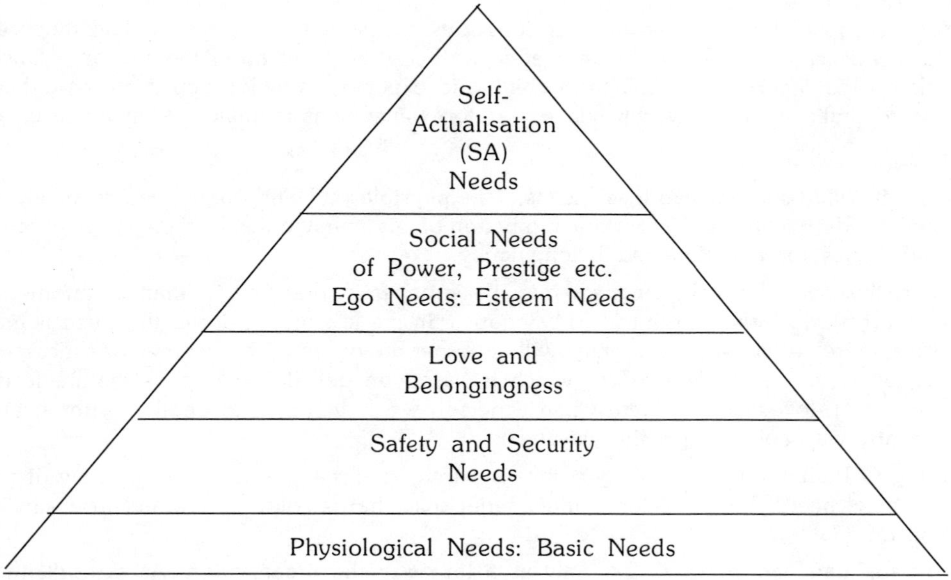

Fig. 7.4 Maslow's Need Hierarchy

Maslow advanced three important propositions about human behaviour:

(*a*) Men are wanting beings. Their needs are unlimited and as soon as one need is satisfied, another appears in its place and this continues from birth-to-death.

(*b*) A satisfied need is not a motivator of behaviour; only the needs which are not satisfied are capable of motivating individuals.

(*c*) Needs of men develop in a sequential order and are arranged in a hierarchical order. Fig. 7.1 illustrates the concept.

Physiological Needs

At the lowest level of his need hierarchy are his physiological needs such as hunger, thirst, etc. When the physiological needs are thwarted, they assume great importance. Consider a man who is very hungry. He may not like to think of status or prestige but would like to find ways and means by which he can satiate his hunger. Maslow, in fact, referred to the potency of needs. Thus, when physiological needs are very potent, other needs like psychological needs are pushed into the background.

Further, it is important to understand these sets of needs are independent of each other. For example, even while an individual is not thirsty, he needs food to satiate his hunger. These sets of needs are also repetitive in nature and reemerge after a short time. To base motivation only on these lower sets of needs will have little meaning in a developed economy because of the fact that the satisfaction of such needs is guaranteed.

Security Needs

When the physiological needs are satisfied, the next level of needs emerge to motivate him. These are the security needs. An individual would like to work for the organisation to ensure continuity of employment. Security needs assume great significance in an organisation where the individual finds himself in a dependent relationship and where he fears arbitrary deprivation. Arbitrary action of management which shows favouritism and discrimination can be strong motivators of the security needs in the work-life relationships.

Security needs can be operative both at conscious and subconscious levels. Too much emphasis on conscious needs can have a disciplinary effect rather than motivating the person. "Unconscious security needs on the other hand result from childhood experiences which depict life as either far too uncontrollable to make initiative worthwhile or far too benevolent to make initiative necessary."

Social Needs

When an individual's first two-level needs, *i.e.*, physiological and safety, are relatively satisfied, then the social needs become an important motivator of his behaviour. He then seeks acceptance by the group and strives for affection and belongingness.

However, this need for belongingness may be stronger in one person than in another. Maslow distinguished the need for affiliation into two categories. In the less mature form, this need is manifested when one tries to relate or seek company with another in order to overcome loneliness or to kill boredom. Maslow called it as "D-love" or which is based on deficit need. In its mature form, which Maslow termed as "B-love," it is evident when a person wants to relate to another without any desire to use him in any way and accepts the way he is.

According to Pathak, "When managers take a purely intellectual and economic view of people by ignoring their social needs, they develop a managerial style that is cold, elusive and insensitive to non-economic concerns."

Quite often, managers perceive this only as a threat to the organisation. As a result, they try to exercise tight control. They constantly see that such informal groups do not emerge and actively try to break up existing groups. When the individuals find that their social needs and even the security needs are threatened, they may become resistant, antagonistic and uncooperative, thereby defeating the organisational objectives.

Esteem Needs

The next level of needs are perhaps of the greatest significance both to the organisation and the man himself. When the physiological, security and social needs are appreciably satisfied, the esteem needs emerge. These needs include those for distinction, achievement, status and independence.

Unlike the other lower needs, esteem needs are rarely satisfied. They are largely unsatisfiable. In a conventional type of management, managers give little attention to these aspects of human motivation which if properly utilised can yield high organisational performance. Some higher social needs and esteem needs are tabulated here for ready reference.

TABLE: HIGHER SOCIAL AND ESTEEM NEEDS

Motive	*Meaning*	*Behaviour Indicators*
Achievement	Desire to excel	Active, exert themselves, set high goals, accept challenges, derive pleasure from trials, strive for quality. They do self-evaluation. They imagine the accomplishments of tasks.
Power	Desire to influence others. Desire to exercise control on others.	Seek positions vested with power. Seek leadership opportunities. Always giving directions to others. Argumentative. Want to be the first.
Extension	Desire to be helpful to others. Desire to serve the organisation, nation or any external agent.	Social workers. Enjoy helping others.
Aggression	Desire to dominate others. Desire to demonstrate strength, at times physically.	Argumentative. Loud-mouthed. pick up quarrels. Want to be winners. Show strength.
Dependence	Need to consult others before deciding.	Seek directions from others. No independent decisions. Need protection. No initiative.
Independence	Desire to do things autonomously.	Autonomous decisions may consult others, but do not seek approval.
Status and Prestige	Desire to be respected in social set up.	Non-violative of social behaviour. Violates social behaviour only when it gives recognition. Selective interaction with others. Authoritarian tendencies. Run for offices.
Recognition	Need to be recognised for one's achievements.	Work hard. Motivation lost if no recognition. Visible, attention-seeking.
Activity	Desire to be always doing something.	Active, hard worker. Opposite of passivity which is a need to relax.

Self-Actualisation Needs

On top of the individual's need hierarchy is the need for self-realisation. It is one of the needs discussed by Maslow about which little is known to the behavioural and social scientist. This is mainly because people try to satisfy these needs in many different ways. It is, therefore, extremely difficult if not impossible to pinpoint or identify the self-actualisation needs. Once the other lower level needs are completely or partly satisfied, the person tries to realise his own potential. Though the identification of these needs is not easy, there are at least two motives which seem to be related to it. They are acceptance and competence.

Self-Actualisation Concept Reviewed

Maslow borrowed the term 'Self-actualisation' from Kurt Goldstein and it refers to the desire for self-fulfilment, namely, one's tendency to become actualised in what one potentially is. 'A musician must make music, an artist must paint, a poet must write, if he is to be ultimately happy. What a man can be he must be.' This need we may call self-actualisation. At the end he shows how nebulous this need is: "Since in our society, basically satisfied people (*i.e.*, people who are satisfied in the physiological, safety, love and esteem needs) are the exception, we do not know much about self-actualisation, either experimentally or clinically. It remains a challenging problem for research."

Maslow has discovered the following six characteristics in seactualised human beings: (*i*) They can accept the way things really are: *(ii)* Afraid to get close to others *(iii)* They are efficient judges of situations, *(iv)* They are creative and appreciative, *(v)* They march to a different drummer and *(vi)* They are willing to learn from anyone.

Rogers has suggested four personal characteristics in self-actualised persons: *(i)* willingness to accept experience for what they are; *(ii)* trust and confidence in their own ability and judgement; *(iii)* greater reliance on self than on society or friends; *(iv)* willingness to continue to grow as persons. McGregor refers to self-actualisation as "the need for realising one's own potentialities." Rensis Likert calls it "the desire for growth and significant achievement in terms of one's own values and goals."

Keith Davis has used the synonym 'self-realisation' for this need and writes, "... which means to become all one is capable of becoming. This need is less apparent than others because many persons have not unleashed it. If to the degree that the need can be unleashed, people will find their work a challenge and an inner-satisfaction." Warren Bennis writes that "the concept of self-actualisation is, at best, an ill-defined concept... (and that) self-actualised man seems to be more myth than reality." Paul Hersey toes the line of other behaviourists and writes, "Of all the needs discussed by Maslow, the one that social and behavioural scientists know least about is self-actualisation. perhaps, this is because people satisfy this need in different ways. Thus, self-acutalisation is a difficult need to pin down and identify... little research has been done on the concept of self-actualisation."

Robert M. Fulmer observes, "Only a few people ever achieve the true concept of self-actualisation." Atchison and Hill have also written about the self-actualisation needs. "Maslow believed that what a person can be, he or she must be. This means that people have a full range of potential (talents, knowledge, emotions and so forth) that must find expression. When people begin to actualise their potential, they begin to perceive themselves, others and the environment creatively, spontaneously and appreciatively." But, these observations are prefaced by the sentence, "the need for self-actualisation is somewhat more complex than the others."

Amongst the very recent observers (1979), Richard M. Hodgetts includes under it "Self-development, and creativity in the broadest sense of the word." But he admits, at the same time, that "of all five needs, the least is known about self-actualisation." As such, this need appears to have defied a correct analysis so far.

Comment

When the lower level of wants are adequately satisfied, the person moves to a higher level and the lower level of wants become less important in his total system of wants. Once the lower level of wants become less potent, the individual is free to realise his higher level of wants which increases in number and variety.

Herzberg's Motivation-Hygiene Theory

In 1959, Herzberg, Maysner and Snyderman reported research findings which suggested that man has two sets of needs: *(a)* His need as an animal to avoid pain and *(b)* His need as a human to grow psychologically.

These findings led them to advance a "dual factor theory of motivation." Since then, the theory has caught the attention of both managers and psychologists. Management training and work motivation programmes have been evolved on the basis of this theory.

The dual-factor theory of motivation was inferred from a study of the need satisfactions and the reported motivational effect of these satisfactions on 200 engineers and accountants.

The first set of interviews asks them to recall a time when they had felt exceptionally good about a particular job, the reasons for their feelings of satisfaction and whether this feeling of satisfaction has affected their performance, their personal relationship and their well-being.

In the second set of interviews, the same subjects were asked to describe incidents in which their feelings about job were exceptionally negative and cases in their negative feeling were related to same events on the job.

Conclusion of Herzberg's Theory

Hypothesis I — Herzberg and his associates concluded from their interview findings that job satisfaction consists of two separate independent dimensions:

The first dimension related to job satisfaction, and second dimension related to job dissatisfaction.

These dimensions are not two opposite ends of the same continuum, but instead represent two distinct continua.

Based on these two dimensions, he classified these job characteristics that are important for and lead to, "job satisfaction" but not to job dissatisfaction as Satisfiers or Motivational Factors, namely: *(a)* Achievement, *(b)* Recognisation, *(c)* Advancement, *(d)* Work itself, *(e)* Possibility of growth and *(f)* Responsibility. They have been found to play an important role in creating a motivation to work on the part of employees. They play an important role in helping people to work more and more.

Similarly, those job characteristics that are important for, and lead to, "job dissatisfaction" but not to job satisfaction, are classified as Dissatisfiers or Maintenance or Hygiene Factors, namely: *(a)* Company Policy and Administration, *(b)* Technical Supervision, *(c)* Interpersonal relations with Supervisors, *(d)* Interpersonal relations with Peers, *(e)* Interpersonal relations with Subordinates, *(f)* Salary, *(g)* Job Security, *(h)* Personal Life, *(i)* Work conditions and *(j)* Status. They prevent job dissatisfaction but do not necessarily ensure motivation. They are essential for people to work.

According to the theory, 'Satisfiers' are related to the 'nature of the work itself', or 'job content' factors and rewards that flow directly from the performance of that work. And it relates more or less to self-actualisation and self-realisation in the work, while 'Dissatisfiers' are associated with the individual relationship to the context or environment in which he performs the work or job context factors.

But recognition and achievement work in both the directions, *i.e.*, they can lead to job satisfaction as 'satisfiers' as well as job dissatisfaction as 'dissatisfiers'.

Hypothesis II — The second major hypothesis is of the dual-factors theory of motivation is that, 'the satisfiers are effective in motivating the individual to superior performance and effort, but the dissatisfiers are not.'

In his recent book, Herzberg (1966) advances the following analogy to explain why the satisfiers or motivators affect motivation in a positive direction. When a child learns to ride a bicycle, he is becoming more 'competent', increasing the repertory of his behaviour, expanding his skills — psychologically growing. In the process of child's learning to master the bicycle, the parents can love him with all the zeal and compassion of the most devoted mother and father. They can safeguard the child from injury by providing the safest and most hygienic area in which to practise. They can offer all kinds of incentives and rewards and they can provide expert instructor. But the child will never, never learn to ride the bicycle unless he is given a bicycle. The hygienic factors are not a valid contributor to psychological growth. The substance of the task is required to achieve growth goals. Creativity will require a potentially creative task to do.

* * *

8 DEMAND MEASUREMENT AND FORECASTING

Demand is a consumer's willingness to buy a product backed up by purchasing power. A teenager wants to buy a two-wheeler, say Sunny. Mere intention to possess a Sunny is not a demand. His parents must have the funds to buy it for him. Besides, the vehicle must be available in the area where he stays. An effective demand thus is based on three components — *interest, purchasing power* and *access*. Basically, demand is of two types — primary demand for a basic product, say, for vehicles or two-wheelers and a selective secondary demand for specific products, say, Sunny. As marketers of new products, the company has to stimulate both the primary demand and the selective demand. Demand is affected by a number of factors like price, demography, income-level, satisfaction, substitutability, competition, and promotional efforts.

❖ How do we Measure Demand?

Demand can be measured for short-term medium term and long-term. Demand can be measured for a customer group (say IV fluids needed by private nursing homes), territory, region and country. Multinationals can estimate demand globally, too. Demand can be measured for each individual product item, product form, and product-line. There can be company-wide estimate, industry-wide estimate and all-sales estimate. These different estimates are made with specific objectives in mind. For example, while setting up a distribution network in a particular region, it is necessary to estimate the regional demand. Short-term demand estimates for a product item may help us in planning our raw material ordering. It may also help us in planning our working capital.

As we have seen, an interest in a product gives us a *potential market.* However, the constraints of purchasing power and access reduce our potential market to some extent. The market thus reduced is called *available market.* Available market may be further reduced by certain restrictions, *e.g.,* adult movies can be seen only by those who are 18-plus or vehicle licence can be given to those who are 18-plus. The market so reduced is *qualified available market.* Out of the total qualified available market, the company may decide to serve only a part, *e.g.,* a bank decides that credit card will be made available in only metros and certain selected cities of India. The *served* market is thus a part of qualified available market. In the served market, certain people actually buy our product. It is the market which we have *penetrated.* These concepts should be appreciated as they are useful for market planning. If a company is not satisfied in its current sales, it can attempt to influence a large number of people in the served market. Alternatively it can change the qualifications of potential buyers, *e.g.*, Sunny's driving licence is available to those who are not 18. The available market can be expanded by reducing prices or by increasing distribution. Vicks Coldrub more than doubled its available market by converting itself from an allopathic to an ayurvedic medicine. Vicks as an ayurvedic medicine can be stocked by grocery stores, panwalas and general stores which do not have drug licence. As an allopathic medicine, it could be stocked only by licenced chemists thus restricting its available market. The potential market can be expanded by effective advertising.

Sale of a product or brand in one country market generates demand in another country – it is called *demand spillover*.

❖ Key Concepts

There are several terms used for demand measurement — predictions, forecasts, estimates, goals and quotas. However, two key concepts in demand measurement are *market demand* and *company demand.*

Market demand is "the aggregate demand of potential buyers of a commodity or service." Kotler defines market demand as "*the total volume that would be bought by a defined customer group, in a defined geographical area, in a defined time period, in a defined marketing environment, under a defined marketing programme.*"

Market demand is thus a function of the given conditions, and is not a fixed figure. It represents marker's opportunity to sell. Consider Fig. 8.1.

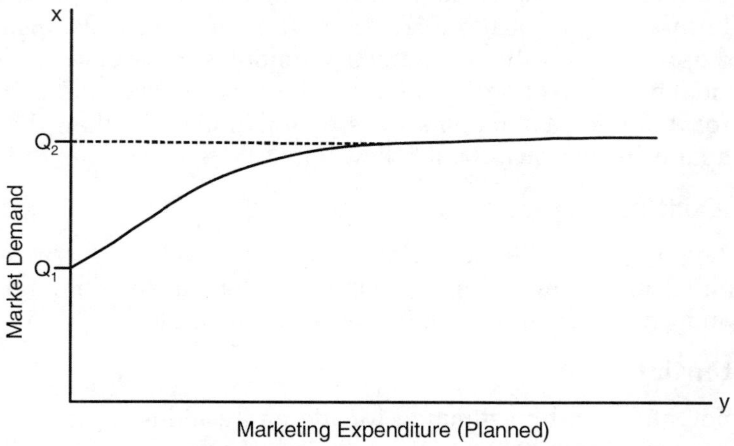

Q_1 = Market Minimum Q_2 = Market Potential

Fig. 8.1

Market demand is plotted on the *x*-axis, and market expenditure is plotted on the *y*-axis. There is a corelation between the expenditure and the demand. The market demand curve (as a function of marketing expenditure) represents estimated marketing demand corresponding to different levels of expenditure. Q_1 represents the minimum sales that will take place irrespective of the expenditure. It is called *market minimum*. An increase in expenditure leads to an increase in demand, first at an increasing rate and then at a decreasing rate. When demand reaches a point of no-increase, inspite of the increasing expenditure, the *market potential* is reached. The distance between Q_1 and Q_2 shows the *sensitivity* of demand. The larger the distance, the more is the sensitivity, making the market *expansible.* The smaller the distance, the less is the sensitivity of the market making it *non-expansible.* In non-expansible markets, a given market size equivalent to the level of primary demand is accepted and resources are deployed to stimulate the selective demand. The level of marketing expenditure of industry that will occur will lead to a corresponding market demand which is called *market forecast.* Market forecast thus represents the expected market demand at a given level of industry expenditure. More-often-than-not, it does not reach the market potential. Hypothetically, if the industry marketing expenditure keeps on increasing, the market potential will be reached in a given environment. An individual company is satisfied only by a share of total market demand, which is called its *market share* or *company demand.* Thus, out of a total market demand worth ₹ 200 crores of toothpaste in India per annum, Colgate has a share of 60 per cent or ₹ 120 crores. It is called company demand. Each company has its own marketing plan in a given environment. It then attains a corresponding level of sales. It is called *company's sales forecast.* Company's sales forecast represents an expected level of sales at a given level of marketing effort.

Sales quotas are administrative devices which define and stimulate sales effort by setting a sales goal for the company or its particular division or its sales representative. The basis for sales quotas are the company forecasts. To stimulate sales effort, the quotas are set at a levels lightly higher than the forecast. *Sales budget* is yet another concept. It means an estimate of the sales volume. It forms the basis of our raw material purchasing, production planning and working capital decisions. Sales budgets are based on sales forecasts and are set a levels lightly lower than the forecast.

As marketing effort increases, relative to the competitors, the company demand rises. When it rises no further, inspite of the increasing effort, we say a *company's potential* has been reached. The upper limit of the company's potential is, of course, the market potential. A company's potential and marketing potential can be equal in case the company enjoys 100 p.c. market. Most of the times, company's sales potential is lower than the market potential because each company has its own loyal following.

❖ Measuring Existing Demand

After acquainting ourselves with the key concepts in demand measurement and forecasting, we are in a position to appreciate the measurement of the existing demand. While doing so, market potential, industry sales and market shares are estimated.

❖ Market Potential

The market potential can be estimated for the entire industry. It represents the higher sales volume an industry can attain in a given period of time, at a given level of marketing effort and for a given environment. Symbolically,

$$\text{M.P.} = b \times q \times p.$$

where M.P. = market potential for the entire industry.

b = number of buyers under assumed conditions.

q = quantity bought by an average buyer.

p = price of an average unit.

Thus, if 5,000 students buy an Advertising textbook once in a three-year B.Com. course at a price of ₹ 100 per book, the total market potential of advertising textbook is:

(5000 × 1 × 100) = ₹ 5,00,000. The trickiest part is our estimation of the number of buyers for a specific product. We start with a total population of students, say, 20 thousand, students in all the B.Com. course for which Advertising has been prescribed. This is our *suspect pool.* Let us say 25 per cent students depend on library books. Thus only 75 per cent of the total population of students are in the *prospect pool.* Out of these, 5,000 students cannot afford a book. Another 5000 students depend upon second-hand books. Thus we are left with a *hot prospect pool* of merely 5,000 students. This value we have put in our M.P. equation above.

Alternatively, we can employ a *chain-ratio method* where a base number is multiplied by several adjusting percentages. Suppose a cosmetic manufacturing firm is keen to estimate the market potential for a new fairness cream. An estimate can be made by the following computation:

Demand for the new fairness cream : Population × Personal Disposable Income (PDI) per person × average percentage of PDI spent on cosmetics × average percentage of amount used on cosmetics that will be used on creams × average percentage of amount that is used on creams that will be used on fairness cream.

❖ Area Market Potential

While selling the products, we choose territories and allocate over marketing budget to them. To do so, we require an estimate of the area market potential. The two methods frequently used to assess the area potential are: market build-up method, and multiple-factor index method.

❖ Market Build-up Method

First, we have to identify our potential buyers for each market. Next, we estimate their potential purchases. Consider a unit manufacturing intravenous (IV) fluids. It has two major categories of buyers — nursing homes (accounting for 70 per cent of consumption) and government hospitals (accounting for 30 per cent of consumption). IV fluids consumption is linked to the number of beds in the nursing homes and hospitals. To assess the area market potential of Mumbai for IV fluids, we have to assess the number of beds available in nursing homes and hospitals in Mumbai. IV fluids consumption per bed is estimated to be between 175–200 bottles per year. In developed countries, bottles per bed are estimated to be 300-500.

❖ Multiple-factor Index

Consumer companies construct an index to calculate area market potential. Ready-made indices like Thomson are used in India. Instead of a single-factor (like the number of beds), a variety of factors are considered. Consumer companies avoid identifying the major buyer groups, since they have a large number of individual buyers. A pharmaceutical company might assume that since 1/6th of population of India is in UP. 1/6th of its pharma sales will occur in UP. Other factors which can be considered are disposable income, the number of doctors per 1,000 population etc. Each factor can be assigned a specific weight.

❖ Industry Sales

Over and above the market potential, the company must know the sales generated actually for the whole industry as such. It means, we must assess the sales of all the competitors and sum them up. Such data are available from the Chambers of Commerce. Against the total industry's sales, we can compare our own actual sales. For instance, if the industry is showing a growth rate of 15 per cent per annum, whereas we are growing at a rate of 10 per cent per annum, we are losing in terms of our relative share in the industry. There are retail audit reports available for some industries where sales for individual brands are estimated. *e.g.*, ORG reports for pharmaceuticals. These enable us to compare the sales of our brand to the sales of the competitive brands. Each company would like to know what percentage its own sales is of the total market/industry sales. It is called its market share.

❖ Demand Forecasting

Forecasting brings to our mind the weekly horoscope predictions of our zodiacal sign in the magazines and Sunday papers. We also remember the weather forecasts being shown on TV at the end of the news bulletin. We tend to take forecasting with a pinch of salt. However, we cannot avoid forecasts, and have to accept them with all their inaccuracies and mystical properties. We make several personal forecasts — what will be the composition of our World Cup team or which team will take away the prestigious and coveted cup? Astronomers forecast the planetary positions a few years hence and scientists forecast the behaviour of a satellite launched in space. Most of the businessmen do make forecasts, knowingly or unknowingly and *foresight* or "vision" is considered to be an essential characteristic of a leader. Decision-making involves some kind of forecasting. Some of these forecasts are quite simple, whereas others are much more complex. Since there are uncertainties involved, the company demand and total demand may not remain fairly stable over a period of time. This itself makes forecasting of demand much more difficult.

Sales forecasts are made in three steps: A *macro-economic forecast*, taking into consideration the parameters of inflation, population, employment, interest, consumer spending, exports, investments both by the consumers and the government is made. In other words, it boils down to GNP forecast. It guides the *industry forecast* of sales. The company then assumes that it would have a certain proportion of total industry sales, giving it its own *company level forecast*.

Sales forecast can be in terms of rupees or physical units for a specified future period. Sales forecasts, thus, can be of three months, six months, one year or even more. Forecasts are thus, short-term (a few weeks — six months — one year), medium-term (one year — four years) or long-term (five years and more, say 10 years). All forecasts are made under a proposed marketing programme and for a given environment.

Sales forecasts are influenced by the company's business environment, both internal and external.

Management scientists have developed many forecasting techniques in recent years to help managers handle the increasing complexity in management decision-making. Each of these techniques, has a special use, and the more you understand about these techniques, the better the chances that your forecasting efforts will be successful. The purpose of this chapter is to introduce you to some of the more commonly used forecasting techniques.

Whether you use one forecasting technique or another, the forecasting process has some permanent features:

❖ Five Steps in the Forecasting Process:

1. Determine the objective of the forecast. (What is its use?)
2. Select the period over which the forecast will be made. (What are your information needs over what time period?)
3. Select the forecasting approach you will use. (Which forecasting technique is most likely to produce the information you need?)
4. Gather the information to be used in the forecast. (Which data will most likely produce forecasts of greatest use to you?)
5. Make the forecast. (Which computational procedures will you have to use?)

❖ Types of Forecasts

There are three basic types of forecasts. Judgemental forecasts based on what people say. Test marketing based on what people do and extensions of past history and causal forecasting based on what people have done.

❖ Judgemental Forecasts

Forecasts when good data are unavailable: We tend to use these kinds of forecasts when "good" data are not readily available. With a judgemental forecast, we are trying to change subjective opinion into a quantitative forecast that we can use. The process brings together, in an organised way, personal judgements about the process being analysed. Outside experts may be consulted, we can convene a meeting of the panel of experts to make a combined forecast or we can ask one of the organised "futurist" organisations (organisations that specialise in the future) what they think about the situation. In each case, we are relying primarily on human judgement to interpret past data and projections about the future.

It is also necessary to anticipate how people will behave under a given set of conditions. We do this by surveying people.

❖ Surveying

We ask the buyers whether they intend to buy a given product and if yes, what is the possibility of buying. This is a useful method if there are a few buyers, *e.g.*, some industrial product. The total quantity expected to be purchased is thus estimated.

❖ Composite of Sales Force Opinions

The sales representatives ask the buyers what quantity of product they would buy. The figures given by the sales representatives are adjusted at the upper levels in the sales hierarchy because sales representative may have given too optimistic or too pessimistic figures, unmindful of the company's marketing plans. There is a tendency to underestimate future demand so that they get sales quotas easily to fulfil. The company's sales executives can prepare their own forecasts by taking into account the opinion of the sales force or on their own on the basis of their specialised knowledge.

❖ Delphi Technique

Expert forecasts without disclosure of majority opinion: As forecasts of the social and economic environment become more and more necessary for managerial decision-making, expert opinion is used extensively to chart out the future. One technique that is used to get agreement among the "experts" is the *Delphi Technique.* Here from a group of experts, their opinions are solicited in an environment in which the majority opinion is not disclosed, to prevent it from influencing anyone unduly.

❖ Everyone Makes Mistakes

Of course, experts are as fallacious as we are. When the first great hydroelectric plant at Niagara Falls, New York, was being conceived, proposals were received for direct-current equipment (a traditional power-generation method) and alternating-current equipment (a new technology). The project promoters consulted England's Lord Kelvin, one of the world's best known power experts, who advised them strongly not to commit the mistake of using alternating current. The decision-makers, however, preferred to disregard the expert and selected alternating current, a decision which has worked out well for about 60 years.

The worst technology predictions of all times are:

- Sir Alan Sugar, founder of Amstrad said that the iPod would never take off (2005).
- Bill Gates in 1981 allegedly said that nobody would ever need more than 640 kilobytes of memory on their PC.
- Ken Oslen, founder of Digital Equipment Corporation (1977) said that there was no need for a computer at home.
- Darryl Zanuck in 1946 felt people would get tired of staring at a plywood box every night and so TV won't last.
- Lord Kelvin in 1883 felt x-rays would prove to be a hoax.
- Bill Gates in 2004 felt spam would be solved.

❖ Panel of Experts

Expert forecasts with full disclosure of information: This technique differs from the Delphi technique in that there is no secrecy and full and free interaction amongst expert panel is encouraged.

❖ Market Testing

In case buyers' behaviour is unpredictable and reliable judgemental forecast is not possible, a direct market test may be useful. It is also very useful to forecast sales of a new product or of an existing product in a new market or a new channel. Market testing is discussed elsewhere in this book.

❖ Extensions of Past History

Forecasts based on the past: When we take history as our beginning point for forecasting, it doesn't mean that we think December will not be different from November and September, it simply means that over the short-run, we believe that future patterns tend to be extensions of past ones and that we can make some useful forecasts by studying past behaviour. Unfortunately, these kinds of forecasts do very poorly when we try to extend them further into the future, because the past, although it is often a guide to the future, does not predict very accurately the point at which rate of interest will show an upward or downward trend, the style of Jeans will pick up, and the demand for mopeds will be maximum in the years to come. All these peaks and valleys are called turning points. Even though turning points are of the greatest significance to managers, extending past history too far into the future is not an effective way of determining when they will occur.

❖ Fundamentals of Time Series

Any organisation must plan for the future if it is to survive and grow. Business organisations must make plans for production, finance, personnel, marketing etc., to meet the variations in the demand for their products. Efficient planning requires foretelling future events that are likely to occur. Foretelling, on the other hand, requires a judicious analysis of past events or data which have been collected at a moment of time. The important method of making inference about the future on the basis of what has happened in the past is the analysis of time series.

"A time series is a set of quantitative readings of some variable or composite of variables arranged in chronological order of their occurrences"[1]. A time series is simply a set of recordings of value of variable quantities measured at intervals of time. "The basic quality of the data from which such series are derived is one of historical fact."[2] Time, in terms of years, months, weeks, days or hours is simply a device that enables one to relate all phenomena to a set of common, stable reference points.

Over a period of time, the observations of a variable record change. The various factors which contribute to the changes over time in some variables are to be shifted. Consider the following example:

AMUL CHOCOLATE COMPANY

Year	*1st Quarter*	*2nd Quarter*	*3rd Quarter*	*4th Quarter*
1989	12,000	9,400	9,500	13,000
1990	13,000	10,200	10,300	15,000
1991	13,200	11,000	11,200	13,700
1992	14,600	12,000	12,200	15,000

From the above table, we notice two things. First, there is a steady increase in sales of chocolate bars throughout the period. Secondly, there appears to be regular seasonal variations in sales. Sales decline during the second and third quarters of the company's year. There may be several causes responsible for increase or decrease from one quarter to another, such as changes in climate, changes in tastes and habits of people etc.

Additional examples of time series are, production figures for a particular product, price of a product, imports, exports, number of passengers travelling by Indian Airlines etc.

❖ Nature of Time Series

The variation in time series can be attributed to a number of causes — natural, institutional; and socio-economic in character. Some of them may be responsible for short-run fluctuations, while others bring about long-run variation. Thus, a time series is made up of a variety of elements or components, which account for the observed variations over a period of time.

❖ Components of Time Series

The commonly used classification of time series is as follows:

(*i*) A *trend component,* which may be defined as long-term growth or decay.

(*ii*) A *seasonal component*, which may be defined as a regularly occurring periodic fluctuation.

1. Lincoln L. Chao, *Statistics: Methods and Analysis,* p. 356.
2. W.J. Reichman, *Uses and Abuses of Statistics,* p. 165.

(*iii*) A *cyclical component* which may be defined as a wave-like fluctuation about trend.

(*iv*) An *erratic* or *random* or *irregular component* which is obviously unsystematic.

For example, at any given time, the sales of an organisation are influenced by the long-term growth of the organisation, by the seasonal nature of demand and possibly by some random shock.

❖ The Time Series Model

If the symbols *T*, *S*, *C*, and E are used to denote the four components of trend, seasonal, cyclical and erratic fluctuations respectively, the time series O, may be expressed as:

$$O = T \times S \times C \times E$$

The above expression is based on the assumption that there exists multiplicative relationship between the four components. In the multiplicative model, it is also assumed that the four components are due to different causes, but they are not necessarily independent and they can affect one another. This is the traditional method and is also easier to use. It enables us to isolate the components.

For example, if in the multiplicative model.

$T = 100$, $S = 1.40$, $C = 1.06$ and $E = 0.90$

then $O = (100).(1.40).(1.06).(0.90)$

"Basic or long time trend may, therefore, be defined as underlying tendency to grow or decline over a period of years." According to Lincoln L. Chao, a secular, or long-term trend refers to the smooth and regular movement of a series reflecting continuous growth, stagnation or decline over a rather long period of time"[3]

❖ Causal Forecasting Models

Forecasts which relate to several variables: If considerable historical data are available and if we know the relationship between the variable we want to forecast and other variables that we can observe, it is possible to construct a *causal forecast.* For example, one causal model regression can be used to relate sales to a number of other environmental factors, including the level of GNP, the price level, personal disposable income, unemployment and population shifts, the number of marriages made during a period, the number of houses constructed, the kilometerage of railway line and roads etc. These models are expensive to use.

Here sales is a dependent variable and is a function of several independent variables like x_1, x_2 till x_n . Computers have made regression a popular model for use in demand forecasting. However, this model has certain limitations. We may miss certain crucial new independent variables. There may be two-way causal relationship amongst the variables. The independent variables may have very high correlation. The model may violate normal curve assumptions. We may select too few observations for this model. All this diminishes the overall usefulness of this model.

❖ Estimating the Market Size

Conventionally, income and price sensitivity data is used for market estimation. Together with these, other demand driving factors are considered. This method, however, is not sufficient to estimate demand for a new product concept. Cross-country data may be used by adapting

3. Lincoln L. Chao, *Statistics: Methods and Analysis,* p. 358.

it to local conditions, but such adaptation is far from satisfactory considering the differences in the development aspects of different countries. Sometimes, the product is developed for only the local market and may not have cross-country data. In such cases, efforts are made to correlate the new product with an existing one and create a surrogate for the income and price sensitivities. A.T. Kearney, a global consulting firm advocates rethinking on this subject. It is necessary to understand the product first and identity features that create value for the customer. Then a surrogate is chosen and it is normalised for consumer and industry differences. Lastly, a demand curve is plotted for sales potential at different price-points. The crucial part is to understand the product as a potential bundle of utilities or values a product can deliver, and price that a consumer might attach to them. The utilities can be tangible or intangible, and when quantified in money, it gives a price-value proposition. The whole process is based on qualitative and quantitative market research. The surrogate bench-mark product must be chosen carefully *e.g.*, for car market it could be Maruti 800. We also have to find a pair of products which are analogous and mimic the cost — functionality relationship *e.g.* for car market these could be mopeds and scooters where large historical data exists.

* * *

9 MARKET SEGMENTATION AND TARGETING

We have already stated that a market consists of people with needs and/or wants, with money to spend and willingness to spend. A target market is a group of customers at whom our marketing effort is directed. We have to select and define our target market so as to develop a suitable marketing mix for it. While selecting the target market, we have to see that it is consistent with our overall goals. Secondly, we have to match our resources and the marketing opportunity. A target market must be cost-effective and must generate enough sales to become profitable. As far as possible, we select a target market where competition is minimal, unless our marketing muscle is very strong, and we have a good competitive advantage.

❖ Market Segmentation

As we are all aware, consumers differ widely in terms of space, time, perception and value. They are not homogeneous. The differences must be studied carefully and suitable products must be offered to suit their varying needs. The market in other words is sub-divided. It is sub-divided into sub-groups of consumer population where each sub-group is identifiable, distinct and homogeneous. Differentiated marketing programme can be developed for each sub-group to improve consumer satisfaction and profitability of business. Thus, the grouping of buyers or segmenting the market is called market segmentation. Market segmentation is the process of dividing the total heterogeneous market into several sub-markets called segments each of which tends to be homogeneous in all significant aspects.

❖ Market Segmentation and Targeting

There are three different approaches. In the first approach, the total market is considered as a single unit or as one mass. This is called market aggregation. There is another approach of adopting differentiation in products while catering to one market. The last approach is to consider the whole market as consisting of smaller, homogeneous segments. This is called market segmentation.

Mass Marketing: In mass marketing, only one marketing mix is offered to all the buyers, hoping it would appeal to everyone. A single product is offered to all the buyers. There is one price structure and one distribution system. A single promotional programme is directed to the entire market. Mass marketing is supposed to be cost effective and creates, therefore, a large potential market. Essentially, this is a production oriented strategy which believes in economies of scale.

According to Kotler mass marketing is the first step in the evolution of marketing. It means one bottle of Coke for the whole world to drink, without caring for those who want sweeter or lighter Cola.

Product differentiated Marketing: Another approach adopted by marketers is to resort to *product differentiation,* where a single product is converted in two or more products, with minor physical variations in size, shape, quality, colour and so on. The basic objective is to offer a variety to the buyers.

Target Marketing: The latest approach is to do target marketing by sub-dividing the market into many segments and then deciding to offer a suitable product to some selected segments. The other elements of marketing, mix, *viz.,* the price and the distribution are tailored to the needs of these segments which are selected. Companies are increasingly adopting target marketing.

These days the companies find it difficult to practise mass marketing, thus initiating a process of de-massification. The total market for most products is too varied or too heterogeneous to be considered as a single unit. There are several sub-markets which differ from each other significantly. The differences arise because of the varying usage of products, different buying motives and such other factors. Market segmentation takes cognisance of these differences. Companies, have increasingly adopted target marketing. There is for instance the segment of light Colas. It is very large. When you get a large segment, it is just camouflaged mass marketing. It enables them to tap marketing opportunities better. Marketers develop a separate product for each target market. They adjust the pricing, distribution and advertising to reach the target market most efficiently. Instead of a shot-gun approach, they concentrate on buyers who are most interested (rifle approach).

❖ Three Major Steps in Target Marketing

There are three major steps in target marketing. These are:

(a) Market Segmentation: The process of dividing a market into distinct buyer groups who may require separate products and/or marketing mix.

Customers are grouped in segments on the basis of such characteristics as income, age, education, sex and so on. The buyer group then becomes a meaningful segment. It helps the company to handle the differing needs of different segments effectively.

The company identifies different ways to segment a market. It develops profiles of these different segments. It evaluates each segment's business potential and attractiveness.

(b) Market Targeting: We as marketers have identified several segments, out of which one or more segments are chosen for entry.

(c) Product Positioning: Here the product is placed in the mind of the consumer in relation to the competitive products.

Target marketing also deals with specialised small segments called niche marketing, local area marketing or cell marketing.

❖ Customer Marketing

It is called one-to-one marketing. Here the product is customised. The promotional message is essentially designed keeping in mind the socio-economic characteristics of the prospect. The approach is individualistic. This type of marketing is common in business-to-business marketing. Panasonic markets bikes and Levis Strauss jeans in this fashion. The basic assumption is the availability of a data-base of the customers and the ease with which prospects can be identified from this data-base. The message is then directed towards this base through a low-cost media. After mass marketing, we moved to target marketing and then to customer marketing.

❖ Market Segmentation

Markets are made up of buyers who differ in their buying habits, buying attitudes, their wants, income, sex, geographic locations etc. All these variables can be used to segment a market.

General Approach to Segmentation: Each customer can be considered a separate segment, *e.g.*, when an aircraft is sold to a limited number of buyers, each aircraft is customised for a specific buyer. However, instead of each individual, a group of individuals is taken as a market segment taking one characteristic that determine the buying behaviour, say, income or age. Sometimes, both the characteristics, say income and age, may affect the buyer behaviour and market can be segmented on the basis of combination of characteristics.

Single and Multiple Segmentation: We have a choice of either having a single segmentation or multiple segmentation.

Single Segmentation: Here one homogeneous group out of the entire market is selected as a segment. The marketing mix is designed to reach this single segment. For example, Johnson and Johnson has directed all its products to a single segment of babies. The company, thus, acquires expertise in this segment. The only risk is that if the market potential declines, the company can suffer considerable losses.

Multiple Segmentation: Here more than a segment is chosen as our target market segments. For each of these segments, a separate marketing mix is developed.

A pharma company can identify the segments of individual patients and institutional buyers. It can develop appropriate marketing mix to reach these segments.

Multiple segments can be served by different product versions or by one and the same product, backed by a different marketing programme. One and the same tonic can be marketed for two segments — youngsters and old people. But the promotional programme will be different. Multiple segmentation strategy is costlier than single segment strategy. But it may generate larger sales volume.

❖ Advantages of Segmentation

1. Segmentation is the basis of better marketing. We make better use of marketing resources.
2. Niche marketing allows a smaller firm to compete effectively with a larger firm by selecting one or two specialised segments. This enables a small firm with limited resources viable.
3. Segmentation results in matching the marketing mix with the needs of the market.
4. Promotion becomes effective, as messages are specifically directed at selected segments.

❖ Conditions for Segmentation

Each segment chosen must be *measurable.* We must be clear about the basis for segmentation. The data about the basis for segmentation must be available easily — it should be *accessible.* Today it is difficult to quantify data about "people who need an eco-friendly product." In a physical sense also, the segment must be accessible, *i.e.,* we should be able to reach it by the existing trade channels, advertising media and sales representatives. Each segment must also be *substantial.* In other words, it should be large enough to be profitable. Measurability, accessibility and substantiality are the three essential conditions for segmentation.

❖ Market Segmentation Techniques

Specialised Segments: First and foremost, it is to be seen whether the market lends itself to segmentation. These days markets have become national and global. Many companies have, therefore, started thinking in terms of demassification as there are less opportunities in mass markets with arguable potential for distinctiveness. These companies become interested in high margin, low volume products. For them, segmentation is an extremely sensible proposition.

To illustrate, we give the following tables of specialised market segments:

Firm	*Product*	*Segment Identified (Niche)*
Block Drug	Sensodyne	The toothpaste for sensitive teeth
	Mentadent	The toothpaste to remove plaque
Block Drug	Dentu Creme	The toothpaste for dentures
Pedigree	Mr. Dog	The up-market dog food for owners of poodles and Yorkshire terriers
Bryant and May	Cook's Matches	Made for kitchen use with a waterproof pack

The simpler the method of segmentation, the better it works. The key is not, however, the method itself, but the *insight* to consider the possible segment options and then to *select* those which are likely to be most promising.

❖ Grid Analysis

Here we prepare a grid covering the most relevant market groups, usage occasions and other characteristics of the market which are relevant. To illustrate, a new insurance service is to be segmented. The following simple grid attempts to do so:

Market Group	*Usage Occasion*				
	Life	*Endowment*	*Medical*	*Travel*	*Specific Benefits*
Men					
Women					
Babies					
Children					
Pensioners					
Single Adults					
Upper Classes					
Lower Classes					
Families					
Travellers					
Sportsmen					

	Usage Occasion				
Market Group	*Life*	*Endowment*	*Medical*	*Travel*	*Specific Benefits*
Houseowners					
Sick People					
Disabled					
Owners of valuable jewellery etc.					
Lecturers and teachers					
Retailers					
Small businesses					
Large quoted companies					
Motorists					
Air-travellers					
Mothers-to-be					
Pet Owners					
Users of Home Computers					
Farmers					

Grid for Segmenting Insurance

This example is, of course, a very simple one. A much more comprehensive gird can be prepared, depending upon the company and its objectives.

❖ Spectrum Analysis

Another method to identify segmentation options is to assess the current product in the same product category. These current products are scaled on each important factor just to find out whether there are any gaps. We give below a spectrum analysis for beers.

Strong	.... xxxx .... xxx xx	Weak
Male	.... xxxx ....xx...... xx	Female
In pubs	.... xxxx .... xx xx	At home
Bitter	.... xxxxx xx	Sweet
Dark Colour	.... x .... xx xxx	Light
Expensive	.... x ...... x .... xx xxx	Cheap
For session drinking	.... xxxxxxx .... xxx xx	For one glass
Young drinkers	........xxxxxxx xx	Old
Fattening	.... xxxx xx	Slimming
Old-Fashioned	.... xxxx .... xxx xx	Modern
International	.... xxx .... xx xxx	Regional
Draught	.... xxx .... xx xxx	In Cans
Drunk chilled	.... xx .... xxx	Warm

Current Beers: Spectrum Analysis

Many more dimensions or factors can be taken. Even in the above example, we find many gaps in the market. To illustrate:

(*i*) a relatively low-alcohol, not very fattening, fairly sweet beer for women to drink at home, (*ii*) a modern very chilled beer for the young,

(*iii*) a dark international sweet beer for older men.

Though these gaps are obvious, it requires market research and market judgements to assess which of these gaps can be exploited. The example just illustrates, how the method produces a spate of ideas?

Market is sub-divided by identifying and applying successive variables.

❖ Hierarchy of Variables

Consider Air India who wants to attract the non-flying public as airline passengers. Here, Air India has considered two segments — users are flying public and non-users are non-flying public. The segmentation base is *user status.*

Non-fliers are further sub-divided on the basis of their *attitudes* to flying — those who are scared to fly and those who are positive or negative or indifferent to flying. Only those who are positive towards flying are further subdivided into those who can afford to fly and those who cannot afford to fly. The basis of segmentation is thus *income* here.

The target of Air India is, therefore, those high income group people who have positive feelings towards flying but have not so far flown. We have successively used three variables to identify our segment — *userstatus, attitude* and *income.* How to identify these variables which can be used?

A sample of consumers is interviewed and a hierarchy of variables is discovered which these consumers make use of while taking a purchase decision.

Many students want books by particular publishing houses and particular authors. It is *a brand-loyal market.* However, if they want a book in a question-answer form, it is called *brand-form* market.

For cars, consumers may buy a fuel-efficient, small-sized family car, say a Maruti. Here the market is a need-size-form-brand market. The need-size-form combination decides the competition. These partitioning variables make us understand the market segments.

❖ Bases for Market Segmentation

Demographic Segmentation. Buyer groups differ in their requirements from the products and their marketing responses, *e.g.,* low-income buyers prefer beedis for smoking. Middle income buyers smoke Wills Filter and high income buyers like 555 cigarettes. This is segmentation of the buyers on the basis of income. Such segmentation can be made on the basis of any relevant demographic variable, such as age, sex, life-cycle stage (single, married, with children etc.) and occupation. Even education, race, religion and nationality can be the basis for demographic segmentation. Marketers generally do multi-variable demographic segmentation.

The following table illustrates the use of demographic variables:

Variable	*Typical Break-up*
Age	Below 6 6-12 Teenage (13-19) 20-30 (Youngsters) 30-35 (Adults) 36-46 (Middle-aged) 47-60

Variable	*Typical Break-up*
	60 plus (Senior citizens) 70 plus (Old)
Sex	Male, Female
Family Size	1-2 members 3-4 members 5 and above
Family Life Cycle (FLC)	Young, single Young, married, no children Young, married, children Young, married, older children, Old couple
Income	Below ₹ 10,000 10,000-20,000 20,000-30,000 30,000-40,000 Above 40,000
Occupation	Professional (MBA, CA, ICWA) Technical (B.E., B.Tech, B.Pharm.) Government Servant Businessmen Farmers Operatives Housewives Unemployed Retired/Pensioner
Education	SSC and less 12th/HSC Graduate Post-Graduate Doctoral and above
Religion	Hindu, Muslim, Parsi, Sikh, Christian, Buddhist, Neo-Buddist
Nationality	Indian, Foreigner

❖ Family Life-Cycle

Concept of Family Life-Cycle: People go through several phases in their lives. Family Life-Cycle (FLC) refers to the series of life stages through which individuals proceed over a period of time.

In other words, FLC describes the process of family formation and dissolution.

To illustrate, a young man or woman marry to form a family, in which children are born and live with the family till they grow up and later move out. At last, the couple grows old and fends for itself. Each life-cycle stage differs from previous stages in terms of (*a*) structure, (*b*) financial position, (*c*) consumption pattern and (d) product need and preferences.

❖ Traditional or Conventional FLC

The FLC is a progression of several stages.

1. *Young and single* bachelor stage. The career has just started. However, in the absence of burdens, they are free to spend as they wish. They tend to buy personal consumption items of food and clothing, are fun loving and buy entertainment, have time to be on vacations and tours, move about on bikes, mobikes and other two-wheelers, read novels and thrillers.

   They buy some basic utensils and furniture.
2. *Newly married couples* have household burdens and go through an expenditure phase in life. They generally buy consumer durables like furniture, wall paints, refrigerators, TVs etc.
3. *Young married with child* directs their income to bringing up the child. They buy toys, medicines, tonics, baby foods, formula milk etc.
4. *Older married with children* are fairly stable income-wise. They like food products, music, educational services and a wide variety of other products.
5. *Older married with dependent children* have a high income, but do rational purchases. There is replacement buying.
6. *Older, married with no children* become interested in self-education, saving, schemes, hobbies, luxury appliances, magazines, health products.
7. *Old, single, retired* people lead an economic life style. They are interested in health care and other services. They have budget constraints.

❖ Revised FLC Concept for the 90s

Conventionally, family was considered a single unit throughout the life time of an individual. However, this assumption is not true these days. There are families due to second marriages, with a legacy of children from previous marriages. There are deserted wives. There are divorcee. Several families are single parent family, where the parent could be either a father or a mother. Again, the ubiquitous working woman makes the traditional FLC model invalid.

Let us consider the following dimensions of Indian families in 90s:

Young, Married with Child and Dual Income: Here both the husband and the wife work and get two income cheques. The pace of the life is faster and there is less time for children and also for one another. The consumption pattern, therefore, shows preference for convenience goods like washing machines, grinder-mixers, rice cookers, grinding mill (gharghanti) etc. Women manage on two fronts — domestic chores and work. Husbands share the responsibilities of running the house to some extent. Instant foods, creches etc. appeal to such families. To compensate for the time babies miss with parents, there is a tendency to buy costly garments for kids, games for kids, prams etc.

Single Parent Families: The single parent family needs security and buys all the products that offer physical and psychological and financial securities — *e.g.,* burglar alarms, teddy bears, insurance, saving certificates etc. When the child grows, he may be put in a boarding school/public school.

Divorced: They buy money saving products, lease or rental housing, child care, time saving appliances, instant foods. They are short of cash.

Older People, Married or Single: They are also cash poor and health conscious. They need security. They also need recreation.

Middle-aged: They buy childrens' lessons (dance, music), dental care, furniture, autos, houses, dining out.

If there are no children, they are interested in luxuries, travels, gift products etc. Their cash position is good.

SEGMENTATION STRATEGY ON THE BASIS OF FLC

Product	*Segment*
(*i*) Cosmetics	Young single and young married women who are cash rich are a potential segment for beauty products like face creams, moisturisers, compacts, foundation make-up etc. Middle-aged families need facials, sauna baths and such related products.
(*ii*) Vacations	Newly married couples are sold vacations at the time of marriage in the form of honeymoon packages. Middle-aged couples with no responsibility of children are the most attractive segment to sell vacations in the form of packaged tours. They are cash rich and free from encumbrances.
(*iii*) Housing	Young, married with children need starter housing. Middle-aged couples need housing — 2 bedroom flats etc.
(*iv*) Education	Bachelors need liberal and professional education. They are career minded. They can be sold courses like private secretary, computers, etc. Middle-aged with children buy education for their children — home tuitions, coaching classes, public schools etc. They buy education for self also to improve their career — *e.g.*, distance education programme of IGNOU.

❖ Psychographic Segmentation

This term was first coined by Emanuel Demby, a marketing researcher some 30 years ago. His definition of psychographics is: the use of psychological, sociological and anthropological factors, self-concept and life style to determine how the market is segmented by the propensity of groups within the market — and their reasons — to make particular decision about a product, person, or ideology. "Psychographics has come a long way since then."

Psychographic segmentation, either singly or in combination with demographic segmentation, is widely used these days, dividing the buyers on the basis of their social class, life-style and/ or personality traits. The point to be appreciated is that people of the same demographic groups are very much different in their psychographic profiles, *e.g.*, young women show different psychographic characteristics.

Social class: In psychographic segmentation, buyers are divided on the basis of their social class, life style and/or personality traits.

Many companies design their product offerings for different social classes, *e.g.*, lower class, middle class or upper class. They build into their product those features that appeal to these social classes.

❖ Life Style Segmentation

Life style segmentation forms the basis of life style advertising. Life style is a mode of living and helps us to understand those who are in the market in terms of their behaviour.

The products which are often sold by this approach are cars, women's clothing, cigarettes, alcoholic beverages, cosmetics and furnitures. An automobile marketer can make a small family car emphasising safety, compactness and economy and a car-freak for sports minded individuals who love maneuverability.

To use this segmentation, data are first collected for developing a profile of the consumer. One such approach is to make use of data concerned with three major characteristics — Activities, Interests and Opinions (called AIO inventories). This is in addition to demographic characteristics.

Consider the following example:

Activities	*Interests*	*Opinions*	*Demographics*
Work Likings, hobbies Recreation Entertainment Shopping	Job Home Food Media Community	Culture Social issues Politics Education	Age Education Income Occupation Family size Life-Cycle Geography

The researcher makes the consumer respond to a number of AIO statements, and then uses statistical techniques to group consumers into similar categories. The grouping facilitates techniques to group consumers into similar categories. The grouping facilitates marketer's job of composing relevant profiles of users/non-users.

For example, the user of a lipstick can be described as:

"Younger, better educated, working woman who is appearance conscious, cosmopolitan and future-oriented."

Thus the marketer gets valuable input for media selection and advertising content. In addition, we can identify likely uses of related products — the products which are consistent with this life style.

❖ Personality

Marketers have identified personality variables to segment the market. Motor-cycle buyers can be identified as "independent, impulsive, macho, ready to change, confident people." Charms cigarettes are smoked by young people who love the spirit of freedom. Lipsticks are for young, out-going, beauty-conscious women. Other products which cater to personality traits are liquor and insurance. The marketers try to adjust the brand's personality to the personality traits of buyers for whom it is meant. Consumers of different brands are subjected personal preference tests to measure their different needs and the differences in personality traits are recorded.

Personality characteristics, especially the self-image which ideally should correspond to the brand image, are the basis of advertising appeals made to certain types of personality. Other personality characteristics used are changeability, adaptability, thriftness, prestige-consciousness, self-confidence, masculinity, conservativeness and sentimentalism.

Since it is difficult to reach targets on the basis of traits like sociability, self-reliance or assertiveness, the classifications based on slots as given above become useful.

Behavioural Segmentation: In behavioural segmentation, buyers are divided into groups on the basis of benefits sought from the product, user status, usage rate, loyalty status, attitude and readiness to use state.

❖ Benefit Segmentation

Here the market is segmented on the basis of the benefits people seek from the product, *e.g.*, lowest price, durability, use on special occasions. Benefit segmentation of toothpastes can be done on the basis a flavour, price, product appearance, brightness of teeth and decay prevention. Forhans is thus for healthy gums, Colgate gives suraksha chakra, and Close-Up fresh breath. Naturally, Close-Up is a craze with young people who like togetherness. In other words, a benefit chosen is a pointer to their demographic characteristic. The benefit segmentation thus requires identification of major benefits which people look for, the kinds of people who look for such benefits and the major brands which offer such benefits. This approach is direct and customer oriented.

Demographic variables correlate positively with purchase behaviour, *e.g.*, income and luxury products. As the market matures, all brands are at the same level of performance and minor benefits distinguish them. Psychographic variables for consumer products offer more promise. The other two variables for segmentation are user rate (light drinker of beer, heavy drinker of coffee) and brand loyalty.

The following table gives Benefit Segmentation of the Toothpaste Market:

Benefit sought	*Demographic characteristic*	*Behavioural characteristic*	*Psychographic characteristic*	*Favoured Brand*
Low Price	Males	Heavy users	Price-conscious Independent	Babool
Decay prevention	Big families	Heavy users	Traditional Health-conscious	Pepsodent
Brightness of teeth	Teenagers Youngsters	Smokers	Outgoing Fun-loving Active	Colgate, Promise
Good Flavour	Children	Mint lovers	Self-involvement	Colgate
Mouthwash	Youngsters Teenagers	Want intimacy and togetherness	Self-involvement	Close-Up Gel
Gentler Toothpaste	Children between 2½ to 7½ years	Loves to taste	Fun Dependent on mother for good habits	Just For Kids

(Adapted from Russel J. Haley, *Journal of Marketing*, July, '63)

Occasions: Buyers can be classified on the basis of the occasion on which they use the product, *e.g.*, talcum powder is used after a bath, after a shave or before moving out for work. Thus a certain brand can be promoted as "something that completes your bath." Occasion segmentation can expand product usage. Formerly, thermos flask were used only to carry tea/coffee to in-patients of hospitals. They are now promoted as picnic companions, office companions, lunch and dinner companions.

User Status: Every product is used by some and not used by some others. The users and non-users are important for the company. Non-users can be the users of competitive products. There can be ex-users for a product. First time users have just started using the product. Many in the target group are potential users — all S.Y.B.Com. students who opt for optional Advertising paper are potential users of this text-book. Marketers are interested in converting non-users into users. Potential users and regular users require different marketing approaches.

Usage Rate: For beverages and liquors, buyers are classified into segments like heavy users, medium users and light users. Heavy users account for volume. Many companies target their marketing effort at this segment. The heavy users have their own profile in terms of demographic, psychographic and media habits.

Loyalty Status: Brand loyalty status is also the basis for segmentation. Hard-core loyalty means constant brand loyalty over a period of time. Soft-core loyalty means loyalty divided over two or three brands. Brand-switchers change their loyalty often. They are non-loyal. Shifting loyals shift from one brand to another, say from *A* to *B*.

In India, razor blades market toothpastes market and to some extent, toilet soaps market are highly brand-loyal. It is difficult to gain market share for new companies. The entry in this market for newcomers is difficult.

A company can make an analysis of its brand-loyal customers to determine its target market. For instance, Colgate buyers are more middle-class, larger families who are health conscious. The study of soft core loyalty gives an indication to the nature of competition. Possibly, Colgate find that Colgate buyers also use Promise. By making use of direct comparison advertising. Colgate can improve its position. Brand shifters indicate our own marketing weaknesses. Non-loyals can be put on our brand by winning them.

Brand loyal purchases may be due to other variables like price, habit, indifference or non-availability of other brands. It should, therefore, be carefully studied.

Buyer Readiness Stage: People at a given point of time are in different stages of readiness to buy a product. They are either totally unaware or aware. Some are informed and some interested. There are some who have a desire to buy or some who intend to buy. The quantum of these groups determines the marketing programme. To create an awareness of cancer is the first step in advertising before people can come forward for a check-up. Later cancer check results are so dramatised that more people desire to have them. Infrastructure is created to handle the motivated individuals for check-ups. In other words, the marketing programme is tailored to the distribution pattern which changes depending upon the readiness of buyers.

❖ Attitude

There are several attitude classes of buyers — enthusiastic, positive, neutral, negative and hostile. Vast reminders work for enthusiastic people. Positive attitudes are reinforced. Neutral people are carefully converted. Negatively inclined and hostile. people are difficult to tackle. The attitudes are co-related with demographic descriptions.

❖ Value-driven Segmentation of Kotler

Customers can be put into four value segments. *Specialised feature segment* of customers have high expectations of the product and expect the product to take care of their special requirements. They visit selective specialised outlets to get such products. Perhaps a branded product suits the specialised features segment well. *High service value* segment demands quality, quick and dependable service and technical support. Such a value group expects the distributors to be service-oriented. *Assortment value segment* expects a wide range of products, and from alternative channels. *Convenience and price value segment* settles for down-to-earth low-priced products which can be easily ordered or routine shopped from a variety of channels and at different price options.

❖ Identifying the Target Audience or Groups

The identification of the target audience is the process of sub-dividing the market on the basis of geographic, demographic, socio-economic, psychographic bases and the market conditions. The most common descriptions of the target audience are in terms of geographic, demographic and socio-economic terms, *e.g.*, our soap is meant for high income bracket people in Western India or our talcum powder is for urban women of cosmopolitan outlook who are on the move. However, these days mere demographic description is considered poor predictor of buyer behaviour, though it is the most common method of identifying the target audience. Of late, psychographic base is used to describe the personality traits, life style, self-image and other psychological variables of the target audience. In Mumbai, Market Research Advisory Services (MRAS) conducted a study of life styles of cigarette smokers in 1975, identifying distinct groups or clusters of customers. Wills Flakes Filter Kings and Four Square Kings are targeted at the same demographic audience. However, qualitative research of customers who were subjected to expressing reactions to 118 psychological statements showed a remarkable contrast between the tall personality of those who smoke Wills and those who smoke Four Square. The table gives illustration of how the Garden Saree buying women are psychologically different from Garden Vareli dress material buying women. Consumer differences extend beyond demographics is the AIO's piece together the total market puzzle.

Table 9.1

COMPARISON OF GARDEN SAREE WOMEN AND GARDEN VARELI DRESS MATERIAL WOMAN

Garden Saree Woman	*Garden Vareli Dress Material Woman*
Older	Younger
Married	Universal, unpredictable
Softer, quieter, intensely feminine	Venturesome
Grace and dignity	Exotic
Dreamer	—

Haley suggest a benefit sought as a useful base for identifying a target audience. It cuts across all other bases. The example of toothpaste users illustrates this. Toothpaste market has four identifiable segments, *e.g.*, one concerned particularly with tooth decay prevention, one with brightness of teeth, one with flavour.

Targeting makes the marketing mix relevant and effective. The product matches consumer profile. The promotional programmes remains in tune with consumer willingness to receive, assimilate and react positively to communication. It is a recognition of the fact that the market is not a single, cohesive unit but it is seething, desperate, pulsating, antagonistic, infinitely varied sea of differing human beings — everyone of them as distinct from the others as fingerprints; everyone of them living in circumstances different in countless ways from those in which everyone of them is living.

In a country of India's diversity, identifying target audience for a product is a formidable task. To optimise targeting, the potential of the market segment, its need, its effective demand and its accessibility must be considered.

APPENDIX

TABLE: TARGET GROUPS FOR DIFFERENT PRODUCTS

Brand Name of the Product	*Company*	*Targeted as*
Fair and Lovely Lotion	Hindustan Lever	Skin care conscious, urban woman.
Liril Cologne Lime	Hindustan Lever	Younger, modern, urban consumer.
Lacto Calamine	Duphar Interfran Ltd.	Skin care lotion for young women between 16 and 25.
Perfect Skin Natural Make-up	Cadila	Women in the age group of 28-40 years who are in the habit of using face masks.
Hot Shot Macro	Photophone Industries	Consumers who are looking for a moderately priced indigenous camera. It is also aimed at a person who owns or uses a camera.
Softel Ice Cream Maker	Convenience Marketing (P) Ltd.	Urban families, especially those with children. The consumer already owns durables such as refrigerators and mixies.
Evita Soap	Godrej Soaps	Women who care about their complexion.
Kwality Sundae (Fruti Punch, Thandai Badam and Chikki Choc)	Kwality	The product is directed towards people who understand what the product is. It is for upmarket kids and working people who have access to ice cream parlours.
Khana Pani Food Container cum Thermos Flask	Jaydeep Delhi	The product is directed at office goers and at the family or individuals when out on a picnic or journey.
Royale Range of Titan Watches	Tata	The older rich.
Jewellery Watches	Tata	Men and women with a strong status and snob value.
Spectra Two Tone Watches	Tata	Watches fit both in office situation and evening leisure activities.

Brand Name of the Product	*Company*	*Targeted as*
Bajaj Sunny Bike — 50 cc	Bajaj	16-18 years old, first time buyer who cannot afford the 100 cc bike.
Wilman Shave Foam	Wilman	₹ 3,500 plus segment.
Wilman Shaving Cream	Wilman	₹ 1,500 plus segment.
EX Accountancy Software	TCS	Indian entrepreneur who have not graduated to using computers for accounting because the hardware and software seemed just too complex.
A.M/P.M. Anti-plaque Mouth Wash	Elder Pharmaceuticals	Consumer over 18 with a monthly household income of ₹ 5,000 plus.
Garden Sarees	Garden Silk Mills	Older normally married women who are softer, quieter, intensely feminine, more vulnerable. She dreams. Her grace and dignity are her mystery.
Garden Vareli (Dress Material)	Garden Silk Mills	Younger women whose aspirations are different from the saree woman. She has a streak of unusual, the unpredictable running through her. She's always ready to venture to new territories, do exotic things.
Magi Cook Ovens	Expo Machiner Ltd., Delhi	Aimed at husbands; uses emotion to sell the concept.
Kandla Free Trade Zone	KAFTZ, Kandla	NRIs, exporters, multinationals.
Aquel Basin Mixer	Velmor Home Decor	Very well-to-do, status conscious people and five-star establishments.
Prime Life Sunflower Oil	ITC	Health conscious people who are in the prime of life.
Snuggy Disposable Diapers	Transelektra	Young women from upper income families. Working women.
Breast-Feeding Concept	Amul	Mothers and fathers of infants.

Brand Name of the Product	*Company*	*Targeted as*
LIC Mutual Fund	LIC	Adult 30 years plus, executives; businessman, self-employed.
Ariel Micro System	P & G	All housewives, household income of ₹ 7,500 plus, with at least school education.
Red Eveready Batteries	Union Carbide	Youth 15-35, with monthly household incomes of ₹ 2,500.
Ray Ban	Bausch and Lomb and Montari	People who consider glasses a basic part of wardrobe accessories. They make the effort of acquiring sunglasses from abroad. They are also directed towards those who use sunglasses of inferior quality without being aware of their harmful effects.
Aqura Range of Titan Watches	Tata	Psychographic niches where the design can resonate with the mood of the target segment — *the young and the young at heart.* They are for the privileged and the young.
Raga Range of Titan Watches	Tata	A fashion accessory for the up-market Indian woman to be worn to match her dress.

Focus:

Al Ries in his recent book *Focus* advocates selection of market segments and niches, rather than a broad 100 per cent market. People tend to be similar in their brand choices, but they also tend to be different. Leaders do not have a different brand to offer to such consumers. A company has to be prepared to sacrifice a segment of the market. A segment chosen can be a quality niche, price niche, safety niche, driving niche, home delivery niche etc. A company has to find a word to own in the mind. While sacrificing, we are defining our positioning sharply. IBM wanted to be a broad-based computer company, but PC business slipped out of this company because competitors with a narrow focus arrived on the scene. A full-line supplier is no longer a specialist. Health care institutions and educational institutions are so far generalists. They will have to learn to be specialist. An educational institute should focus on a single field of study and achieve world class excellence. Law firms will also need to focus. Even celebrities are focused. Tom Peters is remembered for 'excellence,' Hammer for 're-engineering' Porter for 'competitiveness' Crosby for 'quality,' Stern for 'Economic Value Added (EVA), Barker for 'paradigm shift' and so on.

* * *

10 PRODUCT PLANNING

Planning is necessary to cope with the changing environment. Product planning consists of setting product objectives and strategies. Strategy, the end result of planning, helps a firm travel from where it is to where it desires to be. Strategies vest with the firm an advantage over competitors and are therefore, called *deliberate strategies*. Most strategies do not flow naturally from plans. Many experiments are conducted to see what what works out. The unworkable component is modified. Strategies may emerge through trial and error — they are called *emergent strategies*. Plans are used to implement these emergent strategies. Plans are an insurance against the uncertainties of the future. They are an aid to decision-making.

Organisational objectives have a hierarchy. There are a variety of objectives from corporate level to the departmental level. The following diagram illustrates this:

Environmental Scanning
↓
Corporate Planning
↓
Level I — Corporate Objectives
↓
Corporate Strategies

Level II	Production objectives	Marketing objectives	Other Departmental objectives
	↓	↓	↓
	Production strategies	Marketing strategies	Departmental strategies

Level III	Pricing objectives	Promotional objectives	Distribution objectives	Product objectives
	↓	↓	↓	↓
	Pricing strategies	Promotional strategies	Distribution strategies	Product strategies

❖ Objectives

In product planning, we are concerned with the product objectives. Objectives are set for growth in terms of sales revenue and market share. Objectives are also set for profitability. These two are difficult to optimize simultaneously. Increased market share may mean increased promotion, personal selling and reduced prices. When expenditure increases, profit margins come down. There is a trade-off here. Objectives are maximized or minimized subject to some constraints. The objective that is to be maximized is *primary* objective. The constraining adjective is the *secondary* objective. Another product objective could be the cash flow. A number of non-economic and non-quantitative objectives can be followed e.g. quality objective, satisfaction objective, maintaining brand equity. There is, however, a link between these enabling objectives and the economic objectives.

❖ Strategic alternatives

The second step in product planning is to develop the marketing strategy either gain sales or market share or to improve process. Ansoft's matrix provides us four choices to gain sales or market share.

		Present	New
Market	Present	Market Penetration	Product Development
	New	Market Development	Diversification

Product

Fig. 10.1 Product-Market Relationship Matrix

1. Market Penetration: We can gain more sales by improving over market share in existing markets, perhaps by more advertising. There can be line extensions and new applications or new usage occasions.

2. Market Development: We can gain more sales by introducing our current products into new markets – either new segments or new geographic areas. Japanese cars have entered the European and American markets.

3. Product Development: We can gain more sales by developing new products and introducing them in our existing markets.

4. Diversification: We can gain more sales by introducing new products in new markets, e.g. a consumer electronic company enters oil drilling business.

The other strategic alternative is to improve profits. The alternative strategies are to decrease the inputs or increase the outputs.

The decrease in inputs can be brought about by cost reduction or by better utilization of assets at the disposal of the product manager.

The increase in outputs is done by revising prices or by improving the sales mix. The sales mix must be analysed in terms of the contribution of individual products to overall profits keeping in mind the 80 : 20 rule where 20 per cent item contribute 80 per cent to profits. The same analysis can be extended to customers too.

ROI or return on investment is given by the following formula:

$$\text{ROI} = \frac{(\text{Unit sales}) \times (\text{Margins})}{\text{Investment}}$$

We can have better ROI by having better productivity. We can keep the unit sales constant but improve their margins or increase the unit sales. Both of these can be combined.

❖ Positioning Strategy

There are three components of a positioning strategy — whom we are targeting as customers, who our competitors are and how we differentiate our offering.

Positioning statement is a declaration of the position our product will occupy in the mind of our target customers. Complan is the complete food for growing children. This positioning is targeted to a specific segment.

Brand position should assert the advantage of the brand over the competitive brand. This distinction based on a competitive advantage must appeal to the customer and must distinguish the brand from the competitive brands. Our brand can be superior to a competitive brand or at least must be close to it. Tata Indica has the approximate outside dimension of the Maruti Zen, inside space of HM's Ambassador, the economy of a diesel vehicle and is priced around, that of Maruti 800. Its base-line 'more-car-per-car' is Indica's chief weapon to take on the competitors.

Positioning involves some prioritization of the competitors. We learn about competitors by doing situational analysis. A market leader has to defend his brand. A market follower can take offensive stance while targeting the leader. Weak followers try to bypass the leader and seek market niches. Positioning does not require a head-on collision with the leading competing brand. This is quite risky. It is better to manoeuver around the leader's position.

The differential advantage that is communicated to the target customers is often called product positioning. This differentiation can be based either on price or product-service features. Product-service features could include functional as well as psychological benefits.

Several themes could be identified for positioning. They all are examined carefully in terms of meaning, feasibility, competitive strength and furtherance of the product objective. The best positioning is adopted and promotional programmes and marketing programmes to support it are implemented.

Positioning ultimately gives us the *core strategy* or *value proposition.*

A low-cost airline may have the following value proposition:

To provide the travellers the most reasonably priced air transportation with fun-filled enjoyable ambience.

It clearly positions the above airline on the element of price and fun. It sacrifices all frills, catering and faster non-stop travel.

Cost-price strategy believes in low-price differentiation. There is emphasis on volume. All products cannot be volume-driven. Some of them are. There should be focus on availing of advantages of scale. There should be exploitation of efficiencies resulting from learning curve. Over-heads must be controlled tightly.

The component costs can come down to bring the product cost down. *e.g.,* computers and ACs in India.

Wal Mart followed lost cost strategy. Its philosophy is "pile them high, sell them cheap."

Customers tastes can shift thus making low-cost alternative obsolete *e.g.*, old video games. Competitors can catch up, robbing you of the low-cost advantage. We should assess the size of the price-sensitive segment correctly to spot a low cost opportunity.

Non-price differentiation considers product characteristic either tangible or intangible. There is total product concept analysis where there are generic, expected, augmented and potential product components. All functional aspects of the product are generic. *e.g.*, speed of a car, fuel efficiency, engine cc and so on. Expected product gives additional benefits, say warranties, after-sales-service etc. Augmented product really comes to the level of differentiation — all those benefits beyond expectations. Potential product benefits are future benefits or features. A hotel providing free room to a dissatisfied customer is an example of potential product. The following diagram illustrates the total product concept:

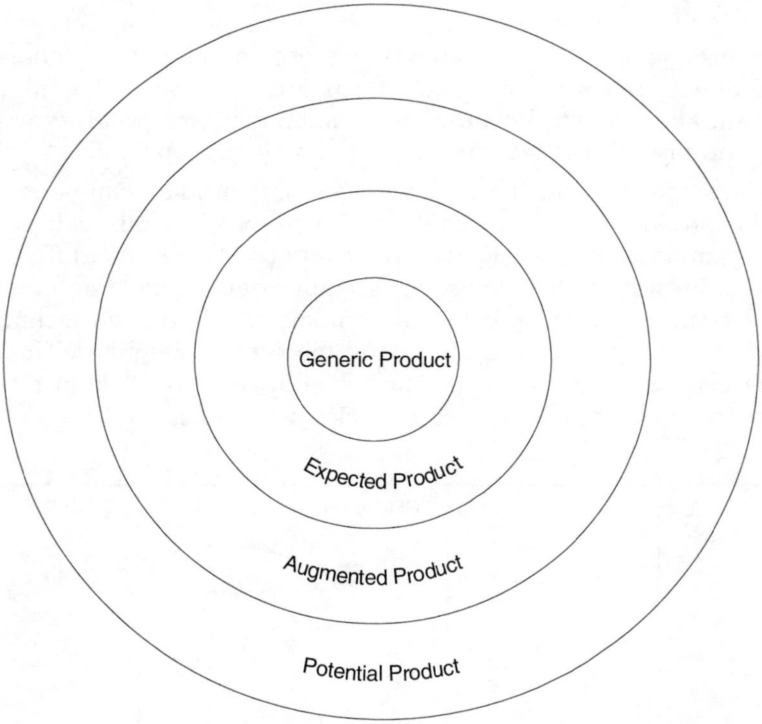

Fig. 10.2 The Total Product Concept

The importance of going beyond usual expectations for providing differential advantage must not be missed. An organization should ask the basic question 'what business am I in?' to focus on the benefits the customers are buying. The differentiation is obtained on the basis of quality, status and image, branding, convenience and distribution channels. A PC becomes a quality product when there is Intel inside. Mercedes has status and image. Branding gives value add-ons e.g. McDonald's and fast food. Customer convenience differentiates a product. *e.g.*, a bank provides cash at home. Courier packages can be tracked and it is the channel advantage.

The differential advantages may not be actual physical product differences. There could be differences based on perceptions. Perceptual mapping is done to appreciate this.

All differentiation can be copied. That is the risk. An organisation has to innovate constantly.

❖ Product Strategy over the Life-Cycle

Each product class as a whole and an individual brand passes through several stages from its birth to its final eclipse.

When the new product is introduced in the market, the sales pick up slowly and the product comes to the notice of the customer due to heavy promotion. Then it is well-distributed. This is called the introductory stage.

Later comes the growth stage, where the sales rise quickly. The cost of distribution and promotion is spread over a large volume and so the cost per unit is low. It is a critical stage from the viewpoint of the product.

The maturity stage stabilises the sales. Competition enters the scene. Due to this sales may be pushed down, unless promotional efforts are increased. The sales, in fact reach a plateau, or a saturation point. Because of additional promotional expenses, profits may decline. Those who are market leaders may need no extra push.

The maturity stage is longer than other stages. The product can be revived at this stage by improving the product and by promotion. A new product mix can be thought of. The product may be eliminated or redesigned. A revival of PLC (Product Life Cycle) extends the life of the product, by starting the stages once again from introduction onwards. The decline stage could be a result of changing consumption patterns, improved technology, availability of better substitutes. The profits take a dip, and the product might die. It can be eliminated prior to that. Or else, its price has to be slashed. But it is also ticklish to reduce the price. When extra promotional effort is needed to jack up the sales.

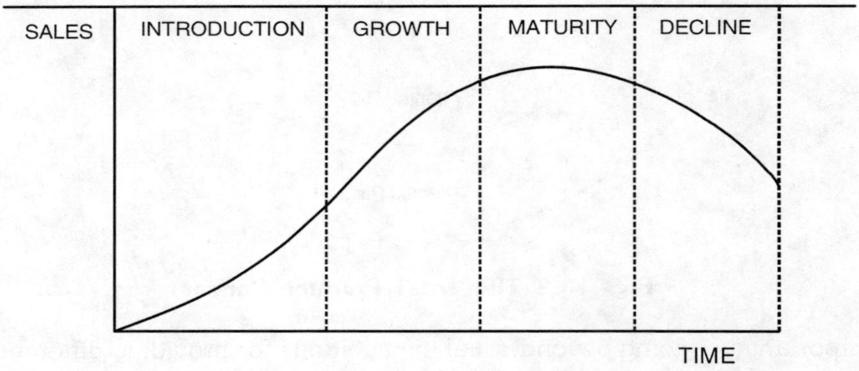

Fig. 10.3 Product Life-Cycle

❖ Revival of PLC

The following considerations are uppermost:

(*a*) Improve product quality.

(*b*) Add new product features, generating additional benefits.

(*c*) Market penetration in new segments.

(*d*) Incentives to trade channels and straightening increasing the channels.

(*e*) Improve advertising/sales efforts.

In a nutshell, innovation is the answer to the revival of PLC. Ultimately, however, if necessary, a product is eliminated. It is, sometimes, difficult for the executives associated with the product for a long time to abandon it due to emotional reasons. This is a pitfall to be avoided.

The PLC for some products, say consumer electronics items and fashionwear, is very short, and for some other products like consumer durables, it is very long. Some products like personal computers (PCs) might have reached a maturity stage in the US, but in India, they are at the introductory and growth stages. The readers should appreciate that the level of advertising effort is related to the stage of PLC of a particular product.

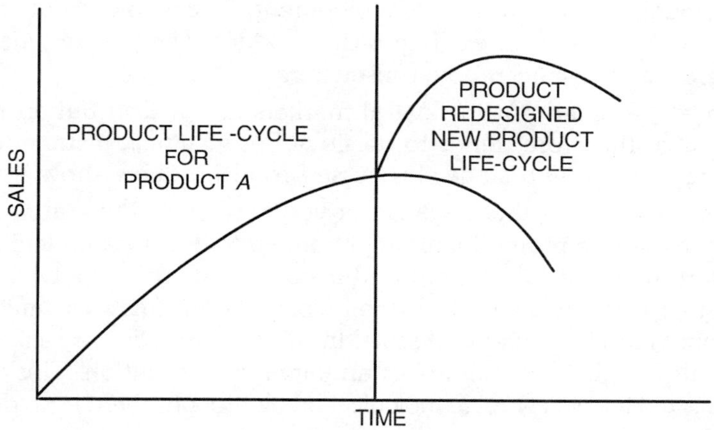

Fig. 10.4

❖ Changing Markets

It is necessary to appreciate that we cannot have a constant market. Markets do change. There are very few markets which are the same today as they were ten years ago. Consumer attitudes, competitive pressures, socio-economic changes all make it vital for each company to keep in its toes. This means that it is certain that once a product is born, it matures and eventually dies. To explain this, a simple product life-cycle technique has been invented. But in spite of this, there are countless examples of 50-year-old or even 100-year-old products or brands growing stronger and stronger each year. Are they not subject to product life-cycle? Does Lux soap have a perpetual life? However, product life-cycle approach and an appreciation of changing markets make us anticipate the changes and respond to them.

No market, in fact, in the world has remained the same as it was ten years ago and will remain the same ten years hence. Until a few years ago, a car was characterised by the image of a car as *an object of aspiration or achievement*. Now, for most people, it is a *functional object*, which has become common place. We have to appreciate such changes also along with the product life-cycle.

Though products have a life-cycle and passes through different stages, how do we account for certain perennial brands like Lux, Vicks, Dettol, Cadburys which are not subject to the dictates of PLC? For understanding this, we have to understand the application of PLC to product category satisfying a basic need, *e.g.*, music, product from *e.g.*, LP, audio cassette, CD and the brand within each product category. Out of these three, product categories are least subject to PLC — our need for music has remained unchanged though the product forms/symbols satisfying this need have ranged from court musicians to compact discs. PLC is more relevant for each product form. Brands, however, can be kept contemporary by a trade-off between continuity and change. Some elements of brand mix can be left untouched, and some have to be changed. Technology may demand the change in the product form of the brand. A brand that adapts to change by changing its form escaped the vagaries of PLC.

We shall examine now in brief, the characteristics of each stage of the PLC and the marketing strategies adopted at each stage.

❖ Introduction Stage

This is the stage when a new product is launched in the market on a full-scale. The new product has gone through all the stages of development. The whole product may be new or it may be an improved version of an existing basic product. The product may be new in the market, but may be an established product elsewhere.

The product must be rolled out in several markets and a distribution network is to be set up. The sales growth, therefore, tends to be slow. For instance, instant coffee took many years before it entered the growth stage. Processed food products show a slow growth.

The profits at this stage are either negative or very low, since there are heavy distribution and promotional expenses. The promotional programme attempts to stimulate *primary* demand rather than *secondary* demand. The target audience consists of those who are the readiest to buy. Prices are higher since heavy costs are to be covered on small volumes and technology of production still cannot reap the benefits of scale. In short, an introductory stage is characterised by high prices, low sales, high costs, net losses and limited distribution. This stage is the most expensive as well as risky. However, for technological breakthroughs there is no direct competition.

❖ Product Marketing Strategies at Introductory Phase

While launching a new product, marketing mix for each variable can be set at a high or a low level. If we examine price and promotion variable of the marketing mix, there are four strategies available.

PRICE \ PROMOTION	H	L
H	RAPID SKIMMING	SLOW SKIMMING
L	RAPID PENETRATION	SLOW PENETRATION

Rapid Skimming Strategy: The product is launched at a high price. Even the promotional effort is very heavy. The firm is inclined to charge higher prices to recover high costs and still get some profit — as much as possible. Heavy promotion is needed to allow offtake of the product even at higher prices, considering the merits of the product. The product penetrates the market due to high promotion. This strategy is successful if there are people who are unaware of the product, become aware of it and buy it at a price demanded. There is a risk of competition and so the firm has to build up brand preference.

Slow Skimming Strategy: Here the product is launched at a high price. But surprisingly the promotional effort is kept low. The higher price yields better profit per unit sold. The lower promotional cost keeps the marketing expenses in check. It gives an additional boost to profits. The limited market size in which there is awareness about the product and an unwillingness to offer price demanded makes sense for this adoption of this strategy. It is perceived that potential competition will not be around right now.

Rapid Penetration Strategy: The product is offered at the lowest possible price. At the same time, promotion is kept at a high level. The objective is to bring about a very fast market penetration. The end result is a larger market share. This strategy is suitable for large markets which are highly competitive. The market is price-sensitive. The company has enough production experience and production costs will show a downward trend as the production rises.

Slow Penetration Strategy: Both the price and the promotion are kept low at the time of launch. Lower prices lead to fast market acceptance of the product. The lower promotional costs keep up healthy profits. Though it is a price-elastic market, it is not promotion elastic. In a large market with high awareness level and price sensitiveness, this strategy makes sense. There is some potential of competition.

An *inventor* develops the product for the first time. He patents it. A *product pioneer* develops its working model. A *market pioneer* is the first to sell the new product category. A pioneer chooses a strategy that goes well with the proposed product's positioning. Market pioneers will be market leaders if they play their cards well. He should select the best markets to enter, by rating each market carefully. He has to decide how different products should be introduced in different markets. He can swap the products later in different segments. First, he is the sole supplier of the product — say, photo credit card of Standard Chartered Bank introduced in India in 1995. The competitors will take some time to build up the infrastructure to introduce a competitive product. It is a stage of competitive penetration. Standard Chartered believes that it has atleast a lead time of 10 months at its disposal. In other words, competition will enter the fray after 10 months. Competition may charge lower prices, compelling a reduction in the price of the leader's product. The market growth stages sees over capacity, preventing the entry of further competition and stabilising the share of all the players. At last, the *commodification* may begin, when the product is viewed as a commodity, with no differentiating features. Throughout the *competitive cycle,* we have to design new strategies of marketing and pricing.

❖ Pioneer Advantage

Pioneers of new products do have an advantage over the followers. The consumers' first-brush was with the pioneer's brand, and once thus satisfied, favour it later. The pioneering brand sets parameters of a product class. Mostly the brand is placed in the middle of the market and has more users. As a result, there are certain technical advantages to a pioneer — economies of scale, leadership of the brand, ownership of assets. All these are entry barriers. However, pioneer advantage can be assailed by late entrants. The late entrants can take advantage of the pioneer's flawed marketing. A pioneer should always be alert to the new market entrants.

❖ Growth Stage

This is a market acceptance stage. Both sales and profit rise up in this stage. The rise is very rapid. The early adopters start buying the product. Even middle majority start buying the product. New competitors appear on the scene lured by the profit potential. The marketer introduces the new product features. Distribution is strengthened. The promotion becomes brand based, as against product based. The prices may come down slightly or may remain stable. The promotional budget is either maintained at the same level or is increased slightly. As sales rise rapidly, the ratio between sales to promotion expenses declines. Profits increase as promotional costs are distributed over a large volume and the production costs dip down faster than price declines owing to experience-curve effect.

The rate of growth, however, slows down. The deceleration in rate of growth must be anticipated, to and strategies must be formulated to overcome it.

❖ Product Marketing Strategies at Growth Stage

The overall objective is to sustain the growth rate. The strategies have the following elements:

(*i*) Product quality is improved. New features are incorporated. The style is improved.

(*ii*) New models are introduced. *Flanker* products are introduced.

(*iii*) New market segments are tapped.

(*iv*) Brand building promotion is resorted to.

(*v*) Prices may be lowered to lure the next layer of price-conscious buyers.

At the growth stage, the firm has to trade-off between the High market share and High current profit. By strengthening promotion and products, it can secure its dominant position. It foregoes the maximum profits it can get right now to secure greater profits further ahead.

❖ Maturity Stage

As we have observed, the sales growth slows down at some point. The sales continue to increase but at a decreasing rate. The product then enters a stage of relative maturity.

This is the longest stage in the life of a product. It is a very challenging stage. As most of the products are at maturity stage, most of the marketing management addresses itself to the mature product.

Even during the maturity stage, there are three distinct phases. The very first phase of maturity shows that the sales growth is declining. The laggards are the ones who buy the product. In the second phase, sales level off as all potential customers have tried the product. Further demand originates from the growth in population or replacement demand. In the third phase of maturity, absolute level of sales falls off and consumers adopt other products.

Over capacity in the industry is a salient feature of this stage. This result from the decreasing level of sales growth. Competition, therefore, becomes cut-throat. Many competitors resort to niche marketing. The prices are reduced frequently and price competition becomes severe. Promotional effort is increased to maintain trade channels and retain the shelf-space. Sales promotion shows an increasing trend. R&D budgets are increased to bring about product improvements and develop flanker products. The profits of both manufacturers and the trader decline. A shake-out throws out marginal producers. The competent and well-entrenched competitors survive the shake-out. Giant firms selling larger volumes survive, since their profits come out of larger volumes and lower costs. Other surviving firms are market nichers who serve small specialised segments at a premium price. The choice, therefore, at maturity stage is between being a leader selling large volumes to earn profits through volumes and lower costs or being a nicher selling to specialised segment to earn profits through a high margin.

❖ Product Marketing Strategies at the Maturity Stage

Several companies think of giving up the product once it turns weaker, committing resources in this way to either more profitable products or new products. Still what is needed is to explore the untapped potential of the old product. Industries like automobiles, TVs, cameras and watches were considered to be mature elsewhere, but the Japanese gave them a new lease of life. They added value to these products and created new customers. Ovaltine has been revived in terms of sales several times over. There are strategies of market modification, product modification and marketing mix modification available to the marketers.

Market Modification: The sales volume is contributed by the number of users and by the consumption per user. A market can be expanded by increasing either or both of these contributory factors. The users can be increased by converting non-users to users, or by entering new market segments or by attracting the customers of the competitors. The consumption can be increased by getting customers to use the product more frequently or by getting customers to use more quantity of the product on each use occasion or by discovering new applications for a product.

❖ Product Modification

A product can be modified to stimulate sales at the maturity stage.

Quality Improvement: Tries to increase a product's functional performance — its speed, taste, durability, reliability etc. New and improved version of a soap, TV, car etc. are introduced to give new life to the product. The ads speak of a bigger or better or stronger product. The buyers have to accept the claim of improved quality. Then, they will pay for this value addition.

Feature Improvement: Here new features are added to the product, *e.g.*, additives, new ingredients, additional weight, accessories, size etc. The aim is to make a more versatile product or a more convenient product. Sometimes, new features improve the safety factor. Introduction of new features is taken as a sign of an innovative company. These features are added and if necessary can be dropped later. They can be made optional to the buyer. A major drawback is the ease with which new features can be copied by others. We should try to be pioneers in introducing new features to get permanent gain.

Style Improvement: Here the product is improved aesthetically, *e.g.*, new car models, colour and texture variations of household products, package re-styling. This gives a unique identity to the product. It is, however, difficult to predict which style variation will appeal to the people. People may still want the old style. *e.g.*, the curvy bottle of Coke and so its discontinuation may result in loss of sales.

❖ Marketing Mix Modification

Sales can be stimulated by manipulating one or more elements of the marketing mix. The following checklist gives an idea of how each element is questioned for modification:

Advertising	:	Should we increase the ad budget? Should we change the theme? Should we modify the copy? What changes can be made in media mix? Is it necessary to change media planning?
Sale Promotion (SP)	:	Should it be increased? At what level? (At the level of consumers, dealers or sales people).
Personal Selling	:	Should we strengthen the sales force? Should we change its orientation? Are any changes needed in territory allocation? What changes can

		be made in sales incentives? Can we improve planning of sales calls?
Price	:	Should prices be cut? How? Should prices be raised?
Distribution	:	How can we improve the display? How can we get more shelf space? Should there be more penetration in our distribution? Can the product be put into new channels?
Services	:	How can we improve delivery? What after sales and technical services can be given to the customers? Can credit be extended?

It is debatable which element needs modification at the maturity stage advertising or sales promotion (SP). According to some, SP will be more effective as consumers have already reached an equilibrium and need financial incentives given by SP rather than psychological persuasion of advertising. SP budget is improved for mature products. However, each brand is an asset, and SP needs advertising support. Ad expenses are capital investments, and yield long-term benefits. Marketers tend to use SP as its effects are quick in the short-term. Excessive SP, however, affects brand's long-term profit potential.

Marketing mix modification strategy is also amenable to copying by the competitors. As firms battle it out in the market place, there may be profit erosion for each firm.

❖ Decline Stage

Most of the products show a decline in sales ultimately, primarily because of a number of new products begin their own life-cycle, and replace the old products. The decline may come fast in the case of fashion products or consumer electronic goods or may be a slow process. Apart from technological advances, another reason for sales decline is a shift in consumer tastes. At this stage, some firms withdraw from the market, especially from small segments. Ad budgets are cut. Those who survive face the problem of profit crunch. Prices are cut which further decline the profit.

Ageing products do need careful handling. Mostly there is sentimental attachment. Sometimes, logical thinking results in the continuation of the product — the declining product contributes to the sales of other products. However, a weak product continued is always as costly proposition. It is not a question of merely accounting costs. It is a question of the weak product's management consuming a lot of precious executive time. Besides, there is less attention to the development of replacement products.

❖ Product Marketing Strategies during the Decline Stage

In order to deal with the ageing products, a company has to take a number of decisions. First and foremost, weak products must be identified systematically. The declining markets are given up on the basis of *exit barriers.* The lower exit barriers make it easier to leave the industry. The survivors tend to remain so as to lure the customers of the abandoning firms. The firm in a declining market can adopt investment strategy in which it either increases investment or maintains it. Alternatively the firm disinvests on a selective basis, first from smaller market segments. Simultaneously, investment in market niches is increased. In a harvesting strategy, investment is recovered as quickly as possible. There can be a total disinvestment by disposing of the assets. In India, in the electronic typewriter market, the portable electronic typewriter segment has shown sales growth, though elsewhere the PC has overtaken the electronic typewriter. Firms like Godrej have, therefore, strengthened their presence in portable ET market. Proctor and Gamble lies to re-stage their brands, rather than abandoning them. While dropping a product, it should be seen whether the product can be sold to a smaller firm to take advantage of the goodwill and the distribution network set up. If there are no buyers, it should be decided whether the product is to be dropped quickly or in a phased manner. Some stocks of spares must be maintained or else past customers will be stranded.

❖ Synopsis of the PLC Concept

The following table gives a quick *recap* of what we have already learnt about the PLC:

Characteristics	*Product Life-Cycle Stage*			
	Introduction	*Growth*	*Maturity*	*Decline*
Costs	High	Average	Low	Low
Sales	Low	Rising	Peak level	Declining
Profits	Negative or low	Rising	High	Declining
Competitors	Few	Increase	Stabilisation	Decline

The following table summarises the marketing strategies followed at each stage of the PLC.

Marketing Mix Element	*Product Life-Cycle Stage*			
	Introduction	*Growth*	*Maturity*	*Decline*
Product	Basic product	Improvements	Diversity of models, brands	Withdrawal of weak products. in a phased manner
Price	Skimming or penetrating policy	Penetrating policy. Lower prices	Competitive parity	Prices are cut
Distribution	Selective Few and Exclusive channels	Intensive	More intensive or broad-cast	Selective Unprofitable segments are left out.
Promotion	Awareness buildup. Heavy promotion to induce trials Emphasis on prestige	Promotion is reduced. Interest building promotion. Brand/value features Emphasis on features	Differentiating promotion. Budget increased. Brand/value Emphasis on price	Minimum Promotion Specialist Selling Emphasis on special applications

❖ Benefits of the PLC Concept

(*i*) PLC serves as a planning tool to the marketers. It allows a marketer a choice of strategies at different stages.

(*ii*) PLC is a control tool which allows a comparison of the launched product with previously launched products.

(*iii*) PLC is a forecasting tool which gives an idea of the likely sales growth of a product and its profitability. However, as there are variations in the duration of each stage, its usefulness as a forecasting tool is limited. Besides, there are several patterns of PLC.

❖ Limitations of the PLC Concept

It is difficult to pinpoint exactly at which stage the product is. The product sales might stabilise and we may think this to be a sign of maturity. However, it may turn out to be a temporary phenomenon and sales might show an upsurge again. There is every possibility of a change in the traditional PLC pattern. Sometimes, the pattern changes due to marketing strategies followed.

PLC is restricted to products and does not take into consideration the overall changes in the markets. It is necessary, therefore, to appreciate both the PLC and the market evolution stages.

❖ Market Evolution

Latent market is a stage where there is no product or service in existence to satisfy the hidden needs and wants. A market emerges after a product is launched by a pioneer. Later, others enter the market, leading to its growth. In a large market, several firms share a market. The new firms can also decide to cater to a market niche. When all major niches are covered by competitors, the growth slows down. At this stage, the market is mature. New product attributes are added to consolidate the firm's market position. There will be competitors who copy the new product's attributes. Market will again fragment. Thus, there is a swing between Market fragmentation and Market consolidation in a mature market. Competition leads to fragmentation and innovation leads to consolidation. When the new technology replaces the old, the market demand declines. It is the decline stage of the market. A marketer has to anticipate attributes that may become winners and are technically feasible. Technological and social forces influence the new attributes which emerge.

❖ Planned Obsolescence

As consumers, though we want new products, we would like to glide over newness in a slow and steady manner so that our habitual pattern is not unduly disturbed. Planned obsolescence is the marketer's attempt to achieve this. As a product policy, its objective is to outdate an existing product and create market for the replacement products. Planned obsolescence has several dimensions. It may be purely technical, *e.g.*, a jet engine made propeller engine obsolete. Sometimes, these technological advances though available are not introduced immediately. They are introduced only when the demand for the present model decreases. In other words, it is a case of postponed obsolescence. Many a time, a new model is just styled differently from the old model. It is a superficial change. It affects the consumers psychologically. They may think that using the old product is being out of fashion. This is style obsolescence. A style is a distinctive manner of presentation or construction. There are styles of writing, singing, clothing, furniture and dancing. The criticism against planned obsolescence is that it shortens the life of the products artificially, creating some sort of disutility.

❖ Fashion

Any style that is popularly accepted and bought by successive groups of people over a period of time becomes fashion. All styles are not fashionable. A fashionable style has wide acceptance. When a style becomes popular for a short time and is not based on any novel feature, it is called a fad. Basic styles remain as they are, but fashions change. Fashions are found in all societies.

Mostly, people are conformists. At the same time, they like to differ from others without offending the existing codes of behaviour. Fashion is a statement they make about themselves. Though there is an urge towards conformity, there is a genuine dislike for 100 per cent uniformity. Monotony generates a desire to change. Leisure helps a movement towards this change. Fashions satisfy recognition needs of the individuals.

Adoption of Fashion: It is a series of buying waves that arise when a given style becomes acceptable in one group, is adopted by the other group and then the third group and so on till finally it falls out of fashion. This wave-like movement is called a fashion cycle. Fashions trickle down through socio-economic classes; they move across the classes or trickle up the classes from lower classes.

Mostly, fashion-adoption is a trickle down. Designer garments are purchased by the elite from departmental stores and are later adopted by the middle classes. They finally move on the pavements for lower classes. Ethnic wear may show a trickle up process, where a Rajasthani outfit of tribals is accepted by the elite later on. However, it is the trickle-across which best summarises the fashion adoption process. Salwar-kameez are sold across the classes, but at each class level, the material, its quality and its price my be different. But the style is basically the same. Market conditions today are conducive for a trickle across adoption. Fashion marketing critics call it a dictatorial style of marketing where the designer calls the shots. However, designers never work in isolation and are influenced by many factors. They have to be creative within the established customs and any departure far from it is not taken kindly.

❖ Managing Brand Equity

There are references to brand equity in product and brand management literature. Brand equity, in simplest possible terms, is the value of a brand. Brand value management is a very important task for any product manager. Brand is as much an asset as any of the physical assets like plant and machinery, land and building, etc. There are many private label brands of retailers and they give tough competition to national brands. However, national brands survive in turbulent environments by improving their brand equity. Brands also face the competition from counterfeit products and pirated versions.

❖ Aaker's Approach to Brand Equity (1991)

Aaker calls brand equity a set of assets associated with the brand.

Which is this set of assets Aaker is referring to, which when associated with a brand lends it equity? Brand awareness, brand loyalty, perceived quality of the brand and brand associations are the four assets which brand managers create and enhance to build brand equity (Aaker, 1991). It is also necessary to realise that a brand is an intellectual property and so patents also form a brand asset. Besides, we cannot undermine the importance of the relationship between a Channel and a Brand. We shall consider these assets one by one.

1. Brand Loyalty

Brand equity concept tends to exclude brand loyalty, as loyalty itself is an outcome of a good equity. However, Aaker includes brand loyalty in the set of assets, because the other assets that make up brand equity and brand loyalty work simultaneously in tandem. A brand manager who conceives programmes to build brand loyalty is actually enhancing brand equity.

Brand loyalty gives us a stable and growing market share. It is reflected in the purchase price. Brands with larger market shares, according to one study, have proportionately larger group of loyal buyers.

Brand loyalty means to retain our existing customers on a continuous basis. It is less costly to do so than to attract new customers. Even when we lure new customers, it does not mean we have to ignore our existing customers. Strong brand loyalty is an effective entry barrier for the competitors.

Brand loyalty can be defined in terms of consumer *behaviour* or consumer *attitudes*. Frequency of purchase is a behavioural indication. Attitude towards a brand is an attitudinal indication. Food products have more brand loyal users. A customer who has found a satisfactory brand resists the promotional efforts of rival brands. Brand loyalty is not necessarily based on perceived differences amongst brands. Brand loyalty is also time-related. Brand loyalty is related to involvement. High involvement leads to extensive information search and hence to brand loyalty.

An organisation can put its customers into loyalty segments — those who are really committed to the brand and those who buy brands possibly due to habits formed. These two categories of customers need marketing support to retain their loyalty. There are non-users of the brand and customers who are indifferent to it.

Brand loyalty develops quite early in family life-cycle. Marketers should not play around with brands having loyal following without considering all the factors. A new Coke formula was not acceptable to its brand loyal customers.

Brand loyalty is enhanced by creating brand awareness, improving perceived quality and establishing a clear identity. To enhance brand loyalty, there can be incentives for frequent buyers, benefits of a customer club and data-based direct marketing. Sales promotion also helps in arresting a declining brand loyalty.

Brand switching is a headache for brand managers. It happens when there are new products with distinct benefits. There is brand switching due to pricing. Sometimes, customers develop fatigue with an existing product-brand. Product line extensions and product-form extensions are sometimes used when brand loyalty starts declining.

Brand loyalty is closely related to brand associations and imagery evoked. These are emphasised in promotion to enhance the brand memory.

Loyalty can be due to lack of reasonably good alternatives. There is circumstantial loyalty because of intellectual property rights. In most of the situations, we select the brand repeatedly due to efficiency motive. A brand minimizes our buying effort. There can be channel-related loyalty when a dealer suggests a product. The strongest loyalty is due to attachment. Here the buyer seeks a product desperately. It almost becomes ritualistic. It may be due to the previous experience. Such dogged selection of the brand insultates it from competitive pressures and promotions.

2. Brand Awareness

We say we are aware of brand when its presence is registered in our mind. The level of awareness can range from mere recognition to recall to top-of-mind to dominant. We recognise a brand on account of past experience. Recognition by itself leads to positive feelings. Familiarity also means that a company is spending money to keep it in our memory. We remember some brands when a product class is mentioned. Thus detergents bring to our mind, Surf, Ariel and Nirma. Though recognition is a positive sign, it does not necessarily indicate the brand's strength. We recognise a weak brand too. When for a product category, we name only one single brand, it is called brand name dominance. Say computers and we remember just IBM. Say copier and we remember just Xerox. However, such dominance may make a brand generic, *e.g.,* Dalda for any vanaspati ghee and Aspirin for any headache tablets. While creating awareness, we make use of advertising, promotion, event management, sponsorships, PR, direct marketing. Some brands have small life, and so it will be uneconomical to incur heavy promotional expenses for them. It is economical to use corporate brand names in such cases. As promotion is expensive, we must have a policy regarding the number of brands which are selected for brand-building. Awareness ultimately enhances brand equity. Some brands should have a different kind of awareness as they are strategic brands. A brand that is promoted over a period of time retains cumulative level of name recognition.

Awareness is a sign of familiarity. Familiarity builds up confidence. A known brand, when selected, provides reassurance to a customer about his choice.

3. Perceived Quality

Perceived quality becomes an important asset for a brand as it is a major thrust area of a business. It affects all other elements of a brand identity. Perceived quality is a result of an understanding of the requirements of customer segments. Perceived quality leads to financial performance. It is a key positioning dimension and often a part of company's mission statement. Quality achieved, however, in an area not considered important by the customers may not pay-off. Perceived quality is based on judgements of quality. It is necessary to understand the cues associated with quality. Perceived quality is not the same thing as actual quality. Suppose the physical quality of the product improves, but the consumers still carry a poor image the product had, the perceived quality will be low. It is necessary to educate the customers about the right parameters to measure the quality.

The building blocks of brand equity are awareness, loyalty, associations and perceived quality along with patents and channel support. Upshaw (1995) call this *identity equity.* There is another kind of brand equity called *valuation equity* which focuses on the financial value of the brand.

Perceived quality could be attribute specific or category specific. HP makes reliable computers, VIP makes long-lasting luggage, Gillette gives clean shaves. A brand can become synonymous with a category *e.g.,* Xerox and photocopies, Kleenex and tissue papers, Band Aid and antiseptic tapes. A brand may have strong price associations, which affect quality perceptions e.g. Mercedes is a high-priced prestigious car. There are thus strong quality associations for many products and brands.

4. Brand Associations

Consumers associate the brand with certain tangible and intangible attributes, a celebrity endorser or a visual symbol. Most of these associations are derived from brand identity and brand image. Each organisation has to carve a brand identity and develop it further to build strong brands.

These associations are subjective and emotional. There could be *personal associations* such as Aamir Khan and Coke. There could be emotional associations where the stability modernity, responsibility are highlighted. The users associations are also important *e.g.,* a suit and business executive. Geographic associations like Champagne and France, Basmati and India, watches and Switzerland are also seen. Collectively, these associations contribute to *brand personality* which indicate situations for which a brand is suitable.

5. Other Brand Assets

Other brand assets such as patents and trademarks are very important for the products.

Brand equity creates value for the organisation and its customers. Brand becomes a short-cut for processing a large amount of information. Brand names can be leveraged through extensions. Strong brands can be easily distributed. Product managers have understood that it is important to build brand equity by taking care of the five dimensions discussed above. This is important for fast moving consumer goods facing the competition of private labels in the organized retail. It is necessary to understand the process of stretching a successful brand. Product manager must view brand equity management as an important task. Aaker provides in *Building Strong Brands* 10 important guidelines for building strong brands:

1. A brand should have a *personality* or *identity.*
2. A brand must have a unique *value proposition.*
3. Brand must be *positioned* appropriately.
4. Brand *communication* programme must be executed.
5. *Consistency* of identity, position and communication must be maintained.
6. A brand portfolio must have synergy and consistency so as to form a *brand system.*
7. *Brand leverage* by way extensions and co-branding must not dilute its identity.
8. Brand equity must be *tracked.*
9. Brand must be managed by responsible *brand management.*
10. There should be *investment* in the brand.

Keith Reinhard, DDB Needham ad network's Chairman and CEO had suggested the following steps to build brands:

(*i*) Have a clear point of view.
(*ii*) Communicate it with passion.
(*iii*) Create a distinct personality.
(*iv*) Support it with money overtime.

To build a brand, the following steps can be followed:

(*i*) Target and segment a brand correctly and focus on it.
(*ii*) Product consistency ensures the same experience from the brand. It helps ion building a brand.
(*iii*) A brand should be associated with one feature or benefit by a large number of people, *e.g.* Volvo and safety or Liril and freshness.
(*iv*) Make a brand credible and convincing by substantiating the claims it makes e.g. tooth-passes recommended by dentists.
(*v*) A brand name that is unique and memorisable.
(*vii*) Promote through advertising, word-of-mouth and PR.

❖ Brand Equity's Diagrammatic Representation (Aaker)

When we say a brand has a high equity, we mean it has a high value as a tradeable asset. This equity may be due to a number of factors. Mostly, brand equity is because of its reputation, loyalty that it commands, the awareness it has, its distribution, patent and other brand associations. David Aaker has diagrammatically represented brand equity as follows:

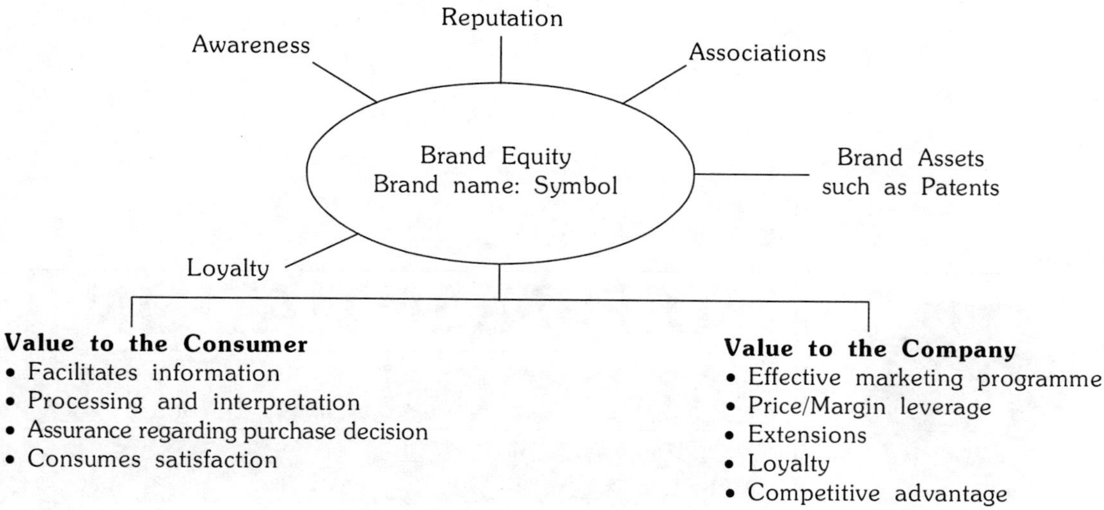

Fig. 10.5 Brand Equity (Aaker)

Adapted after *Managing Brand Equity (N.Y.: Free Press, 1991)*

It is obvious from the Fig. 10.1 that brand equity is captured in the brand name and symbol of that brand, A brand has equity both with the consumers and distributors. Coke is having very high brand equity because it is within our reach anywhere in the world owing to its wide distribution.

High equity brands are preferred by the consumers since they find it easier to interpret what the brand stands for — what benefits it offers and are confident in dealing with it. They do get more satisfaction by using a high equity brand. Such preference of consumers can be leveraged and a company can charge a higher price and can command loyalty and run more effective marketing programmes. (It need not do more sales promotion and can extend the brand). It has a higher asset value.

❖ Measuring Brand Value

Interbrand Group PLC is the pioneer in the field of assessing the brand value. Here current and future cash flows of a brand are assessed and the net present value of the future earnings is computed. The brand is evaluated against two factors — earnings and strength. Strength, a composite of seven variables, represents potential of future earnings. It represents discount rate given by a brand multiple rate given by a brand multiple. Thus brand multiple is brand equity divided by brand profit. In Interbrand approach, we have to arrive at brand earnings and brand multiple (a brand's strength). Young and Rubican model is based on consumer perceptions and evaluates a brand on two dimensions — brand strength and brand stature. According to this model, brand strength is the combination of differentiate and relevance. Brand stature is a combination of esteem and knowledge.

Price premium a brand commands is another method to value a brand. There are many proprietary brand valuation models available in the market. Media conducts surveys such as India's Most Trusted Brands to measure the brand value.

* * *

11 DIFFERENTIATION AND POSITIONING OF PRODUCTS

❖ Product Differentiation

After selecting the target audience, a firm will be able to get the desired price for the product if it is alone in the market. However, a high price and no entry barriers will act as an invitation to the competitors. The consumers will then favour a low-priced product, assuming that all products are more or less the same. To maintain its position, the original firm will have to differentiate its product offering. The more the differentiation, the better are the chances of charging a higher price. Differentiation enables a firm to charge a premium based on the additional value perceived to be offered and delivered to the customers.

The differentiation could be in terms of newness, goodness, fastness or economy. Newness refers to a solution not offered so far. It is not just a minor tinkering. Goodness refers to a better performance than that of the rival products. Fastness refers to the quick results shown or quick delivery. Economy refers to the monetary amount paid which is lesser than the other similar products in the market.

It is advisable for the companies not to rely merely on cost reduction and price reduction plank for differentiation. An economical product is suspect even though it may be good. Cost and price reduction may lead to poor services. The competitors also try to reduce their prices to match our offer. Thus, it is desirable to differentiate products by other ways, too.

The strategies for differentiation are based on operational excellence (DHL Couriers or Citibank Cards), customer intimacy (Kraft) and product leadership (Sony). The winning company has excellent operational back-up, it knows its customers well and is quick to respond to its needs and is constantly evolving better products.

❖ Competitive Differentiation

Each company has to devise a strategy to gain a competitive advantage. In any given industry, a company can differentiate it in a variety of ways. In some industries, there is too much scope for differentiation, whereas in some industries, there is too little scope. Boston

Consulting Group puts industries into four categories depending on the availability of competitive advantages. *Volume industry* offers few opportunities to differentiate, but each advantage is very large. As against this, the *stalemated industry* offers few advantages and even the advantages offered are small. Kotler quotes the case of steel industry as an example of stalemated industry. There is little to differentiate the product. Each company tries to entertain people more lavishly and recruits better marketing staff. But these are marginal benefits. In *fragmented industry*, the chances of differentiation are many, but each advantage is marginal. There are a number of ways by which a caterer can differentiate himself, but each contributes only marginally to this success. In a *specialised industry,* there are not only ample opportunities for differentiation, but there also is a correlation between each opportunity and high profits. The following diagram illustrates this matrix:

Opportunities		Advantage: Small	Advantage: Large
	Many	Fragmented	Specialisation
	Few	Stalemated	Volume

Fig. 11.1 BCG Matrix of Competitive Differentiation

All companies cannot have cost-reduction or benefit-building opportunities to gain a competitive advantage. We have many companies which have too much scope for differentiation, but all these lead to minor advantages. These are easily copied. They are thus volatile. Such companies have to innovate constantly and by a built-in innovative culture, they try to inch their way ahead.

Lele talks of *potential manoeuvrability* of each company along the following dimensions:

(*i*) Change in target audience.

(*ii*) Change in product, place, promotion and price.

The companies freedom to manoeuver is subject to industry structure, and firm's position in this. Each possible manoeuvre is related to possible returns. The highest possible returns are obtained from some manoeuvres. These are called *strategic leverages.*

❖ Bases for Differentiation

For Products: A physical product can be differentiated on the basis of a number of factors. Physical products, on an extreme, can be highly standardised, leaving little scope for any variation, *e.g.*, steel or chicken. Even in such cases, there can be differentiation which is genuine, *e.g.*, tender chicken given by Venkys in India. There are physical products on the other extreme, which can be differentiated in a variety of ways, *e.g.*, cars, furniture, real estate etc. The major product differentiators are discussed below:

Performance: It refers to the operation of the product to perform the basic functions. Consumers compare the performance characteristics of the different brands. A premium can be placed on performance if it does not exceed the higher perceived value. The performance level of a product can be low, average, high or superior. A firm designs higher performance level products that contribute to its bottom-line. However, superior performance beyond a certain level yields diminishing returns, as people are not willing to pay for it. 'Over-engineered' products are not needed. The performance level of the product must match the expectation of the target audience and must be on par with that of the competitor.

Performance level is generally improved over a period of time by constantly improving the product. Some companies, however, maintain a constant quality. Some companies, surprisingly, reduce the product quality to overcome the escalating costs or to improve the current profits.

Features: "Features" refers to the characteristics of a product which supplement its basic functioning. Products can have a variety of features. The *bare version* of the product is the starting point. When additional features are added, new versions of the product come into existence. A car may have additional features like remote-controlled doors and window operations, air-conditioning and auto transmission. Each manufacturer standardises some basic features and others are made optional. Each feature lures some additional buyer. Japanese companies constantly innovate their calculators, cameras, watches, TVs, mobikes by improving their features. They, thus, meet the competition effectively. Buyer feedback is necessary to identify the features that can be incorporated into the products. Companies also think in terms of feature packages.

Durability: The operational life of the product that it is expected to last is what we mean by durability. Durable products are preferred by the buyers. A premium can be placed on durability subject to certain considerations. Products that face fashion fluctuations or technological obsolescence have to change frequently and durability is not an important factor for such products. A video camera cannot claim it will last longer since there is constant upgradation in terms of features and performance level and consumers would rather aspire to have such upgraded cameras.

Reliability: "Reliability" refers to the probability that a product will not malfunction or fail within a specified time-frame. Reliable products are preferred by buyers. A product having less reliability suffers from frequent breakdowns and is expensive to maintain.

Conformance: Conformance quality is the degree to which a product meets the targeted standard. It denotes whether the products made are identical. Let us say a car attains a maximum speed of 100 kms per hour within 10 seconds. This operating characteristic must be met by each car made. It is then said the cars have conformance quality. If, however, some cars fail to meet this characteristic, there may be disillusionment amongst many car buyers.

Repairability: The case with which a malfunctioning or failing product can be of set right refers to its repairability. Standardisation of parts in the case of an assembled product like a car leads to high repairability. Ideal repairability is that when users themselves are able to replace the parts or fix the product. As the next best alternative, it should be possible to diagnose the fault and corrective action to be prescribed over the phone. The worst situation is that when we have a failed product whose servicing takes a long time.

Style: It refers to the buyer's perception of product's appearance. Some buyers may prefer styling to other factors like repairability. Styling makes products distinctive, that are difficult to be copied. Styling makes products appealing, but may not necessarily mean high performance products. Packaging is used to style products these days.

Design: What we have discussed above are the parameters of design. Product design involves a number of trade-offs and hence it is a challenging task. The designer has to decide as to how far one has to commit resources to each of the above factors. A company has to think in terms of a design which is easy to produce and easy to distribute. A customer should have a friendly design which is not only convenient in use, operation, repair and disposal, but is also good to look at. All these factors go into the design of the product. Ultimately, functional performance is the essence of any product. It may, therefore, be necessary to compromise on certain characteristics. Much depends on the perception of the customers forming a part of our target audience.

Many a time, design is considered just a fancy packaging. Designs may be considered wild imagination which may not be practical to implement or which may not find acceptance. Design essentially adds value to the product and design audit measures how for the company is sensitive to and effective about value addition.

In a competitive market, design can be a good differentiator. Design goes beyond product. It also includes process design.

Even the internal design of the product is a part of design. Graphics and corporate logos are also integral to design. Countries have the reputation of a certain design expertise, *e.g.*, German TVs are sturdy and robust, Italian tiles are appealing and Japanese electronic items are having an overall modern design. Design investments do pay off. Good design arrests attention, puts us one up on quality, improve product functioning and communicate value to our customers.

❖ For Services

Services accompany a physical product and can be differentiated, though not as easily as a physical product can. The key factors for service differentiation are discussed below:

Delivery: A product should be well delivered to the customer. Delivery has to take into account the time taken for delivery, the accuracy with which the delivery takes place and the care taken during the delivery process itself. Customers like a good and timely delivery. A supplier is selected on the basis of delivery reputation. The carriers/transporters are chosen on the basis of perceptions about their delivery record.

Installation: The work done to make the product functional and operational at its planned location is called the work of installation. Expensive and heavy equipment must be installed properly. Vendors differ in their installation services.

Customer Training: Equipment handling does require training so that they are properly used/handled. Siemens does not sell only the lithotripsy units to break urinary calculi but also train the para-medical and medical staff to use these machines. Computer training franchisees receive adequate training from the franchiser. Then only they can effectively use the franchise.

Consultancy: Here the seller offers data, information, operating systems/procedures and advisory services to its buyers. A manufacturer may help the retailer selling his products to maintain inventory systems, billing systems and ordering systems. This builds a loyal clientele.

Repair Services: Faster/better repair services for equipment sold is a major consideration for many buyers. Videocon is very quick and efficient in providing repair services for its washing machines, both within the warranty period and beyond that. There should be a team of trained technicians to carry out the repair job.

Miscellaneous Services: Apart from the above, many more services like a longer warranty period, a maintenance contract, patronage awards/credit points etc. can be offered to customers. A hotel can give accommodation and services like extended check out times, accommodation of the spouse free or at concessional rate, free accommodation of children, welcome drink, airport transfers, fruit-baskets on departure etc.

❖ Differentiation on the Basis of Manpower

Manpower which is trained and competent can act as a good differentiator. Citi-bank is known for its customer service rendered through courteous and competent staff. Airlines emphasise the service provided by its air-hostesses. Manpower should be responsive to customer needs. Their communication skills go a long way in understanding customers and communicate to them effectively.

❖ Image Differentiation

In a world, where most of the competitive offers are on par, what distinguishes one company from another is the corporate image or brand image. In India, the Tatas are known for their quality and professional approach. Many companies develop a brand personality by building an identity for the brand. The brand identity is perceived by people and becomes a brand image. Image communicates a message — the major advantage of using a brand. This message must be distinctive. It must establish a link between the Brand and the Customer. Strong images are formed by the creative efforts. Once developed over a period of time, they are conveyed consistently through every media. Symbols like logos, colour, sound/music are used to invoke a brand/company recognition. The chosen symbols are used in promotional efforts. The ambience of the place where brand/services are offered also contribute to the image. An identity is also built by sponsoring certain events.

According to Al and Laura Ries (*War in the Boardroom*), the perception that consumers carry of a brand is what decides whether a product sells or does not sell. Over a period of time, most brands in a category tend to be quite similar. The differences noticed by the consumer are created by the brand (image) themselves.

❖ Positioning Strategy

A commodity is an undifferentiated offer. When converted into a differentiated offer, the real marketing task begins. Every product/service is capable of being differentiated to some extent. Certain products can be differentiated in a number of ways. It is necessary to assess the buyer needs and tailor suitably differentiated offers. A difference worth consideration is important, superior, distinctive, communicable, affordable, profitable and pre-emptive. Video-phones recently introduced in Mumbai may not click because it is not important to see the party talked to; and this benefit does not justify its high cost. Instant film developing cameras are definitely inferior to videography and hence may not succeed. "Differentiation" means meaningful differentiation. It should distinguish a company's offer from that of the competitors. The differences that appeal most are emphasised. This focusing is called positioning. *Positioning thus reduces itself to a differentiated offer/image which occupies a valued space in the minds of the target audience.* Positioning has to choose from amongst the many differences for promotional purposes.

PRODUCT POSITIONING

❖ Introduction

For each segment the company chooses to serve, it has to adopt a positioning strategy. The product positioning is to be built up, and then communicated.

"Positioning" is a popular term in marketing, first coined by two advertising executives Al Ries and Jack Trout in 1972. Mr. Ries, now aged 66 and Jack Trout, now aged 58 are partners in a consulting firm bearing their name for the last 20-plus years at Greenwich,

Connecticut, US far from the Madison Avenue and its environs which they left five years ago. They started writing about positioning in the late 60s. They authored a series of articles captioned 'The Position Era' in *Advertising Age*. Later, they wrote a book titled *Positioning: The Battle For Your Mind* (McGraw-Hill, 1980). According to them, "positioning" is a creative exercise which starts with a product. But positioning is not what you do to a product. Positioning is what you do to the mind of the prospect. In other words, the product is positioned in the mindset of the prospect. The shortest route to the customer's heart is through the mind.

Positioning may lead to cosmetic changes in the product's name, price and packaging. But far more important is the *psychological positioning* of potential products. Also repositioning of existing products is equally important. In repositioning, the four P's of marketing are developed from scratch again so that product attributes appeal to the chosen target market.

Product positioner does something to the product, as well as something to the mind. Our markets are full of me-too products, with little to differentiate them from one another. The messages are over communicated and therefore, the market's task is to achieve distinctiveness in the consumer's mind.

The consumers mentally rank the products in their mind; along one or more than one dimensions. The marketer's task is to be successful in getting his product ranked first along some significant dimension of purchase. The consumers tend to remember number one.

The dominant number one brand can be challenged by playing the game of the underdog, or by tapping another dimension where the brand can emerge as a leader. It is like searching a niche or a hole in the consumer's mind not occupied by someone else. The Unfixed Deposits of the Citibank are the first to be thought of when the depositor wants easy withdrawal of his fixed deposits.

❖ Meaning of Product Positioning

Product Positioning is an attempt to create and maintain in the mind of the target audience the intended image for the product/brand, relative to other brands so that the target audience perceives the product as possessing the attributes they want.

Kotler aptly summarises positioning as the *'act of designing the company's offer so that it occupies a distinct and valued place in the mind of the target customers.'*

Positioning is not merely a statement or a slogan that creates an image. True positioning *distinguishes* a company/product from competitors along some real dimensions which are relevant to customers so that the company/product becomes a preferred one.

There are two sides to positioning:

(*a*) Market Positioning.

(*b*) Psychological Positioning.

❖ Market Positioning

It is a three-step process:

(*i*) Identify market opportunities.

(*ii*) Segment the market and select the right segment.

(*iii*) Devise a competitive strategy.

The whole idea is to meet market requirements better than the competitors can.

❖ Psychological Positioning

It grows out of market positioning. It tries to establish a distinctive corporate or product identity for which it uses tools of communication such as advertising, Public Relations (PR), Point-Of-Purchase (POP) etc. The whole idea is to move the prospects to a buying decision.

Market position is restated in clear, focused language coupled with visuals to put a product into a niche in consumer's mind.

Psychological and market positioning are integrated to achieve success, *e.g.*, research showed *friendly service* as a relevant dimension that distinguishes the airline from other airlines. The United Airline's copy read *'fly the friendly skies'*.

❖ Three Steps of Market Positioning

Market Positioning

- Explore the Market
- Segmentation and Targeting
- Competitive Strategy

(1) Explore the Market: Ask which are the areas where the company has distinctive advantage over the competition. Study the sales potential of the new market and its growth rate. Do financial calculations like cost to produce, profits, pricing etc. Understand market dynamics and channels of distribution?

Put the key factors that may contribute to success on paper.

(2) Segmentation and Targeting: Markets can be segmented on different bases *e.g.*, users' products. Further segmentation could be on the basis of end-use. The marketer targets his product to a particular segment. While doing so, competitors' position is kept in mind by drawing a Product Space Map (PSM).

(3) Competitive Strategy: Identify the competitor's weaknesses and your company's strengths. Emphasise your strengths to differentiate your offer. The company identifies the most important differences to develop a strategy.

Consider factors like:

(*i*) Market share.

(*ii*) Profitability

(*iii*) Product range.

(*iv*) Corporate profile.

(*v*) Financial strength.

(*vi*) Cost position.

(*vii*) Product differentiation.

(*viii*) Quality of management, technology, distribution.

(*ix*) Reputation.

Find out the gaps between You and Your competitors against the above listed factors. *It will give you an offer that distinguishes you — a benefit bundle or value package* consisting of price, distribution and service mix.

These days many products are technologically so similar to each other distinctions are not possible. The other possibilities to distinguish the offer are so that many — warranties, after-sales-service, instalment offers, price-offs, discounts, strong distribution, responsiveness etc.

❖ Psychological Positioning

Basically, psychological positioning is a communication exercise that follows AIDA: Attention, Interest, Desire and Action model. It is derived from market positioning and tells who the company is, what the product does, and what to expect from the purchase?

The brand name, the look and the packaging must complement the psychological positioning.

❖ Perceptual Mapping for Positioning

Perceptual Space Map (PSM) shows the perceived relative positions of products along different dimensions. To do this, the attributes or dimensions of a product are identified by qualitative research like depth interviews. The consumers are then asked to rank each brand along each of the dimensions identified. Statistical techniques are used to reduce a very large number of dimensions to a few significant dimensions.

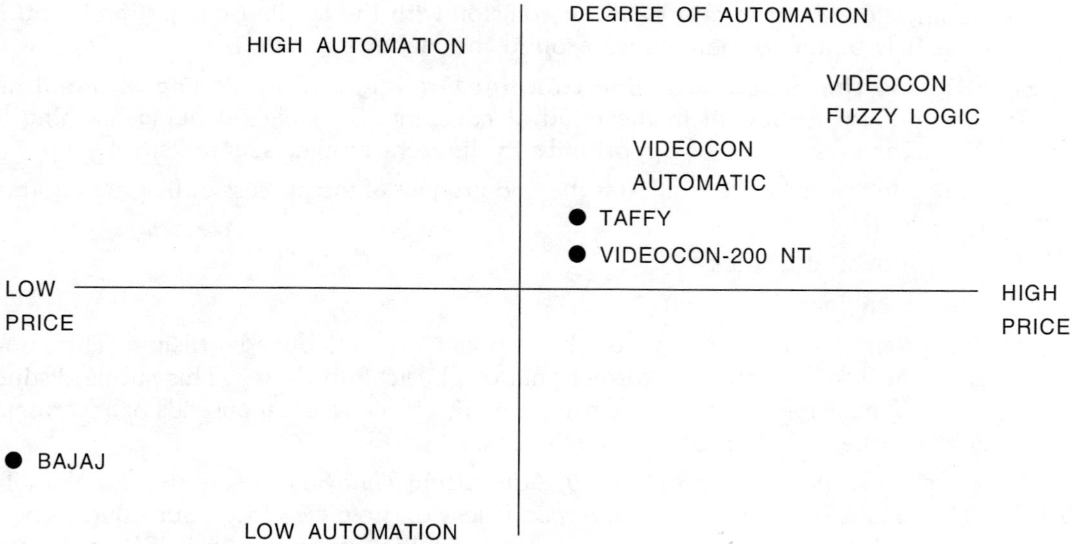

Fig. 11.2

To illustrate, *price* and the degree of *automation* have been identified as the significant dimensions of the washing machines market. The perceptual map showing existing brands along these dimensions is given above.

Consider the following:

1. Videocon semi-automatic is moderately priced washing machine and so is Taffy by Rallies. The closer brands on PSM are competing with each other.
2. Videocon automatic fills a market niche by being high on automation and moderate on price. Videocon fuzzy logic is very high on automation and price.
3. Bajaj is not competing with Videocon and Sumeet since it is low-priced non-automatic manual model.

4. The low price, high automation niche is still vacant and offers distinct possibilities.
5. PSM is used to cluster brands into competing groups to define market segments.
6. When more dimensions are used, a technique called Multiple Dimensional Scaling (MDS) is used. The computer software is now available.

❖ Advertising and Positioning

Research has shown that there is very real limit to how much a mind set can handle. According to George A. Miller, Harvard psychologist, the average human mind cannot deal with more than seven units at a time. Even in high interest product categories, the average person can rarely name more than seven brands. This is where positioning comes in. *Advertising has to establish the brand in commanding position in the mind sets of consumers.*

The image and appeals must be related to the way consumers possibly think about a brand and thus position it in their minds. In order to develop a clear position, the communicator must somehow put together all aspects of product, consumer, trade competition and communication situation in a distinctive way for that brand. Good positions are difficult to maintain, and a company must be prepared to defend its position sometimes at great cost.

The competitors relate their brand to a brand that is in a dominating position.

Positioning doesn't require a head-on collision with the leading competing brand. This is quite risky. It is better to manoeuvre around the leader's position.

Sacrifice is the essence of positioning: For effective positioning, a brand has to stand for one quality or benefit in the mind of consumers, instead of being all thing to all people. This involves sacrifice of opportunity to different market segments.

Positioning in the consumer's mind is the end product of the process of filtering information about:

(*i*) The product attributes.

(*ii*) The packaging.

(*iii*) The pricing and the image of the product created by advertising. This may be different from the product's functional or physical attributes. This subtle distinction is increasingly important in a competitive market place where thousands of advertisements fight for the attention of the consumer.

David Ogilvy while giving *38 Points of Advertising That Sells* wrote in New York Times in 1971: "The results of your campaign depends less on how we write your advertising than on how your product is positioned." The dawn of positioning era in the US is attributed to David Ogilvy, (1971).

In the 50s, there used to be hard-sell, with a focus on product features and customer benefits. The USP became a popular concept, thanks to Ted Bates Ad Agency in 40s. It was later popularised by Rosser Reeves. The Unique Selling Proposition is a unique or specific consumer benefit offered by a brand. It is an integral part of the brand's position. But brand position, however, goes beyond that. It is a fusion of product class, target consumer, brand proposition and distance from competing brands.

In the 60s, attention was diverted to image. Reputation or image was more important than specific product features. As Ogilvy aptly puts it, *"Every advertisement is a long-term investment in the image of a brand."* The result was creative advertising.

In the 70s, as we have already seen, the positioning era dawned. Rosser Reeves discusses this in *Reality in Advertising* (1960).

Positioning is really, to quote Prof. Sen Gupta, a crusade against the slothful marketing philosophy of offering me-too products.

❖ Research for Positioning

Positioning research starts with the study of the market to identify the factors which are most important to various users of the product category. Here we have to ignore all assumptions about product category. How is this done?

First, investigate what consumers do with the products. It reflects their perceptions or understanding of various categories and brands. To illustrate for positioning a cream, ask what people use on their bodies. How various brands are used? When are they used? Last but not the least, the purposes for which the brands are used.

Secondly, attitudinal information should be developed according to the purposes for which the brand is to be used and not just for any two brands. If one brand is used for relaxation and one for refreshment, it is pointless to compare them.

Thirdly, it is important to ask why a product or brand is not being used.

Fourthly, when there are existing brands, it is important to identify where they are placed in the consumer's mind. Early in the product development, it is important to uncover new psychological dimensions. The emphasis then moves to physical attractiveness — how perceptions are related to physical features and what physical features have to be offered to match the psychological positioning.

Lastly, positioning is creative. It is helped by complete information. It is not necessary to carry out always attitudinal and quantitative research all the time. Good strategists do fact gathering research to come up with fairly decent estimates of market perceptions on relevant attributes and location of various brands along these attributes. Once these are identified, alternative positioning strategies could be considered.

❖ One Difference Vs. Many Differences

Should we emphasise one single benefit to the exclusion of all others? Reeves advocates the Unique Selling Proposition: USP concept in which only a single benefit is promoted for each brand. Thus, Colgate gives "Suraksha chakra" and Close-Up "freshness of breath" enabling coming together with confidence. Ries and Tout also favour one positioning message consistently. Many companies prefer to be a leader in respect of one prominent benefit. The strengths on which leadership can be claimed are the lowest possible price, best service rendered, sophisticated technology used, best quality given etc.

Single-benefit positioning, however, may not always work out. Several firms can claim to be leaders on the same strength. Automobiles can be sold on dual benefits like safety and durability. There can be triple-benefit strategy also. Toothpastes can fight bad breath, cavities and can also make the teeth white. There are people to whom all the three benefits are important. They are only to be convinced that the brand delivers all the three benefits. Such a paste caters to three different segments rather than one. When segments are not substantially large, such a strategy may work.

However, as we keep on advancing the benefits given by a product or a brand, the positioning becomes 'hazy' or 'nebulous'. We may risk our credibility. While positioning, we should position it in such a way that there should be no:

- Confused positioning of too many claims.
- Over-positioning giving too narrow an image.

- Underposition vesting the product with no special benefit.
- Dubious positioning which is too hard to believe.

Positioning affects the marketing mix. A high quality positioning makes it necessary to manufacture a superior product, which is sold at a premium through elite dealers and which is advertised in glossy upper-class magazines.

❖ Positioning Strategies

Positioning can be done on the basis of several criteria. Some of them are discussed below:

Benefit Positioning	: Incremin tonic for the growth of children.
User Positioning	: Femina for the woman of substance.
Application Positioning	: Fixit for sticking anything to anything.
Attribute Positioning	: Dove is 1/4 moisturiser.
Quality/Price positioning	: Hong Kong Bank Credit cards, "What you carry tells the world who you are?"
Competitor Positioning	: No one entertains you the way BPL does.
Product Category Positioning	: Don't say ink. Say Quink.

❖ Communicating Positioning

Physical signs and cues must communicate the positioning strategy chosen. For instance, quality of garments must be communicated by its stitching, particularly, at the rims of the pockets. Other elements of marketing mix like price must also communicate quality, *e.g.*, a higher than usual price. Packaging and distribution must support the quality positioning. Promotion should convey the quality image. Corporate reputation also contributes to the quality image.

Sushila Rao, a marketing consultant, states that positioning as a concept is cumulative and takes advantage of the long-term impact of advertising. She further states positioning is a mental set to help consumers deal with the confusion in the environment. In today's marketing environment, it is not enough to merely project an image or trumpet "we are better than X" statements. By developing a position, to help consumers organise the brand's position in their minds, the marketer is making it possible for the consumer to deal with the confusion in the market place.

❖ Positioning Summed Up

Positioning is amenable to the following definition:

1. The position of a brand is the perception it brings about in the mind of the target consumer.
2. This perception reflects the essence of the brand in terms of its functional and non-functional benefits in the judgement of that consumer.
3. It is relative to the perception held by a consumer of competing brands. The competing brands can be denoted as points or positions in perceptual space of the consumer and together make up a product class.

* * *

12 NEW PRODUCTS: PLANNING AND DEVELOPMENT

In any marketing programme, the company has to segment the market, select some segments it will cater to and then determine the positioning of the products it will adopt. The company is now all ready to plan, develop and launch new products. Marketing management has to play a crucial role in this process, though the actual development takes place within the R & D department. In each stage of product development, marketing management has to participate along with other departments.

What exactly is a new product? Are the new models introduced by the audio music companies new products? If a cosmetic company adds an anti-wrinkle cream to its product mix, does it become a new product? Or should an item be a hitherto unknown entity to qualify for being a new product?

There are some categories of new products which have been accepted all over:

(1) ***Technological breakthrough***: That give really a unique product, *e.g.*, an anti-cancer drug, an AIDS vaccine. These products are quite different from the existing products. Nylon or transistors when first introduced were technological breakthroughs. These products are new-to-the world and will create their own market.

(2) ***Significant Improvements:*** These products are significant improvements over the existing products, *e.g.*, instant coffee replaces the usual brew coffee. These have greater perceived value.

(3) ***Modified Products:*** There are revisions in the existing product, *e.g.*, addition of a new flavour or perfume, a new package, a revised size etc.

(4) ***Products New to the Company:*** These products are new to the company but not new to the market. They are imitative products. These allow the company to enter an existing market with a *me-too* product.

(5) ***Repositioning:*** Existing products are targeted to new markets or market segments.

(6) ***Cost-Reductions:*** The products remain functionally the same, but the prices are reduced.

Booz, Allen and Hamilton have given the above six categories of innovativeness of the products. The innovativeness of the products is considered with reference to the company and the market. Market perception of the buyers is the ultimate test of the innovativeness. A new product becomes an existing product after some time *e.g.*, cellular or mobile phones are common abroad. A company has a mix of the above six categories. Really innovative products unknown to the world constitute only 10 per cent of total innovations. Most innovative products are restricted to product and process improvement. It is largely a process of improving the existing product rather than creating new products. Truly innovative products involve the greatest risk and cost. Their innovativeness is yet to be accepted by the market.

In order to survive in a competitive environment, a company must innovate. It is a choice between *innovate* or *perish.* Drucker recognises only two basic functions of an enterprise — marketing and innovation. Many companies get their substantial sales volume and profits through products that did not exist a decade ago. Growth industries are those that are oriented to new products.

Existing products have a life-cycle. These products may be required to be phased out or repositioned or improved. The introduction of a new product at the right time maintains the desired level of company's profits. Shortened product life-cycles do demand innovations on the part of the companies. The advances in technology, globalisation and the changing consumer needs are the factors that support innovativeness. Environmental factors like the conservation of energy, concern for pollution, the green movement, the shortage of natural resources — all these make it necessary for us to innovate new products.

Instead of developing new products by itself, the company can *acquire* existing businesses for adding new products, *e.g.,* P & G acquires Richardson-Vicks. Sometimes, instead of a whole business, a *patent* for a product is acquired. Still there is one more option — be a licensee or franchisee of an existing company.

Those companies which decide to develop new products may do so in-house in their own laboratories or they can contract outside researchers and laboratories.

Some companies adopt both the acquisition and new product development route for growth, depending upon the perception of opportunities by the management.

❖ To Innovate or Not to Innovate Dilemma

If companies decide not to innovate in these competitive times, they are exposing themselves to a great risk. The existing product range needs a change to keep pace with the changing consumer needs, changing technology, the competitive pressures and ever-shortening product life-cycles. Though innovation is necessary, it is not without its risks. The failure rate of new products introduced is very high. Even service industry's products like insurance plans, credit cards, loan schemes and brokerage deals also show a high failure rate. Most of the new products fail at the time of launch. Product failures are defined in financial terms — the products fail to generate the expected profits or do not generate profits at all.

Why do new products fail? Sentimental attachment to an idea being developed is one important cause. The executives find it difficult to abandon the non-viable idea. Perhaps, the idea is viable but it may not have a market potential. Perhaps, the product has certain inherent flaws. There may be problems of marketing mix — poor advertisement, poor pricing, incorrect positioning. New product development costs exceed the budgeted costs several times. Competitors give a tough fight sometimes.

What are the barriers to the successful development of new products?

Lack of Ideas: In certain areas, there are few ideas to develop the products further, *e.g.*, steel industry.

Social and Governmental Constraints: New drugs have to be cleared by FDA. It slows down innovation in pharma industry. Liquors cannot be advertised in press and on TV in India. It is a social constraint.

Prohibitive Costs of Development: Many ideas are screened to select a few viable ideas. The process of development is prohibitively costly. Even viable ideas cannot be researched adequately sometimes due to shortage of funds.

Niche and Fragmented Marketing: Instead of mass markets, these days a company caters to specialised segments which are smaller niches. It means lower sales and profits.

Development Time: Many companies may be working on similar ideas. Only those who can develop these ideas faster than the competitors have a chance to succeed.

Shortened PLC: Competitors imitate successful products thereby shortening their PLC. It becomes difficult to recover the development costs.

Any successful attempt to innovate basically depends upon the type of organisational arrangement made for managing the process of developing the new products.

❖ Organisation for New Products

Any programme of innovation can be successful only when it gets top management support on a continuous basis and this support is not withheld even in the face of failure of some new product development efforts. It is for the top management to define the overall domain of the business for new product development. The top management may spell out the product categories it wishes to emphasise.

Top management has to set out the criteria against which new product ideas will be scrutinised. The top management might say a new product proposal is acceptable if the product can be introduced within three years and has a market potential of at least *A* 100 crore and a growth rate of 10 per cent Further, it should provide a return of 25 per cent on sales and 35 per cent on investment. A very significant decision is about the budgeting of the new product development. Some companies finance several projects at a time, considering the possibility of having a few successful products at the end of different time periods. Some companies allocate a percentage of sales to R & D efforts. Even competitive efforts are taken into account. One may first decide how many successful products a company must have and then calculating backwards the investment needed.

It is common experience for companies that out of several ideas considered for a new product, only a handful pass the idea-screening stage. Each idea reviewed, however, costs a lot to the company. Only 50 per cent ideas of the screened out ideas might survive the concept testing stage and only a half of these might reach the product development stage. There has to be budget for concept testing and product testing stages. Hardly one or two ideas are then launched at an enormous launch cost. They may be successful or may not be. The total cost of developing the new product is thus the summation of the costs incurred at each stage of development. The company has to improve the pass ratio and reduce the costs at each stage to make the whole process cost effective. The average cost of an idea getting converted into a successful product can be calculated. The products needed for a company multiplied by the average cost thus gives the total budget for new product development.

Several organisational mechanisms are introduced to handle the development of new products. There is no 'one-best' organisational structure to do so. Some most widely used organisational structures are briefly explained here.

❖ Product Planning Committee

In several companies, a committee is formed with representatives drawn from the top management for monitoring new product development. The committee usually consists of the chief executives and representatives from the marketing, financing, production and research departments. Once the product is developed, the marketing responsibility is assigned to either a product manager or a new product department. The committee is an effort to pool the combined wisdom of different people. A resulting new product thus has the approval of the concerned administrators who were a party to its developmental decision. Incidentally a committee type arrangement is a time consuming process and is slow to arrive at decisions.

❖ New Product Department

In large companies, a new product department under a senior manager vested with sufficient authority and having access to top management is created. The manager heads a department which is compact, consisting of 4-5 persons. This department spells out the new product programmes. It also monitors the development process of the new product. Once developed, the new product is assigned to the concerned operating department.

New product department in some firms is authorised to contract with outside parties to bring the new product on par with competitive products. New product department can be authorised to farm out ideas to outside specialist firms who specialise in product development process. The new product department keeps track of patents and revives old patents. The products developed may not be of immediate use to the company. The new product department can be authorised to sell-off these products or technology to others at a price so as to cover the R & D costs.

Routinely, all new product departments co-ordinate with R & D, generate and screen new product ideas and test and commercialise the ideas developed.

❖ Product Manager

He may be named as a product manager or a brand manager or a merchandise manager. He is after all responsible for either a product or a group of related products. He mainly plans the strategies for *existing* products. He may be assigned the additional responsibility of developing and marketing and new products. However, as the product manager is over-burdened with his existing load, he may not do justice to the new product. At most, he can do brand or line extensions and slight product improvements. Besides, he may not have the competence to develop the new products. Being too close to the company's existing product line, he is also blinkered to the possibility of exploring new product ideas.

New Product Manager: To overcome the drawbacks of an arrangement whereby new products are made the responsibility of existing product managers, some firms create the post of a new product manager who has to consider only about the development of new products. This professionalises the new product function. The new product manager reports to the Group Product Manager.

New Product Venture Teams: Here the major development work of new products is assigned to a venture team which is a small, multi-disciplinary group organisationally segregated from the rest of the firm. The venture group looks after the whole new product development process right from idea generation to full-scale marketing. It consists of representatives from the operating departments like engineering, production, finance, marketing research etc. The team acts as an entrepreneur, within the organisation, as it is immune to organisational rules and regulations. It reports directly to top management and has a single-minded commitment to enter a new market profitably. The group members are relieved of their other organisational duties. They are given a budget and a time-frame. Once a product is developed, it is turned over to the existing organisational arrangement or to a subsidiary company. The venture team is then disbanded.

Venture teams are organisations within organisations. They by-pass the traditional problems of bureaucratisation and red-tapism. Besides, in existing organisations, there is an inherent resistance to change. The existing arrangements lack the authority or the courage to see the product through all the developmental stages.

Randall (1980) has identified three main types of formal organisational mechanisms used for product innovation: (1) new-product committees, (2) project teams and (3) new-product or venture departments. Souder (1978) has found the following nine organisational trappings behind the formal structure to organise product innovation:

1. New product department.
2. Product committee.
3. Commercial-product manager.
4. Technical-project manager.
5. Commercial-line manager.
6. Technical-line manager.
7. Commercial one-man show.
8. Technical one-man show.
9. Dyad.

Each of these nine systems can fall into one of the three broad categories suggested by Randall. Souder scores by emphasising the power base which could either be commercial or technical. Though useful to understand the structure, still it does not enlighten us about the interactions amongst the participants in terms other than formal power. Stalker (1961) finds that less product-innovator firms use mechanistic structures and active product innovator firms use organic structures. But this explanation is also not satisfactory, because while *implementing,* active firms to exercise far greater control just like mechanistic structures than they do at the initiation stage. Surprisingly, the control was exercised without changing the formal job titles.

❖ Why New Products Fail or Succeed?

It is a baffling question. Some new products fail. Some succeed. For a company, every new product that is developed is a star. But it may fade out. Some of the reasons for this are.

❖ Lack of Organisational Team-work

In most of the organisations, there is a tradition to rely on R & D to come out with a bright idea and research it, which is then handed over to the design and production people. The ultimate end-product comes to marketing department for selling. There are many problems in this segmental approach. The design people may revert to R & D, if they find the product unviable. The production people may ask the design people to redesign if the product cannot be turned out at the budgeted cost. The design people take their own time to redesign. The marketing department ultimately gets a product that is not acceptable to the customers at a price quoted. Perhaps, their needs are not met. Each party places the blame at the door of the other party. The solution to this situation is to have *team-approach*. At each stage, there should be cross-functional approach, *e.g.*, marketing examining the product idea. New products should be linked to a strategic management process and the new product development process should be under an effective organisational arrangement. A stage-gate process of development ensures that the product proceeds to the next stage only when cleared by a cross-functional team of gate-keepers. At each stage, while the gate-keepers decide whether to go further/no go and kill /no go and hold/recycle. The criteria are decided by the project leader for each stage. This is different from the department-to-department approach; where leaders change often. Thus, if marketing research into consumer's wants and needs does not support a product, the product does not go ahead from the *business planning* stage to *product development* stage. *Simultaneous product development* by a cross-functional team turns out products quicker. It may be risky to do so. But where product life-cycles are shorter, quick development of new products offers far more benefits than the risks associated with it.

Technical Problems: Too complicated a product or poor performance of a product that is not superior to any of the existing products may fail.

Poor Timing: Philips was too slow to bring improved generations of VCRs after it put its new product in 1972. In the meantime, Japanese companies put at least three generations of VCRs. Delay in introduction of new products may affect the marketing chances of a company. Even rushing a product in the market too quickly is not advisable. Hima Peas introduced by Lever several years back were not accepted by Indian consumers, who were not ready to accept packaged branded commodities then. In this age of working women, many fast-food items may become acceptable, though it was unthinkable to expect so a few years ago.

Let us now examine why new products succeed.

(*i*) Any product, whether new or existing, has to satisfy a consumer need or more than one consumer need.

(*ii*) The *product advantage* of being superior goes a long way in making the product successful. Xerox — a copying machine succeeded because it copied anything in seconds without any chemical/special paper. Polaroid succeeded as it took a picture, developed it and gave a print in 60 seconds flat.

(*iii*) The product must be competitive cost-wise. It must be compatible with the distinctive competence of a company. It must be supported by top management. The environment should be conducive to developing new products. The management must be alive to new-product opportunities.

(*iv*) The product must have a *marketing advantage e.g.,* Avon is sold door-to-door or Barbie doll can get clothes to drape her in.

(*v*) The product must have a *creative advertising advantage, e.g.,* Maggie's two minute noodles emphasised the two-minute solution to satisfy the hunger of school going children.

❖ Stages in the New Product Development Process

The overall guide to the new product development is the product strategy of the organisation. The development of new product proceeds in the following eight stages. At each stage, the firm has to decide whether to move ahead to the next stage or abandon the product or seek additional information. The eight stages, involved are: (*i*) Generation of new product ideas: (*ii*) Screening and evaluation of ideas; (*iii*) Concept development and testing; (*iv*) Marketing strategy; (*v*) Business analysis; (*vi*) Product development; (*vii*) Test Marketing and (*viii*) Commercialisation. The Fig. 12.1 illustrates the process:

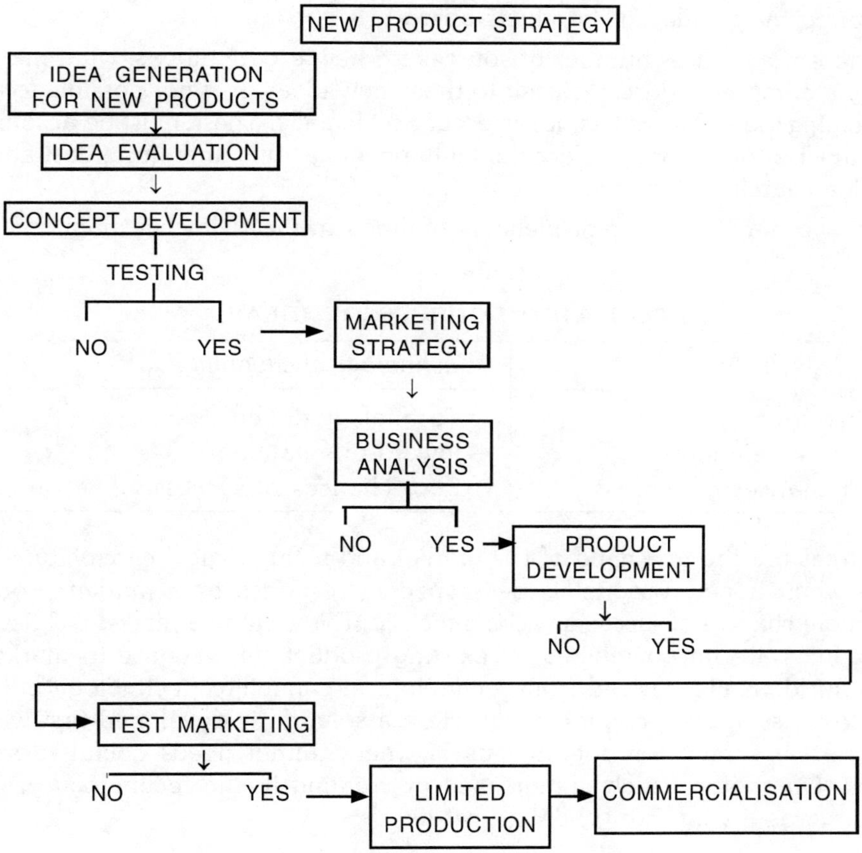

Fig. 12.1 New Product Development Process

The first three stages up to the concept development are the critical steps. These are the least expensive steps. Further steps are escalating in terms of costs and commitment of scarce resources. Most product failures are attributable to an unviable idea or faulty concept development. The stages help us to identify these situations. Activities in the development process can be co-ordinated and controlled by mathematical models like PERT/CPM.

❖ First Stage: Generation of New Product Ideas

Idea Generation: A product that we use today was just an idea sometime back. It is the creative idea that gets eventually translated into the new product opportunity. Where do we find these ideas?

Sources of New Product Ideas: Ideas can come from a number of sources. Ideas can come from the R & D department. The chief executive himself can be a good source of ideas. The marketing people including the salesmen provide certain ideas. Outsiders like the suppliers, the dealers and the distributors, inventors and research agencies are fertile sources of new ideas. Technical people working in the company and outside are a good source of ideas. Companies get ideas from the competitors. The kith and kin of people interacting with the company, *e.g.*, Chairman's wife, may throw up bright ideas. Customers themselves are the most important source of new product ideas. Surveys of customers and feedback from the customers are treasure-mines for the companies. Ideas can be found in our country; or else we can be inspired by people and products abroad.

Though there are endless number of sources for new product ideas, what matters more is how seriously a company addresses itself to those new ideas. It is not possible to anticipate the sudden emerging idea. Sometimes, ideas occur accidentally. These must be accommodated. It is, however, unwise to rely on such accidental happenings. It is, therefore, desirable to have a systematic idea search programme.

There are two major sources of ideas as outlined in the following diagram:

Table 12.1

TWO MAJOR SOURCES OF IDEAS

A Real Problem	*Technological capability*
Market-driven External-orientation Good chances of success	Technology-driven Inward-orientation Poor chances of success.

These sources are the real need of the market and technological capability. There may be a situation when a new product is developed in response to a market problem as a solution, it has more chances of succeeding commercially. This is called a market pull development. Many such products are improvements on existing products in response to market pull. In another situation, ideas are derived from technological capability (technology push). These are less likely to be successful commercially. Here a solution is developed first which seeks a problem. Here we search for potential users where unmet needs could be satisfied at acceptable cost. On spotting such unmet need or creating it, the technology product may sometimes emerge as a winner e.g., 3M's Post-its.

❖ Idea Generation Techniques

There are a number of techniques available to generate ideas. Apart from techniques, two other important factors in generating ideas are perspiration and inspiration.

Brainstorming Sessions

Alex Osborn is credited with this idea generating technique. It is a group exercise undertaken by six to ten people. They study a specific problem for sometime, say an hour. The chairman invites the participants to throw up ideas — any ideas, even the wildest. The emphasis is on quantity. There is no qualitative evaluation at this stage. The ideas flow — one leads to another and then to the third and so on. Within an hour, a few hundred ideas may emerge. To make brainstorming effective, participants are encouraged to formulate new ideas from other participants' ideas, and build upon the ideas of others. Brainstorming sessions traditionally used are extremely rewarding if they are well-planned and conducted properly. The group should consist of people with different backgrounds and from different disciplines, *e.g.*, a brainstorming session on new financial product must have executives from the operational department of the bank, the marketing executives, the computer specialists, the clerical staff in direct contact with the customers, the market researcher and one or two potential customers. They should all be lively, bubbling over with ideas. They should articulate their ideas even at the risk of appearing stupid. They should be properly briefed beforehand. It is only at the end when all possible ideas are squeezed out of the group that it may be worthwhile to examine them critically, see the more promising ones and develop the best ones from just a short description to more of a concept.

Synectics

Synectics is a further refinement of brainstorming. It is developed by William J.J. Gordon. Synectics believes that creative process is not logical. It is more of an accident. Inventions come about when a person has given much thought to a problem, though there is no solution in sight. Suddenly, a solution appears accidentally. It is seemingly an unrelated situation. When Archimedes was having a bath, he found the Archimedes' Principle — a solution to his problem. A falling apple led to the solution of Newton's problem. A mould on agar plate led to the discovery of penicillin.

Synectics was developed at Harvard in the 60s. Many different variations have been developed over a period of time. Whatever the synectic technique, the objective is to find an answer to a given problem through "limbering up," by discussing seemingly unrelated subjects and then by asking the participants to come back to the initial problem and trying to find original solutions through a "force-fit" discussions, *i.e.,* by relating to the original problem words and ideas from completely different word associations and thought processes.

A really expert leader and a group of six to eight suitable intelligent outgoing people will come up with excellent results. A synectic sessions with uncreative people will, however, be useless.

For an important project, it is worth the while to hold several brainstorming sessions and synectic sessions. A number of ideas generating sessions under different environments and with different people go a long way in the generation of viable ideas.

Attribute Listing

All major attributes of an existing product are jotted down. Each attribute is then modified so as to improve upon it. A pencil is round. Can it be made hexagonal for a better hold while writing or while sharpening? A razor is manually operated. Can it be operated by battery-power? The following questions are used to examine the attributes or the product itself. What other uses the product can be put to? Can we adapt the product? Can it be magnified or miniaturised? Can we substitute or rearrange it? What are the possibilities of reversal and combination?

Forced Relationships

A relationship is sought to be established among several objects. An executive desk has several objects — a planner, a clock, a phone, a fax machine, a PC and so on. These can be made available as one product — an electronic desk.

Morphological Analysis

Here the structural dimensions of a problem are examined so as to arrive at relationships amongst them. The problem is to have a vehicle for carrying is the office-goers from the place of residence to the place of work. The important dimension is a vehicle — what type of vehicle (four-wheeler or three-wheeler or two-wheelers or two-wheeler with a side-car), the fuel used — whether petrol or diesel and the characteristics of the vehicle. We may think of a easy-to-start non-geared moped which is fuel efficient and is suitable for the city roads. The attempt is to find some novel combinations.

Need Problem Identification

Here the consumer is involved in idea generation. He is asked to specify his needs, problems and ideas.

Second Stage: Idea Screening and Evaluation

It is relatively easy to find a large number of opportunities in the form of initial ideas. We have to consider now which of them are really worth the while for a follow-up. Which of these ideas are worth commiting the corporate resources to them? These are fairly difficult decisions. Some of the ideas are rejected for obvious reasons like:

(*a*) lousy idea.

(*b*) unsuitable idea for the firm.

(*c*) obvious problems in production and marketing.

(*d*) too little potential.

(*e*) someone else is already exploiting it.

(*f*) others would be able to implement it better and quicker.

(*g*) no long-term potential.

(*h*) other reasons, *e.g.*, unsuitable for the main customers of the company.

It should be possible to reduce the ideas from several hundreds to thirty or forty having some *prima facie* merit. Later, further pruning is done more rigorously. While screening the ideas, the company should not dismiss an otherwise good idea — a drop-error. Carlson's copying machine was a good idea. Xerox exploited it while IBM could not. RCA exploited the radio while Victor Talking Machine Company could not. Too many drop-errors may prove to be disastrous for a company. Its standards perhaps are too conservative. On the other hand, some companies become victims of the go-error — they proceed to the next stage though the idea was worth dismissing. An early rejection proves less costly for the company, since with the progressive stages of development process, the costs escalate. It is wrong on management's part to allow poor ideas to reach so far. Management should not allow ego and arrogance to blind fold itself in carrying forward apparently poor ideas.

A numerical rating of the specific factors is often useful at this stage. A typical rating device is given below:

Factor	*Maximum Score*
Idea is unique	20
Non-copiable	25
Wider appeal	20
Strong enough to induce trials and repeat purchases	25

Factor	*Maximum Score*
Technically viable	25
Not price-sensitive	25
Compatible with corporate policy	25
Little need for consumer education	20
Likely to appeal to current customers	20
Suitable for development considering company's technical expertise	25
Relevant to production resources/know-how	15
Can use company's branding	20
Suitable with the present sales/distribution resources	20
Can exploit other resources (financial, personnel, international)	10
Can be tested in the market place	20
Can be marketed in a given time frame	20
	335

Adapted after Peter Krausher, *Practical Business Development* (1985), *Holt, Rienhart and Winston.*

The factors chosen and the scores assigned are based on judgement and experience. These are useful in prioritising the factors at this stage. A team uses the above screen and arrives at an agreed point of view.

Richman's product-idea rating device lists the factors like company resources, location, corporate personality and goodwill. All these factors are weighted. The company's competence level against each factor is jotted down. The overall rating is the summation of the product of relative weight of each factor and company's competence level. A minimum cut-off point for acceptance is indicated.

The rating devices make idea screening more systematic. However, it is just an aid to decision-making and cannot substitute it.

❖ Third Stage: Development and Testing

Even the best ideas just give an inkling of the final product. Product ideas are just an offer, say a "disposable watch" or a "powder to add to nutritional value of milk and make it tastier" or "a new savings scheme for kids — a kiddy-bank" or "an apple-based drink — an alternative to cola." This initial idea is to be developed into a *product concept* or a *consumer proposition.* The idea becomes a concept when it is elaborated — it covers the consumer or the consumer benefit, the target market and the intended usage. Consumers do not buy product ideas — they actually buy product concepts.

One product idea can lead to several possible product concepts. Each variant is to be examined with care because of all the product stages, the concept stage is the most critical. Hurried and haphazard approach might lead to a loss of an opportunity or heading for a wrong path from which it is difficult to retreat.

Let us take the idea of the disposable watch (the Swatch). First, we should ask who the possible users of this watch could be. The watch could be targeted to children, adults, fashionable women, upper-class people. Secondly, what benefit is to be built into this product is a question to be answered. It could be a time-keeping device, a fashion accessory, a low-cost watch, a gift watch, a disposable watch. Thirdly, one can consider the occasion of the use of this product — birthdays, weddings, festive occasions, daily use, accessory matching the outfits etc. By asking these questions, a company formulates several concepts.

Concept 1 : The ideal gift for children — tough, plastic, really water-proof.

Concept 2 : The modern woman's fashion accessory — in plastic, the material of the 90s. It tells the time, but it is bought for its looks. This is a feminine appeal.

Concept 3 : The tough watch for men who want to tell the time. It should be durable and when faulty, can be thrown off without bothering for repairs.

Concept 4 : The low cost disposable watch for the whole family. Who bothers about expensive repairs these days? It is boring too. We should be able to change it at will.

Concept 5 : The latest gift for upmarket people. Though expensive, they can throw it out when out of order or when it wears out. It should have expensive face and band.

Concept 6 : The new up-market fashion accessory that tells the time. A range of beautifully designed straps for both men and women, made of expensive materials and with a disposable watch face inside.

Many more concepts can be developed around a disposable watch, but the above gives you an idea as to how slight variations can affect a concept significantly. Each concept is likely to be different in terms of the probable product design, the target market and the pricing. Each concept has different marketing implications and technical considerations.

The above concepts may also define a product's category — a children's gift watch will compete with toys and games. A woman's accessory would compete with jewellery, buttons, straps, laces, flowers, footwear, shoulder-bags etc. It is the product's category that ultimately decides its competition.

Suppose, out of several milk additives, we ultimately accept the concept of instant breakfast drink. It then competes with eggs, breakfast cereals, coffee and cakes and other breakfast products. How it stands in relation to these other products is shown in a *positioning map* having time and cost dimensions.

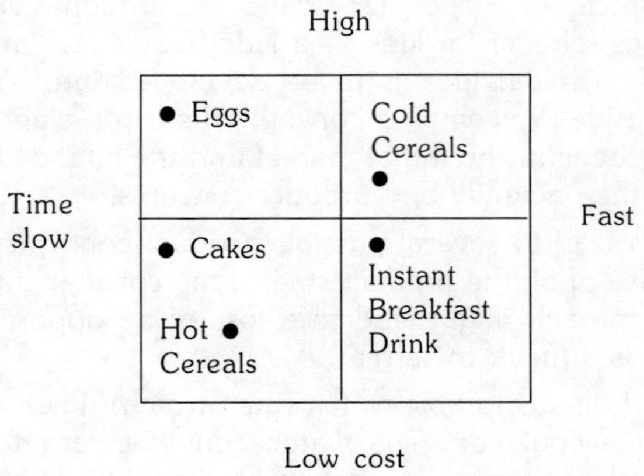

We have positioned instant breakfast drink as quick to make breakfast product which is low cost. Cold cereals are also quick to make but are not low cost. The product concept is then made a brand concept. Let us take three brands of breakfast drink and position them on price and nutritional value.

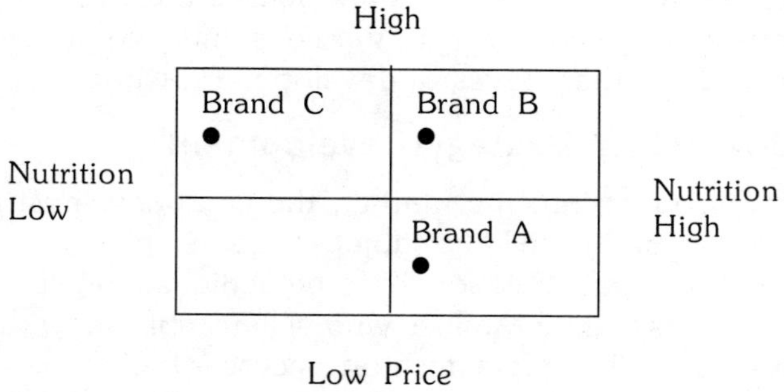

Our brand can be positioned as a moderately priced and moderately nutritive brand or low-priced and low nutritive brand.

Concept in certain markets, however, are relatively ephemeral. Concept is based on image factors rather than on factual service or product differentiation. This is particularly true of cosmetics, toiletries, household chemicals, cigarettes and even alcoholic beverages. Several pedestrian cosmetic products succeed due to image factors. The success of Dettol, Nivea, Marlboro, Brut after shave, Fa deodorants etc. is largely due to image: The image is created by consistent and heavy advertising. However, in the absence of any foundation on product attributes, if an image is built on advertising alone, it could prove risky, because the sales decline as soon as ad budget tapers off.

❖ Concept Testing

Concepts developed painstakingly are tested on target audiences. The concepts are presented symbolically or physically. Maybe, a picture or verbal description suffices at this stage. However, concept test becomes more and more reliable when it is led from abstraction to concrete form. The consumer proposition should be informative. It just can't be like an ad copy "the best ice-cream in the world". It has got to be 'a range of high-priced, high-quality ice-cream made from real cream and only with natural flavours and ingredients for those who like the best US or French ice-creams." The concept maybe backed up by illustrations and product prototypes, illustrating the claims in the proposition. The nearer the concept is to the final product or service, the better. However, in the case of durables, it is most likely to be an artists' impression. It is interesting to learn how much can be shown to consumers without spending money on prototype development. To illustrate, products already on the market can be chosen for comparison. Many straps and bracelets can be shown to the consumers for the watch concepts; without developing anything. It is, however, necessary that the customer understands what is being shown to him/her. Statements on a piece of paper may not be adequate. If the reaction is "it really depends on what the product looks like," the concept visualisation has failed.

Consumers are asked several questions while testing the concept:

1. Are the benefits clear and credible?
2. Will this solve your problem or satisfy your need?
3. Are there existing products which satisfy the same need?
4. Is the price fair?
5. Do you intend to buy the product?
6. Who would use this product and on what occasions?

In the light of these answers, the concepts are polished, revised. The testing and revising continue till the precious concept conforms to the consumer requirements. Once established finally, it is carried forward to other stages of development, without compromising anything.

❖ Fourth Stage: Marketing Strategy Development

In order to put the product into the market, the company must develop its marketing strategy. The strategy developed initially is subject to revision later. The size of the market, the target market and the financial goals sought to be achieved are specified. Thus, the target market for disposable watches will be families who will accept a new disposable watch which shows time, but, at the same time, is a fashion accessory. The watch will be moderately priced. The company initially intends to sell 5 lakh pieces. The profit margin expected is 15 per cent of sales. The company plans to raise the sales to 35 lakh pieces in the next three years.

The second part of the strategy spells out product's price, distribution strategy and the promotional budget for the first year:

The watch will be given on plastic stand and will retail at ₹ 200 a piece. To begin with, dealers will be given one watch free for every few watches bought. To induce trials, coupons will be put in the press, giving a discount of 10 per cent The promotional budget will be ₹ 50 lakhs. The budget will be split between 60 per cent for TV and 40 per cent for press. The theme of advertisement will be to emphasise the watch as a fashion accessory at a reasonable price. During the first year, ₹ 10 lakhs will be spent on marketing research.

The last part of the marketing strategy is to state the long-term financial and marketing goals: The company intends to acquire a 30 per cent market share of the total watch market and intends a rate of return on investment of 12 per cent There will be further improvements in the product — straps and faces to match the current fashion trend. Price will be maintained at a low level. The promotional budget will be increased by 25 per cent every year. Marketing research expenses will be reduced in future years.

❖ Fifth Stage: Business Analysis

We have already developed the product concept and the marketing strategy. It is now time to examine the proposal's business or financial worth. Here projections are made about the sales, costs and profits to see whether these meet our objectives. If yes, the proposal proceeds to the prototype development stage.

❖ Sales Estimation

It is important to know whether the product will generate sales enough to yield a satisfactory profit. Products are classified for such an estimation into three classes, a one-shot product, a frequently purchased product or an infrequently purchased product. The sales of a one time purchase product show a usual pattern. They rise, reach a peak and decline. If new buyers are added, the sales stabilise. Frequently purchased products are consumer nondurables or industrial products. First the sales rise as new buyers are attracted and then the sales fall. If the product is good, repeat purchases stabilise the sales. Infrequently purchased products like cars have two types of sales — first-time sales and replacement sales as the previous products become obsolete or depreciate due to wear and tear.

❖ Estimating First Times Sales

We can use a *build-up* technique in which general estimates of future demand in the segments, likely to use the product are made. These are added to get the total forecast. It is also called a top-down approach.

First *market potential* for a product is estimated. It is the estimation of total market sales. To illustrate, a medical equipment may be sold to hospitals, laboratories and privates nursing homes. The existing facilities are accounted. They are reduced by the purchase probabilities for the new equipment. The sum gives the market potential. This market is to be penetrated. It is the *sales potential* that an individual company expects to achieve out of the market potential.

The company can make use of experience, judgement or statistical techniques to make the predictions.

Since replacement sales are difficult to predict before the product is in actual use, manufacturers base their new product's sales estimates on first-time sales.

❖ Estimating Repeat Sales

This is necessary for frequently purchased products. A high repeat purchase rate shows satisfaction with the performance of the product. We have to estimate repeat purchases in each class, repeat purchase once, or twice or thrice and so on. Some products are abandoned after a few trials. It is necessary to estimate the rise or fall of repeat purchase ratio, and the rate of such rise and fall.

We can make use of the *derivation* method. To illustrate, we are interested to know the replacement demand for car tyres. First, it is estimated how many cars are candidates for the new tyres. Market research shows, on an average, a mileage of 10,000 miles per car per year, and tyres last for 30,000 miles. In 1995, all cars which have three-year old tyres are potential candidates for new tyres. We shall have to get the figure of cars sold in 1992. Further, in 1995, cars becoming 6 years old will be ready for the second replacement. The number of cars are put into age brackets. This number is multiplied by four (tyres per car). It gives market potential of replacement demand for car tyres in 1995. It should be noted that these are averages. All cars will not be driven for 10,000 miles a year.

❖ Survey of Buyer Intentions

Sales are commonly estimated by undertaking a survey of potential customers. The customers are asked whether they would buy a new product, and if yes, how much and how many times. Consumer panels might be maintained as a sounding board for new product ideas. It is to be noted that the consumers just *intend to buy*. It is open to question whether they would *actually buy* it. Perhaps, the survey might show inflated results.

Buyer behaviour may be studied for new technological breakthroughs and hitherto unheard products. What need is satisfied while the consumer may use this product? Products satisfying the same need already existing give an idea of the sales potential. The number of occasions a consumer cleans the toilet is a pointer to the possibility of use of a new toilet cleaner.

❖ Estimating Costs and Profits

The costs are estimated by the marketing department in consultation with the production/ engineering department and the costs/finance department. Afterwords, statements of estimated trading and P & L accounts are prepared for a specified future period, say of three to five years.

Proforma of Estimated Trading Account as on ...

To Cost of goods sold (estimated)	....	By Estimated sales	
To Estimated profit Transferred to P & L	....		
	....		....
	....		....
To Development Costs	....	By Estimated G.P.	....
To Marketing costs	....	By Estmated Other Income	
To Overheads allocated	....		
To Estimated Net Profit	....		....

The net profit estimated is subjected to the *discounted cash flow technique (DCF)*, *viz.*, the present value of each year's net profit is discounted at an agreed rate of discount (say 15 per cent). Alternatively, the company may use *pay-back period* method to know what time it will take to recover its investment. *Break-even analysis* is another technique that is used to know what quantity of sales/production at which the company breaks even — no profit or no loss. *Risk analysis* using optimistic, pessimistic and *most likely* time estimates for a given uncertain variable are made to find out the possible outcomes. A rate-of-return probability distribution is computed, showing the possible rate of returns and their probabilities. The students are advised to consult a good text-book of Financial Management to master the details of these techniques.

❖ Sixth Stage: Prototype Development

On passing the commercial tests, the product idea reaches a stage where it is converted into a physical product by the R & D and the engineering department. So far it was just a verbal or visual entity. Maybe, a crude mockup was made. However, its conversion into a physical product requires commitment of resources on a much larger-scale than that at the earlier stages. The technically and commercially feasible product is developed at this stage. The firm may develop more than one prototypes. Prototype embodies the key features or attributes spelled out in the concept statement. The prototype should perform safely under normal conditions. It should also be made within the budgeted cost. Developing a prototype maybe a short process, hardly taking a few days or it may be a long process, taking several months or even years. In food products, it may take several months to develop a taste that corresponds to a taste demanded by the consumers. Even then, the desired product may become too costly. The prototype not only incorporates the physical attributes but also communicates the psychological aspects of the products through physical features. Perhaps, a green colour is perceived as being cool. A green mouthwash will be considered giving a cooling effect. To communicate that VIP is sturdy, it must be moulded out of the best ABS plastic. Marketing people have to communicate to the laboratory scientists as to what the consumers might expect of the product being developed.

Once the prototype is made, it is subjected to several tests — both functional testing and consumer testing. Functional tests are carried out in the lab and data collected. In the case of pharmaceuticals, there are extensive tests — pharmoko-kinetic and toxicity tests. Consumer testing assumes various forms. The consumers might be invited into a lab. Sometimes, a product is placed at home to see how it is liked by the consumers. Consumer's preferences are solicited by techniques like ranking, paired comparisons and rating scales.

❖ Seventh Stage: Test Marketing

The prototype may come up to the expectations of the firm. Then it is packaged properly, given a brand name and is tested in the market. Branding and packaging are discussed in detail in separate chapters. Test marketing tests the product in an actual market setting. It gives an idea about the reactions of the consumers to the product, the rate of trial and repeat purchases, the reactions of the distributors to the product and the potential market for the product.

All companies, however, do not opt for test marketing, and launch the product directly. Most companies, however, are convinced about the effectiveness of test marketing which enables the company to test the effectiveness of alternative marketing strategies. To what extent test marketing is to be resorted to we have to consider the risk involved in launching a product. The higher the risk, the greater is the need for test marketing. However, the time factor is an overall constraint. If competitors are likely to overtake the firm in putting a similar or better new product in the same category, it is better to dispense the testing. It is a choice between the risk of failure of the untested product and the risk of losing the market to the competitor who overtakes us.

❖ Test Marketing Methods

The following methods are used in test marketing:

Consumer Goods Market Testing: Basically, we have to estimate the first trial purchase, the first repeat purchase, the adoption of the new product and the purchase frequency. All these variables must be preferably at a high level. If it is observed that the consumers are buying the new product initially, but are not coming back to buy it again, then it clearly means that they are not satisfied with the performance of the product. There are situations when they come back for purchasing again, but the repurchasing rate later falls down. Sometimes, the product is adopted but the purchase frequency is less. Maybe, the buyers think that the product is for special occasion only. Though it is necessary to know about the repurchases it lengthens the test marketing period averages for two years. However, it seems preferable to settle for quickening of the time-scale like P & G which insists on one year's test marketing.

In durables, it maybe difficult to measure repeat purchase by means of test marketing.

❖ Sales Wave Research

First, the product is offered free for trial. Then it is offered at a reduced price with an option to accept competitors product. The reoffeing is done three to five times (sales waves). It is noted how many times the company's product is chosen and the level of satisfaction at each wave.

Sales wave research estimates the repeat purchase rate under conditions of freedom to spend money either on the firm's product or the products of the competitors.

Sales wave research can be used to test the advertising effectiveness of various themes of advertising. It can be seen how the theme affects the repeat purchases.

Sales wave research is easy to administer. It, however, is not useful to assess the trial rates, since the consumers are preselected to try the product.

Simulated Test Marketing: The consumers' simulated shopping exercise first exposes them to the ad copies including the one that advertises the new product. The consumers are given an amount to spend. They are invited to buy any items from a store. The new product is given free to even those who do not buy it. The company records how many consumers buy the new product and competing brands. This indicates the effectiveness of the copy to induce a trial. The consumers are later telephonically interviewed to know their reactions. The results can be used as inputs in sales forecasts.

Controlled Test Marketing: A panel of stores participating in the exercise carry a stock of new product. The shelf position, the display method, the point of purchase promotion and prices are all pre-planned by the researcher. The sales results are analysed. This test enables us to know the impact of real-life in-store factors on buyer behaviour. Consumers are later interviewed for feedback. This technique, however, exposes the product to competition.

Selection of Test Markets: Test market ought to be a replica of the national market or full-scale market. Some cities are selected for test marketing — mostly 2 — 6 cities. No city can be an exact replica of the national market. Each company has to develop its own criteria for test-city selection. The city should have enough diversity, media availability, necessary retailing outlets, average competition and should not have been overtested.

Time of the Test Marketing: Test marketing ranges from a few months to several years. The test period corresponds to the average repurchasing period. The competitive activity calls for a shorter test marketing period.

Data Collected in Test Marketing: The data to be collected must be decided. Its cost and value trade-off should be studied. Inventory levels will indicate weekly retail sales. Stores audits indicate retail sales of both the test-marketed product and the competitive product. Consumer panels are used to know the buying habits. Consumer surveys are carried out to collect data regarding attitudes, usage and satisfaction. Trade research is also carried out. Studies to assess effectiveness of promotional campaigns and retail distribution are also carried out.

Action Taken: "Success test marketing" means a high trial rate and repurchase rate. We can move further for a full-market launch. If there is high trial rate and low repurchase rate, it shows the dissatisfaction of the consumers with the product. The product needs modifications/redesigning. If there is low trial rate but high repurchase rate, it shows satisfaction with the performance of the product. But we should motivate more people to buy it by making promotion effective. If there is both low trial rate and repurchase rate, the product should be dropped.

❖ Benefits of Test Marketing

(*i*) It is a value input to a sales forecast. Lower than the targeted sales in the test market indicates the dropping of the product or its modification. Even marketing programme will have to be reconsidered.

(*ii*) Test marketing enables us to compare alternative marketing plans. In each test market, a different marketing mix is used. The data are collected. The most beneficial marketing mix is chosen.

(*iii*) Test marketing may point out defect in a product, distribution problems and the different behaviour of buyers in various segments of the market.

Test Marketing Questioned: Though test marketing is a useful tool it alerts the competitors about a new product. Competitive activity may spoil test marketing itself. Several companies by-pass the test marketing route and resort to other methods of market testing like a launch in 25% of market or a launch in some countries.

❖ Eighth Stage: Commercialisation

Test marketing feedback enables management to take a decision regarding the launching of a product. A product launch is the costliest stage of new product development. The company either sets up the manufacturing facilities for production itself and hires the same. As a precautionary measure, the company may set up a plant smaller than the one demanded by the sales forecast. Apart from production costs, the company has to bear heavy marketing costs — packaging, promotion, advertising, distribution etc. Marketing expenditures are the highest in the year of the launch, reaching in some cases almost 60 per cent of sales.

Timing of the Launch: It is critical to time the entry of the new product correctly. When a competitor is also on the point of launching a rival product the company can decide to have the first entry and establish leadership or to enter the market simultaneously with the competitor or to have a late entry to have the benefit of hindsight. Soft drinks are generally launched in pre-summer months. The text-books are launched at the beginning of the academic section. The most likely question books are launched just before the exams. A product launch may be all delayed to clear first the previous stock.

Coverage: The product may be launched locally or in a region or in several regions or nationally or internationally. Few companies have the marketing muscle and capability to undertake a national launch or a global launch. There is mostly a planned roll-out. They first do the local or regional launch and then expand gradually. Those companies which have national distribution network might launch their products nationally. In roll-out marketing, markets can be rated. In any roll-out marketing, the competitive scene is taken into account.

Target Markets: Each company identifies the main prospective users of its product. These are the prime prospects. They should ideally be early adopters, opinion leaders, be accessible at reasonable cost and heavy users.

❖ Initial Marketing Strategy

An action-plan is put into effect in the roll-out market.

❖ New Product Adoption

The new product's acceptance by the consumers is called its "adoption". It is a six-step process in which the consumer passes through the awareness, interest, evaluation, trial, adoption and confirmation.

Stages	*Activities Involved*
(*i*) Awareness	Person is exposed to the new product. He becomes a prospect.
(*ii*) Interest	He develops interest in the new product, solicits information about the new product.
(*iii*) Evaluation	He studies the merits of the new products mentally.
(*iv*) Trial	He tries the new product in a limited manner. He prefers a small quantity for trial.
(*v*) Adoption	Here he decides whether to accept the new product in a full-fledged manner.
(*vi*) Confirmation (Post-adoption)	The new product is adopted. He needs a constant reassurance about his choice.

The above progressive stages suggest that the marketer of a new product should facilitate the movement of the prospect through these stages. In India, many prospects are interested in a dish washer, say, a Maharaja Whiteline Dishwasher, but there is an uncertainty about its functioning. They may be given a demonstration of a dishwasher. A mail order company selling garments might induce the prospects to place a trial order and may ask the consumers to return the goods if not satisfied within a specified time. A product may be offered on a trial basis with an option to buy if the results are satisfactory. It may be noted that the ultimate adoption or acceptance is a result of the adoption process.

❖ Adopter Categories

Some people accept a new product quickly while others take time. There are some who never adopt a new product. Research studies put adopters into five categories depending upon the time taken to adopt a new product. The following diagram illustrates this:

The adoption process is represented as a normal distribution over time. First, there is a slow start. Increasing numbers adopt it later. The adoption reaches a peak. If then diminishes, leaving very few non-adopters.

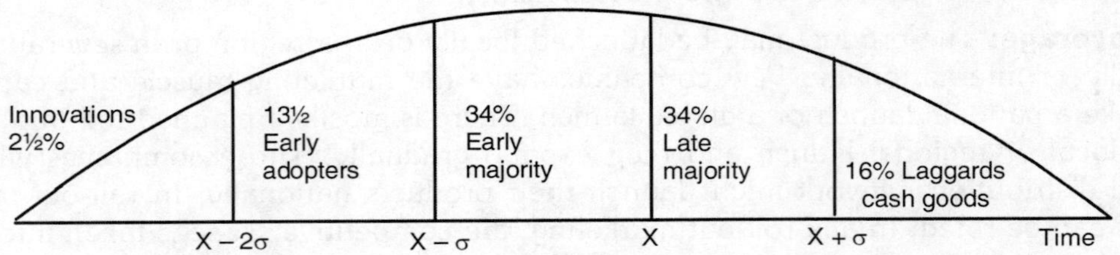

Fig. 12.2 Distribution of adopters of a New Product

Innovators: They are the first who venture to adopt a new product. They are likely to be younger. They may have a high social status. Their outlook is broad and cosmopolitan. They are venturesome to try out new ideas, taking some risk.

Early Adopters: This group consists more of opinion leaders. They are greatly respected in society. They adopt new ideas early but are careful. They are "change agents".

Early Majority: It is a *deliberate* group who accepts an innovation before the average person does so. It is a notch above average group. They themselves are not the leaders.

Late Majority: It is a *skeptical* group who adopt a new product out of necessity or social pressure. They adopt when so many others have done so before them.

Laggards: They are a *tradition bound* group. They are the last to adopt a new product. They are suspicious of new products. When they finaly accept a new product, it may so happen that the innovation might already have been discarded by the innovators. These people are comparatively older. They are at the lower end of social and economic scale.

These slots help the marketers to study the media habits of each slot differently. There is no overall innovative trait in an individual. He may be an innovator in certain areas and may be a laggard in others. A person may be conservative in dress habits, but may accept exotic dishes. Each marketer has to study the characteristics of likely early adopters in a given product category.

❖ Characteristics of Innovation Affecting Adoption Role

According to Rogers, there are five characteristics of an innovation which affect its adoption rate.

Relative Advantage: This is the degree to which a new product scores over the old ideas. It maybe the benefit of a lower cost or some other advantage. The greater the advantage, the faster the adoption.

Comparability: This is the degree to which the new product lives up to the cultural values and experiences of the prospects. A music system may be highly consistent with the life style of an upper middle class home.

Complexity: The degree or level of difficulty in using a new product or in understanding and mastering it. A professional camera may take a longer time for adoption since it is difficult to master its various functions.

Divisibility or Trialability: This is the degree to which a new product may be tried in a limited manner. The hire purchase scheme increases the rate of adoption of an air-conditioner. Central air-conditioning system is having a lower trialability than a new variety of seed which can be tried on a small plot of land.

Communicability or Observability: This is the degree to which the results of the use of a new product can be observed or described. An innovation whose use can be demonstrated to others diffuses faster in the social system.

Apart from the above, personal influences, initial pricing, scientific credibility and social approval also affect the rate of adoption. All these factors must be carefully studied by the marketer and are used as inputs while designing a new product.

❖ Diffusion

Rogers has defined a diffusion. It is the spread of an innovation in the mass of ultimate users or adopters. Diffusion starts from the source of invention or creation and ends with the users or adopters. Diffusion is the process by which the innovation is communicated within the social system over time.

❖ Product Planning Process: Some Observations

There is no normative model of product planning process. It varies from company-to-company. Many companies do not use strategic planning much and so also the marketing research inputs. This holds true especially in the idea generation and demand estimation stages. Criteria to appraise product proposals are neither fixed nor strategic concept testing is an extremely useful tool, but its use is an exception. Business analysis is just too elementary, and little effort is made to do detailed demand forecasting.

Some companies focus too much on engineering and not only marketing. Their over-engineered products may be too expensive for the market.

There is a considerable gap between Theory and Practice, suggesting how complex the whole process is. The process tends to be disorderly, as it involves people with different skills, and varying perspectives. There is a further complication. In the new product development process, we deal with an intangible concept rather than a tangible product. It demands management of creativity. It is easy to become infactuated with technology. Engineers feel too competent to design anything. Scientists in the R & D are enamoured of their technological outcomes. They, as a result, are divorced from market realities. They come out with technological solutions to phantom problems.

The failure to provide strategic direction to the technical staff also results in a too technology-based approach. Creativity is the crux of the new product planning process, but requires conducive organisational climate to flourish. Bureaucratisation stifles it.

A suitable organisational mechanism must be developed to do new product development. Many a time, management fails to provide such a mechanism. Technical personnel may lack a managerial perspective. Undue emphasis on consent rather than conflict also eliminates many potential new product ideas.

❖ Improving the Product Planning Process

According to Feldman and Page, product planning process improvement has three dimensions — strategic orientation, ordering the process and increasing information inputs.

Strategic nature of product decisions must be appreciated. It is essential to set up criteria against which the product decisions will be evaluated. Strategic direction must be given to the entire process. Or else we may venture deep into new product fields. Sometimes, we are anchored to the shallow waters of the current offerings, thus making us staid. The market may want us to brave the new areas.

Systematic product planning process pays-off. There should be a method of evaluation of business proposals. The uniformity in the process should be seen both in contents and procedure. As it is a 'people process', it leads to a paradox. It fosters subjectivity, whereas the process should try to attain objectivity. Very few companies have a formal document spelling out the process. Criteria of evaluation must be carefully determined. The relative importance of these criteria must be known.

In business analysis stage, there is a tendency to equate it with screening while deciding its business viability. It may lead to a superficial appraisal which spills over from the screening stage, failing to understand deeper marketing realities. Marketing research inputs must be increased to improve the product planning process. It should be a continuous integration. It should be used more at the concept testing and product testing stage.

APPENDIX

Prior to launching a new product, a company needs to analyse the relationship between the Product and the Customer. It is this relationship that ultimately determines the level of difficulty in the sale. Generally, all buyer-seller relationships fall into any one of the following categories:

Existing Customer/existing product

This is the easiest sale. Here the customer's needs are known. The customer also is familiar with the product. He has thus known expectations from the product.

Existing Customer/new product

This requires sales and marketing effort. A new product is being introduced to our own customers. The critical task is to figure out what the new product does for our customers and how it addresses this need.

New Customer/existing product

This requires greater marketing effort. It is a new territory. New customers can be from a different industry, from the same industry but not using our product, new needs of existing customers. Many times, these new customers have different terminologies and ways of doing business. Their key concerns may be different. Their problems are unknown.

New Customers/new products

Here a new product is introduced to new customers or market segment. Here we do not know the customers and their ways of doing business. The customers also do not know the track record of the company. This is the most difficult of all sale situations.

Concept Marketing

The idea of the product — the concept — is to be marketed first before marketing the product itself. Certainly any new concept is a risk. It, therefore, requires a *staying power* while marketing concepts.

Pioneering a concept has both advantages as well as disadvantages. The advantage is that the firm is so strongly associated with the concept that it becomes difficult for others to knock it out. The disadvantages are the high cost of generating awareness and acceptance.

The second entrant has the benefit of knowing the market acceptance. He also studies the mistakes made by the pioneer. Thus though Det of Swastika was the pioneer of detergents in India, it was Surf that entered later but outsold Det by educating customers on the use of detergents through demonstrations. Here the second entrant sold the concept better than the pioneer.

Some concept may have worked satisfactorily elsewhere, but Indian market may not be ready for them. "The need the concept satisfies, the salience among consumers and cultural compatibility of the concept are critical." (Arun Shankar). To illustrate, credit cards are accepted today but five years ago, it was not so.

The concept should satisfy a generic need, as opposed to a focused need. Papers thus satisfy the generic need of communication. Home theatre and CDs satisfy generic need of entertainment. The way these generic needs will be satisfied is different. It gives an idea of a new product form by pointing out the gaps.

Acceptance of the concept depends upon regional factors, personal disposable income and psychographics.

The time involved in first marketing a concept successfully and then moving into brand marketing has been compressed. Mostly, branded competition comes as soon as the concept selling starts. For some manufacturers, concept itself is the main line of business, *e.g.*, breakfast foods of Kelloggs. The concept-to-brand marketing process gets fuzzier, *e.g.*, telecom market of mobile phones and radio pagers.

Hima: HLL marketed in the late 60s and early 70s Hima brand of dehydrated foods, which were convenient to use, though slightly expensive. The concept acceptance was too small then since the number of working women was not so large and there was no felt need of convenience on the part of women. Perhaps now the concept may become acceptable. Before pioneering the concept, there should be evidence to suggest that the concept would be acceptable. If we are far ahead of time, the market does not take-off.

Nescafe: The instant coffee was introduced in India in 1964, and for 10 years Nestle just continued educating the customers about it. Petrol pumps were used for direct marketing and sampling. The salesmen there served coffee to the car-owner while the tank was being filled up with petrol. The point driven home was the convenience.

Bru: It was promoted as 'Instant Coffee closest to the filter.'

Coorg: Tata Tea has launched filter coffee in bags which makes it instant.

When competitors enter, over and above selling the concept, we have to protect the brand by devising suitable marketing strategies.

Washing Machine Concepts

Pulsator wash (the Japanese system), tumble wash (the European technology) and the internal wash are the three concepts on which washing machines are based. Since pulsator wash suits Asian conditions better, today 90 per cent of the washing machines sold in India are pulsater wash.

The key in a concept sale is to initiate trials and communication and sampling facilitates this.

Ceasefire from Real Value Appliances

New concept of miniature fire extinguishers was pioneered successfully. The same company has now introduced a vaccumiser which seeks to *create* a need that stretches the imagination in these times of growing health consciousness and the concurrent pre-occupation of food. Vaccumiser concept has no precedent.

Brand Launches

Most of the marketers are today opting for big budget launches, costing several lakhs of rupees. A strong start gives better mileage. Brand launches are not low key affairs. It has to be a noticeable and talked about affair. A theme maybe selected for a launch. Mostly companies prefer innovative launches. They should be made memorable too. Launches provide a strong stimulus to buy and to induce trials, thus making it compulsory for the marketers to make this launch interesting. Launches create strong brand imagery, *e.g.,* Zubin Mehta's concert was sponsored by Seagram, creating an exclusive image for the product. The media blitzkrieg preceding and succeeding the event helps to create a brand image to a wider cross-section of users and potential users. The launch events are a perfect communication tool — they not only register a brand image but also register it to the right target audience. Present-day launches are supported by feedback from MR and test marketing. There is emphasis on launch conference. The launch is not restricted to consumers alone. It also spells out a mission statement for the employees. The event, of course, must not subdue the brand. There should be a connecting link between the brand and the event; *e.g.,* Pepsi sponsors cricket tournament liked by the young generation whose choice obviously is Pepsi or Pierre Cardin sponsors fashion shows. New product concepts require flashy brand launches. Complex products like computer require high-tech launches. The use of event marketing to launch products is a new phenomenon. But making too much noise costs too much.

Brand Relaunches

To begin with, brand relaunches were conventional exercises to make brand contemporary, keeping the product more or less the same. This generates a new excitement. These days brand relaunches have become as important as brand launches because of the multi-brand market scenario and fierce competition. HLL conducts between 15-20 relaunches every year for its 30 brands. Brand relaunches have been attempted as a pre-emptive move to face future competition, *e.g.,* Vicks Vaporub has been relaunched as New Vicks Vaporub, and its position has been restated as stronger formulation for faster to relief.

Similarly, though undisputed leader in Chyawanprash market, Dabur relaunched its Chyawanprash in 1993 to gain a dominant market share of 68.5 per cent. Companies give a radical new image while relaunching a product, *e.g.*, the stodgy Palmolive shaving cream was relaunched for the young consumers of 90s in a new package and with a new ingredient. Relaunch is not a mere cosmetic superficial change in brand. It offers the consumers a better product. The weak spots of brands must be strengthened when they are launched again.

Le Sancy's unique shape and packaging proved its undoing, thanks to India's transportation system which damaged the cake and made it dented. While relaunching, new packaging of cartons was used and variants like lilac were introduced. Margo is another example of relaunching where the soap has been made trendier.

Sometimes, relaunches are resorted to when a brand suffers from image problem. Sometimes, relaunches make the product relevant again. Horlicks, was formerly a milk substitute and Bournvita, a milk additive. New Horlicks is a health care brand and Bournvita has been made a nutritive product.

* * *

13 MARKETING STRATEGIES FOR MARKET LEADERS, FOLLOWERS AND NICHERS

Business environment is undergoing rapid fire changes, mostly inspired by rapid development in technology. All over the world, people are demanding more amenities, thus, turning the whole world into a potential market for every business. The world is becoming competitive. Therefore, marketing strategies are designed, keeping in mind the changing business environment in a competitive world. In this completive world, the firm can play any of these roles.

(*i*) It can be a market leader.

(*ii*) It can be a market challenger.

(*iii*) It can be a market follower.

(*iv*) It can be a market nicher.

A "market leader" is a firm with the largest market share. Next to it stands the "market challenger", in terms of the market share. A "market follower" shows a little less market share than the "market challenger" and tries to maintain its share. "Market nichers" are firms selling to small but specialised market segments, *e.g.*, a publisher publishing computer books only. These segments are currently not being served by the larger firms.

We shall study the marketing strategies followed by market leaders, challengers, followers and nichers in this chapter.

❖ Marketing Strategies of a Leader

A firm having the largest market share in a given market is a market leader, say Citibank is a market leader in credit card business with a share of 60 per cent. A leader influences the competitors in the market. A leader may be liked or despised, but cannot be ignored. Some of the best known market leaders the India are the Colgate (tooth paste), Videocon (washing machines), Reliance's Vimal (textiles), Blow Plast's VIP (moulded luggage).

Only when a dominant firm is a legal monopoly, it lives a secure life. All other firms have to be extra vigilant. Their strengths are constantly under attack by the other firms. Their weaknesses are likely to be exploited. An innovation might threaten a leader's position.

Paracetamol (Crocin) may overtake Aspirin (Anacin). The leader is conservative in spending as it anticipates hard times ahead. On the contrary, the challengers are free spenders. Good Knight mosquito heaters are constantly challenged by Jet, Samurai, Odomos and others who spend heavily on promotion and distribution. The leader may look too traditional against a modern rival, *e.g., Woman's Era* is an old fashioned magazine, facing a challenge from the modern *Savvy*. The dominant firm may be a high cost firm, whereas a market challenger can be economical.

A leader wants to continue its leadership by acting on three fronts — expanding the market, protecting the existing market share and improving the market share further.

❖ Market Expansion

When the total market expands, large benefits accrue to the market leader. If more people buy washing machines, Videocon stands to gain, as it sells over 60 per cent of the country's washing machines. If Eagle, the thermos flask market leader, can convince people to buy more flasks by pointing out more situations when flasks can be used, Eagle will benefit considerably. If Odopik can convince people to use more cleansing powder on each occasion it stands to gain tremendously. In general, a market leader has to concentrate on new users and new applications. It should also concentrate on increasing the present usage.

New users are roped in by inducing non-users to use a product. This is called market penetration. Those who do not fly can be persuaded to use Indian Airlines flight. We can rope in new users in the new market segments, *e.g.,* a baby shampoo can be promoted for adults. We can expand our market geographically to get new users.

New applications can be spotted for the product. A thermos flask was formerly used only to carry beverages for in-patient in a hospital. It is now recommended as a product that is useful for picnics, carrying to office and carrying it during travels. Baking soda has been used in fried products, but its use as a fridge deodorant is now being advertised.

More consumption of the products on each occasion will expand the market. The firm may suggest that we should use 2 tablets of Aspro whenever there is head-ache. Clinic shampoo advises us to use it twice.

❖ Defending the Market Share

Rivals attack a leader who has to hold on. Marketing wars are fought between a Leader and a Follower *e.g.,* Coke and Pepsi, Kodak and Fuji, BPL TV and Videocon TV, HTA and Lintas. Sometimes, the attack is very severe; Amul was challenged by the combined might of multinationals like Glaxo and Nestle. The battlelines in such situations must be sharply drawn.

While holding on against competition, we must keep on innovating constantly so as to remain unassailable. A leader has to show considerable initiative in leading others in terms of product features, prices, quality, distribution etc. A leader remains always competitive and offers value to its customers. To use the military parlance, offence is the best defence. A leader has to exploit a rival's weaknesses and set the agenda for the war. He must guard all the fronts, and should not leave vulnerable flanks exposed to rival attack. All weak spots are taken care of to avoid giving an advantage to the rival. A consumer firm introducing a 14" TV, 16" TV, 21" TV, 29" TV at low, moderate, and high prices is just trying this strategy. This puts an effective barrier to the entry of the competitor. Some terrains are defended even at a loss and some are abandoned with some risk.

"Position defence" means fortifying the current product so that it can resist any rival attack. All resources are put into fortifying the current product. Even very strong products like Colgate are vulnerable to attack and so some diversification is necessary Colgate, in fact, entered late into the gel toothpaste market.

Flanking defence suggests that not only the present territory but also the weak spots must be guarded. Indian car manufacturers never thought of having a fuel efficient car like Maruti.

Pre-emptive defence is launching our offensive against the enemy before it strikes. Lakme may think of introducing a premium range of cosmetics before a foreign firm gets a foothold in this market.

❖ Mobile Defence

Mobile defence makes the leader move to new territories by broadening the market and by diversifying. He makes the innovation work in both these directions. A need oriented definition broadens the market, *e.g.*, an oil company can consider itself to be an energy company, thereby broadening its market to cover coal energy, solar energy, electric energy etc. However, a focus which is too broad is likely to make the company loose focus. Broadening should always be reasonable; *e.g.*, a furniture firm can become an interior decorator firm. Diversification into related industries is O.K. However, diversification is unrelated fields should be carefully thought out. Unrelated diversification, say from, cigarettes to hotels, gives strategic depth to a company. The new areas of business become centres for future offence and defence.

"Counter offensive defence" is the defence offered as an answer to competitor's attacks. The attack can be taken frontally. A leader can also manoeuvre against the flank of the attacker. Attackers' base can be subjected to pincer movement. Frontal attack is necessary when there is a rapid decline in the market share. However, if we have strategic depth, we can withstand the initial attack. The counter-attack can be postponed then to an opportune time. An attacker's weakness must be noticed so that a counter-offensive can be launched.

When a leader is attacked, he may base his counter-attack in the attacker's territory. The attacker has to deploy resources to this territory for defence.

"Contraction defence" involves a strategical withdrawal from too large a territory since the whole territory cannot be protected effectively. The resources realised after such withdrawal are deployed to stronger territories. Planned contraction consolidates our competitive strength in the market.

C. Britt in his book *Predatory Marketing* points out that companies cannot expect in a mature and not so-dynamic market growth to come through entry of new customers into the market. The only way to survive is by tugging aggresively at the competition's market. Preferably not through flanking manoeuvres, battlefield shifting and the like. Instead, one should attack the competitor's core strengths. Predatory marketing is probably, the best route to success. The ultimate goal is to take away as many consumers as quickly as possible.

❖ Market Share Expansion

Expansion of market share serves as a good strategy for market leaders. Each per cent point of market share may be worth lakhs of rupees. Any gain in per cent points makes a significant gain. Market share greatly affects company's profits. Profits however, do not go up automatically when the market share rises. The method to gain increased market share is equally important. The economic cost is always to be considered. Any rise in market share beyond an optimal point may cause profits to fall. The leader is advised to increase the market size, rather than market share at this point. It might be economical for some dominant marketers to reduce their market share selectively in some weaker markets. A wrong marketing mix adopted to gain higher market share may also adversely affect profitability. Higher market shares tend to produce higher profits if unit costs fall with the rise in marketing share or if the premiumness of the product is supported by a premium price which covers the rising cost of premiumness.

In short, market leaders have to expand the total market, defend their turf, and expand their market share at a profit.

❖ Market Challenger Strategies

The runner-up firms who trail a leader can either attack the leader and other competitors taking an aggressive posture (market challengers) or they can play the game placidly by being market followers. There are instances when market challengers have overtaken the market leader, *e.g.*, Toyota, today produces more cars than General Motors. The battle becomes fierce in high cost and stagnant demand industries. We shall examine some strategies available to a market challenger.

What is going to be the strategic objective of a challenger? Mostly, it is more market share which leads to higher profits. The competitor can be subdued or its share can be reduced. Much depends upon the nature of the competitor.

Market leader could be a false leader who ignores the market it serves. The extent and the type of dissatisfaction with the leader provide opportunity to a market challenger to attack him. The leader could be rendered outdated by an innovation. A dry copier may displace a leader who produces wet copiers.

Firms who are weak financially and have limited resources, and are not performing to satisfy consumers fully can be attacked frontally. Smaller firms can be eaten up by stealing their business.

The competitor and the strategic objective thus decide the strategy formulated.

CHOICE OF AN ATTACK STRATEGY

Frontal Attack: Head-on attack or a frontal attack is an attack where an opponent is attacked with our full might. Here the strong points of an opponent are the target rather than its weak points. The winner in this attack is one who is stronger and has more endurance. The opponent's entire set up is matched by the attacker — product, price and so on. To succeed in frontal attack, we must have advantage over the competitor. Instead of a pure frontal attack, sometimes a modified frontal attack is practised — match the competitor in its offer in every respect but cut the price of the product. The Japanese have used this technique widely.

Flank Attack: At a point where attack is expected, the opponent is the strongest. The result is that the flanks and the rear remain the weak spots, which could be chosen for attack. The opponent is engaged at the strong point, but the real attack is at the sides or at the back. This strategy is useful when we cannot match the opponent in terms of strength.

There are two aspects of flanking — geographical and segmental. In a geographical strategy, the area of attack is a market where the opponent is underperforming. In a segmental strategy, a market niche which is not being served by the leader is chosen, *e.g.*, a niche of fuel-efficient economic cars or lighter beers. A flanking strategy is just another name to cover the gaps in the market which are left by the leader's portfolio of products. Flanking is not so violent as the frontal attack and is based on the basic marketing philosophy of need-satisfaction. It has, therefore, a better chance to succeed.

By-Pass Attack: This is not a direct attack strategy at all. In this strategy, we by-pass our opponent completely. We rather concentrate on diversification into unrelated products, or entering into new geographical markets or taking a quantum jump into new technologies to replace the existing products. The challenger may concentrate on R&D and develop the next technology to launch an attack. The battle ground is thus shifted to a territory where the challenger is at an advantage.

Encirclement Attack: It is a comprehensive attack on the enemy wherein the enemy is confronted on all fronts and remains engaged in defending his territory everywhere. An all-out offer is made which is hard to resist. The offer covers everything that is offered by the opponent and goes even beyond that. It is a full show of might of a powerful aggressor to bring the opponent to his knees.

Guerrilla Attack: Smaller undercapitalised firms may resort to guerrilla tactics where small and off-and-on raids are carried out against the opponent to harass him. The ultimate aim is to get a permanent foothold. Both the conventional and non-conventional means are used; *e.g.*, price reductions, promotional blitz, legal action etc.

All the above strategies are broad-outlines. The total strategy is worked out by combining the characteristics of several specific strategies. Some of the specific strategies could be a price discount on a comparable product or offering a cheap product or premium product. A large variety of products can be introduced. Products are innovated or services are improved. A new distribution channel can be tried. An overall cost reduction strategy can be adopted. An intensive ad campaign can be undertaken. Any combination of these alternatives is used by the challenger to improve its market share.

❖ Market Follower Strategies

Many runner up companies copy a product developed by a leader or improve the same product and then launch it. It is sometimes self-defeating to challenge a leader. In the process, some customers of the leader are taken away from him. While reacting to these efforts, the leader may reduce its prices, improve its services and offer additional benefits. In the ensuing fight, both the leader and the runner up firm might lose. The challenger must, therefore, carefully plan its strike. Otherwise, a me-too product strategy works better. In the homogeneous products industry like bulk drugs and chemicals, steel and fertilizers, the opportunity to find a product differentiation is low; and hence this strategy of me-too product works. Each market follower offers a distinctive advantage to its target group in terms of location, credit extended, services etc. A follower is vulnerable to attack by a challenger. Therefore, a follower has to maintain a good quality and offer better services, while keeping the manufacturing costs less. It should take the initiative to enter new emerging markets. Followership is not all about, xeroxing the leader. It only attempts to ward-off competitive retaliation.

A follower can be *cloner* of the leader in terms of products, advertising and distribution. He may graduate to become *imitator* by differentiating. The offer in terms of packaging, pricing, promotion etc. At best, he is an *adapter* who adapts a leader's products by improving upon them. He may thus, grow into a challenger in future. Many consumer electronics firms of Japan are clever adapters.

It must, however, be noted that market followers may not earn as high as the leader and the challenger, though they do not have to bear the expenses of innovation.

❖ Market Nicher Strategies

Instead of being a small fish in a large pond as the market follower is, the firm can decide to be a big fish in a small pond by being a nicher. The small niches of the markets are of little or no interest to the market leader. Niching can be highly profitable, unlike followership. Profitability while niching is attributed to better need satisfaction, by choosing the small target market well. A nicher can charge a higher price than a casual seller. A nicher secures better profits, whereas a mass marketer secures better volumes.

A niche should be of sufficient size, with a growth potential. A nicher has got to be specialist. A niche marketer has to create a niche, expand it, and protect it. An existing niche may weaken, and so new niches must be created. The specialisation of a nicher is based upon customer type, size, end use, vertical integration, geography, products and their features, quality-price combination, services and channels.

New firms may decide to be nichers rather than mass marketers.

* * *

14 INTERNATIONAL MARKETING

❖ International Marketing

Philip Cateora and John M. Hess define International Marketing (IM) as 'the performance of business activities that direct the flow of company's goods and services to consumers/users in more than one nation'. The fact the business is carried on in more than one nation adds many complexities to the marketing task.

These days the companies wish to exploit the whole world as a market and hope to be a *global marketer*. Global marketing has two dimensions:

(1) Foreign marketing.

(2) International and multinational marketing.

The company proceeds in this order or undertakes IM first. However, the logical order is to have domestic saturated markets, enter foreign markets then, adopt IM and multinational marketing last.

❖ Foreign Marketing

Here the whole marketing mix remains the same, but the products are put additionally in foreign environment, so as to increase the size of the market.

❖ IM and Multinational Marketing:

Here the firm changes the marketing mix to suit the foreign environment. It formerly markets from the home country, but later opens subsidiaries in the foreign markets.

The following table summarises the above:

Foreign Marketing	— Marketing within foreign countries
	— Marketing-mix remains the same as in home market
	— No subsidiaries

IM (International Marketing) — Marketing across the national borders
— Marketing-mix adapts to the market abroad
— Subsidiaries develop

Multinational Marketing — Universal marketing approach
— Marketing is not considered foreign
— Marketing-mix adapted to country's requirements
— Co-ordination amongst subsidiaries in different countries.

Marketing on a global level is "the process of focusing resources and objectives of an organisation upon the opportunities and needs that exist globally."

Supplementary Information: There are restrictions in IM. The marketing task is complex with formalities and procedures. There is the presence of trade blocks. There is a sympathetic role of GATT and UNCTAD. Each nation has its trade policy.

❖ Difference between International and Domestic Marketing

The marketing task is common whether national or international but the very fact that you are dealing with other nations gives it certain additional dimensions. The differences arise because the environment in our country and the environment abroad is not the same. The marketing efforts and programmes naturally directed towards different marketing environments and must be different.

The following table list illustrates this point:

Variable	*Domestic Marketing*	*I.M.*
Segmentation	Single market and sub-markets	Many Markets Many sub-markets
Control	Easier (Single market served)	Difficult New variables of culture, religion, govt. policy.
MR (Marketing Research)	MR dispensable	Indispensable
Admn.	Easier	New admn. machinery in each new market for a new market for a new marketing-mix.
Product mix	To increase revenue	Market adaptability and acceptability is an important criterion.
Quality Product Design	Product-price combination of several types Tailor-made for the market	High product quality. Adaptation to different market segments.

Product Development	Product developed to meet needs of the domestic market. Withdrawn on decline.	Products developed to meet international needs. Product at one stage of PLC maybe at another stage in a different market. Can be moved.
Advertising	Media chosen for segments	Adaptation of message. Universalisation of message. Media planning is complex.
Sales Production (SP)	Options known. Predecided.	Options may not be known. MR called for.

❖ Reasons for Going International

Vern Terpestra has identified the following five reasons for going international:

1. Product Life-Cycle

This is a very valid and forceful reason to go international. Different products are at different stages of the Product Life-Cycle (PLC) in different countries. For example, though colour TVs were very common all over Europe and were in the maturity stage, they were introduced in India on the eve of Asiad. Similarly, many products of consumer electronics have entered India late. The steam-heated iron and the light-weight iron were long established elsewhere, but were seen India in the eighties.

The very season for the existence of the multinational firm is attributed to the concept of international PLC. Here, there is emphasis on price and cost changes in the production process.

In the introductory stage, the product is high-priced due to cost overheads which are high. The production process is also job shop in nature. When the product travels to growth stage, the product shows product differentiation in physical terms. The price and cost still remain relatively high since the production process becomes sophisticated to meet the growing demand.

In the maturity stage, however, the market is competitive and therefore the demand and the price are elastic. The product differentiation is psychological. The production costs are lower due to mass production.

The MNCs exploit this price, cost and production relationship by moving the product from one market to another.

Thus while PCs (Personal Computers) are in their early maturities in the American market, they are in their early growth in India. By moving the same product from the US market to India, the companies obtain large returns. This approach is feasible as long as the demand can be created or utilised.

Examples from Indian Context: Many proprietary Ayurvedic medicines are in the mature stage here in India. These are exported abroad and are placed in the growth stage there. Products like Chyavanprash, mritsanjivani, sarpagandha, ashwagandha, shilajit, aphrodisiacs of a wide variety fall into this category.

Marketing of tourism: Places of tourist interest — which are already too widely frequented by Indians can best be promoted abroad to attract flow of foreign tourists, many of whom will be sold on the place for the first time. Recently, the Ganpati Festival in Pune has been promoted abroad. As it is, the festival attracts maximum people from India, showing a mature product, but remains a fresh attraction for the foreign tourist.

A prominent example of international exports due to a stable Indian market is provided by Vicco Turmeric Cream manufactured by Shri G.K. Pendharkar, of Vicco Labs, Dadar, Bombay. The product has registered impressive exports to the US, though in India, its sales have stabilised. Many herbal cosmetics can be placed in this category.

2. Competition

In an effort to avoid competition which may be intense in the domestic market, the firm may choose to go international.

This is an appropriate reason to go international.for an over populated manufacturing scene domestically.

Examples from Indian Context: Indian pharmaceutical industry is a prime example to illustrate this point. Pharmaceutical formulations in Indian market put up by more than 10 thousand licensed firms are mind-boggling. There must be at least 40 major brands of vitamin tonics competing with each other nationally, with a large number of local brands also. In almost all product categories, there are many formulations available. So while we import many essential bulk drugs, Indian pharmaceutical companies prefer to overcome intense domestic competition by exporting formulations to Middle-East and South Asian countries. Thus M.J. Pharmaceuticals' net foreign exchange earnings as a percentage of net sales were 88. 8 per cent in 1988-89. The other Indian companies which export their formulations are Cadila Lab, Ahamedabad; Lupin Lab, Bombay; Cipla Lab, Bombay, Unichem Lab, Jogeshwari, Bombay; Biological Evans, Hyderabad; Zandu Pharmaceuticals, Dadar, Mumbai etc.

3. Excess Capacity

In an attempt to minimise its fixed cost per unit the firm may undertake foreign orders.

In case of several agro-products, this maxim sounds true. Even industries like battery cells which expanded after the transistor boom much more than the market find the exports worthwhile. Exports make the domestic production cost effective.

Examples from the Indian Context: Handicraft items, exquisite jewellery, shoe uppers, vanity and fashion bags, spices and condiments, cardamom, leather products, Kashmiri shawls, Ready-To-Wear (RTW) garments, ethnic dresses are some examples where surplus goods are sent abroad to make the domestic sales economically viable.

Tea of first quality picked up from the gardens of Assam is a regular export item. In the UK, the Herrods has fetched a record price of 5000 dollars per kg for such specially plucked tea, since the aristocrats there prefer it as an item of hospitality on week-ends to the usual brews of Scotch.

4. Geographic Diversification

This is a strategic posture of market development which believes in expansion across the borders rather than extension of product line at home. MNCs are examples of geographic diversification.

Examples from Indian Context: Camel, a company producing writing instruments, stationery and colours, thought of expanding the market by setting plants at Malaysia. Shri Dandekar of Camel has successfully competed with Taiwan and Korea in this market in many South Asian countries.

Asian Paints has set up a plant at Fiji as a part of its geographic diversification strategy.

5. Increase the Market Size

Expanding operations beyond one's own country, a firm goes international. Coke is a legendary example. It is available all over Europe, Asia and Africa. It is predominant in America. It has reached Communist China and Russia.

***Examples from Indian Context*:** Many financial services are being marketed by overseas branches banks or financial institutions. Foreign exchange business, shares and securities, Indian fund floated recently in the States. NRI schemes are examples of business expansion on these lines.

Here the growth is provided to the firms by international business rather than mere domestic business.

Motivations of International Business: The above five are valid reasons for going international. They are substantiated by Indian examples.

Mainly, the "economic criterion" where the surplus is sold and cost advantages are reaped is the underlying cause of internationalisation.

Over and above this, international markets may offer higher profit margins.

Exports are encouraged by the governments the world over.

International markets are a symbol of materialistic society, aspiring to have a higher standard of living.

The socio-political environment of the world is now in favour of a compact international market, with East European countries opening up their economies. However, at the same time the economies which believed in free trade, are closing down to some extent.

MNCs believe in oligopolistic expansion and strategic use of their PLCs.

The emerging trends in post-World War II periods reflect the development of Regional Co-operation Groups, free trade areas, customs union, economic unions and projected political unions and special agreements like GATT.

All this augurs well for foreign trade. In short, Terpestra's reasons are appropriate and sum up the basic philosophy of going international.

Management of Political Risk: The insecurity arising out of political risk especially the risk of loss of investment and information in the foreign lands can be minimised through proper management of political risk. This process can be pre-investment or post-investment planning.

❖ Strategy for managing political risks in Iraq while doing project exports:

Iraq's massive developmental plans, specially after a war ravaged economy, subsequent to its long war with Iran, lasting for eight years, offered tremendous potential for project exports. The fields where opportunities could be tapped were: telecom, roads, bridges, construction, mining, railways, electricity, ordinance, factories etc. Such infrastructural projects on turn-key basis were available, until August 2, when it preferred to occupy Kuwait, a neighbouring oil-rich state and later annexing it as its 19 province. Many economists of our country like Prof. Goyal were in the forefront in planning Iraq's economy.

Here the strategy adopted was that of negotiating the environment by entering into an agreement with the government there, clearly stating the rights and undertakings of each party. These are also called concession agreements. Insurance was also resorted to.

Poland — Tea Exports: Poland has recently set up a democratic government under the stewardship of Walesa. It as an East European nation, where the socialist movement was strongly rooted. Since then, the economy is opening up.

Strategy: Here the exporting firm structures the investment amongst several countries, of which Poland could be one.

Switzerland — Silk Scarves: Switzerland is a very low-risk country as per BERI index. It is, therefore, extremely safe to export silk scarves over there.

As a long-term strategy, it could be possible for the firm to develop local stock-holders by setting up facilities there itself. It will minimise the political risk and in receiving the best treatment.

Thailand — Rayon Plant Investment (In-venture): Thailand is a high-risk country. Rayon is a product which might not be considered very important for the Thai economy by the politicians there.

So, though the plant will be a joint venture to start with, to minimise the political risk, the company should follow a systematic strategy of *Planned Divestment*, where after the payback period, the partnership is continued for some time for cash returns and then the assets are sold over to local citizens.

Hong Kong — Onions: Right now, there can be no hitch for trade between Hong Kong and India. But then, Hong Kong is a British colony and as Britain is to vacate it in 1997 and transfer it to China, the business could be for short-term profit maximisation.

To conclude, the strategies adopted are as diverse as the political environment now prevailing. In future, while dealing with Iraq, we can cash profits through management contracts, without any direct investment there. Perhaps the biggest impact is that of a unified Europe which has become a single market. Perhaps, a product and its price will be a major determining factor in this vast market.

❖ Some Basic Requirement for Successful Exporting

Without researching the markets fully, it is not desirable to venture into exporting. “We shall just tackle the market” is not the right attitude. Many companies in their enthusiasm to export bite off more than they can chew. We have to consider product planning carefully to be successful in exports.

Another important thing is to sell as close to the market as possible by eliminating unnecessary intermediaries. Too much intermediation means less profits for the exporter and higher prices for the consumer.

Export quality should not be just a cliche. We have to assess carefully the needs of export markets and then develop appropriate products of good quality. Can we sell windows opening outwards in a market that prefers windows opening inwards?

Some companies find that their products are not exportable. They should explore the possibility of exporting technical know-how. There is another distinct possibility. We can choose to supply products to other companies who already have an export trade.

No exporter should ignore the following four points:

(i) ***Selling in export is difficult*** and one has to overcome many barriers.

(ii) ***Timely deliveries*** are a must.

(iii) ***Servicing the product*** is equally important as selling it.

(iv) ***Communication,*** both internal and external, should be far-reaching and speedy.

A successful exporter knows his costing and pricing. He has a good grasp of the implications of the latest exim policy. He is aware as to how exports are to be financed. He knows the importance of promotion. He should maintain a good export organisation, with qualified, trained, motivated and adequately compensated staff.

❖ Entry Routes to Foreign Markets

1. Export Indirectly: It is predominantly followed by India. A firm sells its goods to the local agent who then exports these goods. Such indirect exports are done through merchant exporters, export houses, import agencies and even government bodies. Here the firm merely plays the role of a manufacturer. It has no active role in marketing of goods abroad. For instance, leather goods manufacturers in the south adopt this strategy.

2. Direct Physical Export: It is done by the firm or its distributors abroad. Here the firm has to learn about the market. It has higher control of export operations, specially in terms of pricing. However, the method is expensive.

3. Joint Ventures: These are tie-ups, both technical and financial that international companies enter into with their partners in other countries. Some tie-ups are only for manpower transfer arrangements. The risk here is that the local partner may copy the technology in future. Even differences in management practices due to the presence of locals may create problems. However, they are the only options available in certain parts of the world.

4. Licensing and Franchising: The manaufacturer licenses out his technology, know-how and brand to local franchisees and get royalties on the sale. Most fast food chains and soft drink giants choose this route.

5. Wholly-owned subsidiary: The firm owns 100% equity in the company. Many countries do not encourage such a presence.

6. Project Exports: Here turn-key projects are undertaken. The supply, erection and commissioning of the project is the exporter's responsibility.

7. Export of Technical and Management Services.

8. Buy-back Arrangements.

❖ Factors affecting international marketing:

1. Government policy, environmental laws.
2. Monetary system and amounts that can be repatriated.
3. Legal systems.
4. Copyright laws.
5. Currency exchange.
6. Cultural, political and social trends.
7. Consumer profile.

❖ Export Management

Export management is basically a component of international marketing. Here a country or a company is crossing its borders to market its product abroad. Export management is the performance of business activities that direct the flow of a company's goods and services to consumers or users in nations abroad.

Export management is a micro-level concept at the level of a manufacturer or an export house, unlike foreign trade which is a macro-concept. Export management deals with the issues which concern a firm and has managerial perspective — planning, organising, co-ordinating and controlling the export activities. The following activities fall within the scope of export management.

1. Scanning the environment of foreign market: The countries to which we propose to export have different political, economic, social and technological environment. The peculiarities of Gulf nations must be properly understood before exporting to them. Japan and Iraq have vastly different environments.

2. Marketing research: The consumers, the markets, the producers must be studied to assess the needs and preferences of consumers. There should be some studies on how they see a product in terms of its functions and before exporting, the product should be modified in line with this. The pricing pattern and the distribution channel also need a thorough study. MR is thus a useful link that provides information about foreign markets and buyers to the exporter. Market research also helps to identify the opportunities in the foreign markets.

3. Marketing planning: In the light of market studies, export targets can be set. Mostly these are based on the potential of foreign market and our own strengths. Exporters have to focus on certain products and have to identify the characteristics the products will show to satisfy foreign buyers. Specialisation in terms of product is desirable for an exporter.

Quality control and planning are also a major area of attention. Our products tend to suffer due to defective quality. Quality is to be ensured right from the selection of raw materials, design of the product and its processing to the finished product stage.

4. Export pricing: FOB prices are quoted in export trade, and they are based on costs, which have to be curbed and minimised to remain competitive. A high cost economy results in higher prices, and we then do not remain competitive in foreign markets. The price has become the determining factor from 1992 onwards, in the unified European Economic Market.

5. Packaging: Agreeable packaging at an economic price is the need of the hour. Packing standards to be upgraded and have to be evolved for a large variety of products by doing R and D, *e.g.*, rose flowers and their packing.

6. Distribution and warehousing: Exporters appoint agents in different countries. They have to be selected carefully. They are to be supervised also carefully. Personal contacts are important in this context. Sales organisation of an exporter must be efficient and must be manned by qualified and trained manpower.

Overseas storage in the warehouses to ensure proper flow of goods/services is also important.

7. After-sales service: Distribution outlets must carry adequate spares and have technicians expert in repairs and servicing.

8. Promotion: Promotional techniques, including advertising are to be adapted to the environment of the country to which the goods are exported.

9. Export formalities: Being familiar with the technicalities of export procedures/formalities is a plus point in chalking out export strategies.

10. Export Finance: To attract foreign buyers, credit is extended. Credit at pre-shipment/post-shipment stage is an important area of export management.

11. PR (Public Relations): Favourable PR do have a positive impact on export efforts.

❖ Supplementary Information

Export management is closely related to import management. They are two sides of one and the same coin.

Exporting is the basic mode of entry in a foreign market. Later, the firm may license in foreign markets, *e.g.*, Parle soft drinks in Middle East countries. Still later, joint ventures may be set up. Those companies which develop an international orientation start investing in the foreign market and develop their own manufacturing and marketing systems there. There is also a possibility of accepting management contracts *e.g.*, foreign companies managing refineries/petrochemical plants in the Middle East. East India Hotels (Oberoi Group) have taken management contracts in Egypt, Australia etc. So we have the options of indirect export through trading companies, direct export through distributors, agents, subsidiaries and foreign production. Export management, thus, leads to the emergence of multinational firm (MNC).

Viewed narrowly, export management is concerned with the activities of the export department alone.

Export management must also be socially responsible, going beyond mere commercial profits.

❖ Types of Export Organisations

The organisation structure and the export performance criteria give us the following types of export organisation:

1. Merchant Exporters.
2. Manufacturer Exporters.
3. Export Houses and Trading Houses.
4. Entrepreneur Merchant Exporters.
5. Public Sector Export Organisations.

Let as discuss each one of them briefly.

1. Merchant Exporters: They are traders or marketers who buy goods to be exported from local market and sell them abroad. These traders make arrangements with reliable manufacturers for a steady supply. Quality control is exercised by the merchant, in keeping with the requirements of the buyer. The ultimate responsibility regarding the quality is that of the merchant. Vendor selection is, therefore, of crucial importance. The merchant is a marketing specialist and is spared the knitty-gritty of manufacturing. He briefs the suppliers, and then concentrates on managing his export business. His staff is quite conversant with the export trade and its documentation. Merchant exporter gives opportunities to young career-minded students/beginners and provide them adequate training environment in his firm. Merchant exporter slowly graduates to be a manufacturer-exporter in time to come.

2. Manufacturer Exporters: The manufacturer runs his own factory and exports its products directly. Being a manufacturer of standing, he has a substantial presence in the home market. He is marketing abroad a part of his products, either a surplus or to expand his markets. They can do better pricing than merchants in export trade, if they are selling surplus production adopting marginal price technique in the export market.

Companies first ask their domestic or home market sales organisation to look after exports too. Later, they may set up a separate export department in charge of a full-fledged manager. Alternatively, as export committee may be set up, headed by export manger to act as a coordinator. Some companies go to the extent of having a separate export division with a different name. In this case, there is full autonomy and freedom to export the products of other manufacturers also. This can be likened to a merchant-exporter firm.

3. Export Houses: Are certified export organisations dealing in select products manufactured out of technological processes and non-select items or traditional items. The recognition of export house comes to an organisation having export performance of ₹ 3 crores of select product or ₹ 7 crores of non-select products. For SSI's the limits are ₹ 75 lakhs and ₹ 3 crores of FOB for select and non-select commodities respectively.

Trading Houses: Here the emphasis is on innovation for exports, particularly at the level of SSIs and cottage industry. Export houses are recognised as trade houses, once they have shown export capabilities as prescribed and quality control facilities as prescribed. The house must be registered with FIEO, having three years standing and an annual export turnover on an average of ₹ 15 crores FOB of select products in the previous three financial years.

Benefits of Export Houses: (1) OGL imports, (2) Capital goods imports, (3) Non-OGL capital goods imports, (4) Can import specified value designs and documents? (5) Can certify quality of their own export item? (6) RBI allows to utilise 2.5 per cent of foreign exchange of FOB value of total exports for certain specified purposes.

Export Houses of SSIs: SSIs can form a consortium and can apply for the grant of export house certificate (₹ 75 crores select items and ₹ 3 crores FOB non-select items). The recognition is valid for 3 years.

4. Entrepreneur Merchant Exporters: This scheme supports entrepreneurial initiative in exports amongst the small and cottage industries. They are eligible for 5% of FOB value of their exports on additional licences. They are registered with the Export Promotion Council.

5. Public Sector Export Organisations: There are canalising agencies like STC and its subsidiaries, MMTC etc. They are specialised in export marketing. They do the entire marketing of products canalised through them. Some companies like HMT have set up subsidiaries to stimulate their exports.

❖ Functions of an Export Manager

The functions of an export manager and his associates is to identify the main problem areas. They should make their own decisions or seek advice from specialists on the selection of appropriate techniques for dealing with a particular problem area. The export manager should study advantages and disadvantages of a technique and also the use of possible alternative methods and then decide the merits and the demerits of using the control techniques. If a technique is used, the results must be checked and analysed periodically and if necessary, appropriate corrections and changes should be made. There are many management techniques that could be used by the export manager. Before the techniques are examined it is advisable to have an understanding of the concept of control for which these techniques are aroused.

The control process in the export department has four major elements:

1. Setting a standard for export activities.
2. Measuring the performance of the export activity against the standards.
3. Analysing the feedback of the results on the comparison between Actual performance and the Standards.
4. Correction and analysis of any deviation from the standards.

The setting up of standard for the export functions in the office should be expressed in financial, quantitative or qualitative terms.

Financial Standard: This enables to plan the future exports to achieve a target. This specifies financial terms and sales targets.

Quantitative Standard: This is expressed in units which will be used by production department to plan and control the output of units periodically.

Qualitative Standard: This is to examine the trends of activity and introduce a standard accordingly. It means a standard could be set on the number of units being rejected during and at the end of production run or the number of complains and rejection of products by importers.

❖ Skills Expected from Export Manager

(I) He must be thoroughly competent in marketing with a sound grasp of export marketing — mix variable, concepts, tools and techniques. Some of the import factors are the knowledge of:

1. Searching and selecting export markets.
2. Selecting export worthy products.
3. Choosing channels of distribution or selection of agents abroad.
4. Incentives for export production and promotion.
5. Export promotion ideas and planning.
6. Deciding export prices and computing FOB/C&F/CIF quotations.
7. Export inspection and packing.
8. Export procedures and documentation regarding claiming of cash assistances, import licences, rebate of central excise duty, drawback of duty, sales-tax exemptions and government organisational set up.
9. Financial transaction between the Exporter and Importer, foreign exchange regulation regarding export proceedings, Reserve Bank rules and procedure, export finance from banks and other financial institutions, ECGC policies.
10. To co-ordinate with the latest developments or problems in international markets and the new policies or regulations regarding export in India.

(II) He must have a particularly acute understanding and the ability to perceive patterns of consumer behaviour in different countries and the ability to evaluate the essential differences and similarities between markets.

(III) He must have the management skills to organise, plan, co-ordinate and control an operation of considerably greater complex, particularly in its human relationships.

(IV) He must be capable of taking the necessary decisions at crucial times within a short period. Analytical and wise decisions will help the organisation to flourish while hasty and non-analytical decision will perish the business enterprise.

Export Manager's Functions in Export Marketing: The functions of an export manager in developing markets can be classified into mainly four groups:

1. To plan the export marketing activities.
2. To organise the export marketing system.
3. To direct the export marketing operations.
4. To control the export marketing efforts.

The export manager, therefore, should have a clear understanding of these major export marketing functions. Planning the export marketing activities is vital in order to avoid bottlenecks, which are particularly expensive in marketing abroad. Organising the export marketing system requires an understanding of the fundamental organisation concepts and basic organisational principle. The organisational system must be capable of carrying out the export marketing plan. While the plans can be easily adjusted, taking into consideration the latest developments, most organisations are not that flexible. While in the U.S.A. adjustments are made much more easily, these are almost impossible in Europe. This is even more true in Japan. The organisational export marketing system might be viewed as a legal organisational structure, a formal organisational structure and an informal organisational structure. The foreign legal aspects and cultural setting of the export firm play an important role here. The export manager may also keep in mind the following basic ways of organising export marketing operations:

1. Organising the export marketing operations by sub-functions such as pricing, promotion and transportation.
2. Organising the export marketing activities by product groups.
3. Organising the export marketing efforts according to the user of the product, the customer.
4. Organising the export marketing system geographically.

Export organisations very often use a combination of these basic methods. Once the export marketing activities are planned and the export marketing system is organised, the export manager faces the task of directing the export marketing operations and controlling the export marketing efforts. Directing a sales force in Kuwait is quite different from directing a sales force in the U.S.A. Understanding of foreign culture and sociological structure is vital. While autocratic approach might work in Federal Republic of Germany, it is the motivation approach which is successful in the U.S.A. A well developed marketing plan might serve as a controlling device.

Probably, the most important task for the export manager is the development of an export marketing strategy. If we define strategy as a system of plans, then it requires a careful co-ordination and integration of the various sub-plans which must be developed. The sub-plans must be developed for each major export marketing instrument. These sub-plans must be co-ordinated and integrated into an export marketing plan for a given market abroad. Besides horizontal integration, a vertical co-ordination is needed, in order to avoid costly mistakes and to benefit from the experience gained in other export markets. Horizontally and vertically co-ordinated sub-plans and area marketing plans must be brought together in an overall global marketing plan for the company.

To carry out the above mentioned major functions, the export manager must possess (1) Conceptual skills, (2) Human skills and (3) Technical skills and be able to apply these skills effectively to the export marketing situation might be "the export manger's lack of these skills" and therefore, non-performance or perfunctory performance of some of the functions. The export manager, operating in more or less sophisticated markets, must be familiar with the modern management tools. These tools such as concepts, theories, models and methods are intellectual weapons, helping the export executive to make better decisions and to develop a better export marketing strategy of his organisation. They are multi-disciplinary in nature and come basically from such discipline as political science, economics, psychology, sociology and mathematics. The export manager borrows these tools from the so-called basic underlaying disciplines of today's business management.

(Dealing in export markets requires special attention to the ecological structure). Any export organisation operating in a foreign country must be viewed as a system surrounded by such super systems as the political system, the legal system, the economical system, the social structure and the cultural environment. These political, legal, social and economic systems influence the operations of the export manager. He must, therefore, learn to adapt to special circumstances in overseas markets. The export manager is warned not to ignore the ecological structure nor make an assumption that conditions in the export markets are similar to those at home. A major characteristic of export marketing is the presence of a number of international variables, non-existent in the domestic market. Foreign trade policy differs from country to country and, as a result, trade barriers such as tariffs, quotas and exchange controls will affect export marketing efforts differently. There is always the danger of a change in the prevailing exchange rate, increasing the risk factor in export marketing. An advance analysis of the balance of payments provides more insight into a foreign country's international economic activities and helps to minimise the risk factor. Some of the major restrictions on export marketing operations emanate from international trade agreements concluded at the level of governments and collaboration agreements finalised at the firm's level. Thorough knowledge of relevant agreements is vital for effective market planning.

Probably the most important factors in an export marketing situation are the consumers abroad and the worldwide competitors. Major efforts should be devoted in trying to understand the foreign customer with reference to his psychological dimensions, his sociological dimensions and his economic dimensions. The focus must be on the consumer's decision-making processes. This emphasis, particularly in the export marketing field, is important, because the export organisation usually operates in a number of foreign markets with a variety of customers, subscribing to different value systems. In order to develop a successful marketing strategy, a thorough knowledge of the market structure is essential. The factors mentioned above, although basic and relevant, are beyond the control of the export market structure is essential. The factors mentioned above, although basic and relevant are beyond the control of the export marketing system. However, there are a number of factors, which are under the control of the export organisation. These factors are frequently referred to as the marketing-mix variables or the marketing instruments. The controllable factors, which the export manager can manipulate, feature prominent in the export marketing plan. An export marketing plan is the expression of a firm's definite export objectives in relation to specified products and markets and normally should represent the best possible combination of marketing-mix variable in order to ensure the successful operation of the firm in foreign markets. This requires a capital analysis of the marketing instruments and their intra-and inter-relationship. Even with the most careful analysis, an optimal solution may elude the export manager sometimes. However, this is quite understandable because the export manager unusually operates in a probabilistic rather than a deterministic business situation. Subject to this constraint, the export manager should attempt the best possible solution under the circumstances. Exports, however, are difficult. There are certain problems. Let us learn something from the unsuccessful export operations of some companies.

❖ Pitfalls in Exporting

Fear of Failure: Fear of exports failure when psychologically ingrained does lead to actual failure. The company must be confident while exporting.

Policy of Dumping: Export markets should not be treated as dumping ground for the surplus production. This production which could be sold on domestic front should not be sold abroad. The assumption is that such production is unsuitable for foreign markets.

Flippant Attitude: Some companies never take exports seriously. Exports have glamour because they mean stints abroad to a few executives at the company's cost. Exports might be made just to show others that they do export. Exports are taken casually. The business is not developed on proper lines.

Export Marketing is Absent: Export does not mean just supplying the markets abroad. We have to pursue exports seriously. Some hard selling is essential. We have to modify the products, explore new markets, assess foreign buyers' needs etc. Exporting goods of certain value is very good, but who knows we have much more potential. Export marketing is as much important as domestic marketing and a right attitude rubs-off the other exporters too.

Lack of Professionalism: Exporting requires trained professional manpower and so employing amateurs who know nothing about its intricacies means inviting trouble.

Production Orientation: Production orientation tries to pass-off products as they are manufactured in the export market, without modifying them in the light of needs and wants of the customers. The buying preferences of customers are much more important than the convenience of the production of staff.

Passive Approach: Many companies export but feel that it is not worthwhile to go abroad and visit the customers. They expect their customers to come to them. Home customers are to be serviced, but not those abroad. This attitude should be rectified.

Principles of Business Management and Exports: Just as home business becomes successful if we take care of R & D, design, production, marketing, personnel and finance. The same holds true for export business, too. In a small company all these functions may be carried out by a single individual, but in a large company each of these functions are put in charge of a specialist.

Export Markets Vs. Domestic Markets: Exports differ from domestic trade. Domestic trade is generally done in one market; whereas in export trade we may deal with hundreds of markets, where each market differs not only from the domestic market but from one another also, *e.g.*, Gulf market is different from the European market. What is, therefore, necessary is the *constant adaptation* to the local market conditions.

The foundations of an export office staff as regards practices of export are as follows:

1. Customer's liaison: Staff are needed to handle customer liaison in respect of enquiries, quotations and orders. They need to advise, customers on the progress of their orders and ensure that delays do not occur. They are the essential backup to export salesmen, with whom they must work closely.

2. Transport: The actual transport of goods to overseas markets must be arranged, either directly with the carriers concerned, or through shipping and forwarding agents.

3. Insurance: Since it is customary for all cargoes to be insured, staff are needed to ensure this. This is always done, either on behalf of the company or the customer, or by the customer, so that goods are never left uninsured.

4. Finance: This is always a problem area since the work touches closely on that of the accounts department of the company, nevertheless, in an export office. There must be people who decide and operate methods of payment; to deal with the bank whenever necessary with regard to payment; and to handle credit insurance by the Export Guarantee Scheme operated by the government or some other means.

5. Documents: While each section is normally responsible for its own documents, their sheer number means that some form of control has to be exercised so that all the documents for any transaction are brought together and dealt with as required. This means having someone in charge of documentation.

6. Records, statistics and information: In an export office, there must be staff able to keep the necessary shipping and sales records and such statistics as are required. In addition, information must be recorded about methods of transport rates, procedures and while this may be kept by the individual concerned, it must be available to anyone in the export office.

It is normal for certain export functions to be carried out by the appropriate departments in the company, but staff will be needed in the export office to liaison with these other departments. The main areas where this is necessary are as follows:

7. Production: There are two main aspects concerned with the production of goods for export with which the export office staff are concerned. One is the completion, packing and despatch of goods, in accordance with instruction which the export office will have to issue. The second is the planning and production of goods for export and the modification which may be required to existing products for export markets.

8. Research and development: The export staff will have to be consulted on various aspects of research and development, that new products will be considered in the light of both their domestic and export suitability.

9. Legal considerations: Normally, all legal matters in a company are under the control of the company secretary or a special legal department since so many aspects of export have legal implications for the company, the export office staff must work closely with the company's legal personnel.

10. Information and research: All markets have to be studied and the information obtained about them will need to be recorded. Where specific research has to be carried out, staff will be needed to handle this.

11. Distribution: Where various channels of distribution are used, it is normal for this work to be handled by the export office staff and not by anyone on the domestic side.

12. Promotion: This covers all forms of promotion, from the production of price lists to the carrying out of advertising campaigns in overseas markets, it may be handled by the company's advertising or publicity department or it may be looked after by specialists in the export office.

Home Trade	*Foreign Trade*
1. It is domestic trade within our boundaries.	1. It includes trade across our boundaries with other countries.
2. Simple and easy operation.	2. Various difficulties of distance, currency, licence, duties, clearing, payments etc.
3. Procedure is quick and simple.	3. Lengthy and complicated procedure.
4. Factors of production (labour, capital etc.) are mobile.	4. Factors are not mobile.
5. Self-reliance.	5. Essential for LDCs (Less Developed Countries) for growth.
6. Wholesale as well as retail activities.	6. Always large-scale.
7. Limited risk and hence profit.	7. Substantial risk and hence profitable.
8. Not so competitive.	8. Very competitive.
9. Marketing costs are less.	9. Marketing costs are more.
10. Less formalities and documentation.	10. Formalities of licence, clearing, customs. Documentation is a pre-requisite.
11. Voluminous.	11. Not so voluminous.

* * *

15 PRODUCT MIX STRATEGIES

We shall first try to define a product before taking up a serious discussion on product mix strategies.

Philip Kotler defines a product as *"anything that can be offered to a market for attention, acquisition, use or consumption that might satisfy a want or a need."*

Stanton defines a product as a *"set of tangible and intangible attributes... which the buyer may accept as offering want satisfaction."*

Products in the market can be *physical goods* like cars and medicines, *services* like banking and insurance, *persons* like Alisha Chenoy and Baba Sehgal, *places* like Kashmir and Ooty, *organisations* like RSS and NCC, and *ideas* like loss prevention and cancer awareness.

❖ Product Levels

Every product has several layers. The most basic layer is the *core benefit* representing the fundamental benefit the consumer is buying. As Fulmer Wheeler remarked, "Dont sell the steak, sell the sizzle." A travel agency is not selling a 2-week Goa excursion. It rather sells "exotic locales, romance, glamour and rest." Products are also symbols. Credit cards are security blankets. Amusement parks are an escape from reality. Jeans are a sex symbol. Markets see themselves as benefit providers.

Each marketer translates the basic core benefit into a *generic product* which is its basic version. A hotel's core benefit is rest and sleep but its generic version is a civil structure with rooms on hire. Other generic products are a grinder-mixer, an ice-cream maker, a toaster, a shaver, a concert, a medical examination.

The third level of a product is the *desired product* representing the expectations of the buyers while buying the product. A hotel guest may expect a napkin, a towel, a fruit-basket, a welcome drink, an airport transfer, clean linens, a telephone and CC TV. He expects a particular ambience. The hotel that comes close to the desired level is preferred.

The *augmental product* is the level of the product that distinguishes itself from the competitor's offers. A computer manufacturer provides training to the buyer's staff, maintenance services, designs customised software to augment his product. The product augmentation level considers the total consumption pattern of the buyer. The manufacturer gets an opportunity to add to a factory turned out product so many values. However, each augmentation has a cost and we have to see whether it is possible to recover this cost from the customer. There may be a sizeable number of people who will demand a budget hotel rather than a 5-star luxury hotel.

The last level of a product indicates its potential. The potential indicates its possible evolution in future. It is an exploration on the part of the marketer to find out new and better ways of satisfying their customers and make their products stand out.

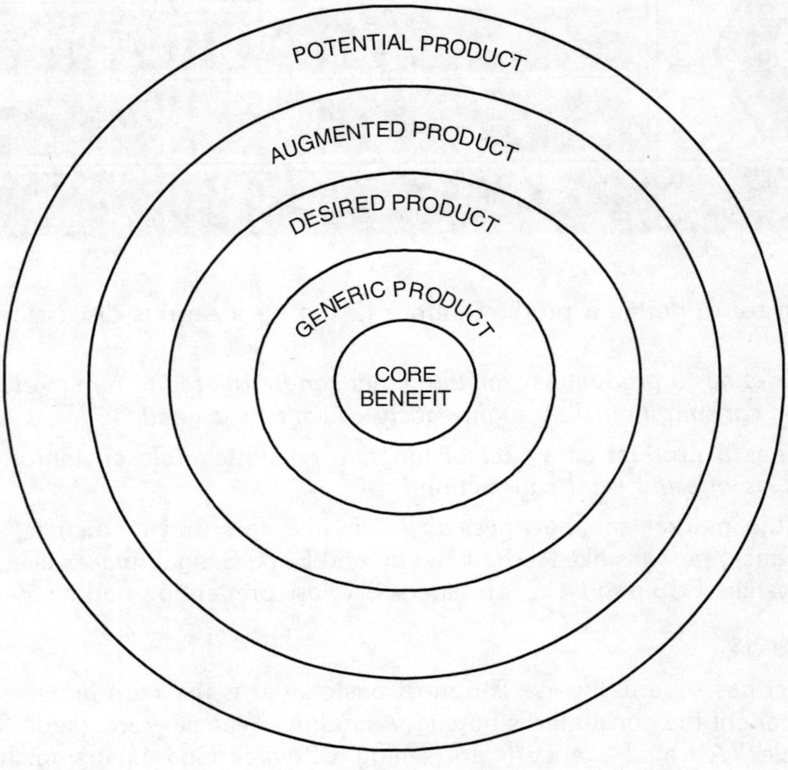

Fig. 15.1 Level of a product

❖ Product Hierarchy

Products are related to each other. A product hierarchy ranges from a core need to a specific product item. If we consider a Kinetic Honda scooter, the following illustrates the product hierarchy:

❖ Basic Need: Transport

Product Family: All the product classes that satisfy this basic need, *e.g.*, two-wheelers and four-wheelers — motorised and non-motorised.

Product Class: A group of products within the product family having a functional coherence, *e.g.*, motorised two-wheeler.

Product Line: A broad group of products for essentially similar uses and possessing a reasonably similar product characteristics constitute a product line, *e.g.*, scooters.

Product Type: Those items within a product line that share one of several possible forms of the product, *e.g.*, non-geared automatic scooter.

Brand: The name assigned to one or more items in the product line that is used to identify the item and distinguish it, *e.g.*, Kinetic Honda.

Item: A distinct unit within a brand or product line that is differentiated in terms of quality, price, appearance, size or some such other attribute *e.g.*, Kinetic Honda scooter (new) Model II.

To illustrate further, health gives rise to a product family of tonics, in which there is a product class of iron tonics (haematinics), of which one line is iron syrup which is offered as a brand called Tonoferros.

We also frequently come across a term *product system* which is a group of diverse but inter-related products functioning with compatibility. To illustrate, a computer company sells a basic computer with software, printers, computer stationery, modems, monitors and other options that constitutes a product system.

Product mix is another frequently encountered term. It is a product assortment. It is a full set of products and items offered for sale by a marketer to the buyer.

❖ Product-Mix Strategies

The product mix or product assortment is a full list of products (all product lines) by a company. To illustrate, Videocon's product mix consists of audio products, TVs and VCRs, washing machines and home appliances like refrigerators, water purifiers etc. The product mix of company may consist of related products or unrelated products, depending upon how diversified the company is.

Each product mix has width, depth and consistency. The width of a product mix is given by the different product lines handled by the company. The depth of the product mix is given by the variants of product items offered in each product line. The consistency of the product mix refers to the affinity of the product in terms of production facilities or marketing or research *e.g.*, GEC has as many as 2.5 lakh products, but they have an overall affinity as all are driven by electric power. The following diagrams illustrate these concepts.

VIDEOCON

Product Mix Width

TVs	VCRs	Home Appliances	Washing Machines	Audio Products

Videocon

Product Mix Depth: Washing Machines

Videocon Semi-Automatic 2.5 kg

Videocon Semi-Automatic 5 kg

Videocon Fully-Automatic

Videocon Fuzzy Logic

Depth

The length of the product mix is given by the total number of items in its entire product mix. Each product line can be assigned an average length by dividing the total number of items by the total number of lines. For instance, if there are 25 items in the product mix of Videocon and there are five product lines, the average length of the product line is 5.

The above discussion enables a company to spell out its product strategy along four dimensions:

(*i*) The company can add new product lines. (widening the product mix)

(*ii*) The company can introduce more product items. (Lengthening the product line).

(*iii*) The company can introduce different product variants, *e.g.*, Videocon introduces Bazooka TV. (Deepening of product mix)

(*iv*) Keep more consistency in product line or less consistency in product line. (Concentration or focus or diversification).

The planning of the product mix is largely a function of strategic planning. The product mix is allowed to expand or contract or maintain or harvest or divest.

❖ Product Line Analysis

A product line is put in charge of an executive. He has to monitor the sales and profits of each item in his product line and see how it fares with the competitor's product lines. Those product items which contribute most to sales and profits should be guarded against competition. A high concentration of sales in a few select items makes the product line vulnerable. Those items which contribute insignificantly to sales and profits are either to be rejuvenated or dropped. Products of competitors are put on a map in terms of their attributes. This enables a line manager to decide the competition of his own product. It also indicates the niches in the market which can be filled up. This has been discussed under product positioning later.

Product Line Length: The product line manager tries to have an optimum product line length. The length is considered short if any addition of new product increases the profits. The length is considered too much if there is a possibility of increasing profits by dropping the items from the product line. Company objectives do affect product line length. Those companies which are committed to high market share and growth have longer lines, even though some items are not yielding profits. Those companies which are obsessed with profits tend to have shorter lines.

Over a period of time, as the company grows, product lines start lengthening. The sales force and distributors pressurise a company to have a full product line to satisfy all the needs of the target customers. The expanded production capacity also acts as an incentive to have product lines length increased. The product line manager keeps on adding product items for having larger sales and profits.

The ever lengthening product lines in their wake bring additional costs, which cannot be allowed to rise beyond a limit. A review of product line is then undertaken. Such a review may reveal many loss-making product items. To improve the bottomline, such items are dropped. From an undisciplined product-line growth, we reach a massive product pruning stage. The length of the product-line is increased by two ways — line stretching and line filling.

Line Stretching: Line stretching consists in going beyond the current range of products. The stretch can occur upwards or downwards or in both the directions.

Downward stretch is resorted to by those companies whose products are all upper end. A downward stretch may *fill up* a market void or may extend the high end reputation of the company to the low end products. A competitor's attack at the highest end may provoke a company to attack him at the lower end. Sometimes, there is low growth at the high-end and so a downward stretch may become necessary. Downward stretch exposes the company to the risk of cannibalisation — the low-end items cannibalising the high-end ones. There is another risk — the competitor is compelled to enter the high-end market as a response to the company's low-end entry. There may be distribution problems. The trade might not like to patronise low-end items for a variety of reasons.

Upward stretch is the entry of the company in the market at the higher end when its current range is located at the lower end. Perhaps, a high growth rate or higher profits are an incentive for upward stretching. It also gives an opportunity to the company to have a complete range. An upward stretch is a risky proposition. The competitor is likely to go down market. Besides, the competitors at the upper end are usually well established. Even customers may not take a lower end company entering the higher end seriously. The trade channel may not have the competence to handle a higher end product.

Two-way stretch is in the middle of the market and can opt for stretching both upwards and downwards.

Line Filling: Within the present range more product items can be added. This is called line filling. There should not be a missing link in the line. It may result in lost sales. Line filling may help to fill up excess capacity, *e.g.*, children's tooth brushes can be manufactured if there is excess capacity in a toothbrush industry. Addition of product items may lead to incremental profits. The gaps are filled up so competitors do not get a chance to enter the market. Line filling, however, should not confuse the customers — each item must have a visible difference. Line filling should not lead to cannibalisation.

Upward stretching is also called *trading up* and downward stretching is also called *trading down*.

Line Modernisation: A company may have an adequate product-line length. But the product-line might be old styled. What is necessary is the line modernisation. In rapidly changing environment, line modernisation should be continuous. Overall modernisation or piecemeal modernisation is an important decision. Modernisation in piecemeal allows the company to assess the reaction of the traders and customers. The disadvantage of such an approach, however, is that it allows competitors to copy the changes. Modernisation should not be too early to affect the sales of existing products adversely or should not too late so that competition goes ahead of us and makes us obsolete.

Line Featuring: One or a few product items are selected by the product-line managers for featuring. Sometimes, low end products are featured as traffic builders. Videocon has selected its ₹ 8,000 worth colour TV for featuring. It attracts customers inside the shop. Its high-end product Bazooka is, however, priced at ₹ 24,000. Sometimes, a high-end product is selected for featuring to give prestige to the entire product line. Sometimes, weak items are selected for featuring.

Line Pruning: A product line needs pruning to eliminate low profit products. There is an attempt to get profits from fewer products. Sometimes, an entire product line is eliminated; *e.g.*, Xerox dropped its line of computers and Gillette its line of digital watches. Line pruning is also resorted to when there is shortage of raw materials and energy. It is difficult to maintain production capacity then.

❖ Product Positioning

We have already discussed the concept of product positioning in a separate chapter. We shall restrict now to examining certain positioning strategies.

❖ Positioning Strategies

1. Positioning vis-a-vis a competitor: Here the position is directly against the competition. It is head-to-head positioning. Liril's position and Cinthol Lime's position of "lime freshness" is an example of head-to-head positioning. This stance may not be suitable for a weak competitor.

2. Positioning by product attribute: Here a product is described in terms of the benefits it offers, *e.g.*, Maruti offers economy, Colgate *"suraksha chakra"* and Pepsodent "fights germs" long after its use.

3. Positioning by price and quality: Up market stores at Breach Candy are reputed for having quality merchandise and high prices.

4. Positioning in relation to product use: Vitamin E has been considered as vitamin for youthfulness and its use has increased tremendously after this positioning.

5. Positioning in relation to a target audience: Baby Shampoo of Johnson was later on repositioned as a mild shampoo for adults required to wash their hair frequently. Light beer is directed to calorie conscious consumers.

6. Positioning in relation to a product class: Either a product is associated with or dissociated from a product class, *e.g.*, 7-Up is an un-cola drink setting it apart from the Coke, Thumps Up and Pepsi. We can have a range of food products in which there no salt.

7. Positioning for social accountability: A product or a firm is identified with a social concern.

APPENDIX

Developing a new brand and launching it is an expensive as well as a risky proposition. As an alternative strategy, companies resort to brand extensions which reduce costs as well as risks. Besides, the values if embodied in a brand are transferred to the extended brand.

There are three types of brand extensions:

Brand Extension

Line Extension	*Vertical Extension*	*Horizontal Extension*
Here the basic product remains unchanged. Variations are created by introducing new flavours, colours and fragrances. They stay within the marketing forces governing these extensions. They help in broadening consumer base, expand market through segmentation and keep the brand's leading image alive.	Though a new product form is introduced, it still falls into the same usage area. Toilet soaps are extended as liquid wash. These are within the category. The new product carries forward the expertise of the mother brand.	Here the brand name is extended to a totally different product category, *e.g.*, men's wear to men's toiletries (Park Avenue). This is the most risky extension. Here there is no synergy between the products. Dunhill — a cigarette brand has been extended to male accessories. These are outside the category. Extended products must carry the same benefit forward, the category must have well-defined leaders and the timing must be right.

Brand extensions occur when firms 'enter markets they had not previously been present.... under the name of one of their existing brands — Jean Noel-Kapferer in *Strategic Brand Management.* In other words, what Ries and Trout call *line extension,* Kapferer calls *brand extension.*

Ashok Jain of Cadbury feels the most obvious reason for brand extensions is corporate ego — having a great brand which can be extended.

The extended product's qualities should not go against the consumer perception of the original brand name. *e.g.,* Camlin's effort to extend the stationery and art material brand name to cosmetics has not proved successful. Similarly, Dettol antiseptic's extension to Dettol beauty soap could not succeed, though after repositioning, there is some amount of success.

Many companies in India have opted for line/brand extensions, *e.g.,* Amul, Maggi, Nirma, Lux, Clinic, Milkmaid, Lakme, Bata.

Brand extensions reduce the initial resistance of the consumers to a new brand since they are already familiar with the original brand. The trade channels also support the extension readily.

There should not be, however, uncontrolled extensions. The danger is to the identity of each brand. The associations get diluted. Sharp association is necessary for a product.

By themselves, brand extensions do not spell out success of a product which also depends upon other factors like quality, price, market characteristics, consumer perceptions and promotional efforts.

Wrong extensions damage not only the extended brand but also the original brand.

According to a study by the US-based Neilsen Company, 40 p.c. of new product launches in the US grocery trade in recent times were brand extensions. No such study exists for the Indian market.

Brand Extensions

Ries and Trout do not favour brand extensions when the company tries to be all things to all people. They lack the confidence to build the brand from scratch. To develop a new brand requires corporate courage which is very much in short supply. Ries and Trout find that brand extensions are never the leaders in the US in any product category, the only exception being Diet Cola segment.

Pond's toothpaste is a very glaring example of an extended brand failing in India. Lakme shaving cream failed to work as brand extension due to Lakme's strong feminine connotation. Similarly, Vicks Hot Sip did not work.

Each brand has certain core values. When brand extension is for dissimilar products, the brand has to draw more on its core values (provided they are present) to be successful. Besides, brand extensions creating new products must be symbiotic — the new brand puts something back into the mother brand and mother brand rubbing-off its values to the new brand. Sometimes, the new brand overshadows the mother brand, *e.g.,* Wipro computers have overshadowed Wipro Oils. We may say that what is considered to be mother brand today may become child brand tomorrow — the composition of the family may change.

In the ultimate analysis, brand extensions are the second-best options to launching a new brand. Given the capacity of invest, one must opt for a new brand name.

Extensions

A single brand can be extended to two markets — from industrial markets to the domestic consumer markets. It increases the consumer base of the industrial marketers. Industrial market products are associated with a specific technology. Ultimately, the markets for such a technology shrinks. It is logical for them then to expand in the domestic sector. The industrial marketers identify the need for gaps and extend their products. The successful extension in India of several such products can be quoted here — M-Seal of Mahindra, Fevicol of Pidilite, Zero-B of Ion Exchange, Cease Fire of Real Value Appliances. Of course, once an industrial marketer decides to enter the consumer market, he has to put in fresh brand building efforts. They may involve new communication strategies, new methods of packaging, changed distribution strategies and selling techniques. The product should be made more user-friendly. However, industrial to domestic transition may not always succeed, *e.g.,* Super Glue. To ward off failure, the industrial marketer might tie-up with a consumer marketer, e.g., Grindwell Norton's tie-up with Lever to supply scrubbers with Vim.

Brand Stretch or Extensions

Brands are stretched to tap the business opportunities in *new areas* where the company believes it has technical, financial and marketing expertise. Brand stretching logic can be better understood within a framework of marketing forces in which they have a better chance to succeed.

There are three types of extension philosophies:

Commercial: There is an opportunity. We have a strong brand. Extending the brand to the new opportunity legitimises it in the minds of the consumers and lessens the ad expenditure to make it familiar. This is an economical option. However, underpromotion may not always work.

Marketing: Marketing viewpoints restrain the wanton extensions. It emphasises brand equity. Ideally, there should be one brand-one product form. Brand equity becomes diluted due to extensions. Brand equity is to be guarded. It is a narrow viewpoint that makes one prone to neglect the marketing opportunities, *e.g.,* Colgate entered the gel category very late.

Naive: Brand is a symbol of quality and promises a particular quality. Brand extension rubs-off brands quality, promise to new categories. Each brand, however, also stands for a host of benefits and expertise in product areas. Cadbury's learnt this when they entered biscuits market.

Successful Extensions

These extend the core brand benefit. They consider the brand's area of expertise. They are timed critically. Had Colgate gel come earlier, it would have been a market leader instead of Close-up. When core brand benefit is reflected in the extended product, the extension becomes credible. Dettol antiseptic was extended to Dettol Soap. The benefit associated with Dettol was that it was a cut and care product whereas Dettol soap is a 'love and care' product, which thus runs contrary to the care benefit of the parent brand. However, Surf becoming Surf Ultra, and Lifebuoy becoming a liquid are examples of the brands remaining confined to their core benefit even when extended. These extensions have strengthened the brand equity. Each brand has an area of expertise. Lipton's expertise in tea would not make it successful in biscuits market. Even category experience counts. Pond's have no category experience in toothpaste market and thus its extension into this area was troublesome. Maggie has successfully exploited its expertise in culinary across different brands. There are hardly any other brands having expertise in areas in which Maggie extended. It has in the process created new categories. Each extension has to be timed properly. Shower gels were unimaginable a decade back. The state of development around must be conducive to the acceptance of the extension.

Line extensions have become popular on account of the prohibitive costs of entry for new products, ranging from ₹ 5 crore for a soft drink to ₹ 30 crore for a detergent. Line extensions, normally, could mean a one third reduction in entry costs.

Experiments in Line Extensions

Product Plus	:	Horlicks' extension into Chocolate Horlicks
Price-linked Extras	:	It is within a product category. A brand is extended to gain niche markets. Pricing is used to differentiate products. The well-known example is that of Johnson and Johnson in sanitary napkins market. Carefree is in belted segment, whereas Stayfree is in beltless segment. Stayfree is available as a regular, double and deodorant. Stayfree silky dry is poised against Whisper. Cheaper line extension, however may endanger the equity of the mother brand. Palmolive Extra Care was launched as a premium skin care soap in 1989 with three colour variants. Colgate Palmolive used skin-typing as a distinguishing factor; white for normal skin, pink for dry skin, and green for oily skin. Lever has three variants of Lux International based on skin typing. Palmolive took the risk of downgrading its product by offering Palmolive regular in the popular segment. It has also three variants based on skin typing.
Positioning	:	Sharply positioned line extensions are also sometimes an opportunity for rejuvenating stagnating brands, *e.g.,* Cinthol from Godrej Soaps. Cinthol is extended to include Cinthol Lime, Cologne and Sandal. Liril's attempt to extend to cologne segment is, however, not so successful.
Using Form	:	Vim has successfully used form to extend line. It was a scouring powder. It became then a liquid cleaner. Now it has become a washing bar.
Product Synergy	:	As already explained, a brand extension should be in harmony with the mother brand. A lack of synergy between the two leads to a near-certain failure, whether there is product-plus or no product-plus. Cibaca Top was extended as Cibaca Lime, but it did not have synergy with Cibaca Top. On the other hand, Colgate Dental Cream (CDC) was extended as a blue gel in the South. The blue gel combined the therapeutic and cosmetic properties of the parent brand (stops bad breath and fights tooth decay). It was further positioned as the confidence product which became its USP. The gel extension gave consumers a reason to stay with the brand name.

(Based on Nandini Laxman, Stretching the Leader Brands, The Strategist Recollected 1993-94.)

* * *

16 BRAND DECISIONS AND PACKAGING DECISIONS

In any product strategy, a crucial decision is about branding. Branding a product means a long-term investment in building that brand by spending on promotion, advertising and packaging. There are manufacturers who manufacture a product but leave the branding decision to the marketers to whom they hand over the product. However, the fact remains that brand name gives power to the firm. Brand name marketers with no manufacturing base are still at an advantage. They can anytime change the manufacturer. Whereas Taiwanese firms remained only manufacturing firms, say, in textiles and consumer electronics, Japanese and Korean firms did both manufacturing as well as branding to consolidate their position. Goldstar TV (now available in India), Sony TV (now made in India) and Toyota are very well built brand names. Brands ultimately command customer loyalty.

❖ What is a Brand?

This word *brand* is quite comprehensive and covers several other narrower terms.

A brand is defined as "a name, term, sign, symbol or special design or some combination of these elements that is intended to identify the goods or services of one seller or a group of sellers. A brand differentiates these products from those of competitors" (American Marketing Association, Chicago)

A brand in short is an identifier of the seller or the maker. A brand *name* consists of words, letters, and/or numbers that can be *vocalised.* A brand *mark* is the visual representation of the brand like a symbol, design, distinctive colouring or lettering. Mercedes Benz is a brand name and the star with it is a brand mark. A *trademark* is a brand that is legally protected. All trademarks are brands and include both the brand name and the pictorial design. Exclusive rights to use the brand in perpetuity are granted by the trademark law, unlike the Patents and Copyright Laws which have expiry dates.

Essentially, a brand is a promise of the seller to deliver a specific set of benefits or attributes or services to the buyer. Each brand represents a level of quality. Irrespective of the fact from whom the brand is purchased, this level of quality can be expected of the brand. A brand is much more complex. Apart from attributes and benefits, it also reflects the following:

Values: The values which govern a producer are reflected by the brand, thus Tata stands for quality, fair price and so on.

Culture: A brand represents a certain culture, *e.g.,* Coke is an icon of American culture, while Shilpa Bindis are typically Indian.

Personality: A brand projects a personality. Had the brand been an animal or an object or a person, what would come to our mind? Videocon suggests a lion, MRF suggests a muscle man and Rin suggests· a lighting flash. Sometimes a brand may take on the personality of an actual person, *e.g.,* Charlie Chaplin and Cherry Blossom.

User: The brand suggests its own target audience. We know what a Garden Woman is. We know that Sunny is for teenagers. We expect a Mercedes to be driven by an executive or a top-class businessman. These users correspond to the values, culture and personality of the brand. Because of the imagery associated with the brands they actually have the power to enhance or limit a consumer's perceived image of self-image.

The above discussion makes one thing very clear — a brand is a complex symbol. It is not just a name. Branding, therefore, involves developing deeper meanings for the brand. The lesser the dimensions a brand possesses, the shallower it is. The more the dimensions, the deeper it is. A brand cannot be just a bundle of physical attributes. Attributes are very easy to copy. Besides, attributes valued today may not be valued tomorrow. Even benefit-oriented brands are not on firm grounds.

Maruti's fuel economy can be attained by other brands. Maybe, the benefit valued today may not be valued tomorrow. A brand becomes enduring by its values, culture and personality. These constitute the essence of the brand. Mercedes stands for prestige, success and high technology. Actually, this should become the building blocks of its brand strategy. We just cannot think of a Mercedes being offered at a price of Maruti. Perhaps, this will dilute the values associated with Mercedes. Remember, it takes years to build these values.

❖ Brand Equity

We have observed already that brands have the power and value in the market place. There are brands in the market which people have not heard about. Certain other brands are fairly well recognised, showing a high degree of *brand awareness.* However, brand awareness is just the first step. As a brand climbs up further, we find people ready to buy it, giving it *brand acceptability*. Brand equity is the intrinsic worth or value of the brand in terms of the kind of money a consumer is willing to pay for it in *preference* to its competitors. These brands are said to have a high degree of *brand preference.* Then ultimately comes what is called an acid test of a brand — *brand loyalty.* The consumer's reluctance to settle for an alternative product is the true indicator of brand loyalty.

Brand equity can be measured against brand loyalty, brand acceptability, brand awareness. Brand equity can be described in terms of its perceived quality, brand associations, channel relations, patents and trademarks. Brand viewed in this manner becomes an asset which can be sold or bought for a price.

A good example of brand equity is Wills Filter Cigarettes which has a 30-year heritage, and which has taken into its stride no less than 28 price increases. It has also faced severe competitive pressures from king-size entries. And yet Wills Filter still holds its own, enjoying immense loyalty and showing sound brand equity. The brand has consistently consolidated its position. The Wills Filter "made for each other" campaign has been nurtured, nourished and continually freshened. Another example of brand equity is Lux, which has consistently followed a strategy of "beauty soap of the film stars" position.

There are several advantages of high brand equity:

1. The marketing costs are reduced as there is a high level of consumer awareness and loyalty.
2. The bargaining position of the company is strong while dealing with the distributors, because consumers expect them to carry the brand.
3. It allows the company to charge higher prices than those charged by competitors because the brand has a high perceived quality, *e.g.*, LML priced its select model ₹ 6,000 more than Bajaj's Chetak.
4. Brand extensions become possible as the brand name carries weight.
5. When a company's brand has strong equity, it can be traded-off at a good bargain, *e.g.*, Parle selling its soft drink brands to Coke for $40 million after building them up for 15 years in India.

Brand equity which is the science of brand building takes all possible contingencies into consideration. In the process of building a brand, a company will have to employ a continuous R & D, skilful advertising, excellent trade and consumer service and other measures. The marketing scenario is analysed to see how it can best be used for the benefit of our brand. To quote Indranil Gupta, if we are "in the business of building brands, the biggest reality we need to face is that we would never go doing so in isolation. That means building our equity better than (the equity of) others." Along with the other needed values and functional benefits of a brand, advertising also helps build brand equity. The impact of advertising in building a brand varies from category-to-category and even from brand-to-brand. But in essence, contributing to brand equity is what advertising is all about. A brand's equity is the effect the aggregate of potential consumer's belief that it will deliver its promise. Thus brand equity depends, to a large extent on *consumer equity*.

David Aaker's classic work suggests the routes to build brand equity:

- Salience of a brand name.
- Its perceived quality.
- Its key image and personality associations.
- Its relationship with the customer.

These lead to the benefits of:

- Brand preference
- Brand loyalty
- Possible price premium or holding on volumes
- Leverage in other categories.

In many companies, we have "brand managers" or "brand equity managers" to build the brands.

Brand equity is measured both in quantitative and qualitative terms. The quantitative parameters are sales, profit earnings, past performance and potential growth. The cumulative effect of these factors taken together makes brand equity worth more than mere sales *e.g.*, Coke's sales are worth $8 billion as against its brand equity of $ 24 billion and Pepsi's sales are worth \$5 billion as against its brand equity of \$9 billion. The qualitative criteria include leadership position of the brand, its stability in the market, its internationality and trend of support and protection. The brand is rated in comparison with other brands in the same market segment. The brand score gives it strength and power. The brand equity is built by improving its rating on each of these parameters.

Brand equity, to begin with, was only a financial concept to be thought of if one wanted to sell-off the brand, just like goodwill. Over a period of time, brand equity expanded its meaning to include all the assets gathered by the brand, especially the intangible ones. As we have already observed, some of these assets are brand awareness, brand loyalty, perceived quality and strong consumer association. Brand equity further includes brand personality, brand bonding with the consumers, user imagery and values.

Different brands hang on different elements of equity and in this sense there cannot be parity of brand equity between two brands. The moment the brand equity of two brands become equal, one of them must fail. The one that creeps into consumer mind first succeeds.

Though all the elements of brand equity are at work, only one or two elements really matter for deciding in favour of that brand. Thus companies identify such *hooks*, and emphasise them. In this sense, brand equity approximates to USP (unique selling proposition) but it is still distinct. "USP is vigorous, whereas brand equity hook is not" (Muhammed Muneer C.P. in First into Buyer's Mind in *Perspectives,* MOS dt. Feb 11-12,1995). USP emphasises a single-point. Brand equity hook is complex, consisting of several elements taken collectively. Brand equity hook can change over a period of time, and is not inflexible.

In India, the *Advertising and Marketing* (A & M) magazine of Spectrum Communications, Delhi conducts a survey to arrive at brands scores, by rating the Indian brands against several quantitative and qualitative criteria.

❖ Branding Decisions

Historically, most products were unbranded. Producers sold goods or commodities to fulfil our core or basic needs like taste, hunger or energy. These products did not have any identification mark on them. The first step towards branding a commodity is to package it, *e.g.*, rice, papad, salt. The company enhances the value of the commodity functionally. Branding started formally when craftmen put trade marks on their products to protect them against inferior quality. Painters started signing their art works. Pharmaceutical companies were the first to put brand names on their products. Today hardly anything is unbranded. Products from unorganised markets like vegetables, salt, fruits etc. are unbranded. But now we have branded salts and atta too. Venky's has branded chicken successfully. Inspite of a brand movement, products have been demanded in generic, unbranded form in pharmaceutical and staple consumer goods sector.

When commodities are branded, they have to counter the retailer resistance, who get greater pricing freedom when they are unbranded. Along with this, there is consumer resistance — a housewife loves to select foodgrains, clean them, get them ground into flour. A readymade Captain Cook or Trupti atta deprives her of all these sentimental actions. However, if we are successful in lessening the consumer resistance there arises a demand. The pull effect compels the retailer to stock the brand and his resistance also comes down. Consumers want a good value for money from a branded commodity.

Functional products and commodities take less to branding than aspirational products. Manufactured products are branded easily, whereas it is not so for agricultural ones. Of course, a commodity can evolve into a brand in stages. Branding evolves through stages —

a commodity, a functional brand, a high value added brand and a premium product. Pads were used as sanitary napkins. The next improvement was belted napkins. It was followed by beltless napkins. We now have dry-weave napkins. The consumers are expected to adopt each of these product versions one by one, as they come in the evolution of brand. However, it may so happen that the aspiring middle-class with high disposable income leap frogs into the high end brands like "Whisper" and "Ariel".

While branding an attempt is made to go beyond mere functionality brand equity is to be built up by advertising appropriately to reduce the initial consumer resistance. The low involvement product can be made high-involvement product by emphasing certain situations *e.g.,* Cease Fire demonstrated how a family's bliss can be shattered by a sudden fire. Sometimes, non-functional elements like fun are emphasised *e.g.,* Captain Cook salt. Textiles are sold on imagery and not on functional appeals. The brand becomes aspirational. Later, textiles are associated with values like machoism, friendship and growing up. Benetton ads do just this. The brand then becomes an icon — it stands for something. However, all brands cannot become icons.

The core need of clothing is satisfied by a set of product classes — jeans, shirts dhotis. If we consider two-legged garments only, we have a choice between Trousers and Jeans. Jeans are denim blue material, with rugged cuts, metal zippers and buttons and is a tough piece of clothing. This product is augmented by giving fancy pockets, double stitching, wider range and designs and is associated with youth and machoism. The augmented product takes the brand name of FM jeans. Brands thus help to make a personality statement. FM Jeans declare your anti-traditional intentions and your desire do find a cause in your life. The onlooker may like this attitude and shares it.

Despite the branding, consumers may treat a certain product as a commodity, *e.g.,* cement, since the price is the same for all the brands and all of them have established the same identity. To begin with, just a little value addition like packaging makes a commodity a brand but when all competitors do the same thing, there is the danger of the brand again switching back to its commodity status. Many consumers prefer lower priced generics which are sufficiently satisfying. Generic products are a challenge to high-priced brands and weaker brands. Some companies cut their prices to compete with generics. It is desirable, however to fight them on the basis of quality — offering greater quality than generics at competitive price.

As we have already observed, branding makes it easier for consumers to identify products and services. Brands ensure a comparable quality when products are repurchased. Brand's simplify a consumer's shopping. Choosing a commodity is far more complex than choosing a brand. Commodity selection is based on rational left-brain logic. Brands have enotive association. They can be chosen on a more holistic basis involving parallel left and right brain processing. The firms find that brands can be advertised. The firms also get the advantage of recognition when brands are on the shelves of the retailers. There is no confusion between branded products amongst consumers. Branding makes price comparisons difficult. Good brands help build a corporate image. Branding gives added prestige to the marketer. Branding also gives legal protection to the seller. Brand loyalty protects a firm against competition. Branding enables a seller to segment the market. The distributors prefer branding as an identification tool for vendors, as a convenient tool to handle the products and as a guarantee of certain production standard. These are some of the factors which encourage sellers to brand their products though branding is a costly proposition, involving the costs of packaging, labelling, advertising and legal protections.

The firms have to carry out two onerous tasks once they decide to brand — promoting the brand and maintaining a constant quality. If these two requirements cannot be met, products are better left unbranded. Branding decision is related to the nature of the product and the trade channel is involved. The sophistication of the distribution channels is conducive to branding. The opening up of a vast national market also augurs well for branding. Brand development and personal disposable income have a positive correlationship.

❖ Who will be Sponsoring the Brand?

We have already discussed why it is advantageous to brand the products. The next important branding decision is about the sponsorship of the brand — whether it is going to be manufacturer's or national brand or it is going to be a middleman's brand. In countries like the US, this is a very important decision, owing to the presence of large departmental stores and super-markets. In India, mass retailing has still to register its presence. Middleman's private brands in India are still restricted to co-operative super-bazars and NCCF (National Consumer Co-operative Federation). Some retailers have brand names in the product category of sarees. In the US, manufacturers may produce some output under their own name and some under distributor's label. Private label brands in the US wage a constant war with the national brands.

❖ Brand Names

The company has to choose its brand name strategy.

Each product can have a separate brand name or one family name can be extended to all the products. Philips follow the family brand name strategy. Hindustan Lever brands the individual products. Let us consider the pros:

❖ Family Brand

(*a*) It is cost effective in as much as it reduces product launch costs and also the promotional expenses incurred on a continuing basis. The success of one brand when well-promoted gives a push to the entire product line. Management of trade channel also is easier. In tyre marketing this approach is highly successful.

(*b*) For products of uneven quality, this approach is a dicey proposition. Even in markets showing variations in consumer profiles, this approach is not useful.

(*c*) Each product is denied a special identity which can go a long way to make it click.

❖ Individual Brand

(*a*) Individual brand invokes associations and imageries. These psychological factors influence the buying decision.

(*b*) Even if the product fails, the effect are restricted to that product only. They are not transferred to the whole product line.

(*c*) Costlier strategy.

(*d*) No benefit to the brand of the organisation's reputation.

❖ Modified Strategy

These days companies tend to brand the products individually, but also give prominence to the company's name or logo in all promotional efforts and product packaging. For instance, A TATA PRODUCT is a legend that goes with every individual brand name of Tata Oil Mills Co. (TOMCO). Some companies adopt brand extension strategy, by introducing similar or dissimilar products, *e.g.*, Nirma toilet soaps. Some organisations decide several brand names of the same product where each brand has its own following. The brands compete amongst themselves. Soap manufacturers follow this strategy. Al Ries and Jack Trout are against brand extensions. In their opinion, brands are not dying — the companies are killing them through mindless line extensions. When a company line extends, it weakens itself. Product categories can be given extensions, *e.g.*, gel pastes, detergent ultras, puri-gerators. Telephone directory reclassified becomes Yellow Pages. It is more than mere positioning. It is creating a new product category with just an extra push. Tinker in the lab and let the brand or product plus emerge, *e.g.*, gel, cologne soap, microsystem, germicheck etc.

The choice of an individual brand name is the next important decision. The choice is not so easy. There are really few good brand names. As a wit has aptly remarked, "Searching for a brand name is like search for a wife — there are lots of choices, but the best ones have already been taken." Sometimes, brand names are based on a person's name, *e.g.*, Honda, Estee Lauder, Khaitan. Brand names can be based on locations, *e.g.*, Indian Airlines, Kentucky Fried Chicken. Brand names can suggest an important product attribute, *e.g.*, Duracell. There are brand names which suggest a life style, *e.g.*, Fleet Footers. EXXON and Kodak have an interesting history behind them. When ESSO found it necessary to change its name, the computer was fed various vowel and consonantial combinations, and 44,990 four-letter and 500,000 five-letter combinations came out. EXXON was finally chosen because it is distinctive and has graphic design possibilities. Kodak was coined by George Eastman in 1888 because he liked the letter 'K' and wanted a name which could not be misspelt.

555 cigarette's brand name is said to have been inspired by a batting record set in 1932 between Percy Hulmes and Herbert Sutcliffe.

❖ Characteristics of a Good Brand Name

A good brand name should possess as many of the following characteristics as possible:

(*i*) *It should be distinctive:* The market is filled with over-worked names and over-used symbols. A unique and distinctive symbol is not only easy to remember but also a distinguishing feature. "Northstar" shoes have a distinct name.

(*ii*) *It should be suggestive:* A well-chosen name or symbol should be suggestive of quality or may be associated with superiority or a great personality. The name *VIP Classic* for travelwares is suggestive of a superior quality for a distinct class of people. *Promise* is suggestive of an assurance of tooth health.

(*iii*) *It should be appropriate:* Many products are surrounded by a certain mystique in the minds of the consumers. *Carefree* is an appropriate brand name of a sanitary towel.

(*iv*) *It should be easy to remember:* It should be easy to read, pronounce and spell. *Tide, Surf, Gold Spot* are examples of such brand names.

(*v*) *It should be adaptable* to new products. Videocon is a good brand name for TVs and VCRs but when it is extended to refrigerators and washing machines, some of the sales appeal is lost. Hotline was a good name for gas stoves, but is definitely not a suitable name for TVs.

(*vi*) *It should be registrable* under the Indian laws of Trademarks and Copyrights.

Mostly a company develops several names for a product and makes a choice later after debate and discussion.

❖ Generic Usage of Brand Names

Sometimes, a brand name becomes so successful that it comes to be associated with a particular product category, *e.g.*, frigidaire is brand name used for any refrigerator, Dalda is a brand name commonly used for any vanaspati ghee. The brand names then do not remain distinct and become generic. Cellophane, nylon, fiberglass, celluloid, kerosene and aspirin have thus become generic. Xerox and Band Aid are not yet legally generic, but they have been so well promoted that many people just use them generically. Though each firm strives to have a popular and preferred brand names, it does not like it becoming generic. It is a tight-rope walk.

To protect against such generic use, a brand name can be combined with a company's name, *e.g.*, Eastman Kodak. A brand name can be combined with a generic name, *e.g.*, Dacron polyester, Dabur Chyavanprash. The public can be given a notice about the copyright of the brand name. Some companies assume the name of the brands e.g. Sony.

❖ Brand Strategy Decisions

A company has four choices in respect of its brand strategy.

(*i*) *Line extensions:* Extend the existing brand name in the existing product category.

(*ii*) *Brand extensions:* Extend the brand name to new product category.

(*iii*) *Multiple brands:* Have new brand names in the same product category.

(*iv*) *New brands*: Invent a new brand name for a new product category.

The following diagram illustrates these four choices:

		PRODUCT CATEGORY	
		EXISTING	NEW
BRAND NAME	EXISTING	LINE EXTENSION	BRAND EXTENSION
	NEW	MULTIPLE BRANDS	NEW BRANDS

Fig. 16.1 Brand Strategy Choices

Most of the new products in the day-to-day use and grocery products are line extensions. A few are brand extensions. A few new brand names appear in both multiple brand strategy and new brand strategy.

Line Extensions: Here the company introduces additional items in the same product category, keeping the brand name same. The additional items may be of a different size (say a 150 gm cake of Palmolive Soap). There may be a new form, say Liquid Lifebuoy Soap. The additional item can be of different colour, say, a lilac soap instead of a white soap. The package may be different, say a satchet of a shampoo. Some additional flavours can be introduced, says Brown & Polson Custard Powder is now available in chocolate and with elaichi flavour. There may be added ingredients, say, Lifebuoy Gold. Lux is available in three skin types, say for normal skin, dry skin and oily skin, making it "your kind of soap for your kind of skin". Line extensions can be innovative, or "me-too" or may be void-filling. Most of the new product activity is of line extension type. Line extensions offer a variety to the customers. An advantage can be taken of consumer's latent need. Or else, a competitor is to be matched in terms of its offer. Line extensions also allow a company to command more shelf-space at the retail level.

Line extensions can be made available through a specific mix of trade channels *e.g.*, lower end products are available at general stores and higher end products at a few specialised outlets.

Line extension, though very popular, is not without its drawbacks. The specific meaning of a brand might be lost by heavy extensions. Ries and Trout are against line extensions. Today, Coke in India means a 300 ml bottle of the real thing. Say, an extension brings a 500 ml and 1 litre bottle. Again, a can may be introduced. Perhaps, there may be a diet Coke later. All this may become confusing. Besides, what is the guarantee that all these extensions will have sales sufficient to cover the costs? Even additional sales may be at the cost of other items in the line. Line extensions work only if the sales are taken away from the competitors. Mostly, they eat up the sales of our own brands.

Brand Extensions: An existing brand name is extended to a product being launched in a new product category. Honda is a brand in the field of motorbikes. The same brand name is given to products in the field of lawnmowers and marine engines. Brand extension works well for rubbing-off the success of established brand names to new products. The new product, therefore, finds easy acceptance. However, if the new product is not satisfactory in performance, it might affect the reputation of the company's other products. Most of the times, brand name may not be appropriate for the new product category. While brand extending, if it advisable to see how the associations of the parent brand are consistent with the extended brand.

Multiple Brands: This strategy is employed to saturate the market. Additional brands are introduced to cater to the different segments, *e.g.,* P & G's Tide is for soiled clothes and Dreft is for gentle clothes. P & G produces nine different brand of detergents. Sometimes, flanker brands are introduced to protect the major brand, *e.g.,* high-priced Seiko watches are protected by introducing low-priced Pulsar watches which are flanker brands. Multiple brands offer us price flexibility. A competitor's 'fighting brands' are so priced that they beat those of the competitor. This way the main brand is protected and its price is not cut. Multiple brand strategy may not allow the company's resources to be focused. They may get dissipated over a large number of brands. Besides, if each brand has a small market share, the overall profitability may get affected. Our brands should affect the competitor's brands and not the other brands of our own. Sometimes, a company gets a legacy of new brands in the process of acquisition. Thus Coca-Cola got the Thums-Up, Gold Spot and Limca brands.

New Brands: To make brand names more appropriate, a company puts a new brand name when it enters a new product category. A new brand again has to be built up and this is quite expensive. It should be considered whether the sales and profits estimated from the new brand justify it.

We shall now familiarise ourselves with the following terms used in connection with the brands — brand positioning and repositioning, brand images and brand personality.

❖ Brand Positioning

The core part of the brand strategy is brand positioning. Ogilvy felt that the results of an advertising compaign depended less on how the ads were written but how the products were positioned. Naturally, positioning should precede advertising. Al Ries and Jack Trout also advocated positioning. To them, positioning was a battle for the consumer's mind. They have concluded that a strong brand has a clear association with a single word or category. Xerox implies photocopiers, IBM mean computers and McDonald's indicate burgers. Marketing and advertising's task is to single-mindedly focus on and build such associations. Brand positioning creates a relationship between the Brand and the Consumer and gives a reason for this relationship.

Even a well-positioned brand may require repositioning in the light of competitive activity or changing consumer preference. The positioning stance taken a few years ago may be too diffused today. Ceat tyres' rhino denoted toughness for decades together. But others have encroached upon the *toughness* territory. Ceat, therefore, repositioned it along the non-functional benefits — the safety plank. Sometimes, even a too focused stance may spell disaster if the new rivals have a general appeal. To illustrate, Marico's *Saffola* refined oil, rich in Poly Unsaturated Fatty Acid. (PUFA) content reduces the risk of heart attacks. Later, ITC *Sundrop* and Lipton *Flora* chose the same health platform but with a light variation. The new brands promised all-round good health, rather than harping on the heart attack alone. *Saffola* thus got reduced to a small niche — oil only for those with heart trouble. Marico found a creative solution. It launched *Sweekar* on a general health care positioning, keeping Saffola a niche brand. This is a wise strategy because any repositioning of Saffola would have contradicted all it has stood for all these years. While repositioning we have to first examine what is wrong with the old positioning and then decide what our new positioning would be. The shift should made gently and without losing the old customers. Management must consider repositioning costs and the revenues likely to be generated after repositioning.

❖ Packaging

Is packaging a component of advertising? Or is it really a component of a product? These are the questions that are most commonly asked. The answers to both the questions are "yes." We already know that packaging is an integral component of a product; but the package also plays an important role in its saleability. It, therefore, becomes partly a component of promotional advertising. Packaging is no longer a mere outer covering for the protection of the product; it is very much a contributing factor to its increasing marketability. Ads after ads feature a beautiful package and the product image in the minds of consumers is, to a good extent, due to attractive packaging. In the case of similar products, the brand difference is only due to differences in packaging. Good packaging covers an idea of the quality of the product; it has a value which is distinct from the value of the product. Attractive packaging is an effective Point of Purchase (PoP) and stimulates gift sales.

As the old adage goes, "Clothes make the man." So, also, does the package make the product. Product are often judged by their packages — particularly for *impulse product*. Perfume is a good example of this. There is a close interrelationship between the Advertising and Packaging components of the marketing mix. Several advertisements feature the product in its package.

Though packaging is primarily a means of protection during transportation and storage, our interest in it is primarily for its use as a marketing and promotion tool. Advertising people are involved because, in addition to being a protective device, packaging is featured as a campaign theme. The package is a vehicle for carrying the manufacturer's name, the brand name, the trademark, apart from the information it provides about the ingredients and direct advantages of product use.

The other marketing significance of packaging is that it helps in achieving product differentiation. Packaging is designed for convenience in the use of the product and may be used to differentiate a brand from the brands of its competitors. Further, packages are designed to have a reuse value. Good packaging will gain for a product more shelf space than for a product with unsatisfactory or unattractive packaging and will result in its extensive exposure to the customers visiting retail stores. This will improve the sales of the product.

A beautiful packaging is an advertisement at the point of sales. In short, packaging is an important advertising medium, carrying varying message from the marketer to the consumer. In view of the advertising and promotional significance of packaging, professionals in this field should have a profound understanding of packaging so as to make it an effective marketing and sales tool.

Packaging as a function has two separate dimensions — the physical aspects related to the science and technology and the behavioural aspect related to the art of product design associated with buyer behaviour and motivational research. It enhances the value of the contents and passes on the impression to the consumer directly or subtly.

In the case of consumer products, package serves as a silent salesman. It performs self-selling tasks. It should attract attention, and tell the product story. It should build the confidence and give a clean and healthy look. It should be convenient in handling and usage, as well as in storage. It must reflect good value.

Packaging research concentrates on the colour of the package and its matching with the product and the consumer. Packaging research also studies the design aspects of packaging — the desirable properties of a container. Graphics and logos are an important part of package design and in conveying the total product image.

Packaging is called 'the trade dress' of a product. 7-6-7 is a peculiar term used in cigarette packaging. In packs of 20s, seven cigarettes are stacked in the first row, six in the second row and seven in the third row. Reuben Rousing is inventor of aseptic packaging and the founder of Tetra-pak.

❖ Packaging and Sales Promotion

Product package has a vital role to play in SP (Sales Promotion). Some of SP techniques used are:

(a) *Money-off Pack:* A message of a reduced price is flashed in distinctive colour on the package.

(b) *Coupon Pack:* Coupon can be made an integral part of the package or can be placed inside it separately. For instance, Johnson and Johnson puts coupons for redemption in its sanitary napkins packages.

(c) *Pack in Premium:* A premium or gift is placed in the package, *e.g.*, charms are placed inside Cibaca Fluoride Paste.

(d) *Premium Package:* It is a specially designed package having reuse facility or a prestige storage value, *e.g.*, instant coffee package doubling as tumblers, tea packages later serving as jars, alcoholic beverages later used as display items.

(e) *Self-Liquidator:* The buyer preserves either packages or their parts as evidence of buying the product. In return, he is given a reduced price at the time of repeat purchase or is rewarded with a different product.

(f) *Other Applications of Packaging as a Marketing Tool:* Shelf-life of a food products is an important consideration. Shelf-life can be increased by using special packaging materials, *e.g.*, tetra-packs. Packaging can be used to avoid direct price comparison with the competing products, *e.g.*, Maggie Ketchup packages 400 gms. bottle which is not comparable immediately to industry wise norm of 500 gms. bottles. Dhara edible oil packages are popular since they are pilfer proof and spare the consumers the adverse effect of adulterated oil.

APPENDIX I

Mascots

For long marketers have used mascots to build a distinctive image for their brands, aid recall and boost sales. By long association, mascots impart character to a brand and represent what the company and its brand stand for. Mascots have well-defined personalities and their positive traits tend to rub-off the brand. Over a period of time, the symbol and the brand become inseparable from each other. Mascots add life to an otherwise low interest product and improves visibility.

A green eyed Onida devil has become a central part of Onida's advertising theme. Even negative traits of a mascot has worked wonders for Onida. Onida marketed its VCR with a chameleon as a symbol of adaptability to environment.

Penguin, the Kelvinator's mascot, is well-established, and inspite of an attempt to modify it by putting a woman in, they have consciously decided to continue with the penguin only.

Asian Paint's *Gattu* has become a marketing legend — he is a mischievous little boy with a paint brush in one hand and a dripping can of paint in the other. R. K. Laxman created this famous mascot.

Goadlass Nerolac chose a tiger as a mascot — a symbol for colour and toughness. The mascot was called *Goody*. However, the company uses it infrequently today. He has been deliberately underplayed. Nerolac — the company name itself is being emphasised. This is an example of what happens when the company name is as prominent as the mascot.

Pepsi's brand 7-Up has a mascot — Fido Dido, who began life on a cocktail napkin. According to the Fido Credo, created by Pepsi, Fido is *cool*. This cool image helped 7-Up stand apart from competing brands. A mascot not only creates an image for a brand, but helps it to stand out in the face of many similar brands.

Kiwi has been used to launch a range of shoe-care products by the TTK.

AI Maharaja

The Maharaja, for one, with his myriad moods has become one of the most enduring and endearing mascots. The Maharaja is always doing things in AI's communication – smiling, frowning, raising an eyebrow, closing an eye-lid, teasing and becoming cheeky.

He is a man of may parts — lover boy, Sumo wrestler, pavement artist, naughty post card vendor, monk, Red Indian, Arab, Chinese and even pregnant.

ORIGIN OF SOME FAMOUS BRAND NAMES

Listerine Antiseptic

Owes its name to Sir Joseph Lister (1827-1921) who introduced the use of antiseptics.

Listerin was first developed in 1879 by one of the founders of William R. Warner & Co. — Jordan W. Lambart (the American pharmacist) who based his antiseptic on the earlier formula by Lister.

Colgate

William Colgate (1783-1857) founded in 1806 a firm by this name as a manufacturer of tallow chandlery and soap. Colgate was an English-born soap manufacturer brought to America as a child. His son Samuel Colgate (1822-97) expanded the business. His son Sidney Morse Colgate (1862-1930) became the chairman of the consolidated Colgate — Palmolive - Peet Co. which was shortened to Colgate-Palmolive in 1953. Palmolive comes from the palm and olive oils contained in the soap.

Nokia

The brand gets its name from a river in Finland.

Castrol

It was originally based on castor oil.

Ray Ban Sunglasses

They were originally created in the 1930's for fighter pilot is of the US Army Air Corps.

Chanel's 19

This perfume is so named as it was launched on Aug. 19, Coco Chanel's birthday.

Sunlight and Lux

First branded soap was produced by William Lever in 1855. All Lever's soaps made by others for him were called Sunlight. Lever shifted his business to the village called Port Sunlight, south of Birtenhead, now in Merseyside in 1888. Lever then emphasied on their own Sunlight brand. The name conjures up brightness, health and cleanliness.

Lux was inaugurated in 1899. To begin with it was called Sunlight Flakes. A year later, it was renamed Lux. It suggests "light" (from Latin Lux). It also suggests luxury. This also seems to have been suggested by W.P. Thompson — Lever's patent agent in Liverpool.

Nivea Skin Cream

It is produced by Smith and Nephew. Beirsdorf in Germany manufactured this original cream under this name, from Latin *Niveus* meaning snowy.

Anne French

It is a name connected with toiletry products by ICC (International Chemical Company). This name was introduced in 1937 on the premise that the 'French connection' is a desirable attribute for toiletries. It was promoted before the second World War on Radio Normandy by a young lady who claimed to be Anne French.

Brylcreem

It is a combination of brilliantine and cream with stylised spelling. "Brylcreem" was first marketed by the Country Chemical Co., Birmingham. The chief chemist developed a product different from existing hair dressing products. The company passed to Beecham in 1939.

Cuticura

Latin "cutis" means skin and "cura" means care. The original Cuticura product was an ointment designed for Newfoundland fishermen whose hands became very sore in the course of their work.

Dacron

It is called Dacron in the US, but Terylene in the U.K.

Max Factor

This is the name of a Polish immigrant to America in 1904. In 1909, he established the firm in St. Louis, Missouri. In 1935, the U.K. branch of Max Factor opened in Bond Street, London. Factor in incidentally a Jewish vocational surname, meaning "agent".

Silvikrin (Beecham)

The name dates back to Second World War. The shampoo was first marketed in 1960. The first half of the name refers to grey or silver hair. The ending 'krin' is from Latin *crinis* meaning hair.

Vaseline (Chesebrough – Ponds)

It is a petroleum jelly. It was first manufactured in 1870 by American chemist Robert A. Chesebrough.

Vaseline may be from German *wasser*. (water) and Greek *elaion* (oil) on the misconception that petroleum is a product of decomposition of water in the earth.

Perhaps the more romantic explanation for "Vaseline" is that flowers were tossed by Cheesebrough from their vase and filled the same with jelly. This inspired the name. 'Line' is a popular suffix in medical names.

Bournvita

It comes from Bournville chocolates also made by Cadbury. Bournville is a place in Birmingham, where the chocolate factory was set up in 1879 by George Cadbury. The name ends with Latin *vita* meaning life.

Vespa

In Italian, it means 'wasp.'

Sprite

This soft-drinks name means 'elf.'

Mercedes

Consul General Emil Jellinek was a wealthy businessman who had a pretty daughter Mercedes who was born in 1889 in Vienna. Jellinek entered Daimler racing car event under the pseudonym Mercedes, and won the first prize. This inspired Maybach the brilliant designer of Daimler to adopt a new design, which was ordered for sale by Jellinek who was confident of its success Jellinek's proposal to name the new design after her daughter Mercedes was accepted. This name became so popular that it came to be used for all Daimler vehicles.

Lakme

High priestess of sacred Indian temple meets English army officer who has unwillingly strayed into holy ground. They fall in love. Her orthodox father vows vengeance. That's the story of Lakme, a 19th century opera written by Frenchman Leo Delibes, from which Simone Tata borrowed the name Lakme (French for Lakshmi, the name of the priestess). Lakme has since then been sold to HLL.

* * *

17 MARKETING OF SERVICES

As we have already observed, the term product also includes intangible services along with tangible physical products. The world of commerce is made up of a basic agricultural sector, a manufacturing sector and a services sector. The services sector undertakes activities which aid the trading and commercial activities, *e.g.* banking services, transportation services, hoteliering, consultancy services etc. There are also personal services like a beauty parlour and a dentist's clinic. There are social services to fight the evils in the society. Let us now distinguish between Goods and Services.

We are now in a position to appreciate the characteristics of services:

Goods	*Services*
(i) Being tangible, they can be created and transferred.	They are intangible and non-physical.
(ii) These can be carried home and can be stored.	They cannot be physically carried home. Only their effects can be carried. Consumption occurs during the process of creation.
(iii) Non-perishable, generally.	Perishable.
(iv) Standardisation possible.	Difficult to standardise.
(v) Equal quality can be ensured.	Equal quality between two offerings is difficult to assess.

❖ Intangibility

As services are not physical objects, they cannot be touched or smelt. Physical goods can be touched, seen, tasted, smelt or heard before they are bought. This cannot happen with the services. We can market services by emphasising the benefits and the satisfaction offered.

Service itself cannot be a primary object of promotion. Credit cards *per se* are useless pieces of plastic. However, the power to buy a variety of things at 90,000 different establishments with this piece of plastic makes it a useful product. Services carry with them an array of perceptions. It is an abstract concept.

However, there are always some tangible elements which enable us to evaluate services *e.g.* in a flight, the tangible elements are the experience at the airport, on-board services and the in-flight entertainment. But these are not comparable to a TV set or a suit where the total product is seen. As services are abstract, they are given reality through tangible elements *e.g.* a law firm is evaluated on the basis of its tunrover, size, track record and location. All these elements create a brand image.

Perishability: A service is perishable to a higher degree. If not used, services are lost forever. Services are not storable. A seat in a plane for a particular destination must be occupied before the flight commences. If it remains unoccupied, it is a waste. An unoccupied hospital bed or unutilised credit facility are thus economic wastes. They cannot be restored or reused.

Inseparability: Services are not separable from the person who provides them. Dancers, musicians, dentists and doctors create and offer the services at the same time. This inseparability of services creates challenges for the service marketers.

Heterogeneity: Services are not easy to standardise because they are heterogeneous by their very nature. Even when the same price is paid for a particular service, the same level of quality cannot be ensured. Services are predominantly performed by people. It is difficult therefore to maintain the same standard. Some organisations try to standardise staff performance by careful planning and control. But then it introduces inflexibility Heterogeneity also provides an opportunity to strenghten the brand by customisation. Moreover, the perceptions of those who provide the service and those who receive it are different. Service output is also difficult to be standardised.

Ownership: The goods change hands on the price being paid. The buyer gets a title of ownership to the goods. However, services are not physical in nature. So we can have only access to them. We can make use of services without any rights to ownership. Thus, medical services at a hospital can be used on payment of a price without any claim on the ownership of the hospital bed. The same is true while hiring a hotel room, or being a member of the swimming pool club. The ownership vests in the providers of the service. First of all, services are intangible. Secondly, even if tangible, things are used while providing these services, there is no transfer of permanent ownership to these tangible things.

Simultaneity: Service providers bring the customers to the point of delivery of service or they themselves go to the user for delivery of service. This puts a natural limitation on the size of geographical area being covered by services.

Goods are produced and then sold and finally consumed. Services are sold first, then simultaneously produced and consumed. The consumer participates in the production process. It greatly influences his perception.

Quality Measurement: It is difficult to quantify the total purchase of a service. We can put a quality rating on hotel food, but the delivery of service by the waiter or the ambience in which the food is served are difficult to quantify. Services are judged on the basis of overall satisfaction of the users.

Physical goods can be checked for quality before they leave the supplies. Service quality can be assessed only when consumers come in contact with the staff. Staff training is an important area for service brands.

Demand Pattern: Hotels show a high occupancy rate during vacations and low occupancy rate in slack season. Transport is also in demand during peak hours, but is underutilised otherwise. Thus services have a flexible pattern of demand.

❖ Concept of Services Marketing

The services are to be sold keeping in mind the interests of the buyers. The interests of both the provider of the service and the buyer must fuse finely. As services cannot be moved we shall have to see how demand and supply can be optimised. The most important factor is the quality level of the services. Services are intangible and the promises made about them get credibility over a period of time. Marketing management covers the marketing of tangible products as well as services. Even non-profit makes organisations like Red Cross, RSS, Lions, Giants and others can profitably use the principles of marketing. Service Institutions can both be profit-making institutions like the banks and the insurance companies or non-profit making institutions like an art museum. Service sector in the economy is growing at a very fast rate. Many jobs are being created in the services sector. Service sector is not as technology-dependent as the manufacturing sector. It gives us an opportunity to make optimal utilisation of valuable untapped resources. It paves the way for capital formation and raises our standard of living. In the US, 85% of the jobs created come from the services sector. Bank marketing in the developed countries have emerged as an important discipline. In developed countries, principles of marketing are applied in areas like education, hospital, communication, tourism, hotels and consultancy. In the 80s the services sector accounted for 40 per cent share in the Indian economy. The developing countries tend to neglect services marketing, as they neglect customer satisfaction. The developing countries are now waking up to the significance of services marketing. Banking, transportation and telecom are not known for their high standards of customer service.

❖ Scope of Services Marketing

Services marketing also depends upon the marketing research and Marketing Information System (MIS). A bank will have to undertake a survey of its customers to assess their needs and aspirations. An airline has to undertake a survey of passengers to assess their expectations about in-flight services. The next step in services marketing is market segmentation and targeting. Marketing mix of services consists of its product mix, price mix, place mix and promotion mix. In services marketing, product mix places great emphasis on the quality of services. The demand from different segments determines the ultimate product mix, *e.g.*, luxury rooms in hotel for business travellers and budget rooms for routine tourists. Product innovation plays a great role in product mix here also, *e.g.*, photocards in credit card markets are an innovation that makes these cards safe to use. Services are to be located so as to be convenient to the buyers, *e.g.* bank sets up extension counters at church premises, college campus and school campus. Pricing of services is a tricky area. Mostly, quality considerations override price considerations. Price setting also takes into account competitive practices. There are legitimate controls over pricing the world over. Promotion in the form of direct mailers, advertising, personal selling and sales promotion plays an important role in services marketing. Indian banks are slowly realising the importance of services marketing, though they are not still as effective as foreign banks. Insurance services are far behind in terms of marketing. Transportation services have undergone a change recently, *e.g.*, open sky policy has seen the emergence of private airlines. Tourism is being marketed, but it has still a long way to go. Indian hotels have professionalised the most. We can trace marketing elements in consultancy services and hospital services. Personal care services like beauty parlours, garments making, hair-cutting saloons, shoe repairing are concerned with transforming the personal appearance of the individual. They are designing a suitable marketing mix now. Education marketing has received a boost with the advent of private computer training institutes. We now have accepted the principle of "pay for your education". Entertainment marketing has witnessed software of TV programmes being marketed to channels and advertisers. Communication marketing has become competitive with paging companies and cellular phone companies vying with each other. Electricity marketing is still a conservative field that needs a review.

The distinction between Products and Services is fast fading. Credit cards from service providing institutions like banks are tangible and standardised products and are branded like other products.

❖ Involvement of Consumers

Consumers are active participants in a lot of the services *e.g.*, in a beauty parlour or a self-service restaurant. Here consumers need to be educated about the extent of their participation.

❖ Consumer-to-consumer Contact

Different services have different levels of consumer-to-consumer contact, for example there is minimal contact in legal services whereas there is high contact in an airline flight. The contact level does affect the consumer perceptions Who likes a boisterous group sitting across the other table in a restaurant? Such groups need separation *e.g.* smokers and non-smokers or economy travellers and business class travellers.

❖ Criticality of Time

Getting the service may involve some waiting time. Consumers do not like to wait for a long time. Organisations try to reduce the waiting time. In a queue system, some reservations can be given to consumers. A receptionist should be able to direct tactfully the demand to off-peak hours. Requests are prioritized on the basis of urgency. Waiting time is made enjoyable or tolerable. In the wating room, magazines are kept and TV is switched on. Some starting activities can be undertaken *e.g.*, filling up the medical details or reading of the menu at a restaurant. Consumers should be informed from time to time that they will be served shortly. They should be assured that they are not forgotten *e.g.*, on telephone hold, the operator time and again explains the cause of delay. Organisations can follow first-come first-served rule by allocating waiting numbers. Even then consumers are ready to accept queue jumping on account of emergencies.

❖ Evaluation of Services

Consumers base their decisions of products and services on search qualities, experience qualities and credence qualities. *Search qualities* are the attributes consumers can identify and assess *e.g.*, price, size, colour, smell, shape or feel. Physical goods are high on search qualities. In a restaurant, we differentiate the service while experiencing a dinner. These offerings are characterised by *experience qualities.* We do not have sufficient competence to evaluate many services like legal advice or surgical procedures. Even after consumption, our evaluation is difficult for such services. These services are characterised by *credence qualities.*

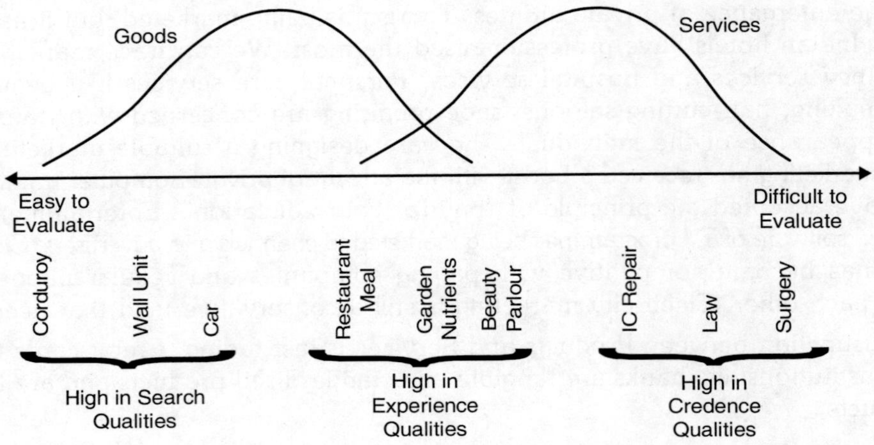

Fig. 17.1 Evaluation spectrum of products and services

In an evaluation spectrum, search qualities are on one extreme and credence qualities on the other, and experience qualities fall in-between.

The greater the difficulty in evaluating a service, the higher the perceived risk. Brands must therefore serve as risk reducers.

The following table spells out the communication strategies to help consumers evaluate service brands:

High Qualities	*Communication Strategies*
Search	Member-get-member schemes. Word-of-mouth publicity.
Experience	Demonstrations *e.g.*, video presentation
Credence	Creative communication, *e.g.*, appreciation of value of a house purchased against housing loan.
	Emphasis on trust element.

❖ Tangibalizing the Services

As there are intangible elements associated with service brands, these brands tend to be commoditized. Service brands are made tangible so as to make their perception consistent and common amongst consumers. The tangibility is imparted by using as many physical elements as possible which could be associated with the brand *e.g.*, staff uniforms, ambience, interior decor, music when customers are on hold, use of colours, stationery brochures, packages, design of physical facilities. These elements must be consistent with the service. There should be a holistic approach. Physical evidence must go well with the brand, convey a consistent message and appeal to the target audience. We should seek the additional opportunities to provide physical evidence for the service.

❖ Manpower and Service Brand

Services are represented by the manpower. In so many cases, they are the only point of contact for the consumer. If the staff is properly trained and well-behaved, the chances of the service brand being successful are greater. Service quality is influenced by the following factors related to the manpower:

Appearance	:	Shabbily dressed staff cannot sell high profile services. Elegantly dressed staff are a must for the service brand.
Responsiveness	:	Manpower should be sensitive to the needs of the consumers. In a cinema hall, a family can be given corner seats. A split family can be made to sit together in a bus.
Assurance	:	If there are snags, the manpower courteously informs the consumers and also inform them about the steps being taken to rectify the problem.
Empathy	:	A crying child is given a choco-bar in a restaurant. Manpower tries to comfort the child.
Reliability	:	Trade record is built by providing reliable service.

Manpower who is satisfied on the job leads to consumer satisfaction. Staff motivation is an area which requires utmost managerial attention. Right from manpower planning to selection to supporting and retention of manpower, the personnel aspects do go a long way in developing the right service brand. Customer service should become the second nature for all employees. Such an organisation culture cannot be created overnight, but it is worth the effort to accept the challenge.

❖ Consumer Participation and Service Brands

Consumer participation, as we have already observed, greatly influences the perception of a service brand. A particular swimming pool may be very good, but a person whose experience with the swimming coach is not good, many complain about the quality of the swimming pool itself.

There are different degrees of consumer participation. There is low participation in restaurants and air flights. Here the consumer's presence is necessary and the whole service is rendered by the service personnel. Even courier services have low consumer involvement. Consumers rarely see their infrastructure. They interact telephonically with the courier company for a short while. We can provide standardised offerings of such services. The procedures are well-defined. In the financial sector, the participation is limited, say in a bank branch, consumer is expected to fill in a pay-in-slip while depositing cash and tender the cash across the counter and get back duly stamped acknowledgement. But the major portion of work is done by the bank staff.

But in a health club or business management school, there is higher level of consumer participation. They take active part in a weight reduction programme. They hold themselves responsible if the results are not satisfactory. They are very happy when the service provider tries to solve the problem. Because of high degree of participation, organisations design customised offerings for the consumers.

Consumer participation is also an educative process. A consumer must master telephone banking or mobile banking before getting its benefits. Even Internet banking is a participative process requiring effort on the part of the consumer. But consumers gain benefits on account of such participation e.g. utility bills can be paid through internet from anywhere.

* * *

18 PRICING DECISIONS

An appropriate price for the product is one of the most important decisions for the marketing manager since a customer reacts more to the price variable than to any other variable. Price does affect the buying decision and the profit margins. Though there should be emphasis on the entire marketing mix, price is that variable which either makes you buy or prevents you from buying.

Though pricing is an important area, many pricing decisions are taken casually and based on cost analysis. Price is treated just as an accounting concept. Prices are expected to cover costs and leave a margin for the marketers. It is not prudent to go below cost. Pricing that is cost-based is easier since it relies more on internal data.

Though costs are important, the customer is much more important. Customer value or the worth of a product to the customer is an important criterion in pricing. Pricing is just not to cover costs. It has to capture the customer value. Pricing thus has shifted from being cost-based to customer-value-based.

These two are, however, not the only factor affecting price. Marketing strategy and competition are two other important factors. In this chapter, we shall study all these four factors in detail.

❖ Marketing Strategy and Price

Marketing mix for a product is set after designing the marketing strategy. As we have already observed, marketing strategy consists of segmentation, core strategy or product proposition and positioning strategy. Strategies guide us in price-setting – whether the price should be low or high.

A marketer can charge different prices for different segments. Even in the targeted segments, there can be differential pricing. These variations are called price bands. It is necessary for a marketing manager to understand the price sensitivity of the different segments. A marketing manager must know the significance of price in the overall purchase decision. Surveys may not suffice. Special techniques like conjoint analysis can be used. It is also necessary to understand how important the product is to the customer. The more it is, the lesser is his price sensitivity.

❖ Perceived Value

Perceived value is an important concept in pricing and in appreciating the customer's reaction to pricing. An industrial product may save money for the customers. A consumer product may provide benefits. These are matters of perception. There is always a comparison between the pricing and the perceived value.

Perceived value can be considered in relation to a market segment or an individual customer. An individual customer perceived value is called customer value.

There are three possible relationships among the perceived value, price and variable costs. These are:

1. Perceived value > price > variable cost
2. Price > perceived value > variable cost
3. Price > variable cost > perceived value

Let us consider each of these situations one by one.

Perceived value > Price > Variable cost

Here the price covers the production cost (or cost of service delivery). But such a price is less than the customer's perceived value. Customers think that this is a bargain. It is also called value pricing.

Price > Perceived value > Variable cost

Here the price covers the costs but such a price is also greater than the perceived value. It is a bad deal. Customers may not buy such a product. Either the company has to improve the customer value or decrease the price.

Price > Variable cost > Perceived value

Here also the price covers the costs. But the perceived value is even lower than the cost. It is a case of product failure. Such products are abandoned in the new product development process. If not, they are phased out of the market later.

The optimal relationship a product manager seeks is

Price = Perceived value > Variable cost

In short, the price must fully cover the perceived value placed on the products by the customers. This equation is not attained in practice always. Besides, it is difficult to ascertain the perceived value. Moreover, it is good to leave the customers with a feeling of a bargain. It is a decision on the part of the product manager where he has to see how much value is to be given to the customers and how much is to be retained. The highest price equals the customer value and lowest the variable cost. The other points in between is value is sharing between the product manager and the customer.

❖ Method of Value Pricing

Value pricing or value-in-use pricing assigns a price to a product based on its value to the consumer in the use of the product. Consider a product like a computer. It can be priced more as compared to its costs. The computer's life-cycle cost is made up by its price, start-up costs, service and maintenance costs. The product can offer more advantages over the basic product, e.g. faster feeding. Value can be assigned to this additional benefit. The following diagram illustrates this:

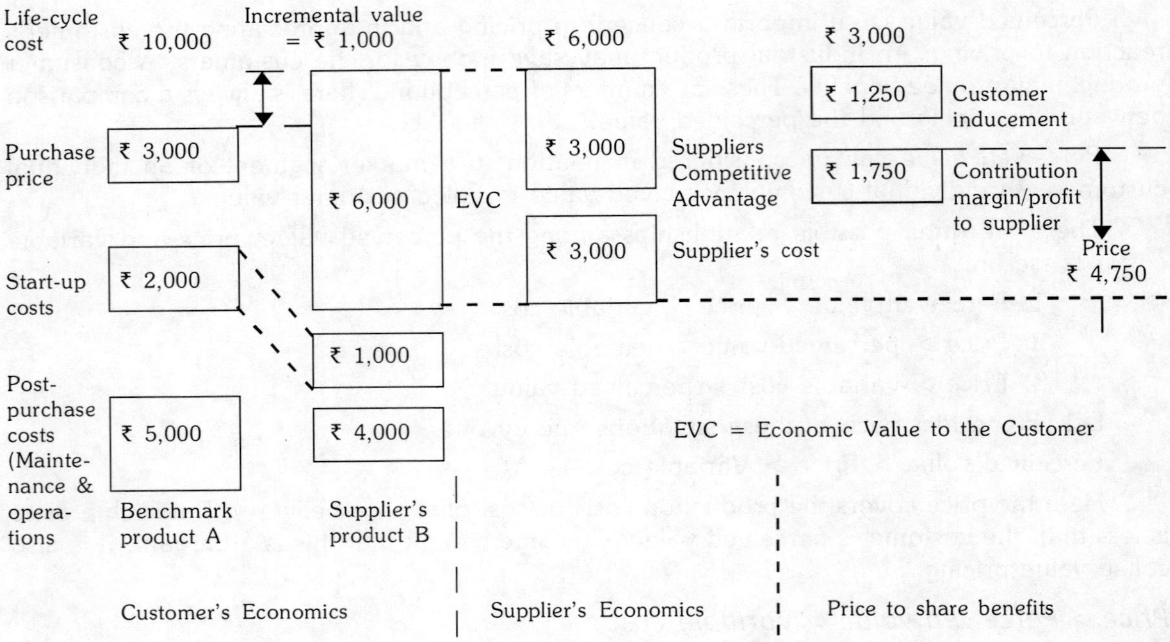

Source: Adapted from Forbes and Mehta, value-based Strategies, Business Horizons, May, 1981 and Anderson, Jain, Chintagunta, *Customer Value Assessment in Business Markets,* Journal of B2B Marketing, Vol. 1, 1993.

The value of the existing current product being used by the customer is first calculated. It is compared with the value of a competitive product and the difference is established. The consumer ought to be indifferent between existing product at prevailing price and a competing product at a different price if the difference is equal to the difference in relative value.

The life-cycle costs of a computer are ₹ 10,000. Our product offers additional benefits. A value of ₹ 1,000 is placed on this. The customer is willing to pay ₹ 3,000 for the basic product, he should in theory be willing to play ₹ 6,000 for our product – ₹ 3,000 basic plus ₹ 2,000 for savings start up and service plus ₹ 1,000 for the additional benefit. This is the customer's viewpoint.

For a supplier, it costs ₹ 3,000 to make the product. Any price above ₹ 3,000 will then be a profit. Any price under ₹ 6,000 will give a consumer a better product than the existing product he uses. The difference of ₹ 3,000 between our costs and value limit is the competitive advantage.

The last section of the diagram mentions one possible price. It is ₹ 4,750. It generates ₹ 1,750 as profit. But it offers an economic advantage of ₹ 1,250 to the consumer over his currently used product. This advantage induces him to buy our product.

Thus the final price reflects the value of the product to the end-user and the amount of inducement (from relative value) the supplier wishes to give to the customer. The consumers make price-performance trade-offs between competing brands.

❖ Simulating Buying Experience

Here shopping experience is simulated and customers are asked to shop and see the promotion in a mall-like situation. Price is manipulated to record the reactions of the people.

❖ Estimating Brand Equity

The brand equity is the price advantage one brand enjoys over another brand. The relative utility of products can be gauged by brand equity analysis.

❖ Using Price Thresholds

Here customer price thresholds are assessed. It provides an overall estimate of customer value. The reservation price is one such threshold. It happens to be the highest price a consumer would pay. The lowest boundary price is another threshold which indicates the lowest price someone would pay. Lower price is associated with lower quality. A customer may not purchase a low-priced product because of the suspicions about its quality. In a market research study, the typical questions are 'above what price you would not buy' and 'below which price you would not buy.' The most acceptable price then can be decided.

❖ Scaling

Rating scales are prepared to assess willingness to pay for a product. The buying intention scale asks the customers to show their intention to buy against a scale of 1-7, where 1 indicates 'very unlikely' and 7 'very likely'. Alternatively, scaling can be done in rupee terms. Here a pair of brands is taken and then the price for the preferred brand is recorded. Each brand is compared to the other brand. The scores are then compared.

❖ Competitive Price

Most of the products are priced at competitive levels. This is generally done when ours is a me-too product, not much different from that of the competitor. This corresponds roughly to the theoretically perfect market conditions, where the products are homogeneous and the buyers are well-informed about the prices. Thus there is no control over the prices at the end for the seller. This is a market-based method of pricing suitable for crude products, products of small manufacturers which are standardised and routine and agricultural produce. This method is also adopted when there is a customary industry norm of pricing. Pan masalas, toffees, chewing gums, chocolates are priced in this manner. When costs rise, either a new customary industry norm is set to enhance the price or the quality is diluted to maintain the price. When prices cross the customary industry norm, there is a sharp decline in demand.

In an oligopoly there are a few sellers whose products are similar and the demand is generally inelastic. An oligopolist prices at market level to maximise profits. On crossing the market price, he faces drastic reduction in total revenue. If the sells below the market level, all other sellers fall in line with him and a new reduced norm is established. Thus price reduction is not beneficial for the oligopolist. It is better to set the prices at the competitive level. However, pricing wars are very common in oligopolistic situation.

Arithmetically, competitive price is simple to arrive at. The going price of the market is assessed. There are usual mark-ups of the middlemen. A the retailer sells a ready-to-wear shirst for ₹ 100. This usual mark-up is 25 per cent. The firm's price should, therefore, be ₹ 75. It is to be seen whether ₹ 75 covers all costs and still leave some profit for the manufacturer. Sometimes, there is a real squeeze; especially when the costs are rising.

❖ Pricing Below Competitive Level

Here the process are set at some point below the competitive level. It is practised by discount retailers, who are interested in large volumes and low mark-ups. Soaps of well-known companies are available below the listed prices at some co-operative supermarkets in India. This is possible due to elimation of middlemen. Sometimes, a cash discount is offered to the customers.

❖ Pricing Above the Competitive Level

In skimming the cream strategy, the prices are set above the competitive level. The product which is new distinctive and prestigious is generally sold by this method. Some retail outlets are elite and charge a price above the retail norm.

❖ Competitor's costs

To arrive at correct decisions of pricing in relation to competition, it is necessary to estimate the cost sheet of the competitors. Reverse engineering can be used to analyse the cost sheet. Competitor's products are dismantled and component costs and packaging costs are estimated. The financial data available in public domain about the competitors can be analysed. The cost of delivery of services are more difficult to estimate. There are fixed overheads and these can be estimated by considering the number of employees, sales per employee etc.

❖ Proactive and Reactive Pricing

During periods of price stability, the decision to change the price can be made. It is a reactive decision when prices are changed in response to competitive prices. The product manager can either maintain the price, or match it with the competitor's price or lower it. Instead, a product manager himself can take the lead in changing prices and be proactive.

❖ Pricing Objectives

Marketing effort keeps in mind certain objectives and pricing is no exception. The pricing objectives must precede the actual price setting process. Pricing objectives can be related to sales like sales increase or maintenance or increase in market share. Pricing objectives can be related to profits like maximisation of profits or having a desired ROI or return on sales. Pricing objectives may seek to maintain the *status quo* like price stability and encountering competition. The pricing objectives must be consistent with the overall objectives of the firm.

Desired Returns: A firm may seek to achieve a certain percentage on its investment or sales and can price its products accordingly. Generally, net sales are considered while calculating returns for short-term. A percentage mark-up on sales is put to cover estimated operating costs and a desired profit for the year. Here, the percentage of profit may remain the same.

The rupee profit varies as per the units of output sold. In trading, returns on net sales are not so high. Manufacturers adopt the desired returns on investments. Mostly, the expected returns are 10-20 per cent. after taxes. The desired return price is advantageous to market leaders who can set pricing objectives without considering the smaller firms. It also enables the evaluation of different divisions of the company.

Profit Maximisation: This is a widely used pricing objective, though profit itself is considered an ugly word; synonymus with profiteering and exploitation. Profits cannot remain high in the long-run, because competition enters the scene, thus increasing the supply, reducing prices and profits. Public opinion also forces the prices downwards. Sometimes, governmental intervention brings down the prices. Firms that introduce new products or enter new markets may offer lower prices to penetrate the market. They are ready to suffer even losses in the initial years. It is better to have profit maximisation on total output rather than on individual items.

Credit card companies do not make any profit on a card till it becomes two and a half year old. Besides, profits come after attaining a critical mass of customers, say, 3½ lakh cards being sold. A part of the output called 'leaders' may be sold by a retailer for lower or no profits so as to attract customers to the store. But other profitable buys offset the losses and still leave a sufficiently high profit. Foreign banks use credit cards to get a clientle for their personal banking activities which are highly profitable.

Raise the Sales Volume: Pricing may be used as a tool to increase the sales volume, *e.g.*, by giving discounts or by cutting prices or by selling under cost at a loss. The objective may be to get a footing in the market. However, this may not always be profitable.

Market Share: One of the major objectives of pricing is to maintain the market share or to increase the existing there. First, the existing market share is assessed. Then attempt is made to increase it, especially if the market is growing. In a growth-oriented market, the desired return goal may not be sufficient since though the company earns what is planned, its market share may actually be coming down.

Price Stability: Market leader sets the prices and other firms follow these prices. Generally, this takes care of wide demand fluctuations. Because pricing today is flexible, smaller firms may not always consider a leader's price as benchmarks.

Competitive Pricing: Prices mostly respond to the competitive product's prices. Generally, there is a parity. It is difficult to cross the market-determined price. In a market of standardised products, if there is a price leader, other firms follow him in respect of prices.

Price Determination: Several factors influence the actual price setting. *Base price* is the price of one unit of product at its point of manufacturing or resale. Here there is no allowance made for discounts, delivery charges or pricing strategy modification. Though one and the same method is followed both for existing products and new products, the pricing of existing products is simpler, whereas pricing of new products is complex. Factors like demand for the product, market share, expected, competition, pricing strategy, other elements of marketing mix and production or procurement cost affect the price setting process.

Expected Demand: To estimate the total demand of the product is an important initial step before pricing it. It is simpler to forecast demand for an existing product than for a new product. In practice, we have to estimate the expected market price and to estimate demand at different prices.

Expected Price: The price at which a product is considered worth, knowingly or unknowingly, is its expected price. The expected price is not a precise price but a range of prices say, "between ₹ 300 and ₹ 400" or say "not exceeding ₹ 100". Customers do price evaluation prudently. However, for those new products for which there are no reference points, manufacturers show latitude while setting prices. Trade reaction also helps to determine the prices. Trade, by its experience, can guide a manufacturer as to which price will be acceptable to the market.

A too low a price than the expected price will result in lost sales. It is erroneous to price Revlon lipstick below ₹ 100. It will make customers doubt the genuineness of the product, and its quality. Some customers will consider it below their dignity to use such a cheap product. In other words, the product does not tally with their self-concept. Higher prices may lead to greater sales, showing an inverse demand.

The method of determing the expected price may consist of trade appraisal. expert appraisal or customer survey. It is also possible to observe the prices of competitive products. There is a possibility of a gap between what the customers say they would be willing to pay and what they actually pay. It is, therefore, advisable to do limited test marketing under different price alternatives.

Expected Sales: It is advisable to estimate the sales volume at several different prices. Previous experience with this product or a similar product is really helpful. In other words, we are here estimating a demand curve at different prices for a product. We also try to estimate the elasticity of demand. High price elasticity products could be priced lower than the price inelastic products. This analysis of estimated sales at different prices lead to Break-Even Point analysis (BEP) considered later in this chapter.

Expected Market Share: A company striving for a greater market share is aggressive in its pricing policy (lower prices, heavy discounts etc). The market share expectation is related to the present capacity of the plant. Some plants may not be able to sustain a larger market share. Sometimes, expansion plans may attract other competitors. The ease of competitive entry determines our expected market share. The easier the competitive entry, the higher the initial prices.

Competitive Situation: Current and future competition affect our base price greatly. The ease of entry and a healthy bottomline are an invitation to competition in future. There are three types of competition:

(*i*) Competition from similar products, Eveready cells and Novino cells.

(*ii*) Competition from substitute products, Metallic vessels and Plastic vessels.

(*iii*) Competition from unrelated products having a claim on the same disposable income of the customer.

Profit-oriented pricing objectives are vulnerable to competitive reaction. A company that just wants to maintain its prices as they are, is most likely to have competitive price parity.

❖ Odd-price Sales

In India, this is better known as 'Bata pricing.' This innovation was pioneered by Melville Stone Publisher of Chicago Daily News to stimulate sales of his one penny newspaper in the late 19th Century. He persuaded Chicago Merchants to price their wares at 1.99, so that the circulation of one - penny increased in the market. He purchased one penny coins from the US mint to increase the overall supply of these coins.

❖ Pricing Strategies for New Products

New products are in the introductory stage of Product Life-Cycle (PLC). The company modifies its pricing from stage-to-stage in the PLC. The first stage *viz*; the introductory stage, is really challenging.

Here there is a distinction between:

(*a*) Pricing a genuine product innovation that is, patented.

(*b*) Pricing a product that imitates the existing products.

Pricing an Innovation: Patented innovative product when launched offers two pricing options to a company: (1) Market-skimming pricing, and (2) Market penetration pricing.

Skimming the Market: Here, a high initial price is set for the new product to 'skim' the market. The American chemical giant Du Pont has followed this strategy by charging the highest possible price for their discoveries — cellophane, nylon and so on. The initial high price is suitable for some segments of the market. Later, other segments of the market are tapped by lowering the price. This strategy enables the company to skim a maximum amount of revenue from the various segments of the market. Polaroid also adopts this strategy by introducing a high-priced camera first, followed by lower-priced versions later to attract new segments. In India, there are many publishers who publish a hard-bound deluxe edition of the book first. Later, they come out with cheaper paperbacks.

Market skimming is relevant when the following conditions prevail:

(1) Substantial high current demand.

(2) Small volume is economically viable for production.

(3) The high intial price will not attract more competitors.

(4) The high price supports the image of a superior product.

Penetration of the Market: Here, a low intial price is set on the new product, hoping to attract a large number of buyers and win a large market share.

Texas Instruments (TI) in the States have successfully followed this strategy. It sets up large plants. It charges the lowest possible prices and gains a large market share. The costs start falling; and with that it reduces the price even further.

This strategy is relevant under the following conditions:

(1) There is a price-sensitive market. Lower prices are an incentive to the buyers for market growth.

(2) Production and distribution costs decline when this experience accumulates.

(3) Low price is a disincentive for competition.

❖ Pricing an Imitative New Product

Initially new product is not a technological breakthrough. Here, mostly it is a question of product positioning. The product is to be positioned here on two attributes — quality and price.

Product Quality	Price: High	Price: Medium	Price: Low
High	1. Premium strategy	2. Penetration strategy	3. Superb value strategy
Medium	4. Over charging strategy	5. Average strategy	6. Good-value strategy
Low	7. Rip-off strategy	8. Borax strategy	9. Cheap-value strategy

Fig. 18.1

In the above figure, we've shown nine possible price/quality strategies.

The newcomer may produce a premium quality product and charge a high price for it (Cell I).

If there is a market leader already doing this then other strategies can be adopted.

(1) Design a high quality product and charge a medium price. (Cell 2)

(2) Design an average quality product and set an average price (Cell 5) and so on.

The newcomer has to take into account.

(1) The size and growth rate of each market in each cell.

(2) The competitors for a particular strategy.

❖ Extra Factors Affecting the Price

The above discussion considered pricing objective and strategies well within the control of either the marketing or product manager. There are some extra factors outside their control which affect pricing decisions.

❖ Psychological Aspects

Customers being rational do consider price information. However, they also consider their buying experience, communication package received and POPs. There are two major aspects relating to psychological pricing — reference prices and price-quality relationship.

Reference Prices: A standard price against which the observed price is compared is reference price. Reference prices may be regular retail prices. Reference prices could be mentally arrived at standard prices. Consumers think in their mid that they are fair prices. These could be the last price paid or average price charged for similar products. It leads to the concept of perceived price which to the customer is the current actual price of the product.

It observed price exceeds the reference price, it affects the buying negatively. A pleasant situation is one in which prices are at reference price level or below them.

Heavy sales promotion price-wise brings down the reference price for many products. The resumption of regular price then affects buying. Reference prices also affect anticipated future prices. Holiday travellers expect the air fares to fall. They can use their discretion to fly during such a fall but business travelers have no such discretion. Students expect cell handset prices to fall when colleges re-open in June.

Price-Quality Relationship: Sometimes a higher price leads to higher demand as customers feel that it is a sign of higher quality. Prestige products can thus be high-priced. Experiential products such as wines, perfumes and professional services are to be experienced to assess their quality. Without experience, it is difficult to assess their quality.

❖ Pricing and Product Life-Cycle

At the introductory phase of the product, pricing could be skimming or penetrative. At growth stage, pricing takes into account competition. At the plateau stage, pricing is reduced or is linked to sales promotion schemes.

❖ Category Conditions

There are several factors with respect to product category that affect pricing. The threat of new entrants is met by lowering prices. The buyer-seller power affects the pricing. The higher bargaining power of buyers depresses the prices and the higher seller power raises them. When there is intense rivalry, there is strong price competition. There is price competition also when there are substitute or alternative products available. Capacity constraints raise the prices and over-capacity tends to depress them.

❖ Decision-Maker

Those who influence purchase decision also affect the prices. In industrial marketing, this has lot of significance. Different functionaries have their own objectives.

❖ Pricing Tactics

There are several tactics available to the product managers for setting prices.

Price Bonding: Here a package of related products is offered to the buyer at a price lower than the sum of their individual prices. At times, this bundle can be priced higher even as it is convenient or attractive. Sometimes, there is unbundling of product components, e.g. a telephone line where the instrument will be bought by the buyer separately. A customer can choose those components of the bundle for which he is ready to pay.

Product-line Pricing: Both a high-priced and low-priced version can be offered. *e.g.* high priced Surf and low-priced Wheel.

Complementary Pricing: Here pricing is for the complementary products such as blades and razors, pastes and brushes, rolls and cameras, cassettes and recorders. A blade company prices razors cheaper than the blades.

Value Pricing: McDonald offers value price based menus. It gives the customer most of the value-cost difference or a good deal. It is related to customer expectations. It offers customers more than they expect. In other words, the price is less than the customer value.

Everyday Low Pricing: Everyday low pricing or EDLP is followed by some retailers. Wal-Mart practices this tactic. It is better than high-low practices off and on in terms of its effect on sales.

❖ Differential Pricing

Price discrimination can be direct, *e.g.*, concessional railway fare for senior citizens. Coupons of discount could be sent to the targeted audience. There could be record-market discounting where excess production is sold at a discount to a market different from the main market. *e.g.*, generic drugs to doctors and hospitals and private labels to retailers. Periodic discounting charges a higher rate at peak times and lower rate at slack times.

Discounts and Allowances: All over the world, giving discounts is a trade practice. It is a deduction given by the seller to the buyer from the listed price. Here the seller could be a manufacturer, a wholesaler or a retailer. He can be even a consumer. Discount acts as an incentive. The deduction on account of discounts in price leads to a reduction in price. Discounts could also be given as a concession, *e.g.*, free merchandise on the size of the order.

Types of Discounts:

There are cash discounts, trade discounts, quantity discounts. These are very common. The other discounts are promotional discounts, seasonal discounts etc.

Cash Discount:

Cash discount is a deduction or concession for cash payment in a given period of time. A cut is offered either for on the spot cash payment or cash payment within a given time period. There is no cash discount if the payment is made after the period specified. The cash discount is calculated on the net amount, after making an allowance for trade and quantity discounts. Consider a buyer has to pay ₹ 3000 net after allowing for other discounts. He may be offered terms of 3/15, n/45 on an invoice dt. 1st January. If the buyer pays by 15th Jan, he may deduct 3 per cent discount. Or else he is required to clear the whole amount within a period of 45 days. Cash discount thus, has three dimensions — the percentage of discount, the specified time period to avail of this percentage of discount and the time period when the invoice becomes overdue. It encourages the buyer to clear the invoice amount in 15 days. He is earning this discount by preponing the payment by 30 days. Those who do not avail of this discount are in effect borrowing money at 36.6 per cent annual rate of interest. (In a 365-day year, there are 12.2 periods of 30 days. It is thus tantamount to paying 36.6 per cent interest for the entire year).

In a high cost economy like ours, marketing and finance people carefully draft the financial terms of any transaction of sale. There is a tendency on the part of buyers to delay payment as long as it is possible. It is a working capital management on the part of buyers. They are using the seller's capital by not paying. To cope with this challenge, we have to devise a suitable cash discount scheme.

2 /	15	net 45
Percentage to be deducted if the bill is paid within 15 days	No. of days from the date of invoice in which payment must be made to avail of cash discount	No. of days from the date of invoice after which it becomes over-due

Fig. 18.2 Components of a Cash Discount

Trade Discount:

Also known as functional discounts, these deductions from the listed price are offered to trade channels for marketing functions they supposedly perform. The quoted price is reduced by the amount of discount, which the intermediary retains to cover his costs and get his profits. Imagine an item costs ₹ 800. The trade discounts for the retailer and the wholesaler are 40 per cent and ten per cent respectively. Thus, the retailer has to pay to the wholesaler ₹ 480 (₹ 800 less 40 per cent.) In his turn, the wholesaler pays the manufacturer ₹ 432 (₹ 480 less 10 per cent.) The wholesaler is, thus, given a trade discount of 40 and 10 per cent. He retains 10 per cent, for himself and passes on the remaining 40 per cent the retailer. Do not club together 40 per cent and 10 per cent to make 50 per cent. Each discount in the trade channel is computed on the amount remaining after the previous percentage has been deducted. Trade discount is deducted from the invoice price. It appears only on the invoice and not in the books of account. Tax is payable on the net price. Trade discount is a cover for middlemen. Higher discounts are used to promote sales.

Quantity Discounts:

The objective of this discount is to encourage the buyers to buy a larger quantity by allowing the deductions depending on the size of the purchase — either in rupees or in units. A non-cumulative discount is based on the size of individual order. A kg. of onion will cost ₹ 10 and 2½ kg. will cost ₹ 22. A schedule of discount may be devised by the seller.

Dozens of Talcum Powder Tins	Percentage deduction from listed prices
up to 5	Nil
6-12	2
13-25	3.5
Over 25	5

Since overheads like billing, order filling and wages of the staff remain the same irrespective of the size of the order, the expenses as a percentage of sales decrease when the orders become larger. These savings are passed on to the purchaser who buys in bulk.

Cumulative discounts can be availed of over a period of time. These establish a sustaining relationship between the Seller and the Buyer. These can be called relationship or patronage discounts. For perishable products, these discounts are helpful. The buyers gets an opportunity to buy fresh supplies frequently.

Quantity discounts enable the seller to enjoy economies both in production and in selling.

Seasonal Discount:

To boost up sales during a slack season, this discount is offered to the customers. We do come across such discounts for seasonal products like ACs, refrigerators etc. These are very much in demand in summer, but can be sold off-season by giving a hefty discount.

Forward Dating:

It is a mix of both seasonal and cash discounts. For instance, fire cracker manufacturers might solicit orders much before Deepavali. Orders before Deepavali keep the production running. The bills are forward-dated and are to be paid once the Deepavali sales are generated. Stationery manufacturers also may adopt this method.

❖ Promotional Allowances

When the buyers perform some promotional functions, these allowances are granted. Hardware manufacturers may offer some free items to dealers who display their items. Or a textile mill meets a part of the promotional expenses for the ad of a retailer that features the mill's product.

❖ Strategies of Pricing: Geographic

Transportation costs are invariably considered when goods are sold by a seller to a buyer and they affect the price quotation. In fact, freight contributes a great deal to total variable costs. There are three alternatives with respect to freight

(i) The seller bears the entire freight.

(ii) The buyer bears the entire freight.

(iii) Both of them share the freight.

The chosen strategy influences:

(i) The competitive position in various markets.

(ii) The geographic limits of the market.

(iii) The location of the plant and facilities.

(iv) The sourcing of raw materials.

❖ FOB Factory Pricing

This is a selling price ex-factory. The entire freight is to be borne by the buyer. The seller does not pay any expenses towards transportation. He only loads the goods on the carrier — hence the term FOB — free-on-board. The amount that the seller receives under this strategy is uniform for similar quantities of goods. However, distant customers are at a disadvantage, as the seller is priced out.

❖ Uniform Delivered Pricing

Also known as "postage stamp price", this strategy quotes a uniform price for all the buyers irrespective of the distance. The net revenue to the seller is either more or less, depending upon the location of the buyer. Here the buyer gets the benefit of "free delivery." This is adopted when the transportation costs are a small part of the overall selling costs. In a sense, nearby buyers pay the same transport costs as those for buyers located far off. *Zone-delivered pricing* divides the market into geographic zones and there is uniform delivering pricing during each zone.

❖ Freight Absorption Pricing

Here the seller shows willingness to absorb some of the freight costs. It is a factor price plus freight costs (which would have been charged by a seller located near the customer).

❖ One Price/Variable Price Strategy

There are two options available to management — a single price or a variable price. One price strategy means the same price to identical customers purchasing identical quantities of the product. Variable price means different prices for similar quantities to similar buyers. Variable price is set after a lot of bargaining. In India, one-price policy has been adopted at the retail level. Though there are minor variations from state to state due to variations of local taxes like octroi, state sales tax and Central Sales Tax (CST). A credit card may be sold to a buyer at lesser price to wean him away from the competitor. It is an offer of reduced price. The same credit card is available at the normal price to others. Even when a buyer shows the potential of becoming a good customer in future, a variable price may be offered. However, this pricing may cause heart-burn when other customers realise that some have been sold the same product at a lesser price, for which they have paid the regular price.

❖ Unit Pricing

Unit price enables the comparison between similar products. As we are aware, a soap cake can weigh 75 gms or 100 gms. When the pack price is seen, we may find it difficult to compare both these packages. Sometimes, two shampoo bottles priced more or less equally, and giving the same appearance may actually contain differing quantities of shampoo liquid. When unit price is adopted, the label mentions two prices — the price of the pack and at the same time price expressed in rupees per unit — say a litre, or a kg. or some other standard measure. Unit price allows the consumers to make "more knowledgeable" purchases. At a retail level, these days a Universal Product Code called Bar Code is printed/affixed separately on the products. The scanner reads the bar code and pricemarking is no longer necessary. When such a code is used, unit-pricing shelf signs become important to provide greater price information to consumers.

❖ Price Lining

Garments are generally sold on the basis of price lining. It means all shirts available of a particular group will be sold at ₹ 100, another group at ₹ 150 and the third group at ₹ 200. Price lining simplifies the buying decision. Higher costs are a constraint on price-lining. The seller will have to revise the price lining or he will continue the old lining putting a squeeze on profits.

❖ Resale Price Maintenance (RPM)

It is an earnest desire of manufacturer that their product range should be available to consumers at fixed or uniform prices. For this, prices are marked on the packages. It contains the artificial rise in prices. When goods are sent to marketing intermediaries, there is resale from wholesalers to retailers and again resale from retailers to final customers. Resale price maintenance refers to a supply which is sold at one uniform price to final consumers at all retail outlets. resale price is a price at which a wholesaler sells goods to retailers, and a retailer sells goods to consumers. This price is fixed by manufacturers. Distributors cannot sell goods at less than this price and more than this price. It can be a maximum resale price, or a fixed resale price or a minimum re-sale price.

In other words, resale price maintenance involves a bond between the manufacturers and his customers. Here it is agreed that there will not be any sale at less than RPM. RPM can be individual by one manufacturer or collective by many manufacturers. It is possible to resort to RPM for branded goods. RPM came up as a measure against price wars. There were malpractices on the price front. Some shopkeepers extending credit to patrons used to charge a higher price. Multiple shops used to charge a lower price. Small retailers were thus always at a disadvantage. It was, therefore, decided to fix a retail price and maintain it. This is how this practice came into vogue.

Advantages of RPM:

1. RPM helps the small retailers. Large parties cannot cut the price.
2. Entry into business is not dictated by price. Business becomes broad-based.
3. Consumers have to pay a fixed uniform price. There is no bargaining.
4. It helps to build the quality and image of the product.
5. There is no question of 'loss leader' selling under the RPM.

Disadvantages of RPM

1. As there is no price competition, the consumers do not get advantage of a lesser price.
2. Retailers lose control over pricing.
3. There is no competition amongst manufacturers and traders.
4. It is possible to do RPM in case of branded goods only.
5. RPM degenerates into a restrictive trade practice.
6. Inflated retail prices may lead to exploitation of consumers.
7. Many countries have not opted for RPM and many are opting out even now.

In India, an agreement restricting the price is considered now as a restrictive trade practice and as such RPM is not practised here. There can be suggestive retail prices, but still the retailer has the freedom to sell the goods below the marked price. Manufacturers cannot withhold supply on this ground. RPM is thus not valid in India.

❖ Leader Pricing

In retailing, prices of some very fast-moving well-known products are reduced so as to attract customers who buy not only the *loss leaders* but other products too, the profits of which offset the loss on account of loss leaders. The total volume of sales increases and so also the total profits.

❖ Magic Price Points

While buying fast moving consumer goods like shampoo, chocolate or soft-drink, we find the prices to be either ₹ 2, ₹ 5 or ₹ 10. These are considered to be popular price points, which no marketer can afford to ignore. Cadbury gets 50 per cent of its turnover from products priced at ₹ 5 or below it. In fact, sachet revolution in shampoo market made marketers recognise the significance of these price points. These days first a price point is fixed and then reverse engineering is done to develop the product. In the innovation process, price point/pack size equation is decided earlier, so that the development proceeds on these lines. If consumers select our brand, but are unable to afford the price, we lose them to smaller rivals which are at the right point on price-value equation. Such price points are also convenient as they coincide with the coin denomination in the country. Besides, round numbers are easy to remember. Coke also sells its chhota version on the basis of price. Fractional prices for such products erode trade margins, since regular consumers expect the retailer to waive the fractional part of the price, say instead of ₹ 5.50, he tenders ₹ 5 to the retailer. Lower prices are also an incentive to trials and help penetrate the market.

Magic price points also enable a company to do away with discounts and free-bies. Discounts and free-bies lower the price. But it is better to give an undiscounted brand of a smaller size at a lower price.

The weakness of these points are their sustainability in the long-run. After establishing the brand at these price points, it is difficult to move to the next price level. Even marginal increases tend to reduce the sales. It is a trap. It has no exit. But over a period of time, the perceptions charge, ₹ 2 becomes ₹ 5 and ₹ 5 get shifted to ₹ 10. Maintaining prices at the original level for quite some time, however, demands staying power on the part of the organisations. While maintaining prices, cost cutting should not lead to compromising the product or reducing the weight.

All marketers cannot take advantage of magic price points, e.g., soaps are to be offered only in particular weight (grammage) by law.

❖ Lower Prices

Airlines have started operating no-frills aircrafts to attract low budget customers. The Taj group of hotels have started budget hotel with no-frills, no room-service rooms for price-conscious people. Hypermarkets offer FMCG and even durables at discounted prices. Sachets have made shampoos and hair-oils affordable. Cell phone tariffs have nose-dived lower and lower. Credit cards are available with free life-time offer. However premium products targeted towards upper classes cannot charge a lower price or else the brand equity will be diluted. Mass markets are driven by volumes. The luxury products are driven by image. Except for the clearance sales, brands like Raymond and Colour Plus do not cut prices. Walmart is known for its 'always low prices.' The price chasm can be bridged by high quality good image and constant innovation *e.g.* Nike is priced higher than the competitors. Market penetration is always at a lower price *e.g.* ₹ 2599 EMI for Maruti 800. Korean electronic firms are known for lower prices. Service companies have higher margins and therefore have better scope of offering reduced prices. Price cuts in mass consumption products such as Tide detergent do not dilute the brand equity.

❖ Cherry Picking

Bargainint by going from store to store to get the best deal is called Cherry Picking.

* * *

19 MARKETING CHANNELS – RETAILING

Prior to commencing the production every organisation gives some thought to the methods and routes to get to the final consumers. We have to develop our distribution strategy and undertake the task of physical distribution itself. Before discussing distribution philosophy further, we shall discuss two important components of the distribution system — retailing and wholesaling.

❖ Middlemen

Organisations and consumers are linked together either directly or through middlemen. A middleman is an independent link between the Organisation and the Ultimate consumers. He facilitates the flow of goods from the producer to the consumer. He may take title to the goods flowing or helps actively in the process of transfer. He negotiates in the buying and selling of goods. Other service organisations like banks and transport companies do help the marketing process but they never take the title or are not involved in the negotiations. A middleman may take upon the functions of storage and transport. However, it is possible that he renders his services without even handling the goods physically.

Merchant middlemen actually take title to the goods but agent middlemen just assist in the transfer of title without owning the goods at all. We come across many agents of reputed organisations.

Merchant middlemen are further divided into: retailers and wholesalers.

❖ Channel of Distribution

Channels of distribution are also called trade channels. Channels are the routes taken by the goods when their title is moving from the supplier organisation to the final consumer. A channel, by composition, consists of the producer, the final consumer and the intervening middlemen. Even agents are part of the channel for the vital role they play in transfer, though they do not take title to the goods. The channel starts with producer and ends with the consumer. The middlemen or marketing intermediaries (wholesalers, agents, semi-wholesalers, retailers, franchisees, stockists etc) are the links between the Producer and the Consumer.

The middlemen do get their profits since they perform many important marketing functions and also take the risk.

Broadly speaking, we come across six important channels.

1. Manufacturer ⟶ Wholesaler ⟶ Retailer ⟶ Consumer
2. Manufacturer ⟶ Agent ⟶ Wholesalers ⟶ Retailer ⟶ Consumer
3. Manufacturer ⟶ His own sales depot ⟶ Retailer ⟶ Consumer
4. Manufacturer ⟶ His chain shops ⟶ Consumer
5. Manufacturer ⟶ Retailer ⟶ Consumer
6. Manufacturer ⟶ Consumer

Importance of Middlemen: It is not always possible to deal directly with the consumers for a producer. Imagine a scene where we do not have our familiar grocery shop or a retail chemist shop or newspaper vendor or a petrol pump. It is true that middlemen can be eliminated, but not the services which they provide. If there is no middleman, someone else, say a producer, will have to perform his functions.

(*i*) Middlemen purchase on behalf of their customers. They are sales specialists for the suppliers.

(*ii*) They provide various financial services both for the suppliers and the customers.

(*iii*) They buy in bulk and sell in smaller lots. They store the goods.

(*iv*) They provide feedback to the suppliers and advice to their customers.

(*v*) They give the customers a wide assortment of goods and services by buying from different suppliers.

(*vi*) Middlemen help in creating time, place and possession utilities.

Retailing: Retailing is selling goods and services to the ultimate customer for personal and non-business use. Retailing is mostly done by small retailers in India, but in some cases, even big organisations can indulge in retailing. Eureka Forbes selling vacuum cleaners home-to-home is indulging in retailing. A Satara farmer selling vegetables at a roadside site is also indulging in retailing. The sale for personal use to ultimate customer whether done by a producer or a wholesaler or a retail outlet is still a retail sale. Retail sales remain retail sale, irrespective of the method and the place of selling.

Retailer or retail store is a business enterprise that caters basically to household customers for non-business use.

Ease of Entry: It is easy to enter into retail trade. A manufacturing set-up requires plant, machinery, investment in materials, recruitment of staff etc. A professional like a doctor or a chartered accountant requires a professional qualification to set up his practice. A worker requires skills of a fitter/turner etc. The retailer can enter the business without a large capital, any special qualification or membership. Such ease of entry is a plus point. But at the same time, retail institutions fail when untrained, under-financed persons and persons without aptitude enter the scene.

Key to Success in Retailing: Entry and exit in retailing are very easy. The survival, however, is difficult. A retailer survives if he plays his role effectively — catering to the final consumer and serving the producers and wholesalers.

Nature of the Retail Market: Retailing is crucial for any marketing company. Whether yours is a multi-brand company or a single-product one, retailing cannot be ignored. The whole marketing exercise ultimately boils down to whether your product moves off the retail shelves.

Urbanisation has expanded retail business. Each retail outlet caters to the needs of the consumers whose profile is different. Retail audit monitors the market penetration data of a company's brand.

Retailing costs are estimated to be about 15-25 per cent of retail sales, whereas wholesale costs are estimated to be about 5-10 per cent of wholesale sales. The higher retailing costs are on account of dealing with the customers directly. Retail customers demand a range of services — packaging material, credit extension, home delivery etc. The per customer sale is lower. The expenses like rent, electricity, taxes, stationery, telephone, salaries of staff are more. Retailing means some amount of underutilisation of facilities, as customer traffic is not constant.

The average profit margin varies depending upon the type of retail outlet — from 10 per cent to 40 per cent. It is lower in the case of necessities like groceries and milk and higher in case of textiles.

The retailing scene consists of small outlets, big stores, single price stores, single product stores, chain stores, departmental stores, supermarkets, shopping centres, speciality stores etc. In a city like Bombay, in downtown area like Fort and Colaba, there are a number of well-stocked shops. These form a part of Central Business District. (CBD). There are prestigious stores like Benzer, Amarsons and Premsons in Breach Candy. There are small shops in suburbs. Some suburbs do now have bigger stores like Shoppers' Stop at Andheri (West), Bombay. In India, retailing has one added element — hawkers selling goods on pavements of Linking Road, Dadar, Pydhonie, D.N. Road, Santacruz and near stations of all the suburbs. The network of retailing outlets mentioned above is called the retailing structure.

❖ Suburban Shopping Centres

In metropolitan cities like Bombay, we find suburban shopping centres which are housed in one single complex. It may be a supermarket, or a cluster of shops or a departmental store. These are big-sized and are miniature markets. The bigger centres may have a wide variety of stores — textiles, ready-to-wear clothes, custom notified shops, footwear, service-oriented stores like an optician's shops etc. Abroad, these centres also house banks, offices, places of worship and theatres. These centres cater to the shopping needs of the customers in their catchment area. Some centres attract customers from far-off areas, too. Parking space is available near these centres. Children can move around freely. The atmosphere is informal. Mostly, they are centrally air-conditioned, and have common security and other amenities. The customer traffic benefits all the stores in one shopping centre.

❖ Classification of Retailers

Retailers are classified on the basis of their size, product-lines handled, ownership pattern and operational method. The following chart explains this classification:

Retailers

Size	Product-lines	Ownership	Operational Method
(i) Mass retailers like superbazars, departmental stores	General stores Departmental stores Limited-line stores	Corporate Partnership Proprietary	Mass retailing Mail-order Direct Marketing
(ii) Small retailers	Variety stores	Co-operative Association	

Fig. 19.1

Small Retailers: Small proprietary concerns or partnership concerns form the bulk of retail trade in India. These firms mushroom all over, because the entry is very easy and does not require any special qualification. Besides, these can be started with a small capital. These retailers maintain personal rapport with their clientele and provide services like credit extension and home delivery. They offer local convenience because they are located near our place of residence. In India, we find large retailers like superbazars, Apna Bazars, Chintamani's, Shoppers' Stop, Akbarallys etc. Still the small retailers hold their own as they are flexible enough to adapt their product lines to the needs of their consumers. It is economical to buy from small retailers, who have no high overhead costs. They create their own identity by adopting a unique decor and layout. Besides, small retailers can always become franchisees by obtaining a franchise to run a business under the name and guidance of a large company, *e.g.*, NIIT, Aptech offer franchises to individuals to run computer classes.

Large-scale Retailers: Large-scale retailers cater to a wide clientele and do mass retailing. Mostly, the stores have a large selling area and in some cases, several storeys in a building are occupied by them. They bring the customers directly into contact with the goods by removing the two barriers which small retailers have — the barrier of the counters and the sales people. Goods can be seen, inspected and chosen by several thousand customers at a time. When the customers choose on their own with some assistance from the sales people if needed, the system is called self-selection. When no salesmen are present at all and the customers pickup their own goods, the system is called self-service. Generally, in groceries section, the system of self-service is in vogue. Cash can be collected by the salesman at the counter which is called decentralised cash collection. But mostly, cash is collected by the cashier and not the sales people who make only the vouchers. This is called centralised cash collection. The goods are delivered against cash paid vouchers from the delivery counter. To facilitate sale by either self-selection or self-service method, all the goods are labelled, pre-weighed and price-marked. Pilferage and shoplifting are kept in check by good security system. The percentage of pilferage is accounted for in the pricing of the products. The inventory is controlled by physical units at the godown level and is controlled by value at the counter level. Large-scale retailing gives the retailer an opportunity to experiment with new products. Their financial strength is better leading to integration, experimentation, purchase discounts, effective promotion and executive specialisation. Large-scale retailing is slowly making an entry in India, especially in urban and metropolitan areas. We have Apna Bazars and Superbazars run on co-operative basis and Akbarallys and Shoppers' Stop run in the private sector. The supermarkets in foreign countries deal in strictly the kitchen-items, whereas the Indian superbazars are in reality the departmental stores. The method of food retailing adopted by supermarkets have been adopted by the chain stores. The discount supermarkets sell food at a discount. The warehouse or box stores are a form of discount supermarket where limited food products are sold on no-frills basis. Convenience stores are small in size, sell limited range of food, are located conveniently and have extended shopping hours.

Superstores handle more product-lines than a typical super market, *e.g.*, personal products, alcoholic beverages, tobacco products, hardware items, sewing supplies, stationery, leisure products and household services. This concept originated in France.

Door-to-Door Selling: It is one of the oldest methods of retailing. Sales people may call in prospects without any advance selection. Generally, prospects are selected in a store or a coupon response or query. Both the retailers and manufacturers can use this method of selling. In-home selling is informal and leisurely. It is always good for products that need demonstration, *e.g.*, a vacuum cleaner. However, a customer may not get an opportunity to compare different products. This method is very expensive as it involves face-to-face selling by a salesman. These days door-to-door selling is extended to tele-shopping — shopping by the assistance of TV and telephone.

Automatic Vending: Slot machines as they are generally called, take the price of products in a slot and the merchandise are dispensed. Though assistance is available, generally the vending machines do not need the presence of sales people. Products sold through vending machines include soft drinks (now in India too), edible oil, hot beverages like tea and coffee, candy etc. These products have low unit value and low mark-ups. These machines sell goods and services at all hours and can be placed at strategic locations. ATMs — Automatic Teller Machines — have been rightly described by Hong Kong Bank, the first bank to use them in India, as "Any Time Money" machines. We can withdraw cash and deposit through ATMs by using a magnetic-strip coded card (like a money-link card of SCB or credit card) and Personal Identification Number (PIN). The operating costs and maintenance costs of vending are high. Vandalism is another problem in a country like India.

❖ Retailing's New Frontier

Home shopping: The original. They sell products on the TV. You have to phone in to buy them.

Infomercials: These are programme length ads. They are used to sell gym equipment and cook wares. Many more retailers may exploit them.

Retailing through Internet: Many retailing sites like Indiatimes.com or fabmall.com sell directly to consumers. This is called e-commerce. The payment is through credit card. The security of data is ensured by encryption and 128-bit security. It is certified by veri-sign.

❖ Departmental Store

A departmental store may be described as a large retail establishment having in the same building a number of departments each of which confines its activities to one particular kind of trade and forms a complete unit in itself and is centrally controlled. A departmental store is really the opening of a number of shops, under one roof and control each dealing in a certain line of goods. The idea of a departmental store is to provide a large variety of merchandise from a pin to a motor car at one place. It aims at providing convenience in shopping and acts as a universal provider. The customers can get all their requirements at one place and need not go from place to place making purchases.

Purchasing in a departmental store may be centralised or decentralised. In the case of decentralised buying, each department has a "buyer" at the head who is responsible for the buying and selling policies of his department. But this checks the concern from getting the advantages of large-scale buying. Hence in order to get the advantages of large-scale and expert buying, the work of making purchases is usually centralised. There is a central purchasing officer who makes arrangements for making purchases for all the departments. The various departmental heads send their requisitions to the central purchasing officer and the purchases are duly made by him.

The departmental store is usually constituted as a limited company, the control resting in the borad of directors. The organisation of a departmental store can be clearly represented by means of the following diagram:

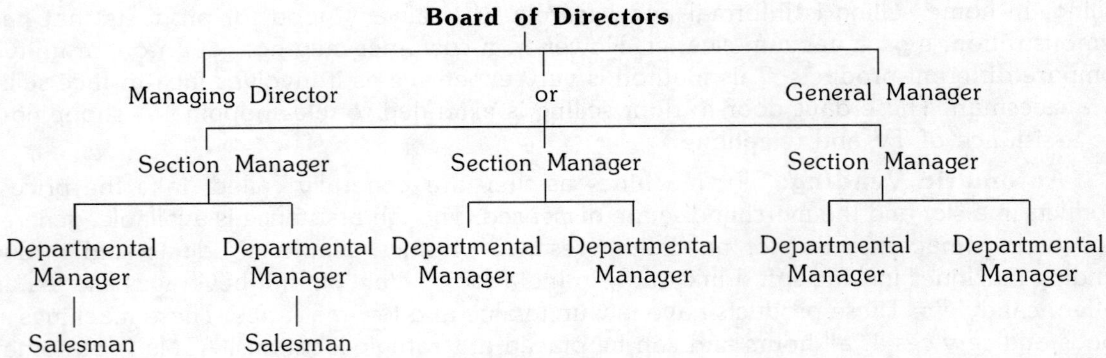

Fig. 19.2

As is clear from the above diagram, the ultimate control of a departmental store rests with the board of directors. The actual management is delegated either to the managing director or to the general manager. The whole organisation is divided into broad sections each under a section manager. A section is a division of the business comprising several allied departments. The section managers are responsible to the general manager or the managing director and their aim is to coordinate the activities of the various departments in their individual sections. Each section is divided into different departments each under a departmental manager. The departmental managers look after the sales of their individual departments and have corps of salesman to help them. The section managers form a board of management. The managing director or the general manager acts as a chairman of this board. The board meets once a week to discuss broad questions of management and to make important decisions.

In order to attract a large number of customers, the departmental store must be situated at a place which is most frequently visited by the rich people. It must occupy a central position. The shop front should be very attractive and there should be window dressing of a high order. It may also provide certain special facilities in order to attract more customers. For example, in certain cases, departmental stores provide writing rooms, resting rooms, libraries, information bureau etc. All these imply a large overhead expenditure. Hence the departmental stores generally charge a higher price than an ordinary retail establishment.

An efficient internal check upon sales is also very necessary in the case of departmental stores. The number of customers being very large, it is always possible that some of the customers avoid payment or some of the money received from them is pocketed by the salesmen. Hence it is necessary to separate the work of selling from that of receiving the price of the goods sold. For this purpose, three copies of cash memos are prepared by the salesman at the counter. One copy remains with the salesman and the other two are sent to the cashier with the goods sold. He, after getting the payment, gives the commodities with one memo to the customer who shows the same at the gate and only then is allowed to go out with the goods. This system ensures payment and provides a check against misappropriations and frauds.

Advantages:

1. Departmental stores provide great convenience in shopping. The customers can get all their requirements from one place and thus are saved the botheration of going from place to place.
2. They enjoy the advantages of large-scale enterprise. Buying in bulk reduces cost of buying. They, because of their large financial resources, can afford to utilise the services of experts and enjoy economies of buying and administration.
3. They can advertise on large-scale and attract a large number of customers.
4. The advertisement of one shop or department is also the advertisement of other shops or departments.
5. Due to the large volume of sales, the selling cost per unit becomes very low.
6. The customers are assured of a higher quality of goods. They can make much better selection of goods while making purchases as departmental stores keep a very wide variety of goods with them.

Disadvantages:

1. The cost of doing business is usally very high in the case of departmental stores. They have to spend a large amount on extra services and facilities in order to attract customers. They also incur a very large amount of expenditure on advertising and window display. Thus, overhead establishment charges in their case are considerable. The prices charged by a departmental store are usually higher than those charged by other small retailers. They may sometimes be even prohibitive. Thus only rich persons can take advantage of departmental stores and poor and middle class people do not take any benefit out of them.
2. Lack of personal contact is another defect of the departmental stores. The large number of customers and the vastness of the size of the store makes it impossible for the proprietor to give personal attention to every customer. Sales are made by salaried staff who may not be interested in securing buyer's satisfaction and goodwill.
3. As the stores are generally located in a central place, they cannot give any local convenience to the customers. People living at a distance may find it costly to visit departmental stores. Thus, people living in suburban areas, belonging to the middle-class find it suitable to make their purchases from their local retail shops.

The departmental stores have not become popular in India due to various reasons. Firstly, they require a large amount of capital for their establishment. In India, there is a great dearth of capital and hence, the departmental stores have very little scope. Secondly, the departmental stores charge slightly higher prices than the other retailers. Thus they cannot be successful unless the number of rich people is quite large. As in India the majority consists of poor people, these departmental stores have very little scope. Thirdly, the departmental stores for their success require a high order of orgnisation, salesmanship and advertisement. This further imposes a check upon the development of departmental stores in India.

❖ Multiple Shops

The multiple shop system of retailing is an attempt on the part of the manufacturers or wholesalers to approach consumers directly thus avoiding the middlemen's profits. A multiple shop system consists of a number of branch shops owned by a single business firm. These branch shops are situated at different localities in the city or in the different parts of the country to provide the consumers with shopping facilities near their residence. All the branches are centrally controlled and have uniformity of operation. Every multiple shop system has a head office, where broad policies are discussed and decided upon. Instructions from the head office are sent to all the branches and almost similar arrangements regarding window dressing shop decoration etc. are made at all the shops. Prices are fixed by the head office and thus the same price is charged at every branch. The head office may be situated at the factory where all the goods which the branches stock are made. The supplies to various shops may be made directly from the head office or from the local depots established in various cities for the purpose. The Bata's and the various retail stores of Delhi Cloth Mills provide a good example of multiple shops in India.

The multiple shop is usually constituted as a limited company. It carries both manufacturing and retailing and thus requires a huge capital which can be collected through joint stock enterprises only. The ultimate control lies with the board of directors. They decide the broad policies and pass instructions to various branches. The head office has various departments like buying, warehousing, selling, advertising and finance. In order to facilitate the work of selling, the whole country is divided province-wise and sales offices under provincial managers are established. Every provincial sales office has a warehouse wherein goods to be supplied to various district sales offices are stored. The Provincial Manager has under him district sales managers who are in charge of district sales offices. In each district, several branches under branch managers are established to facilitate sales.

The ultimate responsibility for making sales, therefore, lies upon the branch managers. As the arrangements regarding window display, shop decoration, etc.— are made according to instructions of the head office, the branch manager is saved much of botheration in this regard. Prices are also fixed by the head office. Sales are made strictly on cash basis. Therefore, the main duty of the branch manager and his salesmen is to provide efficient service to the customers so that a liking for that shop is created in them. The customers should be properly greeted and attended to. The goods should be nicely packed and any difficulty of the customer must be immediately removed. The branch manager is required to deposit the amount of sale proceeds daily in the bank account opened in the name of head office. He cannot deduct anything from the sales proceeds even on account of his expenses. His expenses are directly met by the head office. In order to ensure a check upon the working of the branches and to check any misappropriations by the branch managers, inspection at irregular intervals is done. Inspectors appointed by the head office visit the branches without any prior notice, count the cash in hand and tally the same with cash register and sometimes also check the stock in hand.

The multiple shop system can be successful only in regard to those commodities which are largely demanded. The commodities should be of such a type that a rapid turnover may be expected. Thus, this system is most suited to those commodities which are necessities or semi-necessities and have a constant demand, which are standardised and branded thus requiring little selling effort on the part of salesmen and which are portable type.

The main features of multiple shops can now be summarised as under

1. Multiple shops specialise in only one or a couple of lines of goods.
2. They aim at providing convenience in shopping by establishing branches near the customers' residence.
3. Management and control are centralised while selling is decentralised.
4. The articles sold are mainly necessities or semi-necessities and do not require much of a selling effort.
5. Window dressing and shop decoration is uniform in the case of all the branches.
6. Fixed price and terms cash are observed at all shops.

Advantages:

1. Middlemen's profits are eliminated as direct contact with the consumers is established.
2. Shortage of supplies at one branch can easily be met by transfer from other branches having surplus stock.
3. Fixed price and standard quality help in winning public confidence.
4. Large and rapid turnover means lowest cost of selling per unit.
5. Advertisement is centralised and can be carried on at a large-scale. Besides every branch is an advertisement for other branches. Once a customer is satisfied with the service provided at one shop he is confident and sure to get the same at another branch as well. Thus buyer's preference is gained for all shops and each branch is an advertisement for other branches.
6. Convenience in shopping is provided to the customers as branches are established in very important localities. Customers are no longer required to travel long distances for making purchases.
7. As sales are made strictly on cash basis, there are no bad debts.
8. Uniformity of window dressing and shop decoration at all shops makes identification of the branch shops very easy.

Disadvantages:

1. The owner loses all personal contact with his customers. He cannot attend personally to his customers and remove their difficulties. Thus the whole success of the organisation depends upon the branch managers. If they are responsible persons and take keen interest in their work, only then good results may be achieved. But this is not always possible as salaried branch managers may not be interested in securing customers' satisfaction.
2. Multiple shops have heavy expenses to meet. They have to spend a large amount on shop rent, shop decoration etc. The maintenance of poorly paying branches also means heavy cost.
3. A high degree of specialisation reduces consumers' choice.
4. Absence of credit sales may deter certain customers from having relations with multiple shops.
5. Adaptability to local needs becomes impossible as policies are governed by the head office.

❖ Distinction Between Departmental Stores and Multiple Shops

A departmental store is a large retail establishment which consists of a number of departments situated in the same building. Each department confines its activities to one particular kind of goods. They are centrally located.

A departmental store deals in a wide variety of products and acts as a universal provider. A multiple shop system, on the other hand, consists of a number of branch shops owned by a single business enterprise. These branch shops are situated in the different localities in the city or in different parts of the country but are centrally controlled. They specialise in only one or a couple of lines of products and aim at providing local convenience in shopping. Both the departmental stores and the multiple shops are run on a large-scale and require a large amount of capital. But they are distinct in many respects. The main points of distinction between the Departmental store and a Multiple shop may be stated as under

1. A departmental store keeps a wide variety of products and acts as a universal provider, but a multiple shop specialises in only one or a couple of line of goods.
2. A departmental store is centrally located and attracts some customers towards it whereas multiple shops are established in the various localities and try to reach the customers.
3. Departmental stores cater mainly to the rich people and sell costly luxuries, while multiple shops deal mainly in necessities and cater to the general public.
4. Departmental stores are established for providing everything at one place, whereas a multiple shop system is an attempt at eliminating middle men and establishing direct contact between the Manufacturer or Wholesaler and the Consumers.
5. Departmental stores sell both on cash and credit basis whereas in the case of multiple shops, sales are strictly made on a cash basis.
6. Control over the activities of a departmental store is easier than over those of multiple shops.
7. Departmental stores have greater flexibility as regards sales etc. but the multiple shops lack flexibility in this respect, since quick adjustment according to local changes cannot be made in their case.
8. In the case of departmental stores, the decoration of different departments is not uniform, while in the case of multiple shops, uniformity of shop decoration, window-dressing etc., is observed in all the branches.
9. The same price is charged by all the branches in the case of multiple shops while different departments of a departmental store may charge different prices.
10. Multiple shops usually deal in the products of only one manufacturer, while a departmental store sells the products of various manufacturers.

❖ Chain Stores

Sometimes when a retail shop becomes popular, the retailer finds it profitable to open new branches in the city. All these branches deal in same commodities and are chanined together as they are one of a group of retail stores of essentially the same type, centrally owned and controlled. Chain stores may be defined as retail selling organisation with a number of branches which operated on very similar lines. The purchases are centrally made and thus economies in buying are secured. A chain store system represents centralised buying combined with decentralised selling. The chain store may be a "variety store" when it deals in a wide variety of goods, or it may be "specialised store", when it specialises in a limited range of goods or it may be Fixed Price Chain Store, when the price of goods sold are fixed and varies between narrow limits. The chain stores are organised and run on very similar lines to those of a multiple shop and some authors have used the term chain stores as synonymous with a multiple shop. But whereas a multiple shop is established either by a manufacturer or a wholesaler for establishing direct relations with the consumers, chain stores are established by the retailers for taking advantage of their growing popularity. It is defined as. "An organisation having a controlling interest in two or more establishments which sell substantially similar merchandise at retail price."

❖ Federal Trade Commission

1. The main advantage of the shops is that all matters relating to window-dressing, advertisement, etc. may be made at one place. Experts may be employed for this purpose.
2. As the purchasing is centralised, buying in bulk may be done. It means lower price and other economies of large-scale buying.
3. They may also buy directly from the manufacturers and avoid the profits of the wholesalers.
4. They may also place special order and secure further economies.
5. The policy adopted by chain stores in regard to selling is to specialise in goods most in demand and to eliminate slow selling lines.

❖ Chain Stores Suffer from Following Limitations

1. It is difficult to adjust each store according to the local commodities as control is centralised.
2. It is difficult to obtain first class branch managers and keep expenses down at the same time.
3. The managers cannot adjust merchandise and service according to changes in demand.

❖ Mail Order Business

Mail order business is a kind of retail trade where business is done through post. From the buyers' point of view, it may be described as shopping by post. The seller approaches the customers by post by sending them circulars, catalogues, price list samples etc. by post, When the buyers are convinced, they place orders for the supply of the goods through the post. The goods are usually supplied through value payable parcels. But if the price of goods has been received in advance, then goods are sent by registered post parcel or though a courier. In the case of costlier goods a certain percentage of the price is always required to be paid in advance.

There are certain factors which favour the growth of this kind of business. Firstly, cheap postage facilities are essential for its growth. If cheap postage facilities are not available, this system may prove to be very costly and discourage the consumers to buy through post. Secondary, a vast size of the country with its population spread over a wide area is a pre-requisite for the success if this method of retailing. Thus, this method of retailing has a wide field in new and rapidly developing countries. Thirdly, a highly developed science of advertising is also necessary for the success of mail order business. Mail order business is most suited to such commodities which can be understood fully from description, which can be easily standardised and graded, which possess easy portability and which can be easily described and even represented in pictures. This is so because the consumers purchase goods without inspecting them. They depend mainly on decription given in the advertisement. Moreover, bulky goods, which lack portability will mean a high cost if sent through post. Thus this system suits best to such commodities as contain more value and less weight.

Advantages:

1. Lower cost of marketing is an important advantage of mail order business. A mail order house need not spend any amount on window dressing and shop decoration. It is not required to have the shop in the busy centres of the city. The godown may be situated in one corner of the city and thus much saving is effected in regard to shop rent.
2. A mail order house need not maintain a big salaried staff. As the work of selling is reduced to a mere routine, this can be performed by low grade labour who can be paid very low wages.
3. Results of an advertising campaign can easily be estimated from orders secured as a result of this campaign.
4. It gives great local convenience to customers. They get their requirements while sitting in their houses and are saved the journey to the retailer.
5. There is no danger of bad debts as price of the goods is received either in advance or is collected by the post office before they are actually delivered to the customers.

Disadvantages:

1. Lack of personal contact means that a mail order house has no permanent customers.
2. As customers cannot examine the goods, they may easily be received by unscrupulous and dishonest dealers.
3. A large amount is spent on advertising which increases the selling cost.
4. The causes of failure to effect sales and procure orders cannot easily be found.
5. In small and densely populated countries where a majority of population lives in cities, this type of retailing has very little scope.

❖ Consumers' Cooperative Stores

Consumers' cooperative is an attempt on the part of consumers to eliminate middlemen and to establish direct relations with the manufacturers. The consumers have now realised that the prices paid by them for their different requirements can be reduced to a very great extent, if the middlemen are eliminated and their profits, thereby avoided. Thus they have established their own distribution agencies which purchases commodities directly from the manufacturers and sells them at reasonable prices to their consumer members and others. The profits of the organisations, after making the necessary provision, are distributed among the members on the basis of the purchases made by them. In this way, the profits made through higher prices charged from the consumers are returned to them and they indirectly get commodities at prices lower than those prevailing in the market. The membership of these societies is voluntary and open to all. Anybody can become a member by paying a small fee or by buying shares and by undertaking to abide by the rules of the society. The organisation of these societies is completely democratic as each member has only one vote irrespective of the number of shares held by him. The shareholders are paid dividend, the ceiling of which is fixed. A part of the profits is usually spent on the provision of welfare activities for the members. The stores are usually managed by honorary members, although sometimes paid managers may also be appointed.

Advantages:

1. Costs of retailing are reduced as unnecessary expenditure on advertising etc. is avoided.
2. Consumers get better quality goods and lower prices as middlemen's profits are eliminated.
3. Supply can easily be adjusted to demand as demands of the various consumers are easy to estimate. This brings about greater economic stability.
4. It eliminates monopoly and profiteering.
5. Amount spent on welfare activities like education, medical aid, sanitation etc. does much social good and raises the standard of living of the members.
6. It promotes thrift among members and increases their economic security.

In spite of the above mentioned advantages these co-operative stores have not been successful in various countries. The main causes of their failure may be stated as under:

1. Lack of business training, ability or experience in the store personnel.
2. Want of careful study of members' requirements.
3. Too much dependence on honorary service.
4. Ignorance of the basic principles of the cooperation movement.
5. Credit trading resulting in bad debts.
6. Insufficient loyalties of members.
7. Meagre resources making large-scale operations impossible.

❖ Instalment Selling

In order to facilitate the purchase of costly goods by people of small resources, a system known as instalment selling has been evolved by businessmen. Under this system, the customer is not required to pay the full price of the commodity at once, but is allowed to pay the same in easy monthly, quarterly, half-yearly or yearly instalments. Instalment selling may take two different forms, *viz.*, hire purchase system and instalment system. In the case of the hire purchase system, goods are delivered to a person who agrees to pay the owner by equal periodical instalments. These instalments are treated as the hire of these goods until a certain fixed amount has been paid. In this case, the legal ownership in goods rests with the sellers, until the whole or a certain fixed amount has been paid. In this case, it is not proper to call it a sale as the seller can retake possession of the goods if there is default in regard to the payment of any instalments.

These instalments always include some element of interest as the seller has to wait for some time till the full price is paid. In the case of instalment selling, the ownership in goods is transferred to the buyer immediately after the contract of sale is completed. In this case also, payment is made by periodical instalments but they are not treated as hire for the goods, They are mere part payments and the seller cannot retake possession of the goods even though a default in the payment of any instalment is made by the buyer. He can only go to court of law and claim damages.

Advantages:

Consumer durables such a houses, furniture, cars, typewriters, TVs, VCRs, fridges etc, are made available to middle class people on easy terms. The method tends to encourage thrift. The buyer has to economise in future so that he may be able to pay his instalments for the convenience availed of by the early possession of the goods.

Another advantage of the system is that it encourages trade. People with small incomes are in a position to purchase expensive articles by purchasing them on the instalment basis. The buyer is forced to save the money and thus, gets sufficient incentive to save.

Disadvantages:

The disadvantage of the system is that it frequently induces the buyers to go beyond his means and he may find it difficult to meet all his obligations. His future income on which he depends for the payment of the instalments may decrease. He may find himself financially embarrassed. Similarly, the seller with the temptations of increasing his sales may sell without proper credit appraisal and may have no incur bad debts.

Whatever the merits and demerits of the system may be, it has proved useful to the business community and the general public alike. Consumer durables are sold on instalment basis so that they may be used even after the payments are completed or they should have a resale value in case the buyer returns the goods. The selling price is usually higher as the seller has to take the extra risk and therefore, marks all prices higher. He allows a discount for cash. He may add a percentage to the cash price. While selling on instalment the percentage usually varies according to the period over which the instalments a spread. The longer the period, the higher will be the percentage.

* * *

20 MARKETING CHANNELS — WHOLESALING

Wholesalers are the most hated lot in the distribution channel and there is always a cry to eliminate them. Mass retailing has succeeded, to a certain extent, in reducing the importance of wholesalers, but still they as a whole, continue to exercise their influence on the distribution channel.

Wholesaling is sales to those who buy for resale or for business use. Thus manufacturer to manufacturer sale is wholesale sale, *e.g.*, a tyre manufacturer supplies tyres to an automobile manufacturer. Even a retail institution when it sells to another institution some products for business use, it is called wholesale deal, *e.g.*, a stationer supplies files to a branch of a bank. Wholesaling covers all sales made to any buyer who is not an ultimate consumer, who consumes the product personally and in a non-business way. Thus the purpose for which a product is bought determines whether it is a wholesale transaction or a retail one.

In a narrow sense, wholesaling is primarily considered in the context of wholesalers and not the retailers. A wholesaler is a middleman engaged in wholesaling. They may be merchant wholesalers or other wholesalers like agents and brokers who do not take title to the goods. Sometimes, wholesaler are also called distributors.

❖ Wholesale Trade

The internal trade of a country may broadly be divided into two main classes, *viz.*, the wholesale trade and the retail trade. A wholesaler is the first intermediary in the channel of distribution. He purchases goods in bulk from the manufacturers and sells them in small lots to the retailers. Sometimes he collects raw material from scattered and small producers and sells them in bulk to the manufacturers. He thus stands between the manufacturers and the retailers, on the one hand and between the Producers of raw materials and the Manufacturers, on the other. A wholesaler generally specialized in the purchase and sale of only one commodity. A retailer, on the other hand, is the last link in the chain of intermediaries. He is an intermediary between the Wholesaler and the Ultimate consumer. He purchases from the wholesaler and sells in very small quantities to the consumers. He needs a smaller capital than a wholesaler and usually, carries trade on a cash basis. He does not generally specialise in any commodity and usually carries a large variety of goods in his stock. The main points of distinction between a Wholesaler and a Retailer can be enumerated as under:

1. A wholesaler provides a link between the Manufacturers and Retailers or producers of raw materials and manufacturers, while a retailer provides a link between the Wholesalers and the Ultimate consumers.
2. A wholesaler deals only a large scale but a retailer deals generally on a small-scale. Therefore, capital invested in the wholesale trade is usually larger than the capital invested in the retail trade.
3. A wholesaler generally specialises in one commodity, while the retailer deals in a large variety of goods and caters to the varied requirements of his consumers.
4. A wholesaler need not have his shop in the heart of the city whereas location of the shop near the consumer is very important for a retailer. The wholesaler may have his godown in a corner of the city and can supply orders therefrom, but a retailer in order to attract a large number of customers, has to establish himself in some central place.
5. The wholesaler charges a smaller margin of profit than is charged by the retailer. Unlike the retailer, the wholesaler has not to spend anything on window-dressing, shop decoration etc., and thus he can afford to sell at a lower margin of profit. Besides, large turnover as compared to that of the retailer and lower shop rent also enables him to sell at a lower margin of profit.

SERVICES RENDERED BY THE WHOLESALERS

(a) Services to Producers or Manufacturers

(*i*) He places large orders and thus enables the manufacturers to produce on a large-scale, which means reduction in the cost of production per unit.

(*ii*) He advertises on a large-scale, which is indirectly an advertisement for the manufacturers.

(*iii*) He collects information regarding taste, fashion and liking of the consumers through the retailers and passes it on to the manufacturers. He enables the manufacturer to produce according to the tastes and fashions prevailing at a particular time.

(*iv*) He provides a ready market to the manufacturers and thus relieves them of the botheration regarding storing, advertising and selling the commodity. Manufacturers are relieved from blocking up their capital in the form of stock and from suffering losses due to market fluctuations.

(*v*) He assembles raw materials from various scattered producers and helps the manufacturers to obtain them from one place.

(*vi*) He acts as an intermediary between the Manufacturer and the Retailer.

(*vii*) He also helps manufacturer with money by paying the price many a time in advance.

(b) Service to the Retailers

(*i*) The retailers can purchases the goods from one place and are not required to establish relations with scattered and numerous manufacturers.

(*ii*) They provide credit facilities to the retailers and enables them to trade as a much larger-scale than their means would permit.

(*iii*) They advertise on a large-scale and this provides an advertisement for the products of the retailers as well.

(*iv*) They provide a regular supply of goods to the retailers. The retailers can purchase as much as they like on time to time and need not maintain a large stock of goods.

(*v*) They inform the retailers about the new products form time-to-time.

(*vi*) They bring about an adjustment in the demand and supply, thereby reducing market fluctuations and save the retailers from losses which they might have suffered due to these fluctuations.

(*vii*) He also arranges for transportation insurance and warehousing the goods belonging to retailers.

(c) General Services

(*i*) By keeping a larger stock of commodities, from time-to-time, he controls the price level and reduce market fluctuations.

(*ii*) He relieves both the manufacturers and the retailers from the botheration of storing the goods.

(*iii*) He carries on the import and export trade of the country.

(*iv*) Sometimes, he also arranges for home delivery of the goods and saves the consumers the trouble of going to the shop for making purchases.

Thus we see that both the wholesalers and the retailers render very useful services to the community. But some people nowadays have begun to question the usefulness of the wholesaler. According to them, the wholesalers unnecessarily enhance the prices and makes huge profits. The appointment by manufacturers of their own travelling salesmen and sole agents and the establishment of their own retail stores and distributing centres in different parts of the country, to contact the consumers directly in the first case and retailers in the second, also strengthens this belief. The Royal Commission on Agriculture called "them parasites growing fat a the cost of producers and consumers. Their number is more or less of the nature of superfluous and roadside stations, where the goods are unnecessarily delayed on journey from the producers to the consumers." or But, in fact, the wholesalers neither can be nor should be totally eliminated. They render very useful service to all the manufacturers, the retailers and the consumers. The importance of their function was fully realised in the depression days when the manufacturers were unable to bear the cost of maintaining direct selling organisations. The wholesalers are indispensable in the case of goods produced by a large number of small producers or where the number of retailers was very large. Thus we see that services rendered by the wholesalers are very useful and even indispensable in certain cases and hence the wholesalers should not be eliminated.

Production without sale is of no use. It is a liability rather than an asset for a business enterprise to produce commodities which they cannot themselves sell. Hence it is the endeavour of every businessman to maximise his sales. Selling, however, has become a very complicated affair these days. Direct contact between the Producer and the Consumer no longer exists. Goods are produced not only for the local market but for national and even international markets. Thus the manufacturer has to take the help of various other persons, known as middlemen or intermediaries, to approach the consumers. He sells his goods in bulk to the wholesalers, who in turn sells them to the retailers. These retailers provide the last link in the chain of intermediaries and sell the goods directly to the consumers. If these intermediaries do not perform their functions efficiently, then successful selling would not be possible.

Similarly, if the relations between the Wholesalers and the Retailers are not cordial then also sales would be adversely affected.

Retailers come in direct contact with the consumers. They influence the consumption pattern of their customers to a very great extent. Their suggestions are favourably received by the consumers. Thus, the success of the manufacturer to a very great extent depends upon the goodwill of the retailers. If the retailers wish, they can help greatly in increasing the sales of one commodity in preference to the other. The retailers do not generally deal directly with the manufacturers. They purchase their requirements from the wholesalers. Thus they will favour one manufacturer or the other on the basis of their relations with the wholesalers. If the relations are cordial, they would always purchase their goods and thus the manufacturers would gain and *vice versa.* Thus, it is in the interest of manufacturers to see that the relations between the Wholesalers and the Retailers are cordial.

Retailers, through, the wholesalers, can also supply very useful information to the manufacturers. They study the likes and dislikes of the consumers and by means of such studies find out the future trend of demand. This information can be of great use to the manufacturer in determining his production plans. Retailers communicate to the manufacturers the results of their study through the wholesalers. They will pass on information to the wholesalers only if their relations with them are good. If proper treatment is not given to them by any wholesaler, they will either keep this information with them or will pass it on those wholesalers with whom their relations this cordial. Thus bad relations between the Retailers and the Wholesalers prove detrimental to the interests of the manufacturer, so the manufacturer, always tries to keep the relations between the Retailers and the Wholesalers cordial.

Purchasing in a wholesale concern is a very important activity. The whole success of the organisation depends upon the effective organisation of the purchase department and upon the efficiency and skill of the purchase manager. If a mistake is committed in making purchases, it may prove to be disastrous for the whole concern. For example if these commodities which have no or very low demand are purchased by mistake, the wholesaler will not be in a position to sell them and the whole transaction will result in loss.

The problem of purchasing centres round the questions as to what to buy, how much of it to buy, from where to buy and when to buy. These problems can easily be solved if the head of the purchasing department is an expert and knows his job fully, well he must possess complete information regarding qualities, markets as well as the prices of the requisite products at different manufacturing in centres. Only then can he be successful in making effective purchases. He should also be aware of the future trends of demand and supply and of prices of such products.

In order to decide what is to be purchased, the purchases manager or supplier who is sometimes so-called, must know the tastes and habits of customers for whom the goods are meant to be purchased. If the goods are meant for the rich people, they should care more for quality, packing etc., of the goods rather than for price. But if the customers of the retailer are poor or middle class people, he should see that the prices of such products are not very high. He should always keep himself informed about the prevailing design, style, colour and pattern as also about the likely changes in the same so that any change in the taste or fashion may not effect the concern adversely.

Quantity to be purchased is another important question. If the purchaser makes a mistake in regard to this question, the wholesaler may not be in a position to maximise his profits. If his supply falls short of demand, he may have to incur losses if the amount purchased is much in excess of the market demand. For deciding this question, the purchaser should work in consultation with the sales department and the finance department. The sales department will inform him about the normal sales and the anticipated sales. It will also guide him in matters of style, quality and fashion prevailing at a particular time. The sales department has first-hand information in respect for these things and thus, the suggestions made by it may prove to be very useful. Besides, the ultimate responsibility with regard to the sales rests upon the selling department and hence it is always good to work in consultation with it. Prompt payment of the purchases is also very necessary for maintaining the credit of the firm. Thus, it is equally important that purchases are made according to the financial strength of the concern. The Finance Department will guide the buyer with regard to the financial policy of the organisation, period of payment and as such other related matters. Therefore, the purchaser should formulate his buying policy in consultation with the finance department. He should prepare a buying budget which would serve him as a guide in the matter of purchases. This budget can be modified from time-to-time according to any expected change in demand. He should also fix a minimum and a maximum quantity of purchases. This will enable him to keep a check on over purchasing and under-purchasing of particular articles. The purchaser will normally be made according to the buying budget but when prices are fluctuating the purchaser will use his discretion to limit or increase his buying as the price rises or falls.

If, for example, certain goods which he thinks can be profitably sold in the market are available at very cheap rates, then he can even exceed in maximum limits.

The purchaser should also be very careful in making actual purchases. He should invite quotations from various manufacturers producing such commodities. The various quotations should be compared as regards price and quality of product, terms of sale and period of delivery etc., Now he can place an order upon the manufacturers whose terms are most suitable to him. If possible, he sould try to examine the articles before they are actually purchased so as to avoid any loss due to some defect in the product which cannot be detected by simply examining the sample. After considering all the above mentioned points, the purchaser will place an order. The order must give exact and detailed information regarding the quality, quantity, price and the date by which the goods must be delivered. Having placed the order, the buyer will arrange for the following up of orders, for the arranging of deliveries and for the passing of invoices for payment. He will also see that the goods purchased are properly stored and that there is an efficient internal check upon the receipts and issues of the goods.

Wholesale trade is usually carried on a large-scale. Thus, the wholesaler needs more finance than a retailer. He usually carries heavy stock and grants credit to the retailer. He may also pay to the manufacturers in advance. Thus, the wholesale trade is usually organised on partnership or joint stock company basis. The whole organisation is placed under the supervision and control of a general manager or a chief executive to whom the various sectional heads are responsible. The organisation is divided into three sections, *viz.*, administrative section, the executive section and the cash section. The administrative section and the executive section which are under the control of sectional managers are further subdivided into certain departments. The administrative section has departments like record and filling department, correspondence department and accounts and finance department. The executive section consists of buying department, selling department, publicity department and despatch department. The cash department is usually controlled by the general manager, although sometimes, it may be under the control of separate sectional manager. The following chart will clearly show the organistion of a wholesale firm.

- General Manager or Chief Executive
  - Administrative Section
    - Record & Filing Department.
    - Correspondence Department
    - Accounts & Finance Department
  - Cash Section
  - Executive Section
    - Despatch Department
    - Publicity Department
    - Selling Department
    - Buying Department

The planning function or the functions relating to the formulation of broad policies rests with the board of directors or with the proprietors of the concern. The various sectional managers and departmental heads have to work according to these broad policies. A brief description of the various departments is given below.

1. Administrative Section

(a) Accounts and Finance Department: This department is responsible for maintaining the accounts of the whole organisation. Accounts relating to purchases and sales receipts and payments and debtors and creditors etc. of the concern are kept by this department. This department also prepares the financial budget of the organisation. Financial needs of the various departments are also met by this department. Without the sanction of the accountant or some other person, authorised for the purpose, in this department, no payments can be made by the cash section. The department is under the control of a chief accountant who may have some assistant accountants under him.

(b) Correspondence Department: This department is responsible for looking after the outward correspondence of the business. Receipt of letters and writing of suitable replies thereof is the main concern of this department. Outward correspondence require great care and skill, because tact and tone must come into play in order that each letter is a sales letter. Sometimes, specific replies may be drafted for covering regular matters of routine. This will save time and money but this should not be carried too far. Correspondence that is still in progress, is kept in the suspense file. When the correspondence is complete, the copy of the letter together with the letters received is sent to the filing department.

(c) Records and Filling Department: Preservation of business respondence for future reference is called filing. The main duty of the filing department is to preserve by means of certain devices the correspondence and other useful records of the concern so that if need be, reference thereof may be made in future. For easy reference proper method of indexing is used. Indexing makes it easy to find out the file etc., wherein the letter has been preserved.

2. Cash Section

This section is responsible for the receipts and payment of the concern. It has direct contact with the bank. It is the duty of this section to see that payments are made promptly or on the due dates, so that the credit of the concern is maintained in the market. It also demands payments from the customers and sends them reminders to safeguard against loss from bad debts. There is a petty cashier for making small payments. This cashier is provided with some imprest money out of which he makes small payments and when he has spent the whole amount, he receives a further imprest from the head cashier.

3. Executive Section

(a) Buying Department: This department is in charge of an expert purchaser who has complete information about the various sources of supplies and who is constantly in touch with market conditions and prices. He is responsible to make purchases for the whole concern in the most profitable manner and to look after storage and warehousing. Before making actual purchases, he usually invites quotations and after comparing them with regard to the price and quality of the products and the period of delivery etc., he places orders.

(b) Selling Department: This department is in charge of the sales manager who is responsible for the effective selling of products. He appoints agents and salesmen for assisting him in this work. He conducts market research and keeps himself informed about the prevailing fashions, designs styles and patterns and about the likely changes in them. He passes on this information to the purchaser who makes purchases accordingly. As the sales manager develops relations with the retailers, he is in a position to find out causes of any complaints from them and tries to redress them.

(c) Publicity Department: This department is responsible for advertising the products among the consumers. It carries on a regular advertising a campaign and assists the travelling salesmen in their efforts to secure orders from the retailers of their territories. Advertisement is mainly done through press, circular letters and the direct mail advertising media. This department also arranges for exhibiting the products in various commercial fairs and exhibitions. Registration of trade marks and brand names is also the duty of this department.

(d) Despatch Department: The responsibility of this department is to despatch goods to retailers according to their instructions. This department is responsible for proper packing, marking or labelling of the goods. When an order is received by the selling department, instructions regarding the execution of this order are sent to the despatch department. The department then arranges for the packing and labelling of the goods. If the wholesaler has his own delivery vans, the goods are sent to the retailers promptly. In other cases, this department arranges for the despatch of goods by rail and procures railway receipts for such goods.

Success of the whole organisation depends upon the full co-operation amongst the various departments. Unless there is full co-operation between Buying and Selling departments, goods may not be delivered promptly due to scarcity of supplies. Similarly, if payments are delayed due to inefficiency of the cash department, credit of the concern will receive a setback. Similarly, sales cannot be maximised unless publicity department functions properly. Similarly, unless proper records are maintained and outward correspondence is properly handled, the efficiency of the whole organisation will not be maximised. Thus, full co-operation amongst the various sections, *viz.*, administrative, executive and cash section is necessary for the efficient working of a wholesale firm.

❖ Resale Price Maintenance (RPM)

Resale price maintenance refers to the control by the manufacturer of the price of the sale of goods. Manufacturers of branded goods these days generally elect to set the minimum price at which their goods shall be sold to the public. Fixation of wholesale and retail prices of the products by the manufacturer is technically called "Resale Price Maintenance." This policy is followed to eliminate competition and unfair trading. Short-term market fluctuations are not allowed to affect the prices of goods under resale price maintenance. Whenever a retailer attempts to sell below these prices supplies are discontinued by the manufacturer. The main reasons for resale price maintenance are given below:

1. Many retailers have little conception of what the retail price could be, as they do not know their costs accurately.
2. A uniform price discourages the retailer to resort to price cuts for attracting customers to his shop. The retailer is generally tempted to make especially attractive price on well advertised goods in order that customers may be drawn to his store.

   This spoils the sale of goods by competitive dealers and ultimately proves harmful to the manufacturer. Further, more out priced goods even if of high quality, soon come to be classed as cheap.
3. A uniform price enables the manufacturer to feature the price in his advertisement and gives the buyer a sense of security, as he now knows how much the goods should cost and knows when he is overcharged.

Resale price maintenance is, however, possible in the case of such articles only as are identified by some brand, copyright, trade market or the like. It is so because in the case of branded goods only, the price can be advertised in catalogues and periodicals. But after a resale price has been fixed, it is often difficult to maintain it. The retailers may even then resort to price cutting secretly if competition in that line of goods happens to be keen. In fact, there is no legal binding on the retailers to sell at the price fixed by the manufacturer as it has been held generally by the costs that the manufacturer cannot act and maintain the price at which article will be resold.

Advantages:

(*i*) It protects the small shopkeepers from price cutting by chain stores or supermarkets, which are more capable of achieving a large turnover to compensate themselves for reduced margins then are small retailers who may go out of business unless supported by fixed margins. Since the margin of profit of intermediaries is fixed and they are not required to sell goods at lower prices, it will help small dealers to coexist with big dealers.

(*ii*) Maintenance of quality is a corollary to the maintenance of prices. If prices are left to be determined by free competition, provision for the costs of research to maintain and improve quality of goods may not be available. To cover these costs, sales prices must be maintained at adequate levels.

(*iii*) Selling goods at fixed prices will always add to the goodwill of the product as well as its producer. It will be very easy for him to win over the confidence of his client. Manufacturer can advertise his products with a price which ultimately creates a belief in the consumers that the price is same everywhere and they cannot be cheated. This will educate and will eliminate bargaining and haggling about price.

Disadvantages:

(*i*) Resale price maintenance will allow the small and inefficient shopkeepers to survive and this will add to the cost of distribution of their goods.

(*ii*) It takes the form of semi-monopoly sustained by big manufacturers at the expense of the consumer. It may cause selling goods at higher prices by eliminating competition or by trying to accommodate inefficient dealers.

(*iii*) It discourages enterprise and gives an advantage to the efficient dealer to overrun the efficient one.

(*iv*) Strict supervision and inspection for the maintenance of uniform prices may encourage them to sell substitutes.

For the first time, the policy of Resale Price Maintenance was legally recognised in U.S.A. by the passing of McGuire Act of 1952, Some of the enlightened dealers have also been following this policy in India *e.g.*, Philips Radios, Bata Shoes, Britannia Biscuits, Atlas Cycles etc.,

❖ Classification of Wholesalers

They are classified against three criteria:

(*i*) the product lines handled.

(*ii*) the operational methods.

(*iii*) the markets they cater to.

For the sake of convenience, wholesalers are classified into three broad groups: (*a*) merchant wholesalers, (*b*) manufacturer's depots, branches, offices and (*c*) agents and brokers.

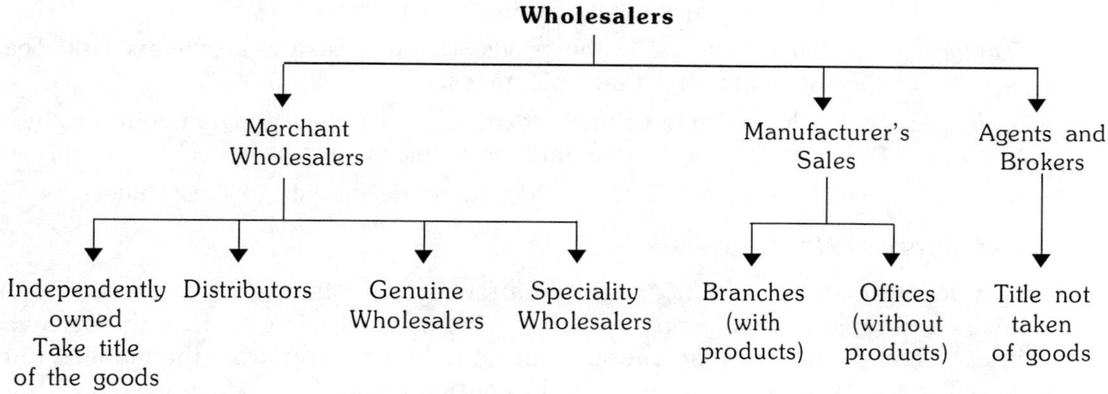

❖ Economics of Wholesale Trade

Their operating expenses are on an average 10-12 per cent of the wholesale sales. They thus take almost 8 per cent from the consumer rupee.

The operating expenses of the merchant exporters are this highest and those of agents/ brokers the lowest. The operating expenses also vary according to the products handled, *e.g.*, lower expenses for a grocer and higher for consumer durable wholesaler. The profits are comparatively lower than those of the retailers. The net profits on an average are 3 per cent to 5 per cent.

❖ Full-Service Wholesalers

These render full-service wholesaling functions and could be called wholesalers or distributors or suppliers or jobbers. They may handle either consumer goods or industrial products.

❖ Services Rendered by Wholesalers

Buying : They anticipate the needs of their customer. They have awareness of the market and sources of supply. They purchase on behalf of their customers. Their customers have to deal with a few wholesalers, rather than a whole lot of manufacturer's representatives.

Selling	: Wholesalers keep their own sales force who reach out to the retailers and industrial customers. Customers repose faith in wholesalers located near them rather than in the remote producers.
Dividing	: Wholesalers buy in bulk — truckloads or wagonloads. They divide the lot into small lots while selling. This is a valuable service both to the producers and their customers.
Transportation	: They transport the goods to their customers while delivering the ordered goods. It saves inventory carrying costs of their customers and reduces their risk, too. They buy in bulk from the producers, thus effecting a saving in freight costs.
Storage	: They keep the goods in their warehouses. It is a valuable service to both the producers and their customers.
Financing	: They extend credit to their customers and thus save their capital from getting blocked. Producers find it difficult to entertain credit proposals from the retailers. They order goods much in advance from the producers and pay in time. This enables the producers to have better working capital management.
Risk Taking	: They take title to the goods. This reduces the producers' risk. They bear the losses and pilferages.
Market Feedback	: They provide valuable feedback to their customers about the styles, trends, price movements, new products, special schemes etc.
Counselling	: They give technical and managerial advice to the retailers.

❖ Limited Service Wholesalers

These merchant middlemen concentrate on a few product lines, *e.g.*, truck distributors call on retailers and replenish the supply of perishable and food items or drop shippers who do not physically handle the consignment but cause it to be delivered from the manufacturer direct to the customers such as lime and cement consignments.

❖ Agents

These wholesalers do not take title to these goods. They handle the goods on behalf of their principal, the producer. They are governed by the Agency Law. Slowly they are being replaced by the wholesaler's sales offices or branches. Agents get commission by way of compensation. They may be assigned a territory to sell. Each agent may take the agency of several competing firms manufacturing related products. Brokers bring the buyers and sellers together and provide information to both the parties. They charge a brokerage for their service. They are prevalent in food items, defence items, complex machinery, plant, technical products, real estate etc. Agent middlemen in food items are called commission merchants. They take goods from producers and provide storage, grading and other services. They find buyers at the best prices and effect sales. They remit the amount of sale proceeds to the producers after deducting their commission, freight charges and other expenses. Auctioneers sell foods at an auction where goods are sold to the highest bidders. Auction companies like Sotheby's and Christie's are well-known all over the world for their auction of antiques and art products. Selling agents market outputs of a manufacturers in the entire market. They take on the complete functions of the manufacturers' entire marketing department.

* * *

21 CHANNEL MANAGEMENT

The most challenging task before a marketing department is to design and manage the distribution channels. Channel dynamics makes it so challenging. It is a known fact that the middlemen are all independent entities and the producer exercises little or no control over its wholesalers and these wholesalers in their turn exercise little or no control over their retailers.

Channels are selected and managed mostly by the manufacturer and therefore, channel discussion is always made from his viewpoint. Still the fact remains that the problems of middlemen are similar to those faced by the manufacturer. Even channel selection, to some extent, is done by the middlemen.

A channel of distribution should form a cohesive unit, and each member of this unit must play his role effectively and efficiently to serve the final customer to his satisfaction. A channel that is cohesive has a distinct competitive advantage. A disjointed channel where each member does not harmonise with other members and treat them as competitors rather than collaborators is counter-productive. Actually, there should be no competition within the channel. Competition should be between our own channel and those of the rival producers.

These days, channel management is handled by a distribution manager in a marketing organisation. The distribution manager plans, co-ordinates and evaluates the distribution channels.

❖ Channel Conflicts

Though what is expected is co-operation amongst channel components, there are conflicts amongst the channel members. Mostly these conflicts are due to institutional changes. Horizontal conflicts occur at the same level of distribution and vertical conflicts occur at different levels of distribution. A chemist having a conflict with another chemist is an example of horizontal conflict. A hardware store and paint-store have conflicts. This also is an example of horizontal conflict.

When channel members who traditionally sell one particular product-line add on other non-traditional lines, there is horizontal conflict. A retail chemist may resent a grocery store selling Aspro tablets. He may then have grudge against such 'unorthodox' selling in a rival channel. The desire to have products on the part of consumers at conveniently located nearest shop which could be one-stop shopping spot results in non-traditional selling.

Severe conflicts in the channel are vertical. A retailer sells to an institution or industrial user and a wholesaler resents this. A producer sells his products directly to the customers bypassing the retailer. Producers cover markets which were so far being serviced by the agents.

Large retailers have considerable freedom to choose their own sources of supply. They dictate their terms. So far only the producers were the channel leaders. This is a production-oriented approach. However now retailers have increased importance as they put the goods in the hands of the final consumers. They have emerged as channel leaders. However, channel leadership is a matter of trade-off. In industrial marketing, traditionally, the products are sold directly to the customer. But in consumer markets, the products are routed through the wholesalers, who are now being by-passed. There are, thus, conflicts between the Producers and the Wholesalers. Mass marketing reduced the importance of the wholesalers as far as customary wide margins were concerned. Wholesalers have to hold their own against large retailers and producers who tend to sell direct. Still the wholesalers have to continue to deal in several lines and cannot afford to concentrate on one styleline. They also resent any cut in their discounts.

❖ Bypassing the Wholesalers

Wholesalers are bypassed by the producers because the producers feel they are not rendering satisfactory services or it is necessary to approach the customers directly due to the peculiar marketing conditions.

❖ Case of Manufacturers

(*i*) Wholesalers are lethargic in promoting.

(*ii*) Wholesalers avoid the storage function and push back storage to manufacturers as far as possible by taking advantage of modern-day transportation and inventory management.

(*iii*) Wholesalers may promote their own private brands.

(*iv*) Wholesalers are expensive, and if producers undertake some of the wholesaling tasks it may be more economical.

(*v*) Producers have a need to exercise greater control over the market.

(*vi*) For fashion products and perishables it is advisable to by-pass the wholesalers.

(*vii*) Mass retailing makes it imperative for the large retailers to buy direct from the producers.

❖ Case of Wholesalers

(*i*) Producers fail to recognise that wholesalers have to cater to the customers primarily, and services to the producers are of secondary importance.

(*ii*) Wholesale margins are not enough to undertake functions like warehousing and promotion.

(*iii*) Wholesalers are used for less profitable segments and products. For profitable lines and segments, producers themselves skim the market.

❖ Options before the Producers

Wholesalers can be short-circuited in four ways:

1. Sell direct to the retailers: When there are large retailers, this alternative can be tried. It makes sense to sell direct to specialty stores like photo studios, textile dealers, shoe stores. Direct selling is recommended when the product is complex, technical, perishable and of high value.

2. Set up sales offices/branches: This is decentralised distribution through a sales force.

3. Sell direct to consumers: It could be house-to-house distribution or mail-order selling. Producers may establish their own retail outlets, *e.g.*, Bata Shoes stores. They may sell directly from their own depot at the point of production, *e.g.*, a retail outlet of a textile mill.

4. Make use of missionary sales force: Missionary sales force makes a call on the retailer to promote the producers' products. The orders, collected are passed on to the agent. Missionary sales people introduce new products and do sales promotion at the point of sale.

❖ Options before the Wholesalers

Wholesalers can improve their position by rendering such valuable services that it is difficult for any producer to bypass them; they can assist the retailers in managing the retail outlet better and this works in their own interest. They can put their own private brands and can form an association with a group of retailers.

❖ Manufacturers Vs. Retailers

There is a conflict between the Manufacturers and Retailers as their ethos are totally different. Manufacturers are mostly growth-oriented whereas retailers like to maintain the *status quo*.

Manufacturers push their products by promotion over the heads of the retailers. They can appoint franchise dealers or set up their own retail outlets. Retailers try to promote their own store. However, it is in their own interest both for the manufacturer and retailer to treat the whole channel as an integrated system and each component of the channel is just an extension of the previous component. Manufacturers should co-operate with the retailers and retailers must reciprocate.

❖ Marketing Systems

Vertical marketing systems are of three types: corporate marketing system in which production and marketing are handled by the same company or administered marketing system in which production and marketing are co-ordinated through a powerful channel member or contractual marketing system in which independent entities are welded together by contract.

❖ Selecting Channel of Distribution

We shall now examine the choice of channels available to a producer and the factors affecting this choice.

The most frequently used channels for consumer goods are as follows:

(1) M ⟶ C **Manufacturer ⟶ Consumer**

It is the shortest channel. There are no middlemen here. It is also called direct sale. It operates a mail order house, or through door-to-door salesmen. Thus Bullworker — Exercise Equipments are sold directly through mail order. Aqua Guard Water Filters, vacuum cleaners etc., are sold by Eureka Forbes through sales people directly. The sales people are paid commission on sales.

In developed countries, there are direct sales through vending machines of products like ice-cream, soft-drinks, milk, butter etc. Here in India, banking services through ATM (Automatic Teller Machines) have started being sold direct.

Direct sale through own retail outlets is also a possibility.

Here, there is complete control over the channel. Marketing feedback is also excellent. As middlemen are eliminated, the prices become competitive.

Here, the major cost is that of promotion — either through personal selling or direct mail advertising. The independent sales organisation is a costly thing to be set up. This channel suits the following conditions:

(1) Local Market, (2) Perishable goods, (3) Finance to set up own distribution system, (4) Premium products with after-sales-back-up, (5) Selective distribution, and (6) Effective control over retail prices and marketing. Avon Cosmetics (USA) does direct marketing successfully.

(2) M ⟶ R ⟶ C **Manufacturer ⟶ Retailer ⟶ Consumer**

It is suitable for large retailers who buy directly from the manufacturers, bypassing the wholesalers in the process. It is a shorter and quicker channel.

(3) M ⟶ W ⟶ R ⟶ C **Manufacturer ⟶ Wholesaler ⟶ Retailer ⟶ Consumer**

This is a traditional channel. Small retailers and small manufacturers find this channel suitable. In this channel, there is division of labour. A manufacturer concentrates on production, and leaves the distribution to wholesalers. It improves productivity and reduces cost. The only disadvantage is that the commissions of the intermediaries raise the price of the product when it reaches the final consumer. This channel suits mass distribution.

(4) M ⟶ A ⟶ R ⟶ C **Manufacturer ⟶ Agent ⟶ Retailer ⟶ Consumer**

Here, the wholesalers are replaced by the manufacturers' agents. They reach the retail market, especially large-scale retailers.

(5) M ⟶ A ⟶ W ⟶ R ⟶ C **Manufacturer ⟶ Agent ⟶ Wholesaler ⟶ Retailer ⟶ Consumer**

Here the agents sell to the wholesalers who then approach the small retailers.

(6) M ⟶ D ⟶ R ⟶ C **Manufacturer ⟶ Depot ⟶ Retailer ⟶ Consumer**

In this channel, the wholesaler has been eliminated. Manufacturers transship the goods to their own sales depots, which arrange to supply the goods to the retailers. In other words, the responsibility of distribution falls upon the manufacturer. Here, he has to develop a chain of retailers, keeping in mind their diverse requirements and operational methods. Here, the manufacturer gains control over the channel, improves his profits, knows the market trends immediately, avoids the malpractices at the wholesale level. But as a result, his concentration gets divided between production and distribution. He has to perform all the functions of a wholesaler and so his cost of operations increase. In pharmaceutical industry, Alembic has many sales depots supplying goods to wholesalers.

(7) M ⟶ C ⟶ S ⟶ C Manufacturer ⟶ Chainstore Consumer

Here the manufacturer takes upon himself the additional function of distribution by setting up his own shops in different parts of the city or even in different parts of the country. He sells his own goods directly to the consumers through these shops. It is the shortest and quickest channel. Here the manufacturer becomes both a wholesaler and a retailer.

❖ Distribution Channels in Industrial Marketing

In industrial marketing, there are four types of channels in vogue. An industrial marketer can use his own sales office or branch to reach the next component of the channel. He may choose alternatively two levels of wholesalers.

(1) M ⟶ I ⟶ C Manufacturer ⟶ Industrial ⟶ Consumer

Large and complex products are sold directly to the users, e.g. air-craft, power generators, heating plants etc.

(2) M ⟶ ID ⟶ U Manufacturer ⟶ Industrial Distributor ⟶ User

Distributors are used by suppliers of components, accessories, building materials, air-conditioning equipments etc.

(3) M ⟶ A ⟶ U Manufacturer ⟶ Agent ⟶ User

Agents are used by those firms whose own marketing department has not yet been set up. It is also useful to introduce new products or while entering the new markets.

(4) M ⟶ A ⟶ ID ⟶ U Manufacturer ⟶ Agent ⟶ Industrial Distributor ⟶ User

When it is not possible to sell directly to the users by the agents, we can make use of the industrial distributor who also provides storage services.

❖ Factors Affecting the Choice of Channels of Distribution

While selecting a channel, we have to keep in mind the three C's — channel *control,* channel *cost* and market *coverage.* A channel is generally selected on the basis of the customers' buying pattern. Some more considerations like the product, the intermediaries and the company itself also affect our channel decisions.

Market Considerations: It is obviously to be seen whether ours is a consumer-product or an industrial product. In industrial marketing, there are no retailers.

Number of Potential Customers: If there are a few customers, the product can be sold direct to the customers by personal selling. The larger the number of customers, the greater are the chances of using the middlemen.

Geographic Concentration: When customers are concentrated in a few geographic centres, we can think of direct sale *e.g.* ready-to-wear garments or textiles. For a nationally marketed product also, there may be some segments that have a high density and it is in such densely populated areas that the sales branches are set.

Order Size: A pickle manufacturer may sell directly to a retailer like Apna Bazaar as it places a large order. However, it may use wholesalers to reach a large number of small retailers.

❖ Product Considerations

Unit Value: Lower unit value of the product means longer channels. However, if a large quantity of low unit value products are sold, the channels can be shortened.

Perishability: Short channels are recommended for highly perishable products or fashion products.

Technical Nature: A complex technical product can be sold directly to the user. Such a product requires pre-selling and after-selling services, which wholesalers are not able to provide.

❖ Middlemen Considerations

Each producer selects the middlemen who provide services which the producer himself cannot provide or cannot provide economically. The availability of the middlemen and the attitude of the middlemen towards the producer are also important considerations.

Company Considerations: A sound firm is less dependent on middlemen. Experience of the trade makes a firm less dependent on middlemen. A new firm may handover the distribution to middlemen. The desire to control the distribution affects the choice.

❖ Use of Multiple Channels

It is possible for a producer to use more than one channel while distributing the products. A paint manufacturer can sell both to the household customers and industries. Here the product remains the same. It is obvious that different channels will be used for different products. It is possible to use dual distribution even for a single market on account of the type of buyers and the density of the market. A food product company can sell directly to Apna Bazaar but sells to other retailers through wholesalers. Some manufacturers use competing channels to sell the same brand to the same market, *e.g.*, Vicks Vapo Rub is distributed through general stores and chemist shops or Bata markets its shoes through its own stores and through other shoe retailers.

❖ Intensity of Distribution

Once the channels are selected, the manufacturers have to decide the number of middlemen to be employed either as wholesalers or retailers. This is called determining the intensity of distribution. Generally, three levels of intensity are adopted, but they are not exclusive of each other. They, in fact, are on a continuum. They range from (1) intensive distribution and (2) selective distribution (3) exclusive distribution.

(1) Intensive Distribution: Mostly used for consumer convenience goods, the consumers demand immediate satisfaction of their need and would rather not postpone the purchase. This strategy is dependent upon the retailers. A manufacturer who introduces a new food product may wish that all retail outlets of groceries and general stores carry it. But retailers may decide to stock only four well-known brands already existing. Intensive distribution thus needs putting advertisements and aggressive promotion. The promotional burden rests mainly on the manufacturer. There is no incentive for any retailer to promote a product that is carried by the competitive outlets.

(2) Selective Distribution: A business selects a few out of a wide variety of outlets. Maybe, a business selects a large number of outlets, but still not all. This distribution is suitable for shopping goods and speciality goods. It is also useful for accessories. This strategy may be adopted after first gaining experience from intensive distribution. The switch over may be due to the high cost of intensive distribution or non-satisfactory performance of some channel members. In this strategy, we can eliminate unviable middlemen. It is a more productive approach. The sales may in fact increase, though the number of accounts handled may be small.

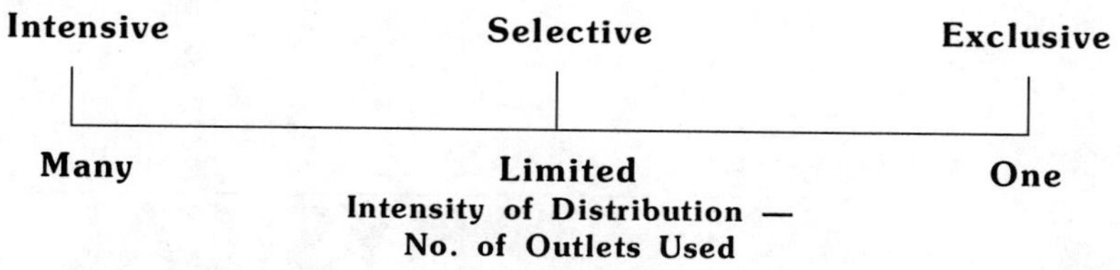

Fig. 21.1 Intensity of Distribution Continuum

(3) Exclusive Distribution: Here one middlemen (either a wholesaler/retailer) is appointed, and is given all the supplies. An exclusive distributor can be a wholesaler or a retailer. He handles the producer's line. Mostly, he is not allowed to carry a competitive line. Such distributorships are common for specialty products. In this strategy, the retailers have to carry a large inventory. Such distributors also provide installation/repair service. Machinery manufacturers generally appoint exclusive distributors.

Exclusive distribution helps a manufacturer to exercise channel control. The distributors may become collaborators in promoting the products. This channel assumes efficiency of distributors. If they are not efficient, the producer will suffer. Exclusive distributors are dependent on efficient manufacturers. If the manufacturer falters, the distributor may suffer. Such distributorships involve a certain level of financial commitment. There is a risk of the manufacturer adopting another level intensity level of distribution once the market is *developed*.

❖ Manufacturer-Middlemen Relationship

The selection as well as the day-to-day working with the middlemen ultimately determine the success of the distribution strategy.

A Perfect Middlemen:

(*i*) Helps the manufacturer to reach the market he wants to reach.

(*ii*) Carries adequate inventory and range of products to be distributed.

(*iii*) Promotes these effectively.

(*iv*) Provides services to the customers.

(*v*) Pays his dues in time and runs the show efficiently.

A Perfect Manufacturer:

(*i*) Should place the right product of right quality at right price in right quantity and at right time in the hands of the buyers.

(*ii*) Should promote these products effectively.

(*iii*) Should assist the middlemen both in promotion and management.

(*iv*) Gives product warranties and provides maintenance and installation services.

It is Utopian to think of a perfect combination of a middleman and manufacturer. Each party should endeavour to perform according to expectations. There should be a good communication system between the Producer and the Middleman. There should be an exchange of information about the marketing data, inventory levels and the marketing conditions.

* * *

22 PHYSICAL DISTRIBUTION MANAGEMENT (PDM)

After having established the channels of distribution, we can pay attention to the physical distribution of goods and services through these channels. By physical distribution, we mean the actual movement of the right quantity of products to the right place at the right time.

In Indian conditions, there are transportation bottlenecks and the size of the country is vast. Physical distribution thus acquires added significance. The expenses involved in physical distribution are substantial, *e.g.*, transport costs and ware-housing expenses. These are the days of energy shortage and high interest rates. It affects our inventory costs. All this needs efficient physical distribution management.

So far, cost reduction has been adopted in both the production and the marketing functions. Now, it is being adopted even in physical distribution management. Savings effected thereby lead to a heathy bottom line. Physical distribution efficiency is closely related to customer service.

❖ System's View

Physical distribution is a matter of logistics. Imagine an army with weapons but no ammunition, or a fleet of vehicles without any fuel. Similarly, a business with orders to fill but no vehicles to transport or a business with overloaded warehouses in Maharashtra but demanding customers in East India could not be considered to be strong enough. It leads to the importance we have to attach to the location of facilities.

Physical distribution is defined as the "actual flow of products." Physical distribution management is the management of efficient flow systems for products. It involves creating and developing these flow systems. The scope of physical distribution covers the flow of raw materials from the sources of supply to the production line and the flow of finished products from the end-point of production line to the final customer. The term also includes flow of goods within a channel (flow of goods onto the shelves of middlemen) and outside the channel (from the shelves to households or retail stores.)

Physical distribution system has five sub-systems:

(i) Inventory location and warehousing sub-system.

(ii) Material handing sub-system.

(iii) Inventory management and control sub-system.

(iv) Order processing sub-system.

(v) Transportation sub-system.

Each of these sub-systems is interdependent. Where our warehouse is located influences our mode of transport. The mode of transport affects the size of consignment. We should consider physical distribution as a total system and should not isolate the individual sub-systems for lopsided treatment. There should be coordination amongst the components of the system. Our long production runs may bring down production costs, but lead to an increase in our inventory costs. The traffic should not consider the freights in isolation. Freights are just a part of the total cost of physical distribution. What good is it to select low freight carriers if they take a long time to reach the destination? Finance always favours a standardised inventory to avoid unnecessary blocking of capital. But marketing needs a wide array of products. That too so located that they are in proximity of the customers. Such conflicting claims affect the flow of products. It is, therefore, necessary to take an overall systems' view of physical distribution and co-ordinate the various sub-systems.

Some problems of physical distribution are addressed by a statistical and quantitative approach. OR (Operations Research) is a helpful tool to a physical distribution manager. It is used in solving the transportation problem. Information Technology (IT) is a greater help in handling the enormous amount of data in this field. The quantitative aspects of physical distribution are outside the scope of this book. We shall concentrate only on the conceptual aspects.

❖ Total Cost Approach

Physical distribution alternatives have separate costs and the alternative that optimises cost-profits for one entire system should be chosen. Each component of the cost should be given thought. Air freight may be costly in absolute terms. But much more costlier it could be to store the goods in warehouses. It is not being suggested that airlines are the best carriers, but what must be borne in mind is the totality of the physical distribution, rather than one aspect of it.

Physical distribution optimisation is a trade-off between the Total cost and the Customer services. Maybe, we will have to increase the physical distribution costs to reach a desired level of customer satisfaction. There are many cost trade-offs, *e.g.*, transport costs and warehousing costs.

❖ Strategic Approach to Physical Distribution

When physical distribution is treated strategically, we achieve lower operational costs and increased customer satisfaction. Physical distribution affects the marketing mix of a firm.

In certain non-differentiated products like chemicals, effective physical distribution improves the level of customer satisfaction and gives a competitive advantage to the firm. Physical distribution when managed efficiently proves to be cost reduction and elimination strategy.

As stock-outs are avoided, both sales volume and customer satisfaction increase. Efficient physical distribution operated at a lower cost passes on the benefits to the customers who get products at reduced prices. This also leads to enhancement of sales. Physical distribution brings about an adjustment in production and consumption. It creates a time utility by storage and place utility through transportation. Physical distribution stabilises prices by strategic use of transport and warehousing. Physical distribution also affects the choice of a channel of distribution. Traffic management ensures fastest delivery and lowest freights.

❖ Tasks in Physical Distribution

As we have already observed, physical distribution consists of five sub-systems which are interdependent.

Inventory Management: There are four areas of decision-making:

(*i*) The size of the inventory.

(*ii*) The location of the inventory.

(*iii*) The material handling.

(*iv*) The transportation of inventories.

The location of inventory and the number of sites from which inventory is supplied affect the total size and the mode of transport of the inventory.

Storage: Storage means holding and preserving products from the point of production to the point of sale.

Warehousing: Warehousing is broader is scope. It goes beyond storage. The other functions include assembling, dividing and preparing products for transportation.

Centralisation Vs. Decentralisation: Whether inventory is to be concentrated at one point or to be dispersed throughout market is a basic question. A centralised inventory is amenable to better control, but leads to increase in transport costs and belated deliveries. Decentralisation leads to lower transport costs and quicker deliveries.

Distribution Centres: It is a new concept in warehousing. Distribution centres are related to the markets and not to the transport facilities. It represents an integrated system for the flow of products. It accepts orders, executes them and effects deliveries to the customers.

Material Handling: We have to select the proper material handling equipment so as to reduce the time and costs in handling. Warehouse architecture takes into account the material handling aspects. Mechanised equipments are used to move materials internally. Containerisation has come to be accepted for facilitating inter-modal transport. A metal certainer can be placed on trucks, on railway wagons and in ships. These containers remain unopened from the point they are transported to their final destination.

Inventory Control: Much finance gets committed to inventory. The objective of inventory control is to reduce the capital blocked and to stabilise the fluctuations in inventories and while doing so, to execute the orders of the customers, on time and with precision. Information technology is of a greater help in the proper management of inventory. The basic input for inventory management is the sales forecast. The accuracy of forecast affects the optimum level of inventory. There are two types of costs associated with inventories *(i)* ordering costs and *(ii)* carrying costs. The carrying costs are expressed as a *percentage*. They include warehousing costs, interest cost, pilferage and losses, taxes etc. Customer satisfaction is related to proper inventory control. Stock-outs result in loss of goodwill and loss of sales. It is also necessary to determine what quantity is to be ordered — EOQ. It is nothing but balancing of ordering costs with carrying costs.

Order Processing: Each organisation must have a prescribed procedure for handling orders. Orders are received and filled. It involves billing, credit extension, invoice making, and collection of dues. There is much heart-burn if there are billing errors or the orders are not properly attended to.

Transportation: Sending or despatching products to customers is a major part of any physical distribution system. The decision is taken regarding the mode of transport and the specific carrier company. The chief modes are railways, trucks, ships, aeroplanes and pipelines. These days, trucks have become a major means of transport, though railways are more economical. The following table compares the various means of transport:

Criterion	*Means*			
	Railway	*Ships*	*Trucks*	*Aeroplanes*
Cost	Medium	Lowest	High	Highest
Speed	Medium	Slowest	Fast	Fastest
Reliability	Medium	Poor	Good	Medium
Locations served	Many, but still many locations are not accessible	Limited	Unlimited	Few
Flexibility (Variety of products hauled)	High	High	Medium	Limited
Products suitable	Bulky	Bulky Low value	High value Short distance	High value Speed is important

Indian Railways offer wagon-load services and less-than-wagon-load called 'road van' services. They also offer container services. If the delivery is not taken in time, railways levy a demurrage charge. After sometime, the railways auction the goods whose delivery is not taken. Railways issue a Railway Receipt (RR) when goods are delivered to them. While taking the delivery of the goods, the RR is to be presented to the railways. The suppliers can negotiate the RR through a bank, where it is sent along with a Hundi or a Bill and an invoice or beejak. Motor transport operators issue a Motor Transport Receipt (MTR) once the goods are given to them. Aeroplanes issue Airway Bill (AWB). Services of freight forewarders can be availed of by the firm who provide valuable services in physical distribution.

* * *

23 PROMOTION MIX

As we have already studied, marketing mix consists of four elements — product, price, distribution and promotion. The last element, *i.e.*, promotion, is the link between the Company and the Outside public. Promotion itself is a combination of advertising, personal selling, publicity and public relations. Together this is referred to as the promotional mix.

Though promotion is the most high profile activity of the marketing mix, it is the most criticised activity, too. Some of the criticism is justified because of the untruthful and misleading advertisements and the bogus discount sales announced everyday in the media. However, it is to be noted that promotion *per se* is not at fault, but one who uses it wrongfully. However, in keeping with the human nature, the promotion as a tool gets blamed. It is like an unskilful dancer blaming the dimensions of the courtyard to cover up her own faults. Or like a bad workman who could not drive a nail straight blaming the hammer. We cannot throw away a hammer for this reason. Similarly, promotion cannot be discarded because it is used wrongfully by some people.

❖ Promotion Mix

Promotion mix consists of five major tools:

Advertising: Any paid form of non-personal communication of ideas, products and services by an identified sponsor.

Sales Promotion: Short-term direct inducements to encourage sales of products and services.

Publicity: Non-personal stimulation of demand for product/service or business organisation as a whole by putting commercially significant news in the media to create a favourable image. It is not paid for by the sponsor.

Personal Selling: For making sales, a salesman interacts orally with the buyer or buyers in the form of a sales presentation.

Public Relations: Markets engage in public relations to develop a favourable image of their organisations in the eyes of the public — public at large, customers, suppliers, employees, government, media, competitors, shareholders and the community around them.

It is to be appreciated that promotion is a broader term while sales promotion is just a part of it. Sales promotion consists of giving direct inducements to promote sales. *e.g.*, a free gift, price off, sales contests, dealer contests etc. In a sense, all marketing activities are in part promotional, *e.g.*, product differentiation, line extensions and branding.

Promotion essentially is a process of communication which not only informs but also persuades. Being persuaded and being informed are two sides of the same coin. It is the job of the marketing manager to make promotion contribute to the marketing mix in such a way that the overall marketing objectives are realised.

In this chapter, we shall define one major element of promotion mix, *viz.*, advertising first and then study how advertising is a tool of communication.

❖ Definition of Advertising

The simplest definition of an advertisement is that it is a 'public announcement.' In earlier times, to 'advertise' meant merely to announce or to inform. Some advertisements today still do just that: provide information about 'birth,' 'deaths,' 'engagements,' with little or no intention to persuade. The majority of classified advertisements provide useful information about jobs, accommodation, sales of second-hand vehicles and furniture, etc. Matrimonial advertisements, recruitment advertisements, and tenders, notices and similar types of public announcements also provide the public with valuable information, which would otherwise be difficult to obtain easily. The earliest advertisements in the first English newspapers published in India in the Eighteenth Century were little more than 'public announcements' about the arrival of ships and merchandise from abroad.

Basically, then, an advertisement is an announcement to the public of a product, service or idea through a medium to which the public has access. The medium may be print (such as newspapers, posters, banners and hoardings), electronic (radio, television, video, cable, phone) or any other. An advertisement is usually paid for by an advertiser at rates fixed or negotiated with the media.

An advertisement is a form of persuasive communication with the public. The communication is usually one-sided, in one direction from the advertiser and to the public. The members of the public are free to respond to it in their own way; the response is at an individual or family level. There is little or no dialogue with the public; advertising forces itself upon the public. At the same time, especially in a democracy with a market economy, such communication is required so that intelligent choices are made.

The American Marketing Association, Chicago, defines advertising as ***"any, paid form of non-personal presentation of ideas, goods and services by an identified sponsor."***

An analysis of each element of this American definition follows:

Any Form: Advertising may be in any form of presentation. It may be a sign, a symbol, an illustration, an ad message in a magazine or newspaper, a commercial on the radio or on television, a circular despatched through the mail or a pamphlet handed out at a street corner; a sketch or a message on a billboard or a poster. Any form of presentation, which an advertiser imagines will fulfil the requirements of an ad, can be employed.

Non-personal: This phrase excludes any form of personal selling, which is usually done on a person-to-person or on a people-to-people basis. If it is a person-to-person presentation, it is not advertising.

Goods, Services, Ideas for Action: It is well known that advertisements are employed to communicate information about products and services. Most definitions neglect the use of advertising to promote ideas. The Posts and Telegraph Department advertising to promote the use of the PIN code for faster delivery of letters is an example of selling an idea for action. The Income-Tax Department advertising to persuade the income-tax payers to pay their taxes before the due date to avoid default is another case of the application of advertising to ideas involving action.

Appointment ads by corporations and employment agencies, the seeking of donations by charitable institutions and political parties and election candidates advertising to "sell" themselves to the public are striking examples of advertising being fruitfully employed for a persuasive communication of ideas for action. In fact, in the presidential election in America — a much-advertised and the most lengthy election in the world — candidates do employ ad agencies to sell "The President 1992." This is not a product, nor a service, but an idea for action. In most social marketing, we advertise ideas for a social cause, may be family planning, prohibition, adult education, etc. The services of ads released by the Loss Prevention Association of India promoting the prevention of losses and the preservation of life are very relevant here. One such ad may highlight the hazards of fire-crackers during Diwali days which may take the lives of children who are somewhat careless. The headline may say: "This year, take that nagging fear out of Diwali days. Teach your children these simple rules of safety."

Openly Paid for by an Identified Sponsor: This means that advertising is openly and directly paid for as against publicity, which is not openly paid for. As it is paid, the sponsor has control over the form, content and scheduling of the ad. The sponsor, too, is identified. The sponsor is identified by his company's name or brand name or both. If, in an ad, the sponsor is not identified and it is not paid for its use of the media in which it has appeared, then the message is considered to be publicity. The publicity material, when prepared, may be paid for by its sponsor; but the newspaper, magazine or radio station that carries it does so free of charge.

❖ Other Definitions of Advertising

John E. Kennedy who was a Canadian ex-Mountie formerly and was a copywriter at Lord and Thomas Advertising Agency described advertising as "salesmanship in print." (1905). Sidney Bernstein (1990) reinforces Kennedy's definition by describing 'advertising as a substitute for the human salesman.' Bob Isherwood, creative director, Saatchi & Saatachi, Australia, calls himself a salesman. According to him, a good advertisement is born out of selling on idea that has been seen somewhere. It is how well the idea is sold that makes the difference, he says.

❖ Advertising as a Tool of Communication

Advertising is as old as man. There is a semblance of advertising in the many activities of a human being, especially those activities which influence others, either favourably or otherwise. A baby crying for its feed, a girl wooing the prince charming, a doting wife desirous of having a new sari are all aspects of advertising. They want to communicate, to persuade, to influence and to lead to some action. All this has been a part of human life almost from the time it took shape. We shall go a step further and state that the persuasive form of communication that is advertising pre-existed human life. Take, for instance, the dancing daffodils or sweet smelling roses which silently invited butterflies to achieve the objective of pollination. There were fruits, flora and fauna all advertising themselves even before man existed. Yes, but advertising informally is interwoven with nature and the evolution of the world. Padamsee, the ex-CEO of Lintas says: "when a man wears trouser-shirt ensemble instead of a dhoti, he is advertising he is westernised. When a woman wears lipstick, she is advertising that she wants to look beautiful. When a *neta* delives a speech, he is advertising that he wants to be noticed. Ads are parts of human nature to be noticed." Perhaps, as a means of formal mass communication, advertising came to be practised by royalty who sent drummers to make an announcement or communicate the will and desires of a monarch to his people.

Advertising, as we understand it today, was not used until about 200 years ago. The form of advertising for the transmission of information dates back to Ancient Greece and Rome. Criers and signs were used to carry information for advertising goods and services well before the development of printing. Even during the Middle Ages, advertising signs were very extensively used. These signs generally consisted of illustrations of symbols of the products advertised. The upsurge in advertising came after the development of printing. When printing techniques were perfected and as this industry developed, the signs were replaced by written words or messages.

Advertising has evolved since the industrial revolution as a tool of marketing communication. It is an art as well as a science. It is a career for many. It is rapidly getting professionalised. Competition, growing marketing expenses, product failures, liberalisation, globalisation, emergence of new electronic media have given an impetus to advertising activity.

Advertising is the most visible marketing tool which seeks to transmit an effective message from the marketer to a group of individuals. The marketer pays for sponsoring the advertising activity. Advertising, unlike salesmanship which interacts with a buyer face-to-face, is non-personal. It is directed at a mass audience; and not at an individual, as in personal selling.

Though marketers use advertising, basically it is a communication process. Here the advertiser is the source who transmits the message which passes through an appropriate medium like press, TV, radio or magazines. The message is decoded meaningfully. It is ultimately received by the target audience for whom the product/service is meant. The ultimate aim of advertising is to make the target audience favourably inclined towards the product or service. In that sense, advertising is not ordinary communication but *marketing communication.* Since it is received by a large number of people, through the mass media it is called 'mass communication.'

Advertising aims at drawing attention to a product. It seeks to create an awareness about the existence of advertised product. It passes on information about the product in such a way that interest is created in the mind of the prospective consumer about the product. Then there is a growing desire to possess the product. There are convincing arguments in favour of the product. All this leads us to a buying inclination.

❖ The Communication Process

In marketing communication, there is a transmission of a message from a sender to the receiver. The end result of the communication process is the understanding of a message. The message is transmitted through media or certain channels. The response to the message is known by receiving the feedback from the recipient of the communication. The communication sometimes fails to accomplish its purpose — creation of an appropriate response or understanding when the message is distorted by 'noise' elements. The following diagram illustrates the communication process.

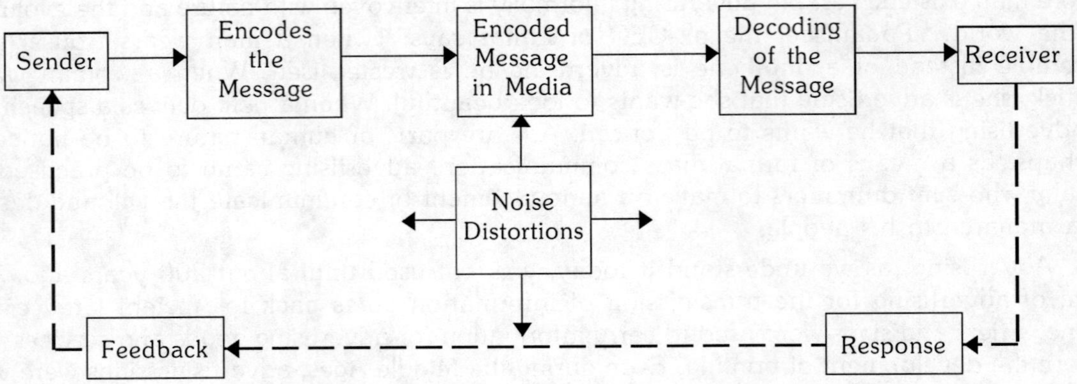

Fig. 23.1 Communication Process

The sender is the source of the message. It puts the message in symbolic form say a letter or advertising copy. It is called 'encoding.' The message is carried by the media, say the postal department or TV or newspapers. The message is received by the receiver who shows a particular response which is communicated back to the sender.

The message must accomplish three tasks in order to be effective:

(*a*) It must gain the attention of the receiver.

(*b*) It must be understood.

(*c*) It must stimulate the needs of the receiver and suggest appropriate method to satisfy these needs.

Senders must be aware of the receivers or audiences they want to reach and the responses they want. They must be skilful in encoding the message, taking into account how the receiver or the audience is going to decode the message. Since the sender wants the receiver to understand the message, the sender must know as much as possible about the receiver before the message is designed. The sender puts the message through efficient media that reach the audience. The response of the audience is known by developing the feedback channels. In this process, noise may distort the effectiveness of communication. Noise includes poor message planning, busy audience members or careless feedback of response.

❖ Marketing Communication

Modern marketing is the management of the four P's — product, price, promotion and place or distribution channel. In a sense the entire marketing process has a large content of communication. For instance, the product communicates a distinctive image such as youthfulness, glamour or prestige. The brand name communicates physical and psychological attributes of the product, *e.g.*, Dreamflower talc. The package communicates to the consumer what the manufacturer thinks of his convenience and sense of beauty. The price communicates the quality of the product. There are communications between Buyers and Sellers, *i.e.*, the distribution channel. Thus each element of the marketing mix either helps or hinders communication and ultimately the sales effort. Marketing communication is thus a broader term than promotional strategy. However, the most important element of marketing communication is the planned promotional communication.

❖ The Process of Marketing Communication

The following diagram (Fig. 23.2) illustrates the marketing communication process as applied to promotional strategy.

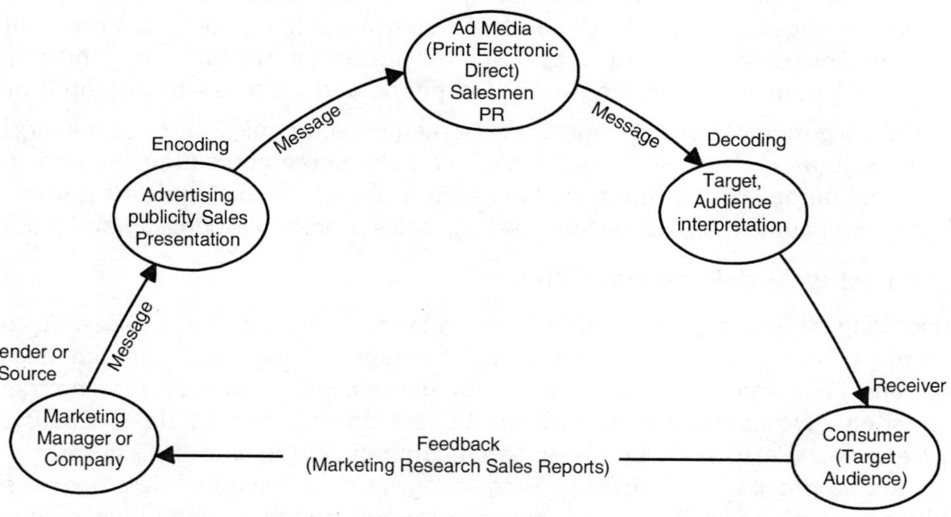

Fig. 23.2 The Marketing Communication Process

The marketing manager or the organisation is the sender of the message. The message is encoded as advertising copy, publicity material, sales promotional displays or sales presentation by sales people. The media for delivering the message may be the print media like press and magazines or the electronic media like TV, radio and films or a salesman who makes a presentation. The decoding step involves the consumer's interpretation of the message. This is often the most challenging aspect of marketing communication as consumers may not always interpret the message the way the sender wants them to interpret. As seen previously, the fundamental difficulty in communication process occurs during encoding and decoding. This may happen because the meanings attached to various words and symbols may differ, depending upon the frames of reference and the field of experience between the Sender and the Receiver.

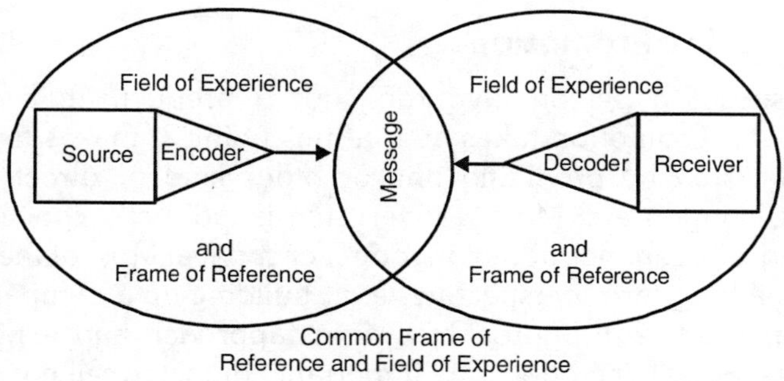

Fig. 23.3 Communication Marketing View

This is explained by the Fig. 23.3. The overlapping of field of experience and frame of reference makes the communication possible. If there is no overlap, communication may be bad or impossible. The consumer or audience response is known by undertaking a market research study or by analysing the sales reports. The noise element is in the form of competitive promotional messages. There may be random noise factor like people fast forwarding a video casette when advertisements are shown. Errors in communication may be minimised by knowing the relevant market dimensions the needs and attitudes of potential buyers.

In total corporate communications, the marketing communications are the most important part. Advertising as we have seen is a part of marketing communication. Advertising as a tool of communication has certain important characteristics which distinguishes it from other tools of marketing communication like personal selling, sales promotion, publicity and public relations.

❖ Advertising and Personal Selling

Advertising is communication with many consumers of products and services. To communicate with a large group, we put the advertising message through mass media like the press, magazines and TV. Advertising is thus one form of mass communication. Advertising communication is non-personal. We communicate with the buyers through the media. There is no face-to-face conversation. Personal selling is personal communication where a salesman talks person to person with a prospect. Advertising aims at a group, *i.e.*, mass while personal selling aims at individuals. Personal selling is not mass communication but individual communication. These days products are mass produced for mass consumption. It is not possible to contact each customer individually. Therefore, advertising a mass communication tool is a must for modern marketer. But industrial products and complex pieces of machineries can be sold better by personal selling where the salesman is in a position to explain the characteristics of the product to the buyer. Salespersons are in a position to tailor their messages according to unique characteristics of each prospect. In modern marketing, the marketing manager decides a judicious mix of advertising and personal selling. It is difficult to measure the effectiveness of advertising, however salespersons receive immediate feedback during their interacting and can see how their messages are getting across. They may, therefore, adjust the message or presentation quickly.

Personal selling is a very intense means of communication. People may skip an advertisement on TV but find it difficult to dismiss a salesperson. It is the most effective communication tool as it is inter personal. But this is its major wektness as well as strength. It is terribly inefficient for mass market producers, where advertising a mass communication tool scores over it.

❖ Advertising and Sales Promotion

Advertising predisposes a person favourably for a product/service/idea moving him towards its purchase. Sales Promotion takes over at this point. It makes the consumer take a favourable purchase decision by providing one or other kind of direct inducement, *e.g.*, discount, price-off, gift, coupon etc. Mostly advertising is indirectly concerned with sales. It either informs or persuades or reminds about a product or service. Most of the times, it is indirect in its approach and has a long-term perspective, *e.g.*, building up a company image or brand image. Sales Promotion short-term approach, a direct approach and expects an immediate response in terms of sales. Sales promotion is an important adjunct to selling. Advertising is more frequent and repetitive than Sales Promotion. Sales Promotion are non-recurrent selling efforts. They supplement the advertising and personal selling. Displays are effective method of sales promotion. Contests are also another effective method of sales promotion.

❖ Advertising and Publicity

Publicity is defined as non-personal stimulation of demand for a product/service/ business unit by *planting commercially significant news* about it in a published medium or obtaining *favourable presentation* of it on radio, TV or stage *that is not paid for* by the *sponsor*. Two significant distinctions emerge. Publicity is not openly paid for. Secondly, presentation is not programmed.

Marketers have less control over publicity than they have over advertising. Publicity is left to the discretion of the media in terms of whether to present it or not, contents of presentation and the format of presentation. Publicity may be negative as well as positive.

❖ Advertising and Public Relations

The ultimate aim of Public Relations is to develop a favourable image in the eyes of the public. It refers to a company's communication and relationships with various sections of the public — customers, suppliers, shareholders, employees, governments, media, society at large. PR can be formal or informal. PR, unlike advertising, is personal.

Advertising is not the only form of persuasive communication. Very closely allied to advertising are sales promotion and public relations. In fact both are important parts of advertising and are often 'managed' by the same people or agencies or departments. All three are vital to the 'marketing' of a product, service or idea.

While advertising is termed 'above ← the-line' communication, sales promotion may be termed 'below-the-line' communication. The ultimate goal of all three is to sell products, services, reputations, projects, programmes, people, politicians, beliefs, ideas indeed everything and anything.

The institute of Public Relations, London, defines Public Relations as 'the deliberate, planned and sustained effort to establish and maintain understanding between an Organization and its Public.' Public Relations is low-cost compared to advertising, for the publicity obtained, say in the press, through public relations is not directly paid for. Indirectly, the expenses involve keeping in close touch with people in the media through press conferences, press visits and press releases. Besides, media persons have to be 'entertained,' and some of them expect 'gifts' from companies.

According to Edward L Bernays, the 'father' of Public Relations and the author of 'Engineering of Consent,' the phrase Public Relations means, 'quite simply, the name of the engineering approach, i.e. action based on thorough knowledge of the situation and on the application of scientific principles and tried practices in the task of getting people to support ideas and programmes.'

There are four elements to the mechanics of PR:

1. The message to be transmitted.
2. An 'independent' third party endorser to transmit the message.
3. A target-audience that it is hoped will be motivated to buy whatever is being sold.
4. A medium through which the message is transmitted.

Advertising and PR are different from the point of view of their objectives. Advertising is an aid to selling and it improves the bottom-line of business.

PR, which is the business of image management, cannot replace advertising. Of course, PR can in some way push up sales because it changes the way consumers perceive the company and hence the product. Adertising and PR are complementary in most cases but sometimes advertising is not necessary. PR can do the job. If a new manufacturing facility is started by a company, it cannot be advertised. A PR effort is more effective.

PR no doubt is valuable. Edit space is far more important than paid ad space. Of course, what has been achieved by PR must be adequately supported by the product and service. If PR is professionally handled, it can achieve benefits for an organisation at a fraction of a cost of advertising.

Advertising has a greater role when we are selling a tangible product. In a service industry, however, PR has a greater role, since the product is intangible.

Advertising and PR can't replace each other. By PR we create a good image. Advertising is necessary to take advantage of that good image for actual selling.

PR has higher degree of credibility since it is not paid for. Advertising, however, creates a brand personality. Only advertisement can add value to a product.

PR has now slowly evolved into an integrated approach called corporate communications.

❖ Corporate Communications

There are papers on corporate communications in American Universities and there are departments of corporate communication in different companies including our Hindustan Lever. In the 90's, business seeks to communicate positively in terms of clarity of identity to a wide range of people — financiers, those in autority, the general public, among others. Corporate communications is not limited to mere PR. It includes crisis communication, e.g., corporate identity programmes, re-imaging, media relations, corporate advertising, sponsorship for image building and communicating during take over. Corporate communications is not restricted to image management but considers corporate philanthropy, media dealing and crisis management.

❖ Communication Model

Marketing communication, especially advertising is meant for a group of users of products called the target audience. After identifying the target audience, we must determine the response desired. The ultimate response desired is of course the buying of the product or service. We must know the decision-making process that leads the target audience from its present position to a higher state of readiness-to-buy.

The effectiveness of advertising depends upon to what extent the advertising message is received and accepted by the target audience. Research has identified that an advertisement to be effective has to (*i*) attract attention, (*ii*) secure interest, (*iii*) build desire for the product and finally, (*iv*) obtain action. All advertisements obviously do not succeed on these counts. This is one solitary reason behind the great divergence between the number of people exposed to the advertisement and those who ultimately take the purchase decisions. At this stage, however, other elements of the marketing mix, especially distribution become crucial.

Advertisement communicates an idea, a message or a belief. An advertisement would be effective only if the media audience accepts that message and is motivated to take the required action. Several models have been developed which have specifically identified the sequence of events which must take place between receipt of the message and desired action.

AIDA Model: A somewhat simplified model based on the identical principle of sequential stages of consumer action is known as AIDA model. AIDA stands for:

A — Attracting attention

I — Rousing interest

D — Building desire

A — Obtaining action

Advertising as a communication medium can in most cases effectively perform the first three functions. In the case of direct-action advertising, it also must translate desire into action, unaided by any other promotional instruments. In the case of indirect-action advertising, however, the action can be aided at the time of purchase by two-way communication between the intending Buyer and the sales Staff.

Let us examine the attention, interest, desire and action components in more detail.

Attention: The layout is the most important factor that directs attention to an advertisement. Typography and colours used in the layout can rivet us. The size of the advertisement also compel us to get attracted to it. Contrast by white space is a good attention-getter. Movement is a vital element for getting attention. Movement can be physical or emotional. The position of the advertisement also adds to its attention value. Celebrities in the advertisement, dramatization, model selection, illustration all this contribute to attention.

Interest: *Ad* seen does not mean *ad* read. Mostly people see the illustrations and do not read the copy. Here illustrations have to work hard. They should together with headlines must provoke further reading. The selection of the illustration and its integration to life are thus very important. Even copy format is important for interest creation. Some people get worked on by a scientific copy and some by a humorous copy. Here there is a dilemma for a copywriter. He has to satisfy maximum number of people and so he has to search for a common denominator of interest.

Desire: The basic purpose of advertising is to create a desire for the product or service being advertised. Appeals used for the motivation of people. Vivid description or copy always helps. Buying motives, physiological as well as psychological, make people purchase products. The copy of the advertisement must kindle these motives. There are certain barriers here — certain reservations in the mind of customers. We have to overcome them. We have to convince by giving evidence, testimonials, endorsements, facts and figures. On arousal, people become prone to buy the product.

Action: The logical end of the desire aroused is to buy the product.

1. Products are associated with the company.
2. The message is repeated.
3. Certain immediate action appeals are used.

The attention stage is the *cognitive stage*. In this stage, the target audience is exposed to the message, which when received by them causes a cognitive response awareness. The interest and desire stages are the *affective stages* which affect the attitudes and bring about an intention to buy. The final action stage is the *behaviour stage*. In practice all the ad copies do not lead the consumer through awareness to purchase. AIDA model suggests only the desirable qualities in an advertising copy as a communication tool.

❖ IMC

IMC supports a common idea of communication across all the communication vehicles. Of late, it had been reduced to a TV executional idea being translated into other communication vehicles. IMC should allow each communication element, to do what it does best rather than 'translating a TV ad'. Grey calls this 'synchronised marketing' rather than translating one ad idea across the media, we should extend the brand idea or the core of the brand. Ad net-works have divisions for each communication element and all such divisions chase their own business goals and emphasises its own primacy rather than pushing the total or best communication package. Integration in a divisive organisation becomes a flawed concept. Cross-activity and geography brand teams are needed in a structure. At present, India lacks that scale and critical mass to avail of such services. It is also felt that one-stop buying of all communication needs was not easy to achieve just because the advertisers would like to shop for the best and avoid the effect of such shopping on brand synergy. A client has to orchestrate while buying services from several sources, since he owns the brand. A crucial decision is who will lead the process from the communication end. Should it be the agency or any of the specialists whose services are sought? The emphasis today is on total communication planning and not just media planning. Agencies see them as integrators in the integration process. But sometimes, the communication is led by DM or PR. It is to be realised that the idea can originate anywhere, not just from mainstream agencies. If there is not proper integration, who is to be blamed? Advertisers blame the agencies. But the ultimate responsibility of integration is placed at their own doors. This responsibility is not to be abrogated to the agency. It is the marketing manager's job to exercise to control over the whole communication package.

Different agencies are attempting to cope with IMC in their own way. Grey India is test running its new synchronised template that has separate departments, not companies O & M is being restructured across consumer need clusters. There are going to be brand teams McCann talks about brand optimisation.

❖ Designing the Message

Advertising as a communication tool concentrates on four problems:

(*a*) What to say (message content).

(*b*) How to say it (message structure).

(*c*) How to say it symbolically (message format).

(*d*) Who should say it (message source).

❖ Message Content

To get the desired response, advertising as a communication tool should decide what to say. Various names have been given to this exercise — use of *appeals,* selecting a *theme* or an *idea,* identifying a *Unique Selling Proposition* (USP). In practice, it amounts to establishing some kind of benefit, motivation identification or reason why the audience should think or do something.

Appeals are broadly classified into three categories:

(*i*) Rational appeals.

(*ii*) Emotional appeals.

(*iii*) Moral appeals.

Rational Appeals: These are directed towards the thinking faculty of the audience. Here the functional benefit of the product is highlighted. Some examples of rational motives are:

(*a*) *High quality*: Consumer durables are expected to have high quality. Many consumer goods are also expected to be of high quality.

(*b*) *Low price*: Purchasing a product paying a lower price which functions as good as or slightly less than the higher priced product is considered to be a rational decision.

(*c*) *Long life*: A bulb lasting several thousand hours before fusing-off is considered to be a rational appeal.

(*d*) *Performance*: of a Luna Moped on city roads and the mileage per litre of fuel is a rational appeal.

(*e*) *Ease of use*: As in the case of Videocon Automatic Washing Machine which cleanses, rinses and dries too.

(*f*) *Resale value* as of Bajaj Scooter.

(*g*) *Economy in operating expenses* as in case of an electronic regulator which saves electricity and pays-off its cost.

Industrial products are sold against rational appeals. Purchases are made more against specifications — technical, physical, chemical etc.

Even when products are purchased on emotional grounds people give rationalisation for their purchases.

Emotional appeals: Here the agitated or excited state of mind prompts us to purchase. There is no deliberate process involved. Emotional motives may be sub-conscious too. Emotional appeals could stir up positive or negative emotions which lead to an interest in the product and its purchase. Let us examine two major categories of emotional appeals.

Negative emotional appeals: Negative emotional appeals emphasise the loss if not heeded. *Fear appeal* is one such appeal. The effectiveness is commensurate with the level of fear it generates. Tooth pastes warning us against tooth decay or bad breath is an example of this appeal.

Positive emotional appeals: These are love, humour, pride, prestige, joy. Mother's love is commonly employed appeal. Parental love is also widely used. Joy and thrill appeal is also extensively used (soft drinks). Humour appeal in Utterly-Butterly Amul and in Mosquito Coils of Bombay Chemicals are well known. Price, prestige and exclusiveness are other positive emotional appeals.

Other emotional appeals could be

(*i*) Desire to be different.

(*ii*) Desire to conform (desire to be in jeans like teenagers).

(*iii*) Desire to attract the opposite sex.

(*iv*) Desire for prestige.

Most of the purchases, however, are on both rational and emotional grounds. You are doing now B.Com. and desire to do MBA later because that will give you social prestige plus you can well be a productive member of the society.

Moral appeals: These appeals are directed to your sense of judgement between the Right and the Wrong. These are mostly used in social awareness advertising.

❖ Advertising Message Structure

Advertising communication effectiveness not only depends on the message content, though it is no doubt an important component, but on its structure as well. The important aspects of message structure are: Drawing conclusions, repetition, one-versus-two-sided arguments, and the order of presentation.

(i) Drawing Conclusion: The question often raised is whether definite conclusions should be drawn for the audience in the ad for quick understanding or should they be left to them. In many instances, it is best to let the receivers of the promotion message draw their own conclusion. Such consumers feel that the message which draws a conclusion is over-aggressive and an attempt at forcefully influencing their choice. Moreover, since conclusion drawing at best assists in an easy comprehension of facts and not in the process of attitudinal change, it will not affect very much the persuasive quality of ads which aim at a change in attitude. When the issue involved is simple and the audience is intelligent, to draw a conclusion will be merely to attempt to explain that which is obvious. It does not add anything extra to the persuasive quality of the advertisement. Moreover, if the communicator perceived to be unworthy, the receiver may resent the attempt on his part to draw a conclusion for him and influence his choice.

When the issue is highly personal, the audience may resent the communicator's interference in drawing a conclusion. A typical example of this is the recent ad campaign sponsored by the Poultry-Farm Association in Gujarat, promoting the use of eggs among vegetarians. Eggs from the poultry farms were given a new name the "Veggs" and recommended for consumption in that segment of society which is fully vegetarian. Since this touches a highly personal issue concerning religious attitudes, the ad was resented, and much criticism was published against it in the Reader's Opinion column in popular dailies. Thus, even though promoters sought the sale of the product in a new segment by drawing specific conclusions, these were not accepted, but rather resented. However, conclusion drawing is favoured where the product is a complex or specialised one. The Farex baby food ad, starting with a sensational headline: " Your baby is born with a 3-month gift of iron. After 3 months, milk alone cannot give him the iron he needs." The ad closes with the conclusion : "Doctors recommend Farex. Baby's ideal solid food for rapid all-round growth." A long body copy goes on to explain that Farex is ideal baby solid food.

(ii) Repetition: Repeating an ad message is often beneficial, for it develops a continuity of impression in the minds of the target audience and may increase the predisposition to think and act favourably towards the products advertised. Everything else being equal, a repeated message increases awareness and knowledge on the part of the prospect. Audience retention improves with repetition and falls-off quickly when repetition is abandoned.

(iii) One-versus-two-sided Communication: This raises the question whether the advertiser should only praise the product or should also mention some of its shortcomings. The most common approach in sales and advertising is a one-sided approach. However, on deep analysis, it is found that one-sided messages tend to work best with the audiences which is initially favourably predisposed to the claims made in the ad message. Two-sided arguments go well when audiences have an unfavourable opinion about the communicator's position. Also, a two-sided message tends to be more effective with educated audiences capable of sound reasoning, particularly when they are exposed to counter propaganda. A two-sided communication produces the greatest attitude change when people are opposed to the point of view presented. Also, a two-sided communication is effective in maintaining the belief level against a counter-attack by competitors. However, it is single-sided communication which is commonly used, for it is difficult for the advertiser to refer to the product's shortcomings and still effectively persuade prospects to buy it.

(iv) Order of Presentation: Whether to put the strongest argument first or last is a part of copy writing strategy. In a one-sided argument, it is advisable to present the strongest point first, for it will result in better attention and interest. This is done with the objective of achieving the primary effect. However, when an audience necessarily requires a two-sided communication, it is better, at least initially to start with the other side's argument and slowly disarm the audience which is opposed to the communicator's position and then to conclude the message with the strongest argument.

❖ Message Format

Message format is an important step in message development. By format, we mean the organisation, plan, style or type of ad message. The message format is the scheme by which the message content and structure strategy are implemented. It is characterised by the type of media vehicle in which the message is delivered. In a print ad, the message format elements are headline, body copy, illustration and colour, whereas, in radio advertising, the format elements are words, voice qualities (speech rate, rhythm, pitch, articulation) and vocalisation (pauses, sighs, yawns). The message format is important because a good message strategy may not click if it is put in a poor format. The message format for a print ad includes such things as the position of the headline, the position of the picture or illustration, the colour scheme, the size of the letters in the headline and the body of the message.

❖ Message Source

The overall impact of the advertising message depends upon how the target audience perceives the sender. Messages originating from credible sources are more persuasive. When doctors recommend a pharmaceutical product, the credibility of the message is very high. Ex-drug addicts may warn the youngsters about the ill effects of drug addiction. Ex-drug addicts have high credibility as they have already gone through the ordeal. Companies use celebrities to endorse the products. What factors are behind the credibility of the source? Three very commonly identified factors are expertise, trustworthiness and likeability. *Expertise* means specialised knowledge which the communicator possesses to endorse the product. The type of expert used depends upon the nature of the product. *Trustworthiness* is related to how objective and honest the source is thought to be. Friends are better trusted than strangers. *Likeability* describes the source's attractiveness to the audience. Beauty, candour, humour, grace, spontaneity make a source more likeable. The most credible source scores high on all these three dimensions.

The following points are to be kept in mind while communicating with an audience:

1. Instead of building a wall around the product, the message should create a bridge to the target audience by being presuasive.
2. Arouse the audience, and give it a reason for listening to you.
3. Make use of questions to involve the audience.
4. Use familiar words and build up points of interest.
5. Use specific and concrete words.
6. Repeat key points.
7. Convince the audience by sticking to facts.
8. Empathise with your audience.
9. Use rhyme and rhythm, for instance when Waterbury's compound is advertised they say 'when vitality is low, Waterbury's brings back the glow.'
10. Make use of Zeigarnnik effect, *i.e.*, leave the message incomplete, where the audience is provoked to complete and close it by pondering over it
11. Ask the audience to draw conclusions.
12. Let them know the implications of these conclusions.

ADVERTISING THEME

The advertisement is built around a core idea; for instance Liril soap advertisement is built around the freshness concept. This central or core idea runs through the whole copy. The same idea is sustained in the entire campaign consisting of a series of advertisements. The core idea is thus the theme of the advertisement. The theme is a specific appeal and is an important unit of content analysis. Several attempts have been made to classify the advertising themes for different product groups. The late Narendra Mohan of IIM-A studied the themes of Indian ad copies and identified the following themes:

Utilitarian Theme: Here, the major emphasis was on the usefulness of the product. Rin and whiteness is a utilitarian theme.

Focussed Theme: This theme is directed to a specific segment of the market. Johnson directs all the messages of its baby products to mothers who love and care for their babies.

Infomative Theme: The theme basically informs about the product. All of you must have seen the informative themes of ad copies of no-frost fridges and micro-wave ovens these days.

Non-specific Theme: This theme is vague and diffused. An advertisement of Rayon states:

Practical people wear it, busy people ride on it, industries depend on it and smart people back on it.

Achievement-orientation Theme: Here the advertiser announces the achievements to its credit like export earnings, export awards, awards for excellence, awards for productivity, any form of acclaims. The ad copy goes beyond the product features. Philips recently announced that it is the company that gave the world the picture tube.

Descriptive and Projective Theme: It is an amalgam or combination of information and achievement themes. The message is built around the advertiser product/service and projects an image/achievement of the advertiser. Telco is thus a movement.

New Product, Service, Scheme or Idea: The new product launches exploit these themes, e.g., launch of an anti-ulcer product like Ranitedene or credit cards.

Each advertisement is thus built around a primary theme but may also have a secondary or perhaps even a tertiary theme.

The advertising themes are based on our knowledge of the market. The target audience, the product features and the types of appeals which motivate the target audience.

❖ Factors Affecting the Promotional Mix

It is for the management to decide an effective promotional mix for the organisation. The following factors affect the promotional mix of any company.

1. The Promotional Budget: Irrespective of the most desirable promotional mix, the availability of the funds for promotion affect the total mix considerably. A smaller firm with less funds cannot afford heavy advertising. They would rather give more importance to personal selling and sales promotion at the level of the dealer. Paucity of funds may force us to use far less efficient method of promotion. For instance, per capita cost of advertising is far less than that of personal selling. Still, a firm with lesser funds cannot resort to advertising.

2. Nature of the Market : In a wider national market, we shall have to resort to mass communication method like advertising. Personal selling is sufficient for a firm with a small local market. Out target audience also determines our promotional method. For instance *e.g.* a pharmaceutical company is prevented from advertising its product through mass media and the doctors prescribe their products to the patients. Therefore, they adopt ethical promotion where the medical representatives personally promote the products before the doctors. The number of buyers also affect the promotional mix. The fewer the buyers, the more is the likelihood of personal selling being an important promotional tool. Besides, a heterogeneous market calls for advertising, as reaching out by personal selling will be prohibitively costly. Even a firm with a national market can have personal selling as promotional method if buyers are concentrated in a few pockets. But if they are widely scattered, it will adopt advertising.

3. Nature of the Product: An industrial product which is complex and technical must be promoted mainly by personal selling, backed up by trade journal advertising. A fast moving consumer product, on the other hand, is promoted by advertising.

4. Product Life-Cycle: Demand is to be stimulated while introducing the product. It calls for heavy promotion. In the growth stage, advertising is emphasised to stimulate brand-specific demand. In the maturity stage, advertising is used as tool of persuasion. In the declining stage, promotional expenses are curtailed.

* * *

24 ADVERTISING DECISIONS

One of the important tasks for the marketing manager is to design a communication package for the product. The following diagram outlines a typical communication package:

Corporate Plan
↓
Marketing Plan
↓
Communication Plan
↓
Communication Objectives
↓
Communication Strategies

Advertising | Public Relations (PR) | Sales Promotion (SP) | Direct Marketing (DM)

Advertising
↓
Advertising Objectives
↓
Advertising Strategy
↓
Advertising Tactics

Fig. 24.1 Communication Package

The above diagram shows the various elements of the communication package — advertising, PR or public relations, SP or sales promotion and direct marketing. It is expected that these elements have harmonized functioning to convey the features and benefits of the product. These functions are handled by different functionaries — advertising is handled by advertising manager and advertising agency, PR by PR manager and PR consultants SP by sales-promotion manager or product manager and the advertising agency and direct marketing could be outsourced. The modern approach is to have integrated marketing communications or IMC. Integrated communications are synergistic and could be planned by the marketing manager. In integrated communication, there is consistency in communication e.g. POP display character and TV commercial display character are the same.

In the integrated mix, the product manager is primarily responsible for sales promotion, advertising and direct marketing.

We shall first consider advertising in this chapter.

Advertising is the most visible of all the marketing activities. In 2012, Indian advertisers have spent ₹ 20,000 crores on advertising. Advertising receives far more attention and sometimes it is at the cost of other elements of the marketing mix. viz. product, price and distribution. Advertising cannot be considered in isolation. It is an integral part of the product strategy. The following table illustrates the role of the product manager in advertising planning:

Stage of Planning	*Contributors*	*Contributors*
Market Plan	Product Manager contributes to the overall marketing plan	It leads to marketing budget, product budget and profit estimates.
Advertising Plan	Product Manager in consultation with the advertising managers briefs the agency	Target audience is identified. Budget is allocated. Advertising strategy and message strategy.
Copy or Message Design and Development	Ad agency, research group, product manager and advertising manager	Finished copy is generated and media planning is done
Execution	Ad agency and media buying organisation	Ads are placed
Feedback	Research group product manager	Ad agency -

The above table highlights the contributions of the product manager in the advertising process. A product manager contributes to the marketing plan which sets the marketing mix. The product manager contributes to advertising budget, advertising planning (identifying the target audience, designing advertising strategy and message design and development. He also contributes to copy development and media planning. However, it is to be noted he does not develop copy himself. Neither does he buy the specific media space or time. Here, we shall consider the important areas of advertising with which a product manager is concerned.

❖ Target Audience

Here the idea is to identify those who buy our product. These buyers will be the target for our communication. The primary target audience influences the decision making process. Advertising target audience could be broader than marketing target audience. Chocolates can be meant for kids, but advertising target audience could be kids and parents together. Computers can be for office staff, but advertising target audience could be the managers. It is expensive to target all relevant groups. It is sensible to have some primary focus target audiences can be described in categories — heavy users, moderate users and light users. They could also be described in terms of current product usage — users of product *A*, users of our product. Such categorization, however, is not useful in media selection.

❖ Advertising objectives

This is an area in which the product manager plays a vital role. He can set customer-oriented objectives, exposure-oriented objectives and other specific objectives.

Customer-oriented Objectives: Advertising has to sell, and therefore sales leading to profits are the most obvious objectives. Ad agencies create ads at great cost to generate demand for the products. Sales objectives are however problematic. Advertising, first of all, is not the variable that contributes to sales. There are multiple variables. Besides, ads show effects after a period of time.

Advertising has to aim at creating interest and awareness. It has to induce positive attitudes leading to an intention to buy. Products could be low-involvement products and marketing efforts including advertising lead to direct purchase. Products could be high involvement products and here product evaluation is a laborious process. There could be either direction action (purchase) or no action. It all depends on product evaluation.

Foot, Cone and Belding (FCB) model examines how advertising works differently for different products.

	Think	Feel
High involvement	LIC Policy ● Shares ●	Perfume ● Cosmetics ●
Low Involvement	Lollypop ●	Odopic ●

Fig. 24.2 FCB Grid

The FCB grid classifies the products into *thinking* and *feeling* products and uses a 2×2 matrix to help direct the communication package. There are low involvement and high involvement products. Low involvement products do not engage customers cognitively or emotionally. High involvement products occupy customers both cognitively and emotionally.

It is also important while selecting ad objectives to understand the target audience – current customers, competitor's customers or non-customers. These different targets influence the objectives chosen.

Exposure-oriented or Media-Planning Objectives: These media-related objectives are expressed in terms of reach, frequency or GRPs. Reach denotes the number of persons receiving at least one exposure. Frequency denotes the average number customer. GRPs or reach multiplied by frequency are the total number of advertising exposures received. Ad these objectives are defined in terms of a target audience.

Reach and frequency are arrived at by assessing the number of exposures needed to make the advertising effective. The overall constraint operating on these objectives is the advertising budget.

Specific Objectives: Ads can aim at increasing the awareness level from *X* per cent to *Y* per cent. They can improve favourable attitude towards a brand by one point on 1-7 scale. They can improve the usage from *X* units to *Y* units per year. They can generate *X* number of enquiries or *X* number of footfalls for a retailer. In terms of exposures, ads can aim at reaching *X* per cent of target audience at least once in a quarter of a year and 7 per cent at least four times.

❖ Advertising Budget

Advertising is big business worth ₹ 16,000 crore per annum. As advertising period is substantial especially in FMCG companies, it is important for a product manager to plan its budget manager to plan its budget. Advertising is not to be treated as an expenditure, but an investment, as it stimulates demand and generates sales.

Money makes the mare go. It drives both the marketing and advertising plan. Advertising must justify the expenditure it makes. Advertising in an investment in future sales. It has a long-range cumulative effect. It builds consumer preference and creates goodwill. Consumers' loyalty is earned. Advertising has a relationship to sales and profits. The higher the advertising budget in consumer goods industry, the higher is the market share. Additional advertising leads to an increase in sales and the effect builds over a period of time, and so consistent efforts are needed. Below a minimum level, ad expenditure will not affect sales. Some minimum sales always result even if there is no advertising. Sales reach saturation in the context of a given market. Beyond that, ad expenses will not lead to an increase in sales.

As sales are affected by a variety of factors including advertising, it is difficult to determine allocation of funds. Before making allocations, the business environment is considered in its totality. A number· of methods are used to determine how much to spend on advertising.

Affordability Method: Here we spend as much as we can afford on advertising. Mostly once all other expenses of the business are made, what is left over is spent on advertising. It is, therefore, also called *residual method*. Though simple to use, it is not suitable in lean periods when sales are low. Actually, these periods do need more advertising activity.

Percentage-of-Sales Method: It is a ratio. It is the percentage of previous year's sales or estimated sales for the next year or a combination of the two. It is a simple method. It is related to revenue. Generally, an industry norm is used as percentage figure. The problem is that we may spend too much or too little. It does not consider the environment or the effectiveness of our advertising effort.

Competitive Method: Here the expenditure on ads is matched to that of the competitor. If the competitor spends one per cent of its expected sales on ads, we also do the same. The assumption is that the competitors always judge the spending correctly. Besides, our spending is not related to our objectives. *Market share* and *share or voice* can be related. Share of voice is the total advertising expenditure. To improve market share, the share of voice must exceed the current market share. The expectation is that it will lead to increased sales. J.O. Packham of A.C. Neilson has developed a formula which states that for a new product to reach a desired market share must have the share of voice 1.5 times greater than it.

Objective and Task Method: It is a logical method. We determine the ad objectives. Each task is at a cost. We budget that cost. The only problem is that it is very difficult to define advertising objectives. It is also difficult to estimate the amount of money needed to accomplish a task. The techniques of measuring advertising effectiveness are still far from perfect.

Additional Methods: Advertisers use experimental method to determine the budget. It is called *empirical research method*. There are computer-models for allocating advertising funds. Some methods adjust the budget to media cost. Some methods advise to use the same amount of money as was spent last year.

The budgeting process requires judgement and experience. As the first step, we consider our marketing and advertising plan. We then consider the budgeting figure against our advertising objectives. While doing so, we have to keep in mind allocation to be made to other tools of communication.

❖ Evaluation of Advertising

It is to be noted that copy development is done by the creative department of an advertising agency and the product manager's role is next to nil in this. However, the product manager has to evaluate the ad campaign before committing large resources to it.

❖ Why to Test

Large sums of money are poured into advertising and the sales results are dependent on the success of advertising campaign. It is, therefore, necessary to test the effectiveness of advertising. Though sales are affected by advertising, advertising alone is not responsible for either an increase or decrease in sales. There are other factors which affect the sales-product quality, price, sales promotion, distribution corporate reputation etc. But it is equally true that advertising is a potent tool for increasing sales and large sums are spent on it.

❖ What to Test

Advertising testing may be done either before the ad has run in the media or after it. When it is tested before, it is called pre-testing. When it is tested afterwards, it is called post-testing.

There are two objectives of testing — to avoid costly mistakes and to predict the relative strength of alternative advertising strategies and to increase their efficiency.

An ad copy consists of several elements such as headline, illustration, body copy, logo and base-line. These together communicate a message. The effectiveness of an ad thus is the cumulative effect of all these elements. Though each element can be tested individually, it is also necessary to test them together. What to test in ad copy? First whether it, secures attention? Whether its communication is proper and effective? Whether it affects attitudes?

Copy testing may .make us conclude whether a particular copy is stronger than another one, but this isolated testing is of little significance. The best ad in copy test may not be the best ad in the medium. This can be tested later when the ad has run for sometime.

❖ Purpose of Pre-testing

Here we attempt to evaluate what performance can be expected from an ad copy (when it finally runs). It gives us an idea about the potential of an ad.

The evaluation seeks to evaluate the following:

(*i*) To spot the errors in the copy.

(*ii*) To make the communication more effective.

(*iii*) To design the ad better.

(*iv*) To reduce wastage in advertising.

(*v*) To ensure that money is spent prudently.

Pre-testing, as Lary Grant puts it, does not create strong advertisements, but it certainly helps to eliminate weak ones. Pre-testing cannot guarantee absolute success. By the time the ad runs, market conditions may change. Maybe there is another similar ad or another similar product.

It is better to know· something about our ads rather than nothing at all.

❖ Purpose of Post-testing

Post-testing, as the name itself suggests, is done after the runs for some time or for its full term. It will be a reflection on pre-testing done.

Post-tests seek to:

(*i*) find out the impact of an ad in terms of its being noticed, seen and read.
(*ii*) find out its credibility.
(*iii*) find out its comprehension.
(*iv*) measure its memorability.
(*v*) assess its effect on buyers.
(*vi*) assess its fit with the promotion and marketing mix.
(*vii*) assess whether it has achieved its objectives.
(*viii*) assess the relative effectiveness of different copies and media plans.
(*ix*) improve future advertising efforts.

❖ Methods of Testing

As we are now aware, ads can be tested before they are run in the media (pre-testing) or after they have been run (post-testing). Both pre-testing and post-testing have a number of methods:

METHODS OF TESTING

Pre-testing Methods	**Post-testing Methods**
Pre-testing of Print Ads	
(*i*) Check-list method	(*i*) Recall tests
(*ii*) Consumer Jury test	(*ii*) Recognition tests
(*iii*) Portfolio test	(*iii*) Triple association tests
(*iv*) Lock Magazine test	(*iv*) Sales tests
(*v*) Perceptual meaning studies	(*v*) Inquiry tests
(*vi*) Projective methods	(*vi*) Attitude tests
Pre-testing of Broadcast Ads	
(*i*) In-home projection tests	
(*ii*) Trailer tests	
(*iii*) Theatre tests	
(*iv*) Live telecast tests	

❖ Pre-testing methods

Pre-tests are conducted before the ads are actually run in the media. The elements of ad copies or the whole ad can be tested. The test can be conducted in a laboratory or studio or in natural environment. Pre-testing can test the relative performance of alternative ad copies.

The following methods are used to pre-test the print ads.

1. Check List Method.
2. Consumer Jury Test

(i) Order-of-merit test.

(ii) Paired comparison.

3. Portfolio Test.
4. Mock Magazine Test.
5. Perceptual Meaning Studies (PMS).

Check List Method: These checklists are used to test the various elements of the ad copy or the copy as a whole.

There are some check lists which test readability or audibility.

Checklists ensure that no important feature is omitted and there is (balance of all the elements.) It is a simple and speedy process.

Example of Check List

1. Is the copy based on briefing?
2. How is the start? Is it interesting?
3. Is it direct uses 'you' and is in present tense?
4. Is it vague or specific? Is it in the idiom of the users?
5. Is the style natural and spontaneous?
6. Are the words picture-words? Are the verbs power-packed?
7. Is there dramatisation of points in relation of their importance?
8. Is it adequate and complete?
9. Is the story line smoothly flowing?
10. Are their pauses and breaks for reading?
11. Does it over-state? (it should not).
12. Will it sell for competitors too? Or for you alone?
13. Is it meant to sell?
14. Does it end interestingly?
15. Is summarisation bold?

Check lists are suitable for body text but not for other elements. The copies can be given a score of all the points, But there can be a bias. So different copies should be rated by different persons.

Consumer Jury Test: Here a group of consumers act as jury to show their preferences for one or two ads out of several being considered, The jury members have to rank the ads. The jury members respond to questions like:

(*a*) Which of these ads interest you most?

(*b*) Which of these ads provoke you to buy the product?

(*c*) Which of these ads received your attention first?

(*d*) Which of these ads are easily readable and understandable?

(*e*) Which of these ads are credible?

Consumer Jury Test is conducted by two methods:

(*a*) Order-of-Merit Rating

(*b*) Paired Comparison.

Order-of-Merit Rating: Here, the advertisements are ranked by a small group of respondents who are potential prospects or the jurors. They are shown some 5-6 ad copies and are asked to rank them. If more than 5-6 ad copies are shown, the accuracy decreases. When all the ads are ranked, score sheets are made and the best ad is found out. But the best may be the best amongst the group of chosen ads which may be the worst ones. Each rank is given points, suppose we are testing six ads and they can be assigned six ranks. The points for the ranks are given below:

Rank	*Points*
1	10
2	8
3	5
4	3
5	2
6	1

The score sheet is given below:

Jurors	*Ad 1*	*Ad 2*	*Ad 3*	*Ad 4*	*Ad 5*	*Ad 6*
11	R 3(5)	R 3 (5)	R 2 (8)	R 1 (10)	R 3 (5)	R 4 (3)
12	R 2 (8)	R 3 (5)	R 2 (8)	R 1 (10)	R 2 (8)	R 4 (3)
13	R 2 (8)	R 2 (8)	R 3 (5)	R 1 (10)	R 4 (3)	R 3 (5)
14	R 3 (5)	R 1 (10)	R 2 (8)	R 2 (8)	R5 (2)	R 3 (5)
15	R 6 (1)	R 2 (8)	R 6 (l)	R 1 (10)	R 5 (2)	R 2 (8)
...						
...						
J10	R 3 (5)	R 1 (10)	R 1 (10)	R 2 (8)	R 2 (2)	R 1 (10)
Total Points	(32)	(46)	(40)	(56)	(22)	(34)

It is obvious from the above that Ad 4 scores the maximum number of points and as such is considered to be the best amongst the six ads.

Paired Comparison: Order-of-merit ranks the ads but these ranks may change if two ads are compared at a time. It is a one-to-one comparison amongst the ads being tested. We consider a pair at a time. The procedure is continued till all ads are paired with one another. Scores are recorded and summed up. The winner gets the highest score. The other ads are rated as per their summed scores. We can compare upto 10 ads in this fashion, but later on, the accuracy decreases. The number of comparisons can be found out by using the following formula:

$$N = \frac{n(n-1)}{2}$$

where n is the number of ads to be tested. Suppose five ads are being tested ...

$$= \frac{n(n-1)}{2}$$

$$= \frac{5(5-1)}{2}$$

$$= \frac{5(4)}{2}$$

$$= \frac{20}{2}$$

The score sheet of the five ads is given below:

Jurors	*Comparisons*			*Value*
J1	(Ad 1) (Ad 2) (Ad 1) (Ad 5) (Ad 2) (Ad 5) (Ad 4) (Ad 5)	(Ad 1) (Ad 3) (Ad 2) (Ad 3) (Ad 3) (Ad 4)	(Ad 1) (Ad 4) (Ad 2) (Ad 4) (Ad 3) (Ad 5)	Ad1 = 1 Ad2 = 2 Ad3 = 1 Ad4 = 4 Ad5 = 2
J2	(Ad 1) (Ad 2) (Ad 1) (Ad 5) (Ad 2) (Ad 5) (Ad 4) (Ad 5)	(Ad 1) (Ad 3) (Ad 2) (Ad 3) (Ad 3) (Ad 4)	(Ad 1) (Ad 4) (Ad 2) (Ad 4) (Ad 3) (Ad 5)	Ad1 = Ad2 = Ad3 = Ad4 = Ad5 =
J10	(Ad 1) (Ad 2) (Ad 1) (Ad 5) (Ad 2) (Ad 5) (Ad 4) (Ad 5)	(Ad 1) (Ad 3) (Ad 2) (Ad 3) (Ad 3) (Ad 4)	(Ad 1) (Ad 4) (Ad 2) (Ad 4) (Ad 3) (Ad 5)	Ad1 = Ad2 = Ad3 = Ad4 = Ad5 =

Advantages of Consumer Jury Test

Consumer Jury Test has the following advantages:

1. It is not time consuming.
2. It is cost effective.
3. It can be conducted without running the ads.
4. Rough ads can be compared.
5. Jurors can be encouraged to give unbiased responses.
6. It can be conducted on a small sample.
7. There are no extraneous influences to distort the ad.

Disadvantages of Consumer Jury Test

It suffers from the following disadvantages:

1. The ads are not tested under real life conditions.
2. There can be an element of bias.
3. The sample may not be representative.
4. It is based on opinions.
5. Different members of the jury do not show consistency in responses.

Portfolio Test: Here some dummy ads are mixed with regular ads. A number of dummy ads are put in a folio along with the ad copy to be tested. The consumer-sample sees the folio. The consumer is then asked about what he has seen in each ads. The ad giving minimum playback is considered the best. It is verified whether the adjudged ad is dummy or regular. In case it is dummy, the actual ad is improved on the same lines.

Another version of this test divides the sample into two groups — experimental and control groups. Experimental group sees portfolio containing dummy as well regular ads. The control group evaluates only the portfolio without test ads. Recall test is later conducted to assess reaction to test ads.

Mock Magazine Test: It is an alternative version of the portfolio test. It does not use a portfolio, but uses a real magazine. It introduces best ads in a magazine to an experimental group to read. The control group is also exposed to the same magazine, but is without test ads. Later a recall test is conducted to assess the effectiveness of test ads.

Perceptual Meaning Studies (PMS): This method uses time-exposure to test the ads. Tachistoscope is an instrument that may be used in this test. The respondent see the ad for a pre-determined time and then are subjected to a recall test-product, brand illustration and the main copy.

PRE-TESTING BROADCASTING ADS

The methods discussed above can be applied to broadcast media also. In addition, some special methods are available to pre-test broadcast media ads — TV and radio ads. The techniques used are:

1. In-home projection tests.
2. Trailer tests.
3. Theatre tests.
4. Live Telecast tests.

In-Home Projection Tests: A movie projector screen at consumer's home tests commercials. He is questioned before and after exposure. The questions are related to ad and the change it causes after exposure. We can assess the strong and weak points of the ads.

Trailer Tests: A real life shopping environment — a departmental store, a shopping centre, a parking place, front and back of shopping complexes is used to measure consumer behaviour. The prospects are invited to the display. The invitation does give some incentive like discount coupons for purchasing displayed brands. Another group is invited, given the coupons, but .is not shown the test ads. The redemption rate of coupons may give an idea about the effectiveness of test ads.

Theatre Test: A captive audience collected for entertainment is administered a questionnaire. The free tickets are later sent to them for the programme where the test ads are run. On viewing these, they are asked to fill up another questionnaire. It assesses product, brand and ad theme.

Live Telecast Tests: Here the inaccuracies of artificial testing environment are not encountered. Here ads are put on air either by narrow casting or live telecasting. These ads are test ads and not the regular ads. Later, viewers are interviewed to know their reactions.

❖ Projective Pre-testing Methods

These are several other pre-testing methods:

Projective Techniques: It is a type of motivation research where a respondent has to project himself into the scene and reveal his feelings or thinking about the ad. In projective technique a *depth interview* can be taken to assess the underlying feelings and motivations. The thoughts are expressed freely, and the interview is not structured. In *word association test*, a respondent has to provide the first word, or image or thought that comes to his mind on seeing an ad. In *sentence competition test*, a respondent is supposed to complete and incomplete sentence about a product. In construction test, story is woven around a scene or picture. The concealed feelings of the respondent in the story provide valuable insight.

POST-TESTING METHODS

Post-testing gives us an idea about the actual performance of the ad in terms of exposure, perception, communication and sales effect. We can assess the credibility and comprehension of the ads.

Recall Tests: In recall tests, the respondent is asked to answer, entirely on the basis of his memory, whether an individual ad has been read or not. Recall tests can be unaided where respondents are not given any help to recall the ad. In aided recall methods, respondents are given certain clues for' recalling the ad.

Recognition Tests: In recognition tests, first individuals have to qualify as readers of a particular issue. This method is relevant for print media, and is not suitable for broadcast media.

Recognition tests are also called *readership tests*. They were first developed by Daniel Starch. It assumes that noticing an ad and buying a product are closely related. But this assumption may not always be true.

Triple Association Tests: Here a respondent is given clues or ideas which he can associate with a brand name. 'Which toothpaste is combination of whiteness and mouthwash?' If the answer is Close Up, the response is correct with respect to the brand name and its advertisement theme. If the respondent associate the product with a company the triple association is complete.

Sales Effect Tests: They measure the various stages of buyer awareness, preference, buying intention and actual purchase in relation to advertising effort. They are also called progress tests.

Sales Results Tests: The additional sales generated by the ads are recorded. It is difficult however to correlate an increase in sales to advertising alone.

Enquiries Tests: These are couponed advertisements of consumer durables. They invite consumers to send back the coupon to seek a demo or more details. The member of enquiries reveal the effectiveness of an advertisement.

Attitude Tests: As we have seen, attitudes show our predisposition towards objects, ideas, people and places. They indicate overall feelings. The change in attitude as a result of advertising is assessed. The assumption is that favourable attitude towards the product may lead to purchases. Most ads are designed either to reinforce or change the existing attitudes. The attitudes are measured by rating scales.

Rating scales can be single-item scales or multiple-item scales.

❖ Single-Item Scales

We can express our satisfaction (single-item) about an airline in terms of:

Very Satisfied +2	Quite Satisfied +1	Can't Say 0	Somewhat Dissatisfied −1	Very Dissatisfied −2

Similarly, our liking can be expressed as:

Like Too Much	Like Fairly	Like Somewhat	Neither Like nor Dislike	Dislike Too Much	Dislike Somewhat	Dislike Fairly

❖ Multiple Item Scales

In multiple item tests, various beliefs about a product are examined by three scales — Thurstone Scale. Likert Scale and Semantic Differential Scale.

In Thurstone Scale, statements, say about family planning are examined in terms of their favourableness or unfavourableness. This scale is mostly used to study attitudes towards social and cultural phenomenon. It is not much used in marketing.

Likert Scale asks the respondents to indicate their agreement or disagreement with a variety of statements related to an object. We can have the five gradations as follows:

Strongly Agree +2	Agree +1	Neutral 0	Disagree −1	Strongly Disagree −2

Semantic Differential Scale plays on the differences in the meanings of words. Bipolar semantic scale indicates two opposite conditions such as sweet-sour, good-bad etc. In unipolar semantic scale, the same adjective is used at either end — sweet-not sweet, good-not good, etc. Thus a health beverage is good product or is not a good product.

❖ DAGMAR Approach

It is felt that the task of measuring ad effectiveness will not be daunting if we clearly spell out the advertising goals. Russel H. Colley (1961) pioneered an approach known by the acronym DAGMAR-Defining Advertising Goals for Measured Advertising Results, where to establish an explicit link between Ad goals and Ad results. Colley distinguished 52 advertising goals that might be used with respect to a single advertisement, a year's campaign for a product or a company's entire advertising philosophy.

These goals may pertain to sales, images, attitude and awareness. Some of the goals are:

- persuade a prospect to visit a showroom and ask for a demonstration.
- build up the morale of the company's sales force.
- facilitate sales by correcting false impression, misinformation and other obstacles.
- announce a special reason for buying now (price, discount, premium and so on.)
- make the brand identity known and easily recognisable.
- provide information or implant attitude regarding benefits and superior features of brand.

According to DAGMAR approach, the communication task of the brand is to gain (*a*) awareness, (*b*) comprehension, (*c*) conviction, (*d*) image and (*e*) action.

Advertising goals should be consistent with these communication tasks. Later performance on these counts and projected goals is compared. For example, a company setting a goal of 15 per cent increase in sales advertises and achieves this objective. Its ad then is successful and effective.

DAGMAR presupposes the understanding of the dynamics of consumer behaviour as without this goals cannot be set. Besides, a thorough acquaintance of market environment is called for. DAGMAR is a planning and control tool. It may guide the creation of advertising. However, as will be appreciated the basic inputs of DAGMAR are not so easily to formulate and may also inhibit creativity.

* * *

25 ADVERTISING CAMPAIGNING AND CREATIVITY IN ADVERTISING

Advertising is too important an activity to be left unplanned. The advertising task is to be spelled out and its contribution to overall marketing effort is to be pre-decided. The advertising programme is planned to fulfil certain objectives which are related to overall marketing objectives. Advertising plan is thus a part of marketing strategy and is co-ordinated with the other elements of marketing mix — personal selling, sales promotion, pricing, distribution and product.

It is better to spell out advertising objectives and define the target audience before undertaking any programme of advertising. In fact, the first question considered is whether to advertise or not. We should advertise only if there is advertising opportunity which depends upon the nature of the market, different products and different brands.

The total promotion mix consists of advertising, personal selling, sales promotion, publicity and public relations. The firm must decide the exact role of advertising in the promotional mix. For instance, in case of industrial products, the role of advertising is not so dominant. In case of ethical pharmaceutical products, it is non-existent.

Advertising plan is based upon research which provides inputs to strategic decisions pertaining to copywriting, scheduling and budgeting. After the campaign is run, research provides data to judge its effectiveness. Research thus provides the feedback mechanism.

Advertising plans are geared to segmentation, targeting and positioning strategies.

❖ What is an Advertising Campaign?

An advertising campaign is an organised series of advertising messages with identical or similar message over a particular period of time. It is an orderly planned effort consisting of related but self-contained and independent advertisements. Though the campaign is conveyed through different media, it has a single theme and a unified approach.

The independent ads used in a campaign are similar to one another and this is deliberate. There is a psychological continuity due to a unified theme. The physical continuity is provided by similarity of visuals and orals.

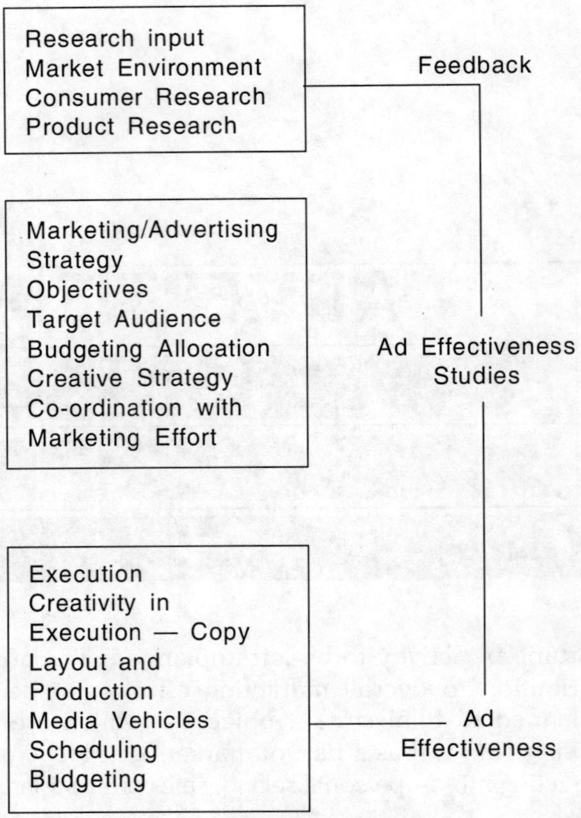

Fig. 25.1 Planning Advertisement Effort or Campaign Planning

In a broad sense, a campaign is a co-ordinative effort of promotion of a particular product/service during a particular period of time to attain predecided objectives.

Advertising effort does not remain erratic or spasmodic or opportunistic when we plan a campaign. It is a concrete advertising plan consisting of several advertisements and has a time-frame of a few weeks, or months or years. All promotional efforts is tied to a campaign and does not come into conflict with it. The campaign tries to accomplish certain objectives or tries to destroy certain objectives.

❖ Why to Advertise in Terms of a Campaign?

Buyers are forgetful of erratically appearing ads. Often due to a clutter of large number of advertising messages, they overlook several of them. It is therefore better to approach them in the form of a campaign which is sustained advertising effort.

Part of our advertising effort goes waste at any given point of time, since some buyers are not real prospects at a point of time the advertisement appears. New prospects emerge over a period of time. Campaigns force us to look an advertising effort retrospectively so as to improve it.

Co-ordination, balance, timing, continuity and performance — all favour for an advertising campaign.

❖ How long should be a Campaign?

Campaigns are of varied length — say a seasonal campaign of cough syrup or Vicks VapoRub or woollen garments or it may last the whole year. The logic behind yearly campaigns is that they co-incide with accounting year, at the end of which sales and profits are computed. There are several advertisers who keep a campaign running without any change for two or even for three years. All of you are familiar with the Lux soap campaign where it is promoted as a beauty soap of cinema stars, adhere the present queen bee of Hindi films endorses it. The factors which affect the duration of campaign are the type of product offered, the nature of advertiser's marketing programme, seasonality of sales, media policies and the competitior's advertising.

❖ Basis of Campaign

The geographical spread of a campaign can be the basis. The campaign can be limited to a local market or one entire region. It can be a national campaign too. National campaign is ruled out for test marketing and for small budget companies.

Pioneering campaigns introduce new products. Competitive campaigns emphasis competitive superiority to retain the present market and to expand it either by increasing the products consumption or by weaning the customers away from a competitive brand.

Campaigns can be classified in terms of media, *e.g.*, direct-mail campaign, newspaper campaign, TV campaign etc.

Campaign's purpose can be the basis of classification, *e.g.*, direct action campaign where a customer is expected to buy a product or indirect-action campaign. Some campaigns promote products, while some build up a corporate image.

❖ Campaign Planning

Campaigns, a term borrowed from military science, is an organised and carefully planned use of paid publicity for fulfilling a definite purpose.

Campaign planning is broader than mere creation of individual advertisements. The basis of any campaign is the consumer behaviour and the market profile. The demographic and psychographic study of consumer constituting a market is a must to create advertisements for the right target audience with the right type of appeals.

❖ Campaigns are governed by the following parameters:

(*i*) The total advertising budget.

(*ii*) The media availability.

(*iii*) The consumer profile.

(*iv*) The product profile.

(*v*) The campaign's duration and its timing.

(*vi*) The advertising and marketing objectives.

(*vii*) The distribution channels.

(*viii*) The marketing environment including pressure groups and competitors.

(*ix*) A review of previous advertising/promotional effort.

(*x*) The creative considerations.

(*xi*) The new plans.

Some factors like the demographic study of the consumers, the media availability and the competitors' activities are uncontrollable factors. They are called the limiting parameters or the constraints.

It is extremely important to plan the advertising of a product, a service or institution, since the costs of advertising are so high. A full-page advertisement in *The Times of India* or *The Indian Express* cost over a lakh of rupees; a 10-second ad before a soap opera on television costs over one lakh rupees. This is, of course, besides the costs of production. Careful planning at every stage of the process (campaign planning, media planning) are essential if the advertiser's budget is to be spent purposefully.

Advertising planning involves making certain what the specific objectives are, what is the nature of the message to be conveyed (the Unique Selling Proposition, for example), and the budget to cover production and media cost. It also involves pre-testing to find out how a sample of the target audience 'reads' the advertisement. Sometimes, an ad can turn people off by its language or illustration; certain negative images of rival products or brands can turn the target audience hostile to the product.

Media planning is the selection of appropriate media or a combination of media for 'placement' of advertisements. Thus ads targeted at women are placed in women's pages of weekend newspapers, though it needs to be remembered that women read other magazines too. For women executives, there is the Executive Women's Digest and for upper class men, monthly magazines like Debonair and Gentlemen. Curiously, products and diets for slimming appear in magazines like Health and Nutrition.

The following points need to be kept in mind while planning an advertising campaign:

1. Identify the Problem: Why have sales fallen? What do you expect from the campaign? Just higher sales or a better 'image' for the brand or the company or the need to educate the consumer? Answers to these questions would help determine the Unique Selling Proposition (USP) and to 'position' the product.

2. The Budget: How much is a client prepared to spend on the campaign? Are his funds limited?

3. Pre-testing: Consumer and product research to find out the habits of consumers, their needs, values, living standards; their present reactions to the product and how it is advertised. What feedback is available from the public or the target audience?

4. Target Audience: Children? Teenagers? Upper-class housewives? Working Women? Middle class households? The Aged and Retired? Yuppies?

5. Media Selection: Which is the most effective medium or combination of media for talking about the product or service? Among the effective media, which particular vehicle (or combination of vehicles) would reach the target audience? Determine the 'media schedule' depending on the advertising rates for each medium.

6. The Language: Hindi and the regional languages are more widely understood than English; why do advertisers still insist on using English? Do not merely translate ads conceived in English in the Indian languages. Would a bilingual ad tell the story more interestingly?

7. The Visual and the Copy: Would they be 'read' as you intend them to be by target audiences? Or, are they too highbrow? How relevant is the use of Western images? The golden rule among ad folk is: KISS (Keep it simple, stupid).

8. Timing and Duration: Choose appropriate seasons for launching new products. (Remember the launch of Go-Kool ice-cream during a cold-wave in the north?). Use 'reminder' ads during other seasons.

9. Post-Testing: This is necessary to gauge consumer reaction to the ad campaign.

10. Effects on Sales: This is the acid test of the success of any ad campaign. The ad might have been 'creative', won many awards, but did it lead to purchase? Look at other marketing factors too.

❖ Why to Plan Campaigns?

Campaigns are to be planned with the following objectives in mind:

(*i*) To determine the market and its potential.

(*ii*) To obtain the consumer profile.

(*iii*) To study the consumer psychology.

(*iv*) To know the frequency or size of buying.

(*v*) To decide about the channels and their statisfactory operation.

(*vi*) To bring about product modifications.

(*vii*) To determine the geographical scope of the campaign.

(*viii*) To do the media planning.

(*ix*) To develop a central idea or core idea around which the selling points revolve. The idea has to be discovered. The strength of this idea forms the basis of effective campaign planning.

(*x*) To determine the fundamental human desire to which the advertisement will appeal.

(*xi*) To determine the type of copy.

(*xii*) To determine the scheduling and space buying.

(*xiii*) To prepare the actual ad copies with a dominant central idea which has been effectively presented and laid out. So that it appeals to the motives. The consistency is maintained.

(*xiv*) The placement of the copy in the media to run the campaign.

(*xv*) To do the budgeting for the campaign.

(*xvi*) To co-ordinate with the general administration, sales staff and other promotional activities.

❖ Basis of Campaign Planning

Information distilled over a period of time from past activities including advertising/selling at the agency forms the basis of campaign planning. The secondary data available and the primary data generated by research guide any campaign.

The three-word recipe for a good campaign as given by Sir William Crawford is *concentration, domination* and *repetition.*

We have not to disperse our efforts or budget. We have to be dominant in either our approach, say an appeal used or in a market or in a media. It is not sufficient to stop after a single impact or to jump from one advertising objective to another or from one set of media to another. The message should be continuous and should remind regularly over a period of time.

Marketing Research provides quantitative guidelines for campaign and motivational research provides qualitative guidelines for a campaign. Research feedback also makes review and retrospection possible.

❖ Three — Phases of Campaign Creation

There are three phases involved in the creation of any campaign: **I.** Strategy Development Phase, **II.** The Briefing Phase and **III.** The Creative Phase.

I. Strategy Development Phase: This phased decided the objectives and contents of communication. It analyses the research data and decides positioning of a brand. The strategy formulation is in modern day's agencies is a team effort. The creative persons form this team. There are brain-storming sessions. The ideas are thrown up by the team. These ideas ultimately make up the strategy. The brilliant in the team pick up one or two ideas from the total idea generated and develop them. Our strategy should give us a competitive edge.

We want the students to appreciate the importance of strategy development phase. If the strategy is wrong, no amount of creativity will help. If the strategy is right, despite the poor creative work, we can sell due to right strategy. However, right strategy and creative campaign is a winning combination. Mere creativity and no strategy never works. To your client, you should tell what you are trying to achieve in your communication.

The strategist is the left-brain oriented, very linear in thinking, very logical in deduction. The strategy formulation leads to an advertising brief.

II. Advertising Brief to the Creative: As a matter of fact, the client has to brief the agency about the strategy. However, most of the time this does not happen. The agency is supposed to brief itself. The strategy formulated is communicated to the creative people. They are briefed about how to create the advertising for the product needs. The strategy should be communicated with clarity. The strategist should be a good motivator for the creative team.

Proper briefing is going half-way as far as creativity is concerned. Bad brief to the creative team results into bad work. Good brief ensures good work.

Within the creative team, the copywriter the and visualiser work together and it is difficult to attribute the final product to either of them. Yes, when they are working, there are personal sparks of creativity. Please appreciate that briefing completes half the job. Creative campaigns are creative due to a good brief.

It is critically very important to question the brief. Very often, a brief is a set of cliches. We have to get the real situation. Creative brief of strategy contains a key consumer insight. If the brief acquaints you with the consumer and how his mind works, it has the seeds of creativity in it. It gives stimulus to the creative team.

Success or failure of the advertisement is largely dictated by the brief.

III. The Creative Phase: Here the lateral thinkers come on the scence. They leap from a single uni-directional idea of the strategist to an advertising idea that will add value to the product/brand. The creative persons are supposed to be right-brained — lateral thinkers; unrational thinkers. They make connections which had not existed before. They rearrange the order of the things. They create abruptions in the consumer mind. There should be a beautiful marriage between the Strategy and the Lateral thinking by the creative people.

❖ Creativity in Campaign

The basic creativity involved in a campaign is the discovery of what is variously called—

(*i*) The sales proposition.

(*ii*) The purchase proposition.

(*iii*) The copy platform.

(*iv*) The campaign theme.

❖ Liril Campaign

The creative film on Liril soap is an outstanding creation of Padamsee of Lintas. It is promoted as 'freshness soap'. A girl under a waterfall is a fantasy used here. Karen Lunell frolicked under waterfall at dawn — and it was a run away success. The USP (Unique Selling Proposition) was freshness concept.

❖ Strategy Review Board (SRB)

At Lintas, this body brain storms every issue concerning marketing and sales before launching a campaign. Padamsee is the Chairman of SRB. He generates a lot of heat in order to produce a single point of light.

ADVERTISING AND THE CREATIVE PROCESS

❖ Creativity in Communication

Communication in an ad emerges from a powerful idea — an idea that is unique and does not get lost in the crowd. Creativity remains an enigma to most people — people think 'we are born creative or we are not'. Creativity is a complex process whose outcome depends upon the forces within the individual and outside. As Pradip Khandwalla, an eminent worker in the field of creativity and now Director, IIM-A, aptly puts it: 'There is no difference in the fundamental workings of the brain of a genius like Shakespeare or Tagore and that of an ordinary man. It is just the habits of the mind are different and the habits of the mind can be changed.' Khandwalla, in other words, firmly believes that creativity can be taught, innovative thinking can be learnt. Creativity is not just giftedness or genius or lateral thinking or permissiveness or intelligence.

I.Q. is not final answer. It ignores the dimension of originality — the ability to give unique responses. I.Q. also ignores flexibility — the ability to see problems from different angles. I.Q. also ignores the dimension of ideational fluency — being able to come out large number of possible solutions. I.Q. ignores the ability to restructure the problem in an interesting way or the capacity to judge the causes/consequences of something. All these dimensions are important constituents of creativity but are left out of the I.Q. tests. I.Q. is only a part of creativity.

Creativity is thus a range of abilities. Yes of course in I.Q. there is a strong genetic factor. However, the genetic factor is much weaker for the abilities that constitute creativity, except for adaptive flexibility — the ability to shift the perspective. Even adaptive flexibility can be built into people. Business schools who have adopted case method of teaching make the engineer/technologist participants who are trained to think of only one right answer to learn to approach the problem by 50 other valid viewpoints. In other words, they are made to learn multiple perspectives. Advertising cashes in on people being able to have different viewpoints.

Creativity is both convergent and divergent thinking. Creative ad people have to overcome the constraints of deadlines and time pressure by developing relaxed atmosphere of working.

Creative people exhibit an ability to go off the beaten track a capacity to respond to reality and keep their feet on the ground.

We give a checklist for exploring the creative element in you:

1. Restate the problem in as many ways as possible.
2. Question the assumptions underlying the problem. You may invert the problem while doing so.
3. Combine the ideas in unusual ways, related with unrelated.
4. Question the problem itself.
5. Have a concern to discover problems. Being too near to them makes you sometimes blind to them.
6. For being creative, learn to relax.

Let us take one concrete example. The promotion of 7-Up as an Un-cola drink is an all-time classic creative promotion. The drink was used as a mixer with hard drinks. To carve out a niche in consumer's mind against the two cola drinks (Pepsi and Coke), they used colas as a frame of reference and announced 7-Up as the Un-cola soft-drink, thus relating the unfamiliar to the familiar. It established 7-Up in a position in consumer mind which was at once:

1. A soft drink.
2. Different from colas.
3. Enigmatic (what's an Un-cola?).

Let us take another classic example. Here there is creative improvisation by restating the product attribute. Leo Bernett noticed that Marlboro filter cigarettes were regarded womanish, and the product's red-tip to mask lipstick smears strengthened this image. It was obvious that the product needed a change of image on the masculine side. The cow — boy was therefore brought in to give it a virile masculine position. The package which was effective-looking due to stripes was replaced by a bold red. The flavour was made more aromatic. The cow — boy ad read: 'You get a lot to like in Marlboro. Filter, Flavour and Flip-Top Box!' The ads projected rugged masculinity. The product image was changed, without disturbing the key physical attribute, the filter but changing other attributes slightly. The given attribute, *i.e.*, filter was communicated differently to do so. The brand has non-functional subjective attributes/ values apart from purely physical attributes. These are the so-called 'added-values'. They are not created on the shop-floor but by the strategist/creative person in the organisation and its ad agency.

Discerning readers will appreciate that creativity and innovation in marketing and advertising are not the same as the creativity of a poet or a novelist or a painter. The marketing or advertising people are creative to the extent it suits the overall marketing objectives and facilitate selling. A novelist like Nayantara Sahgal, niece of Pt. Nehru, can afford to say about her creative effort that she does not aim it at any audience and that it finds its own audience once it is written it does not. She feels that being audience-centred is not a part of her consciousness or responsibility. It is the art for the sake of art and not art for the sake of life. In marketing and advertising, we have to relate to the consumer. As Subhas Ghosal, a doyen of Indian advertising, remarks "Good advertising is advertising that sells. Unfortunately, most of our ads are made with a view to impressing peers rather than the consumer."

Martyn Forrester in his recent book quotes ads full of lovely words, all of them colourful, but totally meaningless and hence not creative at all. Creative ads are idea-centred and not word-centred.

We also invite attention of the readers to a tendency to consider positioning as an exercise in communication like Ries and Trout. However, real positioning starts from the design stage of the product itself.

The product is designed in such a way that consumer needs are best satisfied. This is real positioning. The positioning that starts after the product comes into existence is an exercise in communication — the product is positioned in the minds of the customers regardless of what the product is. For instance, Dettol could be promoted as an after-shave lotion or an antiseptic for cuts and bruises or a food can be promoted as either a breakfast food or health food for the aged. Positioning and its communication in this approach is an afterthought. Creative efforts thrive most in those companies where right from the product development stage, an eye is kept on what the probable product positioning would be, once the end product comes into existence. Repositioning then may involve changes not only in communication strategy but also in physical features of the product and its packaging. Philip Kotler advocates this viewpoint.

The correct positioning stance is taken when it is driven home through every element of marketing mix. In service marketing advertising creates expectations in the customers regarding a desired level of the delivery of service. However, in practice, we come across a rueful clerk on the bank's counter and less-than-courteous and caring employees in the front office of a hotel chain. Perhaps, the ads promise more than the service organisation can deliver. The product restructuring should therefore, be the starting point. It is better to understate the claims and then keep on improving on them.

To wind up the discussion, we quote David Ogilvy, the Goliath of Advertising to emphasise ad that the ad that sells is of more importance to marketers than anything else. He says "when I write an advertisement, I don't want you to sell me that you find it creative. I want you to find it so interesting that you buy the product." Yet who can deny that the Rolls Royce copy by Ogilvy that reads 'at sixty miles an hour the loudest noise in the new Rolls Royce comes from the electric clock' is a best creative effort that sells too?

CREATIVITY IN ADVERTISING

There are two dimensions to advertising creativity, *(i)* Creative strategy and *(ii)* Creative Execution.

❖ Creative Strategy

Advertising planning ultimately boils down to creative strategy and its execution. The advertising message is a response by an agency to advertising goals or campaign goals. The budget acts as a constraint over the creative process. The germination of advertising message takes place from the purchase proposition. The ultimate success of the message is measured in terms of its reception by the target audience. It depends on the product offering and its relevance to the prospect's requirements and mental disposition.

❖ Purchase Proposition

It is the first step in creative strategy. It is a look at the product from the angle of a buyer. Besides, it is not only the product, but a brand that is being promoted. In short, purchase proposition pre-supposes not only the product knowledge but also a meaningful brand identity. Claude Hopkins classic campaign head-line for beer was:

Our bottles are washed with live steam. Perhaps hygiene appealed to audience, when overall standards of hygiene were very low. 'Get rid of film on teeth' is another Hopkins classic purchase proposition for a toothpaste.

❖ Unique Selling Proposition (USP)

The basic philosophy behind USP developed at Ted Bates in early 40s is to announce in every advertisement the specific benefit on buying a product. Thus Colgate's 'Suraksha Chakra' is a USP. USP is unique, since competition does not offer it. USP must be strong enough to move the masses. Creativity and innovativeness do contribute a great deal in devising a sound USP.

❖ Advertising Positioning

Accurate positioning is the most important step in effective selling. Vicks VapoRub has been positioned as a remedy for cold through liberal application on chest, back and neck. This positioning is different from its positioning as a pain-reliever elsewhere. The advertising angle of positioning treats positioning as a change in communication strategy, without altering the product itself.

❖ Creative Execution

This process begins in the advertising agency which has been given a complete brief by the client. The same ad message is run of great diversity. Besides, the clutter of competing messages make creative execution one sure method to get attention. Advertising is pre-tested for its effectiveness. Creative execution pre-supposes thematic brilliance and motivational force of appropriate primary and secondary appeals. Evans has suggested that an effective advertisement must have impact, relevance, single-mindedness, reason, capability, topicality and identity.

Clarke has identified the following process in creative thinking:

Abstracting	: **Market situation provides relevant data about the prospects and media.**
Synthesising	: **Elements are integrated. Ideas are scrutinised to either accept them, reject them or modify them.**
Hypothesizing	: **Ideas are converted in to a working statement.**
Gestation	: **Objections and problems sorted out. There are discussions. There are references to different sources of information.**
Coalescence	: **Ideation is translated to writing.**
Performance	: **Actual writing.**

❖ Lateral Thinking

It is the ability to engage in thinking reasoning that is not obvious. It looks for creative possibilities outside the usual framework of perception. Edward De Bono, Maltese psychologist, physician and writer coined the term lateral thinking. There are three main reasons for the demand of creativity in the market — problem solving, opportunity and simplicity. If one cannot solve the problem, then there is need for creativity. There should be a new way to create new value. Creativity helps in finding simpler, faster, cheaper ways of doing things. There are some differences between artistic creativity and ideational creativity.

Lateral thinking or creative thinking is essential in all contexts. It should be integrated in the logics of a company and in its training programmes. Creative thinking extends beyond select jobs. It is useful in cost cutting, procedure simplification and functional analysis. Inhibition and caution cripple creativity, but it does not mean that uninhibited people necessarily become creative. A lateral thinker moves from one known idea to creating new ideas. The techniques of lateral thinking can be easily acquired. It is a matter of exerting the brain.

* * *

26 MEDIA OVERVIEW

The term media is plural for medium. In advertising terms, medium is a channel of communication, such as newspapers, magazines, radio and television. A medium is a vehicle for carrying the sales message of an advertiser to the prospects. It is indeed a vehicle by which advertisers convey their messages to a large group of prospects and thereby aid in closing the gap between Producer at the one end and the Consumer at the other end. Of course, this is from the viewpoint of advertisers and the audiences. There is another way of looking at the media, and that is from the point of view of the medium itself. Different media are organisations or enterprises for entertainment and information. They sell the product in the form of newspaper, magazine and radio and television programmes. At best, they are service organisations fulfilling the needs of listeners, readers and viewers for entertainment and information. Each medium designs its product to be more and more attractive among its audience. Each medium applies marketing concepts to the designing of the right product, selling it at the right price, distributing it through several outlets and, at times, taking the help of the right promotional means to increase its circulation or improve the popularity of its programmes. Newspapers and magazines work hard to build up their circulation among readers by improving the material they publish, be it local news, national news, special interest information such as business, sports, housekeeping, science, etc. Similarly, television and radio stations broadcast programmes which are designed to attract larger segments of the public. In short, media, too are products who have to market them properly.

Once a medium has been well established and has built up a significant readership or audience, it is in a stronger position to attract advertisers who are on the lookout for such media to reach audiences with their selling messages. Of course, they are willing to pay for this service. Thus, in addition to selling their products in the form of newspaper, magazine, radio and television programmes, the media are selling space or time which, in turn, earns large revenues for them. The money so earned out of selling advertising space and time ultimately helps to make the product itself (medium) cheaper and more attractive among its audience.

It would not be inappropriate to mention here that it is advertising which has been instrumental in the phenomenal growth of the media. In the nineteenth century, publishers of newspapers and magazines were faced with the stagnant circulation of their publications, with the result that profits were limited. This was due to the fact that the entire cost of writing and production was covered by subscriptions and news-stand revenue only. If the circulation was to be increased, it was possible only when prices were reduced. With lower prices, the circulation went up, resulting in a widespread reach of advertisers for their selling messages which, in turn, earned more money for the media. Both the media and the advertisers seem to have been benefited in the process. The publishers increased their audiences, profit and sphere of influence; at the same time, advertisers could reach effectively their prospective customers, making mass marketing possible for them. Today, every medium, be it a newspaper or a magazine, the radio or television, has a department with the responsibility of selling advertising space and time. The media themselves do advertise and promote the sale of their advertising space and time, for this is one of the important activities of the media. For their growth and even for their survival, the media have to be constantly on their toes to achieve an increasingly higher advertising revenue. In this chapter, we shall introduce our readers to the various types of media, their classification, the media selection factors, media planning and scheduling. Here is a list of the various media available to advertisers or media buyers.

1. Print Media

Newspapers
Daily Newspapers
Sunday Newspapers
Sunday/Weekend Sections of Daily Newspapers
Weekly Newspapers
Magazines
General Interest Magazines
Special Interest Magazines
Trade Publications
Institutional Publications
Direct Mail.

2. Electronic Media

Television : DD National, DD Metro, DD Satellite channels, STAR TV (Star Plus, BBC, Star Sports, MTV),

Zee TV, Sony TV, Sahara, Colors, Imagine TV, 9X.

Radio: Primary Channel Vividh Bharati and FM Channel

3. Outdoor Media

Posters

Hoardings

Neon Signs

Sky advertising

4. Transit or Vehicular Media

Mainline Trains
Suburban Trains
Buses and Trains
Taxis and Auto-rickshaws
Private vehicles

5. Speciality Media

T-Shirts, buttons, caps, stickers, badges etc.
Off-beat Approach

We can use some off-beat techniques like rub the finger against the surface and smell a perfume. Our creativity should be put to use to design the off-beat techniques.

6. Point-of-Purchase or In-shop Media

Banners
Hangings
Stickers
Packaging
Painted Signs

7. Miscellaneous Media

Internet: Medium of the new millennium
Cinema

PRINT MEDIA

Despite the TV, print media survives. TV cannot replace it. Yes, TV does affect what we read.

We include newspapers and magazines in print media. These days we have mass magazines of general interest like India Today and Outlook and special interest magazines like Computers@home.

Newspapers have special Sunday editions, whose sales are higher because they are content rich.

Print media allows selectivity. We can reach the desired audience. Every magazine and newspaper has a readership base. We have to compare it with our target audience. National newspapers have lesser selectivity. Magazines have more selectivity. Special interest magazines offer the highest selectivity.

The editorial environment of the print media affects the ad messages. Magazines and newspapers are read for editorial matter and not for ads. If readers are emotionally involved with the edito-chances of the ad being seen or read. Newspapers have news environment. The new creates an impact. Who can doubt the pulling power of a full page newspaper ad? But size alone does not matter.

❖ Requirements of Print Ads

A print layout is not as difficult as a TV storyboard. A layout is the arrangement of the different elements of the ad as they will appear in print. The ad as 'a whole should deliver the strategy and rise above the clutter.' Some prints which make print ads work are as follows:

❖ Simple Layout

A layout should be kept as simple as possible. An elaborate layout with a wide variety of typographical variations and multiplicity of illustrations and cluttered copy would not work. The layout should allow smooth eye movement; not necessarily from top to bottom, but from the most powerful element on the page.

❖ Illustration

Fashion goods are advertised on the basis of visuals only. They may not carry even a head-line. Body copy is mostly absent. Illustration must be evocative. It must carry the brand name. A unique product or package can be used as an illustration.

❖ Short Appeal

The illustration must set the reader thinking. He should ask, 'What's happening?'

❖ Photographs

Most modern ads carry photographs. It improves recall. It scores over artwork, especially where sensory appeals are dominant. Ice-creams and food are better known as photographs. Photos can show a product in use. They are a sort of visual evidence. Before-and-after photos are more effective than copy. Cosmetic companies always photos. Captions under photos attract more readership. A captioned photo can itself become an ad.

❖ Benefit headline

Self interest is the strongest motivating force. It is for this reason that head-lines incorporate a major benefit of the product, which is made obvious, and easily accessible. Headline sometimes give news Head-lines have one major function ¾ to capture the reader's attention by a believable promise. Headlines must communicate ¾ whether they are long or short is immaterial. Some short headlines which fail to communicate are no good as compared to long headlines which do communicate.

Headlines can be topicalized and personalized.

❖ Long Copy

We tend to ignore the long copy. But there are occassions to use it. High involvement products like a computer or a car do require adequate information before buying decision can be taken. Ad copy should not be made fatter by empty rhetoric. It must be repute with facts and figures. It should be simple, without any operational jargon. Long copy should be properly laid out. So as to improve readability.

❖ Readability

Consider a good magazine or newspaper. See its typography. It is classic. It does not have wide typographical cariations on one page. They avoid block caps. They use serif type, rather than sans serif. Reverse is used to the minimum. There is no overprinting on tints, or tones or photos. This is to facilitate reading. Good copy should facilitate reading.

❖ Campaign Planning

Every ad should be complete by itself, but should remain connected to a campaign made by a series of ads by adopting a basic theme or proposition.

❖ Off-beat Approach

We can use some off-beat techniques like rub the finger against the surface and smell a perfume. Our creativity should be put to use to design the off-beat techniques.

❖ Match between Creative and Media

An ad should be designed for a specific media. One and the same ad may not work for a daily newspaper and a tabloid. Sometimes companies just reduce the size of a bigger ad to a cramp if in a smaller space. This is not the way. We should also consider the editiorial environment and design our message accordingly. The paper used by the media also affects the creative. Glossy magazines score in colour reproduction over coarse newsprint using dailies. An ad copy must be seen in the context of the media, rather than as a stand-alone.

❖ Production Cost Optimisation

Most of print production is now electronic and so even roughs are closer to the finished copy. Cost control is exercised by understanding what each step is going to cost Outdoor shoots, expensive photographers, weekend or night shoots, special effects, child models - all these will contribute substantially to costs. Production budget should be made in advance and be approved, prior to the allocation of more.

The use of artwork should be agreed upon. Are we free to use a photo for print runs only for a specified time? Can we use the same for promotions?

ELECTRONIC MEDIA: TV

TV has been introduced in India for the last four decades. The Satellite TV appeared in India when CNN started beaming in the wake of the Gulf war between the allies led by the US and Iraq after the invasion of Kuwait. STAR TV and Zee TV which was a Hindi channel in the bouquet of star channels are beaming in India through satellites since 1992, and thus almost a decade of satellite transmission has been computed in India. Though there are more than 500 satellite channels now, the major players are Star, Zee which has since started independent operations and Sony. We have a variety of TV channels ¾ entertainment channels, music channels, news channels, education and knowledge channels. In the days prior to the arrival of satellite channels, DD ruled the scene with monopoly terrestrial transmission through high power transmitters and a series of low-power transmitters to cover the length and breadth of the country. As DD was the only channel available followed by DD2 or Metro, the coverage and reach of DD was phenomenal. Some programmes like the Mahabharat commanded a rating of 80 per cent The audience was not fragmented, as it is now amongst the several satellite channels. A viewership of some 10-15 per cent is considered to be very high. As so many channels have appeared on the scene, software development became the key to success. A shake- out will drive away channels weak in programming and poor in viewership. DD formerly had the increasing share of advertising revenue, but that was later shared with satellite channels.

With such a clutter of channels, it is increasingly difficult to get the viewers to watch our commercial and its message. Commercials are made using the latest filming techniques to capture the attention of the viewers. But what is necessary is a meaningful strategy backed up by a strong creative idea.

❖ Involve the Viewers

We can involve the viewers so as to make them watch our commercial. Our message should provide them the information they want, a solution to their problem, a situation with which they can identify and entertain them.

Good advertising is always relevant to the needs, interests, values and life-style of the people.

❖ Story Board

In the script of a TV Commercial, we have a combination of audio (words) and video (scenes that go with the words). A viewer thus sees and hears what has been presented as drawings below which the action of a commercial has been worded. This is called a story board. The following example will make this concept clear.

Story Board for Amul Butter Film/TV Script

Video: Man with broken heart on the ledge of a sky-scraper. Deliberately falls-off.
Audio: Sad violin music whispers.

Video: A falling man sees Amul girl buttering a slice, as he passes a window.
Audio: Man yells as he falls.

Video: Man pedals furiously and stops in mid-air. He then shoots up.
Audio: Screeching sound of car breaks. Man slows down.

Video: Man jumps and sits on the window sill. Boy and girl run on buttered slices.
Audio: (jingles) Utterly, Butterly, Delicious.

A commercial can be visualized by imagining the drawings which will accompany the audio-video parts. A story is created. We can also prepare a script without the drawings by putting the video on the left side and the audio on the right side of the paper. A few technical terms like CU or close-up, BCU or big close-up or zoom etc. are used in the script.

A story-board should deliver the strategy *e.g.*, stain removing properties of a detergent. If it does not, it will fail. It should also involve the viewer and communicate the strategy.

❖ Significance of Video

TV is a visual medium, and is essentially to be viewed. It is of utmost importance to film the commercial so as to convey the message through the pictures. When sound is muted still the message in the commercial should be obvious.

❖ Virtual Symbol

A commercial should have a frame that captures the essence of the whole message effectively.

❖ Arresting Attention

A commercial must open in such a way that further viewing is ensured. A commercial must have a firm grip in the first five seconds.

❖ Focus

Elaborate and complicated script is not necessary. A simple message which has a clear focus is necessary. A 10-second commercial has to tell the whole story. It packs drama, demo and action. There are 15 second, 30 second, 60 second commercials to overcome the constraints of a 10-seconder. But an advertiser must first explore the possibility of packing the message in a 10 second commercial. If an advertiser fails to deliver the message in a short time of say 10 seconds, he is perhaps not focussed.

❖ Product Consciousness

A commercial may make an impact but the consumer may not know for which product it was. This is very true if the product is new. Brand names should be such which are easy to memorise.

❖ People Oriented

A commercial which makes people talk on the camera becomes memorable.

❖ Benefit Shown

We can show the benefit that the product offers. A pimples cream can give blemish - free screen. A model with clear is shown as proof. BPL Mobile shows how a child can talk to a grandpa, thus touching an emotional chord.

❖ Brand Personality

Our message should support brand personality and must be consistent with it.

❖ Brevity

The less we say, the better. If the commercial is crowded, perhaps the key benefit will be buried under unnecessary foliage.

❖ Campaigning

A commercial should be a part of a campaign that builds up a theme.

❖ Dramatic Forms of the Commercial

We can convey our message by several dramatic techniques like demonstration, story telling or slice-of-life. Each technique has its merits and it depends on the market and the brand which technique will be more appropriate. Techniques can be combined to suit our purpose.

❖ Testimonials

These lend credibility to the message. Someone who has experienced the product first hand testifies about it. A testimonial must have the support of a sound product idea and concept. Dove soap is not only a soap, but also a moisturiser, which makes dry skin glow. A seven day test proves it. A real life person provides legitimacy and authenticity to the claim made by the product. Some testimonials are given by experts. A dentist talking about tooth-care and a paste is an example of expert testimony.

❖ Demonstration

If you an advantage, flaunt it. Demonstration is a very strong technique. An adhesive can show its strength when a man dangling precariously from a bridge does not fall down in a commercial just because there was a container of the adhesive kept on TV set itself. Humour and drama put together ! In a symbolic way, we have made a point. A demonstration must substantiate a key benefit of the product. A soiled kurta can be made new for an occasion by soaking it in a particular brand of detergent. The cleaning power of the detergent is proved.

❖ Presenters

Presenters are just brand ambassador. They can be stars, sportspersons, celebrities or created personalities. One who presents not only the message but also builds the brand image is a good presenter. Sharukh Khan was used to announce the entry of the Santro car and to emphasise its features. Sharukh Khan enhanced the attention value of the commercial. A CEO of a company can be used as a spokesperson. A grandma who is quite knowledgeable and experienced is used as a spokesperson for Ayurvedic concepts. It is an example of created personality. There is a match between the product and the personality. Celebrity endorsement has its own risks. Celebrities may run into disrepute. Of late this is the problem with our cricketing stars. They may overshadow the brand.

❖ Animation

Cartoon animation is popular these days, especially for children products. Animation can be combined with live action.

❖ Slice-of-life

It is a dramatic technique in which the characters enact a role contributing to the development of a small story. They involve people with the brand while enacting the role. Generally, this format follows problem-solution model. The solution is emphasized more than the problem. An effective slice culls from real-life situations to which the audience can relate.

❖ Comparative Advertising

Two detergent cakes are compared on the basis of their whitening power. Two colas are compared in a test. Generally, this approach works when we can establish the edge our product enjoys over the competitive brand. Viewers must not be confused about the brand being advertised and the brand being compared. A market leader has no need to compare its product to other products. However, market followers can adopt this approach.

❖ Music

Music and jingles are very much important in developing commercials. Music is eveocative. Jingles are poetic way of conveying the message. We can compose music and jingles first-hand use. Alternatively, music from the vast repertoire of popular tunes can also be used. Even jingles can be set to tune on popular numbers. These adaptations must enhance the core idea. Music used from second-hand sources can be used by others too and so it is not exclusive for commercial.

A commercial also contains non-musical sounds such as clapping of hands, sounds of sore-throat, sound of door-slam, chirping of birds, flowing of water etc. When these sounds are combined with music, we get what is known as 'sound design'.

❖ Sex and Humour

Humour is entertaining, and sex is helpful in selling. But they must be relevant They should not distract the viewer from the main message. They should emanate from the consumer benefit. They should not be just an appendage. Humour fades out fast, and so constant renewal is necessary. Though humour is commonly liked, we should remember people find it difficult to buy from jokers.

❖ Production Aspects

A commercial has to pass through three stages — pre-production, production itself and post-production.

❖ Pre-production

In pre-production, we select a story board in keeping with our strategy and decide about casting. Mostly, the cast consists of models considered suitable to enact the roles envisaged. Cast can be picked up from established actors and actresses. But it will shoot up the production budget. Even the common people can be used in casting. After the client company approves the story board, it is sent to TV channel for clearance. Mostly it is cleared if it does not violate the broadcasting code set by the channel.

The production company submits a production estimate to the ad agency. It is called budgeting. It includes expense heads like pre-production expenses, recce expenses, casting fees and expenses, production salaries, unit salaries, electrical unit expenses, camera equipment expenses, art department's costs, studio charges, location shooting costs, laboratory costs, post-production costs, insurance and miscallaneous. Animation production expenses and mark-up are added to the total expenses to give the total production cost.

Production is generally set at 10 per cent of the media budget. But it may go to $^1/_3$rd of the media budget. Premium costs can be controlled if we know-how all the elements contribute to the costs. Besides, one must always try to have a strong idea rather than celebrity endorsements and fancy special effects. Over-time also adds to the budget. We have multiple bids from several production companies to select a cost-effective bid. Most commercials are shot on film and later edited on tape.

❖ Production

The actual shooting of a commercial is a matter of cinematography. It has a time schedule of generally one to three days. The actual time taken depends upon whether it is hot in a studio or location, the complexity in terms of lighting, the camera movements and the action involved. The whole process is well-planned to avoid time over-run, produced and aired very economically. We can select mornings to air coffee commercials. Drive-in listening is good to promote automobile products and cellphones.

❖ Post-production

In post-production we generally include editing special effects and dubbing video-tape editing is simpler and faster than film editing.

❖ Last Word

Great commercials are built around strong ideas. We should not produce lousy commercials, and waste resources. We have to spend our budget effectively.

ELECTRONIC MEDIA: RADIO

Radio is still an inexpensive medium to reach a large number of people nationally or locally. As it is a mobile transistor that is being mostly used by people, it becomes its greatest strength. In India, radio was not made commercial in the fifties and sixties. Radio Ceylon was in those days popular. It was only since 1967 that Vividh Bharati, the commercial services of radio started in India. Radio is an instant medium. TV takes more time, since the paraphernalia of the camera and other things are to be sent to get the visuals.

Radio was the sole entertainment medium previously. But since the advent of TV and proliferation of other media, radio listening has undergone a sea - change. The leisure time available is very limited. Radio must create a word picture for the listener who has to visualise mentally what is being described.

Radio is one-to-one medium. We have to anticipate the activities of the audience while receiving the message. The audience is doing something or the other while listening to the radio. Radio, as McLuhan, feels provides a 'private experience' to a person.

FM radio has now attracted the youngsters, especially the teenagers. Radio allows time-wise targeting. We can select a listener and talk one-to-one.

We give here some basic principles of radio advertising:

❖ Editorial Environment

Each programme has its own context and a commercial played is interpreted differently accordingly to the context of the programme. We have selected the appropriate programme to dir our commercial.

❖ Focus

We have to be direct and clear, since there are no moving images to rivet the attention of the listener, who get distracted easily.

❖ Supplementation

Radio can be a good supportive medium especially to print and TV. If it supports a TV commercial, we can use the same jingle or music to maintain consistency in strategy.

❖ Imagination

We can stimulate the imagination of the listener by putting sounds and voices and put people in an ambience we would like them to be in.

❖ Topical

We can customise our message keeping in mind the season, the time of airing, the station from which the commercial is being aired and the listener profile. This topicality is possible as radio commercials are produced and aired very economically. We can select mornings to air coffeee commercials. Drive-in listening is good to promote automobile products and cellphones.

❖ Brand

Radio does not show a product or brand. We have to sink in the brand name by making the listeners hear it.

❖ Music

Music is evocative. Jingles capture the salient points of the brand. We can use the track of a TV commercial or produce special music or commercial for the radio.

❖ Sales Promotion

Sales Promotion efforts can be advertsied through radio. Thus we hear many buy-one, get-one-free commercials or radio.

❖ Commercial in Context

A commercial is listened either while driving or cooking or reading or talking. We have to see how a commercial is affected in different contexts.

❖ Formats of Radio Copy

A radio copy, like the one for TV minus video, can take many formats — humour, drama, straight sell, educational, demonstration, skit of a short play, testimonial, real-life situation, a musical etc.

OUT OF HOME ADVERTISING

Outdoor billboards or posters or hoardings is one important advertising medium. Transit advertising (inside the buses, outside the buses, on taxi-cabs, on suburban railway coaches) is another example of out-of-home advertising. The audiences of both outdoor and transit advertising are different.

Hoardings are controversial since they disfigure the environment. But they are extensively used. Automobile products, beverages, fast moving consumer goods, retailers, fashion goods and movies are the frequent users of outdoors are the first stepping stones to an upcoming artist.

Outdoor copy should arrest the attention quickly. Outdoor advertising is the oldest form of advertising. The modern outdoor media include outdoor advertising in several forms - such as posters, bill-boards, hoardings, non standardised signs, highway advertising and at rail road and bus terminals.

Outdoors are all static, fixed on highways, with increasing number of automobiles, the dispersion of population to the suburbs and the greater mobility of the people, the outdoor ads will be seen by more and more moving people. Outdoor has the possibility of greater exposure-this is the burden or remark. When you are moving on a highway, you are very unlikely to miss a big billboard or sign. There are no big messages in outdoor ads. They are basically the shortest possible, but they are most visible and eye-catching. The matter is to be grasped in a jiffy. Otherwise, it is a waste. The ideal poster uses symbols universally recognised.

Outdoor is not only to be seen. There is no editorial matter here. So no effort is required here on the part of the viewer. It is the audience who goes to the message while doing other activities. Outdoor messages offer repeat opportunities for looking at the ad message.

There is Traffic Audit Bureau (TAB) on the lines of ABC to measure the number of persons passing a particular outdoor during a given interval of time (in some countries).

Outdoors are purchased in terms of coverage, say a 100 outdoors cover an entire mobile population per month.

Indoor and outdoor ads have one vital distinction. Indoor ads themselves circulate amongst viewers/readers. Outdoor ads themselves do not circulate amongst masses. People circulate around them-people in motion. This is an advantage. Outdoors are seen while doing some other activity. For indoor ads a special reading/viewing is called for. Outdoor ads provide a two-fold advantage to see/read message and to continue to move, walk, travel.

❖ Poster Advertising

Posters are of great value in developing countries like India with a great deal of diversity of languages and problems of illiterarcy. It is a visual medium par excellence most of the times. Even when words are used they are pithy.

Mostly posters remain in position for a period of time, say several weeks. We therefore, say that they enjoy 24 hour exposure and long life. The fact is that audience gets only a fraction of a second to view the advertisement. But this is compensated by repetition of viewing. The repetition, as Jefkin says, is ideal for sinking the name or registering a slogan or sales point or pack design in the mind of the audience. The task of a poster is though simple but is an insistent one.

Posters communicate with a large number of people at the same time. Coverage could be according to our choice. It is a real mass medium. It gives exposure to one and all. They may be on their way to office, work, play, shop and so on. Its message delivery is dependent upon the passer-by-traffic. It acts as an impulse-trigger.

❖ Neon Signs

Neon signs are conspicuous at Delhi's Defence Colony flyover or Bombay's Marine Drive. They are electronically controlled; move and form patterns. Once seen in part, we desire to see the whole sequence. In neon signs light emitting diodes, computer cards and curtain backgrounds are used.

Brite Neon Signs, Delhi is one such company that manufactures neon signs. Neon signs are especially useful as an ad medium in those cities which have a night life (a place like Chowpatty, where people can meet in the evenings). These days the emphasis is on special effects (e.g., Milk food ice-cream signs on the Defence Colony Flyovers). The Charms cigarette sign shows a bird flying with the brand name flashing on it. This sign was first introduced in Bombay. Champion Neon signs also operate in this field. These signs are authorised by local administration or are put on private buildings. There are problems with neon signs - power shortage, security hazard as they might collapse if the board on which they are installed is small, traffic hazard. The cost to the companies include the rental to be paid to the landlord. Neon signs add definitely to the beauty of the city. However, they are an eye-sore during the day.

❖ Essentials of a good poster

Outdoor is a popular medium; at the same time it is powerful too. Outdoor media must draw attention to it, or else it fails totally. This is important since the audience is moving. The other essentials is that communication must be immediate. Some principles on which posters are made:

1. Identify the product. It should resisgter quickly.
2. Use short copy. But effective too.
3. Use short words, but crips enough.
4. Be visible and legible. Capitals are scaled almost to a height of 41 cms and lower case letters to a height of 30.5 cms.
5. Use large illustrations.
6. Make use of bold letters.
7. Keep the background simple.
8. The three major elements of layout are identification, copy and illustration.

❖ Essentials of a Good Poster

Outdoor is a popular medium; at the same time it is powerful too. Outdoor media must draw attention to it, or else it fails totally. This is important since the audience is moving. The other essentials is that communication must be immediate. Some principles on which posters are made are:

1. Identify the product. It should register quickly.
2. Use short copy. But effective too.
3. Use short words, but crisp enough.
4. Be visible and legible. Capitals are scaled almost to a height of 41 cms and lower case letters to a height of 30.5 cms.
5. Use large illustrations.
6. Make use of bold letters
7. Keep the background simple.
8. The three major elements of layout are Identification, copy and illustration.

For identification, a logo or a slogan is used. New products are named in the copyline. Contrast is essential in outdoor.

The use of flat colour areas create tremendous impact in a poster design. Brevity is a pre-requisite. Words of copy must communicate the basic idea. A good visual helps you to economise on words. The copy must be readable from a distance. Lettering is a crucial aspect. Open spacing helps legibility.

❖ Sky-balloons or Sky-writing

This is an aerial method of advertising. Painted balloons are floated in the sky by the advertisers. It is called balloon advertising. The balloons are gaudily coloured. They carry a brief ad message or a logo or an illustration. Its exotic nature draws attention.

Sometimes banners are trailed overland. This is confined to the beach area. Tourists can read the banners trailed by air-craft over the sea. On roads, they are not permitted as motorists are distracted. In Germany, advertisements have been projected on clouds. Goodyear airships are used as aerial communicators for public announcements. In U.K., this is not permitted but when the Royal Wedding took place in 1981, greetings were spelt out and seen (even by TV, the viewers). Sky writing or aerial advertising or aerial advertising serves as a reminder advertising.

In UK, the 1961 regulation forbid sky-writing. In India this form is not in vogue. However, there is a party in Bombay who has designed a balloon for advertising purposes. In Germany, night flying air-crafts have had advertisements picked out in lights on the underparts of their wings.

❖ Sandwich Boards

Sandwich man is a man who walks on the streets between two advertising boards. Here the walking medium is a human being who carries the ad message. There are two advertising boards which are joined at the end to form a V-shaped board. The man places himself between them. The persons to the left of the man see the contents of the left side of the board and those who walk on the right side see the contents on the right side. The sandwich carrier dresses funnily and repeats slogans in a megaphone. Sandwich board is a very old medium. In India in mofussil area, this medium was being very successfully used by cigarette companies, especially Cavendars. These days the medium is almost defunct.

Two slices of bread stuffed with some relish in between form a sandwich. Sandwich so-called after the Earl of Sandwich (1781-92) who ate such slices at gambling table to play non-stop. Sandwich man perambulates the streets between two boards of advertising.

❖ Mural Advertising

Mural publicity refers to wall-paintings or to painting on similar surfaces. In its extended form, even posters and printed bulletins pasted on walls become mural publicity. Mural publicity is a supportive medium. It attracts the passers — by. In towns as well as in villages this form has been used considerably. In Maharashtra most of students must have seen advertisements of coaching classes and political messages on the walls. Besides, Sapat Lotion and Ointment and Bytco Blacktooth powder have advertised in Maharashtra considerably by mural publicity.

Mural is a cheap outdoor medium. It is by its nature very big in size. Illustration is a dominating element of layout in murals. Murals are boldly coloured. This form is suitable for eye appealing products. Mural advertising is localised. Mural defies the walls of private owners sometimes in an unauthorised manner.

INTERNET: THE MEDIUM OF THE NEW MILLENNIUM

Internet is the network of computers world over. A group of computers are networked through a server and a modem. Such networks combine together to form a bigger network. Internet is thus a network of networks. Right now, it is accessible on a PC, a mobile phone and hand-held devices. It is going to be accessible on a large variety of devices, once the suitable software is developed and world-wide acceptable language like XML is put in place. Microsoft has formed a dot Net exactly for this purpose.

Information is available on the Net as web pages on the World Wide Web (WWW). An individual or organization can register a site or a domain name. It becomes the identity on the Net, *e.g.*, www.citibank.com. The tag at the end can be 'dot com' indicating commerce, or 'dot org' indicating organization or 'dot gov' indicating government or 'dot in' indicating a country like India.

A web page is written in HTML (Hyper Text Markup Language) which is then read with the help of a browser - Internet Explorer or Netscape Navigator. The document is made interactive by DHTML (Dynamic HTML) or Java applets. Graphics and layout are designed by using editing software like FrontPage (FP) or Dreamweaver

The computer we use on the Net to access information is called the client and this is connected to the Internet Service Providers' server and other computers. A web designer has to know 'client' side languages and 'server side' programming.

World Wide Web follows TCP-IP Protocol. TCP stands for transmission control protocol. IP (Internet Protocol) gives the identity of the computer connected to the Net.

Internet now has millions of computers. There are portals which deal with a wide variety of subjects. There are specialised miche portals. There are search engines to search the required information from the World Wide Web.

Internet has given birth to E-commerce and E-business. There can be two types of transactions — business-to-business (B2B) and business-to-consumer (B2C). Right now, B2B has become fairly common. With the passage of time and the development of secure payment system, we can expect even B2C transaction to grow. On-line shopping of books, fast moving consumer goods, music etc. will be possible.

Internt as an advertising medium is an attractive propostion. It is a suitable medium to access a worldwide clietele. It can be used to acess client overseas, e.g. an Indian company wishes to reach NRI's. Internet ads are cost-effective considering its wider reach. Internet can facilitate direct marketing by putting direct response ads on the Net. Internet ads can provide selectivity depending upon the site chosen and its patronage. The message can be made selectively at certain times of the day.

Generally, banners that carry a short massage are used on Internet. We can measure exposure by counting hits. However, there are some practical problems in the measurement.

Internet can be used to build brands and corproate image. Internet companies which are click-and-mouse companies, can by themselves be great brands. Or else, they can support the physical world's brick-and-morter companies.

❖ Measuring Terminology

Hits: They represent the number of elements requested from a given page. It thus provides no information on actual web traffic. For example, when a user requests a page with five graphical images, it coutns six hits.

Click Through: It is a measure of the number of page elements (hyper-links) that have actually been requested — 'clicked through' from the banner ad to the link. It is typically 1 to 2 per cent of hits.

Page Views: These are defined as the pages (actually the no. of HTML files) sent to the requesting site. It also does not indicate the number of visitors. 1 lakh page views in a week may mean 10 people reading 10 thousand pages or 1 lakh people reading one page or any variation in-between.

Visits: These are the number of occasions in which a user *A* interacted with site *B* after time *C* has elapsed. Usually *C* is set to some standard such as 30 minutes. If there is no interaction in 30 minutes, then a new visit will be counted.

Users or Unique Visitors: The number of different people visiting a site during a specified period of time.

New Users: User's status is determined from the user's registration with the site.

Log Analysis: Measurement software that provides information on hits, pages, visits and users. It also lets a site track audience traffic within the site.

Internet as a medium is still evolving. We cannot ignore it as we are living in the Internet age.

THE CINEMA

While it is comparatively easy to keep a tab on exposure of ads on television, radio and the press, it is next to impossible to check whether a company's ads are being regularly screened in cinema houses. The Blaze organization is the sole distributor in the field of cinema advertising and advertisers have to take its word that their ads are screened at the shows and theatres contracted for.

A further disadvantage of advertising in cinema theatres is that the movement of prints from one place to another and from one theatre to another, is very slow and the theatre owners are often careless in handling them. The result is that poor quality prints are shown to the public. The expense of producing slides and high-quality film advertsiements is thus not compensated.

Yet, cinema remains the most popular medium of entertainment in India. It is also patronised by the rural folk especially those who live near small towns. Another clear advantage is that in cinema advertisers have a captive audience; the distractions of home viewing of video and cable are kept out from the theatres. And unlike the print media, films appeal to the literate and the illiterate, children and adults. A further advantage is that 'segmentation' is easy, since cinema films are classified for 'adults', general audiences and PG (Parental Guidance; that is, accompaniment of an adult is necessary).

❖ Merits of Cinema

- *Cinema ensures a captive audience:* People visit a hall to see a movie of their choice. This choice ensures a higher degree of concentration (as compared to TV Viewing). TV cannot command the complete attention of the viewers.
- *Cinema is the ideal media for niche marketing:* Here the advertiser can be segment-specific, market-specific, right down to a particular district, city or even a theatre.
- *Advertising on cinema is economical:* The cost of screening an advertisement film in a theatre of average seating capacity with 50% attendance or 10000 audience in towns of over 10 lakhs population would just cost ₹ 300 a week.

* * *

27 ADVERTISING BUSINESS

Every business entity, irrespective of its size, ownership and kind of business, does take the help of advertising — the push that makes things happen. Advertising is a function of marketing and pushes the product in the market for bigger sales. The different kinds of advertising have been discussed in the introductory chapter. Here, we shall be concerned with the study of the organisation that plans, produces and places advertising campaigns in the media and the internal organisation of the advertising department. When a firm has decided upon an advertising programme as part of its overall promotion mix, it needs to have a system and an organisation to implement it for the attainment of the desired objective. Firms do have an advertising and publicity department to manage the advertising function. In some small firms, there may not be a separate department in the name of advertising, but the function is either looked after by the marketing manager or the chief executive. The company's advertising department usually relies on outside experts, often the advertising agency which prepares the advertisement messages, selects appropriate media and arranges to release them. The advertising department of a company has only a limited creative function, primarily a supervisory one. This department is merely a liaison point in the company for the agency, though it is responsible for the advertisement budget and supervises the performance of the agency. An advertising manager has to co-ordinate with the marketing and sales function, so that the advertising efforts may be fully integrated with the firm's marketing and sales strategy. He has also to perform the managerial task of formulating advertising strategy and planning an advertising through the advertising agency. The agency often assists the advertising manager in programme formulation.

❖ The Advertising Manager

The advertising manager usually works under the marketing manager for effective advertising. However, in some organisations, he may function directly under the higher management. Whatever may be the hierarchical levels, the advertising programmes should be in conformity with total market planning. Product managers and brand managers have also to co-ordinate with the advertising department for appropriate advertising efforts, so that a particular product or brand may receive an adequate promotional support. The hiring of an advertising agency is a function of the advertising manager. If the agency has to be changed, the recommendation to that effect is made to the higher management by the advertising manager.

In a large corporation, the advertising staff are employed for different product/brand line. Product or brand managers develop the advertising and promotion needs of their products or brands. Similarly, sales managers determine the kind of advertising support they need for sales and distribution managers inform it of the advertising support they require. All these requirements are co-ordinated by a manager, who is known as the advertising manager. He sets the advertising objectives and communicates them to the agency. In a typical, large-size organisation, the advertising manager reports to the vice-president in charge of advertising, sales promotion, publicity and public relations with a view to determining an effective total promotion mix. An organisation structure of such a comprehensive advertising department is depicted in Fig. 27.1. The advertising manager and his department work closely with the agency in the preparation of the ad budget, the media schedule, the creation of individual ads and the schedule of their release. Very large organisations may hire the services of more than one ad agency to cater to the varying nature of their advertising jobs.

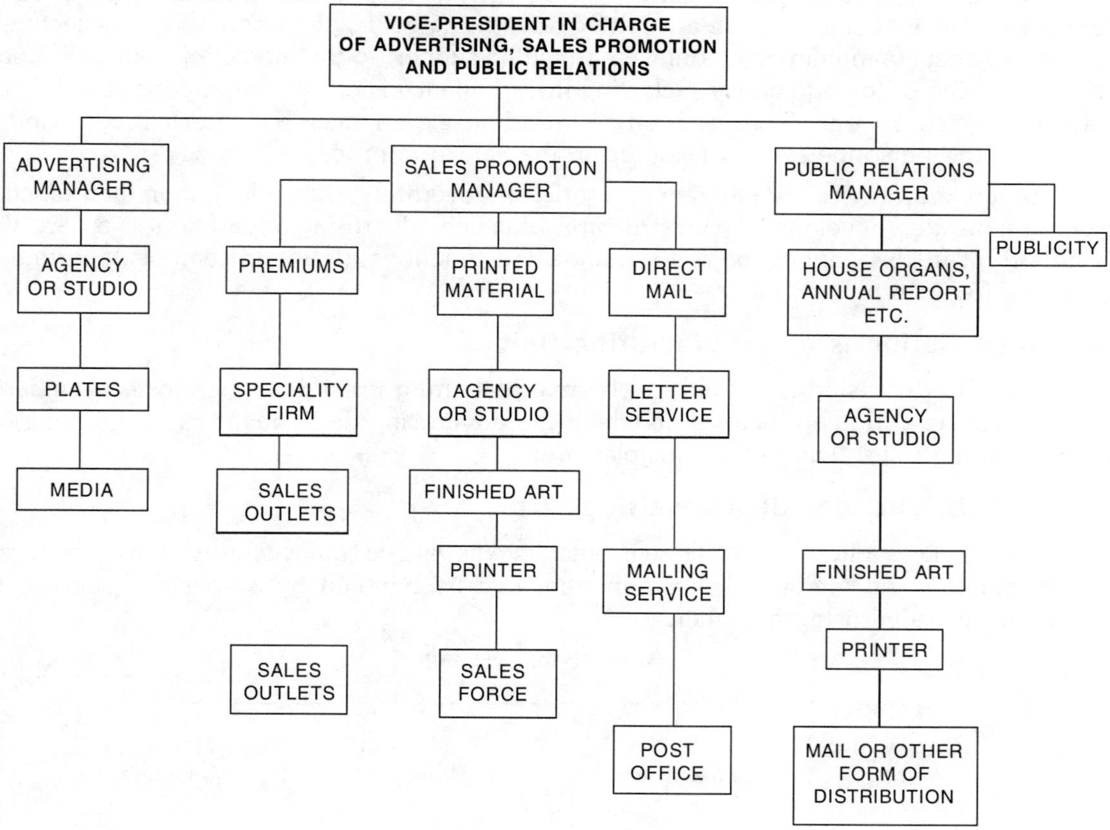

Fig. 27.1 Organisation of a typical advertising department

Retail advertising, though very common in the USA, hardly exists in our country. American newspapers and radio stations are full of retail advertising. In fact, these media would not be able to exist without retail advertising, which is their important source of income. Retailers, such as department stores, advertise their goods in the local market through the local media in the form of brochures and newspaper inserts. In fact, people do look at such newspaper inserts for a good buy of their choice products. Retail advertising is different from a manufacturer's advertising in the sense that most retail firms do not employ the services of an advertising agency. One of the important reasons for this is the non-payment of commission by media to the agency, whereas in the case of a manufacturer's advertising, the media pay about 15 per cent commission to the agency to compensate it for the services it renders. This is why retailers have an advertising department which does all activities of advertising, unlike a manufacturing firm.

❖ Organisation Structure of Advertising Department

All major advertisers maintain an advertising department. The structure of the department however may vary from one organisation to another, as each one tries to develop a form which is most suited to one's requirements. The principal forms of organisational structure are based on (*i*) sub-functions of advertising, such as copywriting or artworks, (*ii*) communication media, (*iii*) geographical spread, (*iv*) product and (*v*) end users.

Irrespective of the specific form, the advertising department has to perform several functions. Principal among these are setting advertising goals, plans and budget, selecting the outside ad agency, maintaining contacts, providing support to the marketing staff and monitor the functioning of the ad agency. Selecting the ad agency is one of the important tasks of the advertising department. Several criteria, including experience, size, track record and the quality of the personnel, are considered in the selection process.

As you know, there are different categories of advertisers. Depending upon their functions, each organisation develops its own structure, of which advertising department is a part. What is important in this connection is to analyse the functions an advertisement department is expected to perform?

❖ Organisation is a Manufacturing Unit

Bulk of advertising is carried out by manufacturing firms. It is therefore, necessary to understand the various principles on which the advertising department can be organised in manufacturing units. The basic principles are:

(a) By Sub-functions of Advertising

Advertising as a function can be segmented into its various components, such as, Copywriting, Art Production and Media. Each component can be handled by a specialist who in turn reports to the advertising manager.

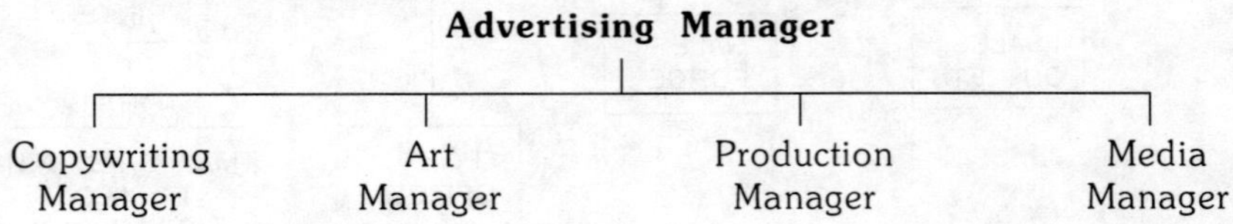

Fig. 27.2

(b) By Media

This structure would involve segregating the total man load on the basis of the media to be used, such as Newspapers or TV (Chart 2).

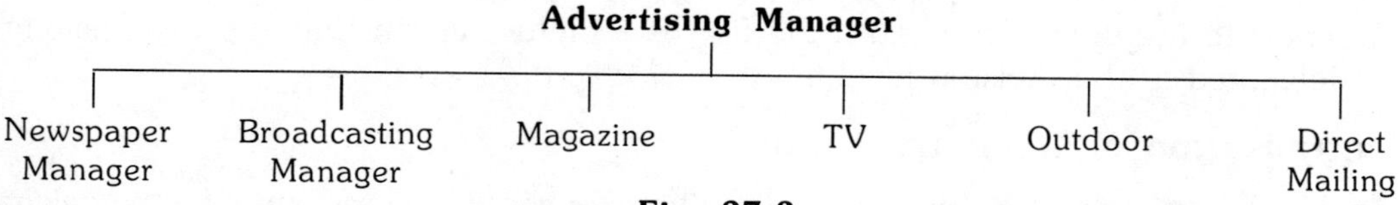

Fig. 27.3

(c) By-Product

In a large multi-product firm, the advertising department may be organised focusing on a product/product group. Each manager would be given the responsibility of one brand or several brands (Chart 3).

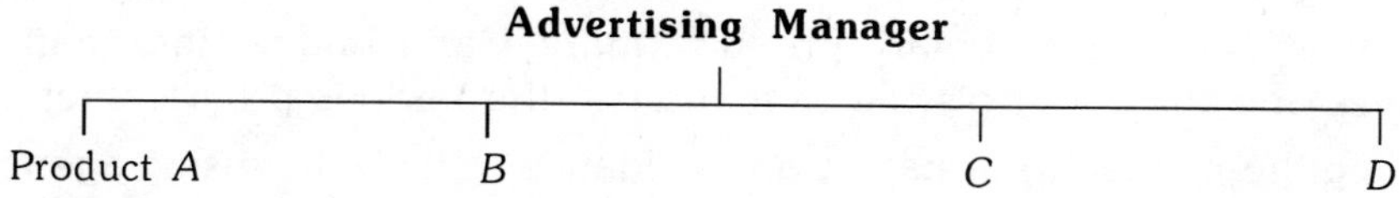

Fig. 27.4

(d) By Geography

If an organisation has distinctly different regional marketing problems and plans, including advertising plans, it may follow a structure based on geographical location of markets (Chart 4).

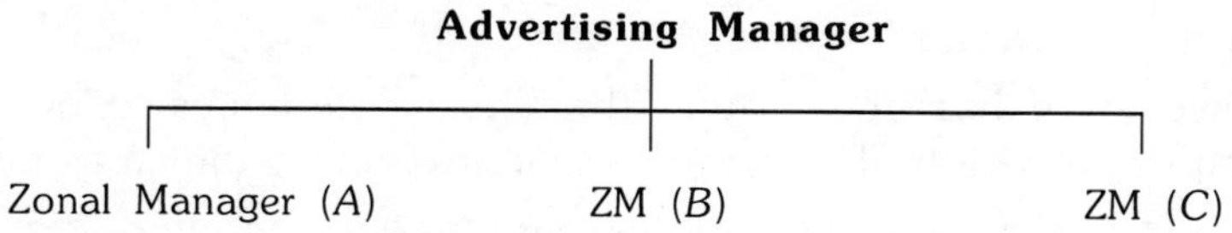

Fig. 27.5

(e) By-End-Users

Sometimes, the same product may be sold to different market segments and it is necessary to plan advertising to take care of the divergent buying behaviours of the different segments. In such a situation, this organisational structure may be desirable (Chart 5).

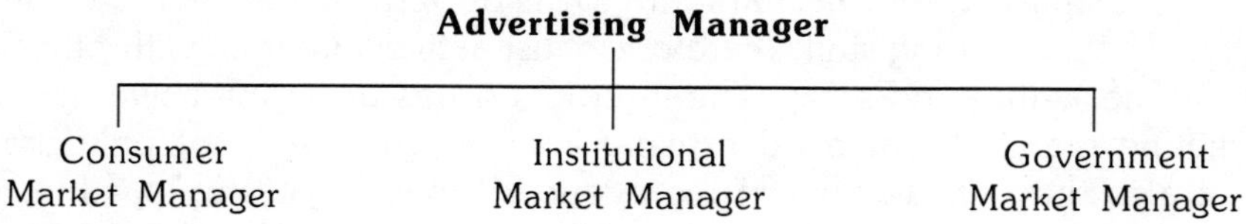

Fig. 27.6

❖ Reporting Structure

The advertising manager has to report to somebody who is higher up in the organisational structure. To whom the advertising manager would report depends upon how much importance advertising is given in the total operations of the firm. There are several alternatives. These are:

(*a*) report to the Chief Executive (Chairman/M.D.).

(*b*) report to the Director (Marketing).

(*c*) report to the divisional head if the firm is a multi-division firm and responsibility is delegated at the division level.

❖ Centralisation or Decentralisation

Should advertising be done on a centralised basis or should the responsibility be delegated to lower levels — say product or geographical divisions?

A Centralised Advertising Activity has been defined by M.E. Ziegenhagen, Director of Advertising and Public Relations, Babcock & Wilcox Co., as that which— is located at or directed by corporate headquarters, reporting to a corporate sales or marketing head or in top management.

In operation it gets the necessary product, market and budget information from the divisions it serves and then controls the execution of the various programmes by —

(1) providing the needed information and guidance to the advertising agency and other services.

(2) then reviewing and approving the completed work before getting division approval. [See Roger Barton (Ed.), Handbook of Advertising Management, 1970].

A Decentralised Advertising Activity is operated and controlled by individual units located in each major division, usually reporting to a division head or to a division marketing or sales head. The division advertising, sales and marketing people and control both the 'what' and 'how' of the advertising job, getting only advice and counsel plus miscellaneous services from a central advertising function.

In practice, however, it has been found that most companies follow the centralised pattern of advertising organisation. There are at least two important reasons for it.

(1) It is difficult to transfer the tasks of preparation and execution of creative advertising from the few to the many without loss of efficiency to a great extent and (2) Most companies entrust their advertising work to outside agencies and it is more convenient to deal with them in a centralised way.

❖ Interface with other Departments

Advertising and, therefore the people, manning the advertising department, do not function in a vacuum. Advertising is a tool of marketing. It is done to achieve a specified short-term or long-term goal. The advertising staff, therefore, must actively interact with other departments most importantly, marketing and sales. The interaction has to be intensive to draw up a co-ordinated marketing plan, of which advertising is a part. In fact, not only the advertising department, but also the outside advertising agency it may have employed, would have to be actively associated with the formulation of the marketing plan.

In companies, which realise the importance of advertising in its proper perspective, the advertising department gets useful inputs from sales, product and brand managers; from marketing heads, general managers and top management and also from many others in the engineering and manufacturing departments who provide valuable advice in respect of appeals to be focused and also other advertising matters.

❖ Functions of the Advertising Department

Just as the organisational structure of an advertising department varies, the activity profile also is subject to change from one organisation to another. Kleppner has identified 14 activities which include all the major functions and advertising department in a manufacturing organisation is supposed to carry out. These are:

1. Determine in consultation with top management the advertising goals, the advertising budget, the advertising plan.
2. Help select the advertising agency.
3. Set up a plan of activity, allocating which work is to be done by the agency and which by the advertiser. Establish with top management the internal division of such non-commissionable duties as sales promotion, research and public relations.
4. Transmit the policy and problems of management to the agency; keep it informed of changes in marketing strategies and other related areas.
5. Decide upon the proportion of the appropriation to be assigned to different tasks in the advertising programme depending upon the importance of these tasks.
6. Approve the plans for advertisements by the agency and by others who work on the advertising problems.
7. Prepare, purchase and issue sales material — point-of-purchase displays and direct mail, including receipts, dealer advertising service, premiums (unless company has separate premium departments).
8. Prepare, issue and control billing of corporate advertising.
9. Keep the sales force informed of forthcoming advertising.
10. Prepare portfolios of advertising for the salesman's use in showing advertising to the trade and to other distributors.
11. Work with the sales department in preparing special programmes.
12. Prepare instruction manuals for those who will sell and use the product; all in all, do everything possible to make the most effective use of the advertising investment.
13. See that all mail enquiries are answered with mailings as required.
14. See that all bills are properly checked; keep an account of funds and prepare proper reports for management.

The ad manager in charge of an advertising department has both managerial and operational functions. He is responsible for interacting with agencies and the media. He pays attention to outdoor aids. He takes part in campaign planning and media planning. He frames an ad budget, and allocates it. He is responsible for broadcast media. He gets POP prepared. He is the man behind SP and merchandising. He maintains press relations and PR functions. He brings out a housejournal. He is appointed on the basis of his knowledge of advertising and journalism, his knowledge of the industry, his management background and his marketing background. He maintains a good client-agency relationship so essential for the success for the campaigns.

To summarise, the advertising manager performs the following functions:

Advertising Functions	*Managerial Functions*
1. Making the ad budget	1. Admission in general
2. Co-ordinating with the agency	2. Goal setting for advertising
3. Making the ad strategy in collaboration	3. Making advertising understandable
4. Determining the ad efforts	4. Participation with higher-ups about his function
5. Evaluation of the advertising	5. Representing the organisation
6. New developments in advertising	6. Creative thinking with respect to his functions

❖ The Agency

A modern advertising agency offers specialised knowledge, skills and experience which are required to produce an effective advertising campaign. It has writers, artists, media experts, researchers, television producers, account executives, etc. These specialists work together to understand fully the advertiser's requirements of an advertisement campaign and develop suitable advertising plans and strategies. By creating advertisements and delivering them through appropriate media, the agencies implement advertising plans and strategies. A modern advertising agency is the fountain-head from which flow most of the advertisements we see and hear in the national and regional media. An agency represents the core of the advertising profession. Madison Avenue, an area in New York where several large agencies are located, has become a symbolic name for advertising.

❖ Evolution and History of Advertising Agency

The first advertising agency was started as a space broker in a newspaper by Volney B. Palmer in Philadelphia in 1841. He acted as a simple agent, selling space for his client newspaper on a commission basis. He made no effort to help the advertiser prepare copy, design a layout and provide the many specialised services now performed by a modern agency.

Since then, the nature of an agency has changed considerably, but the method of compensation in the form or a fixed percentage of advertising billing continues in spite of the inherent defect of the system, for the agency generally recommends only a higher media budget than may be appropriate.

It was only by the beginning of this century that the agency started to prepare advertisements and deliver them through the advertisements media. Lord and Thomas was probably the first agency in the USA, with a reputation for creative work in advertising. It hired copywriters, who did a marvellous job. One of the famous advertisement deliveries of this agency was for a new washing machine. Other agencies also started adopting the new services and soon many advertisement agencies had established departments for copywriting, art work, layout design, media selection, etc. Over the next several decades, the advertisement agency improved the quality of its services, besides offering additional new services at extra charge. Agency growth has never looked back since then. It has grown in size and influence through the years, demonstrating an ability to create effective advertising. Towards the end of the first half of this century, there were several large agencies, offering a full range of advertising services. They produced effective advertisements by taking into account consumer psychology and human needs and wants. Creative advertising appeals effectively influenced consumers to buy the advertised products and services. In fact, advertising at this stage, became a part of the overall marketing mix, furthering the sales and marketing strategy.

An advertising agency is shortened as ad agency. Ad agency is a team of experts appointed by clients to plan, produce and place advertising campaigns in the media. They are called agencies, because literally they are agents of the media who pay them the commission, and the media thus becomes the principal. Media pays commission to only accredited agencies (IENS accreditation). The agency works for the client, but draws its sustenance from the media (nearly 75 per cent).

❖ The Working of Ad Agencies

To begin with, the agencies started as one-man agents who booked space in the media. Even today, in our country, there are so many one-man agents who book space in the media. Soon the space-booking was handed over to the contact-man, and the actual construction of the ad was undertaken by creative wordsmiths adept at sloganising.

In the course of years, the ad agency became service-oriented, and was able to offer every possible service including marketing, Market Research (MR) and Public Relations (PR).

Ad agencies have evolved over a period of time. These days we have mostly studio-based agencies, some industrial and specialised agencies and hot-shops who only plan creative campaigns by engaging the services of free-lancers.

At Madison Avenue, most of these large agencies of the world fiercely compete for new accounts, resulting in a shift of millions of dollars of billing from one agency to another. *Advertising Age* is an official publication of the American Association of Advertising Agencies (AAAA).

In India, advertising business is worth ₹ 10,000 crores. There were only 62 advertising agencies in 1958, which increased to 168 in 1978, more than 2.5 times the numbers in 1958. There are more than 500 ad agencies today. One of the oldest and largest advertisement agencies in India is Hindustan Thompson Associates Ltd. The second largest advertisement agency is Lintas. Dattaram is the first advertising agency that set operations in India in 1905. In 2005, advertising has completed 100 years in India.

Mumbai is considered to be the Mecca of Indian advertising. These days agencies are also being set up at Bangalore, Madras, Hyderabad, Ahmedabad and Delhi.

In India, the ad agencies are sole proprietary concerns, partnerships or private limited companies. But in America and UK, the leading advertising agencies are publicly quoted companies.

Many agencies in India have come of age. Ulka (billing 12 crores) started in 1961 and celebrated its silver jubilee in 1986. It has played a pioneering role in rural advertising. It has tapped media like folk theatre and professional story tellers. It also did a campaign for family welfare.

Lintas India turned 50 in 1989 it is now called Lowe.

O & M became 60 years young in 1989. Its film, 'Spread the Light of Freedom' featuring 24 sports people running with lighted torches in different locales must have been enjoyed by many of you on TV. Was it not beautiful to see the golden girl P. T. Usha gracefully striding with a cute deer loping along in the background? O & M also made 'One Tune' (Ek Sur) commencing with Bhimsen Joshi interspersed with Lata, and ending with Amit, Jeetu and Mithun and a host of Indians. Very well-made for national integration. O & M did proud to Indian advertising by doing a campaign for social awareness about cancer.

It is better to operate agencies on professional lines, rather than as a family. It is good to instal MBO (management by objectives). An agency must necessarily plough back at least 75 per cent of its profit into business.

The advertising agencies are shifting from the creative mode to the marketing mode. Today the onus is on the agency to supply the client with data on his industry; the days of the clients briefing the industry are almost over. The agencies are expected to maintain industry data base. There is a learning towards software for optimising media usage and computerisation of studio functions.

In India, the legal structure of ad agencies is that of a small proprietary concern or a big partnership. Sometimes, they are private limited companies, either big or small.

Indian advertising is a fragmented business. There are over 400 agencies accredited to INS. The top 25 account for 50 per cent of all billings. In addition, there are many unaccredited agencies.

It is the top 25 agencies, most of which are headquartered in Mumbai, that set the pace and define the shape of the industry.

Agencies like HTA, Lintas, Clarion and O & M have shaped the entire advertising industry in the country.

Many Indians firms are coming up, by importing Western ad techniques.

Many agencies die a premature death. Most people do not appreciate that an agency — like any other business — must be properly managed. It is simply not enough just to have great ideas. In recent years, there has been a healthy trend towards sound management practices, especially financial planning and control.

This is a highly paid profession. It is a conspicuous wage island. People operate on high profile. Their life-styles are opulent because of high expense accounts of entertaining clients. They got their elitist image due to this reason. But high salaries and freedom are necessary to attract talents.

Women have been an integral part of this profession. We have examples of Rhoda Mehta (O & M, Media Director), Nargis Wadia (Interpub, MD), Usha Katrak (ASP for many years), Tara Sinha (Tara Sinha Associates Delhi; Formerly, Clarion).

❖ Madison Avenue

Madison Avenue, an area in New York, is considered to be the Mecca of advertising. It is not that a row of agencies dot this avenue. Actually, many of the agencies are to be found in nearby Lexington Avenue and surrounding areas. Madison Avenue has always been a prohibitively expensive piece of real estate. It is in fact known more for its antique shops. Randall Rothenberrg in his latest book *Where the Suckers Moon: The Life and Death of an Advertising Campaign* (Vintage) describes Madison Avenue as " the well-spring of high ambition and low art, of fast deals and boozy lunches, of national neuroses and corporate cynicism." The creativity has shifted to places like Portland, Seattle and Los Angeles and there is a consequent displacement of Madison Avenue as the navel of advertising world.

❖ Satellite Agencies

Bigger agencies these days form smaller subsidiary agencies called satellite agencies. Tony Miller calls them a "delicious irony." It is a sensible way for a big agency to offer nimbleness and personal service of a small shop. The first such subsidiary in India was Acil, which was formed by Clarion Advertising Agencies. Hindustan Thompson Associates (HTA) in 1979 set up Contract Advertising which has now taken over by Grant Kenyon & Eckhardt.

Acil has since broken away from Clarion and is now an independent agency. After Contract, there was a spate of satellite agencies; O & M, Ulka, DaCunha, Everest and more recently Lintas have set up subsidiaries. Lintas has set up Karishma as its subsidiary. The umbilical cord with the parent agency helps the subsidiaries in terms of a few initial accounts and talents to create good copies. Subsidiaries can have fresh, creative approach and can cater to smaller accounts. Subsidiaries can also take up a competing firm's account. If HTA has Lux soap, the Contract sells Mysore Sandalwood. HTA has the Niky Tasha account and Contract has Hotline's.

Edge is an Everest-backed satellite agency. Subsidiaries consolidate business and improve market share. Ulka's subsidiary Interface handles many small accounts. There is a break-away thinking in a subsidiary. But it can also draw on the parent agency, say, by taking advantage of its clout as a media buyer. DaCunha's Victa dabbles into advertising that is a little bolder than normal. Artig, an O & M subsidiary, gets into fields complementary to their business and away from main-stream advertising communications, public relations, direct response advertising. The tax benefit that the formation of subsidiaries gave is no more of any consequence. Forming subsidiary does not mean partitioning a little office space and putting a new sign-board. It must be totally independent resource-wise. Agency spin-offs can also be a way to retain restless.

Table 27.1

Satellite Agencies

Parent Agency	*Satellite Agency*	*Year Founded*	*Key Account*
Saatchi & Saatchi	Team One	1987	Lexus (Toyota)
McGann-Erickson	Merkley ISAS	1991	GMC Trucks
Lintas	L_2	1993	IBM PC Co.
Omnicorn Group	Merkley Newan Hosty	1993	Word Perfect
DDB Needham	Berlin Wright Cameron	1993	Volkswagon

FUNCTIONS OF ADVERTISING AGENCY

❖ Accounts Executive or Director: Key Executive of Agency

The agency's key executive is **Accounts Executive** (he is accounts director when he is a member of the Board in case of a limited agency).

Account in advertising parlance means a client. Thus Hindustan Lever is an account for Lintas, or ITC is an account for Lintas. This accounts executive is a link between the Agency and Client.

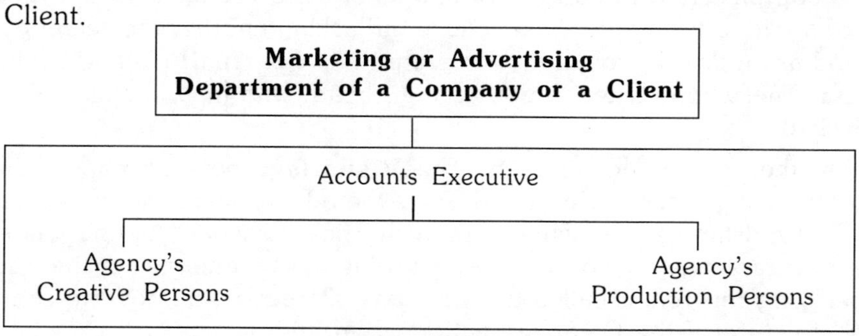

Fig. 27.7

❖ Functions of Accounts Executives

He understands what the client wants. He has to get this done through his agency. He is briefed by the marketing or sales or advertising department of the client. He communicates this to the agency people. He is also called client service executive.

❖ Account Planning or Client Servicing

An ad agency's primary function is to create advertising and account planning function provides a basis for this. Account Planner has to perform a number of functions —

1. Planning the objectives of the advertising: Here he makes use of skills of analysis, synthesis, logic and insight.
2. Selecting and evaluating research feedback on the basis of which the team makes judgments and takes decisions.
3. Making the objective and the feedback relevant and stimulating to the rest of the team — particularly the creatives.

The account team may or may not be headed by an account planner. But the above function should be attended to. It is better to invest a separate person with the composite responsibility. The positive use of research is establishing a dialogue between the Creative team and the Consumer is a valuable contribution that a planner can make.

Planning in agencies conforms to brand responses — the desired responses that a brand's advertising should generate. But when we advertise, apart from brand responses we also generate advertising responses, — effects on our target audience like amusement, education, entertainment, moving effect etc. Many times, these advertising responses are an essential part of what the brand is offering the consumer. Failure to see advertising responses make our planning remote and ineffective.

Modern days agencies have two major sections.

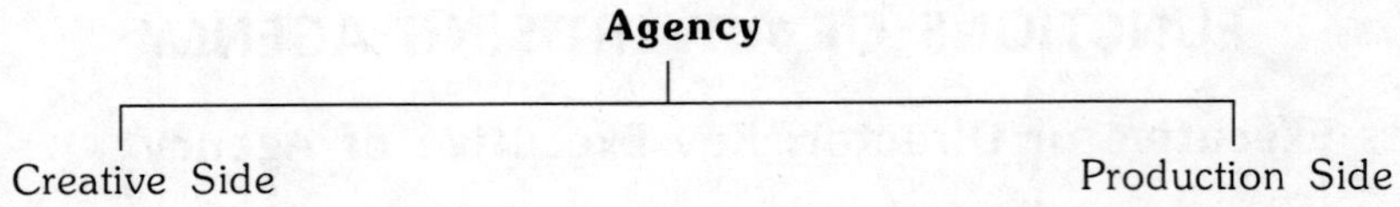

Fig. 27.8

The two sides are supplementary to each other. Now the creative section has a team of bright, talented copywriters who do the wording of an advertisement. Copywriters contribute to the theme of an advertisement, like a college girl asking another the secret of her flawless complexion, and as an answer coming to know that it is **Clearasil** Cream. Now this is called **Copy platform**. These copywriters report to their head, who may be called **Copy Chief** or **Chief Copywriter**.

But merely the copy is not enough. The **Visualiser** puts on paper what has been thought out by the copywriter. He in fact designs the ad. He takes the help of layout artists, typographers and finishing artists who prepare the final artwork. As you will see, creative energies of copywriters must be co-ordinated with the design energies of the visualisers. The person who performs this role is called the **Creative Director**. So now we can put here the organisational structure of the Creative Section of an ad agency.

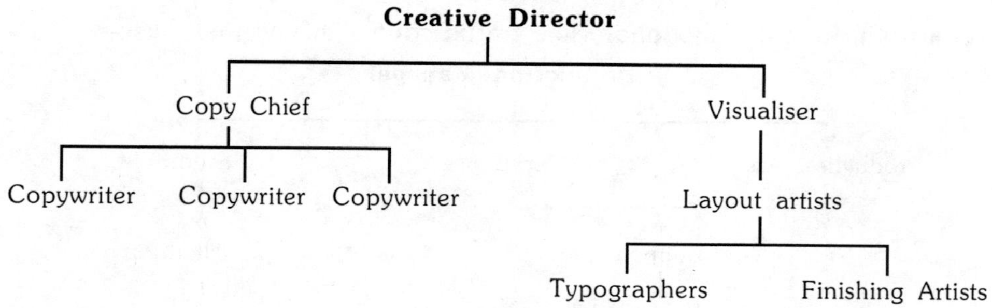

Fig. 27.9

Now we shall come to the studio-based **production department** which delivers a complete approved ad copy. This department is in charge of the **production manager** who has several assistants. For print ads, these people do typography, lettering, blocks, stereos, electros. They also supply text and artwork for photogravure process. Production manager organises the work-flow (copy and artwork proofs and corrections → final copy as per time schedule). In larger agencies this work-flow is under the control of a traffic controller. Some part of the production work can be bought from free-lance sources.

Let us now see the organisation structure of a production department.

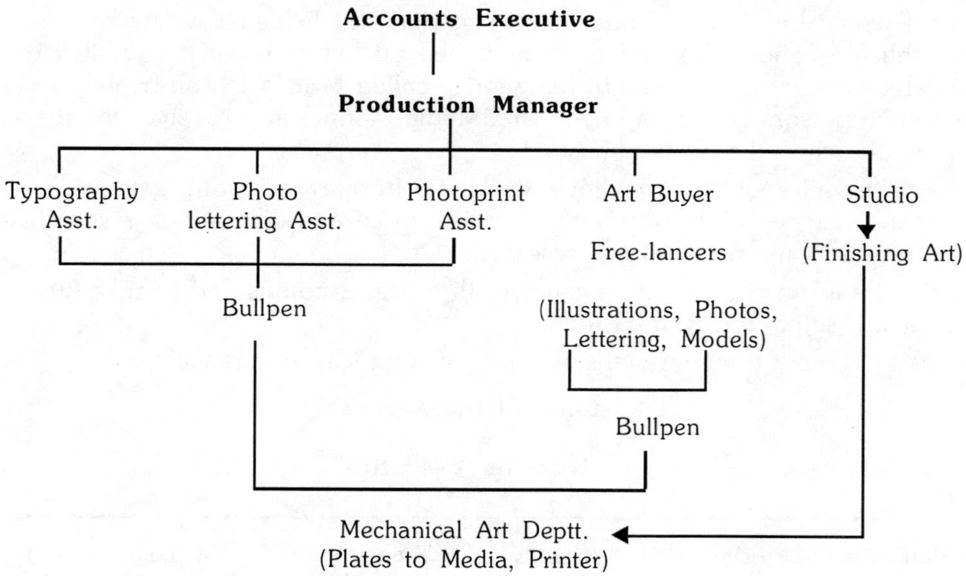

Fig. 27.10

The chart with a staff functionary like traffic controller will look like —

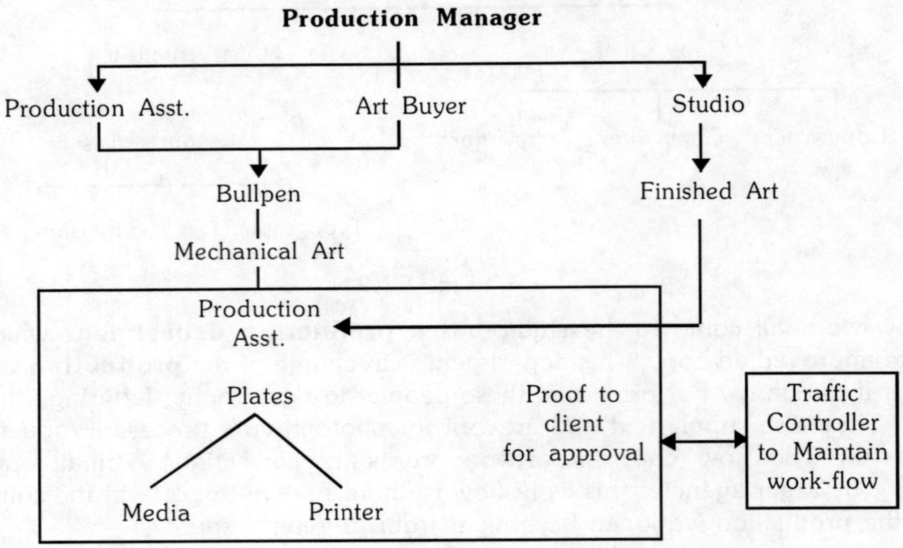

Fig. 27.11

The two important sides, creative as well as production, have been discussed. Now the finished ad is to be sent to different media. Here the first question is what is the total budget, then how it would be allocated on different media, which media would be selected, what would be the frequency, size and position of the ad, when it will be published. All these decisions are taken by a specialist in the agency called **Media Planner**, who is assisted by media research personnel, media buyers etc. Media Planner also receives the tear-off copies from the media when the ad is published.

Most of the ad agencies now have Marketing Research Department who does product research, consumer research, positioning studies, price and distribution research, sales and packaging research and motivational research.

Then there is administrative manager, with office, accounts and finance function. Some agencies have a separate PR department.

Let us have now a comprehensive chart of a typical ad agency.

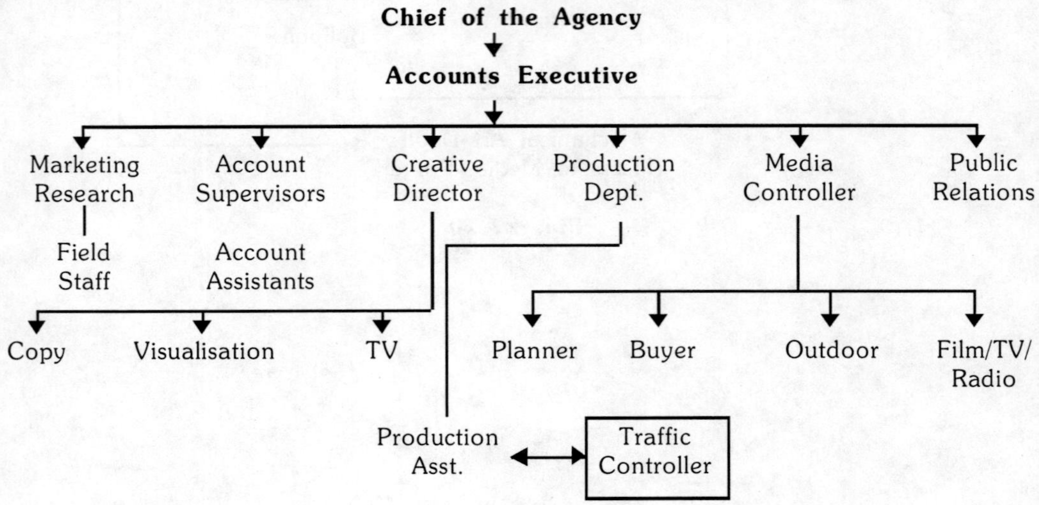

Fig. 27.12

Let us now discuss the top management of the agency.

There are two mechanisms at the top. There can be PLANS BOARD, which consists of a committee of department heads [Accounts Executive, Media Controller or Planner, PR Manager, Creative Director etc.]

The Board takes meetings and plans campaigns by consensus. The client may attend the meeting. The other mechanism could be REVIEW BOARD. Here it reviews or criticises a campaign, which it has not planned or created. In some organisations there is **creative group system**. Each group is responsible for one or more clients. The group is headed by either a copywriter or a visualiser. This system is adopted while launching a new product.

There is only one PLANS BOARD. But in the second system, there could be several independent creative groups operating simultaneously. PLANS BOARD is suitable for a medium-sized agency. Creative Groups are good for a large size agency. The overall structure as the students will appreciate now of an integrated modern agency would be:

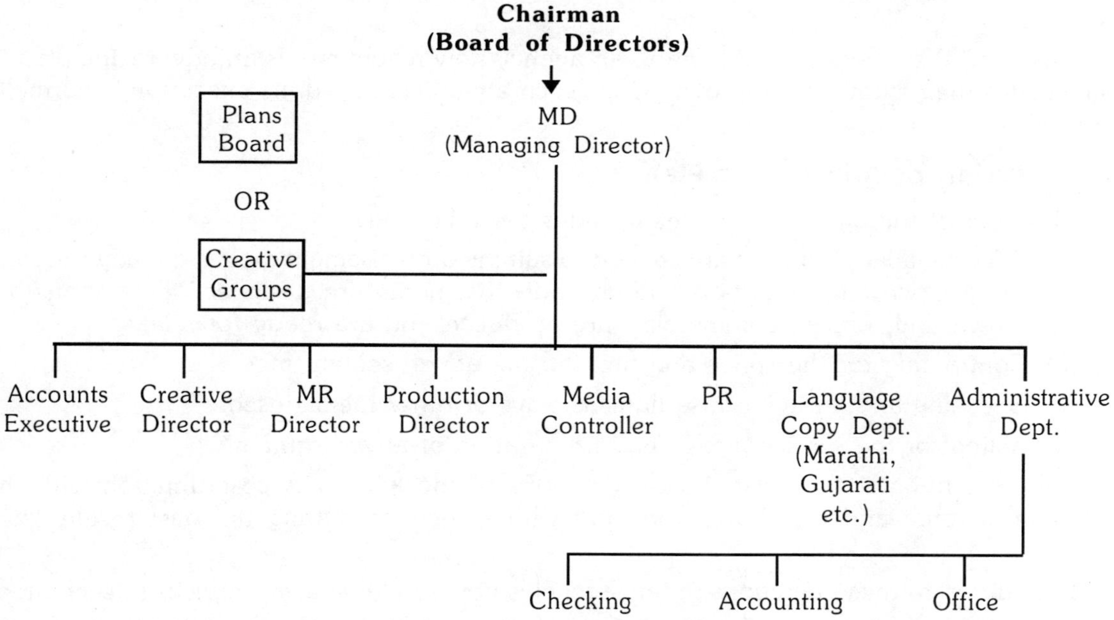

Fig. 27.13

❖ Utility of a Modern Agency

An advertising agency today broadly performs the functions of marketing and advertising, for which a good understanding of the market and the merchandising problem of the advertiser as well as knowledge of media, consumer psychology and advertising appeals are required. However, agencies vary in size and the services rendered by them to a considerable degree. In size, they range from a one-person agency to a large firm employing a few hundred; in services, they range from being agents for advertisement space booking to writing copy, designing advertisement, selecting media for advertisement delivery, preparing advertising programme and market research.

The American Association of Advertising Agencies has outlined the services performed by its member firms to their clients. They are detailed as under:

❖ Advertising Plan

The agency prepares or helps in preparing advertising plans and programmes for its client. This activity necessarily requires a thorough study of the client's product or service, and its advantages and disadvantages, particularly in relation to competitive products. Then comes the information on the present and potential markets for the client's product. Market studies are conducted to have data on who are the buyers, when and where they buy and the clues to why they buy a particular product. Effective advertisements at appropriate times are important for a successful advertising campaign.

The agency should also analyse the marketing methods and channels of distribution used in the past by its clients and their competitors.

The agency then should know fully the various media available and such information on them as their character, influence, circulation, audience and cost. Each medium has its impact on a segment of the market and the availability of space time in an appropriate medium.

Based on the above available data, an agency now recommends an advertising plan to its clients for their study and approval. Once such a plan is okayed, its execution is normally entrusted to the agency.

❖ Execution of Advertising Plan

This part of the agency functions includes the following:

(*a*) Effective advertisements are created to suit the advertisement media, already selected. Copy is written, layouts are made, advertisements are designed, illustrations are drawn and, finally, commercials are produced and are ready for release.

(*b*) Contracting for the space and time on the advertisement media.

(*c*) Checking and verifying insertions/displays or other means used.

(*d*) Billing for the service, space and preparation of advertisement.

The last, but not the least, of the functions of the agency is co-ordination with the client's sales force and distribution network with a view to getting the best results from advertising.

In addition to these functions, many agencies now render special services in such areas as market and sales research, the preparation of product literature for sales-catalogues and leaflets designing product displays and publicity. Some agencies also provide specialised market services, such as product analysis, package designing, sales training, consumer behaviour research and the development of new products.

❖ Organisation of Advertising Agency

All the functions described above are not necessarily performed by all the agencies. They vary widely; and so does their internal organisation. The size of an agency determines its organisation. There are variations and adaptations in the organisation structure of the agencies to suit their individuality. However, one of the two basic types of organisations is found in every agency; the group type and the department type and both organisations have been successful. The selection of a specific type is determined by such factors as the size of the agency, the functions performed by it and the personnel involved in it.

In the group type of organisation, we have a group of individuals servicing a client. The group comprises an account executive, a copywriter and a layout artist and it contacts clients and does creative work for them. It uses other central units, such as media research, mechanical production and accounting, as it needs them. Some groups serve more than one or two clients. The idea is to make a team of trained individuals for specialised work and let this team work on some problem for the same client or other clients. Basically, this type of organisation is more suited for large advertising agencies.

Some authors have referred to the group type of organisation as a matrix-type organisation.

The department type organisation is based on the principle of a separate department for each major advertising function. Each department is headed by a specialist in that particular

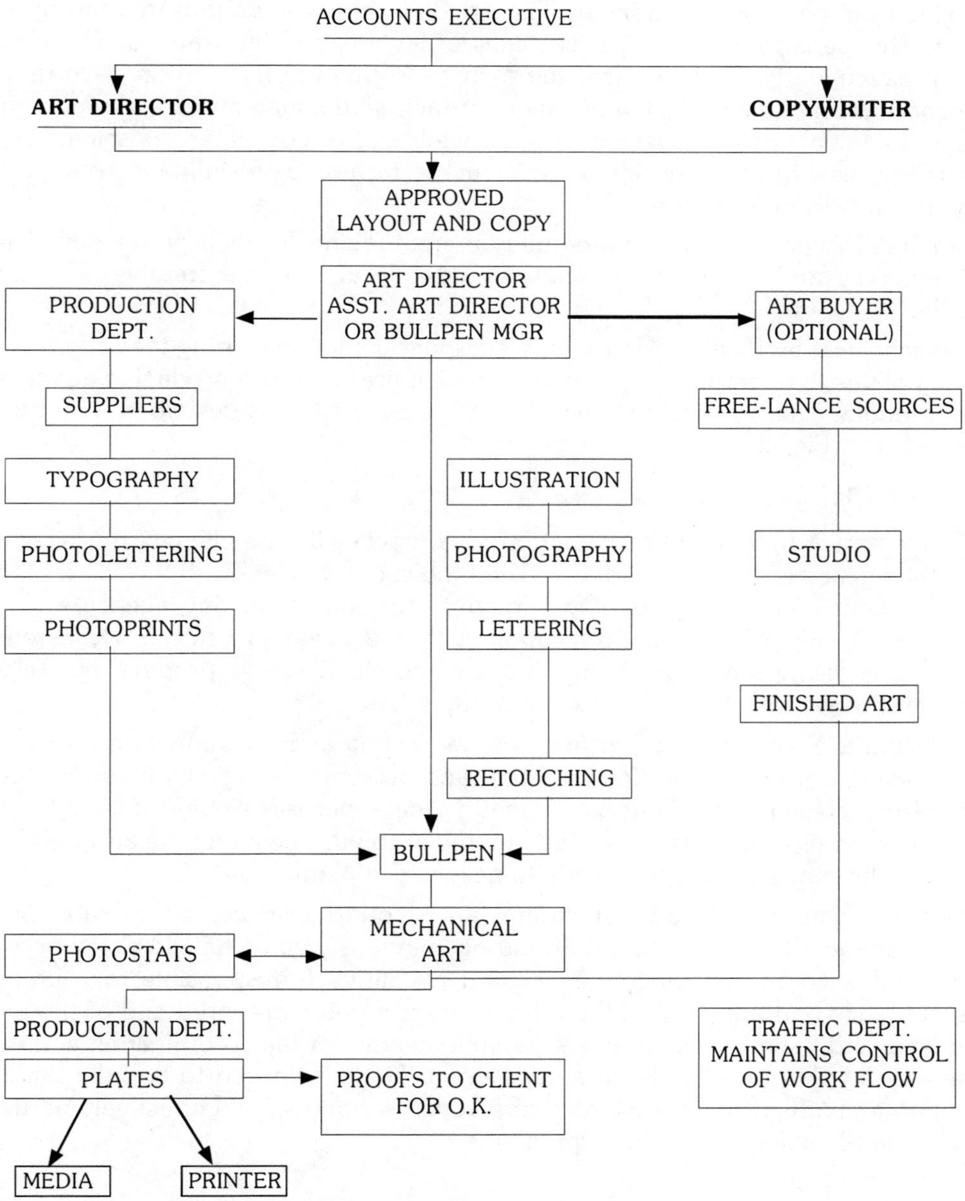

Fig. 27.14 Production in a typical agency

field. Each department serves the clients, unlike a group of individuals serving a client in the group type of organisation. In the department organisation, say, a copywriter works for four or five accounts and writes copy for four or five different products. The persons in each department are responsible to the head of the department rather than to an accounts executive.

The creative services offered by an advertising agency include copy, art, TV and radio production and mechanical production. Some consider the copywriting department to be the most important one in an agency. This is so, if it correctly interprets to prospective buyers the product or service that is advertised in terms of its wants-satisfying ability. The copywriter is assisted by research in determining the effectiveness of the various appeals and the medium through which the copy should appear. The art department adds the dramatising value to advertising. This department develops sketches of layouts and illustrations. The function of the account executive is to co-ordinate the activities of all the parts of an advertisement so as to present it as an effective selling message. In fact, all the employees in the advertisement agency should have an art consciousness as well as the consumer consciousness. Their objective is to present the selling message in such a fashion as to influence one or some of the motivations of the consumers.

Radio and TV commercials require quite different talents for their production. Therefore, agencies doing TV and Radio commercials would have a separate creative department for these media.

The mechanical production department is responsible for converting the copy and artwork into printing plates, typography and materials, which are used in reproducing advertisements in the print media. The production process in a typical agency is described with the help of a flow diagram in Fig. 27.14.

❖ Account Management

We have earlier mentioned the function of contacts with the client. After all, the entire activity of the agency is so performed as to keep the client satisfied with the services rendered to him. The client's satisfaction is of paramount importance for any agency and, for this purpose, a good liaison and communication with the client are absolutely essential. An account, in advertising language, is nothing but the client whose product and service are advertised and to whom other services are rendered.

The accounts executive also performs the marketing and sales function for the agency. He is the salesman of the agency for the client and presents the agency point of view to the client. He also represents the client by presenting the advertiser's point of view to the other members/departments of the agency working on the account. The job of the accounts executive is primarily of liaison, which calls for tactfulness and diplomacy.

Apart from liaison and communication, an accounts executive does sales promotion work for the agency. He has to maintain old accounts as well as develop new accounts. In the function of account servicing, the account executive is responsible for obtaining the client's acceptance and approval of the advertising campaign prepared and of the individual advertisements and the media plan. He is the contact man for the co-ordination and execution of the advertising plan that has been agreed upon. He is supposed to be fully familiar with the marketing and advertising problems of the advertiser and should effectively participate in offering acceptable solutions to those problems.

❖ New Business

The agency, like any other business organisation, has something to sell. The business of the agency should, therefore, grow so that, at any stage, its volume of business may justify its facilities for the services that are offered by it. Moreover, growth is one of the desirable requirements of any business. It is, therefore, logical to have a separate cell in the agency which is responsible for the growth of business. This growth may be achieved either by increasing the business with the present accounts or by getting new accounts. The first is within the jurisdiction of the account executive, while the second may be looked after by him in a small agency. In large agencies, the top management assumes this responsibility. It has a few executives who are exclusively hired for developing new accounts. Some agencies aggressively solicit new business by themselves engaging in advertising. They highlight the agency's competent personnel, the resources and the facilities at their disposal, the influential accounts they service and the successful advertisement campaigns they have handled.

❖ Development of New Agency System

Agencies grew in size, offering more varied and specialised services. Later, in order to cater to the needs of overseas clients and as more multinational corporations came into being, advertising agencies acquired a multinational character. Simultaneously, some other forms of agencies came into being. They are the boutique agency, the *a la carte* agency and the *in-house* agency. Copywriters and art directors, instead of being tied up with a single agency, set-up their own shop to sell the creative function at a fee. These shops have come to be known as creative "boutiques." In an *a la carte agency,* each service is sold on an optional basis at an individual fee. The in-house agency, as its name implies, is owned by the advertiser. In fact, this is nothing but the advertising department of a company. Large corporations have in-house agencies which operate and control the entire advertising programme by themselves. For example, Reliance has Mudra, Malhotras have Bharat Advertising, Golden Tobacco has Govan Advertising and Lohia Machines have Shrishti. By contrast, Lever which promoted and owned Lintas Worldwide diverted its holdings and in India too, the Hindustan Lever followed suit. As Sajid Peerbhoy rightly remarked 'An in-house agency can hardly be sacked.' Here, objectivity and creativity may also suffer. When corporations have a variety of products and services to sell and have a multi-divisional set-up, the in-house agency is very economical to have.

Before we go into a discussion of agency compensation, one more salient point regarding the agency's organisation structure deserves detailed description. This is the facility of the art studio within the agency. A small agency or space-broker may not have an art studio. The artwork in that case is done by hiring an outside artist. But, in our understanding of the modern agency, everyone has a well-developed art studio. It is worth mentioning here that many large pharmaceutical companies do have their own art studios, where product literature is prepared for distribution among medical professionals. The organisation of a typical art studio is shown in Fig. 27.15.

❖ Client-Agency Relationship

As competition increases, companies are demanding more from their advertising agencies. Hence, client-agency relationships are more prone to stress and strain than ever before. There must be a compatability among the client, the agency and the brand. Some clients have a rating method for their agencies, whereas others continue their search for the right working relationship with the right agency. Some clients tend to change agencies when

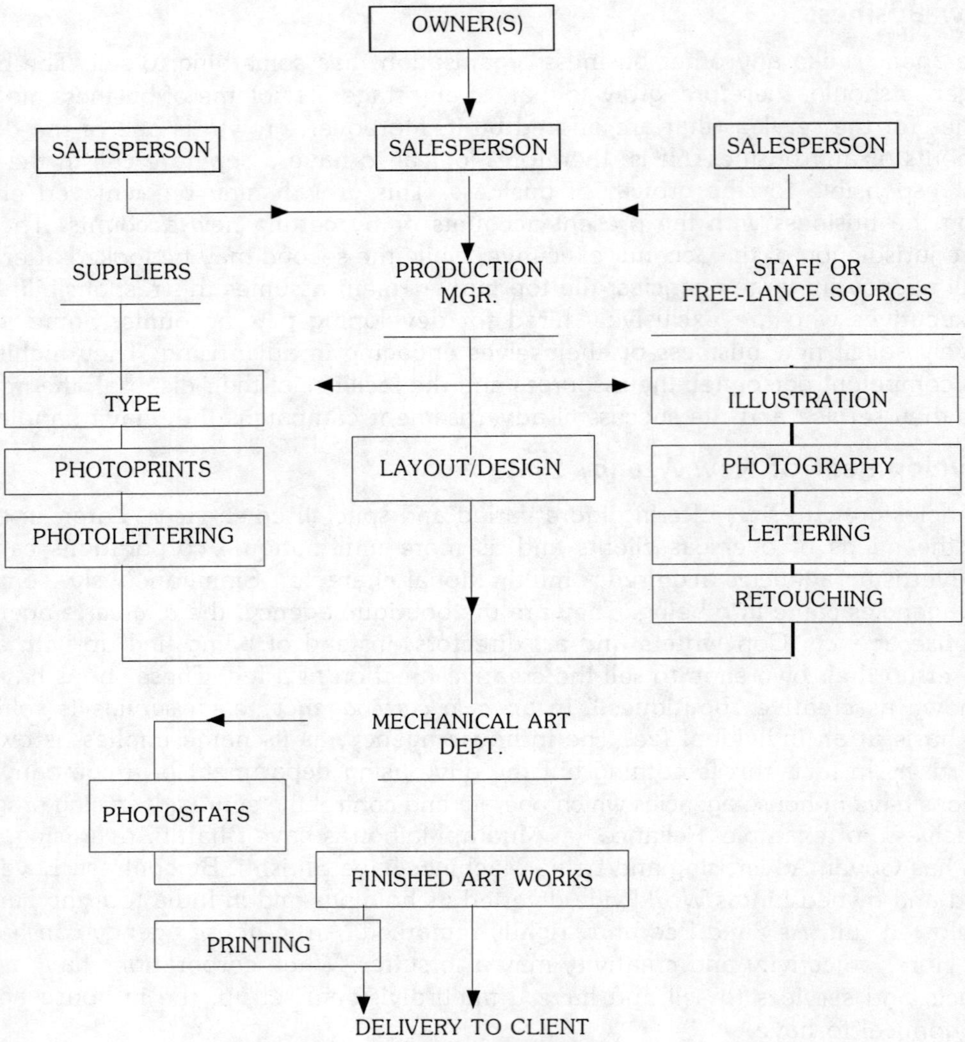

Fig. 27.15 The organisation of a typical art studio

another agency gives an alternative marketing theme, *e.g.*, Ajanta Pharma's Thirty Plus was positioned by previous agency as an aphrodisiac, but was repositioned by another agency as a vitality product which is a cover for virility. Some clients form an enduring relationship, *e.g.*, S.K. Beecham and HTA have an association spanning over 60 years may be due to international alignments. However, international alignments are not always the criterion. Some clients spread their budget on more than one agency. Some clients prefer on appraisal system for the agency. Clients sometimes switch over to a new agencies when the creative team of the old agency move out to a new agency just to maintain 'brand continuity.'

❖ Client-Agency Relationship (CAR)

The classic to-and-fro shuttles between a Client and an Agency are comparable to the matrimonial dithers of Elizabeth Taylor which show 'on-again and off-again' refrain. Many times accounts shift to a new agency and again come back to the old agency. The client-agency relationship may break due to any of the following factors:

(*i*) International alignments may cause a change.
(*ii*) Management changes.
(*iii*) Product conflicts with mergers, takeovers or new product introductions.
(*iv*) Disenchantment with each other.
(*v*) Brand failures.

There can be a variety of minor reasons like payment disputes, differences of opinion about communication strategy etc. Most of the reasons for break up also become the reasons for a win-back account. The break-up may not be for professional reasons, but for personal and cultural reasons. In future, CAR will be much more professional than emotional.

❖ Basic Principles of Client-Agency Relationship (CAR)

These principles are:

(*i*) The agency avoids advertising a close substitute competing product. The client, too, avoids engaging the services of another competing agency.
(*ii*) The agency receives the green signal from the client for all the expenses incurred on his advertising.
(*iii*) The agency keeps the media commission for itself and the client undertakes, to foot the bill promptly.
(*iv*) If the media grants any cash discount, it is passed on to the client.
(*v*) The agency is not taken to task for media lapses in terms of scheduling, positioning, etc.

❖ Basic Principles of Agency-Media Relationship

These principles are:

(*i*) The agency alone is responsible for payment to the media.
(*ii*) The agency does not allow any cut from the commission received from the media to go to the client.
(*iii*) The media do not discriminate amongst the agencies dealt with and follow a uniform policy for all the agencies.
(*iv*) The media do not alter the advertising material without the prior consent of the agency.

❖ Selection of an Advertising Agency

First and foremost, the agency must be **known**. Previously unknown agencies are not preferred.

Secondly, the agency must have **creativity**. Creative people are a little crazy, non-conformists. Creativity does not follow any logical pattern. Creative people are like naughty children. The secret of creativity is **simplicity**.

Thirdly, the agency must have a sound track record, a good deal of **experience**.

Fourthly, the account executive must have ability to **understand the client's problems**.

Fifthly, you may look at the **accounts** they handle and the accounts they have **gained** and **lost**. In other words, the work they have produced for other clients does matter.

Sixthly, the **personal equation** of the client with the agency also matters. If you know them personally, they are **compatible** with you.

Seventhly, their **ability** and **presentation** may make you opt for them. Premier Auto (the company that makes Fiat cars) was **shopping around** for an agency to launch its 118 NE. It invited presentations from various agencies and then shifted its account from its old agency Sistas to Ulka. More and more clients prefer to invite presentations for campaigns of new products and then award the campaign to the agency who they think has made the best presentation.

Lastly, there are some unique considerations, some prefer a small, some a medium, some a large agency. Increasingly, clients prefer to fragment their business, giving different products to different agencies.

Other factors that need consideration is the staff of the agency and its calibre, its flexibility, practical and consumer-oriented approach, the use it makes of MR, its media understanding, the attention it gives to the client, its growth, the ability to handle below-the-line publicity and its international tie-ups.

So creativity, commitment to client and the quality of its top-management go a long way in the selection of an agency. Unfortunately, many think 'creativity' is just another way of saying, 'I like the agency.'

❖ Client-Agency Relationships (CAR)

The average tenure for a client-agency relationship is 9-10 years in India, and about 5-7 years in the developed countries. The frequent client-agency breaks now are attributed to more involvement of top management in ad decisions, and more changes in the top management itself. Global alignments also affect the local accounts. Some clients keep separate agencies for handling different categories worldwide. A client may walkout whenever there is brand or creative fatigue: Creative agencies generally have shorter tenures, because they tend to continue a particular creative even when the market situation changes. When agency is changed, generally a brand is repositioned, *e.g.*, Thums-up was a fun brand. Then it became a taste the thunder brand. Now it is 'I want my thunder' brand. While such repositioning is done, the core values of the brand are kept constant.

❖ Client Turnover

When an advertiser leaves one ad agency and switches over to another, it is known as client-turnover. The various reasons for client-turnover are:

(*i*) The account is not profitable.

(*ii*) The advertiser is interested in a new medium with which the present agency is not familiar.

(*iii*) The client and agency perceive the ad strategy in a drastically different manner.

(*iv*) Lack of co-ordination between the top Executives of the client and the Agency.

(*v*) Change for the sake of change.

(*vi*) Staff changes also lead to client-turnover.

(*vii*) Perceived unreasonableness of the other party.

(*viii*) Loss of confidence.

(*ix*) When the client does not like the ad programme conceived by the agency.

(*x*) Politics and nepotism result in client-turnover.

(*xi*) Separation of client and agency is an easy thing to bring about.

Researchers have identified as many as 40 factors which influence the sale of a product, advertising being one of them. But the Agency is almost always blamed if something goes wrong and the relationship terminates. There are three reasons for this:

1. It is very difficult to measure advertisement's contribution to the success or failure of a product.
2. Legally, it is so simple to terminate a relationship (*e.g.*, a few weeks' notice).
3. New people in the client's office might like to have a change.

Again, sometimes creative people leave an agency. The client therefore naturally changes to a new agency, because the people who worked for him are not there.

Many times, there is a change for the sake of change. Clients prefer an agency that is currently popular. Sometimes, the agency itself voluntarily resigns from an account. Maybe, there are differing perceptions. Maybe, the agency is accepting another competitive account. Agencies also abandon a consistently losing account. Agencies also resign when the client is over-bearing. Many ad people resent the diktats from the client about their own professional work.

Agency Compensation: The method of paying the agency has been a subject of much discussion nowadays at almost all the meetings of advertisement agency associations and advertisement clubs. There are, basically, three methods in practice. They are:

(*a*) *Commission System:* This is the most common and the oldest system of remuneration. The agency is paid a fixed commission by the media on the advertising bill for the advertisement space bought by the agency. This fixed rate of commission is 15 per cent in the USA as well as in India. Though the rate varies from country-to-country, the rate of 15 per cent is almost universal. For example, an agency places a full-page advertisement in a magazine, which costs, say, ₹ 10,000/-. After the advertisement has run, the magazine (the medium) will bill the agency for ₹ 10,000/-, less 15 per cent. This means that the agency will pay to the medium ₹ 8,500/-. The agency, in turn, will bill the advertiser for ₹ 10,000/-. Thus, ₹ 1,500/- will go towards the efforts made and the services rendered by the agency in the preparation of the advertisement and its delivery in the medium. Indian and Eastern Newspaper Society (IENS) accreditation earns the agencies 15% commission and 60 days of credit from the media. Non-accredited agencies have to pay the media in advance and get 10% commission which in real terms translates to a miserable 5 per cent. The popular criticism of this method is that the agency is always tempted to recommend for several deliveries through expensive media in order to draw a larger remuneration.

(*b*) *Fee System:* The system came into effect following a controversy between an Advertiser and an Agency. The former argued that 15 per cent commission was too high a rate, whereas the agency took the stand that it was unremunerative for the many services rendered to the client. The fee system is used in TV advertising; when once the commercial is created, it may be used over a long time. A flat fee is paid to the agency for the specialised services performed by it.

(*c*) The third type of compensation consists of *service charges.* These are added to the cost of materials and services bought by the agency for the client in artwork, photography, typography, plates, etc. Normally, it is cost plus 15 per cent.

In practice, one of the above systems of compensation or a combination of the fee-and-media-commission plan or a method by which commissions granted by the media are credited against professional fees, is used.

Industrial advertising, involving the preparation of catalogues and sales materials and retail advertising, point-of-purchase materials for advertising and direct-mail prices do not usually involve a commission. Here, the fee basis of compensation is mostly employed. When a new product advertising is involved, the agencies are remunerated on a special fee basis.

The agency-advertiser relationship is like the physician-patient or the lawyer-client relationship; the patient pays the physician's fee, whether he gets relief or not. However, the quality of the physician's services will be ultimately reflected in the number of patients visiting him or the volume of business he has. But there is no direct link between the fee paid and the effectiveness of medical treatment to an individual patient. As a patient, he is entitled to get an effective cure in return for the fee he has paid. The lawyer, too, takes the fee, irrespective of the judgement in the case. However, he faithfully argues the case for his client. This raises the question of the efficacy of the remuneration method of advertising. The ideal and desirable method must relate compensation to its effectiveness in some form or the other. Only such a method will have a greater acceptability among the advertisers. Not only this, such compensation method will encourage the growth of a greater measure of professionalisation in advertising. This, however, looks simple but difficult to implement, because the necessary condition for the success of any such compensation plan is to find methods for measuring advertising effectiveness. Once this has been achieved, it would not be difficult to correlate it with the compensation payable to the agency. We shall discuss the method of evaluating advertising effectiveness in a separate chapter later on. The possible future methods of compensation, using suitable scales for measuring the effectiveness of advertisement, can be devised. However, till other alternative methods are available, we have to continue with the existing methods.

❖ Trends in Compensation of Ad Agencies

Several multi-brand advertisers are going in for bulk media purchases through a single source (either an ad agency or an in-house outfit). Here the agency is appointed as AOR; Agency On Record. AOR creates and releases its own advertising. In addition, AOR releases advertisements created by another agency. Thirdly, AOR releases the software it has invested in. Generally, when two agencies are involved, the releasing agency gets 21 per cent and the agency that provided creative gets 12.5 per cent. In case of a software, the situation is complicated.

Some clients may opt to purchase creative work on a flat fee and negotiate media commission on the basis of volume with AOR.

Compensation at the rate of 15% of billing is called billing-based compensation. Compensation on the basis of costs is called fee-based compensation. Internationally a third option has emerged — performance-based compensation whereby a performance falling below expectation will earn the agency only 14% commission and a performance which is successful will earn it 16%. However, this is too subjective.

❖ Commission System

Though lousy, there is, no better alternative to commission system. 'Payment by results' is experimented with. But still commission system is not a dinosaur. It may not be the best, but it is the 'least worst'. Fees are okay to sell time, but advertising agencies sell ideas of unlimited value. Commissions put a value on an idea. The media spend is an index of the value the client attaches to the idea. Commissions however cannot relate efforts taken by the agency and the rewards earned. There can be a combination of fee-based system and commission. There can be several variations of commission — fixed scale commission, sliding scale commission.

❖ Undercutting by the Agencies

Advertising now competes with sales promotion and Direct Marketing (DM) for funds. There is no breakthrough in advertising theory ever since the concept of *positioning* materialised. In fact both these facts are not responsible for the not-so-healthy bottom-lines of the advertising agencies in the States. The culprit is the higgling and haggling over the advertising commissions by the clients. US Agencies have been receiving less than the prescribed 15 per cent since long. In a way, it is a pricing strategy for an ad agency to attract its clients. The subject of commission negotiation is an amathema to Indian agencies. Unconfirmed reports suggest that even Indian agencies have started offering kickbacks to the clients. However, it is not done in a transparent manner and so becomes unpleasant and unethical. With transparency, no one will deny this basic marketing right to manoeuvre price in this manner to the agencies. Lower prices may damage an agency's reputation for quality. High prices may be an associated with quality, but if it is an illusion and the delivery does not match the expectations, there can be a rapid decline in business.

Let commission negotiations be open. This will be conducive for growth in the long-run. The bottom-line will be healthier, if extravagance shown by the ad people is curtailed.

All said and done, 15% commission is ideal.

❖ Agency Of Record (AOR) Concept

Media buying is being centralised by heavy spenders. They appoint a single agency to buy space-time for all its brands, *e.g.,* Unilever has appointed HTA as the central media buying agency for the Unilever group of companies, though the creative work is executed mainly by Lintas. HTA, in its turn, has set up an Agency Of Record (AOR), Fulcrum which aims to deal with Lever brands exclusively. Media marketers now negotiate with the big buyers and that is the basis of the concept of AOR. AOR starts investing in updated and accurate data and sets up system which otherwise were taken for granted. It bargains for a bulk amount and is not taken for a ride by the intermediaries. So far only media planning function was given some thought, but now clients have accepted that media buying is also equally important and is a specialised activity in its own right. However, AOR sings a requiem to 15% ad agency's commission. It is still a moot point how far an AOR can do justice to the client.

There is a lack of qualified people in this field. We do not have specially trained media buyers in India. They are just negotiators.

❖ Future of Advertising Agency

"The competition would be keen and intense in the advertising business in India in the coming years, but it need not pose a problem of survival if Indian advertising agencies show enough resilience to exploit emerging opportunities." This view was expressed at the All-India Advertising Convention held in Chennai in April 1982. The future of the advertising agency seems to be bright. Opportunity awaits the agency to broaden its scope of services in spite of the various emerging challenges on the advertising scene. These challenges pertain to market, media, motivations or putting messages across to the audience.

The biggest challenge to Indian advertising professionals today is the negative public image which this so-called image building industry of advertising has projected of itself. False and misleading advertising does often take consumers for a ride. This was highlighted by the Sachar Committee in its report. The Second Press Commission has also adversely commented on the advertising sector. It has suggested the imposition of the news-to-ad ratio and made several other sweeping recommendations which, if implemented, will create many problems for the agencies. Voices have been raised to clamp ad censorship or to enact punitive legislation against misleading advertisements, false presentation, unfair sales promotion contests, etc. The other disturbing aspect is the steep rise in the rates of TV commercials, radio and press ads. Now comes the conflict between Generic Promotion and brand advertising. Today, there is a demand for greater accountability to the client for the money spent on advertising.

With mushroom growth of agencies, several unethical practices to wean away clients raise their head. In-house agencies are a problem. Even then, the 70s were years of turmoil, the 80s an era of consolidation, the 90s a decade of big agencies and the first decade of the new millennium has made the agencies the custodians of brand. Many medium size agencies will become big in due course. Advertisers will be after a total communication package, advertising being only one part of it.

❖ Conservative Ad Industry

To Ruper Howell, the managing partner of an agency bearing his name, and industry, *i.e.*, perhaps the most conservative industry, with the possible exception of the medical profession. He says that banking is more innovative than advertising is. Agencies in future will have to embrace the total concept of marketing. The commission system keeps the agencies working on narrow margins. This has to go if agencies are ever to be taken seriously. The agency and business should have a serious partnership. The agency should receive a bonus if the clients bottom line improves. Agencies of future should be leaner and fatter. Agencies of future will be concentrating on brand management and holistic marketing.

Communication Package: So far big agencies concentrated only on one aspect of marketing communication — advertising. There was no concentration on other components of marketing communication like public relations, direct promotions, launching of new products or rejuvenating the old. The specialist units have now come up on the scene to cater to these diverse communication needs. They are small non-agency backed units. The following table illustrated this point:

Unit	*Area of work*	*Remarks*
Select Direct, Mumbai	Direct Marketing	
Event Creation and Marketing, Mumbai	Special Projects	
Party Cruisers	Corporate impression management company	Involved in launches and promotions
Cause Celebre	Social marketing and advertising	Diversification in event marketing
Modi creata	Sales Promotions to SP.	Thematic approach
A1 Media	Unconventional promotion from city	Special buses to Shopper's Stop

Bigger agencies have also started setting up specialised divisions to cater to other aspects of marketing communications.

* * *

28 MANAGING SALES PROMOTION AND SALES DISPLAYS

"Sales Promotion" (SP) is a technical term in marketing and is used for measures which are direct inducements to sales. In a sense, the whole of marketing is sales promotion, but we restrict SP to promotion schemes directed to the three target audiences:

1. Consumers.
2. Trade (distributors, retail chemist shops etc).
3. Sales force (Sales representatives, sales supervisors etc).

Sales promotion is a short-term exercise whereas advertising is a long-term brand building task.

The budget for SP has increased of late. As of 1991, almost 60 per cent was spent on SP and the remaining 1/3 was spent on advertising in the US. Similar trends seem to be emerging in India in the last few years in some categories. SP requires a *schematic* ad campaign whereas advertising requires a *thematic* ad campaign.

❖ Managing Consumer Promotions

Consumer promotions are incentives to consumers to improve product usage at the level of consumer. Such schemes include over-the-counter give aways (say, key-chains), price-offs (say, a reduced price for a pain balm), quantity-offs (reduced price for a large bottle of shampoo), sampling (shampoo sachets or Ariel detergent sachets), container premiums, self-liquidating premiums, coupons (Stayfree Napkins), personality premiums, refund offers, trading stamps, contests (Amrutanjan Pain Balm Contest) and lucky draws (Medimix Soap Lucky Draw Scheme).

The scheme chosen in pharmaceutical field is restricted to over-the-counter products and cosmetics. Its success depends upon creativity in designing and implementing the scheme.

Since doctors as prescribers are indirect consumers, many SP schemes in pharmaceutical industry are directed towards them for ethical products. These days the schemes have evolved from a simple give-away gift of a ball-pen to costly give-away gifts of gold jewellery and household items. Many consumer durables like TV's and cars are also on offer to the medical profession. Some companies also promise a package tour to exotic Indian and foreign locales.

Some check-points for SP schemes for consumer promotion:

The basic aim is to increase consumption usage. The incidental aims are:

1. To make slow moving products fast moving ones.
2. To regularise sales fluctuations.
3. To overcome seasonal recession.
4. To clear unsold stocks of old products.
5. To effect sales of a specific pack size (Vicks large size bottle) or in a specific market(s).
6. To help launch a new product (say Cello instead of Hello on telephone and get the gift, identify independent personality and get the Alphanso mangoes).
7. To meet a competitor's strategy.
8. To build goodwill by sharing the gay spirit.
9. To improve products visibility on the shelf.
10. To encourage trade to support the product.

❖ Scheme Selection

The scheme must be novel and innovative. It should not be easily copiable. To illustrate, in-pack premium is better to promote sales of a specific pack while price-off is better to clear unsold stocks.

The scheme's are all product specific. What succeeds for one product may not succeed for other products. The same holds true for markets. The time also determines the success. What has succeeded may not necessarily succeed in future too?

The company must make sure that the benefit of the scheme should reach the consumers for whom the scheme is meant. Unscrupulous traders and transportation bottlenecks may hamper the scheme. Many were aggrieved when they did not get Madonna's audio cassette on Pepsi drink's crowns.

Secondly, the premiums advertised must be readily available at retail points during the entire period of scheme. Here proper forecasting and sourcing are important. The common problems are non-availability of the premium/differing quality of the premium item.

❖ Scheme Execution

The target market area is to be carefully selected and should include the neighbourhood satellite markets to avoid leakage, given the fact the tax structure is not uniform over the states.

The accountability of redemption of coupons or refunds and rebates should be properly fixed.

❖ Promoting the SP Scheme

Promotional support is a must for any SP scheme. The campaign should be directed to the consumers for whom it is meant. It should also take into confidence the trade channels. The sales force should know its role and be motivated to do its best.

❖ Follow-up

The market is to be assessed soon after the scheme begins. The monitoring covers brand/premium availability, brand visibility, movement of the brand at the retail outlets on a day-to-day basis, competitor's countermoves etc. Timely intervention in the form of reminder ads, additional deployment of sales force, additional POP material etc., may sometimes be and necessary.

❖ Consumer Contest

The contest invites consumers to participate by exercising their creative skills. They are generally open for a period of five weeks (or more). *Inter alia,* they aim to generate greater awareness of the brand/sponsor. Some epecific objectives of consumer contests are:

1. To revitalise a tepid brand.
2. To increase product usage.
3. To introduce new products.
4. To familiarise consumers with unique/specific aspects of brand or its usage.
5. To measure ad effectiveness.
6. To generate mailing list.
7. To generate overall goodwill.
8. To generate slogans to promote the brand.

Legal aspects of the contests must be carefully considered. These are governed by the Prize Competition Act, 1955. The permission of the District Collector/Competent Authority is a pre-requisite. This contest should not attract the penal provisions of the MRTP Act.

The four important factors on which the success of the contests depend are: the type of contest, the prizes offered, the promotion of the contest, the rules governing the contest.

❖ Types of Contest

The contest should not be too difficult. It will restrict the participation and hence the very aim of contest will be defeated. The contest should be easy but still stimulating giving mental satisfaction to the participants.

Reason-why, sentence completion, brand name, slogan/essay writing, special skills like cookery etc., could be the theme of the contest.

❖ Prize Schedule

The first prize is bumper one. There are a few second prizes. There are more third prizes. The contest these days have many consolation and early bird prizes. Prizes offered are well-known brands or their money equivalents. The closing date is to be strictly adhered to. Extensions are always seen with suspicion. The result announced and the closing date should not be spaced. The pre-fixed date for results and the media for their announcement are desirable.

❖ Promotion of the Contest

Media advertising of the contest, support by trade and sales force is a must. The ads should be periodically repeated. There should be reminder ads towards the close of the contest. The Entry Forms can be made available in the media/at the dealers.

❖ Rules

The rules should be clear and unambiguous. The panel of judges should have a balance of persons selected on the basis of their social status and persons selected on the basis of their technical expertise. Their decisions should be final and binding. The rules should specify how and when the winners will be notified. They should also declare the ownership rights over the entries. The employees of the sponsor/ad agency are not allowed to participate.

❖ Managing Trade Promotions

The distribution channel is offered sales inducements to motivate them to support a brand by providing it more than their usual push.

Many of these schemes are dealer loaders, *e.g.*, merchandise deals, discounts, buying and selling allowances, shelf-space incentives, display contests sales contests, coupons, gifts, trade allowance, premium or push money and POP materials.

The trade promotions help build a customer traffic at the retail outlet. They improve sales/profitability. They build up buyer-seller relationship.

❖ Organisation

There are certain inherent conflicts. The parties should be clear about goals and role of one another. The manufacturer must appreciate the trader's interest. Similarly, traders should be responsive in terms of performance.

The basic considerations in trade promotions are:

(*a*) The capabilities of the parties. The retailers are poor in the administration of complete schemes, whereas wholesalers are poor at generating primary demand. The sponsors, therefore should carry out these tasks.

(*b*) The terms/schemes should discourage unscrupulous trade practices on the part of trade.

(*c*) Scheme should be properly communicated. Results expected must be clearly stated.

(*d*) Regular supplies of products/gifts during the pendency of the scheme.

(*e*) Booking of shelf-space of prominent dealers must be done sufficiently in advance.

(*f*) The gifts should be good quality and useful.

(*g*) Sales contests/display contests.

1. Proper selection of dealers.
2. Assistance to these dealers.
3. Communication of the team of judges and criteria of judging.
4. Prizes and consolation prizes.
5. Target assigned must be in relation to trading area potential. Prize on zonal basis.

(*h*) POP material and its display need supervision. Only 15% POP material supplied is displayed and that too for half of its useful life.

(*i*) Retailers who launch their own schemes can be persuaded to provide a special support to the company's products.

(*ii*) MRTP provisions must be respected. The discount period should not be less than 10 days. The original price and the bargain price must be stated. The quality must be specified. The maximum and minimum discount must be stated.

❖ Managing Sales Representatives' Level Promotion

SP is offered at the level of sales representatives or the sales force. It consists of incentive programmes or sales contests.

❖ Sales Representatives' Incentives

These are motivational tools. These are rewards or performance. The four methods to offer these are:

1. Rewards linked to unit sales on actual basis.
2. Rewards to those who cross a specific percentage of sales quota performance.
3. Rewards for individual performance.
4. Rewards for special achievements (as spelt out by the marketing department.)

Rewards may be in cash or in kind or a mix of the two. These are cost effective motivators and improve Sales Representative's productivity. Some basic reasons for their intensive use are:

1. Moral boosters.
2. Increase units sold per sales representative.
3. Increase sales per sales representatives.
4. Launch new products.
5. Increase sales on average per account.
6. Boost recession — period sales.
7. Upgrade existing accounts to high ticket products.
8. Revive old products.

The managerial considerations are discussed along with sales contests.

❖ Sales Representative Contests

Here SRs are made to compete amongst them to motivate them to achieve higher goals and benefit the organisation used. Positively they are SRs.

Over-enthusiastic SRs may resort to dumping, overloading inventories, cheating and neglecting of customer service. It is therefore, crucial that these contests are handled properly.

❖ Themes

The themes could be creatively chosen. Direct themes could be obtaining new accounts or improving the market share. Novel themes the focus is on recreation and fund linked with the current sales scenario. Some novel themes could be:

1. Let's hunt for the hidden treasure (find new customers).
2. Make your customer fat (sell more to existing customers).
3. Planting the gold (sell more profitable product mix).
4. Healthy customer, healthy sales (more profits per customer) etc.

Themes must be measurable objectively and be relevant to company's sales curve. Then only can they ensure wider participation.

❖ Rules

Everything must be specific. What constitutes a sale — whether an order or a delivery or payment received? What constitutes a new order? What about sales returns after the contest period? Every achievement must be rated in terms of points. All these will help avoid hard and bitter feelings later.

❖ Participation

Large-sales force with a hierarchical order call for contests for different groups and eligibility criteria restrict the participation to each group. In a contest, individuals should not be pitted against each other. A variety of contests/a variety of prices do help in this direction.

❖ Promotion

SR level promotion must have an element of excitement and also should be capable of entertaining the participants. Mostly in-house journals, circular letters, personal letters, motivational letters, reminders are used to promote the contests. Later, the announcement of a few more prizes, photos, writing of reminders etc. generate an air of expectancy. On the close of the contest, wide publicity is given to the achievers and their photos are flashed. Personal meetings with the executives are arranged. Soon, thereafter, further activities are planned to avoid dipping sales later after the close of the contest.

Some pitfalls which the management must guard against:

1. The goals must not be unattainable.
2. Rewarding just one person is to be avoided.
3. Sales volume should not be the only goal of each contest.
4. Some prizes for each contest are to be avoided.
5. Sometimes, staffers other than sales representatives should be included in the contest.
6. Year-end contests are seen as poor planning to make up deficiencies, and hence are better avoided.
7. Contest is not an intelligence test, and so it should be absolutely clear.
8. There is no 'fair' or 'just' contest. Sales contests have goals to accomplish. Some goals are easier for accomplishment for some than for others. (*e.g.*, territory potential may be different and hence high potential leads to easy accomplishment of goals).

❖ Evolution of SP

SP is to be measured by pre-testing it, monitoring it during implementation and by post-testing.

Pre-testing ascertains cost-effectiveness of various alternatives. It also assesses the most preferred terms on which to offer scheme. Pre-testing is done by panel method or by mail survey or by a field-study.

While monitoring during the implementation, collect data on the following:

1. Product movement.
2. Territory-wise sales.
3. Outlet wise sales.

4. Goals set Vs. Past results.
5. Competitive moves.
6. Market mood.
7. Problems encountered.

Post-testing is basically analytical. Here performance is measured with respect to:

1. Redemption rate of coupons.
2. Sales attained.
3. Cost effectiveness.
4. Redemption of trading stamps.
5. Sales turnover of special packs or self-liquidators.
6. Number of entries received for the consumer contest etc.

Post-testing is done by:

1. Market research studies.
2. Observation method in the stores.
3. Desk-analysis of collected data.

Direct measurements, if possible, relate to the figures of this period to the previous period and find out the incremental sales (rather than gross sales).

Studies on SP give us the following guidelines:

1. Short purchase cycles mean short-term effects.
2. The earliest redemptions are incremental sales.
3. Incremental sales are difficult to obtain for brands having a large market share.
4. Coupon with a sample is twice as effective as a coupon alone.
5. Hidden costs of promotion are:
   (*a*) High level of inventory with trade.
   (*b*) Competitors rise up their sales promotion.
   (*c*) Discount offered during promotion period become the base-line for future promotions.
6. SP designed to suit local market conditions is more effective.

❖ Role of Sales Representative

Sales representative can contribute to make SP a cost effective effort. They also give constant feedback on the market to the company. They monitor the market when SP effort is on and make the trade receptive to it. They discover room for expenditure control.

The budget for SP has inceased of late. As of 1991, almost 60% was spent on SP and the remaining 1/3 was on advertising in the US. Similar trends seem to be emerging in India in the last few years in some categories.

SP requires a 'schematic' ad campaign whereas advertising requires a 'thematic' ad campaign.

❖ Strategic Objectives of SP

1. SP can be used to *convert* customers of other brands and make them switch to our brands.

2. SP seeks to *attract new customers* to the product category.
3. SP tries to *maintain* the present base of customers against competitive onslaught.

❖ Sales Displays

Retail chemists do have facilities for displays, through mostly in urban areas. To attract the customer traffic, many over-the-counter products are displayed in chemists' shops.

Displays are in store presentations. They may be relevant information accompanying the display. The products on display arrest attention and increase the interest of the customers in them. This leads to sales. Diplays have become a part of a retail chemist's atmosphere and have great promotional value.

Technical Representatives have to help the chemists when the products are displayed. They have to motivate them to arrange the display.

Display perform the following functions:

(*i*) Products are exposed extensively.
(*ii*) Products look better.
(*iii*) Products invite attention and kindle interest.
(*iv*) Product information is highlighted.
(*v*) Facilitate a sale transaction.
(*vi*) Impulse products get additional sales.
(*vii*) Remind customers about their buying intentions.
(*viii*) Ensure product security and storage.

Displays, to sum up, have a three-fold task —

(*i*) to motivate the passers-by to stop and take notice of the product, and then to motivate them to step in.
(*ii*) once the passers-by are in, what is emphasised is the product exposure irrespective of whether they buy or not.
(*iii*) those who come as buyers are motivated to buy a large quantity on the strength of smart display.

Displays help the manufacturing organisation as well as the retail outlets. They project a retail outlet and a product's personality. They create an ambience, provoke a desire and trigger a mood. They are thus silent.

❖ Display Aesthetics

Sales representative or the dealers or both of them who design the displays follow certain aesthetic principles. Some of these are given below:

Unity gives a unified whole appearance to different display units. *Balance* leads to harmony amonst them. *Formal balance* means just — apposing the right and left by the same weight, height or number. It is symmetrical. *Informal balance* leads to a novel attempt and hence attractiveness which is due to asymmetry. *Proportion* is related to the relative sizes of display units. *Dominance* means a specially prepared larger size product/pack, *e.g.*, a Vicks bottle or a tonic bottle larger than the original. *Dominance* can also be achieved by special effects. *Contrast* uses differing light shades, product offering and product of different sizes, different colours *etc.*

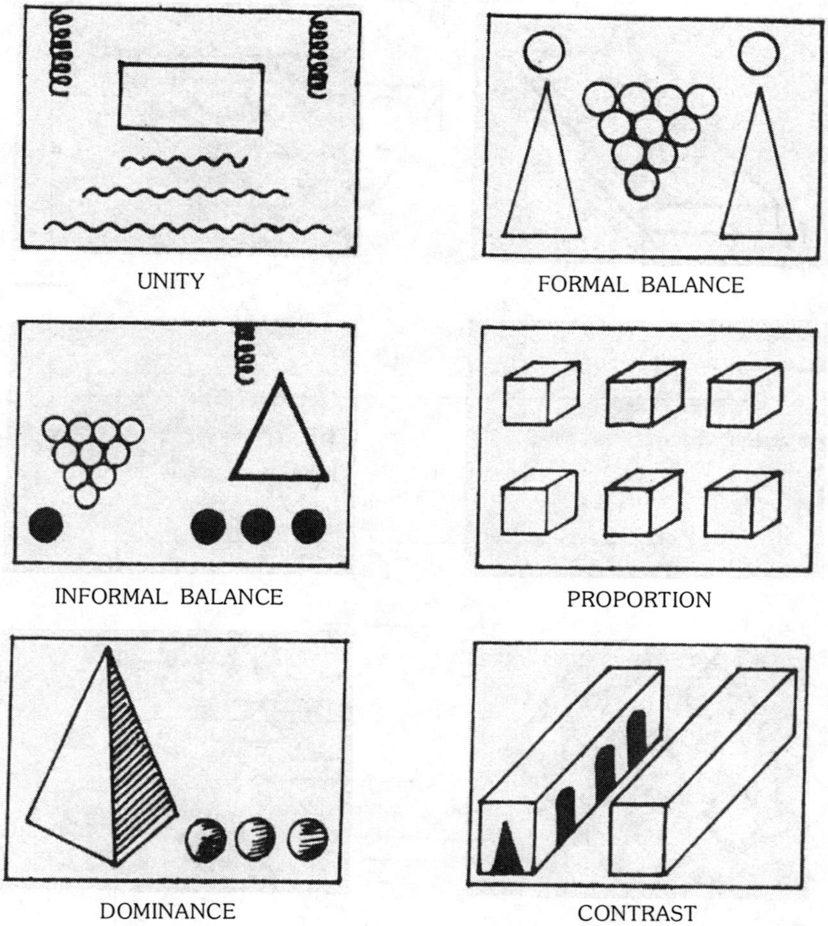

Fig. 28.1

❖ Popular Display Patterns

Popular display patterns are given in Fig. 28.2.

❖ Types of Display

The displays are traffic builders and raise the sales of displayed items and other items too. How to display effectively is the main problem these days. A good display is a creative task. The basic displays are classified in the following table.

❖ Managing Displays

Displays are to be planned and executed properly. Display planning involves utilisation of space, economising, ensuring maximum exposure, aesthetics and how they suit the existing layout and changes to be made.

Execution of displays involves ensuring adequate stock of items being displayed, area allocation, display materials and fixtures, advertising the retail outlet where display has been arranged and training of staff. While executing the display, the windows used, the signs used, the lighting used, the ambience created are to be attended to.

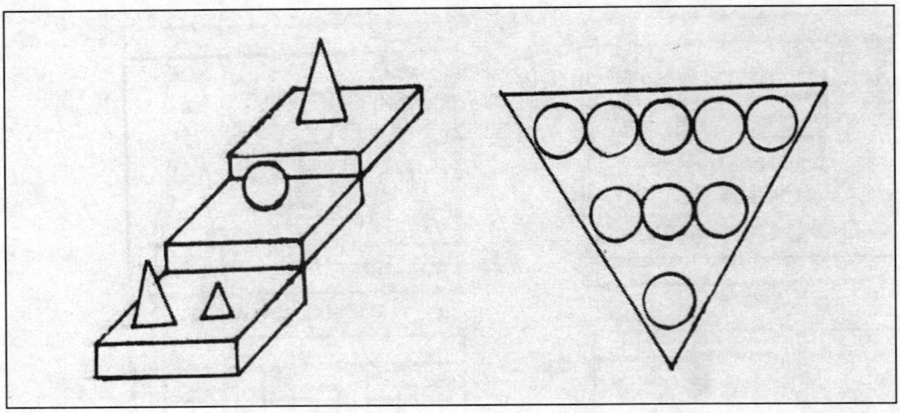

STEP PATTERN
Multi-tiered placing of trays, resembling a series of steps

FAN PATTERN
Basic is heavy. Widens drastically as the height increases

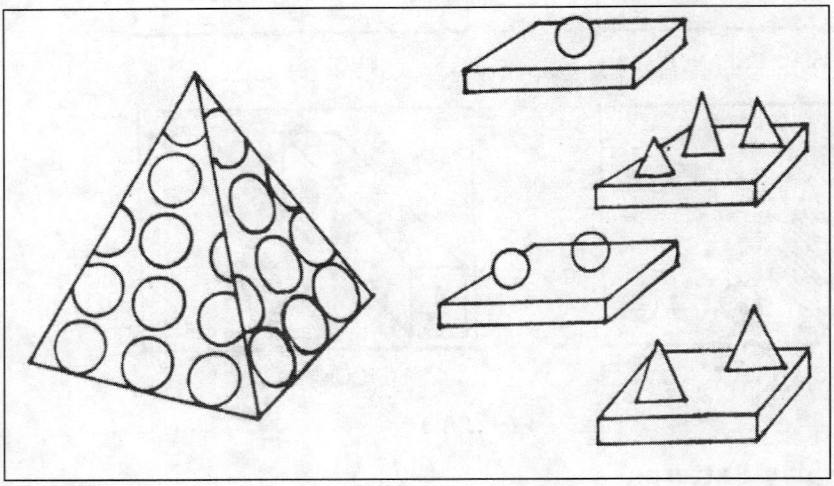

PYRAMID PATTERN
Three-dimensional pyramid, each side representing an attractive triangle

ZIGZAG PATTERN
Combination of step and pyramid. The merchandiše sems zig-zag along the way

Fig. 28.2 Display Patterns

Display management should have an element of creativity. Maybe, outside experts can be of help here. The displays are changed. It has, of course, the budgetary constraint.

Displays at retail chemist shops can be arranged by them on their own or with the help of the sales representatives of the company. The displays sponsored by the company must be sold to the chemists. Their co-operation is of utmost importance. The chemists should be convinced about the objectives of the display and should be trained and motivated.

❖ Why Dealers Show Poor Interest?

Maybe, the rewards are not attractive. Perhaps the space available and the display requirements do not match. There is the monotony of repeating the same pattern time and

Display types	*Remarks*
Assortment Display	A wide variety of merchandise put on display. *Open variety:* The customer can try the product. *Closed variety:* Products are enclosed in glass windows or are pre-packed.
Theme Display	They create a proper atmosphere. Theme related to a national, international or local event; or festival. Many more creative themes can be identified, *e.g.*, ethnic image to promote herbal cosmetics.
Life-style Displays	Focus on AIO: Activities, interest and opinions of target audience.
Rack Displays	Products (mostly household) are neatly hanged from a rod. They can be mobile too.
Ensemble Displays	Focus on selling a concept rather than a product. It is suggestive selling mannequins are used.
Unit Displays	Units looking similar are displayed as a unified whole.
Classification	Depth and width of product line exhibited.
Dominance Displays	Arranged on product basis. Products are placed vertically on walls, floors or all over.
Videotape Displays	The pre-recorded tapes are used to talk to shoppers.

again. Sales represents or the company do not help the chemist in arranging the display, chemists are not given the infrastructure like the display material and kits.

❖ Suggestions to Dealers

1. Visibility must be ensured. The preferred position is the front door.
2. The display should give an opportunity to inspect the product physically.
3. Displays hung from the ceiling should be low enough.
4. Displays should not conceal the merchandise.
5. Displays should be well-illuminated.

❖ Motivating the Dealers

The sponsoring company can motivate the dealers by:

(*i*) Providing display fixtures and materials (on special terms).
(*ii*) By promoting the retailer in co-operative advertising.
(*iii*) By organising a display contest.
(*iv*) By showing one, effort to others through a photo or video clipping.
(*v*) Visit of mystery shoppers who evaluate the displays and reward the outstanding ones.

To illustrate, Food Specialities Ltd. and Vicks Vapor Rub have succeeded in establishing their brands by motivating chemists/retailers and by hiring out premium display windows.

* * *

29 DIRECT MARKETING

Direct marketing has a long history, dating back to the 15th century when an Italian printer was using it to sell books, coinciding almost with the introduction of printing in Europe. Dr. Johnson in 18th century summed up the essence of advertising and direct marketing in his two statements: "Promise. Much promise is the soul of advertising." Consumers are interested in knowing what the product *can* do for them, rather than what it actually *is*. Printing and further innovations has given a boost to direct marketing. It has made the mail order catalogues economical. Literacy is a great boon for direct marketers. Kennedy's apt description of advertising as 'salesmanship in print' is equally applicable to direct marketing. Advertising in general and direct marketing in particular must build an added value into the product beyond its physical constituents. Brand image, as we shall learn shortly, is an emotional construct but people still have to rationalise their choices. Rosser Reeve's USP is comparative. Our product is compared to all competitive products. One feature is then identified which the others do not offer. It is our USP. However, it is difficult to identify a USP for technologically similar products or for complex services such as American Express. Many times USP relies upon some trivial point of difference.

(i) *DM is not just posting a brochure with a letter:*

DM is not limited to direct mail; there are other media like direct response ads, telemarketing etc. Still direct mail is the most popular method. However, don't think it means just posting a brochure with a letter. We have to define the correct market segment, lay our hands upon the correct database, plan the direct mail package, give good follow-up and so on.

(ii) *Envelope is not to be neglected:*

An envelope should not be a barrier. It should be friendly with the receiver.

(iii) *Mailer and letter go together:*

A personal touch covering letter accompanying a mailer goes a long way in establishing a rapport with the prospect.

(*iv*) *Don't neglect the offer:*

It is the heart of the DM. Think of innovations here. It should be action-oriented. Time tested offers are:

(*i*) Free trials.

(*ii*) Inspections without any obligation.

(*iii*) Incentives for early birds.

(*iv*) Discount offer within a limited time period.

(*v*) Gifts in contests.

(*vi*) Incentive on filling up the coupon.

(*v*) Gifts for slogans.

(*v*) *Check the quality of the database:*

Verify the credentials of the database company if you happen to hire it. Just check how the database has been compiled and what results it has given in the past.

(*vi*) *Retain the initiative:*

The sender must retain the initiative right from the beginning to the end. This is done by being persuasive, innovative, using prepaid envelopes and follow-up through reminders.

(*vii*) *Follow-up the Mailers:*

No matter how persuasive you are, your first mailer might fail to enthuse the buyer unless given a good follow-up by reminders. That saves the initial investment from going waste.

(*viii*) *DM is mostly complementary/supplementary:*

DM works on its own for very few products. Mostly, it has a supplementary/complementary role.

❖ What is Direct Marketing?

Drayton Bird, Vice Chairman, O & M Direct Worldwide, defines it as "any activity whereby you reach your prospect or customer (read doctor) directly as an individual — or they respond to you directly."

DM is not simply another form of advertising. It's a way of marketing. Advertising can initiate a sale but it cannot close it. DM has the capacity to close the sale and build a dialogue.

DM is like opening a store in print. And then managing it. (Dick Shaver)

DM and Sales Promotion (SP) offer the twin benefits of helping the marketing manager establish a cause-and-effect relationship between her/his actions and results on the bottom-line and offering advanced data bases which can be exploited to target promotional activity of any kind at an entirely fine-tuned audience.

At a recent seminar organised by MAA Communications in Bangalore, the Regional Director of Kobs & Draft Worldwide's division K. D. Asia Ms. Deborah Coulson spoke on how DM is different from general advertising. The preconceived notion that they — advertising and DM are mutally exclusive is not valid.

❖ Relationship Marketing

One time communication does not build a relationship. We have to get married to our customers in DM. We have to monitor purchases of the customers between two sales points. The amount generated per customer is calculated. Suppose it is 100 Rupees at a profit margin of 25 per cent. We have made ₹ 20 per customer. If the DM programme costs Rupees 5 per mailing, still it is worth.

❖ Qualities of Direct Mailers

1. In terms of overall looks, they must look the best in the category.
2. Writing is very important and writing letters is not easy. Copywriters in direct marketing should write passionately and then edit carefully.
3. High impact DM should not be thrown out by secretaries. It is interesting, innovative. It puts across a message in a cut-throat way.
4. It also reinforces the company's brand image. Our advertising, letter-heads, DM and business cards must project a consistent image.
5. Customers often complain that when they open a DM package, lot of stuff falls out. This is great news because the fallen stuff is picked up and is invariably looked at.
6. For certain products, a mere brochure will not build a relationship. We have to send a personalised letter.
7. Provide a good response device. The order form must be carefully designed — it is so very difficult to do so. Even a child should be able to fill it. It should not turn off the consumers.

❖ Costs

Direct marketing is relevant only when margins in the business can afford the cost of sustained contact. Cost per thousand is much higher. First we lose money but every time the losses come down. The future value and life-cycle value are of much more importance. It is a relationship marketing and that is where profits are.

Increased research costs are paid back in the first year or less than that by mailing less waste mail.

The attempt should be to curtail monthly mailing by eliminating wasted mail.

The cost of computer processing is also dropping rapidly. It will give a further boost to direct marketing.

❖ Clutter Problem

Imagine several thousand mailings received by Indian doctors. The clutter is too much.

❖ Direct Response Ads

If the advertising is designed and its specific purpose is to generate an immediate enquiry or an order, it is called Direct Response ads.

BE (Breaks-Even) analysis of these ads is possible. All costs are divided by the number of responses to get break-even. Even 2 per cent response rate may be good if you are making money at half per cent.

Conversion is the number of sales divided by the number of leads. To have a good conversion rate, we should back our DM by employing a supportive sales force. It can give even a 90 per cent conversion rate.

In print media, Direct Response (DR) ad may generate a low initial response which rises up by the end of the month. Many look for 50 per cent response rate. But people tend to retain the DR ad for future.

General Advertising	*DM*
Reaches a mass of buyers in broad groups, shares common demographic and psychographic profile. Selling a product whose benefits do not include distribution to the customer's door.	Sells to individual customers definable by name, address specific purchase behaviour. Selling a product whose value added lies in distribution to customer's door. Time of purchase and amount of purchase in a particular time period are more important. Medium itself is the market place. It gives comprehensive information to buy the product. Product is controlled all the way through delivery. Enquiry generating advertising or order generation advertising is DM (Direct Response ads)

There is a rapid movement towards database marketing where we are targeting the smallest consumer segment — the individual. Database marketing goes by different names — relationship marketing or one-to-one marketing. But it all amounts to keep an individual customer in focus by collecting mountains of information about him and using the same to design a marketing message. There is a shift from mass market (that vast, undifferentiated body of consumers who received identical messages for mass produced products) to market segmentation (dividing consumers into homogeneous groups with common demographic/ psychographic characteristics) to still smaller niche marketing, aiming for the smallest consumer segment of all the individual.

Direct Marketing: DM is not simply another form of advertising. *It is a way of marketing.* Advertising could *start* a sale but it fails short of *closing* it. DM closes a sale and builds a dialogue. *"DM is like opening a shop in print and managing it".* (Dick Shaver).

In DM, we have to plan the database keeping in mind the target audience. While constructing a database, voluntary information from people must be tapped so as to avoid the charge of intrusion on privacy. It may not always be necessary to mail to a large database — ensuring a large reach. Reach is a concern of advertiser and not of a direct marketer. DM is not just putting advertising into envelopes.

In the States, three percentage of GNP is through direct marketing. Houses, autos and food are not sold by direct marketing. Though there can be traffic building programmes, but a sale is not closed by DM for these products. When we take-off these three categories, DM accounts for 27 per cent of GNP.

❖ Junking

Direct marketers fear the junk mail which is nothing but *ineffective* direct mail. The following factors lead to *junking:*

1. Wrongly targeted direct mail.
2. Unattractively produced direct mail.
3. Wrongly timed direct mail.
4. No *impact* whatsoever on the receiver.

5. No capacity to incite curiosity in the receiver.
6. Improperly constructed database.

It is better to be imaginative about the envelope that carries direct mail by putting a suitable phrase on it as an envelope opener. It is creative headline or envelope opener alone that avoids junking at the envelope stage itself. The covering letter is the next stage at which there is a possibility of junking. It has to be *personalised* by addressing a person by name. There should not be feeling that the receiver is just one number on the mailing list. The receiver is to be led into the letter without being aware of it. If we get across to the right person and get him past the envelope and right through the covering letter, the mail is unlikely to be junked. The chances of junking are at earlier stages and not at later stages.

❖ Direct Marketing

Direct Marketing is an attempt to approach the customers directly. It is a personal approach to consumers. This direct approach may be through sales letters and circulars. It may be through leaflets, folders and brochures. All these are routed through post and so are called direct mailings. Distributors are bypassed in direct marketing. For demonstrations, sales people may call in on the prospects.

Several companies cut their advertising budget and increase the direct marketing budget, *e.g.*, Hewlett Packard, the computer company cut its advertising budget to $ 20 million from $ 40 million and spent $ 40 million on direct marketing.

In US, there are very large direct marketing agencies, with a high profile roster of clients, *e.g.*, American Express, AT & T, Bell Systems, British Airways, British American Tobacco, Burroughs Wellcome, Diner's Club, Du Pont, IBM, General Electric, Newsweek, Philip Morris, P & G. In 1993, the gross spendings the world over on direct mail has increased by 7.2 per cent over 1992 to touch $ 27 billion (₹ 89,000 crores). DM thus remains the world's most-preferred ad medium.

There is a huge opportunity for direct marketing in India. Direct marketing may exploit new technologies like E-Mail, TV etc.

Direct Marketing depends upon the database of the market. The basic challenge in the Indian market is to develop database management skills. The kind of lists now available are not databases at all. They are available for one rupee per name and address while good databases cost anything between ₹ 8 and ₹ 75 per name and address. Building up database is a time consuming process. It takes anything between 3 - 5 months to build databases.

It is difficult to say what is the ideal ratio of general advertising to direct marketing. It varies so much by product categories. General advertising is preferred for packaged products; direct marketing accounting for less than 20 per cent. For satellite TV, cable TV, selling subscriptions, it is mainly direct marketing.

Direct marketing does make sense for small advertisers like a small company or a departmental store. To make direct marketing effective we select a 20 per cent sample of population which accounts for 80 per cent of sales.

Direct marketing effects can be easily measured. Many Indian agencies have opened up direct marketing divisions. Corporate Voice Direct has tied-up with Kobs and Drafts (K & D).

Direct Marketing can make use of personal selling and promotional literature. Mail order advertisements are a form of direct marketing. It is cheaper than personal selling. Sears & Roebuck in America was the pioneer of mail order in the US. In India, the first company that made a success of mail-order business was Bullworker. Mail order advertisements have their merits and demerits. The cost of sales are low since no marketing and distribution networks are required and no margins have to be paid to intermediaries. The disadvantages is only one product can be sold at a time. There are diminishing returns, since every additional advertisement brings a lower response than the previous one.

Direct marketing is slowly coming of age. In India today, we get mail order advertisement ranging for a wide variety of products from music cassettes to saving schemes to holiday packages.

Even computer software companies like Microsoft has commissioned Contract Direct to promote its MS DOS 6.0. It seeks to reach its target of EDP managers and general users via direct mail and advertising.

So far, direct marketing outfits in the US believed that an effective TV commercial for direct marketing should be approximately 90 seconds long in order to demonstrate brand's qualities and to get in a call to action, with the telephone number repeated as often as possible.

However, mainstream agencies deviate from this norm and create shorter, faster and leaner ads. Right now in the US, direct marketing is mostly used by services, charities and travel but many new growth areas are fast opening up. Direct marketing agencies have become more television-literate to keep up. Direct response TV is coming into mainstream — and clients cannot ignore its pulling power.

❖ Direct Marketing in Pharma Industry

The innocent-looking red letter-box of any street corner is the world's most widely used advertising medium. In the West, more and more money is being spent on direct mail advertising. In the US, a significant 11% of total ad expenses are being spent on direct mailings.

The most important constraint on direct mailings in India is the lack of data-bases of good quality. A data-base or a mailing-list is the list of the names and addresses of specific target segments. *e.g.*:

(*i*) Doctors of category A, B, C.

(*ii*) Dermatologists.

(*iii*) Gynaecologists.

(*iv*) Surgeons:

- (*a*) General.
- (*b*) Specialist.

(*v*) Clinical/non-clinical labs etc.

There are few efforts in India to organise data bases. The lists do not have even minimum demographic details. O & M has set up O & M Direct for direct marketing since 1987.

Let us remember that direct is though a still new media for other businesses has been quite established in the pharma industry.

Direct marketing is much more demanding in terms of detailing at every stage than any other method of promotion.

Acolytes of direct marketing herald it as the new messiah and the panacea of all marketing evils. Others are less generous and call it derisively as 'junk mail.' All said and done, it is true that direct marketing is the 'in' thing today. What Ries and Trout did for positioning, Rapp and Collins seem to have done for direct marketing? Does direct marketing work? Sure it does. At least 40 per cent success in direct marketing can be attributed to getting the target (database) right. The rest, say 30 per cent depends on the communication offer (or the incentive) and another 30 per cent on the creative communication of the offer to the identified individual/doctor.

❖ Quality of Data Base

The simplest thing we expect the database to possess is the element of correctness. The names/addresses need constant revision. The organisation has to sanitise or clean the lists while working with them. When lists are merged, there should be an effort to eliminate duplication. Some names need discarding. Even then, no database is 100% accurate. A certain percentage of mailers do get returned.

Sometimes, there can be wrong targeting, *e.g.*, literature of sanitary napkins going to menopausal women.

Software is an essential thing to maintain a quality database.

The quality can make a difference of upto 600% in the results of a direct mail campaign. But still it is not the only factor of success. There are other factors like creative execution, pricing and persistence.

Using the inadequacy of the existing lists as an excuse is a sign of laziness. Only the lethargic product managers may rely upon them.

❖ Professional Vendors of Databases

Data bases may be complied by a vendor for his own private use, but can later be sold to parties who are interested, *e.g.*, Computer Society of India selling the member list to a computer manufacturer or a medical council selling its list of members to a pharma company. Datamatics Direct possesses a huge number of names and addresses. The raw lists which the organisation buys need further refinement, *e.g.*, doctors of a certain area, certain speciality and certain level of practice. The quality of database is much more important than its size. Datamatics Direct has been set up for the specific purpose of selling marketing databases.

❖ Response

A response of 6-7 per cent on an average is considered excellent. Cost/contact is high. Direct mail response should not be considered the isolation. It has to work in collaboration with the medical detailing and SP. Direct mailing is a never ending process, unlike a campaign. Once the responses come in, the result has to be assessed. What is the cost/order? How does it compare with an MR going out to take orders?

Mostly in pharma industry the mailers are traffic builders. Very seldom they are expected to close a sale. The same is the case of the liquor industry where there is ban on mass advertising. Even direct mailing to consumers is illegal. Direct mailers are sent to build traffic with the legend. For restricted circulation in the wine and spirit trade only!

❖ Our Own Database

Most pharma marketers build up their own mailing lists. They can pick up lists from colleges and professional associations. Then they fine tune them to do the target marketing.

We have to approach people directly for information. The tendency to underplay practice exists all over the world, only more so in India. There is a research technique to bypass this problem. We can ask doctors the number of patients they receive and treat in ranges rather than in absolute figures. It is a slow evolution.

A marketer's own list of doctors/chemists/hospitals is probably the pharma company's most productive audience. Yet, a company will consider lavishly spending large amounts on 'cold' mailings to rented lists. It has to spend more time and effort to resell itself and its products to its own existing set of doctors.

The richest source of in-house data for direct marketers are field reports of Medical Representatives (MRs). The realisation of the worth of an 'owned' (*Vs.* rented) database is now drawing among marketers too.

In TV ads, a phone no. is given requesting consumers to dial it for more information. This proves to be an interesting way to build up database.

❖ Post Office

The post office will certainly redefine its mission. They are today just the deliverers of message. Tomorrow they could view themselves as an advertising medium.

❖ Other Deliver

Alternative delivery system may spring up locally. Many couriers would enter the business. There is going to be telemarketing for OTC products.

In direct marketing, we have to track down the reaction of every single doctor. It is much more vigorous. It is definitely less glamorous.

❖ Database Marketing

Database marketing makes use of databases, of customers, suppliers and others to prospect them or to sell to them or to establish relationship with them. The database is built carefully and then maintained by proper updating. A database is a strong source of intimate customer knowledge. Database marketing has two components — data warehousing and data mining. Data warehousing is a storehouse of total customer information. Data mining is a set of techniques applied to the data to segment the customers. It facilitates targeting. It helps the customisation of products and tailoring of the communication mix.

Database marketing also helps in measuring the value of a customer. It is a good method to cross-sell the products. For instance, a customer who has availed of car finance can be sold vehicle insurance. Database marketing is these days considered an investment.

In India, Diners Card was the pioneer of database marketing. Before the card was acquired by Citi, it was issued by the Agarwals Firms used. Diner database to market shares and securities. Even today, credit card companies and mobile phone users are good databases.

A database is different from a mailing list. A database is refined data that provides valuable information — customer spends, life styles, buying frequencies and quantities, demographic characteristics and socio-economic characteristics. The data is extended to cities, states and age-groups. Database is focused. A mailing list has a price, whereas database has value.

The crucial inputs of database must be constantly updated. Outdated and irrelevant data must be eliminated. The basic quality of data must be good. Data available must have been verified and filtered. But it is also true that a perfect database is myth.

Database marketing also shares information on consumer transactions. It should be seen that this does not violate the consumer privacy.

* * *

30 MANAGING THE SALES FORCE

Sales are an important ingredient of any business organisation. Most job opportunities are available in the selling field. Yet, personal selling is considered to be a low-priority area, and it is at times difficult to recruit talented people to do the selling job. Sales force management is a very onerous task. However, the effectiveness of the sales force contributes a great deal to the effectiveness of the entire marketing activity of the organisation.

❖ Personal Selling

The ultimate objective of the marketing function is to increase the sales of want-satisfying products and services, thus leading to a healthy bottom-line. Of the several tools available to stimulate sales, one most important tool is personal selling. Advertising may support careers of a few thousand people. However, those employed in personal selling can be counted in hundreds. Several companies spend 8-15 per cent of the net sales on personal selling as against 1-3 per cent spent on advertising. Selling needs a considerable sum considering the salary bill, allowances bill, travelling costs and operating expenses of the sales branches or offices.

❖ What is Personal Selling?

It is a method of communication — a sales person communicates on an individual basis with a prospect. It is opposed to mass communication like advertising where the organisation communicates with a body of customers. Personal selling is person-to-person communication. It is thus inherent in the very nature of personal selling that the communication is tailored to the needs of the prospect. It is also possible to get immediate feedback in personal selling by observing the reactions of the prospect and thus communication can be modified on the spot. Personal selling effort has the least amount of wastage. Advertising may be received by those who are not our target audience. Personal selling is focused directly on our target audience.

Personal selling may lead to action — the actual sales. Ads can attract customers, create an awareness in them and may arouse a desire to possess the product. But they generally fall short of the buyer's last step — the actual buying. Besides, while doing personal selling, a variety of other tasks like collecting data about credit worthiness of the customers or their preferences can be performed. Personal selling can address to the grievances of the individual customers.

Personal selling, however, is a costly proposition. Though the target audience is reached most effectively by this method, the cost of managing the sales force is substantial. One more drawback is the difficulties in attracting the right type of people to do the selling job. In mass retailing, for this very reason, personal selling has been replaced by self-service and self-selection.

❖ Special Characteristics of the Sales Job

There are several distinguishing features of a sales job:

A salesman is an ambassador of his company to the external world. He leaves a lasting impression on those with whom he interacts and form an opinion about the company from his behaviour. By no stretch of ingination, we can consider the production staff or, for that matter any other staff of the organisation wielding the same influence as the salesman does.

A salesman is out in the field, with no direct or little direct supervision. Other employees have to work under close supervision. Field duties involve hard physical labour and are never a bed of roses. Besides, selling demands creativity, doggedness and initiative. Thus, a successful salesman should have a combination of brain and brawn. As he is to be self-directed, he needs strong motivation.

A salesman needs human relations skill much more than others. As he interacts with a variety of people in diverse situations he must show diplomatic skills and composure. He should show tact and intelligence while dealing with his customers.

A salesman is authorised to spend company's money for his lodging, boarding, travelling and entertainment. Very few in the company are so authorised to use the company's funds.

A salesman cannot enjoy family life like people in other walks of life do. He has to travel his territory while servicing it. Besides, selling is a high pressure job. All this makes him prone to stress. Thus a salesman has to brave all kinds of adverse situations, while being away from home. It is, thus, a very tough job.

❖ Sales Planning

A salesman has to plan sales within an assigned territory. He is not under direct personal supervision. He has been given a product mix to promote. The prices of the products are all determined by the company. He has been trained by the company. He has to plan his selling effort so as to achieve the goals of sales volume set by the higher management. He has to decide about his target audience, his communication with this audience and his emphasis on promotion of particular products.

❖ Types of Selling Jobs

We can see a very wide spectrum of selling jobs — ranging from mere order taking as in the case of a softdrink salesman to a technological presentation as in the case of a sales engineer selling complex products like industrial machinery, aircraft and computers. Selling jobs can be classified on the basis of the creative input needed to perform them.

Just Delivery: Several sales people just fill in orders by giving delivery of the product — a driver of a van of softdrink bottles, a milk vendor or persons at the petrol pumps.

Order Takers: The salesman behind the counter of a grocery store or a book store listens to the requirements of the customers and serves them with the right product. These order takers may be found in the field also *e.g.*, salesman selling hardware items.

Missionaries: They are the persons who build an image of the organisation and generate goodwill for it. Those selling beverages or pharmaceuticals (medical representatives) are the missionaries.

Sales Engineers: These are the sales people who have a good technical knowledge of the product.

Creative Selling: These salesmen make people alive to their needs or impress upon them how an innovation can work in their favour. They may sell creatively the trangible products like vacumizers, computers or aircraft. They may sell creatively the intangible products like insurance, consultancy services, advertising services etc. Selling the intangibles is the most challenging of the selling tasks.

❖ Personal Selling Process

Personal selling is based upon a good understanding of behavioural science as it involves an interaction between the Buyer and the Seller. There should be a matching between the Customer and the Sales person. The sales person must have credibility. A prospective buyer should be made to view a sales person favourably. Personal selling consists of 5 stages called 5 Ps of personal selling.

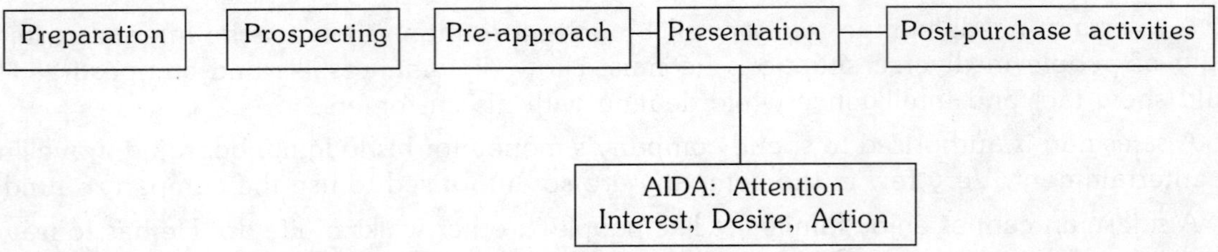

Fig. 30.1 Personal Selling: 5 Ps

(1) *Preparation Prior to Sale:* Every sales person must be fully prepared before he can start the selling process. He should have a good product knowledge. He should be aware of the market conditions and the competitive scene. He must have mastered the techniques of selling.

(2) *Prospecting:* It is locating the prospective buyers. A sales person spells out the buyer's profile. He understands the characteristics of the buyers from the past and the present records of the buyers. He gets from this profile a list of those who could well become the customers of his firm — his potential buyers. He may rely upon the list of prospective buyers prepared by the sales managers. He updates the list by the inputs from his fieldwork. A liquor salesman finds his prospective buyers from the licence vendors' list maintained by the prohibition and excise department.

Pre-Approach: A salesman is expected to call on the prospects. Before doing so, he collects information about his prospects, their buying habits and preferences. In the light of this information, he can adjust his sales presentation.

Presentation: A salesman is now face-to-face with a prospect. He has to attract his attention first. After doing this, he has to sustain the customer's interest and simultaneously, create a desire to possess/use the product. At last, the sale is closed. While interacting with the prospect, the sales person answers any querries that the prospect may have and clarifies his objections satisfactorily.

❖ Attract Attention

In order to attract the attention of the prospect and to open up the presentation several approaches are tried. The most common approach is to greet the prospect and inform him who you are and what you are selling. If the sales person has approached the prospect through a reference the presentation may start by mentioning the name of the reference that "Ramesh sent me to approach you." Product benefits may be highlighted by making a startling statement. A taxation consultant may say that he knows how to reduce his client's tax liability by 50 per cent. While dealing with the new products, a sales person may just allow the customer to 'feel" the product by placing it in his hands. The sales presentation might begin while the prospect is inspecting the product.

❖ Sustain Interest and Create Desire

Once the attention of the prospect is attracted, a sales person tries to sustain his interest and creates a desire for the product in the interaction itself. No ready-made formula can be given for this step. Perhaps, a product may be demonstrated. The emphasis is always on what benefits will flow to the prospect if he uses the product.

Most of the times, a sales person delivers a "canned" sales talk. The same presentation is repeated in calls to different prospects. Though not so creative, it can work effectively. Even in a "canned" talk, a sales person can put the stamp of individuality. All the points must be covered. As time-honoured and tested techniques are used, the sales training is becomes easier.

❖ Clarify Objections and Close the Sale

Once the explanation about the product and the benefits that it gives are over, it becomes necessary to close the sale and take the order. A hint to close the sale may be given to ascertain the prospect's willingness to buy. Some alternative questions can be put across to bring the presentation to its logical end. Maybe, a sales person asks "which colour would you like to have" — the green or the purple? Maybe, he asks whether the customer wants to pay cash or charge his card. These hints are in the nature of a trial close. It gives an inkling of the prospect's mind. Sometimes, a sales talk that is too verbose may be self-defeating. Initially, the prospect might be in a mood to buy but might change his mind if the talk gets prolonged. At times, a sale may be lost because the sales person fights shy of asking for the order.

Buyers may have queries and objections. These should be encouraged. There are enough opportunities to classify and meet these objections. Unspoken objections however, may be too difficult to tackle. It is a matter of inference for the sales person. A prospect that needs "time to think" also poses a challenge. There are chances to lose the sale if the sale is not closed.

A sale is assumed by a sales person in many situations and thus the closing questions are when the prospect expects the delivery and so on.

❖ Activities After the Sale

A sale does not end with an order. We have to build goodwill for the company after that. That paves for a permanent relationship with the customer. Post-sale activities might include installation and maintenance. All activities which reduce the anxiety of the customer after making a purchase — psychologically called "cognitive dissonances' — are post-sale activities. Dissatisfaction with the purchase decision creeps in as certain disagreeable features are noticed in selected alternative. He needs an assurance about the correctness of his purchase decision. He wants to avoid a feeling that the discarded alternative would have worked better. A sales-person has to reduce this dissonance. He assures the prospect by summarising the benefits of the product, emphasing its superiority over the not-choosen alternatives and highlighting the amount of satisfaction the customer will derive by the use of the product.

❖ What is Sales Force Management?

Sales force management has three dimensions — planning, implementing and evaluating the activities of the sales function. The process starts with sales planning and budgeting, followed by fixing of sales territories and setting quotas for the sales people.

In order to meet the planned targets, we must recruit and select the sales people, train them properly supervise their work, compensate them and evaluate their performance against the targets set.

Sales force management is a part of marketing management and planning, which itself is a part of strategic corporate planning. Sales force planning is a component of promotional planning in which we also have other components like advertising, publicity and sales promotion. The strategies adopted in sales force management depend on the promotional mix — we have separate strategies of sales force management for a firm which lays emphasis on advertising and a firm which lays emphasis on personal selling.

The overall marketing planning also affects companies' strategies of sales force management. A company may increase its sales volume by expanding its market geographically or by penetrating the existing market intensively. In both the cases, there will be a different set of sales force management strategies.

❖ Operating a Sales Force

Urwick remarked, "Business is made or broken in the long run not by markets or capital, patents or equipment but by men. Selecting good sales people is the key to successful sales management. We must have the right people, at the *right* time in the *right. quantity.* If we do not have the right quality of sales people, which our competitor may have, we may suffer. Right selection makes other activities like training and supervision easier. A well-selected sales force is a productive asset for any organisation."

Selection process starts with the determination of the number of sales people and the type of sales people an organisation requires. Hence written job descriptions are prepared and job specifications are drawn out spelling out the qualifications needed to perform the job.

❖ Recruitment

Once a company has determined the number of sales people it requires, the next step in the selection process is *to get the right applications in sufficient numbers*. The activities involved in getting the right applications are referred to as "recruitment." Recruitment, however, does not include the selection process whereby the applications are evaluated. The availability of job does not ensure the inflow of applications. Therefore, most enterprises engage themselves in active recruitment. The following are the sources of recruitment.

❖ Sources for Recruitment of Sales-persons in India

Most frequently tapped sources in India are outlined below:

❖ Advertisements

The companies notify the sales vacancies in the appointments columns of newspapers, magazines and trade journals. This is the most effective method of reaching a largest audience at a very low cost. However, this advantage is offset by the screening involved of a large number of applicants, many of whom are not suitable at all.

These ads of recruitment sell the job to prospects. They carry some basic information about the company, about the job, about the specifications and the compensation. The quality of applicants and response to the ad may vary on account of the information given, and statements made in the ad. Even the media affects the response. These ads, therefore, require careful drafting so that they attract the right talents.

Some ads do not reveal the identity of the company, but mention the box number. This decision needs careful consideration. The scheduling, the layout, the typography, the copy, the illustration — all these elements have a direct bearing on the quantity and quality of response generated.

❖ Employment Agencies

Many companies use private placement services to recruit sales people. Here the final selection is made by the company, but the preliminary stages of selection are all handled by the agency. The agency is to be carefully selected and client-agency relationship affects the success rate a great deal.

❖ Educational Institutes

For an entry level position in sales, academic institutions like colleges, vocational institutes and universities serve as a good sources. For example, hotels approach hotel management and catering institutes for their sales people because the position involves expert knowledge in this area. For routine selling jobs, colleges are approached. Even those companies who have good formal training departments like the pharmaceutical companies approach general colleges for getting graduates. The young talents are eminently suitable for moulding. The main limitation is lack of experience and so a compulsory training. They, however, reach a desired productivity level after some time. To exploit this source profitably, a close rapport between Academia and Industry is necessary.

❖ Salesmen of Non-competing Companies

Those who are already handling the selling jobs in non-competing companies are good prospects. Some of their selling experience is transferable. Those employed in related industries have the additional plus point: They are intimate with the product and the market. Since recruits from this source possess experience, they need less training. However, before accepting manpower from this source, the reasons for switch over should be carefully analysed. Outsiders sometimes may be less loyal than the promotees from within.

❖ Salesmen of Competing Companies

One of the most widely used sources, though considered unethical is personnel from competing firms. From an economic standpoint, there is a strong case for such recruitment since the manpower we get is trained, and is in a position to reveal many trade secrets of the competitors. Job hopping, however, is pretty common amongst salesmen to build up career. The "hijacking" organisation pays higher salary. Some companies do not like such head-hunting, on grounds of questionable loyalty. Job-hoppers may hop again from the recruiting organisation, given some additional incentives.

The most pertinent question that needs consideration is the reasons for leaving the previous organisation. The reasons may be attributed to emoluments, or to personality conflicts or instability. However, job dissatisfaction does not always mean that the employee is at fault. If the applicant has cogent reasons to leave, he may be considered and his readiness to be put to immediate productive work can be exploited.

❖ Internal Transfers

Those employees of the company who are working in other departments of the company may be transferred to sales department. In selling jobs where the product knowledge is a very desirable attribute, transfers may prove a very good source. Besides, as these transferred employees are familiar with the company's organisation, they can start work straightaway. Factory and office employees may prefer a transfer to the sales job. The suitability, however, of these employees for a sales career must be examined carefully by putting them under observation.

❖ Recommendations of Present Salesmen

The existing sales force is a good source. It leads to new recruits. Sales people interact widely with people on and off the job. They may be in the know of persons suitable for a sales career. Since sales people know the requirements of the job and the company, they may recommend accordingly. The problem is however, that they may recommend their friends with no selling aptitude. The firm should screen, therefore, the recommended candidates through the selection process. On rejecting a recommended candidate the salesmen recommending his case should be taken into confidence. Salesmen servicing a particular territory are in a better position to recommend sales people belonging to that territory. They know the territory more intimately than in-office executives.

❖ Selection Process for

(a) *Office Automation Products:* These are expensive durable products. Sales approach has got to be rational. The product knowledge also should be uptodate.

The applicants can be subjected to psychological testing. They can be subjected to a structured interview.

The job specifications may suggest a proven track record in this line as a qualification.

(b) *Hard Drinks:* The personality test of a sales person is a primary requirement. He should have outgoing personality.

During the interview, the salesman must be rated on attributes like sales drive, judgment, enthusiasm, attitude etc.

The good source could be sales persons' recommendations and sales persons from competing firms.

(c) *Encyclopaedia:* Good institutions can be approached to select some first-class students interested is selling knowledge to others. The candidates can be subjected to a written test; having items of G.K., verbal and quantitative abilities etc. The personal interview should be a free non-directed one, where the candidate reveals and unfolds his personality.

(*d*) *Gems and Jewellery:* Connoisseur items as these are, the sales must have expert product knowledge. They should also know the latest fashion and design trends. They should have knowledge of customer psychology.

These sales people should be selected through a comprehensive process — application, screening, written test, semi-structured personal interview.

References should be checked properly. Their honesty and integrity should be of a very high order.

❖ Selection

After receiving applications from prospective candidates, the selection process starts. First there is processing of application or preliminary screening to weed out those who do not meet the basic requirements.

The selection process in a step-by-step procedure where several hurdles are created as screening devices and at each such hurdle, the applicant can be dropped. The following illustration outlines the selection process:

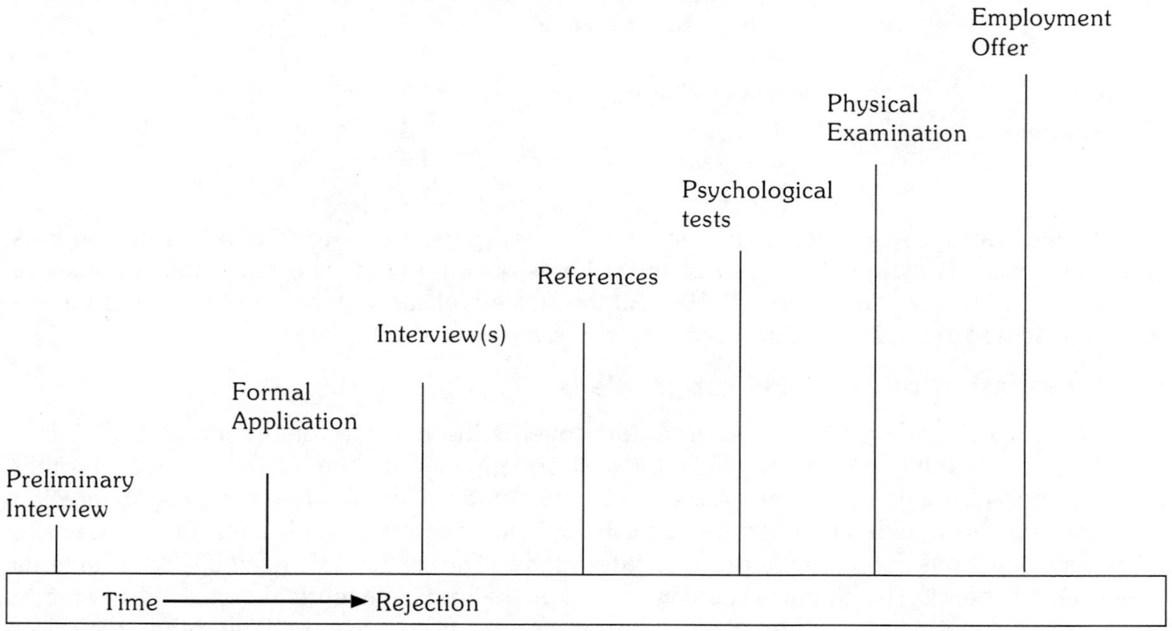

❖ Selection Instruments

The commonly used instruments for selection are as follows:

Application Blank: It is a fact-finding sheet in the form of several questions. It provides important information about the candidate and his capabilities and can be of help later at the interview stage. Application blanks can be short or detailed.

❖ Short Application Blank

It is an initial screening device. It calls for certain basic facts about the candidate. Its main is to eliminate the unsuitable candidates. It includes personal details, educational qualifications and experience. Mostly, the first short application is made by the candidate in his own handwriting to a company. He may be asked to send a brief bio-data, along with a covering letter. Alternatively, the company can provide the form to the candidate.

❖ Detailed Application Blank

It is extensive in scope and covers all the points of relevance in detail. It is designed by individual companies according to their requirements. The facts stated on this form are probed further in an interview.

❖ Scoring the Application Blank

Little is known about the predictability of the items that are included in the application blank. It is also not easy to determine what items should be included and how much weight should be assigned to them. In order to bring objectivity, however, companies assign an objective score to each item to determine the total value of the candidate. The maximum possible value for each item according to its nearness to the ideal.

Illustration:

Education:	**Maximum Score**	**10**
	High School	**5**
	Diploma in Pharmacy	**8**
	B.Sc. (Bio Science)	**9**
	B.Pharm.	**10**
Selling:	**Maximum Score**	**15**
Experience:	**1-2 years**	**5**
	3-5 years	**15**
	5-7 years	**10**

To illustrate, a pharmaceutical company has ten personal history items on its blank. A maximum value is assigned to each of these items on the blank. The maximum total score is 150 points, and the cutoff score is 100. All the successful sales representatives hired by this company scored over 100 when hired and the rest were disqualified.

❖ Information on the Application Blank

The objective of getting the information governs the informational content *e.g.*, if it is to act as a screening device, it could be a short application blank. The choice of other selection tools also guide its format. If we are to use a patterned interview later, the application blank can be shortened. The need for records for reference purposes it may be necessary to ask many questions for verification at a later stage. The nature of the job also affects its design and content. The initial screening in many small pharmaceutical companies is made by the sales supervisor and hence short forms can be used because later other tools like interviews can be used extensively. In medium and large-sized pharmaceutical companies, the prospective sales representive submits a short application and gets interviewed by a Regional Manager, whose decision is later ratified by the headquarters of the company, after an extensive interview if necessary.

Those companies which keep on recruiting sales representatives frequently design a standard application blank and collect the additional information at the time of interview.

❖ Interview

It is the most extensively used selection tool for selection of sales respresentative. For most of the companies, it costitutes the entire selection system. Many companies use it as a screening device in the form of preliminary interview. Companies also use it in later stages of selection *e.g.*, final interview.

The basic objective of the interview is to match the candidate with the job. Interview is a conversation with a purpose. The company treats it as an occasion to give information about its activities and the job to the candidate. It also tries to seek data about the suitability of the candidate for the job — the data which are not available from other sources. This enables the company to take the placement decision. Thus, interview is the most satisfactory tool to assess the communication skills, general appearance, presentability and behaviour, personality traits etc. It also helps to verify the information submitted elsewhere.

The candidate, for instance, might have quoted as his experience sales representative in another company. He can be probed for his responsibilities, his territory, his achievements, his selling skills.

An ideal interview is never a one-way traffic. It is a two-way communication. The organisation comes to know about the candidate. At the same time, it offers information about its ethos, work culture, the job on the offering, the training needed and the compensation package. The nearer the organisation is to hiring a candidate as sales representatives, the more information it gives about itself. Even if the candidate is not to be employed, the interview should serve as a means for creating good feeling towards the company.

To increase the effectiveness of interview, the interviewers should know the job description and the job specification. It helps them to seek the relevant information from the candidate and to give relevant information to him. The interviewers keep the file of the candidate with his bio-profile ready on the table. The interviewer(s) should put the candidate at ease and allows him to freedom to talk. Leading questions are avoided. The interviewer should record the facts during the interview itself and his own impression/judgements immediately thereafter. He should be aware of his own prejudices and should avoid their influence on his judgement. He knows how and when to close the interview.

❖ Interviewing Decisions

The management has to take three important decisions regarding the interview.

Who and Where: Who will be the interviewers? Where shall the candidates be interviewed? In a large pharmaceutical company which is sufficiently decentralised, the interview is conducted at the local level by the sales supervisor/district manager and at the regional level by the regional sales manager. In medium-size companies, the first interview is conducted at the regional level and final at head-office level. In small pharmaceutical companies, this responsibility is carried out by the top people in sales/marketing.

How Many: The more complex the selling task is, the more number of formal interviews held. Some companies put their prospective sales representative through three interviews, including the local, regional and H.O. levels.

When: It may be used to screen the applicants at the initial stage so as to eliminate certain unsuitable candidates. The detailed interview is used at the later stage of selection process. It calls for competent interviewers who can assess the candidate.

❖ Techniques of Interviewing

Patterned/Structured Interview: Here the interview is structured by giving a series of organised questions which the interviewer puts in three major areas: Work history, social history and personal history. Each candidate answers these questions and his responses are recorded on standardised form.

Since all applicants face the same questions, different interviewer can examine the applicants at different places and still the results are comparable. To ensure simultaneous interview of a number of candidates, this method can be used.

The interviewer's rating of the applicant is summarised in the form of total score obtained by subtracting the number of unfavourable answers from those judged favourable.

The forms prepared for structured interview must be validated in company situation.

Non-directed/Non-structured Interview: Here no set format is followed. It is a relaxed conversation. The candidate is given full freedom to talk. He talks about his track record, his domestic life, his academic career, his future plans and also on some remotely connected issues/problems. The interviewer keeps the ball rolling by asking a few questions. Here, the person unfolds himself in a truthful manner. We get insight into his attitudes, interests, opinions and activities. However, this probe requires skilled and experienced people.

❖ Semi-structured Interview

The above two types of interviews are extremes and real-life interviews fall somewhere between them. The interviewer keeps in mind the topic he has to cover. He also allows deviations from the set plan to probe the candidate.

Stress Interview: Here, stressful environment is created by the interviewer deliberately. The candidate is interrupted, challenged and criticised by asking his solutions to tricky problems. For instance, a pharmaceuticals company can put a product into the hand of the candidate, and ask him to promote it. As he starts doing so, he faces many unreasonable objections. The method is especially useful for selecting sales representatives who have to work under stressful selling situations. The stress interview requires the help of trained people.

❖ Psychological Testing

The rising costs of selection and training, the large size of sales representative team and rapidly developing methods of testing — all these have led to the use of psychological tests, though in a limited manner for the selection of sales representatives.

Here the candidate is asked a series of objective-type written questions in a given time to identify and measure the various aspects of his personality *e.g.*, intelligence, achievements, aptitude and interest traits. The design of a test battery is a skilled job, undertaken by a team of psychologists.

Tests of mental ability, tests of special abilities like sales aptitude tests, tests of habitual characteristics, attitude tests, personality tests, interest tests and achievement tests are some major types of psychological tests.

The test battery is validated, in the sense that it actually measures what it is supposed to measure. The tests should be reliable also, which means test scores should be consistent.

Tests are never the exclusive selection tools, but are used along with other instruments. The score on a test does not mean that the person will be the best sales representative. It only means that the man is qualified for the job.

❖ References

The application blanks sometimes elicits this information. The references are checked by personal visit, telephone or letter. The purpose is to verify the bona fides of the candidate.

❖ Physical Examination

A sales representative should be physically fit to do the onerous job. Minimum physical qualifications are to be met, failing which the candidate is not selected on medical grounds.

❖ Concluding Remark

Recruitment and selection policy should be carefully formulated. Good selection matches the right person and the job. Job satisfaction improves. High sales representative turnover can be reduced.

❖ Training and Development of Sales Force

Soon after the selection, the sales person is placed on the job. He is then subjected to his first training called induction training.

❖ Induction Training

This initiates the man into the work environment. The man is introduced to his job. He comes to know about the company, its product line, the rules and policies. He meets the executives and colleagues. He is informed where exactly he is placed in the total scheme of things. A carefully planned orientation induction programme helps the new employee to identify himself with the organisation and its procedures and gives him some feeling for the significance of the work he will be doing and thus helps him to overcome the fears and anxieties that are bound to arise on the new job. It also makes him feel a part of the group.

Induction training is the beginning. But a sales person needs training on a continuous basis. So training programmes are arranged periodically. For each training programme we have to decide about the training faculty — whether inside line and staff executives or outside experts or a combination of both. The content of a training programme must be carefully chalked out. There should be emphasis on communication skills, presentations, product knowledge, selling techniques. Some companies believe in on-the-job training where the representative accompanies in the field a trained and experienced sales representative or supervisor as an under-study. He is called back for class-room training later. Some companies, however, prefer class-room training first before sending him out in the field. Training may be centralised or decentralised. Decentralised training can be conducted near the place of work. Such programmes cost less than those which are centralised.

The following training methods are in vogue these days.

❖ Training Methods

There are two methods in vogue for training medical representatives: (*i*) On-the-job methods and (*ii*) Off-the-job method.

❖ On-the-Job Method

Here, the sales representative has to accompany the sales supervisor and perform the selling job in his presence. He is made aware of the problems in practical situations and is trained by the supervisor by suitable briefing before and after each call. Sometimes, the supervisor himself demonstrates what he preaches. He gives oral and written explanations to the sales representative being trained. Tape record may be used to give voice training.

❖ Demonstration and Examples

The supervisor makes the sales presentation and explains later why, how and what he is doing. Demonstrations are supported by lectures, visuals, discussions etc.

❖ Off-the-job Method

Here training is not in the field, as a part of every day activity. It may be conducted in a class-room of a company's training centre. An outsider organisation may be involved to impart such training.

❖ Lectures

These are delivered on specific topics by qualified trainers/instructors. It is most widely used method to teach theory and concepts. The lectures are supplemented by group discussions, question-answer session, film shows, case-studies role-plays etc.

❖ Conference Method

According to a well-decided plan, a conference is held to discuss problems and to pool different ideas to tackle these problems. Buzz sessions divide participants into small groups. These report back to the whole group with their inference and questions. It makes the participants learn from each other and to reduce dogmatism. They also help in modifying attitudes and in developing conceptual skills.

❖ Seminar

Here a paper is presented on a topic which is later discussed. The paper is authored by a trainee sales representative.

❖ Case Study

A real or imaginary situation is presented to a group. The group is asked to identify one problem and discuss alternatives to tackle them. Each alternative is analysed to arrive at the optimum decision. The trainer only guides the discussion. It promotes analytical thinking and develops problem-solving ability. This method is more suitable for supervisory/managerial training.

❖ Role Playing

Here the trainees have to enact a role which is given to them *e.g.*, one trainee becomes a medical practitioner and another trainee details before him. The role players have to quickly respond to the emerging situation. It is a method of human interaction.

❖ Programmed Instruction

It has two important components:

1. Step-by-step series of bits of knowledge, each bit/unit building upon the previous ones.
2. A mechanism of presenting the series and to check tainee sales representatives' knowledge.

Programmed learning is done through manual or independent worksheets. It is primarily used to teach factual knowledge such as pharmacology, biology etc.

❖ Compensation of the Sales Force

Any field force of sales representative needs adequate compensation to keep its morale high and to put in the best of efforts. The direct salary and the allowances that most companies offer are similar. However, indirect benefits like the incentives and perks do differ from company-to-company. There is a trend to enhance these indirect benefits.

A sales representative is an ambassador of any company. He projects the company's image. To build up a team of competent sales representative is a formidable task. However, more challenging is the task of maintaining this team by proper compensation packages and by keeping them motivated.

❖ Direct Compensation

As has been observed, the direct compensation more or less remains the same for most of the companies. However, some salespeople who handle difficult lines like bio-medical equipments may be given higher start keeping in mind the complexity of their work.

The direct compensation package of as is made up by:

Basic Pay + Allowances including travel and entrainment expenses.

There is one set of allowance for headquarters. There is another set of allowances for 'away from headquarters and back to headquarters (with no overnight stay.)' There is a third set of allowances for 'away from headquarters and overnight boarding and lodging.' All these allowances are budgeted and controlled in accordance with sales representative route and cycle of travelling. The sales representative has to submit vouchers for reimbursement of expenses.

The basic pay and allowances are subject to revision from time-to-time. They increase with the promotion of an sales representative from grade-to-grade. Much more important than the direct benefits are the other benefits made available to a Sales representative.

❖ Indirect Compensation

There are both financial and non-financial incentives.

Financial incentives could be salary plus commission or salary plus a share in profits. Salary plus profits is not a prevalent method in pharmaceutical industry.

❖ Salary Plus Commission

Here, the sales representative gets a direct salary plus a commission on sales above a certain amount. Each has to achieve a fixed quota per territory, per product. The commission is paid on achieving this targeted quota. Further commission may be paid on sales above the target. The sales representative is motivated to put in hard work.

Non-Financial incentives like training programmes for sales representative either at companys premises or at an outdoor locale and awards. recognition and prizes in exotic locales are generally given to the sales representative.

❖ Factors Affecting Compensation Packages

Some factors have a major influence on the structure of the compensation packages.

❖ PLC (Product Life Cycle)

The selling effort put in has a relationship to the stage of the PLC. Compensation is related to the selling effort.

At the introductory stage of the product, aggressive selling is necessary. The sales representative have to travel a lot and meet many prospects to convince them. They should be able to counter objections and are expected to be up-to-date in their product knowledge. At this stage, sales representative need adequate compensation to keep them motivated. The direct salary may be on the higher side. It may not be necessary to introduce indirect benefits at this stage.

At the growth stage, the sales representatives have to sustain the tempo of sale. They have to work with renewed vigour. They have to explore new opportunities. This is the right stage for the introduction of incentive schemes.

At the maturity stage of the product, the sales representatives do expect a respite from the dull routine. Other indirect benefits like training programme at an exotic locale, foreign trips and promotions are needed at this stage. Mature products do need dealer support and so SP schemes are introduced. SP schemes are introduced for customers too. Regular increases in salary and perks are given as per schedule.

At the decline stage of the product, fresh incentive schemes are introduced.

The PLC as related to compensation package is illustrated below:

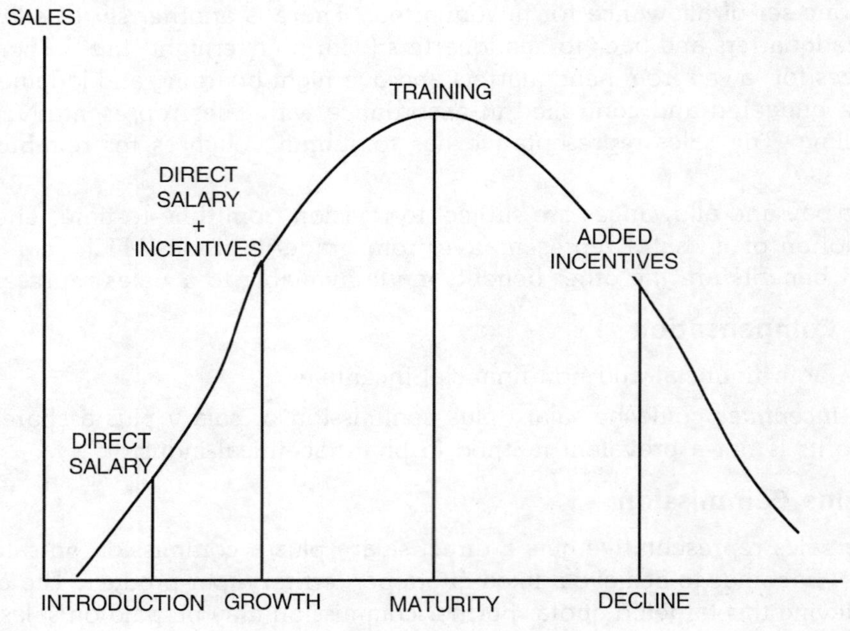

Fig. 30.2 Compensation-related PLC

❖ Supervising the Sales Force

It is a difficult task to supervise the sales force as they are out in the field and are not under direct supervision as the office staff is. However, supervision is important to keep control over the sales people, to motivate them, to develop them, and to guide them. It is a device to see that the sales persons carry out the policies of the company. Sales supervisor or field sales executive is a link between the Sales force and the Higher management. Sales force is supervised, both personally through a sales supervisor and impersonally, through reports, correspondence and meetings.

❖ Monitoring and Performance Evaluation

However well-organised a sales department is, its efforts are to be controlled and planned for effective functioning on a regular basis. Sales reports from the basis for monitoring sales representative. Organisations need regular sales information in terms of products, customers, geographic segments. Most companies also appraise their sales respresentative.

❖ Need and Objectives of Monitoring

The Sales Manager has to know whether and sales representative is putting in the sales effort on the expected lines. A monitoring system sales representative consists of field visits by supervisors and periodic reporting. It is a formal feedback system. It controls the sales effort. It forms an input in the appraisal of sales representatives. *Reports are the basic tools used for monitoring* sales representatives. The sales manager comes to know from these reports how the sales representatives are performing. A good monitoring system enables the management to take decisions to improve sales representatives' performance. Even a sales representative individually benefits from regular monitoring since he gets a chance to compare his present performance with a corresponding performance in the past. It is a method of self-evaluation. A good monitoring system serves the following purposes:

1. It facilitates Market Research.
2. It facilitates the decision-making of a sales manager.
3. It facilitates the performance appraisal of sales representatives.
4. It facilitates the corrective action, in case there are deviations.
5. It facilitates the planning of a sales representative's work.
6. It is a mechanism to record consumer's/doctor's reactions and complaints.
7. It is a mechanism to record competitor's activities and matters of topical local interest.
8. It facilitates the building up of a good database.

❖ Parameters Used to Monitor Sales Representative

The monitoring of sales representative is closely related to the monitoring of sales. One depends on the other. The performance is measured against a number of criteria, some of which are listed below:

(*i*) Calls per day.

(*ii*) Average cost per call.

(*iii*) Direct selling expenses.

(*iv*) Sales per sales representative per dealer, per product.

(*v*) Expenses to sales representative.

(*vi*) Number of accounts.

(*vii*) Number of customer/doctor/chemist complaints.

(*viii*) Profit contribution analysis.

In other words, the day-to-day activities of a sales representative is the basis for monitoring.

Two most important methods of monitoring are:

(*a*) Through sales reports.

(*b*) Through field visits by the supervisors or field sales managers.

The details required in reporting vary from company-to-company. A company with a large number of sales representatives and wide geographical market needs more detailed reporting than a company with a few sales representative and a limited geographical spread. The greater the autonomy the sales representative enjoys in planning/scheduling his sales effort, the greater is the need for detailed reporting.

❖ Contents of a Sales Report

A variety of sales reports has been designed by different companies. However, many of the following components are to be commonly found in the reports of all organisations. These components are:

***(a) Work-plan Component*:** Usually for a week (or a month) in advance, the sales representative is expected to submit his schedule or work-plan. Here he lists the prospects he is going to call on, the dealers he is going to visit and the routes he'll take. He also lists the non-selling tasks he will undertake this reports helps the sales representative himself and the company too which keeps track of his whereabouts. It also helps to evaluate the sales representative's achievement against the plan made.

(b) Progress Report: It is a report on the day-to-day work done. It is prepared after each call or collectively for calls made during a specific time period. It provides information about company's position in each territory and for each account. The progress reports indicates the response of prospects of different categories, extent of competitive activity.

(c) Expense Component: Sales representatives are given reimbursement of expenses incurred or else they may be put on expense account. Most reports have an expense component to keep a check on the nature/extent of his expenses.

(d) Complaint and Adjustment Component: This component is related to the specific complaints the doctors/the chemists have in relation to the company, its products, its policies and the presentation of the representative sales. Attending this component improves the products, services and distribution.

(e) New Business or Potential Business Component: Here the sales representative informs the new customers won over recently and those who have the potential of becoming our patrons in future. It gives the information about the prospecting capability of a sales representative.

(f) Lost Business Component: We may lose certain prescribers who start prescribing competitive products. We have to consider the improvements in product, service and training of sales representatives to take care of this component.

❖ Performance Appraisal

Every sales manager has to evaluate the sale representative on a continuous basis, either informally or formally. To make evaluation more effective, the appraisal has to take care of these three dimensions.

(*i*) Sales representative's skills, habits, aptitudes and attitudes.

(*ii*) Sales representative's selling record — his efforts and achievements.

(*iii*) Direction that development function has to take.

Sales performance varies from situation-to-situation, and hence is difficult to measure. Besides, sales representatives have varied personal traits and selling ability. Even geographical diversity of territories and their differing potential make appraisal difficult. Sales representatives work in the field and away from the roving eye of an immediate supervisor. A good monitoring system, as we have already seen, is the basis of the appraisal system.

Appraisal has to set both qualitative and quantitative standards. These are to be compared against actual performance. The contribution is then judged. Appraisal is found useful in developing sales representatives, in motivating them and in indentifying the training needs. It helps us to restructure the territories and work assignments, in improving sales planning and in introducing sound compensation plans.

❖ Some Basic Issues

1. Mere quantitative evaluation is not enough. Relations with prospects do not lend themselves to quantitative definition. Selling ability is a matter of many qualitative factors. A judicious mix of quantitative and quantitative criteria is to be evolved.
2. Since work environment differs, there should not be man-to-man comparison.
3. Realistic norms and standards of performance are a pre-requisite for effective appraisal.
4. Period of evaluation should not be of too short-term or of very long-term.
5. Appraisal should not be based merely on accounting data.

PERFORMANCE STANDARDS
(Quantitative)

Standard	*Definition*	*Remarks*
Sales Quotas	Sales target assigned to a specific sales representative (in terms of rupee value or units). Based upon sales forecasts.	Most widely used. Shows desired levels of performance for sales volume, gross margin, NP and expenses.
Net Profit Ratio or Gross Margin Rate/Territory	NP to sales ratio. Gross margin to sales ratio.	Decided for sales territories. Attain higher sales or reduce expenses. Sales people concentrate on profitable products.
Sales Expenses Ratio	Selling expenses to sales volume. (some companies include indirect and direct selling expenses) (Some companies use only direct expenses on which sales representatives have control).	Manage the ratio by controlling expenses or by making sales or both. May show low profits, despite a good ratio.
Sales Coverage Effective Index	No. of customers Total prospects in one assigned territory.	How a sales representative covers his territory?
Call Frequency Ratio	No. of sales calls or a particular class of prospects (doctors). Total no. of prospects (doctors) in that class	Direct sales effort accounts that lead to profitable sales.

Calls/Day	Norms set taking into account the territory.	To know whether calls are too many or too few.
Average Cost/Call	Different norms set for different classes of customers.	Importance of making profitable calls.
Multiple Quantitative Measures	Market share. Sales quantity. Sales value. No. of calls. No. of orders. Value of orders. Value of order/calls. Gross margin. Selling expenses. Sales Margin. Average inventory. Average credit. W:C locked up. Marketing ROI/ (Direct sales margin) Working capital New product performance. No. of customer complaints. Competition.	A few are selected. Weightage given.

❖ Qualitative Performance Criteria

- Detailing effectiveness.
- *Espirit de corps.*
- Goodwill external in one teritory.
- Cordial dealer relationship.

APPENDIX-I

SALES QUOTAS

Concept

A sales quota is a quantitative goal assigned to a sales unit, relating to a particular period of time. A sales unit may be a sales representative, territory, branch office, region or distributor.

Rationale

Sales quotas are used as planning and control mechanisms. They enable an evaluation of sales activities of a company. They provide a source of motivation and a basis for incentive compensation. They help to appraise a sales person. They reveal the strengths and weaknesses in the selling structure of an organisation.

Reasons for Assigning Quotas

Sales quotas serve a variety of purposes. The main objectives are:

Providing Goal and Incentive

They indicate a performance level to a sales unit and motivate it to attain the level determined. Quotas are generally linked to commissions/bonus when they are crossed or surpassed. The recognition of superior performance comes through quotas. To be fair enough motivators, the quotas fixed should be realistic and attainable.

Controlling Sales Persons Activities

The sales effort could be directed through quotas. Sales persons can be made responsible for a certain minimum number of calls per day, calls on new accounts, a certain number of demonstrations and recoveries of companies dues. On failing to achieve these, the company can take corrective action.

Performance Appraisal

Sales persons can be rated against the quotas and their strengths and weaknesses are noticed.

Controlling the Sales Expenditure

Selling expenses are kept within manageable limits by the use of quotas. The criterion of reimbursement in some companies is a particular percentage of the sales quota. Some tie expenses to compensation. Expense quota leads to profit quotas.

Marketing Effective Compensation Plan

Quotas does have a bearing on compensation plan. Crossing the quotas is an accepted criterion of commission payment. It may also serve as a basis for payment of bonus.

QUOTAS FOR THE CASES GIVEN

Door-to-door salesperson selling vacuum cleaners

A company like Eureka Forbes which markets amongst other products like Aquaguard, also markets vacuum cleaners. They are a high-value durable product meant for upper middle class and upper class customers. The company has adopted direct marketing method and sends door-to-door sales people to demonstrate the product to the target audience and on conviction book them for order.

Quota Suggested

Each salesman of vacuum cleaners is assigned a territory. He has to *attain a sales volume quota* per unit of time and a particular number of vacuum cleaners are to be booked. Since sales representatives are expected to give demonstrations, a quota for a number of demonstrations made could be fixed. Here 5-6 demonstrations a day may be given as a quota.

He has to visit more number of households to attain his demonstration quota, because some may not be interested. Besides in the first call, he has to take an appointment. *So calls per day* can be fixed as a quota.

Order-call ratio also can be set as a quota. It is also called batting average and indicates the number of orders booked in a given time frame against the number of calls made. It is an evidence of salesman's effectiveness in identifying the right kind of customers and in securing orders on the strength of presentation and demonstration made. In short, a physical target combined with activity quota will be a rational system for this sales person.

Medical Representatives (Salespersons of a Pharmaceutical Company)

Salespersons are technically referred to medical detail men who provide the necessary technical information about the drugs/medicines to the medical profession comprising of various doctors in different specialisations. The doctors are persuaded to prescribe the medicines of the firm which the medical representatives, maintain contacts with chemists see how the prescriptions flow, making products move about. They book the chemists' orders and pass on to the distributors.

Quotas Suggested

Rupee sales volume quota is fixed for each medical representative since it reflects his performance in multi-product from the pharma company. It is combined with unit sales quota for certain special categories of products like Protinex tins, (a protein hydrolysate of Pfizer) or a general tonic. Besides the above, the following quotas are generally fixed.

Number of calls made per day on an average: The medical representative is expected to visit a certain minimum number of doctors for detailing. Here the company expects him to call on *A, B* and *C* category of doctors. The doctors are classified on the basis of their practice and market standing. It is now to be seen that each category of doctors are called on at a determined frequency. It is, therefore, of utmost importance for a pharma company to fix *call-frequency ratio*. It indicates the relationship between the number of Calls and the number of Doctors. Mathematically, it is —

$$\frac{\text{Number of calls on doctors in category } A \text{ or } B, \text{ or } C}{\text{Total Number of doctors in category } A \text{ or } B \text{ or } C}$$

in the assigned territory. Here, the company can control the interval between medical respresentive calls upon each class of doctors. It also helps to redirect from medical representatives less profitable to more profitable categories.

Another important activity quota for the medical representative is *number of dealers (Chemist shops / pharmacy stores)* called on.

The quantity of a quota is result of market share calculation and Thompson Index, indicating the potential of a territory.

Salespersons Selling Computer System Involving Higher Capital Outlay

When mainframes and midis are sold, there is a heavy financial commitment. The decision to buy a system of computers is complex and the salesperson has to interface with the people at the top and provide them with technical specifications, relevant detail and their problem solutions. Prior to buying, there are many calls made. It is a long-drawn out buying process and generally a group decision. Considering the above, the sales people are given a *financial quota*, to determine the net profit and to control the sales expenses incurred.

After the sales, what matters is the after sales service. So one activity quota could be *number of service calls made.*

Conclusion

Depending upon the nature of the product market, selling tasks are required to be performed as well as selling challenges faced. Some companies find it useful to set quotas in combination of two or three types as illustrated in the above three examples.

APPENDIX-II

SELLING YOURSELF

To be a really successful salesman you have to do a double job of selling.

The sale of your products is of course the final objective. But even before this is done, you have an equally important function to perform, *i.e. Selling Yourself.*

Your customer is very important to you. His opinion and his views will influence him to buy from you, even favour if he thinks well of you. You will, therefore, understand how necessary it is for you that your customer likes you, that you sell yourself well.

There are many ways do this effectively. Here are a few *Golden Rules.*

1. The Dress

It reflects the character of the wearer.

(*a*) It must be clean.

(*b*) It must be proper.

(*c*) Avoid wearing garments of loud colours.

(*d*) Shoes should be well polished and the socks properly rolled up.

A well dressed man gives the impression of having clean habits and being well disciplined.

2. Grooming

It reveals the inner-characteristic of the salesman.

(*a*) A timely haircut may not be artistic but makes one look trim.

(*b*) Periodical washing to wipe-off a greasy face helps to keep fresh.

(*c*) An everyday shave is a must in selling.

(*d*) Proper cleaning of teeth.

(*e*) Have well cut nails and clean hands. You may have to shake hands with your customers.

3. Smile

When you meet your customer, it will bring him closer to you. The message of the smile is clear in any language.

4. The Hand-shake

Avoid it unless the customer extends hand or you are sufficiently friendly with him. If you must shake-hands, extend your hand and give a firm friendly shake. Avoid bone-crushing or lady type delicate or even the cocktail type hand shakes. Normally a *Namaste* serves the purpose.

5. Sincere Attitude

When greeting or talking to your customer, look straight at him. Don't try to hypnotise him or knock him with a cold stare or bore him with a blank expression. Just be pleasantly natural.

6. The Right Name

The sweetest sound to a man is to hear his own name. Make sure you know the name of our customer and you say it correctly.

7. Praise

Always praise your customer, never flatter. Praising is sincere, flattering is false. The right form of praise earns friends. Any type of flattery looses them. Showing appreciation works wonders.

8. Avoid Bluntness

In selling "To Call Spade a Spade" does not usually pay. Bluntness is an excuse for rudeness.

9. Never Criticise

The easiest way to lose a customer is to criticise him. Avoid it as far as possible, but you must tune it down.

10. Pocket Your Temper

If you must give vent to the bad side of your temper, do so when you are alone. Never shout or display any outburst of temper to your customer.

11. Good Manners

"Manners Make a Man" Good manners show the polish of a man.

(*i*) 'Thank you' are words which must never be missed even for small favours or gestures.

(*ii*) Take your hat off when entering a premises.

(*iii*) Avoid smoking in the presence of your customer. If you are a nicotine addict, seek his permission before smoking. Needless to say offer him a cigarette.

(*iv*) Don't sit when your customer is standing, unless you are told about it.

(*v*) Give way to your customer.

(*vi*) Politeness and courtesy will pay rich dividends.

12. Appointments

If an appointment is made, make sure you keep it. How irritating it is when the other fellow is late? To avoid giving excuses start early.

13. Apologise

A man usually earns respect of others when he apologises for his mistake. "I am sorry" are magic words, which turn a losing battle of sales to victory and can be rewarded with an account.

14. Promise

Never make a promise you cannot keep. Always keep your promise.

15. Importance

Give your customer the importance he deserves. Everybody like to feel important and your customer is no exception.

16. Little Favours

Be a friend to your customer. Little favours go a long way to bring big accounts.

17. Cheerful Disposition

Everybody likes to see a cheerful fellow. Being grumpy, it may put your customer also in a bad mood and you may lose your customer's account.

18. Side Stepping

Never side step the little fellow. He may be influencing the customer.

19. Mannerisms

Avoid bad habit mannerisms. They only help to distract and annoy the customer.

20. Ears

Always listen to your customer. Give him a chance to talk equally. Constant interruptions are bad manners.

21. Loyalty

If you show disloyalty about your company or your bosses, your customer will doubt your loyalty to him.

THIS IS THE WAY YOU CAN SELL YOURSELF

DEVELOPING YOUR PERSONALITY

Your personality is your future. You have the choice to develop it and build yourself up.

An involved person is a determined man. He is determined to improve himself and to develop his personality because he knows the self-improvement is an essential step if one is to climb the ladder of progress.

It is in your hands to develop a good personality.

You have already seen how you can sell yourself to your customer. Now you will see some other qualities and requirements which help to better selling.

The following personality builders will help you.

Health

Every bit of training and all your efforts will go down the drain unless you are physically fit. Like an athlete you have to keep fit by sober habits. Regular exercise, proper nutrition and timely clearance of the inner system helps you to keep healthy.

Breath

A salesman always comes in contact with people and a man having bad breath can never be popular.

Postures

A sloppy postures gives a poor impression. Besides, it only makes a person dull and lifeless.

Voice and Speech

There is a magnetism in good voice. A voice which is hoarse, too loud, monotonous or high pitched is offensive to the ear. A pleasant voice can be developed and holds the attention longer. The diction must be correct. Conversion is an art which can be cultivated.

Accuracy

The habit of being accurate must be cultivated. It is better to say you get ₹ 13,370 after three years rather than about ₹ 13,000 when counted.

Alterness and Observations

A salesman has always to keep his eyes open. By being alert and observant you may be able to find ways to help. Your customer or you may be able to gather important news of competition or you may be able, through observation, to bring out a new selling point. All these could help you to get more accounts.

Memory

A good selling memory is a great asset. It helps to create goodwill, it helps to serve better and it helps to increase your accounts.

Initiative and Resourcefulness

Many times in selling your progress is halted by certain circumstances. A man with initiative and resourcefulness can find other ways to circumvent such situations. The man with *initiative* does the right thing without being told. Failing that, he does the right thing when told one once. The man who has initiative goes further than the one who looks it.

Job Liking

How can you sell your services if you don't like to sell? Selling is the most challenging job. You have to like to be salesman to be successful in selling.

Self-Confidence

If you don't have confidence in your bank or in yourself, you can't convince others.

Cheerfulness

Everybody likes to see a cheerful face.

Ability to Meet People

To sell is meet people. Not only do you meet them, but learn to like them. If you like people, they will like you.

Tact

To do the correct thing at the correct moment is important. A wrong word at the wrong moment can be offensive.

Co-operation

This quality is necessary not only from the customers' point of view, but also banks. Co-operation is a two way flow. If you co-operate with your employers, the better you will receive co-operation and which will enable you to give better service.

Enthusiasm

One of the most dynamic forces is enthusiasm. Enthusiasm is contagious. If you are enthusiastic in selling/serving, your customer will be enthusiastic in buying your services. No man can achieve success in selling the services unless he can maintain his enthusiasm throughout his career.

Mr. Tack has quoted a letter received from a salesman. Here is an extract from it.

"My enthusiasm for the job will not let me rest. I can hardly think of anything else. It gives me the satisfaction, however, of knowing that I am doing all that I can possibly do, and no other human effort can improve on this.

My first days out have quickly proved to me that if I fail to sell successfully, I might just as well give up selling entirely because there is nothing else that I can possible succeed with."

What a magnificent way to start a job? This sort of burning feeling helps to get you to be a star salesman.

Remember you have to be *enthusiastic* to make others feel the same way.

Honesty

A basic character requirement for every walk of life, particularly for a banker. Honesty is the best policy. A liar or a cheat cannot command respect. He is bound to be found out at some stage.

Loyalty

A disloyal man is seldom honest. It is better to leave a job than be disloyal. You have to be loyal to your customer and to your ideals.

Gratitude

Everybody likes a man who is grateful. A customer, like the bank, appreciates a grateful man.

Sincerity

In all walks of life, sincerity pays. Sincerity is a character worthy of pursuit. It is easy to be insincere. It is equally easy to lose a good customer through insincerity.

Ability to Work Hard

Selling is wonderful job, but, it is hard, sincere, conscientious work and to be successful salesman, you have to work hard, very hard and accept what is given to you like a cheerful soldier.

Ability to Fight

Selling is not a bed of roses. You have to be able to fight with grim determination. You cannot throw up your hands at the slightest opposition. You have to fight hard to win your sales battles.

If you want to be a top salesman, if you want to come up in life, develop your personal qualities.

To sum up, personality implies everything that makes a favourable impression on the doctor. Every personality has two dimensions — the innate and the acquired. The acquired attributes makes a medical representative become professional. It is his *professional personality* that makes him click. A professional sales representative has the knowledge of his products which he communicates successfully to the doctors.

When a medical representative meets a doctor, he sizes him up. Two senses come into play — sense of sound and sense of sight. An medical representative is not only visible, he is also audible. A doctor sees him and listens to him. Frankly, the doctor sees what a medical representative really is. If he carries a favourable impression, and if he likes what he sees and hears, he will allow you to tell the story. *You have to sell yourself before promoting your products.* Success in selling yourself the instant you meet the doctor creates doctor-assistance, instead of doctor-resistance! It makes your job easier, more pleasant and more fruitful.

Poise

One element that is so basic to make a good impression is poise. A doctor sees misery day in and day out. He does not like an additional burden of a sullen medical representative. A medical representative has always to be pleasant. His smile represents his optimism, friendliness and confidence.

Personal Attitude

A medical representative must be energetic when he talks. It is easier for the doctor to agree with the energetic medical representative than to disagree with him.

BASIC QUALITIES

Products and Trade Knowledge

Knowledge in this highly competitive market is an essential ingredient for success. You must have not only product knowledge, but trade knowledge — knowledge about practices, personal traits, interests and needs of doctors and chemists. Our general awareness should be high. Medical promotion becomes efficient on the strength of knowledge only.

Enthusiasm

No medical representative succeeds if at the end of the day he does not feel a satisfaction of having a day well passed. Enthusiasm is contagious. It is knowledge on fire. While communicating with the doctors, you must be enthusiastic.

Imagination

A conversation that is dull and drab is not effective. Our conversation with doctor should rouse his interest. A medical representative's visit should not be a routine colourless event.

While detailing, we can be monotonous if no new ways are discovered to present our story. Imagination also helps to anticipate the needs of doctors and present our products attractively to the doctors. An imaginative medical representative stirs up the doctor to the point where he can actually see himself enjoying the benefits of the product being promoted.

Confidence

Confidence in our product by others is brought about by our own confidence in our product. Our lack of confidence puts them off the products.

Perseverence

There is a resistance to change always. It is hard to break down this resistance. A good follow up is necessary for any doctor worth being on the mailing list. His refusal to co-operate must be probed and efforts resumed to break his resistance.

Human Relations

How to get along with people is an art? It is also a key to success. To make people interested in us, we have to first get interested in them.

The five cardinal principles of Human Relations are:

1. People are too engrossed in their own problems and their solutions.
2. People like those who are interest in them. They need a sense of importance.
3. Our own happiness is a result of how others behave with us.
4. People have the same attitude towards us what we have towards them.
5. We have to take the initiative by being friendly or doing a good deed before expecting others to act.

TABLE: TYPES OF CUSTOMERS

Type	*How to Deal?*
Silent	Do not be embarrassed by his silence.
Price	Assure him about how right your price is and the level of quality you offer at that price.
Scientific	You have to be scientific too.
Over-friendly	Respond to his friendliness.
"I-Know-everything"	Do not try to win an argument. Build up his confidence, but keep it directed to your products.
Timid	Speak softly in assuring tones.
Be backs	In the Us, sales staff calls 'Be backs' to those customers who say they will return to purchase an item, but obviously have no intention of doing so.

Each customer is, therefore, a key-hole. You have to find a right key to open up.

* * *

31 MARKETING ORGANISATION

So far we have learnt the principles and practices of marketing from the short-term as well as long-term perspectives. These principles and practices are implemented through the mechanism of organisation. In this chapter, we shall study the current trends in a corporate organisation and the organisation of marketing department. We shall also study the interface of the marketing department with other departments.

❖ Current Trends in Corporate Organisation

As we have seen, business environment has undergone drastic changes in the last few years and continues to change further every year. Instead of a bi-polar world, we have a uni-polar world, with the decline of the totalitarian ideology and the disintegration of the USSR. The European Economic Community has formed one economic bloc. GATT has come into force. Economies are opening up. There is a trend towards globalisation Rapid strides have been made in telecommunication. Service sector is emerging as a major contributor to the GDP. Companies have started reorganisation and re-engineering. They are examining their core competencies and are developing core business. New opportunities are being picked up by smaller companies. Larger companies, therefore, have started encouraging entrepreneurship within the company by forming small venture teams. There is a trend towards mega-mergers. The companies try to reduce the administrative distance between the Top layer of the organisation and the Final consumer. There is a case for flat organisations, rather than tall organisations. Instead of a hierarchical pattern, there is a trend towards matrix-formation and team-building. Teams are formed around core business processes. We shall now consider how the marketing department is organised.

❖ Re-engineering

In this turbulent environment, change is to be managed pro-actively to remain competitive. Maybe, we can re-structure or re-design or re-organise. Recently, however, we have another tool — to re-engineer. Re-engineering symbolises a full *range of change* initiatives, from the lowest operation to the restructuring of the whole business. Re-engineering is just not tinkering or superficial, but is fundamental in its approach. It means fundamental reshaping and realigning business processes, technology, people, infrastructure with customer needs so as to maximise the organisation's performance. It is a re-think on the way an organisation does business.

Strategies of the 90s will emphasise team-work, customer focus, marketing speed and quality management. We will have to design strategies for new markets, new alliances and new customers. Globalisation has become the cornerstone of business strategy.

Business processes need improvement. All processes should add value. Business structure formerly which was functional should now be process-oriented. The cardinal principles of this process-driven organisation are service delivery, customer satisfaction and product development.

Technology that is new will have to be applied to new methods, rather than old methods. There are opportunities to re-tool. Retail dynamics will change. There will be EDI, bar coding and scanning. Information technology will bring about changes in the financial market. Technology, however, would have to be matched to people.

The people component, the most critical, is found in the organisation structure, job structure and content, career planning and management, performance appraisal, organisation culture. All these can change. All these above components — strategy, processes, technology and people — are inter-dependent, and so re-engineering needs careful co-ordination.

❖ Key for Successful Re-engineering

(i) Top management commitment and involvement.

(ii) Customer focus.

(iii) Long-term goals. Continuous measurement of performance.

(iv) Review of all processes. Elimination of non-value added activities.

(v) Operations developed around customer-driven business results.

(vi) People empowered with knowledge, tools and authority.

(vii) Continuous improvement.

Each organisation decides its agenda for change. Then, there should be simultaneous alignment of technology, processes people, so that each of them support the overall strategy.

❖ Re-engineering

This term has its origins at the Massachusetts Institute of Technology (MIT) in the early 80's. It was coined there to signify the changes in business practice likely to be produced by IT (Information Technology) revolution, with rapid information flows, instant and direct communications and automation of business process.

Re-engineering has technological roots in an information network. In the recession, re-engineering is driven by hard-cash rather than by computers.

❖ Evolution of Marketing Organisation

To begin with a company has only a sales function, along with other important functions like finance, personnel, production etc. The sales manager manages a team of sales representatives. However, when the company grows both in terms of market and product mix it adds more functions to the existing sales function, *e.g.*, marketing research to assess the needs and wants of the customers and sales promotion to induce sales. Slowly, we see the emergence of a separate marketing department with functions like marketing research, advertising, sales promotion and customer service. The sales function and marketing function remain separate in the beginning, but integrate later to convert into a modern marketing organisation. The presence of a marketing department however, does not mean that the company is marketing-oriented. A marketing-oriented company keeps consumer in the focus and all its functions, be they production, finance, personnel or marketing, revolve around the customer. All these departments work towards fulfilling the needs of the customer. Marketing ethos pervades the whole organisation.

The following diagrams illustrate the evolution of the marketing organisation:

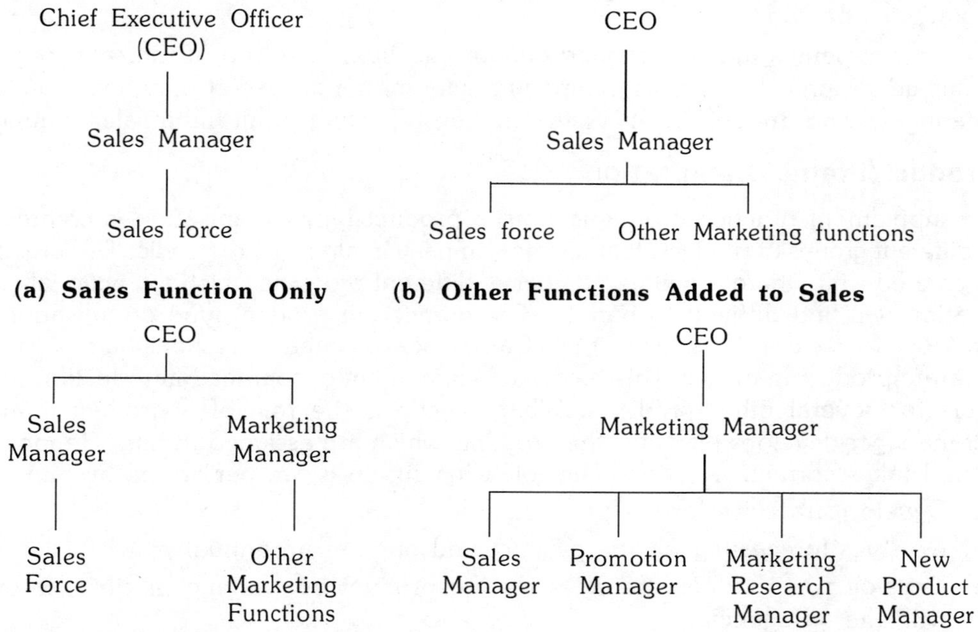

(a) Sales Function Only **(b) Other Functions Added to Sales**

(c) Emergence of a Marketing Department **(d) A full-fledged Marketing Department**

Fig. 31.1

❖ Internal Organisation of Marketing Department

As marketing has a broad spectrum of functions to be accomplished the marketing department as a whole is put under a marketing manager, to whom the other functional specialists report.

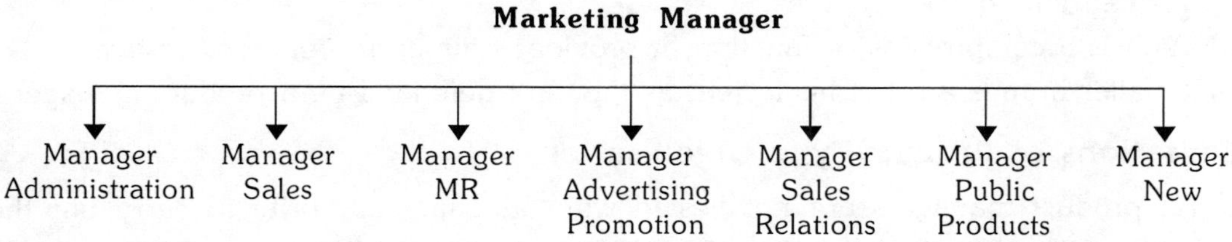

Fig. 31.2

Marketing manager is on par with other functional heads like personnel manager, finance manager, production manager and materials manager. Marketing manager reports directly to the chief executive officer of the organisation. In some companies, a marketing manager becomes a member of the Board of Directors (BOD) and then he is designated as marketing director. A number of functional specialists report to the marketing manager, depending upon the business size, nature of business and the markets served. We can have customer service manager, marketing planning manager and Physical Distribution (PD) manager.

The functional organisation forms the backbone of any further improvement. The limitation of this structure is the co-ordination problem among functional specialists. There is also a lack of focus as products keep on increasing and markets keep on expanding. Each functional specialist also tries to appropriate as much of the total budget as he can and assume as much of the status as he can.

As the company's markets expand geographically, the set-up of the sales organisation reflect this geographical reality. A company having national market may have four regional sales managers who are specialists of that region reporting to all-India sales manager.

❖ Product/Brand Organisation

To supplement functional organisation, a product type organisation is created to take care of different groups of products that a large company is supposed to handle. This organisational layer is created when there is a large number of different products which a functional marketing organisation will find difficult to handle. The pioneering product-type organisation was by P&G in 1927 to restore the sales of their Camay soap. Camay's responsibility was assigned to a separate product manager. This successful experiment encouraged introduction of product managers for several other products. What exactly is the role of a product manager? A product manager develops plans for the products which are assigned to him. He monitors the results and takes corrective action. The following six tasks are performed by him:

(*i*) Develop strategies for the product.

(*ii*) Do sales forecasting for the product and prepare an annual plan.

(*iii*) Develop promotional strategies for the product by working in close co-operation with the ad agencies.

(*iv*) Render assistance to the sales force and distributors to sell the product.

(*v*) Collect marketing feedback.

(*vi*) Think of product innovations.

❖ Advantages of a Product-type Organisation

(*i*) The product manager can concentrate on developing a marketing mix for the products assigned to him in a cost-effective manner.

(*ii*) He can take quick decisions.

(*iii*) As it is a comprehensive function, it provides training to young executives.

(*iv*) Smaller brands are not neglected, as they are defended by a product manager.

❖ Limitations of Product-Type Organisation

(*i*) All product managers are not vested with adequate authority to carry out their expected functions. Though in the text-books they have exalted functions, in practice, they become mere co-ordinators. In the absence of authority, they have to rely on their persuasive powers to get thing done.

(*ii*) Though product managers know all about their products, they do not have mastery over all functions they are supposed to execute *e.g.*, advertising. When the success of a product depends upon such a critical factor like advertising, such a situation does not bid well for the product.

(*iii*) Product managers get over-burdened and demand assistants. This makes the whole concept a costly proposition.

(*iv*) Product managers do not stick to the same product group for a long time. They either move vertically upwards or horizontally to other product groups. This affects the long-term planning of the product or brands.

To make the post of product managers effective, we must have an appraisal system for them that takes into account their role, a mechanism to sort out conflicts between Line and Staff and a sound job description of the product manager's post. Some organisations have instead of an individual product manager, a product management team. Generally, a hierarchical team consisting of a product manager and his assistants is formed. A triangular structure consisting of a product manager, a marketing research manager and a communications manager can also be formed. At times, we may have a horizontal team of several specialists, *e.g.*, sales, engineering, design, laboratory, marketing research, finance etc. Team-approach encourages group decision-making for a product plan. Product managers for minor products can be eliminated, transferring their products to the remaining product managers.

In India, Reckitt & Colman broke down their brand management structure into four regions. The costs shot up. In each region the brands were sold in a different way. The marketing manager, working under their GMs, had a clash of roles because both looked after strategic brand management and the sales function. This decentralised experiment was then modified by splitting the sales and marketing responsibilities within each regional team. Each region assumed overall brand management responsibility for one brand and provided tactical support such as local promotions, local language, advertising for all the brands. Though this worked well, serious brand management problems continued. The brand management function does not seems to lend itself to decentralisation process. A sales driven business has a better chance of making decentralised marketing a success.

❖ Market-type Organisation

Instead of the products, here a market is chosen as the basis of organisation. Generally it is a good structure for a multi-market organisation. A chief market manager can have several market managers. They are also called market development managers. For a major market we can have separate functional specialists. Or else, the market managers draw upon the existing functional services.

❖ Functions of Market Managers

(*i*) They develop long-term and short-term plans pertaining to their market.

(*ii*) They constantly monitor the market trends and decide upon the introduction of new products.

(*iii*) The performance criteria for them is the market share.

Xerox has adopted this type of organisation. Heinz, a food company, was formerly organised on the basis of products. It has now reorganised itself on a market basis — institutional buyers market, restaurants market and groceries market. Even in one market, we can have several sub-markets, *e.g.*, institutional buyers could be hospitals, prisons and academic institutions.

❖ Combination Product-type and Market-type Organisation

A multi-product multi-market company requires product managers who are conversant with divergent markets or market managers who are conversant with divergent products. In each case, a matrix-type structure best serves the purpose. DuPont is a typical example of a matrix of product/market managers. DuPont produces several synthetic fibres like nylon, dacron, rayon etc. There are product managers for each of these fibres to plan sales and profits of these respective fibres. At the same time, there are market managers for their major markets like women's wear, men's wear, industrial markets and home furnishing. They try to develop their own respective markets, without emphasising the type of fibre. The plans of both product managers and market managers are integrated. This is a costly and conflict-creating structure. However, it has its own benefits.

❖ Corporate Marketing Organisation

A company grows in terms of products, markets and size. Then some large product groups or market groups get converted into divisions. Each such division has its own functional organisation. The divisionalised company has to decide what marketing functions should be retained at the corporate level. Some companies may not have a corporate marketing department at all. Some companies have limited corporate marketing department for environmental scanning, assistance to divisions and creating marketing ethos. Some companies opt for a strong corporate marketing function. These departments then do environmental scanning, provide assistance to divisions and create a marketing ethos. In addition, they provide services like advertising, sales promotion, marketing research, sales administration and so on to the divisional marketing set-up.

Companies keep on experimenting with their corporate marketing function — they either strengthen it or prune it or eliminate it altogether. Mostly those companies which have weaker corporate marketing function reinforce it further. Later, some functionaries from the corporate function are deputed to the divisional set-up. Once these divisions have a strong marketing set-up, they expect less from the corporate marketing staff. The corporate marketing department may then become redundant.

Corporate marketing function provides an overall corporate focus, is economical in providing marketing services on a centralised basis to different divisions without an overlap, and brings about a strong marketing culture in the entire organisation.

❖ Interface of Marketing with other Departments

As a matter of fact, all departments of business must work towards the achievement of the common objectives of business. However, in practice, they tend to have their compulsions, pulls and pressures. At times, the departments run in different directions. Most of the times, the perceptions of what is in the interest of business are different amongst them. Ultimately, it is a matter of co-ordination and balancing the interests of the department and the company.

Marketing philosophy is based on customer satisfaction. All departments of business should be guided by this philosophy. It is the task of marketing manager to manage his own department and to co-ordinate with the other departments of business. Though every business decision is to be tested on the touch-stone of customer satisfaction, there is resistance to such an orientation from the other departments, as they think that their own authority is undermined. Each department has its own concern and its own list of priorities. Each department addresses the problems from its own viewpoint and finds the solutions accordingly. The marketing manager has to accomplish his task by being communicative, persuasive and rational in his dealing with the other departments. He cannot afford to be an over-bearing individual. Let us study the points and counter-points put forward by each department.

❖ R & D

Marketing success, as we have already observed in the Chapter on New Product Development, depends to a large extent on our innovative products and the department with whom marketing interacts to develop the new products is R & D. R & D has highly talented scientific manpower. They need an open participative people-oriented leadership style. They are driven by research objectives, unmindful of costs. As against these visionaries, marketing manpower is seasoned, practical business-oriented. They would love to have product features that are acceptable to the customers, and are priced reasonably. Marketing perceives R & D staff as those who are away from realities, and are sitting in ivory towers. According to them, R & D emphasises the technical aspects, without bothering about customer expectations. At the same time, R & D people perceive marketers as men of straw, who know nothing about the rigours of science. According to them, marketers are interested in sales and have no appreciation for technological quality. In technology-driven companies, R & D bears the brunt of new product development. Though they come out with a few successful products, the overall success rate is low. In market-driven companies, the R & D responds to market requirements while developing new products. Though the success rate is high, mostly we have product modifications in such a set-up. In a balanced company, the technology and marketing trade-off result in a better rate of success for innovations. Here the responsibility of innovation is shared jointly by both the R & D and the marketing people.

We can have better R & D and marketing co-ordination by holding joint seminars, team approach to innovation, R & D's participation in the marketing efforts and mechanisms of conflict resolution.

❖ Production

Production turns out an output of the right products from a plant in right quantities, at the right time and for the right costs. They are familiar with Production Planning and Control (PPC), maintenance — both preventive and curative, materials planning and worker management. In their view, marketing people are lay people not conversant with plant economics and working. Marketing people have grievances about insufficient supplies, faulty delivery schedule and lack of customer orientation. It is, however, ignored that the input for any production plan is the sales forecast, which if faulty, might make topsy-turvy the whole production exercise. Besides, marketing people expect product features which are not technically feasible.

The basic problem is the marketer's pre-occupation with the customer who requires goods in time, at reasonable costs, and without any defect. Customer service, however, comes about at a price and there are additional production costs involved. Thus, there is a conflict between Production interest to keep the costs low and the Marketing interest which tends to shoot the costs up.

In the production-oriented companies, the production takes precedence over marketing. The ultimate aim is to have simple products in mass quantities and narrow product lines. In market-oriented companies, marketing considerations overwhelmingly subdue the production considerations. Production follows marketing dictums. Sometimes, there are uneconomical lots. There are heavy production costs, too. A balanced company tries to integrate marketing considerations with production considerations. The bottom-line of a company depends upon cordial working relation of production and marketing people. Marketing people must appreciate the working of a modern plant. Similarly, marketing strategy of excellent quality, for example, calls for a suitable production strategy. Design of a product, production capacity etc. do respond to marketing strategies.

❖ Engineering

Production processes and product designs are the two areas which are looked after by the engineers. The technical specifications of the products, standardisation and cost reduction are their primary concerns. Marketing people, on the other hand, demand variety and many models of the product, instead of standardisation. To the engineers, marketers desire unnecessary trinkets on the products rather than superb functional performance. They think that marketers have no concrete ideas and keep on changing their position. To overcome these conflicts, some companies have marketing managers with basic engineering degrees; followed by management education. Such technocrat-managers do have better appreciation of the engineering realities.

❖ Materials

Materials managers are responsible for procuring the right materials at the right time in the right quantities at the right price. Marketing people like to extend product lines and depths. This disturbs the materials planning function. Marketing also over-specifies the material quality. Marketing forecasts are full of errors. That again disturbs materials planning.

❖ Finance

Marketing costs are rising day-by-day. Marketers need larger budgetary allocations for meeting the rising costs. This is not palatable to the conservative finance managers. Finance managers think marketers do not make a proper analysis of costs and also a proper allocation of funds. Marketers attempt a price competition. This is also not well-taken. Marketers think finance as a stumbling block. They think that finance people have no understanding of their market development efforts. Many a time precious opportunities are lost due to conservatism of the finance executives. It is necessary to subject all managers to a basic course like "finance for non-finance executives." On the other hand, finance will have to learn how its tools can contribute to the overall marketing objectives.

* * *

32 EVALUATION AND CONTROL OF MARKETING FUNCTION

Marketing plan is worked out by the marketing department. Marketing has to see whether the planned targets are being achieved, and if not, why the deviations are occurring. Besides this, a marketer has to control profitability, and efficiency of the marketing function. The profitability control gives us an idea where the company is making profits and where it is losing. Profitability can be studied in terms of products, customers, channels, segments, territories and order sizes. Efficiency control is exercised over major items of expenditure to see that the expenditure generates desired outputs. We have to examine the efficiency and effectiveness of advertising and promotion, the sales representatives and the distribution channels. Marketing audit is a tool of strategic control which indicates how best the marketing practices are being observed.

Marketing control thus is a comprehensive exercise which compares the marketing performance against goals set and identifies the discrepancies to initiate the corrective action. It includes control of the marketing plan, profitability, efficiency and strategy.

❖ Tools Available

Basically, five tools are employed to control marketing function:

(*i*) Sales analysis.

(*ii*) Marketing cost-analysis.

(*iii*) Market-share analysis.

(*iv*) Financial analysis.

(*v*) Tracking customer satisfaction.

❖ Sales Analysis

Sales analysis consists in comparing the actual sales to the targeted sales. Variance analysis — a tool of cost accountancy comes handy to a marketer. A detailed product-wise, territory-wise, salesmen-wise analysis also gives an idea of the underlying problems.

❖ Sales Budgeting

A budget is a financial plan. In a sales budget, resources are allocated to achieve the sales forecast. It is tool of planning as well as control. Sales forecast and sales budget are intimately related. Sales budget also helps to evaluate the sales efforts. The direction of efforts like substantial segments, customers and products is determined. Once the budget is accepted, against its criterion, the actual results are compared. The variances are noted which could be either favourable or unfavourable.

❖ Methods

The popular method set sales budgets are:

• What is affordable?	Capital goods companies and small companies set their budgets by this method.
• Rule-of-thumb	It may be a certain percentage of sales.
• Competitive parity	Pharmaceuticals companies to consider the budgets of similarly placed other pharma companies.
• Objective and task method	First sales objectives are determined. Then the selling tasks are identified to achieve these objectives. Last, the cost of each selling task is calculated.
• Zero-Based Budgeting (ZBB)	The budget for each year starts from the scratch (zero-base). Each expense will have to be justified conventions may be discarded.

The companies use a combination of budgeting methods.

❖ Preparation of a Sales Budget

Three basic budgets are to be made:

(*i*) The sales budget.

(*ii*) The selling expense budget.

(*iii*) The administrative budget of the sales department.

To accept the sales forecast the budget is the starting point. The steps in the preparation of budget are:

1. Background of Marketing Environment: Here bottom-up approach to planning is used. Each department predicts sales volume and expenses and their contribution of overhead. These are summed up at the district level, regional level and final national level sales budget. The sales budget is integrated to the marketing budget. The following are the common items of expenses —

1. *Salaries:* (sales representatives, supervisors, administrative, support).
2. *Direct Selling Expenses:* TA, DA, entertainment.
3. *Commission:* On sales, bonus.
4. *Fringe Benefits:* Medical, LTC, retirement benefits, insurance.
5. *Office Expenses:* Post and telegraph, telephone, office supplies, miscellaneous cost.
6. *Sales Promotion Material:* Selling aids, contest awards, samples, catalogues, price lists.

2. The sales goals should be communicated to the marketing organisation. Fund allocation to realise these objectives is the primary task of the sales executives.

3. Allocation of Resources and Selling Efforts: Realistic allocations product-wise, customer-wise and territory-wise.

4. Top management support is a must for its successful implementation.

❖ Implementation and Feedback

Each item of the budget is a standard or quota against which comparison is made. If there is a variance between what is Budgeted and the Actuals, there are two options.

(1) To see whether the variance is because of poor performance by sales representatives. Corrective steps to streamline the selling efforts are then taken.

(2) To revise budgeted estimates in the light of ground realities, *e.g.*, revise travel expenses figure in view of the fare hike.

Budget consciousness is a necessary part of a sales representative's functioning. The executives keep the figures within the budget limits by constant monitoring. The following diagram gives a sales budget (quarterly):

SALES BUDGET
(Quarterly)

Item	*January*			*February*			*March*		
	Budgeted	*Actual*	*Variance*	*Budgeted*	*Actual*	*Variance*	*Budgeted*	*Actual*	*Variance*
Sales									
Expenses: Salaries Commissions Bonus Medical Retirement									
Travel: Lodging Food (Boarding) Entertainment									
Office Expenses: Mail Telephone Misc.									
Promotions: Samples Catalogues Price-lists Visuals									
Advertising									

Source: Professional Sales Management by Anderson, Hair and Bush (p. 104).

A particular percentage of selling expenses can be earmarked for a larger percentage of achieving the sales forecast figure. (Say 40% expenses can be incurred if 60% sales which have budgeted are realised.)

Sales shortfalls require thorough reviewing. The reasons for shortfalls may be distribution problems, lack of detailing effectiveness, competitive activity, less number of medical representative's, wrong pricing, less competent medical representative's, delays in innovation etc.

❖ Flexible Sales Budgets

Flexible budgets score over traditional budgets by making use of standard costs (historical/judgemental) for different revenue forecasts. Continuous monitoring in terms of standard ratios then become possible.

To illustrate, we can spend on samples ₹ 10 for every ₹ 100 sales or a ratio of 0.10. If the company spends ₹ 800 on samples for ₹ 4,800 worth of revenue, the ratio rises to 0.20. Here some curtailment of expenditure will be necessary.

All these adjustments are necessary in a dynamic and changing market.

❖ Sales Control

It is the responsibility of Sales Managers to exercise control over sales results and the performance of selling activities. It is a continuous process. It indicates the level of sales achieved, the variance observed and the corrective steps taken. The objectives of sales control are to remedy the situation and to revise the sales policy. The productivity of sales representative's may need improvement. The quality of quotas must be improved. The overall sales function must generate profits.

❖ How to Control Sales?

1. Key Result Areas (KRA's) are identified and activities within each KRA are specified.
2. Standards are set against which performance will be measured.
3. The actuals are observed.
4. The actuals and standards are compared.
5. Remedial action which is need-based is taken.

To implement sales control, the Sales Information System (SIS) must give the following data:

1. Sales by unit.
2. Sales by value.
3. Sales by customer.
4. Sales by sales representative.
5. Sales by territory.
6. Sales by a distributor.
7. Sales by cash/credit.

Reporting system provides the necessary input.

❖ Sales Control Methods

There are three methods in vogue:

1. Sales analysis.
2. Marketing cost analysis.
3. Sales management audit.

❖ Sales Analysis

Here had examine sales volume:

1. by territory.
2. by medical representatives.
3. by customer.
4. by product line.

The underlying principle is that the trends of aggregate sales volume hide more than they reveal the ground realities.

Mostly, the Pareto's principles 80:20 operate. 20% sales is generated by 80% orders/customer/products/territories. Conversely 20% of the selling units account for 80% of volume.

The volume is like an ice-berg — it reveals 10% of market but hide 90% of it.

Sales analysis, therefore, is a must.

❖ Sales Analysis by Territory

Sales are scanned territorywise. The assumption is that quota allocation to each medical representatives was based on each territory's potential. The territorial challenges may affect sales adversely.

TERRITORIAL SALES ANALYSIS

Territory	*Quota*	*Actual*	*Value in '000 rupees Performance*
East	1650	1700	103%
West	1500	1500	100%
North	1780	1740	98%
South	1700	1840	108%

Adaptation: Professional Sales Management, R.E.Anderson (page 483), Hair and Bush.

The North region is the only deficient region. All other regions met the quotas or exceeded them. Why is there a shortfall in North? It can be further investigated.

❖ Sales Analysis by Sales Representatve

Let us take the North. All performing sales representatives are considered. Maybe 8 sales representative's are working. Some 4 have either achieved their quota or exceeded it. Others might have missed. One sales representatives is far below the expected quota.

NORTH TERRITORY: SALES BY MEDICAL REPRESENTATIVES

Sales Representative	*Quotas*	*Actual*	*Performance as % of quota*
Sharma	190	186	98%
Sandhu	230	234	102%
Singh	220	218	99%
—	212	220	104%
—	216	214	99%
—	220	224	102%
Rajan	260	212	82%
Reddy	232	232	100%
—	1780	1740	98%

❖ Sales Analysis by Product Line

Maybe sales representative is a poor performer. Even then his performance should first be analysed in terms of product lines.

Shri Rajan, Sales Representative's Sale by Product Line

Product line	*Quotas*	*Actual*	*Performance as % of quota*
Antibiotics	44	46	104%
Anti-inflammatory	56	56	100%
Antacids	60	12	20%
Antidiabetics	48	48	100%
Ointments	52	50	96%
	260	212	82%

Shri Rajan has done well, except the product line of antacids where he has achieved only 20% of quota allotted. Perhaps, a customer-wise break-up may throw further light on Shri Rajan's performance.

❖ Sales Analysis by Customer

Shri Rajan's Customerwise Performance for Antacids

Product line	*Quota*	*Actual*	*Performance as % of quota*
Doctors (Dispensing)	4	4	100%
Big Hospitals	2	2	100%
Nursing Homes	2	2	100%
Retail Chemists	48	0	0%
Govt. Depts.	2	2	100%
Canteens	2	2	100%
	60	12	20%

One important segment, *i.e.,* retail chemists account for his poor performance. Maybe, the competition has effected a price cut and promoting their brands has become lucrative. Shri Rajan has to seek the assistance of his sales executives.

2. Marketing Cost Analysis

At what costs the sales volume? Here sales are not enough, but sales at budgeted profits are.

Marketing cost analysis involves a detailed examination of the costs (organisation and administration of the sales/marketing) and their impact on sales volume. Here a good accounting system is a great help. The following merit attention:

- Profit/rupee of sales.
- Profit/segment, channel, territory, product pack, sales representative etc.
- Cost of goods/rupee of sales.
- Average cost/orders.
- Average value of orders.
- Total value of orders.
- Sales volume and turnover of receivables.

- Stock turnover.
- Profitability related to turnover.
- Enquiries generated/call or direct mail.
- Total operating/functional cost: productwise, regionwise etc.
- Sales/call ratio.
- Expense/sales ratio.
- PC (Profit Contribution).

❖ Sales Management Audit

The previous two techniques — Sales Analysis and Cost Analysis — are operational. The third audit technique is strategic. Audit is comprehensive, systematic, independent and periodic audit of sales policy, objectives, strategies, organisations and procedures.

It examines the basis of sales function. It examines the integration of sales to the changing environment.

The following deserve special attention:

1. Adequacy of selling objectives.
2. Sales integrated to promotion and marketing.
3. Sales representatives' force: Its size and work-norms.
4. Personnel aspect of medical representatives.
5. Quotas, budgets, territories.
6. Quality of sales representatives' appraisal, training and development.
7. Productivity of sales representatives.
8. Sales planning and control system.
9. Commercial Procedures — SP used.

The audit is an evolving field. An outsider may be appointed to take a detached view. Sometimes, audit may suggest a change from a line system to product management system. Sometimes a change in distribution policy may be necessary. Some sales functionaries might be superfluous and redundant. Audit may bring out these redundancies.

3. Market Share Analysis

Companies use four different types of measures to arrive at the market share. The *overall market share* is expressed as a percentage of the total sales in the market. Thus, out of 100 crores of toothpaste market's total sales, a company has 10 crores worth of sales per annum, its overall market share is 10 per cent of the total market. Served market share is expressed as a percentage of the total sales to its served market. It is a share of the company in its chosen segment. Premium cars are meant for a specific segments. A company can have a 60 per cent share in this segment, but its overall sales in the total market may be small. *Relative market share* is expressed as a percentage of the combined sales of the market leader and two market followers. If the company has 20 per cent market share and two of its competitors has 15 per cent and 10 per cent of the market shares, then the relative market share of the company is 20/45 = 44.4 per cent. Relative market share above 33 per cent is considered to be strong. *Its Relative market share to a leading competitor* is a percentage of the leading competitor's sales.

It is easier to use the overall market share figures which are easily available. Relative shares are difficult to arrive at as competitors guard their data on market shares. Market share movements are studied closely in terms of regions, customers, product lines etc.

4. Financial Analysis

Generally ROI is Studied

Profit Margin	×	Assets Turnover	=	Return
(Net Profits/Net Sales)		(Net sales/Total Assets)		on Assets (Net Profits/Total Assets)

Return on Assets x Financial Leverage (Total Assets/Networth)

= Return on Networth (Net Profits/Net Worth)

We can improve returns by increasing the ratio of net profits to total assets or by increasing the ratio of total assets to its net worth. The Asset analysis — current and fixed — is done to see whether they can be managed in a better way.

❖ Customer Satisfaction Studies

The studies described above were quantitative. It is also necessary to undertake qualitative studies to assess the attitudes and levels of satisfaction of the external public — the customers, the shareholders and the distributors.

We shall now acquaint ourselves with the marketing audit which is a tool to study the overall effectiveness of the marketing activity.

❖ Marketing Audit

On account of the rapid changes in the marketing environment, each company tries to assess from time to time its *marketing effectiveness* through a control technique called the marketing audit. Kotler defines marketing audit as follows:

"A marketing audit is a comprehensive, systematic, independent and periodic examination of a company's:

— Marketing environment.
— Objectives.
— Strategies.
— Activities.

with a view to determining problem areas and opportunities and recommending a plan of action to improve company's marketing performance."

❖ Characteristics of Marketing Audit

From the above definition, the following characteristics of the marketing audit become obvious.

Comprehensive: Marketing audit is not a lop-sided study of any one marketing activity but covers all marketing activities.

Systematic: Marketing audit follows a systematic procedure: (*i*) Scanning marketing environment; (*ii*) Scanning the internal marketing system; (*iii*) Examination of specific marketing activities; (*iv*) Diagnosis of the problem and (*v*) Corrective action plan — short-term proposals, long-term proposals.

The ultimate aim is to 'improve organisation's overall marketing effectiveness.

Independent: There are six different routes to marketing audit's conduct: (*i*) Self-audit; check lists are used. It lacks objectivity, (*ii*) Audit from across, (*iii*) Audit from the top, (*iv*) Task-force for audit, (*v*) Auditing office: 3M uses this method and (*vi*) outsider as auditor: they take a detached view.

The steps are examined hereunder and the marketing research input that may be used by the decision-maker at each step is indicated.

Periodic: Audits are undertaken after problems crop up. Generally, audits should be conducted periodically so as to have preventive use. Periodic audits help improve the performance even if things are satisfactory.

❖ Procedure of Marketing Audit

To begin with, the organisation and the auditors meet to decide the objectives, coverage, data collection, reporting and time period of the audit. A plan is chalked out to collect the primary data in the most cost-effective manner in given time-frame. The sample chosen is broad-based — employees, customers, dealers, outside-groups. The collected data is processed and a report is presented along with findings and recommendations. The audit report is discussed and debated.

❖ Components of Marketing Audit

Six major areas are studied:

(*i*) Marketing environment audit.
(*ii*) Marketing strategy audit.
(*iii*) Marketing organisation audit.
(*iv*) Marketing systems audit.
(*v*) Marketing productivity audit.
(*vi*) Marketing functions audit.

The following table illustrates the typical questions that are put in the above areas of audit.

❖ Marketing Environment Audit

Demographic: (*i*) What changes are envisaged in the population size, number, age, education? How do these changes offer opportunities or pose threats to the company? (*ii*) How does the company expect to meet these changes?

Economic: (*i*) What changes are occurring in income, price, savings and credit extension? (*ii*) How does the company expect to meet these changes?

Ecological: (*i*) What is the environment pollution potential of the company? (*ii*) How the company expects to prevent the pollution? How does it expect to reduce the pollution to accepted limits? (*iii*) What resources and energy are needed?

Technological: (*i*) What are the thrust areas of technology? Do they affect the firm? (*ii*) What changes are expected in product and process technology?

Political: (*i*) What laws are on the anvil? Will they affect the firm? (*ii*) How the state policy affecting the firm?

Cultural: (*i*) What changes are expected in the life-styles? What are the public attitudes? How these will affect the firm?

Markets, Customers, Competitors, Distributors: (*i*) What are the changes in the market place? (*ii*) What are the market segments? (*iii*) How do customers view a firm? (*iv*) How do they behave? (*v*) Who are the major competitors and what are their strategies? (*vi*) Which is their productivity?

❖ Marketing Strategy Audit

Mission: What business are used in?

Objectives Goals: What are the overall corporate/marketing goals and objectives? Are they clear? Are they appropriate?

Strategy: (*i*) How is it formulated? Is it suitable? (*ii*) How is the segmentation done? (*iii*) Is the positioning right? (*iv*) Is the marketing mix appropriate? (*v*) Are the resources enough to implement the strategy?

❖ Marketing Organisation Audit

Formal Structure: (*i*) What is the authority of the marketing executive? (*ii*) Is the structure appropriate?

Efficiency: (*i*) What is the role of communication system? (*ii*) Is the product management system in operation? How?

Interface: What is the level of co-ordination between Marketing and Production, Marketing and R & D, Marketing and Finance etc?

❖ Marketing Systems Audit

MIDS: (*i*) How is the internal reporting system? (*ii*) In which way marketing research being used? (*iii*) How is forecasting done?

Planning: (*i*) Is the market plan well formulated? (*ii*) How sales are forecast? How market measured? (*iii*) How sales quotas set?

Control: (*i*) Are the controls adequate? (*ii*) How is control exercised over products, channels, territories and markets?

New Product Development: (*i*) How is the new product development function organised? (*ii*) How are new product ideas cleared for further development? (*iii*) How are the new products launched?

❖ Marketing Productivity Audit

Profits: (*i*) What is the bottom line for different products, markets, territories and channels? (*ii*) In what way can the company expand/shrink the different segments/markets?

Costs: (*i*) Is there enough cost control? (*ii*) What cost reduction methods are in operation?

❖ Marketing Functioning Audit

Products: (*i*) What are the objectives of a product line? Are they being met? (*ii*) Should we extend the product line? Should we phase out certain products? (*iii*) What is the consumer feedback products?

Price: (*i*) What are the pricing objectives, policies and strategies? (*ii*) Do these offer value for money? (*iii*) What is the perception regarding elasticity? (*iv*) Are the pricing policies in harmony with the needs of distributors, government agencies and suppliers?

Distribution: (*i*) What are the distribution objectives and strategies? (*ii*) What is channel effectiveness? (*iii*) Is it necessary of change the channels?

Promotion: (*i*) What are the advertising objectives? (*ii*) What is the advertising budget? How is it set? (*iii*) How are the creatives developed? (*iv*) What are the policies for choosing the media? (*v*) How is that advertising/publicity department organised? (*vi*) Is SP satisfactory? Are PR and publicity satisfactory? (*vii*) What are the objectives of the team of sales representatives? (*viii*) Is the sales force adequate? Is it properly assigned to territories? Is it being compensated properly? What are the incentives given to them? How are they trained? How do that fare with the competitor's sales force?

* * *